First published in 2009 by Designer's Eye

A CIP catalogue record for this title is available from the British Library.

ISBN 978-0-9564250-0-3

The policy of the publisher and printer is to use natural and recyclable papers
produced from wood grown in recognised renewable forests.
Published in the UK and printed by 1010 Printing International Ltd., for information or enquiries email
infodesignerseye@aol.co.uk

Book layout and design,
Cover design & illustration
Alison Berry

AIRPORT–
EXCLUSIVE!

To Emma,
With very best wishes.
Hope you enjoy it!
Ray Berry
2010

RAY BERRY

Designer's Eye

Bibliography

Selwyn Lloyd D.R.Thorpe; Jonathan Cape

Winston Churchill – The Struggle for Survival 1940-1945 Lord Moran; Constable & Co;

Full Circle – the Memoirs of Sir Anthony Eden; Cassell

Hangmen of England Brian Bailey; W.H.Allen

Jane Russell, an autobiography; Sidgwick and Jackson

Slip-Up Anthony Delano; Coronet Books, Hodder and Staughton

Heathrow George Hayter, Pan Books

Tallulah Tallulah Bankhead; Harper Brothers, New York

Trevor Howard, "A Gentleman and a Player" Vivienne Knight; Muller, Blond & White

The Great Spy Scandal Research by Donald Seaman, edited by John S.Mather;
A Daily Express Publication

Chronicle of the 20th Century; Longmans

Great Balls of Fire Myra Lewis with Murray Silver; New York Quill Books and
Virgin Books, London.

Killer Jerry Lee Lewis and Charles White; Random Books

Bevan Michael Foot; MacGibbon & Kee

Greetings, Carbon-based Bipeds! Arthur C.Clarke; Harper Collins

Forte The Autobiography of Charles Forte; Pan Books, in association with Sidgwick Jackson

The Eddie Chapman Story Frank Owen; Panther Books

Picture Credits

Wherever known, credits for pictures and other illustrations reproduced in this book are shown adjoining the subjects concerned.

Every effort has been made to trace the unaccredited illustrations. The publisher will be pleased to rectify such omissions and errors in future editions.

ACKNOWLEDGEMENTS

My thanks are due to a number of people for their encouragement, expertise and practical help over many years, without which this book would never have become a reality.

These friends include former colleague Sylvia Goldberg, for all her advice on publishing, and whose original "Publishers' Proposal" now forms the substance of the synopsis and biographical notes on the wrap-around covers of "Airport–EXCLUSIVE!" The Proposal was described by one publisher as the "best I have ever seen" though even this did not persuade him to commission the book.

Thanks to "tall-ship" sailor and author, Jenni Atkinson-O'Sullivan, also a former colleague, who was the first to persuade me to follow-up a half-formed plan to write of my experiences, and on my behalf, aroused the interest of her own publisher. Both friends have waited a long time to see the result of their efforts.

I thank my niece Linda West for her enthusiasm and advice, and her husband David for his advice on British and German jet engine design. Many former colleagues, particularly the photographers I so frequently worked with, must be thanked for the pictures that are included here; pictures which – I have to admit – so often helped to "sell" my stories. In this context too, I thank Steve Meller, Brenards' last remaining reporter, who inherited the rights and reputation of a re-born Air News Services, for waiving his historical copyright fees.

But my special thanks must go to my daughter Alison for her expertise, her design proposals and innovations and for the many months she has slaved over her Apple Mac and hot scanner, remaining ever patient when responding to my lack of technological understanding and imagination. She was also responsible for tracking down and selecting many of the pictures used in these pages.

Finally, but significantly, my appreciation goes to news magazines, individual newspapers and groups such as Express Newspapers Ltd., The Tribune, The Daily and Sunday Telegraph, the Financial Times, the Co-operative Press for Reynolds News, D.C. Thomson on behalf of the Sunday Post, and the Herald and the Evening Times of Newsquest (Herald & Times Ltd), Glasgow. Each of these generously waived their reproductions copyright, as did overseas media such as the New York Times, the New York International Herald Tribune and the wire service, Associated Press of America.

My thanks are also extended to other British newspapers, such as the Daily Mirror and Sunday Pictorial and its successor the Sunday Mirror, and to groups such as News International Ltd., for permission to reproduce items from The Times and Sunday Times, the News of the World, the Sun and its predecessor, the Daily Herald, and Associated Newspapers Ltd., for reproductions from the Daily Mail, the Daily Sketch, the Sunday Dispatch, the News Chronicle, the London Star evening newspaper and the London Evening News. I am also grateful to the Guardian newspaper for similar assistance, and I am happy to accede to their requirement for reproductions to be acknowledged with the phrase: "Copyright Guardian News & Media. 1963."

Dedication

In memory of Harry, my late brother and mentor, for his invaluable advice, guidance and encouragement throughout my many years as a reporter;

and

to my lovely wife Angela, also known by her Swedish name Gunilla, for her forbearance and strength in enduring several years of semi-solitude during my long and sometimes bad-tempered hours of research and production of this book.

"When one considers that Mr. Sherlock Holmes was in active practice for twenty-three years… it will be clear that I have a mass of material at my command. The problem has always been not to find, but to choose…"

The words of Dr. Watson, the detective's colleague and chronicler, as recorded by his creator, Sir Arthur Conan Doyle, in *'The Adventure of the Veiled Lodger.'*

CHAPTER ONE

prologue

To Heathrow Airport it was a routine call from Hollywood, just one of many seeking assistance for a proposed screen production. Instinctively, public relations officer Iain Burns reached for a filming application form as the caller said: "…we may want to film some scenes at Heathrow."

The American went on: "But first, we need to know what the airport looked like 30 years ago – when Jerry Lee Lewis arrived in London with his young wife back in 1958."

Iain hesitated for a moment as he remembered a similar call of some weeks earlier from a film researcher. And he responded cheerfully: "You've come to the right place. On both counts. We've someone here who was present at the time. In fact I believe he was very much involved."

He gave the caller a name and suggested a time to ring back. And he left a handwritten note for his manager telling him to expect the call.

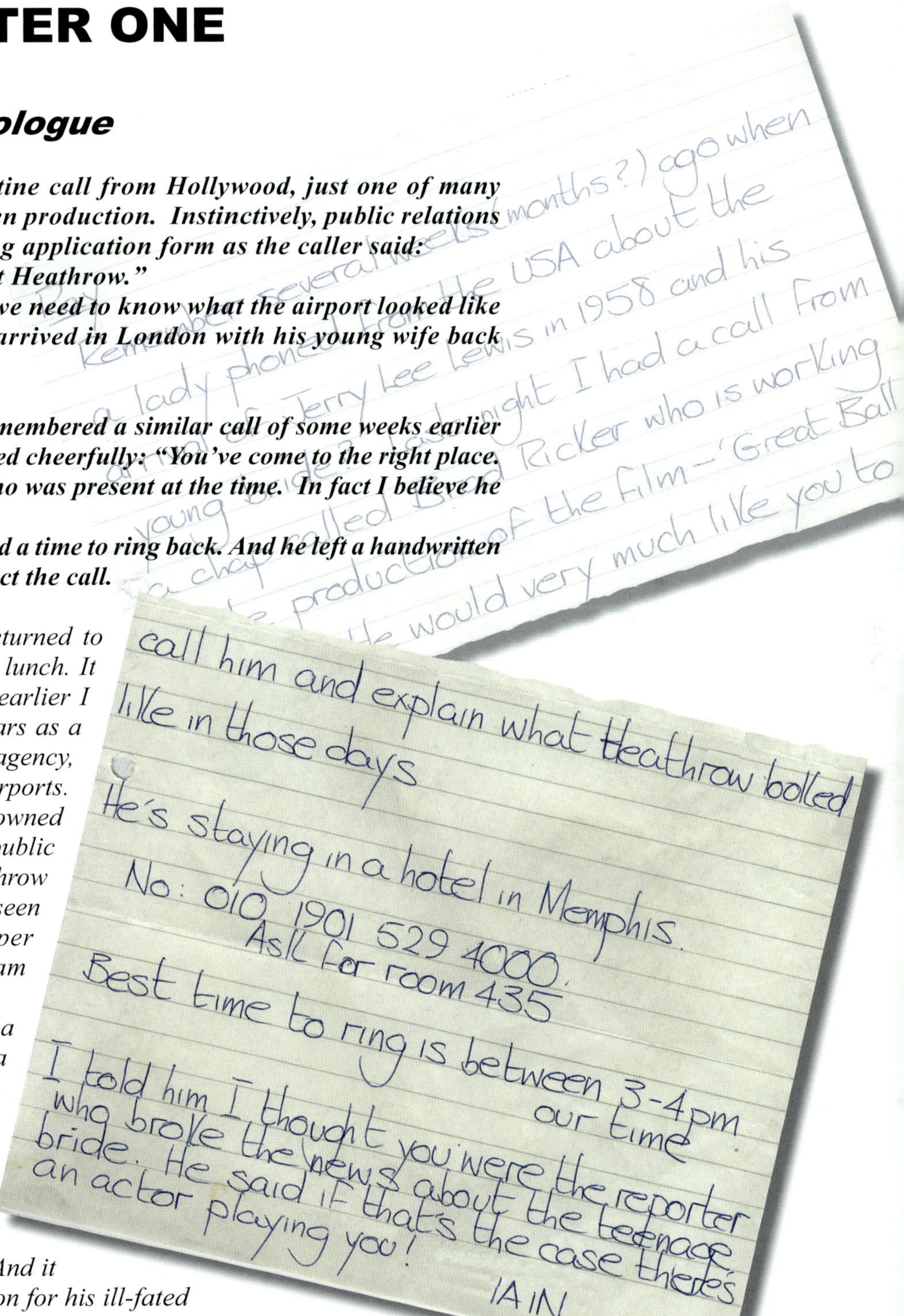
months?) ago when
the USA about the
Lewis in 1958 and his
night I had a call from
Ricker who is working
of the film – 'Great Ball
He would very much like you to

call him and explain what Heathrow looked like in those days.
He's staying in a hotel in Memphis.
No: 010 1901 529 4000.
Ask for room 435
Best time to ring is between 3-4pm our time.
I told him I thought you were the reporter who broke the news about the teenage bride. He said if that's the case there's an actor playing you!
IAIN

Parts of Iain Burns' original handwritten note alerting me to the call from Hollywood, in the late 1980s. By the time the film was released I had retired.

The note was on my desk when I returned to the public relations office from an early lunch. It was August 1988. Some fourteen years earlier I had switched careers, ending my 30 years as a reporter for a national freelance news agency, gathering news from Britain's major airports. My new role was with the publicly-owned British Airports Authority as deputy public relations manager for London's Heathrow Airport – a change understandably seen as a classic poacher-turned-gamekeeper conversion. Iain Burns was one of a team of five public relations officers.[1]

Within the hour I was talking on a transatlantic line to Brad Ricker, a production assistant for ***"Great Balls of Fire,"*** *a planned biopic of the rock'n'roller Jerry Lee Lewis. From his hotel room in Memphis, Tennessee, Ricker told me that the film was based on a book of the same name by Myra, the singer-pianist's former wife. And it focussed on the arrival of Lewis in London for his ill-fated and disastrous British debut.*

"We want to re-create the scene of his arrival at Heathrow thirty years ago… because this is where his career was shattered and almost destroyed," he said, "But of course we need to know what the airport looked like – I guess there have been a few changes since then…"

Briefly I confirmed his guesswork. My mind went back to Heathrow's beginnings. I pictured again the sprawling prefabricated huts of the airport's old north terminal. I described its stark Customs shed, ramshackle arrivals hall and tiny passenger lounge with its hard, cold floor cushioned by layers of fitted brown carpet. I told him of concrete girders and asbestos fibre walls so gallantly disguised under constant coats of pastel gloss paint.

[1] He was to become head of communications for British Airways but, with his boss, resigned from the company some seventeen years later following an alleged air fuel surcharge scandal.

I explained that though the more familiar permanent terminal of the airport's central area had opened in 1955, transatlantic and other long-haul flights had continued to operate to and from these primitive buildings until well into the next decade. "But now its all long gone," I added, "The present terminals bear no resemblance to the original one. Those buildings no longer exist. They were torn down years ago."

Ricker seemed disappointed. I tried to be positive. "There may be nothing Heathrow can offer you which would re-create your arrival scene," I said, "But there are almost identical buildings still in use at Northolt airport, just a few miles away.

"It's now an RAF station, so you'd have to approach our Defence Ministry for permission to film there. But it could save you a lot of problems, to say nothing of the costs of studio space and a mock-up stage." In the meantime, I said, I could fax some pictures of these former north terminal buildings for reference – and I added: "I'll also do a sketch for you of the old arrivals barrier where I first met Myra and Jerry Lee..."

*"**You** met him?" Ricker broke in with a gasp. "So it's true? You were there – on the spot?"*

"Oh yes," I replied. " Sorry, I thought you knew that. I was a Press reporter then – and I broke the story of Jerry Lee Lewis's child bride. I found her and was the first to talk to her, though she claimed to me that she was fifteen and didn't admit to her true age of thirteen."

The American was puzzled. "But according to Myra, the British Press were there in force," he said. "How can you know it was your story?"

"Because I was the one who sought her out and asked her the questions," I said, "And I was the only reporter doing so. There was a crowd at the barrier, but they weren't all meeting Jerry. And those that were seemed to be fans or photographers. I wasn't even aware of any other reporters."

Commented Brad with a laugh: "Well our movie revolves entirely on this arrival in Britain and the consequences of your questions. We have a British actor playing you. But I'm afraid we show a horde of Press at the barrier. I guess you'll have to put that down to dramatic licence."

We chatted for some minutes about Lewis's downward career from that point. Ricker liked the idea of the Northolt setting and said: "We have a British unit working on these scenes. I'll put it to them." Finally, we signed off as I dismissed his appreciative comments with the half-joking words: "You can remember me when you have your London premiere!"

A week or two later came yet another telephone call – this time from Pinewood Studios, just a few miles from Heathrow. Costumier Rosemary Burrows was seeking help on airport uniform designs of the late 'fifties. When I commented: "Ah, Jerry Lee Lewis," she was momentarily lost for words. I told her of my conversation with Brad Ricker, and mentioned my suggestion for filming at Northolt.

Dismissively, as if the studio had independently come up with the same thought, she replied: "We are already in touch with the Ministry of Defence over the possibility of a Northolt location..."

*

My first view of London Airport was from the front seat on the top of a Number 81 double-decker bus. I almost missed it.

There was not a single aeroplane in sight. Just row upon row of blue-grey or khaki-camouflaged ex-RAF caravans. Leyland and Bedford three-tonners with box bodies; they rested almost axle-deep in mud, shrouded in a heavy mist which cloaked any view beyond.

Two bus stops passed before my mind finally registered. It must have been a brief glimpse of the sign "Departures," suspended above a porch door of one of the barrack-like buildings facing the Bath Road a few miles west of Hounslow. In a momentary panic I sprinted to the stair head. The bus was pulling to a halt alongside The Old Magpies, a thatched, sixteenth-century inn just a hundred yards from the airport entrance gate.

This was November 1946. London Airport had been open to civil airliners for less than a year.

The first service with passengers had operated the previous January. Officially it was a route-proving test flight with only guests and aircrew aboard. Years later it was admitted that fares for the handful of passengers *had* been charged. The Central Terminal area and its linking road tunnel were still some years off. Passenger activity, such as it was, was confined for now to this cluster of single storey huts, prefabricated from fibre panels bolted to a concrete skeleton. Their comparative luxury had just recently replaced a storm-blown village of muddy brown Army canvas.

Until March that year the airport had been known only by its location name. The hamlet of Heath Row had already vanished under the advance of wartime airfield developers. Then the Government of the day decided that foreign travellers would find it difficult to get their tongues round "Heath Row." Henceforth, they said, it would be named "London Airport."

The picturesque, sixteenth-century *Old Magpies* inn, which once stood on the airport side of the A4 Bath Road boasted a "priests' hole". Ironically, it was said to have been used by the highwayman Dick Turpin, a regular patron. It was demolished in the early 1950s – some believe quite unnecessarily – to make way first for a car park and later for the M4 spur road.

Pictures courtesy of historian and author Philip Sherwood

One hundred yards to the east of the thatched *Old Magpies* and adjoining the original entrance to "London Airport," *The Three Magpies* has so far managed to survive at the airport boundary, albeit with extensive refurbishment, unlike its once-neighbouring near namesake. Now this 250-years-old coaching inn is also threatened by further airport development.

Twenty years on, this was no longer a consideration. "Heathrow" was revived as a secondary name, now as one word – to avoid confusing those same foreigners when a new decision designated Gatwick, some fifty miles away to the south, also as *London* Airport.

But now my bus was pulling away from the stop, and I had to leap for the kerb. As I headed back towards the airport gate, I passed a second pub. It stood beak by jowl with the first and was similarly and intriguingly named *The Three Magpies.* Next to it, as if claiming the airport entrance as its own, was a small shop-fronted cottage with a ramshackle appendage of corrugated iron.

Though the building boasted the more formal "Airport Cafe," a hand-painted sign over the annexe proclaimed, simply: *"Ben's."* Once it had been a typically unpretentious pull-in for lorry drivers. Now its marble-topped cast-iron tables and junk-dealers' assortment of stools and chairs had become an unlikely and incongruous dining place for a new clientele – the aircrews and ground staff of international airlines.

Blue-uniformed young women – the glamorous airgirls of the day – with their nattily-dressed male colleagues, looking for all the world like naval officers, perched precariously on waist-high stools as they sipped from cracked cups, the rain dripping on them through the battered and rusted roof. The sight was disconcerting.

Up to that time my knowledge of airfields was based on the films and newsreels of the cinema and my limited wartime experiences as a young evacuee in East Anglia. I suppose I expected to see constant aerial activity, with dozens of aircraft at haphazardly spaced dispersal points being fuelled up for take-off. Perhaps even a glimpse of flying heroes in bomber jackets lounging in deck chairs, awaiting a call to "Scramble!"

I remembered witnessing the evolution of the bomber at Wyton aerodrome near Huntingdon, then a county town. Following on were the ungainly Whitleys and Hampdens of the early 1940s, which in turn were succeeded by the smoother lines of the Blenheim and that stallion of the night, the worthy "Wimpy" Wellington. Then their four-engined successors, the huge Stirlings of the thousand-bomber raids on the Ruhr and Rhine, the later Lancasters and Halifaxes; the arrival of the showbiz-like US Army Air Force with their B17 Flying Fortresses, and film star flyers Clark Gable and James Stewart, visiting from another East Anglian base.

Even closer acquaintance with these early leviathans had come when a friendly RAF "erk" at nearby Alconbury airfield showed a wide-eyed ten-year old and my even younger sister over a twin-engined Wellington, already bombed-up and ready for take-off for some mystery target. I still remembered too the shouts from that airman's sergeant when he spotted us being shown back to the road through our hole in a hedge.

A few years on from my first visit to London Airport. The signs above the widened and rebuilt doorways have been repainted to reflect the changing traffic patterns. Flower beds have been provided to greet the arriving passenger...

This was now peacetime. But surely, there should have been some form of checkpoint at this airport gate, with at least a striped barrier and policemen to give directions? Here there was no such concession to the un-informed, nothing to direct the visitor or to tell him what to expect.

Those few buildings I had seen from my seat on the bus turned out to be flat-roofed and single-storeyed. They were signposted "Arrivals" and "Departures," but in spite of a roughcast coat of fresh cream paint, offered the same drab, dejected appearance as those hurriedly constructed barrack blocks of a few years earlier. "Abandon hope all ye who are leaving" quite realistically could have replaced the "Departures" sign greeting the expectant traveller.

Both pictures from author's collection

...and, with the transfer of airlines from nearby Northolt Airport, a new dedicated check-in area has been provided for the ever-increasing short-haul continental departures.

I couldn't have known, as I asked directions at the airport post office, one of the equally cheerless adjoining buildings, that these huts and their eventual successors, the airport central terminals, would become a familiar second home to me for half-a-lifetime. Six months earlier, just before my sixteenth birthday, my days at school were coming to an end, and not too soon for me. Along with some eighty others I was awaiting, with not much expectation, the results of my Schools Certificate exam – the old 'O' levels.

It was careers time. But few of us, apart from the inevitable embryo bank clerks, had made up their minds what to do with their lives. After all, ahead of us we had possibly our last long summer holiday hadn't we? There was plenty of time...

Splinter thought differently. "Splinter" Wood was senior English master at Highbury County Secondary School in North London (later to become Highbury Grove Comprehensive, cradle of controversial headmaster and erstwhile Tory Education Minister Dr Rhodes Boyson, but in my day a hotbed of crusading young Socialists).

He was also our fifth form teacher and careers' counsellor, charged with giving us some aim in life.

"By now," he pronounced coldly, "You should have all thought of a career." And condescendingly he informed us that if we put forward some proposals, he was prepared to find speakers to tell us about various jobs and professions.

There was a flurry of conversational activity and enthusiastic, anticipatory noises from the budding lawyers, engineers, civil servants and (fittingly for a leading school in Highbury) footballers, followed by a despairing lull as ideas petered out. Who did *I* know who had a CAREER? And was that what I wanted?

A sudden inspiration. My brother Harry was back in Fleet Street trying to pick up his pre-war chosen career as a journalist after an enforced stay in the Far East as a guest of the Imperial Japanese Army. I had always cherished copies of articles bearing his name. It had to be the height of achievement to see yourself in print.

I threw up a hand and asked brightly: "What about journalism, sir?"

Looking back, I suspect there was an element of bravado about the challenge. For challenge it proved to be, and I should have known instinctively what Splinter's reaction would be. But not one of us could have been prepared for the vehemence of the reply.

There was a moment's silence; a hush of expectancy as the response was awaited. Splinter was visibly frozen and grey, his facial muscles rigid. Then, suddenly, through clenched teeth the offensive word finally spewed out like steam from a safety valve.

"Journalism?" he exploded. And again: ***"Journalism?"***

A further, deafening, hush. Then, his voice almost trembling with enraged contempt, he sneered:

"That's not a career. It's a mindless activity."

Another pause. Slowly the rigid muscles of his jaw relaxed as he regained his composure. At last he dismissed the subject and me with a derisory brush of the hand.

"Never mention the word again in my presence," he said.

The discussion was ended. The subject was closed.

Up to that moment I hadn't even considered myself as a future journalist. Harry's achievements and my admiration for them were something remote from my own life. All *my* endeavours had been directed, somewhat reluctantly, towards an "artistic" career, whatever that was likely to mean.

One school memento was a letter of introduction from my art teacher. It informed whoever might be concerned, that after his two years' expert coaching I would make a good "improver."

As I was only one of three pupils taking art in that year, it wasn't a very difficult conclusion for him to reach anyway. I wasn't too sure what an improver was, but it hardly endeared me to seeking employment as a commercial artist. Particularly, I told myself at the time, as I was a free spirit unable to draw or paint to order but only when the fancy took me. (Of course, later I realised this was my self-consoling excuse for not being able to draw well enough anyway.)

But now my mind was made up. I could think of no higher recommendation for a career than a condemnation by Splinter Wood. And English was, after all, my best subject.

Splinter and I had never seen eye to eye. Our mutual dislike of each other was obvious on each and every occasion we were obliged by circumstances to make contact, something, which was unavoidable in view of our relative positions. That particular aspect of our relationship was, I suspect with experience, at the root of the trouble. I could never accept that as my senior English teacher he might perhaps know better than I the arguable points of grammar. I would frequently question, for example, his parsing and analysis definitions. Perhaps an earlier, more enlightened teacher who encouraged dissent if only to promote discussion, had spoiled me.

He in turn made his dislike of me patently obvious with his constant sarcasm. *He* was unable to accept that someone who failed to appreciate the finer aspects of rugby football or couldn't tell the difference between the responsibilities of a soccer inside right and a left back could possibly write a readable essay. (His marginal comments in this area varied between *"Too clever by half,"* and *"Such an interpretation of the subject matter is unacceptable.")*

Of one thing I'm certain. If someone else had suggested journalism as a potential career, Splinter would at least have called for some supportive argument before dismissing it. At best he might even have admitted he knew no journalist who would have been happy to come and talk about his job to one misguided enthusiast.

For enthusiast is what I became from that moment. Looking back, it's ironic that I owe the most satisfying, most exciting and most rewarding years of my working life to his response to my half-serious enquiry.

Within weeks I was walking in Fleet Street in search of my first job, a determined 16-years-old. No end-of-school break or summer holiday for me now. I had a target.

I had learnt pretty quickly that the recognised formal route into a journalistic career was through training with a local newspaper, and I had already applied in vain to my local *Islington Gazette* and *Hornsey Journal.* Both reported "no vacancies" and told me to keep trying.

But I was impatient. I had something to prove and I feared my enthusiasm might go off the boil. I would have to start at the top – Fleet Street – and work down. On Monday I took the tube.

From Aldwych Station I walked to Temple Bar. But for some reason it seemed more logical to begin my enquiries at the other, far end of the Street after a thorough reconnaissance. Notebook in hand, I carefully surveyed every entrance, every nameplate along my route eastwards, periodically dodging buses and taxicabs as I crossed the road and retraced my steps to cover both sides of the Street.

Some of the gloomier and less imposing doorways, I soon discovered, served several newspaper offices or the London bases of provincial or overseas publications. Some of these portals boasted notice boards. A few even displayed "Vacancy" signs, for all the world like seaside boarding houses.

Making a note of each prospect, I passed on. No point in not surveying the field.

Now I had reached Ludgate Circus. It was time to start knocking at doors and being respectful to commissionaires. From the *PA-Reuter* building on the south side I began working my way back to my starting point. Crossing and re-crossing the road, I knocked on every glass-panelled door and entered every reception office I could find that appeared to have the slightest association with the world of newspapers. The side-roads – Bouverie Street, Whitefriars Street – would have to come later.

Hour after hour was slipping by. I stopped at the Black and White Milk Bar for a snack. Wondering if it might one day become a regular haunt (it never did), I recalled another Black and White I had frequented with my cronies at Dulverton, in Somerset in the 'forties, during my annual school agricultural camp on Exmoor. Casually I wondered if the two were connected.

The *Black & White Milk Bar* in Fleet Sreet, pictured in the late 1930s.

I moved on. In some front offices I was told to wait, false hopes raised temporarily. In others I was asked to leave my name and address. Yet others simply, but sadly it seemed, offered only a shake of the head.

In only three of those offices did anyone in obvious authority come to see me. One – the *Daily Express* – invited me, under escort by a medal-bedecked sergeant-at-arms, up to the newsroom, compensation indeed for not being offered a job on the spot. Finally, by late afternoon, I was almost back at Temple Bar. Now even **my** optimism was being sorely tried as I turned into the doorway of the old *Manchester Guardian* London office. Then I remembered. Here was one of those vacancies I had noted earlier. After a few minutes someone came down from the first floor to see me. A brief chat and my day's search was over.

I found myself saying: "Yes, please. I'll start tomorrow if you like."

*

Now I had my first full-time job: a copy boy in the London office of the *Guardian's* sister newspaper, the *Manchester Evening News.*

For the next few months I revelled in the enthralling atmosphere of Fleet Street, even if my lowly status made the experience a limited one. My duties, occasionally shared with another junior, a sickly youth who only appeared spasmodically, and who consequently I hardly got to know, consisted of monitoring the teleprinter machines.

These supplied a stream of copy, or news stories, from around Britain and the world. The flow originated from the notebooks of reporters and correspondents, almost always anonymous, contributing to and working for the major news agencies, the *Exchange Telegraph, Press Association, Reuters, Agence France Presse* and the American wire services of *Associated Press* and *United Press.*

A few feet away, shielded from the constant chatter of these machines by a clear glass screen, sat a copy taster, selecting stories for publication and onward transmission to the Manchester offices of the *News* or the *Guardian* over the company's private wire, a ticker tape. My onerous responsibility was to tear copy from the machines at appropriate breaks and place it before the copy taster.

I soon became aware which stories were more likely to be selected for forwarding. I saw how the copy was marked up for the ticker tape operator and I remember some of the major news events running at the time. I watched every word of the Nuremberg trials of the Nazi leaders being avidly devoured, much of it close to afternoon edition times. I also saw my first picture agency photographs, before the prints were wired to Manchester on yet another magical machine.

The introductory codes of agency tapes became familiar. And the significance of the catch line – often just a single word description of the subject matter of a story – revealed itself. I learned that "SNAP" on the *Press Association* tape meant that the copy was a news flash (and wondered why they didn't use the more obvious "FLASH"). And I soon discovered that "FULL" meant that nothing more would be forthcoming on that particular report.

For my own satisfaction, I began to devise a personal system for dealing with what I considered to be the most important items of news.

Urgent reports and stories which I concluded might be of interest to a Manchester evening newspaper I placed at the copy-taster's right hand. Lengthy stories or those which seemed less immediate were placed at his left. And when I knew that edition times were pressing I carefully spaced the tearing and placing of copy to reduce time wasting.

No one told me not to. But no one offered a word of appreciation either. It did not occur to me that as a very junior copy boy I might not have much idea of what news would be considered important. It's also perfectly feasible that no one noticed my efforts, though Ian Cross, one of the more sympathetic copy-tasters, gave me a quizzical look on occasions. Which could have meant anything.

I simply felt that I had to show some initiative in a task which could otherwise have been sheer tedium.

And I *was* learning. For the first time I took a personal interest in national and international news stories. How they were written. How the entire essence of a report could be contained in the first paragraph, the first sentence, and usually was. How the briefest description of people, of scenes, of events could provide the mind's eye with a detailed picture.

I felt too that I had a personal hand in the production of the newspaper. Wasn't it down to me that an important flash from *Reuter's* man in New Delhi was safely transmitted to Manchester, and not lost down the back of the wire machine? After a month's trial my pay was increased by five shillings a week to the princely sum of 35s. As a smoker I was unable to save. And after paying my daily fare from Finsbury Park to Aldwich on the tube, I couldn't afford to patronise that elusive Black and White milk bar. So I spent my lunch break getting to know the byways and bomb-scarred surrounds of Fleet Street and the Temple while munching my homemade sandwiches.

A high spot was an occasional lunch with Harry in the staff canteen of the *Star*, the London evening newspaper in Bouverie Street where he worked. He would point out various reporters and writers on both his paper and its "sister," the daily *News Chronicle.* Few of the names meant anything to me then, but I did recognise a visitor (trespassing?) from the Sunday newspaper *Reynolds News* (or was it *The People*?), the legendary Hannen Swaffer. And later I had reason to remember another name – that of Roy Nash, the *Star* features writer who had co-contributed to that paper's memorable jubilee issue.

It was during one of these lunchtime breaks that my future, and coincidentally, Harry's future too, was unexpectedly, and undramatically established, though neither of us knew it at the time.

Harry had brought along a copy of *World's Press News,* then the journalists' trade paper. He pointed out a small box advertisement on the classified pages.

"Have a look at this," he said. "It could be just the job for you."

West London news agency requires junior for Newsroom. Opportunity to train as reporter. Apply Box No:...

The response to my application came within a week. Typed on blue notepaper headed with the company name *"BRENARD AIR NEWS SERVICE,"* the message was terse and gave nothing away.

"Come for interview," it said. The address was London Airport.

*

Three steps led up to the standard narrow door of the caravan, one of a number in a long line. To the left, suspended above the faded red, white and blue of an RAF roundel, was a freshly painted signboard in bright blue, its white lettering identifying the occupier.

I rapped on the board, the hollow back of its frame magnifying the sound against the camouflaged metal panel of the vehicle's rear bulkhead.

A blast of hot air, reeking with paraffin fumes and stale cigarette smoke engulfed me as I opened the door and stepped through in response to the abbreviated invitation: "Come!" As my eyes adjusted to the gloom, the figure hunched over a portable typewriter just inside the door swivelled round.

"Hello. You must be Berry. Pull up a chair."

I opened up a folded wooden chair and placed it awkwardly at the end of his desk. He added, as if to confirm the signature above the words "News Editor" on his letter:

"I'm John Gullick."

My "interview" was minimal, like the invitation. I had the clear impression there were no other contenders for the job of editorial assistant (a title I thought much more respectable than "newsroom junior") and in no time at all I found myself agreeing to start work the following week, on the first Monday in December 1946. My pay, at £2.10s a week, was fifteen shillings (75p) more than I was earning at the *Manchester Evening News*, but the job did involve shift work and any increase would go on extra fares.

With luck and what he called "the right attitude" I could be out reporting, under guidance, within a matter of weeks. But he was making no promises. It depended...

Now with duties and prospects explained, John Gullick became suddenly, and as I learned later, uncharacteristically more communicative. In answer to my questions, he had already described the role of Brenard Air News Service as a freelance news agency. Through its team of reporters it supplied news on aviation matters and the comings and goings of the famous from a number of airports around the country. Its clients, or customers, were British national and provincial newspapers and other news agencies supplying an even wider network of British and foreign publications.

Now, glancing at his watch as if needing to kill time, he volunteered a potted history of "Brenards" – the name by which the company was already familiar in Fleet Street.

The agency had been launched by former RAF Squadron Leader and fighter pilot Bill Brenard on his return to journalism at the end of his war service. But it had seen its beginnings much earlier, in the 'thirties at Croydon Airport, where Bill's father, Robert Brenard, had been airport manager.

Bill and his brother Arthur, who later in the 1950s was to become air correspondent, then news editor of the *Sunday Express*, began their journalistic careers as "airport correspondents" before moving to staff jobs in Fleet Street.

It was Bill, however, who returned to the airport scene after his RAF service, setting up the news agency first at Croydon, then at London Airport. For the next forty years the company was to provide an invaluable service to the world's news media. It was also to set me on the road to a reporting career.

My "lesson" from John was suddenly at an end. The door through which I had entered some forty minutes earlier crashed back on its hinges as a gargantuan figure in a sheepskin flying jacket and calf-length fur-lined flying boots carefully eased its way through the narrow frame.

Bill Brenard was a big man with a big personality. He was an extrovert with a big belly laugh and a sense of humour to match. His thinning, blond ginger hair and huge handlebar moustache made him stand out in a crowd. The moustache, a popular fad of many wartime flyers, he retained as a trademark throughout his life, later adding a beard. He was loud and sometimes vulgar. Strangers were wary of his apparent brashness, and occasionally found him overwhelming.

Those who knew him were soon aware of a softer, more sentimental side. He was a generous man in every sense and was always loyal to those he trusted. Years later I was to remember him not just as the best of employers, but also as a good friend.

I tried to rise from my chair as the newcomer towered over me, but in my cramped position against the wall could only half-lean and half-stand between the chair and the desk. I looked up expectantly at the ruddy complexion above me as John spoke.

"Bill," he said, "This is Berry."

Before I could say anything or put forward a hand, Bill turned away, and with a sudden kick of each leg shook loose his boots. The effort sent them flying, first one, then the other across the office, crashing into the opposite wall. Then he spoke.

"Humph," he said. And then: "What's your brother like?"

I was perplexed. I could think of no connection between my applying for a job as an editorial assistant and my brother. Which brother, anyway? I had two, both older. and what did he know of either of them? I dodged the question.

"Why do you ask, sir?" I replied, "What is you want to know?"

Bill Brenard tweaked the ends of that huge moustache, a mannerism which was to become very familiar. He didn't suffer fools gladly, and he obviously thought I was being particularly thick. Impatiently he repeated: "I want to know what he's like. He's written to me asking for a job." Then, as an afterthought: "And don't call me 'sir'." [1]

Author's collection

Bill Brenard, in familiar pose, discovers a German sense of humour at Hamburg passport controls as he arrives as one of a group of Press guests of British European Airways aboard an inaugural Comet 4B jet service from London.

Momentarily embarrassed, my mind raced ahead. So it *must be* Harry. How did he connect us? How did he know we were related? I set aside my own questions. It was obviously neither the time nor place to wonder. Hesitantly I told him of Harry's pre-war job in the features department of The *Star*; of his return there after four years in Jap prisoner-of-war camps only to find that his old boss had moved on and he would be getting fewer opportunities to write.

It went without saying that he was good, didn't it? After all, hadn't he been chosen by the *Star* as one of only two young journalists to write for their Jubilee issue special "Youth Week" feature in 1938, when he was only twenty-one? [2] And hadn't he produced, single-handed, a secret newspaper for his fellow prisoners in Singapore, where the only "news" immediately after its surrender was rumour?

I continued in this vein for some minutes until Bill apparently thought he'd heard enough. He had no further questions. Two weeks after my baptism as an editorial assistant, Harry, almost fourteen years my senior, joined Brenards as a reporter. He had written to the company directly after hearing of its growing reputation, unaware that it and the "West London news agency," whose advertisement for an office junior he had carefully

[1] *Many years later, complaining about the shortcomings of the youth of the day, Bill Brenard commented to me: "They don't even look up when I enter the room. In your day you would have stood up." It's not a familiar scenario to me…*

[2] *The other was Roy Nash , one of those writers I'd seen at the Star, of whom, more later.*

selected for me were one and the same. Harry could always say he found me my job with Brenards. I always responded with equal relish that if it hadn't been for my glowing recommendation...

*

My first eight weeks in my new job were spent alternately shivering and sweltering in the grandly named "copy room" of the Brenard caravan.

The Leyland vehicle – in appearance resembling a small removals lorry – was designed when stationary to expand to three times its driving size, providing two annexe "rooms" alongside the interior. The floors and roofs of these annexes were hinged to the exterior of the box van. The extension floors could be lowered into position, while the roofs were raised like wings above them, supported at each corner by anchored posts.

Author's collection

The rear entrance to an ex-RAF caravan identical to the Brenard 'offices' at London Airport in the late 1940s. Note the wheel-arch height from the ground and the suspended, canvas-clad 'extensions' on each side. This one was rented by BOAC, who presumably needed quick access to a public call box; we, of course, had our own phones!

Each annexe, its floor now at wheel-arch height from the ground, was then accessed through doors in the outer wall of the van.

The outer walls of the extensions were merely heavy-duty military canvas, normally stored aboard. It would be hooked at intervals to the roof and floor to form a continuous wall on three sides of each annexe, the fourth wall being the exterior of the caravan itself.

One of these annexes, furnished with folding tables and chairs, was the copy room. It offered its occupants about as much protection from the elements as a badly pitched tent. Gales, that seemed to blow constantly for weeks on end over the flat expanse of the airfield, found their way in through every fold, every loop, every gap in the canvas. And that was in the summer.

When I forsook the relative luxury of my Fleet Street office to take up my new duties, I soon learned that the only answer to the multi-directional airport draught was to turn up the wick of our small Aladdin oil-stove until every air-hole was smothered by the outpouring toxic fumes. At which point, of course, to avoid being choked ourselves, my fellow sufferers and I would have to turn off the heater fully to permit a complete change of air. Then the cycle began again.

There were two copy-roomers on duty at one time ("editorial assistant," I now discovered, was a euphemism reserved for the vacancy ads.). With two shifts to give a 7 am to 11 pm cover daily, this meant, with days off and holidays, a minimum of seven juniors, something that was rarely achieved and maintained for long.

Reporters usually dictated their stories to the caravan by telephone from the passenger buildings nearby. The copy-roomers' main function was to take down those stories on an ancient Royal typewriter, via huge crystal set-style headphones. If the news desk in the caravan's central office next door were manned, the frequently half-legible copy would be taken in for checking or "subbing." If not (i.e. when the *Bricklayers' Arms*, later renamed the *Air Hostess*, on the adjoining Bath-road was open), the story was circulated, dictated again by 'phone, to each of the newspapers named by the reporter as his intended market.

With an important story and a large market, this could take some time. In those early days, London alone had three evening newspapers. Provincial groupings, eight or nine national dailies and up to five agencies had to be regularly served as well.

Between taking and dictating copy, answering constantly ringing telephones, trying to track down reporters or photographers to pass on newspaper "orders" and making new entries in our daily diary of newsworthy travellers or events, there was little time to practice our new-found skills of two-finger typing.

Reporters came to dread a new junior in the office. Similarly, long-experienced copy-takers at the newspapers failed to appreciate that punctuating your reading orally and literally with "caps," "paragraph," "quote" and "unquote," did not come easily on the first day, any more than phonetic spelling of difficult words or names.

This inexperience led to some strange transmissions, not always picked up until the final copy reached some unamused Fleet Street news desk (and on occasions perhaps, not even then). One Freudian spelling was *"au pere"* (to Father) for *"au pair"*. A phrase beginning ".... caught her airliner in" became "caught her hairline in...." A well-known socialite was described as a "social light."

A prominent actress of the day landed at Heathrow and climbed into "her Rolls Royce Centimetre," which turned out to be "a Rolls Royce *sent to meet her.*" The words "...in Paris" became, imaginatively, "imperious." A prominent politician was quoted as saying: "There was a certain illogic hallity about General de Gaulle's words," which led to one newspaper sub asking innocently: "Was he trying to say the General had bad breath?"

On a quiet day, notwithstanding the occasional howler, at least one junior on duty was expected to peruse the previous day's newspapers for items that might be of interest to reporters, particularly references to coming events which could have an echo at the airport. This was by far the least productive area of our endeavours. Despite constant reminders from Bill Brenard in the form of vague but nonetheless sinister threats, the stack of uncut newspapers steadily grew, while our room for manoeuvring in the confined space of the copy room diminished at an equal pace.

Once in a while reporters would visit the newsroom to write up their own copy. This was in the main body of the vehicle, the central office, which boasted fitted furniture in the form of simple desks at diagonally opposite corners. Movable furnishings comprised a few chairs, filing cabinets and cupboards. Additional trestle tables covered the wheel arches on each side, and shelving lined the walls.

Other than in the cab, the van boasted only one window – at its rear. Glazed skylights provided the only other daylight throughout the vehicle, apart from the gaps produced by loops in the canvas walls. As the second of the annexes served as a primitive darkroom, it was necessary to disguise this design oversight with an interior lining of yards of wartime blackout material.

My first direct encounter with a Brenard reporter was on my second day. Bill Brenard had seated me in the newsroom at a portable typewriter and given me something to copy as a test, not of speed but of accuracy. He had left me to it, saying he would return in ten minutes.

Moments later an aggressive newcomer was demanding immediate access to the typewriter. He had, he said, editions to catch. And in any case I should be in the copy room. I was sorry, I said, but I had to finish what I was doing for Mr Brenard.

There was no way I was giving up the typewriter until he returned.

One day on and I hope I would have recognised the priorities. This time I was saved from the wrath of chief reporter Dennis Forknell by the return of the boss, who decided in his wisdom that "Forky's" claim to the typewriter was perhaps the more valid.

Further introductions were more pleasant. Within a couple of days I was surprised to learn that two acquaintances and former fellow juniors from Fleet Street had preceded me to Brenards' and were even now working alongside reporters as trainees. Ralph Churchill and Brian Coates, as copy boys, had shared the same teleprinters with me. But as they worked for the *Manchester Guardian*, we had only met as they took over from me each day to cover their evening shift.

They had left the *Guardian* a few weeks after I started at the *Manchester Evening News.* Now here they were – and already almost fully-fledged junior reporters. There was hope for me yet.

My chance came even more quickly than I expected. It was every copy-roomers' dream to join the reporters and "see the action" in the airport terminal, and each of us in turn pestered the lives of successive news editors to be allowed to try his hand at "doubling-up" on a story.

My own requests were reinforced with cuttings. For some months, initially under Harry's encouragement and guidance, I had been telephoning the news desks of the London evenings with snippets of information, mainly about cancellations and delays on the London Underground.

I discovered that payments from the newspapers for these tip-offs were larger if they didn't suspect you were a pro (or even an aspiring one) but merely a naïve reader with a news sense.[1] On the few occasions I was asked to dictate my information I would say: "I'd rather tell you."

But when a promising story meant making a few enquiries or chasing some facts, I was only too happy to write it up and take my chances on payment. So when my local telephone kiosk, one I had frequently used to phone in my titbits, was mounted by a runaway car, killing a woman waiting outside, the *Evening Standard* gave it a two column head on an inside page. It was complete with quotes from a student who told me he'd been trapped inside.

From all three evening papers my payments that day totalled some six guineas – more than twice my weekly wage.

At the end of January, John Gullick suggested I could try a piece on the preparations for a visit to the airport the following day by the then Princess Elizabeth. The Princess was to name the ill-fated Avro Tudor, Britain's first post-war airliner.

I jumped at the opportunity, convinced I knew just what was required. This was far better that the usual training procedure of sending a junior out to hang on to the coat tails of a reporter (to the embarrassment of one and the impatience of the other).

An hour or so later I returned to the office and proudly sat at a typewriter in the newsroom. Eventually I produced about four hundred words of flowery prose on flags, striped awnings and bunting, and one sentence of original fact.

The Princess, I had learnt from airline people overseeing the preparations, would pour champagne over the nose of the airliner from a silver plated tankard because breaking the traditional bottle on the aircraft might damage it. On 31 January, above the by-line "*Star* reporter," The *Star* published just 130 words *(left.)*

PRINCESS CHRISTENS NEW AIR LINER

"Star" Reporter

BRITAIN'S first post-war four-engined air liner, the Tudor I, was being christened Elizabeth of England by Princess Elizabeth at London Airport today.

Princess Elizabeth's own standard was flying from the 20ft. flag pole which had been erected on the edge of the tarmac.

Luxurious carpets were laid in the airport's new reception hall, from where a striped awning led to the dais.

It had been arranged that the Princess should christen the new air liner by pouring champagne over its nose from a beautiful 18th century silver beer mug. The departure from tradition was purely logical—to break a bottle on the aircraft would damage it.

Elizabeth of England and others of the new Tudor fleet will be in service soon on many of the Empire routes.

The Star *January 31 1947*

Out had gone most of the detailed description I had laboured over. But what was left was mine, all mine. My first publication from Brenards' and after only two months. I was on my way!

Publication taught me my first lesson of professional reporting – be brief. And there were many more such lessons to be learned over the next few weeks. I realised that the continual exhortation to "Cut those newspapers!" steadily growing like stalagmites in the copy-room had another objective: to get us to read those newspapers. Until then I had simply skipped through them, absorbing just those items which interested me.

I started to question, to analyse news items, to compare different newspaper reports of the same events. As I spotted identical phrases, sentences or words in otherwise differently treated stories, I began to recognise when those stories in different newspapers had originated from one source, a "stringer" or correspondent, or even a freelance news agency. And I thought how unfair it was for the newspaper to print the story under a by-line – the name of one of their own staff reporters.

Sixty years on that still rankles, whether or not authorship was fully recognised in payment or not (and frequently it was not). Anonymity is often seen as the principle disadvantage for the freelance or news agency reporter. In general, I found that publication of my stories over a wide range of newspapers in Britain and overseas was ample compensation for the lack of a by-line. But I could never come to terms with someone else getting the credit in print for my story, particularly when hardly a word of the original had been changed.

About this time another school-leaver joined us in the Brenard copy room. Tony Hewson was a local West London lad with an ever-cheerful disposition and an outrageous sense of humour. After his stint as a junior, he chose not to take the accepted road of cub reporter, but to become Brenards' first photographic trainee, as an assistant to Bert Rees and Eddie Lawson, then the agency's only two photographers.

Tony's photographic schooling was undertaken in even more primitive surroundings and conditions than his editorial initiation. His company camera was an unreliable "spare," totally rejected by the incumbent photographers.

The "dark" room where he spent most of his working hours during those early months as he tried to memorise which lemonade bottle held hypo, was that canvas-walled extension

[1] *Newspapers deny this. I had always assumed it was part of newspaper policy to encourage reader participation!*

of the office caravan. Ever present was the threat of fogged negatives as the constant airport winds tore gaps through which daylight stabbed like a sheath knife through silk.

In spite of these pressures (or perhaps because of them) Tony went on to become a top-rate news cameraman, first in stills, and later in cine-film and video when the agency expanded into television. He was a craftsman in the technology of the darkroom, where most of the miracles of photographic journalism were produced. He and I worked as a team on countless stories over succeeding years with many front-page scoops in which words and pictures were totally compatible.

Resisting several tempting Fleet Street offers, Tony was, like me, bitten by the "airport bug" and chose to stay on with Brenards. He progressed to Chief Photographer, then Photographic Manager and even on to Photographic Director before his untimely death in 1983 from a second heart attack at the early age of 52.

Few of my copy-room contemporaries were as memorable as Tony. Indeed only one name of that brief era even comes to mind, though many were to follow later. "Gizzy" Ghisletta (he declined to tell us his Christian name) was as proud of his singing voice as he was of his Italian antecedents. He soon forsook the Brenard copy-room in favour of a job, as he told us, as editor of *Dance Band News*.

It was, he said, an influential and respected voice in the world of modern music, an epithet he no doubt expected to be applied equally to its "editor." Brenards, nevertheless, did become something of a preparatory school for many familiar and successful media names from the late '50s onwards.[1] This was all in the future; I was more concerned with the here and now. And my first major assignment away from Heathrow was to be disastrous.

"Bren" called me in one day after my early-duty sortie into the Heathrow arrival and departure lounges to tell me he was looking for a replacement at an outstation. Brian Coates, the former *Manchester Guardian* editorial assistant who had preceded me to Brenards the previous year, was due for his annual holiday, and someone was needed to cover for him. "How would you like to take over from him?" he asked.

I was flattered. I was excited... and I was fearful. I had hardly been left on my own as a reporter and now I was being asked to move into digs and cover the comings and goings of BOAC flying boats at Poole Marine Airport in Dorset. At 17 I would virtually be my own boss in a job I hardly knew, paying my own way and trying to get to know and rely upon airport and airline staff for information while expecting them to trust me to handle that information responsibly. "Yes, please," I said. How could I say "No"?

"Fine," said Bren. And as if sensing my inner doubts: "Just remember that every passenger has a story."

It was something every junior reporter heard from Bill Brenard. And in those early days of civil aviation it was not a great exaggeration. Holidays abroad were not the norm they were to become from the '60s. Except perhaps for the wealthy – who were often of interest to the news and gossip columns in their own right anyway.

So most travellers had a good reason for flying, particularly on longer, more expensive journeys. And many of them were only too happy to talk about it.

Not that it made it any easier for me to approach ordinary people, interrupt their conversations to introduce myself and ask them their business. It was something I never really conquered without making some quarter-truth excuse, like: "We're conducting a survey/doing some research...."

Even more difficult was explaining to the potentially newsworthy whom you were representing. If you simply said you were from "The Press," it begged the response: "Oh, yes. Which paper?"

To this ingenuous question there were several possible answers, most of which would invite time-consuming explanations and more questions. The name of "Brenards" meant nothing to the general public and invariably led to a lengthy description of the agency and its relationship with the newspapers. There was the danger of ending up becoming the interviewee, not the interviewer. The simplest solution, fortunately acceptable to the newspapers concerned especially when a particular story had been ordered in advance, was to say, "From the *Daily Express"* (or any specific newspaper, daily or evening, depending on the time of day).

[1] *See p.160 - 162 (prominent colleagues)*

Such a deliverance left me wondering what the subjects of the interview thought the next day on finding themselves splashed across the pages of up to three London evenings and eight national dailies, when they may have visualised an "exclusive" in one newspaper.

Sometimes, of course, with VIPs such as Government ministers and international statesmen, it was important to promote the name of Brenards, even if that meant spending a little more time than desirable.

Invariably with airport interviews, time is against the reporter. The arriving passenger is impatient to be on his way. Departing travellers are constantly on the alert for the call to their aircraft. A delayed flight is not always an advantage if edition times are pressing. Then the reporter is as anxious as the passenger for the 'plane to leave.

Now, away from London, I would have to make up my mind which identity to take on. Would it be more acceptable to represent myself as a freelance, which was a perfectly correct description of my agency? Most of the passengers I would be interviewing would be news nonentities. Unless, of course, something emerged which altered that...

*

Poole Marine Airport, in those early post-war days, was the flying-boat base for the long-haul services of British Airways predecessor, BOAC, to Singapore, Hong Kong and Australia. Long haul they certainly were – taking up to five days to reach Sydney. When the list of stops en route was announced at departure, across Europe, the Mediterranean, the Near East, India and southeast Asia, it sounded like the index to a Baedeker guide. (And seemed to take as long to announce as it does at the present time to fly the 12,000-miles entire one-stop route to Sydney.)

The Short "C" Class flying boats, originally built in the late 1930s for BOAC's predecessor, Imperial Airways, had seen service throughout the war years. For a brief spell after the war they had then competed with the Americans on the North Atlantic. Now they were being succeeded by an extended version, the "G" Class, and also by converted Sunderlands originally built for the RAF. Depending on the route, they carried a maximum of 24 passengers, which, together with an explicit passenger list, made it difficult for the publicity-shy to avoid contact with even the most unobservant press reporter.

BOAC's timetable for its flying boat services at Poole earned no marks for my convenience or Press edition times, however much it suited operations, or even the passengers. With an arrival at 6am and a departure at 6pm each day, I found myself working in two shifts, with many long hours of idleness in between.

My digs in Parkstone were within easy walking distance of the marine terminal, a mock-Tudor former hotel at a small inlet at Lilliput known as the Blue Lagoon, on the edge of Poole's huge harbour. Although extensively rebuilt, the building still survives as the clubhouse to a boat yard. Until the mid-eighties, its lounge bar still boasted the wicker chairs and round, light-oak coffee tables which once graced the airport departure lounge.

The early morning arrival and the departure in the evening (frequently extended because of delayed flights) made for a long working day. Had I been more experienced, I might have filled many of the long hours in between, getting to know the friendly and sympathetic BOAC staff, or learning more about the running of the terminal, digging out the occasional news story.

Instead, the net result of my month's high summer at Poole was probably no more than half a dozen stories, all "on the diary" – newsworthy departures or arrivals we had been advised of. And not one of those has been worthy of recall.

My only lasting memory of a news event at Poole was an hour's flight on the short-lived six-engined French flying boat, the Latécoère 631, which was being demonstrated to the British aviation press and to BOAC, a potential buyer.

Between glasses of champagne I interviewed the French Captain – the only reporter who did, or so I was assured. I also spoke to the senior BOAC man on board, who of course was totally noncommittal. And I talked to two or three passengers (the bubbly was very pleasant). One of them finally revealed he was the air correspondent of a leading French newspaper, but only after he'd given me a detailed description of the aircraft's design faults.

Picture courtesy of Jean-Claude Caillez, aviation historian

Although small by today's standards, the fuselage of the new but ill-fated French flying boat, the Latécoère 631, was larger and appeared roomier than most passenger flying boats of the 1940s and '50s, carrying up to 50 passengers. It was distinguished too by its unusual twin tail fins and 6 Wright R-2600-c14 engines carried on a high wing.

Later, I did wonder if he was really well informed or if a mere leg-pull was unintentionally prophetic. The prototype 631 and the first production model both crashed within weeks of that cross-Channel visit and Latécoère abandoned the design.

My south coast assignment at last completed, I flew back to London. I hitched a lift on a BOAC York airliner being ferried from the airline's maintenance base at Hurn, near Bournemouth, something I had been able to do most weekends. Flying time was half-an-hour. Bus and tube from Heathrow to my home in North London took about three times as long.

*

It was late summer before I returned to London Airport, anxious to restore my shattered self-confidence. I badly needed a chance to make up for my unproductive seaside posting.

By now, Brenards could boast a strong reporting team with Denis 'Forky' Forknell, Vera Nash, Helen Swain, my brother Harry and the two juniors, Ralph Churchill and Brian Coates. The single passenger terminal on Heathrow's north side was fully covered between the hours of six a.m. and eleven p.m.

Compared with later years, it seems now to have been an excessive number of reporters, even allowing for days off and holidays, when set against a total of only fifteen to twenty flights and a mere six or seven hundred passengers a day. But production was high, and the Heathrow-based reporting staff was frequently called on to travel out to other airports.

Neighbouring Northolt, Bovingdon in Hertfordshire, Blackbushe in Surrey and even Bournemouth's Hurn airport, were the principal diversion points for London-bound flights whenever bad visibility threatened Heathrow. And that was a constant peril in those days before the clean air laws dramatically cleared the smog. Manchester and Prestwick, too, took a fair share of ad hoc traffic at these times. Both were too far to drive in the time it took to divert an aircraft – but at the Scottish airport Brenards were represented. Manchester, too, would come later.

Midsummer saw another addition to the news team. A blond, blue-eyed discovery of Bill's from Christchurch, Hampshire, he had made a name for himself on the *Bournemouth Echo*. Ray Watts was soon to become the mainstay of that team, justifying Bill's foresight and eventually succeeding him as news director of the company.

His name became synonymous with Brenards and with Heathrow in every major newspaper office in the country and in news centres throughout Europe and America.

Ray Watts's favourite beat at Heathrow was to be Terminal 3, first opened in the early '60s. Throughout the next 25 years the terminal was the London base of all non-European intercontinental airlines. It was said that those airlines rarely took a decision about their London operations without consulting "Wattie" to learn if the decision was good for their image – though I'm not sure if it was Bill Brenard or Ray Watts himself who perpetrated that notion. Wattie was tragically killed in a late-night road accident in the mid-1980s.

With such a wealth of experience around me, life could have been daunting and difficult for a raw junior with no grounding at that time in local newspapers. In practice I was ever impressed by the encouragement I was given and the patience of unemotional newspaper people as I naïvely probed methods and motives in their newsgathering. It was only later I appreciated what a delicate area this could have been to trespass in. Only the wise fear to tread.

Contacts – the reporters' equivalent of the detective's informants or "narks" – were to a large extent, shared. Or at least the more "public" ones were. My secret dread, of being fed false, but seemingly reliable information, thankfully never became reality. Throughout the years I was never aware of having been intentionally misled.[1] Quite the opposite. I always found ordinary people willing to help with information, anxious to share their knowledge, even though "talking to the Press" was a disciplinary offence for so many airline and airport employees.

I was still somewhat surprised, and not a little flattered, when Hilary Watson, a BOAC sales representative whose prime responsibility was looking after the CIPs (those regular travellers who were judged to be commercially important to the airline) approached me one day. He chose to tell me, rather than a senior colleague, an interesting tale.

A group of airport porters, employed not by BOAC but by the Ministry of Aviation, at that time the owners and managers of the airport, had approached him. They were expressing their concern that the Prime Minister, Clement Attlee, was flying to Washington that weekend by the national airline's major rival, Pan American.

NARA picture

The post-war Prime Minister, Clement Attlee

The porters seemed to think that Hilary should be able to ensure that a British Prime Minister flew British. After all, on an almost daily basis he was regularly greeting the world's famous as old friends.

As a salesman, Hilary could have declared an interest. If he were able to show that he was influential in persuading the Prime Minister, of all people, to switch flights to BOAC, it could presumably only help his career. But he needed someone to work the miracle for him – and advised the porters that the best bet was the Press.

"Why don't you come along and talk to them?" he then asked me.

I was happy to do this, even though I half-thought that Hilary may have prompted the porters' view himself. But if he had, they gave no indication of it. Of the small group standing in the baggage hall, waiting for the next influx of passengers, I already knew one or two as useful contacts who almost certainly would have approached me or a colleague anyway. For these were the heady days of "the workers." The euphoria over a Labour Government which had swept to power with a huge majority after the war had not subsided. Labour Ministers and politicians were enjoying the kind of mass adulation usually reserved today for a pop star.

But for the moment Labour's MP's were the pop stars... and they were themselves ordinary people. And as the Labour Government was a government of the people and for the people, so was the publicly-owned BOAC the airline of the people, even if few of them could afford to use it. For the airport porters' own Prime Minister to fly the Atlantic on an American airline, the very symbol of capitalism, was totally alien to them.

I wasn't sure I could do anything, and I said so. I already had the essence of a story **("Airport Porters Protest as Labour PM Spurns BOAC"...?)** but it wasn't enough. Perhaps if Attlee knew of the protest and changed his flight? That would be a better story. It would also improve my standing as a Press reporter and impress the porters and Hilary Watson.

My problem was that I didn't really know what I could do, or how to go about doing it. With more experience, my first call would have been to Downing Street to establish the facts of the proposed trip. In the end it was probably my naivety that came to my rescue.

I was aware that Attlee was going to America to give a lecture, but whether as Prime Minister or as Labour leader I had no idea. It was late afternoon and I had little time to catch people at their offices. But I telephoned the Labour Party at Transport House. There, a press officer told me Attlee had been invited to the US by the Americans, but he hadn't any details to hand. The only person who knew all the background, he insisted,

[1] *With perhaps one exception - see Chap 6 (p138).*

was Morgan Phillips, the Party's General Secretary. Was he available? No, he'd gone home for the evening. I could have his telephone number. But he wouldn't be home for an hour or two.

I took the number with great delight. It was the first VIP telephone number to go into my "contacts" book. Then I impatiently waited for the hour to pass. At last I was able to dial. A woman's voice answered. His wife? A secretary?

"Could I speak to Mr Phillips?" I asked, identifying myself as "the Heathrow Press Room." To quote a senior civil servant of a later age, this was perhaps an economical truth. But I privately hoped that if there were a problem, it might be assumed my call was from an official press relations' office. I was asked to hold on – until the voice of Morgan Phillips with its recognisable Welsh lilt came on the line.

This time I carefully explained who I was and why I was calling. I told him how the airport porters felt. I emphasised the publicity value on both sides of the Atlantic to the airline carrying the Prime Minister. Photographs would show him mounting or descending steps to or from an aircraft where every riser displayed the airline's name, painted there just for that purpose. Of course, I had no axe to grind, but it was likely that the image of Britain's national carrier would be unfairly tarnished if the PM chose to fly American.

I hinted too that I knew BOAC had held a seat for Mr Attlee in the hope that he might switch flights at the last moment. But that would be a confidence between us.

The Labour Party General Secretary heard me out without interrupting. At the time I suspected he liked the conspiratorial touch. At last he said:

"Well, I understand the point and to me it seems a reasonable proposal. But I don't know that it's possible to do anything.

"Mr Attlee is a guest of the Americans; they are paying his fare. And of course it was they who booked him with PanAm. It might be discourteous to ask them to change it."

But would I leave it with him? And could I hold off any story until we'd spoken again?

"Call me tomorrow afternoon at Transport House," he said. "Go through the press office. I'll tell them to expect a call from you. And if I'm called away, I'll leave a message with them for you."

I reported back to the two or three porters I could find still on duty. I'd made a few telephone calls, I said, and hoped to have some news for them the next day – the eve of the PM's departure.

The following day I could hardly contain my impatience. I was fearful that somehow the story I was wet-nursing might leak, particularly if the Americans were involved. Perhaps I should have been satisfied with the original "protest" story. Then I consoled myself with the thought that PanAm were not likely to announce they had lost a VIP to a rival, particularly if they didn't know why.

It wasn't until lunchtime that Hilary buttonholed me. He was looking very pleased.

"You heard the news?" he asked, then went on: "We've done it, old boy. Clem…" (the abbreviated familiarity seemed to come naturally to him) "... has transferred to us. I heard an hour ago."

Then, before I could speak he added: "I've told the porters. They're delighted. And you have your story, don't you? Who did you speak to? Clem?"

I told him: "Not exactly." I wasn't going to explain further, but he forestalled any further comments of mine by adding:

"Of course, I could have asked him myself. But it would look as if I was touting for business. And we have an unwritten rule that we never poach each other's passengers.

"So you won't mention my role in this, will you, old chap?"

I reassured him and thanked him for the story.

"But it will have to wait until I get official confirmation from my sources," I said, "And I'm sure you won't object if I say that BOAC were only too pleased to offer a seat when approached?"

Later that day I called Transport House. Morgan Phillips was at a meeting. But he had left a message for me as he had promised.

"The Prime Minister's hosts have agreed, at his request, to switch his reservation from Pan American to BOAC. The departure time of the BOAC Monarch flight is more convenient."

That was all.

"But what about the porters and their appeal to the P.M.?" I asked.

"Sorry" said the Party's press spokesman. "Mr Phillips doesn't feel he can comment on that. But he does appreciate their motives for the request."

I dictated my story, such as it was, to our copyroom, marking it for circulation to "all dailies, *PA, Ex-Tel, UP* and *AP*." I was well aware that the American wire service coverage would carry my report to the United States, where in an abridged form it would not appear significant. I was more annoyed that the General Secretary's carefully worded statement virtually killed the real story, the reason for the eleventh-hour switch, for the British papers as well.

For that was to prove the case. Newspapers in London briefly reported the change of plan, interpreting the Labour Party statement to mean that it was simply a matter of convenience. The link with a bunch of London Airport porters, which my opening paragraph revealed, was apparently too tenuous for them. If only I'd been satisfied with my original story...

Nevertheless, my ego was riding high again. Story or no story, a 17-years-old cub reporter, I had been instrumental in changing a Prime Minister's plans. So this was the power of the Press!

*

Many years later, at a retirement party for a long-serving airport supervisor, I was chatting with one of his colleagues, Gordon Pankhurst, who had also worked at the airport from those early days. Reminiscing, he suddenly said: "Did I ever tell you how we changed a Prime Minister's mind?"

Before I could say: "I think I know what's coming...." He went on:

"It was in the days of the 1945 Labour Government – the first one after the war. The Prime Minister, Attlee, was flying to America...."

I couldn't resist interrupting and finishing the story for him, adding my sequel to his party piece. Unknown to me at the time, Gordon had been the porters' immediate supervisor and knew of their approach to the Press. As any activity of that kind was strictly against the rules, he couldn't become involved, so in his turn he was unaware of my part.

Strangely, Gordon had become a good friend and contact, and a constant source of information himself in later years. Gordon died in the late eighties. But not before I was able to tell him that Morgan Phillips's widow, Baroness Phillips, remembered the incident well.

She and I were fellow guests of honour at a Metropolitan Police lunch one day in 1983, and I mentioned the story to her. Surprisingly, she recalled:

"I remember taking your call. Morgan took your request very seriously. He called Clem immediately and I heard him advising the PM that the porters were quite right; he should change to BOAC if it could be arranged.

"That was typical of Morgan," she added, "But he would have been very sorry not to be able to give them the credit they deserved. That might have embarrassed the PM's hosts."

CHAPTER TWO

By mid-1947, Northolt Airport, only four miles from Heathrow by air, was already the busier of the two major West London airports.

The former Battle of Britain RAF fighter station was on loan to the Civil Aviation Ministry until permanent facilities for all airlines could be provided at the developing London Airport. Temporary prefabricated buildings offered arrival and departure accommodation on the newly developed southern side of the airfield, alongside the A40 Western Avenue at South Ruislip. The Royal Air Force retained a base adjoining the wartime aircraft hangars on the north side, where Transport Command set up a VIP reception point for British and foreign government special flights.

The civil terminal at Northolt became the principal London home of British European Airways and a number of European airlines, and its growth rapidly outstripped that of Heathrow. Because of the range of destinations and frequency of its services, Northolt was potentially a news centre as important as, if not more important than the No.1 London airport for a time.

Brenards' already boasted resident reporters at Prestwick Airport in Scotland, and at Shannon Airport in the Irish Republic, both busy transatlantic terminals. Now it was obvious that full-time coverage at Northolt was essential. It was also a major element in the company's case for convincing newspapers and other clients that monthly retaining fees were the only insurance against them missing out on the big airport stories.

Bill Brenard's solution was to ask Harry to take on Northolt – to set up a full-time base there. It was a move that was to prove valuable to the fortunes of the agency, significant for my brother and momentous for me.

Civil Aviation was very much a junior department of Government, and in practice was still the RAF in a demob suit. At both London Airport and Northolt, the men chosen to oversee and nurture the infant industry were retired RAF "top brass"– Air Marshal Sir John D'Albiac at Heathrow, and Air Vice Marshal "Simposh" Simpson at Northolt sharing the archaic title of Commandant of their respective territories.

Though quite different personalities, they shared a skill in welding together teams of civil servants recruited from such diverse departments as the Air Ministry, the Ministries of Works, Information, Food, Agriculture and Fisheries, the War Office and the three services to organise and plan the development of the civil airports. But their attitudes to the news media were far from similar. Sir John, ever sympathetic and understanding, saw the need for an enthusiastic and supportive Press. His opposite number at Northolt viewed media needs and activities as a barely necessary intrusion.

Because of its long-distance services the major focus of Press attention was inevitably aimed at Heathrow. In addition to Brenards (we quickly lost the possessive apostrophe), staff reporters from the London *Evening Standard* and the *Daily Telegraph* were originally based there, as were two or three photographers, principally from the international photo-agency of *PA-Reuters.*

The Ministry of Civil Aviation's response to this interest was to install a Press Officer at Heathrow and provide a "Press Room." A windowless office just off the Arrivals Hall measuring some ten feet by fifteen, it boasted a table, two threadbare armchairs and a telephone extension from the airport's manual switchboard – strictly for on-airport calls only.

Harry's first request at Northolt was for a similar Press Room and telephone. The AVM's deputy, airport manager Leslie Green, (later to become manager, then General Manager, at Heathrow) was already having difficulty meeting the accommodation demands of newly-emerging airlines at Northolt. Even so, he offered a military caravan, smaller but similar to many caravans still serving as Heathrow private offices.

With its camouflage paint and army insignia only partly obscured by a fresh topcoat of some anonymous muddy wash, it bore over its central doorway the proud name-plate "Press Office." The caravan appeared one dawn on a patch of grass alongside a block of cream-painted prefab offices – and was promptly claimed by a squatter. Humphrey

Downes was the first press spokesman for British European Airways at the airport, and one of many non-operational airline staff still waiting to be housed.

"I'm the Press Officer, old boy," he said, pompously, when Harry, finding him ensconced, protested. "And that," pointing to the sign, "that says 'Press Office.' So it must mean me.

"Possession, old boy, is nine points and all that. I'm here and here I stay."

He meant it too, turning a deaf ear to Harry's protests: that "Press Office" was a mistake and should have read "Press *Room*,"[1] a subtle difference which had escaped the Ministry's sign painters; that Downes could easily check to see if his airline management had signed a tenancy agreement for a caravan.

It was only after Harry finally appealed to Leslie Green that the obstinate squatter was evicted. I don't believe Humphrey ever recovered from the trauma. It was certainly some time before BEA finally gave him his own Press Office. And he didn't bear any unjustified grudges. He and Harry were soon on good terms again when he realised how much free publicity BEA could get from a good relationship with the resident Press man.

Brenard Press picture

The cub reporter filing copy (dictating) from the Northolt Airport press room to Brenards news desk at Heathrow (circa 1947-48)

With his capacity for making friends and building contacts, as well as his instinct for a good story, Harry very quickly put Northolt on the map in news terms. This was to the confusion of newspaper copy-takers and sub-editors who either didn't know the difference or couldn't believe that more European destinations were served from Northolt than Heathrow. Some regularly and mistakenly substituted "Heathrow" for "Northolt" when a VIP was the subject of a news item.

In no time, the value of Northolt as a news centre became overwhelming. Long hours of coverage were needed to meet the demands of the evening and daily newspapers, to say nothing of Sunday newspapers and the big agencies. Most of these clients were by now paying Brenards a monthly retainer for a regular service. A second Northolt-based reporter was essential. And who better to provide a back-up to Harry than his kid brother? Or so I concluded when the offer came from Bill for me to join him.

I welcomed this new opportunity. Now I could learn my trade from someone who would have the patience and the sympathy to answer my constant questioning, who wouldn't be jealous of sharing "special" contacts. Someone who might happily encourage me to take over his story ideas and take the credit for the end result! I was soon to learn that some news stories might have their darker side...

*

The muffled voices gave nothing away as I strained to learn the identity of the caller. It was still light on an early autumn evening and so far my father and I were the only ones home from work. The rush hour had still not peaked in North London and there were few people on the streets. It was an unlikely time for visitors.

The flat, hollow thud of the cast-iron knocker on the heavy door had been loud and demanding. "All right. I'll go," grunted my father as he rose from his chair.

I had come in just a few minutes earlier after completing a 20-mile journey by tube from Northolt, and was pouring myself some tea from the still steaming pot. I was aware of the receding patter of his slippered feet on the linoleum-covered floor of the empty hallway. The latch turned.

A mumbled question and answer exchange drifted back. It seemed to last for several minutes. Then the footsteps returned alone. My father seemed perplexed, annoyed, as he re-entered the room.

"There's some evil-looking character asking for you," he said, "And he won't go away until he sees you."

I must have frowned with puzzlement as I pushed back my chair. Then I caught his intense look.

"What have you been up to?" he demanded irritably. "I don't like this kind of situation. I don't want you bringing trouble home – you can leave this sort of thing behind you at work." I didn't attempt an answer. I didn't know what "this sort of thing" was; though an uncomfortable suspicion was already beginning to take shape. I hurried to the door my

[1] *A base or assembly area provided for reporters and cameramen.*

father had closed in the face of the caller. My heart thumping, I opened it gingerly.

There in front of me, a triumphant, almost malevolent half-smile on his lips, one foot already poised to block the door at its threshold, stood the man I thought I'd left behind me two hours earlier on the other side of London. The man who had sought me out at the airport, pleaded with me, then threatened me. The man I thought I had been quick-thinking enough to outwit and escape so easily.

Now suddenly here he was, on my doorstep, invading my world. On foot, by bus, by underground train with its two interchanges, he had obviously followed me every step of the way. And I had been completely oblivious of him.

"Why have you come here?" I stammered. Ignoring the challenge in my tone, he thrust a threatening finger under my nose.

"I warned you," he snarled. "I warned you there would be consequences if you wrote anything about my friend. You wouldn't listen. You could have made some money for yourself. But you threw it back at him...."

*

Harry decided we should very quickly split the Northolt coverage between us, with two daily shifts from 7am to 3pm and 2pm to 10pm. The hour's overlap enabled us to exchange information on running events, and me to seek advice on the best way of presenting a particular story picked up earlier in the day. It was Harry who showed me how to get the best out of any story; how an "angle" or a turn of phrase could mean the difference between publication or the sub's spike, even with the most staid of "quality" newspapers.

He also showed me how, in interviewing, the questions were as important as the answers. That often those answers depended on the way the questions had been put. That not infrequently the subject welcomed the words the reporter was apparently putting into their mouths – not everyone is as articulate as they think they are or would like to be.

I began building my own contacts, among airline staff, the airport police, Customs, even the secretive immigration officials and their more laid-back colleagues sharing the passport control desks, the officers of Scotland Yard's Special Branch.

It was from one such contact I had my first "refusal." This is not simply a description of a passenger's response to my attempts at interrogation, although this was also the case on this occasion. It is also the colloquial term for any visitor to Britain who is turned back at the passport control entry point.

The official terminology was more explicit in those early years. "Undesirable alien" or "papers not in order" were phrases frequently used for the apparently innocuous traveller who is unable to satisfy immigration officers that he or she is a suitable and welcome visitor to Britain. "Refused permission to land" is less offensive and less specific.

In the aftermath of war there were hundreds of thousands of refugees prepared to try their luck at breaching national frontier controls. They had, after all, nothing to lose.

My Special Branch acquaintance moved to my side as I stood thumbing through a news magazine at the bookstall in Northolt's departures lounge.

"Don't look now," he said softly, "But there's someone over in the corner you might like to tackle. Immigration have refused him. He's being sent back on the next flight to Vienna."

He briefly described the man, but to my question he would only say: "Can't tell you why. You'll have to ask him. But he's not a nice piece of work at all."

And before I could ask him for more information...even a name...he moved away simply muttering; through the side of his mouth: "I didn't tell you a thing."

No, I thought to myself, you didn't. Where would I start? I turned and looked the man over. To me he looked totally inoffensive. He could have been a middle-aged bank clerk, or the proprietor of a corner tobacconist shop. Dressed in a grey herringbone overcoat and soft felt hat, he seemed resigned, at ease, as he calmly awaited the flight that was to take him back to Austria only an hour after his arrival in Britain. Shortly afterwards I approached the man and identified myself.

He shot out of his seat like a frightened rabbit looking for an escape hole. His lips quivered and he stammered:

"You won't do this. You cannot...."

And he pleaded: "I beg you. If it is known I have been turned away my life will be in danger. You must not publish this."

My instinctive response would have been to say: "Hold on, I don't know anything. You don't have anything to fear," but I realised I must let him believe the opposite, and hope that something would emerge if I could keep him talking.

"Why do you think you think you've been refused entry?" I asked, implying that I knew the secret. But he ignored the question. And simply repeating, "Don't do this," he suddenly thrust both his hands into the pockets of his overcoat and pulled out handfuls of currency notes, pushing them at me, cramming them into my hands and jacket pockets. As some inevitably fell, crumpled, to the floor at our feet, I realised they were US dollar bills of several denominations, twenties, fives and singles. There must have been three or four hundreds in value, a small fortune to me.

I stepped back, horrified, dropping more bills, pulling others from my pockets. I was being bribed!

"But you don't understand," I said, "It's too late. I've already filed... phoned in... a story. I can't stop it now." And, I added intrepidly and somewhat tardily: "Your money can't help you. I don't want it."

I had indeed filed a brief report to Brenards' news desk only 15 minutes earlier, just before making my approach to the man. The first editions of the evenings were going to press soon after 8 am, and I was anxious to catch them with a simple paragraph on a "mystery man barred." It might whet their appetites for more though I didn't really expect that a chat with the passenger would add anything to a relatively unimportant item. But I did wonder then, and have wondered since, whether journalistic ideals or my non-existent bank funds would have won the day if my story hadn't already been actioned.

In the event that was the end of my "interview." My victim decided silence was his best escape. Quickly he gathered up the crumpled notes around his feet, turned and scuffled away to a far corner of the lounge. For me, I thought, it was also the end of the news story. There was nothing I could add.

But somehow, after I left him behind in the lounge, the visitor had succeeded in making contact with an associate who was to have met him on his arrival in Britain, and who was still on the airport. Within minutes of my return to the Press Room to ponder on whether I could provide an "add" to my earlier copy without referring to a personal involvement, this associate had sought me out and was barging in on me. He thrust back the door without knocking and with no pretence at introductions, snarled:

"I hear you've been upsetting a business friend of mine."

His loud check overcoat and rakish pork pie hat hardly supported his implied claim to be a respectable businessman himself, when I demanded to know who he was and of whom he was talking. He soon made his interests clear, but gave no personal details, simply insisting that I withdraw my story about his "friend's" problems with the British Home Office.

My retort that the story had no great significance and that as a news item it would fade away once his friend's aircraft had left, failed to satisfy him. He demanded that I telephone my "editor" so that he could speak directly to him. I told him I would be happy to pass on any message for him, but began to wonder why the incident was apparently so important.

My revived interest must have become obvious. He suddenly changed tack again. "You'll be sorry you're not being very co-operative," he announced finally. And with a parting: "Have it your way," he marched out just as quickly as he had arrived a few minutes earlier.

I sat and pondered this development. At last I decided enough was enough. I had no essential details apart from the mystery passenger's surname (won from a helpful airgirl) and the information that he was "stateless." Immigration officials would never tell me the reason for refusing the man permission to enter the country, other than that unforgiving tag of "undesirable alien." Anything I wrote would be desperately short on facts and would pose too many questions to which I had no answers.

My Special Branch man was still on duty, and I sought him out. Even this took time, as I had to catch his eye from a distance between departing flights, and hope he would leave his desk to join me. Eventually I was able to tell him of my exchange of views with my caller. He seemed unsurprised by the development, but insisted he knew nothing of the background. He would only offer to "have a quiet chat" with his Immigration Office colleagues that evening. With any luck, he said, he might be able to give me a follow-up the next day.

I wasn't convinced. I had the impression that he was regretting his involvement, and I decided to call it a day. I wanted to be home early, and I had a long journey in front of me: a half-mile walk to a bus stop, followed by at least an hour's journey on the Underground, with two changes to get me to North London. By the time I reached there I had skimmed through three evening newspapers. My story had made a brief in only two of them and I brushed the incident aside. Despite that glimmer of suspicion, I was still unprepared when my father told me of my unexpected visitor.

The figure framed in the doorway had stepped forward. His pointing finger was inches from my face as he accosted me. I recalled my father's "evil-looking character," thinking how apt the description was. He was hardly the essence of benevolence. I broke in and halted his tirade. I had no wish to be seen arguing with him on the doorstep. I certainly had no intention of inviting him inside. Just telling him to go wasn't likely to be effective. As calmly and quietly as I could, though I was feeling a coldness in the pit of my stomach, I said, "We can't talk here. Let's go to the pub."

The Duke of Edinburgh, only a hundred yards from my home, was geographically if not colloquially my "local." But neither my father nor I was particularly familiar with the place. In my case it was probably because I had only recently turned eighteen. If I'd wanted to indulge in under-age drinking it would have been wiser away from my own doorstep.

As we took a seat a few feet from the bar, however, I wished fervently that I could have addressed the barman by his first name. A regular customer might reasonably expect some level of protection from a landlord. Even some familiarity between us might inhibit any unfriendly intent.

In reality I needn't have worried. Over a pint of mild my pursuer appeared to mellow. It may have been because I was able to act calm and coldly undisturbed (in truth I was concerned and angered at the invasion of my privacy; an irrational response for a reporter). Or possibly it was his satisfaction at successfully trailing me all the way across London.

It was certainly strange that in no time at all he was apparently accepting my assurances that his unhappy associate was no longer news, something I'd been trying to tell him from the start. I did not say I had milked the situation dry, or that there was a very slight chance of a follow-up the next day. Neither did I allow him to think I was looking for an escape route.

As he was obviously not prepared to fill in all the gaps in my knowledge or respond to my constant cross-questioning on why the incident was so important (I was growing bolder by the minute), there was nothing more to print. He finally reached this conclusion himself, and with a curt "Right," suddenly stood up, turned and left, looking quite pleased with himself. This time there was no parting threat.

The experience, coupled with the explanations and guarantees I had to give my father, who didn't hold with mixing it with criminals (his words) destroyed any lingering thoughts about following the mystery further. A year or two later and I might have dug my heels in. But my journalistic career was still too fragile to be risked on a Hollywood-style adventure. And I hadn't yet heard of investigative journalism.

When I spotted the same man a few months later in a departure hall at Heathrow, he was with a group of three or four others. I called the airport's Special Branch office. My contact there wasn't available, but after a brief explanation from me referring only to my earlier encounters, a colleague of his hurried along to join me at a nearby buffet. I pointed out "my" man.

"Hmm, that's interesting," mused my companion. "You know who he's with?" He indicated a smaller man with greying fair hair in a smartly cut grey suit. "That's Cyril B-----. We think he's the leader of the Ladder Gang. But I don't know your man. He's a bit flash, isn't he?"

The Ladder Gang had earned a reputation in the preceding few months for raids on wealthy homes in the west London suburbs. Their modus operandi was to use ladders borrowed from building sites, always forcing entry at an upper level.

My visitor made another appearance at Heathrow a year or two later. This time he seemed to be a close confidant of someone I did recognise, and had met on a couple of occasions. His new companion was London gang boss Jack Spot, would-be rival of another self-styled king of the underworld, Billy Hill and the up-and-coming Kray twins.

Brenard Press picture

The reporter's notebook seems to worry some people, so mine stayed intentionally out of sight when I approached London crime gang boss Jack Spot, (seen here in dark glasses) at Heathrow as he was about to board a flight with an "aide." On this occasion the reputed organiser of the great airport gold bullion raid of the late 1940s understandably had nothing to say to me and just ignored my questions.

(also see Chapter 14)

Spot (aliases "Benny the Kid," Jack Comer, or Comacho) was thought at one stage to have been involved in an international money-laundering and currency-smuggling ring. No charges were ever brought. But my undesirable alien's pocket change could have been dirty money in more ways than one.

In these years before the huge increase in asylum seekers and illegal immigration attempts, it was not often that we were able to establish the reason behind "refused permission to land" decisions made by the Home Office or its immigration department officers. The subjects themselves nevertheless often appeared willing to talk to us. Some, like the young "photographic models" who regularly flew to London from the Continent in search of work, expressed bewilderment and anger at their treatment. They invariably protested about being held in a "prison cell," though the detention rooms at the airport were usually carpeted and comfortably if sparsely furnished.

Some refusals were philosophical, as if they were expecting to be barred, like the monocled, elderly French woman, who would only shrug and repeat, "C'est la vie," when I questioned her. Then there was the young Danish student who arrived with no money, no return ticket and no contact address in Britain. When, unprotesting, he was told he couldn't stay, he forgivingly presented immigration staff with two dozen fresh eggs and an assortment of a dozen Danish cheeses before re-boarding his Copenhagen flight.

Occasionally, the Immigration staff seemed sympathetic… but still unbending, as in the case of the pretty 23-years-old girl, also from Copenhagen, who had flown to London on a whim. For five years she had worked alongside her mother in a family sweet shop, but ran out after a row. Stopped at Heathrow, she was escorted aboard a homeward bound flight in tears. "I was told I had to go back because I had no work permit," she sobbed to me. "I begged them to send me anywhere but Copenhagen. I can't bear to face my mother again.

"They said they were sorry, but they had no choice."

It took the immigration authorities a little longer to come to a decision in the case of a senior Greek priest. It was a full four years after his appointment as Archimandrite of the Greek Orthodox Church in London that a deportation order was issued on the orders of the Home Secretary. The priest, Kallinikos Macheriotis, 42, was put aboard an Athens-bound flight after being escorted to London Airport by Scotland Yard officers.

A Home Office spokesman told me the deportation was ordered "in the public interest," but declined to give further information. One police officer travelled all the way to Athens with Macheriotis, who as Archimandrite ranked just below Archbishop in the Greek Orthodox Church. Neither his parishioners nor his colleagues in the London church knew of the deportation order or the reasons for it, and were not aware of his detention until after the flight had left Heathrow.

The deportation made Page One leads in both the *Evening Standard* and the *Evening*

News, though I could only claim part credit for that, as much of the background was contributed by staff reporters. But there appeared to be one glaring conflict between my story and information attributed to the Home Office in the *Standard.* I reported that the priest was escorted on the flight to Athens by one of the Yard officers, a point confirmed by the passenger list. The Home Office apparently told an enquiring Fleet Street reporter that the deported priest had left without an escort.

Evening Standard

41,058 TUESDAY, JUNE 12, 1956 Twopence

LONDON PRIEST DEPORTED BY AIR TO GREECE

'Decision in the public interest'

Evening Standard Reporter

On the orders of the Home Secretary, Mr. Lloyd George, a priest of the Greek Orthodox Church, who worked in London, has been secretly deported "in the public interest."

He was put on an airplane bound for Athens at London Airport last night.

His name is Kallinikos Macheriotis. He was Archimandrite (an office roughly equivalent to archdeacon) at the Greek Orthodox Church of All Saints in Pratt Street, Camden Town.

No escort

"The order for his deportation was made by the Home Secretary in the public interest," said a Home Office official.

"The priest left without escort. The Home Secretary has powers to make such an order if he considers it necessary."

It is understood that Scotland Yard officers visited the Archimandrite at his home

"The priest left without escort. The Home Secretary has powers to make such an order if he considers it necessary."

There were 41 passengers aboard the Viscount. The Archimandrite and his escort were the only people to go as far as Athens; the rest of the passengers left the plane at Milan. The plane landed at Athens at 9.35 a.m.

FLOWN BACK TO ATHENS

"Evening News" Reporter

A 42-YEAR-OLD Greek, Kallinikos Macheriotis, in charge of the Greek Orthodox Church in Pratt-street, Camden Town, has been deported by order of the Home Secretary.

A Home Office spokesman said Macheriotis was put aboard a plane bound for Athens last night.

His deportation was ordered "in the public interest," the spokesman said

Macheriotis came to this country about four years ago. He bore the title of Archimandrite—which in the Greek Orthodox Church ranks below the Archbishop.

The bearded Greek was escorted to the plane by Special Branch officers. Yesterday Scotland Yard officers went to his flat in Camden Town.

SWIFTLY

Secretly

The Archimandrite left London Airport at 1.45 a.m to-day aboard B.E.A service No. 132.

There were 41 passengers aboard the Viscount. The Archimandrite and his escort were the only people to go as far as Athens; the rest of the passengers left the plane at Milan. The plane landed at Athens at 9.35 a.m.

(above) Evening Standard, part Page One lead, and (right) Evening News, part Page One lead, (both) June 12 1956

Note the difference in the enlarged paragraphs. My story, the passenger list and the Evening News paragraph all contradicted the Home Office spokesman.

When a new detention block overlooking the tarmac was opened in the administrative offices of the Queen's Building at Heathrow in 1956, it became temporary quarters for a Jewish Rabbi and his family of eight. The family, Rabbi Brief, his wife and their daughter, Mrs Berkowitz and her five children, had arrived from Tel Aviv via Brussels and announced that they planned to spend two weeks in London with relatives. They were refused permission to enter the country.

After their passports had been checked and immigration officers had questioned them for more than an hour, they were told they would be returned to Brussels on the next flight that evening. When the Rabbi protested that as orthodox Jews they could not travel on the Sabbath, due to begin at sunset – they were taken to the detention rooms to spend the next 24 hours.

The Home Office refused to say why the family had been barred, but they did allow them to spend a short time with relatives who had driven to the airport to meet them. One of them told me: "We spoke with the immigration office but they wouldn't tell us a thing.

OUT FAMILY OF 8 BARRED

A RABBI, his wife, his daughter and five grandchildren were banned from staying in Britain yesterday.

Rabbi Brief, his wife, his daughter Mrs. Berkowitz and her five young children landed at London Airport in an airliner from Brussels —and were still there 12 hours later.

(above) Daily Sketch
(right) Daily Mail
(both) Sep 29 1956

Rabbi banned at airport

By Daily Mail Reporter

THE recently opened detention block at London Airport this morning housed a Jewish family of eight who had earlier been refused admission to the country.

The family, Rabbi Brief and his wife and their daughter, Mrs. Berkowitz and her five children, arrived from Tel-Aviv via Brussels early yesterday, planning to spend two weeks in London with relatives at Stoke Newington.

After their passports had been checked and they had been questioned they were told that they could not enter Britain, and must return to Brussels on the next plane.

Seats were found for them on a British airliner leaving at 3 p.m., but Rabbi Brief immediately protested that as orthodox Jews, they could not travel on the Sabbath—which began at sunset yesterday.

So airline officials arranged for the family to spend the night under police guard in the detention block.

They were allowed a few minutes talk with a relative, whose wife said last night: "There was no question of them settling over here. We cannot discover why the authorities are sending them back."

Rabbi and family of 7 sent back

BEARDED Rabbi Israel Brief, his wife, daughter and five grandchildren came to Britain for a fortnight—and were hustled back to Brussels last night after 36 hours.

They landed at London Airport on Friday, and the immigration men who examined their passports wanted to send them back by the next plane.

But Rabbi Brief protested. "We are orthodox Jews," he said. "We are not allowed to travel on the Sabbath, which begins at Friday sundown."

So their names were hurriedly struck off the outward passenger list, and the family trooped to the new detention block, spending the night in apartments furnished like a first-class hotel suite.

The Home Office refused to say why the family were not allowed to stay.

The People *30 Sep 1956*

There was no question of the Rabbi settling here, so we don't understand what the problem is."

The Rabbi may have *wanted* to leave Israel. Former RAF wartime flyer Peter Arton, on the other hand, opted to make his home there, though only under protest. Like others suddenly expelled from Britain, the 32-years-old Czech-born businessman was escorted by Scotland Yard detectives to his Tel Aviv-bound airliner at Heathrow. He had been held in Brixton prison for three weeks after his detention but was released a few hours before his departure so that he could be married, and was escorted to a London register office by a detective.

Arton was accused by the Home Office of passing information about Czech exiles in Britain to the Communist regime in Prague. As he was stateless himself, he was allowed to choose his destination on deportation, and he chose Israel, which agreed to take him. His 26-years-old English-born bride, Claudia Michaels of St John's Wood, had approached newspapers about her fiancé's treatment by the authorities, so the wedding was well publicised. But it was my story of the departure from Heathrow, which had the best coverage – thanks to Claudia who went into exile with him.

Her parting gesture was to stick out her tongue to airport staff as she proclaimed: "I am English to the core and downright ashamed of it. Sending Peter away has ruined both our lives."

Arton, too, was still proclaiming his innocence of the charges. He claimed a statement he had prepared for the Press had been taken from him by police, and added: "The charges made against me are ridiculous. I haven't even mixed in Czech circles since I left Prague before the war, and I haven't passed information about Czechs to the Czech Government or anyone else.

"If the British Government want to put me on trial I would happily come back and defend myself. But they haven't any evidence."

The girl who put her tongue out . . .

BRIDE PUTS OUT TONGUE

Daily Sketch Reporter

PETER ARTON, former R.A.F. navigator, was married in London yesterday — and five hours later was put aboard a plane, to be deported to Israel.

His bride, formerly Miss Claudia Michaels, aged 26, flew with him.

Her parting shot was to put out her tongue to airline staff after saying:

"I am English to the core and downright ashamed of it. Sending Peter away has ruined both our lives."

I'M NO SPY

Earlier, in his father's £15-a-week luxury flat in Portland-place, W., Arton, who is 32 and was born in Czechslovakia, said:

"I am not a spy or a traitor. I have never betrayed anyone.

"If at any time the British Government think they have a case against me I will come back and gladly stand trial."

Thirty wedding guests sipped drinks and chatted in undertones.

Arton, in a grey pin-stripe suit, grey check tie and white shirt, looked tired and pale. He has been detained in Brixton, awaiting deportation, since last month.

He said: "The suggestion that I have given information to Communist embassies is ridiculous. I have not given information to anyone.

"The police have followed me since 1952. They have never said anything definite against me."

(above) Daily Mirror picture
(right) Daily Sketch
(both) April 21 1954

The evidence for a considerable number of refusals however, particularly in the case of visiting show-business entertainers who were stopped at the passport control desks, was usually quite clear. In most cases they were simply unable to produce a work permit, an essential piece of paper in those days for anyone planning to do a job of work for payment in Britain. For others with temporary residential status here, a re-entry certificate was essential.

Prima ballerina Nathalie Leslie was returning to London after completing a tour of Canada with Anton Dolin and his British Festival Ballet. At Scotland's Prestwick Airport, where her aircraft made its first UK touchdown, immigration officers asked for her re-entry permit. It was not in her passport. She was given "permission to land" and allowed to fly on to London while further enquiries were made. But at Heathrow she was detained for a further three hours. She was finally freed after officials discovered that her application for re-entry, which had been lodged in the United States, had been held up at the American Embassy in London.

Beautiful, elfin-eyed French actress Yvonne Monlaur was a frequent working visitor to Britain, spending many months here filming in the late 1950s. But that apparently meant little to the Immigration department when she returned in 1960 to make ***"Terror of the Tongs"*** opposite Britain's Christopher Lee.

As revealed by my *Daily Express* story, elevated to page one with a first class accompanying picture by Brenard photographer Peter Ward, Miss Monlaur on this occasion got as far as the passport checks at London Airport only to learn from Home Office staff: "Sorry, you can't come in." The reason: no work permit.

The 22-years-old actress, who had flown in from Rome accompanied by her mother, Countess Bedot de Monlaur, protested. The work permit had been applied for weeks earlier, and should have been waiting for her. Immigration men agreed to consult with representatives of Yvonne's intended employers, Hammer Films, and with the Ministry of Labour, who were dealing with the application.

But this would take time. So the actress and her mother were taken back to an arrivals transit lounge, still technically outside Britain, to await a decision. There, as my colleague captured Miss Monlaur's bewilderment on camera, she told me:

"I feel like a robber. Never in my life have I had troubles like these. In France, in Italy, in Spain, in Germany, I am allowed to travel without all this filling of forms." It was more than an hour and half before the Immigration officers returned. There had been a hitch.

Equity, the actors' union, had lodged an objection to the application for a work permit. They thought Yvonne's role should be given to a British actress. But the Home Office was prepared to compromise. Yvonne would be allowed in on a two-weeks visitors' permit. And a Hammer Films man told me: "We think we've a good case for employing Miss Monlaur. If we can get the union to agree, we may be able to obtain a work permit within a week."

"Terror of the Tongs" was successfully completed. Miss Monlaur starred as planned.

FOR 90 MINUTES SHE IS BARRED FROM BRITAIN

Never has horror girl Yvonne met such troubles

Express Staff Reporter

THERE she sat for 90 minutes last night, barred from Britain—the chestnut-haired, elfish-eyed actress Yvonne Monlaur.

And she is a countess too—in the widely dispersed French aristocracy.

She flew into London Airport from Rome so happily. Her mother, Countess Bedot de Monlaur, was with her.

Yvonne had come to start work on a new British horror film, "Terror of the Tongs."

She stepped, smiling, to the immigration desk. And then—no more smiles. No work permit!

Home Office men shook their heads sadly and told 22-year-old Yvonne: "You can't come in."

A hurried consultation with representatives of Hammer Films, Yvonne's intended employers, followed. An application had been filed for a working permit, they said.

Waiting

Immigration men checked with the Ministry of Labour. But the inquiry took time.

Yvonne and her mother were shown into a lounge OUTSIDE the Customs barrier—and still technically OUTSIDE Britain.

Said Yvonne: "I feel like a robber. The officers they were very kind, so charming.

"But never in my life have I had troubles like these. In France, in Italy, in Spain, in Germany, I am allowed to travel without all this filling in of forms."

At last the Immigration men came back. There had been a hitch, they said. Equity, the actors' union, had lodged an objection to the application for Yvonne's working permit.

But they were prepared to compromise. Yvonne would be allowed to land on a two-week visitors' permit.

Said the film company: "We were due to start work on Monday. Miss Monlaur has already made three films here.

"If we can get the union to agree we may be able to get a working permit through by next week."

And Yvonne? She smiled again—for a photographer.

Brenard Press picture by Peter Ward, Daily Express

It was more than the simple lack of a work permit that led to the barring of a 16-years-old American who stepped from a transatlantic airliner at Prestwick Airport in March, 1963, soon after the start of my posting there. Lovesick Danny Pritchard had flown more than 3,000 miles from his home in Idaho on a whim, just to look up his pen-pal, 17-years-old Cathie McPhee of Plockton, Ross-shire.

Trouble was he hadn't been invited, wasn't expected, and had made up his mind that (unasked) he was going to stay indefinitely, with Cathie and her family, mother, father and 8 brothers in a small isolated croft.

Immigration officers at the Scottish airport took a long look at Danny, and noted his grimy baseball cap, his shabby, ill-fitting clothes... his one-way ticket from New York, and the mere £8 he had in his pocket. All his possessions were in a small bag he carried. They decided to ask the Ross-shire police to make "further enquiries."

A Plockton village policeman set out to contact the McPhees. At last, while Danny waited, he reported back. Cathie's father, said the policeman, "...knows nothing of Danny Pritchard except as someone his daughter writes to." And what was worse, for Danny: "Cathie McPhee says she doesn't want to see him. She never asked him to come and she thinks he's taking a liberty.

"She now says she wants to forget all about him. She has already tried to stop him writing."

For the Immigration officers to settle the matter, Danny would have to return to Idaho on the first available flight. He was escorted to a detention room to await the return flight of his BOAC airliner the following day. And it was in the departure lounge that my colleague Chris Bramwell found him. Danny told him: "Cathie told me in a letter that she had ten brothers and sisters and one more in the house wouldn't make any difference. She practically invited me over. I thought I could soon get a job here."

The story tickled the fancy of the Glasgow evenings and the Scottish nationals. The *Scottish Daily Mail* and the *Scottish Daily Express* each gave it twelve inches on an inside page while the *Daily Record* made it their second lead on Page One.

By the mid-sixties, Home Office secrecy about "refusals" was more relaxed. Concerned, perhaps by frequent publicity, charges of inhumanity and an apparently cavalier attitude to some cases by individual officers, spokesmen began to replace their standard "no comment" response to enquiries with positive and more explicit information. When an American teen-age couple who also flew into Prestwick were honest enough to tell the immigration staff that they were on a busking tour of Europe and were planning to "sing for our suppers," they were quickly informed that they would not be permitted to land in Britain.

Arrangements were made to hold seats for them on the first

Daily Record MON MAR. 4 1963

3D SCOTLAND'S NATIONAL NEWSPAPER No. 21,010

No love for the roving Romeo

DANNY PRITCHARD wanted a girl-friend—so he flew more than 4000 miles to find one.

But when 16-year-old Danny stepped from a plane at Prestwick Airport at the week-end, immigration officials took a long look at him.

They noted his peaked baseball cap and ill-fitting clothes . . . his one-way ticket from New York . . . and the £8 he had in his pocket.

They asked him what his means were. He thought the British Government would give him money till he found a job.

He had come to woo pretty Cathie McPhee, 17, who lives in a croft near the village of Plockton, Ross-shire.

'Double-crossed'

A phone call was made to the local policeman at Plockton, who contacted Cathie's father. He said he knew nothing about Danny.

AND LAST NIGHT THE ROVING ROMEO WAS HOME IN IDAHO COMPLAINING: "I WAS DOUBLE-CROSSED."

DANNY PRITCHARD

But Cathie McPhee said: "If he writes to me again I'll throw his letters in the fire. I never took him seriously."

The youngsters first got in touch through a pen-pal club run by a teenage film magazine.

Drawled Danny: "American girls won't have anything to do with me because of my complexion. I have been looking for a girl-friend for three years."

He claimed Cathie had told him that as her father already supported her 10 brothers and sisters he could easily manage one more.

Cathie, a senior pupil at Plockton Secondary School, said last night: "We started writing a year ago but I never took him seriously."

Her father said: "I told the immigration people I knew nothing about him apart from the fact he was Cathie's pen-pal."

Her mother, Mrs Katie McPhee said: "We got an awful surprise when we heard he was here in Scotland. What possessed him to come?"

Lonely

The Italian mum of a teen-age girl asked the same question LAST summer when Danny flew on a one-way ticket to Modena from America.

To pay for his latest jaunt Danny plans to sell his collection of firearms. "I've got revolvers and rifles and two heavy machine guns," he said.

"I'm so lonely for a girl friend," he added. "Guess I've just wasted three years."

Daily Record (above)
(all) March 4 1963

Police end Danny's flight to romance

SLENDER 16-year-old Danny Pritchard arrived back in the United States yesterday after a vain attempt to see a Scottish pen-pal.

HERALD REPORTER

Danny, wearing slacks, a light jacket and visored baseball cap, got as far as Prestwick Airport when he was turned back by police.

Danny, of Idaho, said he was willing to become a British subject to be near his pen-pal, Cathy McFee, 16, of Craggen Cottage, Plockton, Ross-shire.

He quoted Cathy as saying in a letter that she had 10 brothers and sisters, and one more person in the house would make no difference.

Disappointed

But Cathy's father had different ideas.

Danny was flown to New York on the first available plane out of Prestwick.

Last night dark-haired Cathie said: "I am very disappointed.

"But I am not upset. We did not know each other well enough for that, and I did not know he was coming."

"But it would have been nice to meet him."

Danny had only £8 when he arrived in Scotland. This was the second time he had gone to Europe in search of a pen-pal.

Last year he flew to Italy, only to come back a few days later disheartened by his inability to speak Italian and the fact that his girl-friend went to school so early in the morning, he never had time to see her.

Danny said he preferred European girls to American when he arrived back yesterday.

"American girls think they're too good for you," he told me. "All they want is Rock Hudson. I'm no Rock Hudson."

Danny insisted he would have been no burden to Cathy's father, because he was ready to scrub floors and wash dishes for the chance of seeing her every day.

"But I couldn't even talk to her on the phone," he sighed.

Daily Herald

YOUTH FLOWN BACK TO U.S.

An American youth was flown back to the United States early yesterday after being refused permission to land in Scotland by Prestwick Airport immigration officials on Saturday.

The youth, Daniel L. Pritchard (17), from Idaho, arrived at Prestwick with a one-way ticket, little luggage and money. He told officials he was paying a surprise visit to a pen friend, a girl in the North of Scotland.

©Glasgow Herald

'Sing for supper' couple are sent home

available flight back to the US. And the Home Office in London told us: "The couple were refused because they had insufficient means of support, one-way tickets and no work permit.

"If the first two conditions are met, and if they give us an assurance not to work in this country, then we may re-consider their position in the morning."

After being given breakfast, one of the couple, 19-years-old Peter van Arsdale, was given permission to contact his father, a New York psychiatrist. And he told us: "My father has promised to cable us 1,000 dollars. The money should be here by tomorrow."

He and 18-years-old Nancy McConaughy, from Pasadena, California, had met in Mexico when they were both visiting friends. Her only relatives were her grandparents in California. She said she and Peter had planned to hike round Europe, hoping to eke out a living by collecting and singing folk songs.

"We never dreamt there would be a problem. We spent 3 months touring Mexico and America the same way. But it seems in Britain we need a labour permit."

Peter spent the night in a detention room at the airport. Nancy was given a bed at a private boarding house nearby. The couple were re-united at the Immigration office later, and Peter was ready to produce a cable from his father confirming that a thousand dollars was being transferred to an airport bank. "But then the immigration officers told us that we were being allowed in Britain after all. They didn't even ask if we were able to get some money. They gave us back our passports and said we could stay a month. But we won't be allowed to work."

And Peter added: "We are far from destitute anyway. We have £150 in cash between us and a similar amount in travellers' cheques. Now my father has given us the name of a family friend in Edinburgh who has offered to put us up."

The story gave us more than fifty column inches in the Scottish nationals and Glasgow and Edinburgh evening newspapers. The copy was backed up by our own oversize pictures, "action" shots of pretty, brunette Nancy and her bearded friend talking on a public telephone to New York, reading the cable from Peter's father, and getting travel directions from an airline official as they finally left the airport.

(left) Daily Record
(below) Scottish Daily Express,
(both) Oct 19 1964

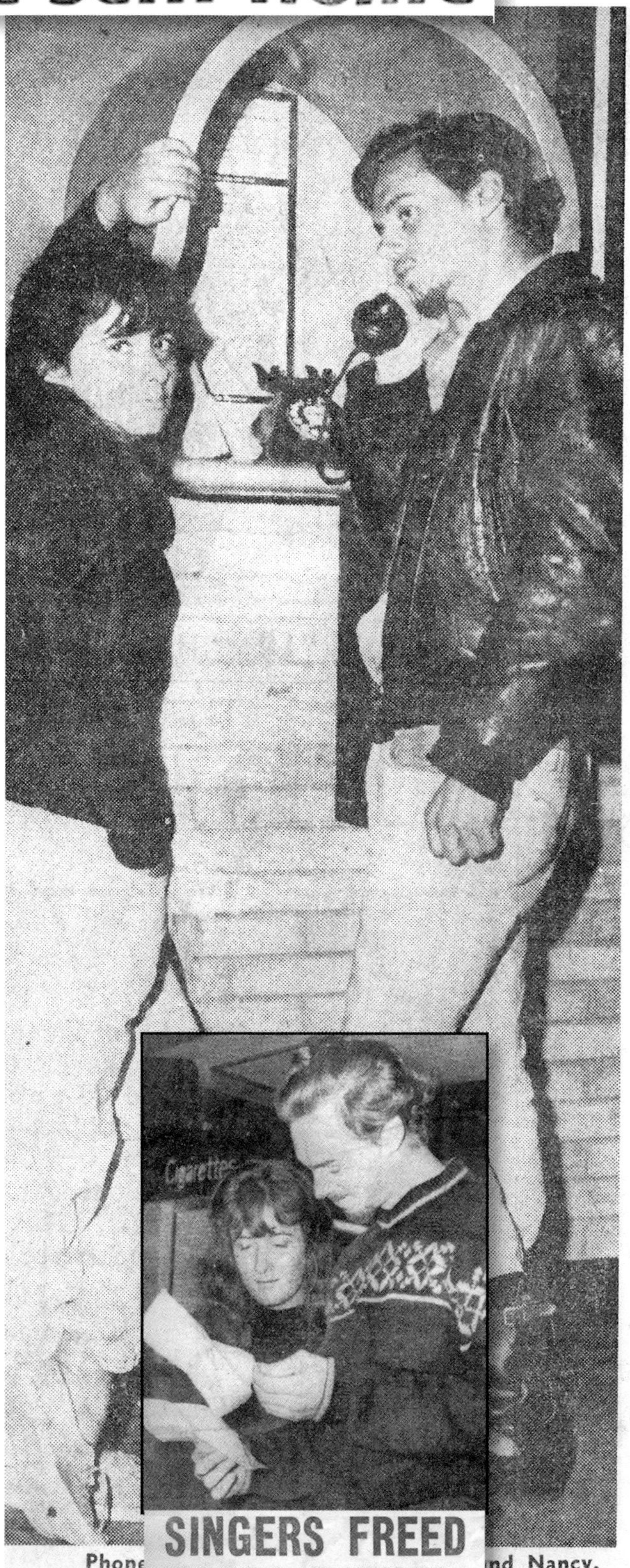

Phone ... nd Nancy.

Brenard Press pictures

U.S. couple fly in . . . to trouble

A TEENAGE beatnik couple were taken into custody when they stepped off a jet from America at Prestwick Airport yesterday to start a "busking" tour of Britain.

And last night 19-year-old guitar-toting Peter Arsdale was being held by Ministry of Aviation police at Prestwick, and his girl friend, 18-year-old Nancy McConaughy, was staying in digs nearby.

In a frantic effort to save themselves from being sent back to New York, the couple cabled Peter's parents in New Jersey asking for 1,000 dollars to be wired to them.

Hoping

Last night a Home Office official said: "The couple were refused permission to enter this country because they had insufficient means of support, no return ticket, and no work permits.

"If the money for which they have wired is forthcoming, and if an assurance is given that they will not work in this country, we may be prepared to reconsider the position.

"Otherwise they will have to be sent back to the United States."

Peter and Nancy were allowed to phone the U.S. consul in Glasgow, and to send cables home from the airport post office.

Said Nancy: "We can only hope that Peter's parents send us the money first thing in the morning."

Peter, a bearded student of anthropology, whose father is a psychiatrist, said: "I gave up my studies at university for a year so that I could travel and see a bit of the world."

SINGERS FREED AFTER FATHER CABLES CASH

TEENAGE American folk singers Peter Van Arsdale (19) and his 18-year-old friend Nancy McConaughy, barred by immigration men at Prestwick Airport yesterday, are to be allowed to remain in Britain after all.

Glasgow ©Evening Times, Oct 19 1964

Sometimes a Home Office ban resulted in despair for the individual concerned. In March, 1958, an 18-years-old German student who was refused entry at London Airport tried to kill himself when left alone for a moment.

The student, Michael Hellermann from Loerrach, near Baden-Baden, had flown in from Paris on a one-way ticket. After interrogation, he was told of the ban, and was escorted to a nearby detention area to await the next flight back to Paris. His escort left him when Hellermann asked to be allowed to go to a washroom. A few minutes later a shot was heard.

When the door was broken down a gun was found and a handful of photographs lay scattered on the floor around the injured man.

His escort, airline man Sidney Thatcher told me: "He asked me for paper and an envelope and said he was going to write a letter. Then he asked to go to the toilet.

"A few minutes later I heard a bang. I had no idea he had a gun with him. I broke the door down and found him curled up on the floor."

Police and a doctor were called and a .22 revolver was found nearby. The student was rushed to hospital and later recovered from "a minor gun shot injury."

And a year or two later a stateless refugee slashed his wrists when he too was barred at London Airport after his arrival from Switzerland. The man, 37-years-old Raimonds Murnieks, was unable to satisfy immigration officers on his identity and was escorted back to the airliner which had brought him from Zurich. Minutes later he was found wounded and lying on the floor of the aircraft. An ambulance took him to hospital where his cuts were treated.

Then he was held at the airport for several hours while the Home Office considered what to do with him. When he finally left, a spokesman told me he was being returned to Switzerland to collect documents, which he claimed, would establish his refugee status.

There was at least one refusal who found the experience challenging, if not wholly welcome. He claimed celebrity status of an entirely different kind from those personalities who had suffered the indignity before him. We had been alerted to the expected arrival of *SS Standarten Fuhrer* Skorzeny by several interested newspapers. Few people who had lived through World War II could have failed to be aware of the exploits of the former Hitler protégé and Nazi commando. The most notorious of these had been the rescue of Italian dictator Mussolini from the mountain top where he was being held prisoner by Italian partisans near the end of the Italian campaign in 1943.

Misguidedly, Otto Scorzeny had been invited to London to speak of some of those wartime activities. When he failed to appear at the Customs barrier where we awaited him, a photographer and I thought we might spot him at a passport desk if we made our way through to the airside arrivals area.

In fact we found him in the "halfway house" transit lounge beyond the control point. He was easily recognisable from the vivid facial scar which twisted his mouth, giving him a permanent sneer. From experience we knew that to find an expected arriving passenger booked to London seated in the Terminal transit lounge could only mean that he was awaiting a flight back to his point of origin, in this case, Switzerland. He must have been "refused."

Unaware if Skorzeny spoke or understood English I approached him hesitantly, wondering how I could indicate my suspicions by sign language. My photographer held back. His opportunity would come later.

Thankfully, communication wasn't a problem. In broken English, the German himself confirmed that he had been halted at the passport control desk. He said that he had been politely but firmly advised he would not be permitted to enter Britain. It was irrelevant that he was at that moment sitting in a chair in a British airport, on British soil. Technically, like other refusals, as he hadn't cleared passport and Customs controls, he was not officially in Britain.

And far from being concerned about his predicament, Skorzeny obviously relished the potential publicity for his just-published autobiography. He arrogantly protested his innocence to me, interrupted frequently by the back-up commentary of his more intelligible companion. He appeared to find the whole situation amusing.

"Do these people really think they could keep me out if I was determined to come to England?" he asked contemptuously, unconsciously mimicking the sentiments of his late master. And no, it didn't worry him that he was being dismissed as "undesirable." He had been accused of far worse things… this with an evil sounding laugh that implied: "probably with some justification."

The "interview" continued for a few minutes in the same vein, but I was happy when it was cut short. An airline official arrived to escort Skorzeny back to the same aircraft that had brought him to London only forty minutes earlier. I hurried away to dictate my copy, leaving the photographer to take his pictures. This was one "undesirable" I couldn't find an ounce of empathy with. So much for the objective reporter.

We were able to track down Skorzeny because after being barred at the arrivals' passport controls, he had been required to await his return flight in the transit lounge. As the name implies, this area is usually reserved for passengers changing 'planes, and at that time was a "no-man's land" buffer area, conveniently situated between airside arrivals and departures.

We always made a point of passing through it when looking for a particular passenger, as it was readily accessible to passengers arriving or departing. We, of course, were primarily interested in the departing passenger. Our rules of engagement with the control authorities, Her Majesty's Customs, and the Immigration Branch of the Home Office, allowed us as resident reporters into airside departure areas to interview outgoing passengers and into airside arrivals' areas only to "view" arriving passengers.[1]

Immigration staff favoured the transit area for refusals awaiting an imminent return flight because it adjoined the arrivals' passport controls, and was relatively under-used. And that was where I found Nadia, seated in exactly the same corner as the Nazi S.S. leader a year or two earlier. Yet, until I spoke to her, I had no idea she was being deported.

Dark-eyed and photogenic, which helped us to promote her case in the nationals the next day, beautiful, red-haired Nadia Bourquen, was an 18-years-old Swiss national, who just six weeks earlier had been allowed into Britain to study. Then she made the mistake of leaving her hostel in Eltham, London to join her parents on a three-day visit to Munich.

Her mistake? When she returned, she was told that the cash she carried in her bag wasn't enough to live on, and Nadia was barred.

"Your officials didn't believe a word of my story," complained Nadia to me, "Whatever do they think I am? I only went away for a short holiday. This is my home now, and I am never short of money. My family sends me money every week. It is due any day now. The hostel will vouch for me."

As ever, the Home Office declined my invitation to justify the refusal order. "No comment." was the official response to my request for an explanation. And the next day, after photographer colleague Peter Ward's photograph of Nadia appeared in most of the nationals alongside my story...

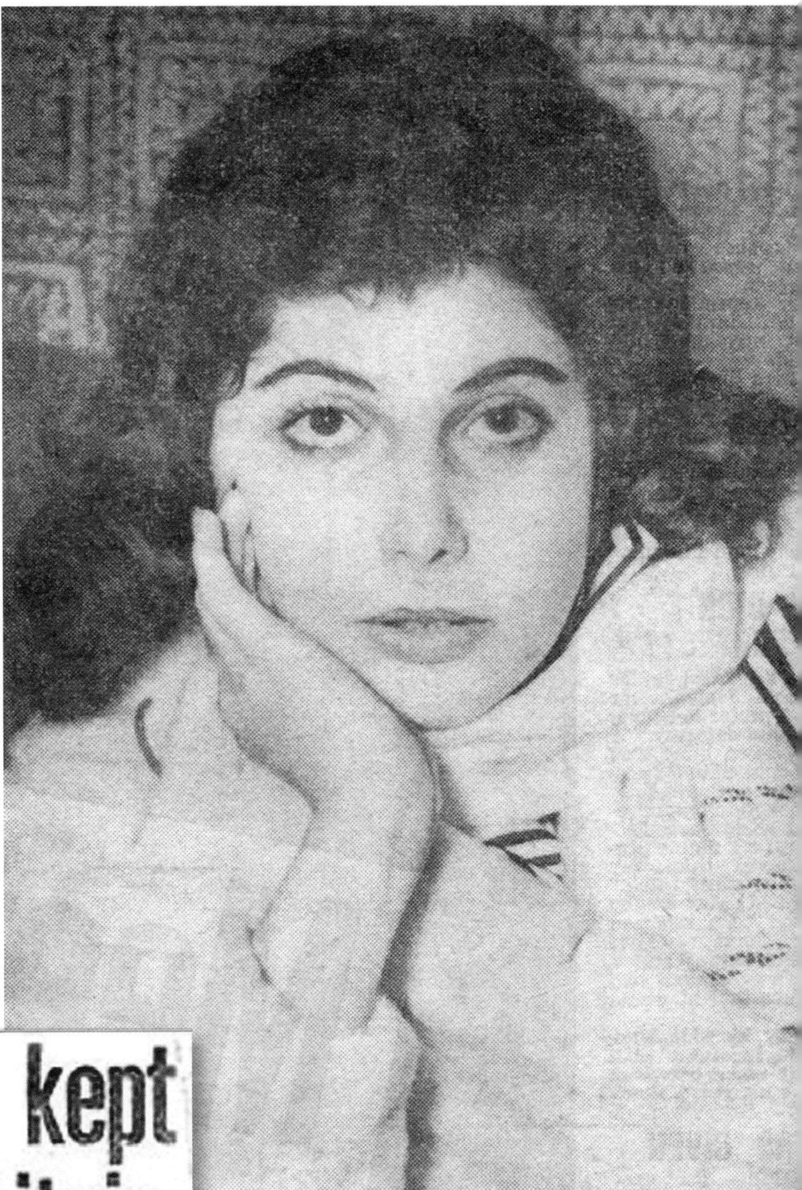

Brenard Press picture

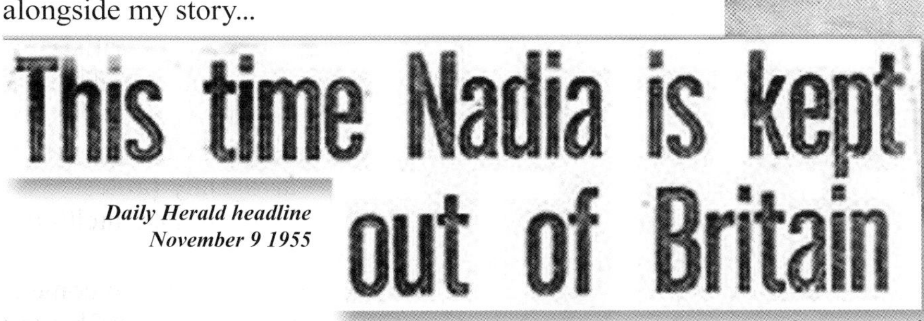

This time Nadia is kept out of Britain

Daily Herald headline
November 9 1955

[1] *Photographers were permitted to take pictures of arriving passengers – but not to make contact with them!*

Beautiful but banned

THAT was the position 18-year-old Nadia Bourquen found herself in last night when she flew into London Airport.

Immigration officers detained red - haired Nadia, refused her permission to land, and told her she would be put aboard the next airliner for Munich.

Nadia protested: "My home is in England."

The girl in the off-white duffel coat explained: "I'm a student, and I've been living in England for a month. I only went to Munich for a three-day holiday with my family.

"Now they have left for Paris, and I have no friends in Munich."

Nadia gave the address of a student hostel in West Park, Eltham, London. "That is my home and all my belongings are there. I'm in England studying languages.

"Home Office officials said the £12 I had with me wasn't enough. But my family send me £25 every month."

Before she boarded the plane Nadia phoned a friend in London. "I know he would have vouched for me, but I could not reach him.

"And your officials don't believe a word of my story. What do they think I am?"

(above) Daily Sketch
(both) Nov 9 1955

AIRPORT BARS GIRL

She is sent home on the next plane

AN attractive Swiss girl student who claims that her home is in England was refused permission to land by immigration officials when she arrived at London Airport last night.

Mlle. Nadia Bourquen

Red-haired, 18-year-old Mlle. Nadia Bourquen had just flown in from Munich. She was sent back.

Meanwhile she waited in a curtained-off section of the departure lounge.

There she explained: "I am a languages student and have been living in England for a month. I only went to Munich for three days' holiday with my family. Now they have left Munich for Paris and I have no friends there."

Mlle. Bourquen, wearing an off-white duffle coat, gave officials the address of a students' hostel at West Park, Eltham, London.

Said she: "That is my home."

Home Office officials had asked her how much money she possessed.

"When I told them I had about £12, they said it wasn't enough. But my family send me £25 every month. It is due any day."

(right) Daily Express

...a senior official of the Home Office 'phoned the Airport Commandant, Sir John D'Albiac, and demanded that my airport "credentials" be removed because I had dared to interview a passenger before she had cleared passport controls. In response to his call to me, I told Sir John that the Home Office was technically correct – but I pointed out that I couldn't have known at the time that the passenger had been refused entry.

"She was seated with other departing passengers about to board an aircraft," I said. "We are permitted to interview departing passengers in airside areas. Are the Home Office saying this passenger was not departing?"

Typically and sportingly, Sir John accepted the argument. He told Immigration that they only had themselves to blame by placing the unhappy Nadia in an area to which the Press had access, *with their agreement*. There was, he said, no justification for withdrawing my credentials.

Inevitably, at the end of another, distant, day, the immigration men won the argument. When the time came to review the resident press facilities some years later, they simply insisted that the goal posts be moved. They would only agree to our future access to the departure areas provided it was made clear that "no person under detention by Customs, Police or Immigration" could be interviewed. This rule ever after was invoked by the Immigration service and police on every occasion it suited. And deliberately ignored by both whenever it was considered that publicity was desirable, for whatever reason.

*

International relations, particularly between the former wartime Allies of East and West continued to be at a low ebb throughout the 1950s. The mutual suspicion between the great powers, reinforced by the spread of Communism across Europe, had led to a great deal of globetrotting by statesmen and diplomats from 1946 onwards.

A probably insignificant departure for Moscow by the Soviet ambassador in London made front-page headlines for me in the London evenings, as if the large typeface itself could contradict his assertion that the visit was "just routine."

The Communist coup in Czechoslovakia and the Berlin blockade a few weeks later also meant that delegates travelling to the United Nations' sessions attracted disproportionate media attention, even for the obligatory attendances of the most junior of delegates.

Britain's Labour Foreign Secretary, the blunt, often ungrammatically eloquent Ernest Bevin, was to travel thousands of miles before his retirement in 1951, meeting his opposite numbers around the world. His attitude to the Press outside the formality of Foreign Office news conferences frequently appeared whimsical, as if he were permanently surprised that his off-the-cuff comments, so often symbolic of airport news items, might have a news value.

Service Ministers, and those with special duties like the Minister responsible for the British-occupied Zone of Germany, Lord Pakenham, (later the Earl of Longford, better known as "Lord Porn," because of his anti-pornography campaign) were constant travellers, usually on special aircraft handled by RAF Northolt.

Though always polite and pleasant, his Lordship was a rare animal among politicians of his day. I do not recall a single occasion when he had anything of interest to say… and I must have approached him, notebook in hand, a dozen times during that period. It's an impression which seems hardly credible considering the forcefulness of some of his unpopular views on controversial issues in later years.

On the other hand, there were several of his Government colleagues who would regularly make well-rehearsed speeches as they waited to board or disembark from aircraft, even if they contained little hard news. One of these, Air Minister Arthur Henderson, took full advantage of his term of office as civil "commander" of the RAF to make regular visits to overseas bases. Returning from one such visit to Cyprus, he presented me with his own story of his tour, handwritten in the third person on embossed Ministry notepaper, with the words: "Thought I'd save you the trouble of taking a note." The full text of the statement reads:

"Mr Arthur Henderson, Secretary of State for Air, returned this evening from his tour of RAF units in the Middle East and from visits to Jordan, Israel and Greece.

"Mr Henderson told reporters on his arrival at Northolt that throughout the Middle East the morale of the RAF was high. Accommodation on the whole was satisfactory, but at one or two places improvements would have to made, and the provision of further married quarters was still a matter of urgency.

In reply to a question about his visit to Israel, Mr Henderson said that he was most hopeful that eventually a settlement would be reached between Israel and her neighbours. Israel was now an established fact, and in co-operation with her neighbours could make a vital contribution to the future economic and social development of the Middle East.

In all the countries he had visited he had found a common recognition of the dangers of the international situation, and an acceptance of the obligation to play a part under the charter of the United Nations in the maintenance of world peace."

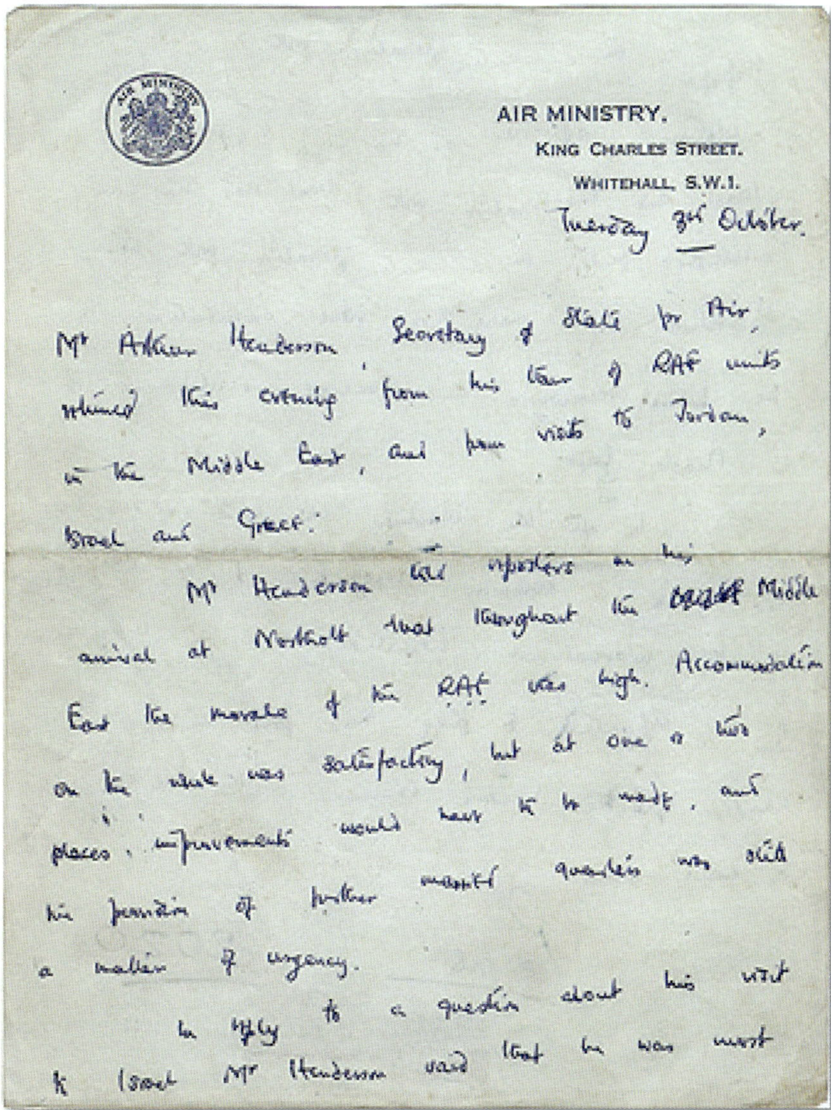

AIR MINISTRY.
KING CHARLES STREET.
WHITEHALL, S.W.1.
Tuesday 3rd October.

Mr Arthur Henderson, Secretary of State for Air, returned this evening from his tour of RAF units in the Middle East, and from visits to Jordan, Israel and Greece.

Mr Henderson told reporters on his arrival at Northolt that throughout the Middle East the morale of the RAF was high. Accommodation on the whole was satisfactory, but at one or two places improvements would have to made, and the provision of further married quarters was still a matter of urgency.

In reply to a question about his visit to Israel Mr Henderson said that he was most

One Government Minister whose ambition, it seems, was to be a journalist! He wrote this statement on blue Air Ministry notepaper and handed it to me as he disembarked from his RAF aircraft at Northolt with the words: "I thought I'd save you the trouble... and you can quote me!"
Author's Collection

On another occasion, the same Minister unwittingly made the front pages without writing a single word. His four-engined RAF York transport hit a 14ft landing-light pillar as it came in to land through a thick ground mist at Northolt. Neither he nor members of the crew were hurt, but a hole three feet in length was torn in the under-belly of the aircraft. This time I had no assistance in writing up the story.

Military leaders too, British and American, though more circumspect in their dealing with reporters, were always newsworthy. General Sir Brian Robertson, who as British Military Governor in Berlin was negotiating with his Russian opposite number on an almost daily basis, had to be as much diplomat as soldier *(see over)*.

AIR MINISTER IN FOG MISHAP

PLANE HIT LIGHT

An air liner carrying Mr. Henderson, the Air Minister, from Germany hit a 14ft sodium-light post as it approached the runway at Northolt in a thick ground mist. A large hole was torn in the fuselage.

Daily Telegraph *Nov 12 1948*

Hit landing light

Mr. Arthur Henderson, Secretary of State for Air, returning from Germany last night, had a narrow escape when his plane hit a 14ft. sodium landing light in the mist at Northolt.

The metal post of the light tore a hole a yard long and two feet high in the fuselage of the plane—a four-engined R A F York—and the hull was ripped and scratched for several feet. No one was hurt.

A few months earlier the same Minister had been involved in a landing incident at Northolt. He made no statement, written or verbal.
Daily Herald
Nov 12 1948

DAILY HERALD

No. 10124 ONE PENNY

Three Western Germany chiefs in London

BEVIN CALLS C-IN-C

By W. N. EWER, Diplomatic Correspondent

GENERAL SIR BRIAN ROBERTSON, British Commander-in-Chief in Germany, flew to London yesterday to see Mr Bevin.

One may deduce that with no Moscow meetings likely for a day or two, the Foreign Secretary wanted the advice of "the man on the spot" while both sides are taking stock of the position before making any further decisions.

Major General George P. Hays, United States deputy military governor in Germany, and Major General R.M. Notret, French deputy military governor are both in London.

The "Berlin Committee"—Sir William Strang and the American and French Ambassadors— was sitting again yesterday.

URGENT CALL TO GERMANY C.-IN-C.

SUMMONED TO LONDON AT HOUR'S NOTICE

ADVICE SOUGHT ON RUSSIAN PROPOSALS

DECISION THIS WEEK-END ON MOSCOW TALKS

Daily Telegraph *August 14 1948*

Robertson flies to see Bevin

Express Political Correspondent

GENERAL SIR BRIAN ROBERTSON, British Military Governor in Germany, was recalled at short notice yesterday to advise the Government on the last stages of the four-Power Moscow talks about the Berlin blockade.

He flew to London, and last night saw Mr. Bevin. He is expected back in Berlin today.

Robertson is here again

By Daily Mail Reporter

URGENT recall of General Sir Brian Robertson, British Commander-in-Chief in Germany, for consultation with Mr. Bevin indicates that the Moscow talks on Berlin have reached the crucial stage.

Coupled with General Robertson's sudden air journey to London yesterday, a clue that the negotiations with the Soviet have proved even more strenuous than was expected is the fact that the meeting of the Western envoys with Mr. Molotov on Thursday failed to be decisive.

GEN. ROBERTSON FLIES TO SEE MR. BEVIN

PREPARATIONS FOR 3-POWER OCCUPATION STATUTE

The Evening News

NO. 20,666 LONDON, WEDNESDAY, DECEMBER 29, 1948 ONE PENNY

ROBERTSON FLIES FOR TALKS

Reporting To Mr. Bevin On West Germany Government Talks

MILITARY BOARD PLAN READY

Opposition to Ruhr Pact

GENERAL SIR BRIAN ROBERTSON, British Military Governor in Germany, arrived at

December 20 1948

Tuesday, July 13, 1948

THE STAR LATE EXTRA

C-in-C FLIES BACK TO BERLIN

No. 18,728 One Penny

The General's comings and goings made frequent headlines but rarely produced "copy." In this selection are Page One leads in the *Daily Herald*, *London Evening News* and the *Star* as well as the *Daily Telegraph* of various dates in 1948. Most of them carried the minimum of information.

***Daily Herald* (right) August 14 1948**

***Daily Express* (right)**

(above right) *Daily Mail* (both) August 14 1948

***Daily Telegraph* December 30 1948**

July 13 1948

As with Lord Packenham, I can trace no evidence of Sir Brian ever contributing anything to my notebook on the half dozen or so occasions I met him during this period. But because of the sensitive part he played in the besieged former German capital, his regular flights back to London were guaranteed to produce Page One leads in daily newspapers as well as the evenings – with only a paragraph or two of copy to justify the large type used.

Not so reserved was Sir Brian's superior, Field Marshal Viscount Montgomery, who revelled in the attention we gave him on his frequent air trips as Deputy Allied Commander in Europe. More than once he asked the reluctant C.O. of the RAF base at Northolt, Group Captain Hodgson (who for his own part had no time for the Press) to "find the Berry Brothers" if, for some reason, either of us was late meeting his special aircraft.

We knew, of course, that Monty wasn't going to reveal any military or even political secrets to us. But he was well aware of the impact of human interest stories, and readily took a cue from Harry who had asked him on an early meeting what souvenirs he'd brought back from an overseas trip.

I hope he was pulling our legs when on every subsequent occasion he met either of us, he dismissed most of our questions in favour of itemising every present, every gift he was carrying for his family and friends. For Monty knew very well what made news, and would sometimes delight in implying there was more to his coming and going than met the eye. He would say conspiratorially:

"We must play the significance of this trip down. People might jump to the wrong conclusion."

Or he might ask, with mock concern:

"How did you find out about this visit? No one was supposed to know."

This regular banter paid off some years later. The familiarity meant I was able to win an exclusive from Monty. His comments on the "Churchill telegram" made front-page leads in *The Star*, the *Evening News* – and the radical Sunday newspaper *Reynolds News*, with similar solid coverage elsewhere.

Further Page One leads were provided in my exclusive interview with an old acquaintance – Field Marshal Lord Montgomery – for ***The Star, the Evening News*** **and the radical** ***Reynolds News*****. Shorter versions were published in the** ***News of the World*** **and the** ***People*****.**

WORLD'S LARGEST EVENING NET SALE

The Evening News

NO. 22,709 LONDON, SATURDAY, DECEMBER 4, 1954 THREE-HALFPENCE

MONTY TO SEE SIR WINSTON

He Says: I'm Going Home to Look for Telegram

(above) 4 December 1954

'YES, HE DID SEND ORDER'

FIELD MARSHAL VISCOUNT MONTGOMERY said at London Airport to-day that he was going straight home to look for the Churchill telegram.

Monty, Deputy Allied Supreme Commander in Europe, had flown in after his visit to the U.S. and Canada.

At once he was asked about Sir Winston's message asking him to collect and stack German arms to meet a possible Russian advance at the end of the last war. The Prime Minister referred to it in a speech at Woodford last month.

Said the Field Marshal: "I am now going home and will look through my papers and documents and see whether I have a copy of that message.

"Having looked through my papers and documents I will go and see the Prime Minister and say whether I have it or not."

DOCUMENTS

'Enormous Number'

He added: "I have an enormous number of documents, diaries and papers to go through, so it may be quite a task."

He reaffirmed that he had received a message from the Prime Minister in May, 1945, concerning the retention of German arms.

But, he declared, "The really important question is what did I do after receiving Mr. Churchill's message.

"As regards that, I shall act on Mr. Shinwell's advice and display a 'remarkable exhibition of reticence.'"

To the question of whether the Prime Minister's message referred to the stacking or retaining of German arms he replied: "I shall have to look it up."

Saturday, December 4, 1954

THE STAR

No 20,712 Three Halfpence

Monty Says It Again— 'I Did Get A Telegram'

4 December 1954

MONTY WILL SEARCH NOW

FIELD-MARSHAL VISCOUNT MONTGOMERY will spend the week-end quietly at his Alton, Hants, home, searching for instructions about German arms sent him by Sir Winston Churchill in 1945.

He said so yesterday when he arrived back in London from the U.S. and Canada.

Asked if he thought the telegram from the Premier was at his home, Viscount Montgom...

The People 5 December 1954

REYNOLDS NEWS

2½d. GOVERNMENT OF THE PEOPLE, BY THE PEOPLE, FOR THE PEOPLE and SUNDAY CITIZEN

DECEMBER 5, 1954 No. 5439

That telegram—the Field-Marshal starts searching

MONTY REPEATS 'PM DID SEND IT'

5 December 1954

Winston Churchill, by this time Prime Minister again, first referred to the telegram in a speech at his Woodford, Essex, constituency in November 1954. He said that at the end of hostilities in Europe he had telegraphed a directive to Monty requiring him to stack German arms "...so that they could easily be issued again to German soldiers with whom we should have to work if the Soviet advance continues."

Such a command would not have seemed so outrageous in the 1980s after forty years of Cold War. But in the 1950s, even after the experience of the previous few years of tension, the extent of Churchill's antagonism towards and mistrust of our previous comrades-in-arms was shocking to many. *The Times* joined the left-of-centre *Daily Herald* and *Daily Mirror* and, of course the Communist *Daily Worker* in a storm of criticism (though curiously, the *Manchester Guardian* was conciliatory).

The Russians themselves were understandably furious. And questioned in the House, even the Prime Minister seemed to have second thoughts.

"It may be that the telegram was never sent," he said, "At any rate it hasn't been traced in official records."

But on his return to London from the US a week or two later, Monty told me categorically: "I *did* receive such a message. That is a fact."

And he revealed: "While I was in Los Angeles I heard from the PM asking me if I could send him a copy of the telegram. I am going home now to look through my papers, and I will tell the PM if I have a copy."

I asked him what he had done about the original order. But as I wrote at the time, the Field Marshal was more cautious with his response.

"That's my business," he replied with that familiar grin. Then he added: "I gave the same answer when the Americans asked me that. I got away with it there...."

My rejoinder did not go into my copy. "It may not be enough of an answer here," I volunteered hopefully. Monty, wisely, did not take the bait.

What was the truth of the matter? As far as I know Monty never did trace the telegram. Or if he did, he chose not to reveal it. And Churchill's doctor and friend Lord Moran later said that a search had been made for the original order three years earlier when the war-leader was preparing his Second World War memoirs. No trace was found. It was concluded, said Lord Moran, that the PM must have decided not to send it.

It seems likely to me that at some stage Churchill told Monty that he had considered sending him the telegram, but had changed his mind. Monty may have been reminded of the intent after the Woodford speech, but like the PM himself, had forgotten that the proposal had been dropped. Both of them should have been well aware by then of the public outrage that would follow the revelation that he was ready to re-arm such a recent enemy to assist in making war against a former ally.

Circa 1952: Labour Foreign Secretary and Deputy Prime Minister Herbert Morrison, in this London Airport "northside" picture, gives me an exclusive as he returns with his departmental officials from an overseas conference ***(see opposite)***

Author's collection

Regular or frequent contact with the same newsworthy people is usually only experienced by reporters or correspondents who specialise in areas such as international affairs and politics, sport or show business. But the airport reporter and photographer come across some travellers so frequently they can become almost confidants, and on first name terms.

This was certainly true in the case of those politicians and some show-business personalities who may have had good reason to make friends and influence Press people. But I would like to think that the *bonhomie* was not always based on self-interest.

It was usually the politician preferring to keep his relations with the news media on an informal basis as much as possible, even when in office, who tended to form these personal contacts.

Some even appeared uncomfortable in the more serious surroundings of the formal press conference.

Herbert Morrison,[1] Bevin's successor as Foreign Secretary, probably spent less time travelling, surprisingly perhaps for the ex-London County Council leader who was said to have coveted the Foreign Office from the first days of the Labour Government.

Brenard Press picture

Airliners rock these homes

Looking for loose tiles in this bathroom is the Minister for Civil Aviation, Mr. Lennox-Boyd.

With him is Mrs. Eleanor Burden, of Cranford Cross, near London Airport.

She is one of the residents who complained that vibration from low-flying airliners is damaging homes.

Mr. Lennox-Boyd visited the houses for two hours yesterday — and promised: "I will take whatever action is possible in the near future."

News Chronicle

However, he shunned the formal press conference at the airport, preferring to answer questions "on the hoof" or in the relative informality of the VIP Suite, as did several Cabinet Ministers over the years. Alan Lennox-Boyd, Colonial Secretary at the height of the Cyprus troubles, was one who called me into the old north side VIP area at Heathrow, the original Royal Lounge, to tell me about his planned overseas visit, then invited me to join him in a glass of wine. I had met him on several occasions in his earlier role as Minister of Civil Aviation, even touring some noise-blighted homes near Heathrow with him. The conversation now inevitably turned to the latest outrages of EOKA, the Greek-Cypriot terrorist movement.

PLANE SHOOK TILES INTO WOMAN'S BATH

A GIANT airliner roared over Mrs. Ellen Cowdray's bungalow between the parallel approach lights to London Airport while she was taking a bath. The vibration caused the white tiles round the bath to fall on to her legs.

Tiny, greying Mrs. Cowdray, a widow, of Malvern-road, Cranford Cross, Middlesex, told Mr. Alan Lennox-Boyd, Minister of Transport and Civil Aviation, about it yesterday.

She said: "I was so frightened. I though it was a man breaking in through the trap-door.

"Now I suppose I shan't be able to have a bath unless there's fog about to stop planes landing."

Daily Herald (part)

Suddenly the Minister announced, partly to me and partly to a senior airline man standing with us, in a room relatively crowded with out-of-earshot Colonial Office staff: "Do you know they put a bomb in my hands the other day?" He might have been acknowledging the delivery of a bouquet of roses.

"I'd just had dinner when the doorbell rang," he said. "I answered the door myself. A delivery man or a messenger placed this small package in my hands. I don't remember if I signed for it.

"But when I tried to open it I found what seemed to be a piece of wire in the way. It was only then that I wondered..."

When the police were called, he said, they discovered the package contained a small explosive device.

"They told me that if I'd pulled or broken that wire, it would have exploded. And I wouldn't have been telling you this now."

It was at this point that Lennox-Boyd realised I'd pulled out my notebook. Pointedly, he said: "Now, you can put that away and forget everything I've said.Or I will have to deny it all."

My pleadings and arguments were for nothing. The police, he said, were sworn to secrecy, and no one at the Colonial Office knew of the incident.

"I don't intend to give the terrorists any comfort," he added by way of explanation, "And I want to keep the story for my memoirs."

Those memoirs were never written, or at least never published. My only witness, the airline man, is long dead. I have no reason to believe he would have broken a confidence anyway. And I doubt if any of the civil servants overheard. So the story of the Government Minister who claimed he'd held a terrorist's live bomb in his hands never appeared in print, until now.

MINISTER SEES DAMAGED HOMES

PLANE COMPLAINTS

Daily Telegraph Reporter

Mr. Lennox-Boyd, Minister of Transport and Civil Aviation, spent nearly two hours yesterday touring 10 homes near London Airport to hear residents' complaints and assess damage caused by low flying and taxi-ing aircraft. He was accompanied by Mr. Reader-Harris, Conservative M.P. for Heston and Isleworth.

Afterwards the Minister said to residents: "I feel very naturally distressed at the complaints I have heard." He promised that whatever action was possible would be taken soon.

DailyTelegraph (all) October 30 1953

George Brown, deputy leader of the Labour Party under both Hugh Gaitskell and Harold Wilson throughout the 1960s, was notorious for sharing confidences. He once whispered to me, blissfully unaware that I was testing out a portable tape-recorder at

[1] *Grandfather of Peter Mandelson, later Lord Mandelson, First Secretary in Gordon Brown's Government.*

the time: "Don't tell anyone I said so, but..."

He then proceeded to slander a Tory opponent below and beyond the call of party politics. One confidence I am *not* repeating for these memoirs. The gentleman concerned is still very much alive.

Harold Wilson himself, as Prime Minister, relished the airport press conference, which in the 1960s, with the growth and influence of television, became so familiar. He would patiently repeat statements and answer questions individually and repetitively for ITN and BBC TV news crews, then BBC Radio as well as a persistence of newspaper and agency reporters in turn. Many of his predecessors would only give one interview for everyone to share.

Yet on one such occasion in the Queens Building conference room at Heathrow, scene of so many world news events, he told a BBC reporter as the cameras began to roll: "Where's the Brenards' man? I'm not starting without Brenards."[1]

Aneurin Bevan, though understandably wary of what he saw as a hostile Tory press, was still a great disappointment to me for a different reason. A hero of my teens, he epitomised what I believed to be rare in politics, sincerity and consistency.

Then I learnt from an elderly relative that an increase in the widow's pension he had so proudly announced as Minister, had resulted in a corresponding reduction in her National Assistance (social security) benefit.

"Nye" was due at Heathrow from Paris the following day. I had the opportunity to take my aunt's problem to the top and perhaps collect a few lines of copy on the way. My question to him as he cleared the Customs barrier in Terminal 2 (he was travelling as an ordinary passenger) must have appeared antagonistic. His reply was certainly defensive.

Wikipedia Commons *21 Sept 1954*
Founder of the National Health Service, Aneurin Bevan.

"The increase in the pension has been welcomed by most people," he said, "They would rather have the money as an entitlement than as a charity."

I was aghast. "Charity?" I said. "Are you saying that National Assistance is charity?"

"No," replied Nye quickly and defiantly, "I'm not saying that. But that is how many people think of National Assistance. This way we are putting right a wrong.

"There will be some who do not gain," he agreed, "But to those not on Assistance, the higher pension will mean they are better off."

I considered this for a moment. Then I asked:

"So those who need it most won't get the extra cash. Is that what you are defending?"

But there was no reply. Nye Bevan, founder of the National Health Service, who with Harold Wilson had resigned from the Attlee Government in protest against the introduction of prescription charges, had moved on to his waiting limousine. Did I report the conversation? I did not. For in spite of my earlier intentions, I had sacrificed my right to a story for voluntarily prefacing my questions with the words: "Off the record, Minister..." to excuse what I declared as "my personal interest."

A fatal error? Would I have received the same answer if I'd had my pencil poised? Who can say? And would I have been so protective of a Tory Minister?

On the Tory side, there were similar contrasts in attitudes towards the news media. Duncan Sandys, son-in-law of Sir Winston Churchill, was bumptious and aggressive at airport press conferences, and twice accused an *ITN* reporter of asking "impertinent" questions.

"I didn't come here to be insulted," was his time-honoured protest on one occasion. Twice he broke off a filmed interview, only agreeing to carry on after telling the reporter: "You can ask me about ...and ... But nothing else." Almost needless to say, the "interview" was not screened.

Anthony Eden and Edward Heath were among those who were always courteous and gentlemanly. Even during the difficult days of Suez, when he was being constantly vilified for bad judgement and his health was failing, Eden never shirked an interview, although it might be only to say: "It's too early to formulate an opinion yet."

Only once did the mask, if that is what it was, seem to slip. And that was my doing. After one brief exclusive interview on his return from a West Indies convalescence three years after his resignation as Premier (which won wide coverage), I asked him to

[1] *Circa late 1975;* ***I*** *was present... but as a Heathrow PR manager and no longer "the Brenards' man."*

WINSTON SEES HIM OFF

Evening Standard Reporter

Mr. Anthony Eden, the Foreign Secretary, left London Airport in a Royal Canadian Air Force airplane to fly to Boston, Mass., for a third gall bladder operation.

With him went his wife and his surgeon, Mr. Guy Blackburn, of Guy's Hospital.

Sir Winston and Lady Churchill saw Mr. and Mrs. Eden off.

Mr. Eden, wearing a lounge suit, walked from the car which brought him to the airport to the airplane, but he took the steps up into the airplane slowly.

He was pale, but he waved to the large crowd which gathered at the junction of the main road and the side road used by Mr. Eden's car to get to the aircraft.

Sir Winston and Lady Churchill entered the aircraft and spent some time with Mr. and Mrs. Eden saying farewell.

Among others who wished Mr. Eden farewell and a quick recovery were Sir John D'Albiac, airport commandant, and Air Commodore Martin Costello, air chief of the Canadian Joint Staff in London.

When Sir Winston and Lady Churchill left they were greeted with cheers and hat waving fro mthe crowd.

Police guard airplane

Mr. Eden's airplane was parked all night, with a heavy police guard, two miles from the main passenger departure point on the far side of the airport.

So elaborate were the security measures — an airport official said they were

Evening Standard 7 June 1953

As Foreign Secretary, and later as Prime Minister, Sir Anthony Eden suffered from poor health, which worsened during and after Suez, leading to his retirement.
These examples of many exclusive interviews were separated by months and years.

EDEN FLIES OFF TO BIG 4 TALK

'I hope Molotov and I can work together for peace'

The strictest security measures were taken at London Airport to-day for the departure of Mr. Anthony Eden and his Foreign Office staff to the Four Powers' Conference in Berlin.

A cordon of plain clothes and uniformed security officers and police surrounded the turbo-prop Viscount airliner as it stood on the tarmac.

A senior official checked the secret labelling of every Foreign Office despatch box and private luggage as it was stowed in the hold.

Not until three hours before departure did BEA reveal which aircraft was being used for the special service.

Important

Before boarding the aircraft Mr. Eden said: "I am glad that our efforts to bring about the conference have succeeded so far. You will see for yourself that this an important occasion.

"We hope and want to see a free election throughout all Germany, because it is only by means of a freely elected, all-German Government that a peace treaty can finally be concluded—that we can have negotiations that can bring about a peace treaty.

"I do not expect to resolve all these difficult German problems at one

● Back Page, Col. Five

Evening Standard Jan 22 1954

'Peace hopes'

● From Page One

meeting in Berlin, but it would be real encouragement to the world if we could make some progress with them.

"Austria is a less complicated issue. Given goodwill and a real desire for real agreement, we should be able to make progress with that."

"If, as a result of the re-emergence of a united Germany the Soviets wish to discuss the problem of European security, we should be ready to join in such discussions.

"If a united Germany is re-created, they may ask about the future of European security, and that is the kind of question which we shall be perfectly ready to discuss.

War and peace

"I hope nobody will expect early and spectacular results. Such results are not possible. A conference like this must take time.

"For my part, as long as we are making any progress at all, I am ready to devote any time that may be necessary."

Mr. Eden, who was seen off by his wife, continued: "I look forward to meeting Mr. Molotov. We did much work together in the war. I hope this time we can work together for peace."

Libraries and Archives Canada picture
Anthony Eden in June 1954

Eden is home—with a warning

SIR ANTHONY EDEN and Lady Eden flew back to London today after their three-month holiday in Bermuda. Sir Anthony, looking fit and well, is in England for the first time since the publication of his book Full Circle, offered a word of warning about optimism over relations between the East and West.

"At the moment," he said, "I would not like to offer a comfortable word about the world problems.

"I feel the problems are not getting lighter but rather becoming more acute in many spheres. I don't think we can indulge in easy optimism."

Asked about criticism of his book, particularly the passages dealing with Suez, Sir Anthony said: "I haven't a word to withdraw or a line to add. It is not an uncontroversial subject, you know.

Ben Gurion clash

"I was speaking for the British public and our Allies, the Free Peoples."

Was there a possibility of another book on the same subject? Sir Anthony replied: "Not as far as I'm concerned."

But he was still working on his second volume — his memoirs from the time he entered the Foreign Office up to the end of the war.

Sir Anthony left the airport with his wife by car for their home in Wiltshire.

Before setting out Sir Anthony commented on the fact that he had arrived at the airport 20 minutes after the Israeli Prime Minister, Mr Ben Gurion, flew in.

"It's a pity I missed Mr Ben Gurion," he said. "I would like to have shaken him by the hand."

Mr Ben Gurion, who also flew from New York, was greeted by more than a hundred Arab students with giant banners proclaiming "Not Another Suez" and "No More British Arms For Israel."

Police linking arms pushed and hustled the students off the main roadway from the airport on to the footpaths.

Evening Standard March 1960

Autographs (from top)
US President Jimmy Carter (May 1977)
Sir Anthony Eden (March 1960)
Edmund Hillary and Sherpa Tensing (Everest conquerors, June 1953)
Charlie Chaplin (1952)
Bing Crosby (1977)
and best-selling author Jackie Collins (1983)

autograph a copy of his book "Full Circle" for me. He agreed unsmilingly, and, I thought, almost grudgingly.

Concerned, I questioned an aide later. "He would never have said anything to you," she replied, "But he would have felt that you were using your privileged position as a reporter to ask a favour. He wouldn't approve of that."

And of course, I *had* realised that, almost from the moment I asked. It was something I had always been wary of, and had frequently refused requests to collect autographs for others for that very reason.

"It wouldn't be right," I would argue. It was also a matter of not wanting to voice the autograph collector's cliché: "It's not for me..." Perhaps that's why, when it *was* for me, I made the odd exception to my principles. I also asked Charlie Chaplin, Bing Crosby, Emil Zatopek and Hillary and Tensing among others for autographs. But I failed with Churchill. I was advised quite firmly that such a privilege was reserved for those who had performed some personal service for the great man!

Ted Heath was always ready to bring me up to date on his delicate negotiations over Britain's proposed entry to the Common Market, as the EC was naïvely (and politically?) termed in the days when he was the Government's main advocate. During that period I must have been one of the best informed journalists on the subject… for about an hour at a time. On a half-dozen occasions he unhesitatingly invited me into the secluded balcony-level section of Terminal 2's VIP Brabazon Suite at Heathrow, responding readily to questions I had mugged up from the newspaper reports of the previous few days.

Enthusiastic and good-humoured, always ready to chuckle politely (with those familiar heaving shoulders) at my rather poor jokes about de Gaulle's intransigence, he was a very different personality from the bitter figure he became from the seventies onwards after he lost the leadership of his party.

His predecessors, Sir Alec Douglas Home and Harold Macmillan were again very different leaders. As a former Foreign Secretary (who was to become so again in Ted Heath's government), Sir Alec talked freely to the airport Press. But he tended to be rather humourless, and though sincere and ever polite, his comments were rarely newsworthy.

Macmillan, like Wilson, welcomed the media attention, and appeared to thrive on it. My first meeting with him was in the 'fifties, soon after the RAF had taken back the former civil airport facilities at Northolt and built a new VIP lounge there.

Then Housing Minister, he had introduced a policy of allowing council tenants to buy their own homes. And to some extent he overcame counter-arguments about the loss of a national pool of houses by seeing his target of building 300,000 new houses in a year achieved.

In appearance, however, he was a perfect foil for the cartoonists. His dress sense and demeanour was Edwardian, but he hadn't the panache of the ever-elegant Eden, his predecessor as Prime Minister. As we spoke, he stood, a glass in one hand, a cigarette in the other, constantly dropping ash down the front of a stained waistcoat. One quarter-inch of ash, I recall, lodged on the bulky watch-chain stretched across his middle, threatening to fall or to be further crushed at his every breath.

His heavy white moustache, stained with nicotine where the ends constantly brushed his upper lip, seemed to encourage the lisp, which became a feature of his oratory in later years. But this was before Tory Central Office took him in tow. His dress awareness began to improve, it is true, during his spell as Foreign Secretary. It wasn't until he succeeded to the Premiership in 1957 that the metamorphosis was completed.

Anyone who doubts that such a radical change to a public persona was deliberate, need only study the cartoonists of the era, Cummings and Vicky in particular. The trimming of that rogue moustache, the snipping of the hirsute head and the switch to tailored shirts and suits contributed in their own way to Vicky's "Supermac" image that was to come. Mac's often-misquoted, "Most people have never had it so good," could have been inspired by his greeting to the bathroom mirror.

It may have been Mac's self-assured, posturing, sometimes patronising style of media attention-seeking which set the pattern for those airport news conferences.

They were not without their hazards. Indeed it has been suggested that it was not so much the winter of discontent itself which saw off Jim Callaghan in 1979 as it was his oft-misrepeated Nelsonic "Crisis? What crisis?" response at Heathrow on his return from a summit conference.

His successor, Margaret Thatcher, vowed that she would never fall into the trap of off-the-cuff remarks or even formal statements at airports after a tiring flight. In all her years as Premier, I do not recall her setting foot inside an airport press conference room. She would not even pass the time of day with reporters lining barriers near her aircraft steps, something she was quite confident to do in the quieter and more familiar surrounds of Downing Street.

In this respect she emulated her great hero, Churchill, who also avoided such confrontations with the Press, in spite of his love of the "public occasion." Both in Opposition and as peacetime Prime Minister he would reject the opportunity for instant headlines by way of the casual remark on the steps of a VIP lounge.

Even so, we suspected sometimes that the complex arrangements which were made on his behalf to enable him to avoid all those tiresome procedures such as baggage check-in, ticketing, Customs and passport controls were the outcome of over-zealous reaction by officials.

On more than one occasion when media access was not only discouraged but actively halted, the later explanation was that "Sir Winston had asked for no fuss."

As far as I was concerned, one fortunate aspect of this absence of direct contact was the challenge of finding an "angle" which would make up for a lack of quotes in the story. It meant lengthy enquiries among airline staff, sorties into forbidden baggage areas and careful observation of everything relating to an actual departure.

So I was able to fall back on such world-shattering titbits as "...among Sir Winston's 30 pieces of luggage was his easel and several prepared canvases." On another occasion: "The Prime Minister's personal dispatch boxes accompanied him." It was either that or nothing. How much we had to try to make up for a dearth of hard information!

On one such flight to Nice, Sir Winston travelled incognito, but was accompanied by his daughter and son-in-law, Mr and Mrs Christopher Soames, booked, revealingly, under their real names. More than once he flew on a scheduled service as the last passenger to board. He was of course watched eagerly by fellow passengers as they peered out from and thrust cameras up to the windows of the waiting aircraft, attracted by that "no fuss" activity on the ground as the VIP car drew up.

This predilection for driving directly to the foot of his aircraft steps gave Winnie little opportunity to observe the long-established reminder to ordinary passengers leaving an airport building which begins: "Please extinguish all pipes and cigarettes..."

And with the short memories of newspapers, my colleagues and I were able to report the story of the still-smouldering Churchill cigar at the steps of the aircraft on almost every occasion.

NARA picture

Sometimes the familiar cigar wasn't even alight. But not always...

BUT NO ONE SAID 'NO SMOKING'

IT was one of those moments that make airline officials shudder. Everyone knows that, from the time they leave the airport lounge until the aircraft is safely airborne, passengers are not allowed to smoke.

Yet when Sir Winston Churchill went out to join his Comet at London Airport yesterday—en route to a Monte Carlo holiday—he was wreathed in clouds of smoke from a fat cigar. Nobody said a word.

At the plane Sir Winston stood, still puffing happily, under one of the Comet's giant wings, an overflow fuel pipe almost directly above his head. Still nobody said a word.

Then Sir Winston was helped up the steps of the plane. At the top, he paused and flicked his still-lit cigar 15ft. to the ground. It bounced in a shower of sparks. A photographer trod on the stub. Still nobody said a word.

Then an indulgent police officer explained: "We always keep a close eye on Sir Winston's cigars—but no one would dream of telling him of the dangers of smoking."

Daily Mail August 22 1961

"It's all right, it's not alight," an airline manager insisted to me on one such departure, only to be confounded by a sudden puff of smoke.

On another, Winnie himself must have recalled hearing of the "no smoking until after take-off" rule. As he reached the door of his Comet jet he paused immediately below a fuel overflow pipe, took a final puff, then deliberately threw the butt some fifteen feet to the ground in a shower of sparks. Ironically it was down to a photographer, for once within physical as well as focal range, to rush forward and stamp on the still-glowing butt. Sir Winston and Lady Churchill took their seats apparently unaware of the suspended breaths outside. The incident gave me and the photographer concerned a centre-page spread in the *Daily Mail*, among others. No quotes were necessary.

*

Czechoslovakian Airlines was one of the first European airlines to open services to Britain after the war. With the Communist coup in Prague, it then became for a time, along with LOT, the Polish airline, one of the only two direct links between Britain and the eastern bloc.

Many of its pilots and other flight deck crew members had served with the RAF as free Czechs and had flown against Germany in bombers and fighters. Their affinity with England and with their British allies made it difficult for them to stay silent about their opposition to their new Communist bosses, and over the next few months they were gradually replaced by crews ostensibly more sympathetic to the new regime.

The airline was handled at Northolt by British European Airways, but had two Czech nationals based at the airport as station manager and as aircraft engineer. Manager Vladimir Becko was in an unenviable position. Thoroughly Anglicised himself – he too was a former RAF flyer – his family was still in Prague. He couldn't afford to put them or his job in danger by expressing any anti-Communist sentiments, though he was thought by many to be closely associated with the dissidents.

He was happy, indeed anxious, to tell Harry and me this, while at the same time assuring us of his desire to stay in the West. When the call finally came to return to Prague "for consultations," as he knew it would, he confided:

"I have to go. If I don't I will lose my job."

Then he added, bitterly:

"If I do go, I'll probably lose my job anyway. They think they are aware where my sympathies lie. But at least I'll be with my family."

In the circumstances Harry and I should have been almost the last people to confide in. If we had published his comments he certainly would have been in trouble. But as he had also confided in Special Branch officers at the airport in exactly the same way, he may have been preparing a case for political asylum at some future date.

The Special Branch men were not so sympathetic (or gullible?) as we. Quietly, we were warned: "Don't be convinced by his protests. We don't believe he's as innocent as he makes out."

Vlado did indeed return to Prague, as I reported for *The Star*, with the explanation that all managers in Europe had been similarly recalled. A month or so later he returned to Northolt and his old job as the airline's manager. Special Branch thought their suspicions had been justified; the Communist regime would never have allowed him back if they hadn't trusted him, they pointed out.

Several weeks went by. Those familiar ex-RAF Czech crews were gradually replaced. Some, we learned, had been grounded. Many more had deserted, seeking jobs with other airlines throughout Western Europe. Then one day Vlado came up to me in the departure lounge as I sipped a coffee at the passenger buffet. He was obviously feeling very pleased about something.

"I am very happy," he confirmed when I commented on this. "My wife and children have escaped from Prague. I don't have to pretend any more."

He and his family had been planning their move for months, he said. First he had worked on convincing his Communist masters that he was politically "reliable." At the same time he set up an elaborate scenario involving some friends in Switzerland, one of whom was to be a "close relative" who would suddenly fall seriously ill. Mme Becko would seek permission for a compassionate visit to the relative's bedside while her children were on holiday with other friends in Czechoslovakia.

At the last moment she would learn that the friends at home wouldn't be able to have the children, so she would apply for them to accompany her to Switzerland.

The ruse had worked.

"Now I am leaving the company and joining my family in Geneva," said Vlado. "Beyond that we have made no plans. But who knows… we may ask to be allowed to come to England."

His engineer at Northolt was somewhat less vulnerable. He had no immediate family in Czechoslovakia to worry about, and the bosses of the new state airline apparently

Czech Air Chiefs Told To Return

MR VLADIMIR BECKO, the Czech Airlines representative in London, said today that all the line's representative in Europe had been recalled to Prague for an urgent conference.

Although Mr Becko (one of those ordered to Prague) said that the conference had been called merely to discuss the new summer schedules, Northolt Airport officials believe that there may be some connection with a coming crisis in the airline's affairs.

"Since the incident of the 22 pilots who 'mutinied' while travelling from Prague to Bratislava," an official said, "individual members of the airline's crews have been deserting all over Europe.

"Changes in many of the crews have already been noticed."

There are rumours that the airline will soon cease operating. The number of passengers using the line has gradually dwindled since the Communist coup.

The Star *May 1948*

didn't see him as a potential subversive of any influence. Frantisek Macek, always known, inexplicably as Peter, thought his situation amusing.

"They don't think I'm bright enough to organise a Government in exile," he joked to me in his halting English, "So for the moment I'm happy to keep my head down." It was something that proved easier to affirm than to achieve. Within days of Vladimir Becko's return to Prague, Peter was facing a crisis of political conscience. He came along to the press room to tell me about it.

He waited in silence at the door as I finished a telephone call. If I was surprised, I tried not to show it. Peter had never before come to the office to see me. We regularly passed the time of day as he waited at the edge of the tarmac for the daily arrival of the CSA flight, and he occasionally passed on tit-bits of information. Northolt of those days was like that, a close-knit community. But we were hardly confidants.

Even so, I turned to him with a "Hello Pete," as though it were the most natural thing in the world for him to join me there. And after returning my greeting he suddenly blurted out:

"I have trouble. I not know what to do. I come to you for help...for advice."

The CSA flight from Prague had touched down at Northolt on time about an hour earlier. After the passengers had disembarked, Peter had gone aboard as usual to take over the controls and single-handedly taxi the American-built DC3 nearer the departures building to re-fuel and prepare for its return flight to Prague later that day. But before he could switch on his starter engine something had caught his eye.

Above his head, leading from the control panel in front of him over the bulkhead separating the flight deck from the passenger cabin were two steel wires. Running back to the Dakota's tail, these were the control cables for the aircraft's rudder and tail-plane stabilisers or "flaps." And they were moving.

He paused to allow this to sink in.

"You know what this is?" he asked, "Somebody is in there. Somebody is in my aircraft pulling on those cables."

"But where?" I asked him. "Where could anyone hide?"

Patiently, Peter explained. At the rear of the DC3, where the fuselage narrowed between the toilet and the tail fin, was a small space, measuring … he held out his arms … some three feet by three feet through which the cables ran. It was accessed through an inspection panel, normally locked.

"I know someone is hiding there," he said, "but he can only be a stowaway who is leaving Prague without permission; *they* would say illegally.

"If I let him out he will be free to ask for political asylum. But then I will be in trouble with Prague. As a loyal Czech, I should leave him where he is and allow him to return home to face arrest. I don't want that on my conscience."

For some minutes we discussed the problem and we dismissed any fanciful solutions. At last I concluded:

"There is only one thing we can do," (it seemed I was now part of the plot). "We must take a policeman into our confidence and let him 'discover' the stowaway. He could say he heard noises coming from the tail and insisted you investigate."

Peter was still unhappy about this, though he couldn't say why.

"I must go back and think about it," he said. "But I can't wait for long. My stowaway will be suffering."

Giving him a few minutes head start, I followed him back to the edge of the tarmac. I could go no closer. As a reporter I was not normally allowed into aircraft operational areas. In the event it wasn't necessary; I could see everything I needed to see. The Czech engineer was carefully unscrewing an inspection panel in the Dakota's belly, just forward of the tail. Overseeing him were two officers of the Ministry of Civil Aviation constabulary.

None of us could have been more surprised when the panel finally swung down on its hinges. From that tiny cavity squeezed not one but two young men, along no doubt with half a cubic yard of some very stale air. Their feet touched the ground one after the other and they both immediately collapsed in front of the two policemen, their tired muscles unable to support them.

For at least five hours, three in the air and two on the ground at Northolt, the two

TWO HIDE 5 HOURS IN PLANE

TWO Czech stowaways were found crouching in the tail compartment of a Dakota at Northolt last night, two hours after it landed from Prague.

The men, both under 21, had spent more than five hours in a space 3ft. high and 3ft. wide, unable to move.

Normally the compartment is not unlocked at Northolt, and they might have gone back to Prague.

The men were put in a detention room for the night. Permission is sought for them to stay here.

Daily Express

TWO FLYING STOWAWAYS

TWO Czech stowaways were found hiding in the tail compartment of a Czech air liner at Northolt airport last night, two hours after it had landed from Prague.

They had spent more than five hours crouching with their knees up, unable to move.

After questioning by Home Office officials the men, both airline engineers, under 21, were taken to the London Airport detention room for the night.

Daily Herald

STOWAWAYS IN CZECH PLANE

YOUTHS HID IN TAIL

Daily Telegraph Reporter

Two Czech youths were discovered crouched in the tail compartment of a Czech Air Lines Dakota at Northolt Airport last night, two hours after it had landed from Prague.

They were ground engineers at Prague Airport and earlier in the day had bribed an official there to lock them in the compartment, which is less than three feet wide and three feet high.

They were only discovered when an engineer making a last-minute check of the plane for the return journey found that a tail control cable, which passes through the rear compartment, was moving.

Normally the compartment is not unlocked at Northolt and the stowaways might have been flown back to Prague.

After two hours' questioning by Home Office officials the men were escorted to the London Airport detention room for the night. Permission is being sought for them to stay in England.

Daily Telegraph
(all) August 19 1948

2 Czechs flee in Dakota's tail

By Daily Mail Reporter

TWO Czech stowaways were found in the tail of a Czech Airlines' Dakota two hours after it had landed at Northolt airport from Prague last night.

The two men, both under 21, had paid an official at Prague airport to lock them in the tail compartment, which was less than 3ft. high and 3ft. wide.

They had spent more than five hours crouching with their knees up, unable to move.

The two were discovered when an engineer, making a cockpit check before the plane left for its return journey, noticed that a tail-control cable was moving.

Normally the compartment is not unlocked at Northolt, and the stowaways narrowly escaped being flown back to Prague.

After two hours' questioning by Home Office officials the men were escorted to the London airport detention room for the night. Permission is being sought for them to stay in England.

Daily Mail (above) *Daily Mirror (below)*

Two Czechoslovak stowaways were discovered crouched in the 3ft. high, 3ft. wide tail compartment of a Czech Air Lines plane at Northolt Airport last night, two hours after it had landed from Prague.

stowaways had been seated on a metal strut, side by side in total darkness, their knees tucked under their chins in the cramped space. For most of that time all they could hear was the roar of the Dakota's engines and the howl of the slipstream.

At last the police officers were able to escort their catches to an immigration office where they spent the next two hours being grilled. From the police I learned that Peter had recognised the two stowaways. They were both aircraft engineers from Prague airport. They had bribed a colleague to lock them in the tail compartment shortly before the aircraft took off for London.

They gambled on both being able to attract Peter's attention at Northolt and on his releasing them, as they had no idea where his political sympathies lay. But when he opened the hatch, his surprise at finding two colleagues was so genuine he was able to convince not only his bosses back home but also the stowaways that their discovery was an accident. He had, he said, been looking for a fault in the control cables. The police presence was purely fortuitous. (Peter told me he used the word "chance.")

The story published in all the dailies, the *Mail* and the *Telegaph* giving it the best space. But I was slightly disappointed. I felt it justified an even better showing. I was to learn in later years that this could frequently happen when a disproportionate amount of time and effort has gone into a story against the few hard facts shown at the end of the day. Perhaps if I'd been able to tell the full facts it would have won a bigger showing. But once the stowaways had been taken into custody and moved into detention at Northolt to await a decision on their future, neither Peter nor I heard anything more of their fate.

The two defectors were not the youngest to make their way to London from Czechoslovakia that summer. In June I reported the arrival at Northolt of a ten-years-old and his eight-years-old brother. Mila and Jan had left their home in Prague a week earlier to go "for a walk in the country," and found their way across the frontier into the American-occupied zone of Germany.

The boys had been living with their grandparents after their parents left for England. American authorities arranged for them to join their mother and father, a major with the former free Czech army in Britain. And as I reported: "There were tears of joy at Northolt as the family were re-united."

There were many more escape tales. We learned from Czech Airlines crews that hundreds of refugees of all ages and persuasions were taking their lives in their hands to dodge military patrols and find their way through unofficial border crossing points.

There were lighter stories too. One pilot told me of a rally of 100,000 schoolchildren for an annual sports festival at Prague's Masaryk Stadium. When the Communist President Gottwald mounted the rostrum to the accompaniment of the national anthem, the children aged between five and twelve, began chanting: "Long live President Benes."

President Gottwald, I was told, hesitated a few moments, then simply waved to the children, as if in acknowledgement. He had snatched power from the last democratic Czech leader only a few weeks earlier.

Later an announcement was made on the state-controlled radio apologising for the incident. No blame, it was said, could be attached to the children, who were "too young and innocent to appreciate the political changes which have taken place."

That story, amounting to no more than three paragraphs, was offered as an exclusive to the "*Peterborough*" diary column in the *Daily Telegraph.* It was used the next day as the column's tailpiece, traditionally a wry or humorous anecdote that needed no background or further verification.

Such verification on many of the stories Harry and I were picking up from the Czech air crews was of course impossible. We couldn't attribute them and we had no way of checking the facts. Fleet Street, and in particular the *Press Association*, understandably insisted that some credibility, in the form of attributable back-up "quotes" was essential for most of these stories. So few of the dramatic revelations about the Communist regime's outrages reaching us were ever published.

Si Jeunesse Savait . . .

FROM Prague I hear that 100,000 children, ranging in age from five to 12, recently gathered in the Masaryk Stadium to celebrate the annual sports festival.

As the new Communist president, M. Gottwald, stepped up to the rostrum, to the accompaniment of the national anthem, the children cried out: "Long live President Benes." M. Gottwald hesitated a few moments, then waved to the crowd.

Later an announcement was made on the radio apologising for the incident. No blame, it was said, attached to the children, who were "too young and innocent to realise the political changes which have taken place."

PETERBOROUGH

"Peterborough" Daily Telegraph ***July 1948***

With no scheduled services operating at the time between Moscow and London, the occasional appearance of a Soviet aircraft was always of interest. It might be a military transport, with its distinctive red star, or an airliner of the civil Aeroflot fleet, recognised by its Cyrillic inscription and red-flagged tailplane. These special aircraft invariably carried Soviet Government VIPs such as Foreign Minister Molotov, his successor Andrei Vyshinsky, or other diplomatic delegates. Less equal comrades permitted to visit the West had to travel the more circuitous route via Helsinki or Berlin or across land boundaries.

As potentially newsworthy personalities, these VIPs vouchsafed little to excite the headlines. On the rare occasions the head of an official delegation or mission indulged himself with a statement it was usually so full of platitudes or diplomatic obscurity it was of no news value. So it was simply the event, rather than the individual which made the news.

Although the mere departure of the Soviet Ambassador in London would provide a ready made front page lead, with most visitors from the Eastern bloc we found we had to rely on finding an "angle". It was the only way to guarantee publication of any sort of story beyond a single paragraph or a line in the "news in brief" columns.

Thus when a large wooden crate, measuring some four feet by three, was jealously guarded by the pilot of one Soviet aircraft as it was unloaded at Northolt, my story had to centre on this "Soviet box of mystery." RAF ground staff, who normally unloaded such aircraft, were waved away, and the Russian crew themselves loaded the crate into an Embassy van.

None of the Russians would talk about it, and the only guide to the contents of the box was an inscription that a Russian-speaking Foreign Office man interpreted for me as "Don't tip up." I decided this did not detract from the story, at least as far as my nose and notebook were concerned. And it was the only item on the arrival of the Russians to win any column inches the next day.

My photographer colleague, Tony Hewson, with two orders from national newspapers to meet, tried to brighten up the proceedings when a delegation of Russian women arrived to attend an international conference of "women for peace." The women looked as if they were determined not to enjoy being in the decadent West. Suspicious and wary, they huddled together for mutual protection as Tony tried to arrange them for a group picture. At last, in a desperate bid to get them to unbend, he appealed:

"Come on girls, smile – it's your birthday!"

Possibly something was lost in the translation. There was still no thaw in their returned stares. Then suddenly... a blinding flash, a loud explosion like a dozen champagne bottles popping and the solid phalanx of Mother Russia womanhood collapsed, as they scattered, involuntarily crouching for cover, in every direction. Tony's magnesium flashbulb, the size of a domestic 100-watt lamp, had shattered, showering the visitors with splinters of

The Star March 9 1951 *Brenard Press picture*

At the height of the Cold War, Mother Russia's representatives, a group of Soviet housewives, arrived in London to attend a two-day conference. They seemed a little unsure of their welcome. And that was before the Big Bang...

glass as it disintegrated.

A moment's silence, a hurried check to confirm no one had been hurt, and then the ice, like the flashbulb, was broken. Now the women were concerned human beings, concerned not for themselves, but for an embarrassed Tony, reassuring him with good-humoured backslaps, grins and jokes in their few words of broken English. It was Tony's turn to be relieved. "It was nothing," he said at last, "Anything to oblige."

Sadly, the newspapers failed to appreciate the humour of the situation or perhaps I failed to convey it. The only story to be published was as cold and forbidding as the accompanying picture *(left)* – the one before the "big bang."

"Seeing reds under the beds" was the kind of comment frequently made against extreme right-wing elements in America who appeared at times to be paranoid over the threat of Communist infiltration. But some of our own defenders of democracy and freedom could be just as sensitive.

When Harry reported the arrival at Northolt of a number of military aircraft carrying the Soviet delegation to Four-Power talks, and referred to the armed Russian guard that had been mounted on them overnight, there was uproar in newspaper editorials and in Parliament.

What were armed Russians doing in a peaceful country? Why were we allowing Russian soldiers to endanger lives with guns when even our policemen at the time went about with nothing more lethal than a truncheon? No one apparently thought to ask if the Russian guns had live bullets in them. Still less did anyone question the need for the guns carried by military police at bases run by our American allies.

Indeed, the Government took the easy way out. They simply denied there was any truth in the story. "There are no armed guards at Northolt," they said.

The denial was accepted, even though Harry agreed, reluctantly, to prove the truth of his report by conducting a national newspaper representative to the edge of the tarmac at night. Using the headlights of his soft-top Morris 8, the aim was to try to pick out a Russian soldier carrying a hand machine gun. The attempt failed because of poor visibility and the distance of the parked aircraft.

Life wasn't all Russians, revolutions and refugees, however. That year of 1948, my second as a cub reporter, presented me with a huge variety of news, from interviews with film stars and world statesmen to "silly season" stories about flying pigs and day-old chicks.

When I spotted three US Army Air Force officers wearing red bedroom slippers with their uniforms as they boarded their military transport aircraft to fly to Hamburg, one of them told me: "Last night we put our shoes outside our hotel bedroom doors for polishing. Today they'd vanished."

A less than conscientious bellhop? I 'phoned their London hotel. The manager

Airman off to Germany in bedroom slippers

AN American pilot and navigator, bound for Hamburg, boarded their plane at Northolt yesterday in borrowed footwear—one in red bedroom slippers.

They had arrived on Monday bringing American Servicemen from Germany, and in the words of the navigator, Lieutenant Wilkinson:

"We stayed at a London hotel, and put our shoes outside the bedroom door to be cleaned.

"Later we found they had vanished."

A representative of the hotel said last night:

"Their shoes may have been taken as a practical joke, because a third member of their party who at first could not find his shoes this morning later found them hidden"

Daily Mirror

Short Stories

RED bedroom slippers were worn by two United States Army pilots and a navigator in their aircraft at Northolt yesterday.

They explained: "Last night we put our shoes outside the bedroom door at our London hotel; this morning they had vanished."

Daily Herald *(both) Dec 12 1947*

disclaimed responsibility. "There were other airmen in the hotel who later found their shoes hidden," he claimed, "One of them must have been playing tricks."

Three men in a balloon, in those days a rarity, caused a minor alert as it "escaped" from its mooring on a Denham Studios film set, and drifted into the air lanes between Northolt and Heathrow. I chased it in a taxi from Northolt when callers warning of "flying saucers" suddenly jammed the switchboard. The balloon just managed to clear rooftops before coming to rest in a recreation ground at Hayes, Middlesex.

Out jumped three grinning Frenchmen, insisting they had Air Ministry permission for the flight. "Not so," the Ministry insisted when I called them, "We understood it was to be moored throughout the filming."

Both stories made "silly season" snippets in most dailies.

I also reported my first workers' strike. It involved BEA catering staff who regarded a refusal of double pay for Sunday working the last straw in what they saw as poor working conditions. The outcome was a compromise fudge and the dispute was one of many I was to follow and try to understand in the next few years. Some were politically motivated, but most were not part of some big Communist plot. Based on reasonable grievances, they were so often the result of poor communication and misunderstanding. But more of this later.

The first airport bomb scare to come my way was as long ago as 1948. It was caused by the discovery of an unmarked wooden box on a British European Airways flight from Athens. A stewardess came across the box on a passenger seat as passengers disembarked, but no one claimed it. Coolly, she handed it to a ground receptionist, less glamorously known in BEA as traffic clerks, with the words: "You'd better take this. It may be a bomb."

As I then reported: "Customs Officers decided it probably was a bomb, for when they opened the box a small metal canister was found."

The box was taken to a grassed enclosure and roped off. But after a further examination, the Customs men finally decided it was harmless. The metal canister was empty. My story concluded: "The box was removed to the lost property office."

For all I know it is still sitting somewhere on a dusty shelf, with the inscription "Not a bomb" over a Customs officer's scribbled clearance symbol.

Naïve people, if trusting and stout-hearted, worked at airports in those times, particularly as only a few weeks earlier the hostess on an Irish airliner from Dublin had been injured by a vacuum flask exploding in her hands. An ambulance took the young woman, 28-years-old Maureen O'Neill, to hospital with cuts to her hands and wrists. The incident led to a stronger vacuum flask designed to withstand the change in air pressure at altitude.

Northolt's cargo sheds could usually be relied upon to provide some snippets of news when the passenger buildings were unproductive. Harry impressed on me the need to include BEA's import and export managers when making the daily rounds of routine calls. Cargo space in what were still relatively small aircraft – twin-engined Dakotas and Vikings – was of course very limited. Bulk consignments were still carried by sea.

Speedier deliveries and simplified procedures of air transport were important, particularly with the carriage of live animals. Breeders in Britain were quick to benefit from the need to re-stock depleted flocks and herds on war-ravaged farms throughout the Continent. In some parts of Europe every chicken, duck, goose and even turkey must be descended from British stock, judging by the millions of day-old chicks and fertilised eggs carried on those early passenger flights.

National economies, as well as rural industries, were also in need of re-vitalisation in the late '40s, and this was evidenced by the frequent carriage of that international currency, gold bullion.

At Heathrow, an early gangland attempt to steal a mere £250,000 of bullion was thwarted by BOAC security and Scotland Yard whose officers posed as supposedly drugged cargo staff to catch the gang red-handed. Though aware of the stake-out, our Heathrow colleagues had to agree to keep quiet, then found that the success of the police action meant that much of the story was *sub judice*, and would only come out in court!

At Northolt we were seeing much more valuable consignments of bullion, mostly en

'BOMB' IN AIRLINER SCARE

A MYSTERIOUS wooden box, at first believed to contain a bomb, was found on a seat in a British European Airways plane which landed at Northolt from Athens last night.

The box, which no one had claimed, was handed to a traffic clerk by the stewardess, who remarked: "You, should take this. It may be a bomb."

A few minutes later Customs Officers decided that it was probably a bomb, for when the box was opened a small metal canister was found inside.

The canister was immediately taken to a corner of the public enclosure, roped off by police and put under guard.

Experts later decided that the canister was harmless, and took it to the lost property office.

Daily Mail

SUSPECTED 'BOMB' AT AIRPORT

HARMLESS CANISTER

Police roped off a corner of the public enclosure at Northolt Airport last night after a mysterious wooden box had been found in one of the passenger seats on a British European Airways plane which landed from Athens.

No one claimed the box, which was handed to a traffic clerk by the stewardess. She said: "You should take this. It may be a bomb." A few minutes later Customs officers decided that it probably was a bomb, for when the box was opened a small metal canister was found inside.

The canister was taken to the public enclosure and roped off. Later Customs officers again examined the canister and came to the conclusion that it was harmless. They removed it to the lost property office.

Daily Telegraph (both) Oct 16 1948

Was this one of the first airport bomb scares?

route to Swiss banks, and it was understood we would only report the arrival or departure of bullion when it was well clear of the airport. Jokingly I asked one cargo handler where he'd hidden the £1 million of gold (about £16m at today's prices) I knew was due to leave. I was a little dismissive when he cheerfully and casually pointed to a heap of boxes outside the Export shed doors.

He wasn't joking. The crates, measuring some fifteen inches by eight or nine inches, each contained a number of gold bars, the gleaming metal clearly visible through the wooden slats. They were stacked on the concrete just a few yards from a road leading directly to the A40 Western Avenue.

"Don't look so shocked," laughed my friend, "No one knows it's there apart from us. And it's just about to be loaded." The aircraft it was destined for was parked at least 200 yards away.

The incident could have given me guaranteed "Gold Scandal" headlines. But a one-day sensation would also have ensured the immediate loss of all our cargo contacts, and a certain black-out on news stories from the freight sheds for months to come. I quietly advised BEA cargo managers of my sense of public responsibility.

An even bigger gold consignment, worth more than £2 million, was being loaded on a series of flights to Helsinki over a period of one week, and BEA had agreed to let me know when the operation was complete if I kept quiet until then. But I was not over-pleased when, as I waited in the arrivals hall for a newsworthy passenger, the airline's press officer, an ebullient Humphrey Downes, burst in on me to announce loudly with an extravagant wave of his hand:

"Release the gold, release the gold! It's all safely away."

I could have kicked him. Heads in the crowded lounge turned in astonishment at this strange pronouncement. But what worried me more was that I wasn't alone. Waiting with me was a rival, a staff reporter from the *P.A.* news agency, Reg Garner, who was immediately on the alert.

"Gold?" he asked, "What gold? What's this all about?"

Fortunately Humphrey realised his gaffe and tried to play the situation down.

"Oh, it's nothing, old boy," he stammered, "Just a little thing we've been dealing with together. I promised I'd come back with an answer."

Reg was a good sport. He must have seen the glare I'd given Downes, and didn't press the point. Next time we met I told him the story.

Curiously, few of the many stories over this period earned the space they really justified. But with a severe shortage of newsprint, newspapers of the day were very small, and even the major reports were curtailed. When four bananas labelled: "Urgent. To save human life," were flown from Northolt to Prague for a ten-months-old baby, the story made only twelve lines in the *Evening Standard*, and only a paragraph in *The Star*. And this after a desperate search of London shops for the then scarce fruit.

Even stranger was the small space, some two centimetres of a single column, the Daily Mail devoted to my following piece (though I take no responsibility for the sentence construction):

THE OPEN DOOR. — When, shortly after leaving Northolt Airport last night the door of a luggage compartment of an 18-seater air-liner flew open, a passenger lay full length on the floor and held the door in position.

The plane circled the airport twice, made a perfect landing, and the door was secured.

Daily Mail June 9 1948

A few years on and an item like this could have made several inches, not just "top of the briefs."

But the shortest story ever must have been the *two lines* I was awarded in a "One Minute News" column, again in the *Mail.*

ONE-MINUTE NEWS

Dr. Richard Strauss left Northolt Airport for Switzerland.

Daily Mail Nov 1 1947

Why did I keep it? Even two lines are better than none!

It was, after all, at a time when newsprint was severely restricted, resulting in very thin newspapers. And there was one major exception to this outbreak of linage deficiency, with a sombre origin. In July 1948 two aircraft, one civil, one military collided as they both approached Northolt. The result was one of the worst air disasters civil aviation had experienced in Britain at that time.

It was a Sunday afternoon, and a miserable, dismal day. Inevitably it was raining, with low cloud cutting the light and making visibility difficult even at ground level. Harry and I had found we could take turns at covering the airport at weekends. Saturday's evening papers were mainly sport, and the Sunday papers went to press early, so the working day was usually short. As there were no evening papers to consider on Sunday, it too was a short day but still an important one, as Monday's papers were frequently short of news.

The time was shortly before four o'clock in the afternoon, and normally I would have been thinking of making my way home, more than an hour's journey on the Central or Metropolitan and Piccadilly tube lines as I've indicated elsewhere. But the *Press Association* had ordered a story on the arrival from Kuala Lumpur of Britain's High Commissioner in Malaya, Sir Edward Gent. He had been recalled for urgent discussion with the Government on Communist activities in what was then a British colony and was due in shortly. Later it was reported that he also intended to resign his post.

It may only have been the depressing weather. But I experienced a sufficient sense of foreboding to remark on it to an airport policeman who greeted me as I ran out through the teeming rain to my cab.

"I don't like this one bit, Paddy," I shouted, "I feel something's going to happen – and I don't know what." He was to remind me of this time and time again in years to come, particularly when the weather was bad.

Author's collection

'Paddy' the PC, 1948

We drove out of the main gate and turned left on the A40 towards London, and a few minutes later turned left again to continue towards Ruislip. We were heading for the RAF VIP base on the north side of the airport, only half-a-mile away across the airfield, but almost two miles by road. As we reached the narrow entrance gates to the RAF station, we had to stop short of the guardroom to permit a service fire tender to exit. I thought nothing of this. Fire tenders and ambulances frequently left the airport for practice runs in the surrounding area.

Seconds later we reached the VIP base adjoining one of the huge aircraft hangars, by this time used for BEA aircraft maintenance. The taxi was going to wait for me. Sir Edward Gent's aircraft, a four-engined RAF York transport, was due at any time, and I expected no more than a "No comment" from him. I would soon be able to leave.

But in the RAF Operations room I was told convincingly: "The aircraft's been delayed. The last we heard it was waiting to land. But it could be a little while. Cloud base is too low at the moment."

I decided to give it half-an-hour. It was only just four o'clock, and there could be other aircraft waiting to land. After a few minutes I thought I'd call the newsroom at Heathrow to let them know of the delay. The agency's then news editor Doug Shillito, a cousin of Bill Brenard, answered my call.

"Thank heavens you've rung," he said, "We've been trying to find you. We've just heard that your RAF York has gone down at Northwood. Have you got a taxi? You have? Then get over there straight away and give us a call as soon as you can."

He had no further information for me and I knew it would be useless trying to get something out of the RAF at this stage. If they knew anything, as they almost certainly did, they weren't going to tell me anything yet, and I might learn something at the crash site, wherever that might be. I dashed back to my cab and with a brief explanation told my driver to "Step on it!"

Northwood is just beyond Ruislip, about six or seven miles away. I was not at that time very familiar with the area, but I knew it was not densely populated, and there was quite a bit of open space, mainly woods and parkland. I had no idea at that stage how we would be able to find the aircraft – it was a huge area and the visibility was getting worse.

Then we had a piece of luck. As we turned out of the gates of the airport, another fire tender suddenly overtook us and rushed through. It turned left towards Ruislip – and I remembered the one we'd passed ten minutes earlier. "Follow it," I said to my driver. "We've nothing to lose while we're going the same way."

We followed the tender, sometimes, it seemed, at breakneck speeds, along suburban and country roads for miles, finally ending in a cul-de-sac, with a few houses lining one side of the road. The tender continued through a gateway into a lightly wooded area, and disappeared from view along a track. A number of vehicles, including a police car and a couple of trucks in RAF blue were parked near the gate, so we pulled in behind them.

"It can't be far from here," I said, "I'll walk. Hang on for me, will you? I can't afford to spend too long."

A minute or two later and I was gazing at a scene of utter devastation. I had seen aircraft crashes during my days as an evacuee in East Anglia. Bombers which had been shot-up over Germany frequently crashed on landing after limping home, and I had witnessed at least one Stirling bomber blow up in a flash of fire when its damaged undercarriage collapsed on touch down. But that had all seemed so impersonal, and from a distance, almost unreal.

Here, the sheer scale of the disaster engulfed me as I stepped through the gloom of the rain-drenched surrounding trees into the sudden misty daylight of open space. A clearing, I suddenly realised, which had been scooped out by the falling aircraft crushing and slicing through those trees as it sank into a jagged underbed of shattered and splintered branches.

Firemen and rescue workers, several of whom I recognised as general services' and other ground staff from the airport, were working all around me. Grubbing through the flotsam of aircraft cargo crates, smashed suitcases and their scattered belongings, they tore at the huge chunks of jagged metal with bare hands in their search for victims. The contorted, obscene pyre still smouldered; its capping of snow-like fire-damping foam reducing all that remained of the four-engined RAF airliner to nothing more enduring than the smouldering ashes of a huge bonfire in some breaker's yard.

I managed to ask one of the rescue team if they had found any survivors, biting my lip at the necessity of the stupid question, then learned before I was moved back by a policemen that three bodies had still to be recovered from the wreckage. I realised I had no idea how many would have been aboard the aircraft with the High Commissioner. I hurried back to the car.

"Must just find a phone. Then I'll be with you," I told the driver.

I looked up and down the road to try to spot telephone wires. About fifty yards back was a telegraph pole, its wires running to an adjoining house. I raced back, crossed a gravel-strewn drive, and rang the bell.

A young woman answered. I showed her my NUJ Press Card.

"I believe you have a phone," I said, "May I use it please, for a transfer charge call?"

Without a word she ushered me into the hall and pointed to the phone, as if providing communications for reporters was an everyday experience. I dialled for the operator. Within minutes I was dictating everything I knew to a Brenard copy-taker at Heathrow. As I wound up, Doug Shillito came on the line.

"Er... yeah, old chap. That's fine," he said as he scanned the copy in front of him, "But what about the other one?"

He responded to my bewildered protests by explaining that the RAF York had apparently collided in mid-air with a Swedish airliner. From all accounts both had dropped like stones, so it too must be nearby...

Shouting my thanks to the householder, I rushed from the door back to my taxi. "There's another one," I gabbled, jumping in beside the driver, "just drive off – I can't waste time here. The ground teams may not know where it is."

Once again, almost miraculously, my luck held. We reached the main road just as a police car shot by, its bell clanging. "Right. Let's follow that!" I cried, and once again we were hurtling along narrow lanes into more woodland. This time we were able to get closer to the scene, which was just a few yards into a heavily wooded spinney.

Now the devastation was even more pronounced. A thick, choking pall of black smoke hung over a plateau of wreckage strewn, it seemed, for hundreds of yards back through the trees and flattened undergrowth. Now there was the heartbreaking evidence of families, their personal belongings and mementoes scattered like chaff among the torn and ravished furnishings and fittings of a luxurious modern airliner.

Much of the fuselage of the American-built Douglas DC6, a brand new four-engined airliner just introduced into service by ABA, the Swedish airline, was still recognisable, though twisted and battered by the impact. A door to the passenger cabin was lying partly open at an awkward angle just a few feet from where I stood. As two oilskin-clad rescue workers reached down to shift the still gleaming polished aluminium saucer, I glimpsed the twisted and obviously lifeless body of a young stewardess in her dark blue uniform. A small army of other rescue workers and firemen swarmed over the wreckage between the stumps of smashed trees, the huge tail-plane of the aircraft towering over them.

But then the similarities ended. Here there was something else; an all-pervading, all-penetrating smell of burning flesh, human flesh. Here the fires had obviously burned even more fiercely, more destructively, before the fire tenders had been able to reach the scene. And the rescue teams were only just recovering the remains, all that remained, of those who perished on board.

One group of five struggled past me, tramping down the waste-high brambles and splintered tree shafts under the weight of their gruesome burden, only partially concealed in its red-stained canvas body bag. I recognised the leading member of the group as an airport tarmac worker, his navy blue battledress uniform mud-covered and drenched through with the unrelenting drizzle.

We acknowledged each other with a nod, but my look must have been questioning because he volunteered:

"We've only found a few so far. There must be quite a number under that lot."

There appeared to be no one in authority, not even a police officer or a fire-chief for me to talk to, and everyone else was fully occupied. But I doubted if there was anything anyone would or could say at that time. I set off to look for a 'phone, and again found one in a nearby house within a few minutes. After dictating my description of the scene, conscious that I had an audience in my host household for every word, I told Doug that I was going to return to the airport to see what I could pick up there. The doorbell rang as I replaced the telephone.

I was standing by the front door, so it seemed quite acceptable for me to open it. Before I could say anything, one of the two callers facing me spoke up.

"Sorry to trouble you, sir," he said, "But we're from the *Daily Mail*. We wondered if we could use your 'phone?"

"Certainly," I replied brashly, "I'm from Brenards. And I've just finished with it."

I remember very little about the rest of the day. When I arrived back at the airport, I found Harry dictating from the Press Room 'phone. He'd been called in on his day off to cover the airport end of the story, which among other things meant finding the relatives or friends of passengers waiting to meet the ABA flight.

It must have been Harry who "...secured a useful beat with the Swedish passenger list," for which Doug Shillito gave me the credit in a letter a few days later.

"You are to be congratulated for putting in some very good work both in the area of the crash and at Northolt," the letter ran, "Conditions for working on the story were very bad and we are pleased with your efforts. A bonus follows..."

But then Doug pointed out: "Without detracting in any way from the above, however, your copy could have contained more descriptive detail...."

And he gently drew my attention to the story in, of all papers, the *Daily Mail*, where, under the names of two reporters was the vivid description:

"...crocodile shoes... a dented can of processed cheese... a child's doll... lay broken against the skeleton of a wing... the tail-fin which reared high against a tree like a giant tombstone."

Perhaps if I hadn't been quite so cocky, I might have learned something from those *Mail* men. But Doug, for his part, must have thought there was some hope for me. His letter concluded:

"If in future you proceed as you did on Sunday, at the same time probing a little more into 'colour,' you will have developed a really first class technique for crashes...."

I am glad to say that I never did regard such a specialist ability as one of my career objectives, neither then nor in later times. Coverage of air disasters is a fortunately infrequent, and far from welcome part of the airport reporter's experience, and not simply because of the sensitive and emotional implications.

It is possible, I learned, not to become over-involved emotionally in such situations,

Souvenirs

Firemen picking about on the edges of the hot metal wreckage retrieved the charred souvenirs which the York's crew were bringing home to wives and relatives in England. They made only a small pile.

There were a pair of brown wool-lined bootees, a crocodile handbag and crocodile shoes, a woman's blue blouse, and a coconut still in its outer shell. The heat had burst it open.

Other searchers brought in a towel, a tie, two flare pistols, and a dented can of processed cheese.

Several victims were trapped under the plane's main spar. This had to be cut with an acetylene torch before they could be brought out.

Behind the firemen as they worked stood the coroner's officer, in plain clothes, to see that any possessions, documents, or identity discs were not lost.

Hundreds of men, women, and children filtered through the guard of R.A.F. men dispersed among the trees, to be sent back by police on guard against souvenir-hunting.

Broken doll

Little more than a mile away there were similar scenes as firemen and police searched among what remained of the DC6.

Only part not blown to pieces was the tail fin, which reared high against a tree like a giant tombstone.

Pieces of clothing, still smouldering, were caught in the bare branches of trees, and the working parties could do little more than collect a few charred relics—shoes, including children's, women's handbags, hundreds of airmail letters, and bits of Swedish newspapers.

Most pathetic of all was a child's doll. It lay broken against the skeleton of a wing, its hair singed and porcelain face scorched.

Dr. A. Drucker, who lives in Ducks Hill-road, said: "I was picking raspberries in my garden

Daily Mail (extract) July 5 1948

however understanding and sincerely sympathetic any normal observer must be in witnessing human tragedy and heartbreak. At the same time I was aware that to be completely detached, cold and without feeling, would be counter-productive. Nothing is so transparent in writing as indifference or impassivity.

In simple professional and practical terms, coverage of major disasters of this kind I rarely found satisfying or rewarding. Of the many column inches devoted to this air collision the next day, I could not honestly claim any obvious input, though the agency's contribution was well acknowledged in newspaper payments at the end of the month. So many of the hundreds of words I had dictated from the crash scene and later from the airport during the many hours I was on duty simply disappeared under the by-lines of staff reporters.

A total of 39 lives were lost on the two aircraft, a fraction of the number of probable victims if a similar disaster had occurred just a few years later with much larger aircraft, but a major incident at the time. The court of inquiry, which sat some months, failed to find the exact cause, and concluded that the accident was "probably due to human fallibility," though no blame was directed at either aircrew.

There was some criticism of ground control radio procedures, and there was speculation on misunderstanding or misinterpretation of radio messages. But the most significant conclusion was that the minimum height separation of 500 feet for two or more aircraft in force at the time "provided an inadequate margin of safety."

The court's recommendation that this normal height separation be increased from 500ft to 1,000ft, was adopted immediately by the aviation authorities. It subsequently proved to be one of the most important air safety measures ever introduced.

Excerpts from front pages *(reduced)* **of the** *Daily Mail (below)* **and the** *Daily Express (opposite)*, **on Britain's worst air disaster to date** *(see also p51)*

Daily Mail

NO. 16,268 ONE PENNY * FOR KING AND COMMONWEALTH MONDAY, JULY 5, 1948

39 KILLED IN BRITAIN'S WORST PLANE CRASH

NO SURVIVORS

From GEORGE HILL and LAURENCE WILKINSON

NORTHOLT, Middlesex, Sunday Night.

TWO four-engined airliners, an R.A.F. York and a Swedish DC6, collided as they circled Northolt Airport in grey rain-clouds this afternoon. Both crashed, killing all 39 people on board. It was Britain's worst plane disaster.

For an hour the York, in from Malta, had droned round and round at 1,000ft. waiting to land. The pilot of the DC6 decided that the weather was too bad to make the attempt. He radioed that he was making for Amsterdam.

As the 48-seater plane swung off on her new course, mischance took her across the path of the York. The two sliced into each other with a crash that was heard all over the town. The voices of the two radio men talking to Northolt control ceased abruptly.

Then, in a shower of riven aluminium and splintered plywood, the shattered planes crashed through the clouds. They hit the earth a mile and a quarter apart.

The DC6 disintegrated in an explosion which blew plane, 25 passengers, and crew of seven, into pieces. The York blazed with a fierce intensity that fired the trees in the spinney into which she fell.

Sole passenger in the York, with its crew of six, was Sir Edward Gent, High Commissioner for Malaya. He joined her at Malta on the last lap of his journey home to discuss the troubles in Malaya. There were reports that he intended to offer his resignation.

Comment

DEATH

TWO large planes collide in mid-air. Thirty-nine persons, among them SIR EDWARD GENT, High Commissioner for Malaya, lose their lives. It is one of the worst disasters in British air history.

Empty shell

It was at 3.55 that a handful of Sunday visitors to Mount Vernon Hospital, Northwood, waiting in the drizzling rain for their buses home heard the crash directly overhead.

The DC6, a Scandinavian Airlines aircraft on the Stockholm-Copenhagen-London run, fell at Ducks Hill, Northwood, narrowly missing houses in Ducks Hill-road.

The York hit the ground in Battlers Wells Wood, Harefield. Her severed tail landed on the flat roof of the night sisters' sleeping quarters at Mount Vernon.

Scores of people ran to the two wrecks. But the heat drove them back. When firemen arrived with foam equipment there was no hope of saving anyone.

Force of the impact ripped everything—seats, instruments, and fittings—out of the York, leaving the hull an empty shell. All on board had been flung into a huddled heap in the nose. They were burned beyond recognition.

Dr. A. Drucker, who lives in Ducks Hill-road, said: "I was picking raspberries in my garden when I heard two crashes. At first it sounded as though planes were having shooting practice, and I looked up to see a huge plane diving out of the clouds.

"Then I saw a second plane. They appeared to be recoiling from each other. The first plane—it was the DC6—turned over and over, as if doing aerobatics, and then dived to earth. She fell into the wood across the road from me.

"The trees had caught fire and we could not approach because of the heat."

The work of salvage went on under lowering clouds. But as the last human remnants were taken from the wreckage of the Scandinavian plane, the sky cleared and a watery sun broke through.

This official announcement was issued tonight:

"The Air Ministry announce with regret that the York aircraft MW 248 of Transport Command, arriving at Northolt from Malta, collided with a DC 6 of Scandinavian Air Lines about 4 o'clock this afternoon near Northwood, Middlesex. It is feared that all on board the York lost their lives. Next of kin are being informed.

"The Colonial Office announces with regret that Sir Edward Gent, High Commissioner for the Federation of Malaya, was a passenger in the York."

Sir E. Gent a victim

SIR EDWARD GENT, High Commissioner in Malaya, killed in the R.A.F. plane, had been called to London for consultations. It had been reported that he intended to resign.

Sir Edward, who was 53, was regarded as the "perfect Civil Servant." He went to the Colonial Office after the first world war.

He was the only passenger in the plane. The members of the crew were: Flt.-Lieut. C. R. Coates, Flying Officer F. Momrie, Flt.-Lieut. W. Trotman, Signaller A. G. Lewis, Flt.-Engineer I. Rees, and Flt.-Lieut. C. Ingleby.

Three British people were in the Scandinavian plane: Mr. and Mrs. Gordon Charles Newman, aged 31 and 29, who worked for the British Legation in Helsinki, and Mr. Douglas Pobjoy, 54, who was associated with aero-engine design for a British firm.

Another passenger was Count Thott, a friend of King Gustav and Master of the Royal Hunt.

Worst air disaster in this country was near Hull in 1921, when the airship R 38 caught fire and broke in half with the loss of 44 lives.

In October 1930 48 died when the R 101 crashed into a hillside near Beauvais, France.

39 die in biggest air crash

Giant planes collide in mid-air

DOOMED DC6 AIRLINER WRAPPED ITSELF AROUND A TREE

DAILY EXPRESS

No. 14,995 Lighting-up: 10.18 pm to 3.51 am MONDAY JULY 5 1948 Weather: Fair, cool

ALL lost as planes collide in the air | **BEVAN attacks Tories for 'bitter days'** | **BERNADOTTE puts new 2-State plan** | **RAIL leaders seek one big union**

AIR COLLISION KILLS 39

Planes circling airport ram each other

'I QUIT' CHIEF DEAD

Express Staff Reporters

TWO planes collided in the air yesterday afternoon, above the woods and homes of Middlesex. Both crashed and were burned out. Thirty-nine people died. Not one man or woman survived. It was the worst air disaster ever known over Britain.

Just before the crash, five planes were circling Northolt Airport in heavy rain, waiting for permission to drop through low-lying clouds to land.

One was a York of R.A.F. Transport Command, which had flown 7,840 miles to bring one man to London. It circled for an hour. Then it was told: "Go south to Hurn Airport in Hampshire."

About the same time, a Swedish Skycloud airliner, headed for Northolt from Copenhagen, radioed: "Don't like the weather. Am returning to Amsterdam."

It set its course east. And the crash came, at 3.59 p.m., rolling like a gigantic thunderclap over the rain-sodden hills.

RIPPED TAIL OFF

The planes met almost immediately above the Mount Vernon Hospital at Northwood. The Skycloud smashed into the York, ripping off its tail. Below the clouds, people could hear three quick explosions.

Down dived the York, with its one passenger and crew of six, straight into Battler's Wells Wood, off the Northwood-road at Harefield. Its tail fell a mile away. Half a mile further on, the Skycloud, a sheet of twisting flame, crashed into the hill known as Mad Bess.

Sole passenger in the York—No. 248, last call Malta—was Sir Edward Gent, 53-year-old High Commissioner of the new Federation of Malaya. He was flying home, it was said, to resign because he disagreed with Service chiefs on how to deal with trouble-makers in Malaya.

Sir Edward and the six R.A.F. men with him were shot into the nose as the four-engined York crashed. Fuselage and wings were torn apart. Only the nose caught fire. There, the seven men were found huddled together. None could be identified.

Firemen made a pile of the salvage from the wreck—much of it intended as gifts for relatives of the crew: a pair of women's fleecy lined bootees, a woman's crocodile-skin shoe, a crocodile bag, a dented tin of cheese. . . .

SEARCH FOR DOCUMENTS

A few yards away, among smouldering leaves, was the silvered surround of the plane's escape exit, which there had been no time to use.

And scattered in a trail across the fields were fragments of paper—so many that R.A.F. rescue teams set to gather them were still searching when night fell. Early this morning the paper-trail was being guarded by airmen. For it is believed that the fragments are from secret documents brought by Sir Edward Gent to justify his decision to resign.

On Mad Bess Hill, up the lane from Duck's Hill-road, the passengers in the Swedish plane died in their seats. Their safety belts were fixed—ready for the landing that the weather postponed. Three of the 25 passengers were British. Two of the crew of seven were girl air-hostesses. Two women, one in a red coat, were found clasped in each other's arms.

As the blazing plane crashed, the wood on the hill caught fire. Trees burned in the rain like torches.

Firemen, smothered in mud, again found the pathetic remnants of disaster—two pairs of silk stockings wrapped round a tree trunk, a zip bag ripped open, a reel of cotton. . . .

There were charred cheques and letters, mostly in Swedish. There was a gold wrist watch and a clock—both sets of hands stopped at 4 o'clock.

And there was a passport bearing a woman's name and a Kensington address. But no woman of that name was known to be in the plane.

WAITING FOR FIANCEE

In the Skycloud were 31-year-old Charles Gordon Newman and his 29-year-old wife Irene. He was a radio operator in the British Embassy at Helsinki. Yesterday morning he and his wife caught a plane to Stockholm, transferred to the Skycloud—on their first trip home since the war.

The third Briton in the plane was Douglas Rudolph Pobjoy, aged 54, a Daimler engineer who spent most of his life helping to design plane engines.

With them died Count Stig Tott, Sweden's largest landowner, and a Swiss girl, Elizabeth Baumann. Waiting for her at Northolt Airport was Captain Lucodi, of Coleherne-court, S.W. They were to have been married.

From the homes of Northwood, where kettles were beginning to boil for afternoon tea, hundreds of men and women rushed to the woods where the planes crashed.

There was nothing anyone could do.

At Mount Vernon Hospital visitors were leaving friends and relatives in the wards, queueing for buses to take them home. Wreckage from the collision rained down—on the roof of the hospital, in the grounds, on the road. They, too, ran to help over barbed-wire fences, through knee-high bracken.

In the back garden of his house in Duck's Hill-road, Dr. Alfred Drucker was picking raspberries with a friend.

Out of the rain and cloud—as low as 500ft.—dropped the Skycloud, "spinning like a huge toy."

The two men ducked into the raspberry bushes, for the airliner seemed to be heading for them. Then they saw it nosedive on to Mad Bess.

A mile and a half away, Mr. A. C. Harewood, an ex-R.A.F. officer, saw the tail-less York spin nose down into the wood. There was an explosion—"it made my house vibrate."

Tree drives through crashed York's wing

AS the York hit the ground in Battler's Wells Wood, one wing was ripped by a tree and came to rest with the tree thrusting up from its centre. Steam and smoke are seen rising from the wreckage.

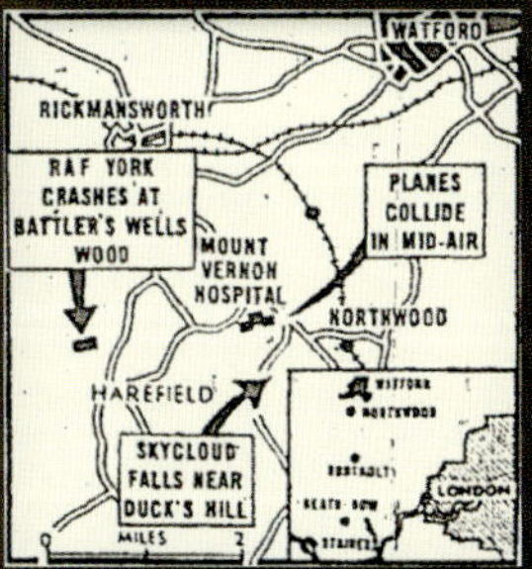

SIR EDWARD GENT

D.S.O., M.C. Aged 53. Became first High Commissioner of the Federation of Malaya, set up on February 1. Had been Governor and C.-in-C., Malayan Union, since 1946.

He left Singapore last Tuesday for consultations with the Colonial Secretary. He had differences with the Service chiefs on measures for dealing with terrorists in Malaya.

Sir Edward, son of a judge, married in 1923 and had two sons and two daughters.

CHAPTER THREE

Just four weeks after that air disaster, I celebrated my eighteenth birthday. And suddenly I woke up to the thought that now I could be called up for my National Service.

I had no desire to become a soldier. I had served with the Army cadets while still at school, and could find nothing in favour of marching up and down a square to the unintelligible ranting of a bully with stripes on his arm.

In any case it seemed just a ridiculous waste of time, my time, when I was at the threshold of my career. I earnestly believed I was the last person my country needed. The War Office, I knew, would regret enticing me away for eighteen months. I didn't want to think of the RAF as an alternative; that would have been a form of masochism. And as for the Navy – I would have been an even worse sailor.

No, if I had to go, it would have to be the Army, and something far removed from aeroplanes. I applied for the Tank Corps. That way, I reasoned, I wouldn't have to walk into battle. It proved to be a fortunate choice, at least in some ways.

The summer passed... then autumn. In November, just when I was vainly hoping that perhaps somehow, I had been overlooked, my invitation finally arrived. Early in January, marching orders despatched me to the Royal Armoured Corps training centre at Catterick Camp, Yorkshire.

Three RAC regiments were based there in 1949, the 14/20th King's Hussars, the 17/21st Lancers and the 8th Royal Tank Regiment. With typical Army logic the first two of these were still cavalry regiments, though equipped with tanks. The 8th RTR was a tank regiment, and it too was equipped with tanks, though I wouldn't have been in the least surprised if it had been saddled with horses.

I was posted to the 8th Tanks. I was glad to find that horses weren't involved. Somehow it seemed preferable to start immediately with tanks rather than to jump from a saddle into a turret.

As any former National Serviceman will understand, I remember little of my five weeks' basic training other than the obligatory "fatigues," spit and polish and square bashing. The last was obviously an alliterative description of the noise made by hundreds of ill-fitting, feet blistering, hobnailed boots crashing down on gravelled asphalt of the barrack parade ground. It also took the form of before-dawn exercising on that same wind-swept and frost-covered square in shorts and singlet at minus 5C.

"Fatigues" was army slang for both punishment duties and the overalls for carrying them out. Spit and polish was literally the science-into-art process of mixing spittle with boot polish and applying it, preferably with a heated tea spoon handle, to a pair of leather boots. The military objective here, it seems, was to remove the surface dimples of the unyielding leather, thereby converting the boots, by a form of introduced osmosis, into a pair of superbly polished reflective black appendages.

There was nothing else to remember, except my letters home, bearing my personally symbolic sender's address *"Catterick Camp/Yorkshire moors"* on the back of the envelope. This did absolutely nothing for the postman, but as the "oblique" symbol could also be read as "oh, bleak," it gave me a kind of perverse, if immature, satisfaction. (Somehow the computer equivalent "forward slash" doesn't have the same dignity.)

Then there was the accommodation. We were airily informed on arrival that we should think ourselves lucky. We were among the first to use the brand-new "Monty Blocks." These were apparently former barrack rooms which had been divided up to provide smaller rooms housing just three or four recruits. Each room boasted its own coke-burning stove; each bed had a switched bedside lamp and its own built-in locker and bookshelf.

Field Marshal Montgomery had ordered the redesign of barrack rooms when he became Chief of the Imperial General Staff – the supreme army commander. My understanding was that he meant *all* barrack rooms to be divided this way. But after our basic training we were moved on, to permit the next intake to savour the little luxuries. Bedside lamps that failed to work (but whose use was not permitted anyway after "lights out"), bookshelves which had to be kept clear of books, lockers without keys, stoves that ran out of fuel. Then we moved into the more familiar dormitory blocks with just two coke stoves between 20 or 30 young trainees, and overhead lighting under 'coolie hat' shades, and a single light switch at the entrance door.

The next few weeks were to be devoted to our training for an Army "trade." Hypothetically, every recruit was given a choice here, but it was limited by the role of the Army unit concerned. In practice, civilian trades or aptitudes were simply interpreted (or in most cases misinterpreted) into a military equivalent.

My commercial artist friend, Mike Noble, was directed to the regimental sign-writing office. His immediate chum, young silversmith and metal artisan David Mellor who, a few years on, was to gain world recognition for his work in stainless steel, joined him there. No one could think of a more appropriate role for someone who was to win prestigious awards for designs ranging from pillar-boxes and telephone kiosks to new concept table cutlery. But another young recruit from that era, the son of General Sir Brian Robertson, the same Sir Brian I'd tried so often to interview in my previous existence, was almost immediately packed off to an officer cadet training unit.

If I was a reporter in civvy-street, I must be a pen-pusher. So I could only be an Army clerk. In reality, this meant going back to the classroom for the next few weeks to study Army forms, to know their reference numbers by heart, and to learn when and how they were to be used. My heart wasn't in the learning or the application. I simply spent the learning time making a ready-reference alphabetical list, with my own notes alongside on the occasions or situations when I thought they might become appropriate.

Catterick Express

ISSUE No. 75 PRICE TWOPENCE

FRIDAY, AUGUST 26th, 1949. Fortnightly

Catterick Express;
"The only newspaper in Britain published by, and for, the troops themselves."

Most of my efforts were directed towards finding some role I could play which allowed me to develop a journalistic capability. Robert Brenard, Bill's father, had given me an introduction to Sydney Redwood, news editor of the British Army News Unit, which produced among other things, *Soldier* magazine. He in turn suggested I went along to see the editor of the local Army newspaper, the *Catterick Express*.

The newspaper had been the brainchild of an earlier district commander, Major General R.T.O. Cary, and its proud boast was that it was the only Army newspaper published by and for the troops in Britain. Unlike its overseas counterparts, it had no War Office financial backing, and was obliged to be self-supporting. Its editor, in name at least, as he had no journalistic background, was the Catterick District entertainments officer, a civilian. Its main income, advertising, was the responsibility of his Accounts clerk, another civilian.

Editorially, production of the newspaper was down to its "staff" of young National Service journalists – one full-time news editor and, when available, two or three part-time correspondents among the dozen or so regiments which made up the 20,000 population of Catterick Camp.

I very quickly found my way to Catterick District HQ to introduce myself to the editor, Charlie Childs, and the incumbent news editor, Taffy Lewis, formerly a reporter with the *South Wales Herald.* A Royal Army Medical Corps sergeant, Iorwerth J. Lewis, from Maesteg in South Wales, had only recently taken over from his predecessor in the post, and was already looking for a potential successor himself. With only eighteen months National Service at that time, and the first few of those taken up with formal military training, it was essential to find someone to take over when "demob" approached.

Taffy was soon accepting stories from me on my unit's activities, and other odd items picked up on my rounds of the garrison town. Pat Nicholson, a mate in the 8th Tanks who had been a reporter with the *Kentish Mercury* in south London and I launched a "Press Club" for young journalists serving at Catterick. It rapidly expanded to include a photographer, a printer and a commercial artist (my sign-painter chum Mike Noble) to make up a quorum to justify the "club" title!

It was, of course, simply an excuse to earn a few guineas in linage from *World's Press News,* which respectfully published my periodic reports of our "activities." At one meeting we counted eleven members, but we sadly ran out of steam and cash after only a few weeks.

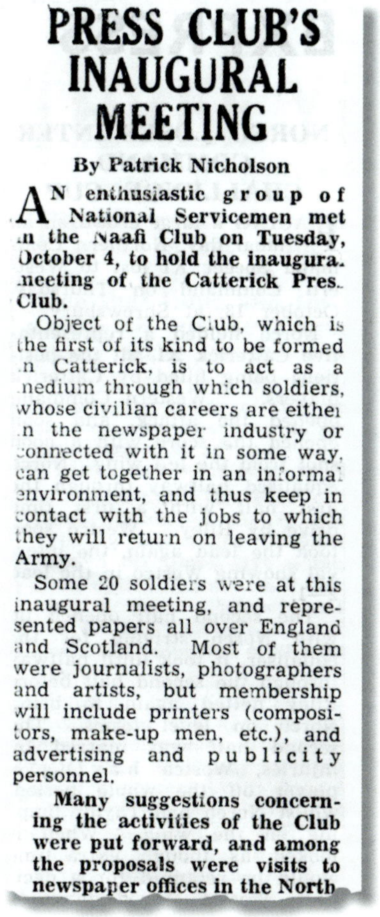
PRESS CLUB'S INAUGURAL MEETING

By Patrick Nicholson

AN enthusiastic group of National Servicemen met in the Naafi Club on Tuesday, October 4, to hold the inaugural meeting of the Catterick Press Club.

Object of the Club, which is the first of its kind to be formed in Catterick, is to act as a medium through which soldiers, whose civilian careers are either in the newspaper industry or connected with it in some way, can get together in an informal environment, and thus keep in contact with the jobs to which they will return on leaving the Army.

Some 20 soldiers were at this inaugural meeting, and represented papers all over England and Scotland. Most of them were journalists, photographers and artists, but membership will include printers (compositors, make-up men, etc.), and advertising and publicity personnel.

Many suggestions concerning the activities of the Club were put forward, and among the proposals were visits to newspaper offices in the North

We launch a Press Club.
October 21 1949

"TAFFY" IS LEAVING US

NEWS Editor of the "Catterick Express" from December, 1948, until January this year, Welsh-born Iorwerth J. Lewis, whose name will be well-known to all our readers for his outspoken Editorials and colourful features, is leaving Catterick.

A National Service Sergeant in the RAMC, Lewis is being 'demobbed' early next month with Group No. 136.

LEWIS — By Avo

Until call-up in June 1948, a reporter for the S. Wales Herald, Lewis, whose home is at Nantyffyllon, Maesteg, has been offered an appointment with the Glamorgan AdvertiserSeries as assistant Art Editor.

Remembered for his work on the editing of the 1949 Catterick Fair 80-page programme, Lewis has been spending the last few weeks of his Army service compiling the Catterick Camp, Richmond, and Barnard Castle Directory, the publication of which will shortly be announced.

On completing it, Lewis laughingly claims, he will know more about the Camp and the neighbouring district than anyone before him. Readers, we know will join with his colleagues in wishing him every success in his life in Civvy-Street.

Lewis is succeeded as News Editor by Ray Berry of the 8th RTR, who has been acting in that capacity for the past two months.

Catterick Express *Feb 16 1950*

An earlier facial caricature from our files (though I added in the battledress uniform) was by "Avo," the paper's brilliant cartoonist, also a serving soldier.

In December I was invited to join the *Catterick Express* on a full-time basis. But there was a problem. The only reason I hadn't been posted abroad to another tank regiment was because the "Eighth," a training unit, was desperately short of clerks, and I had already been taken on its permanent staff.

In the event, my transfer needed the signature of the general himself, because the 8th RTR was not enamoured of the idea of me remaining, unproductively, on their strength whilst employed "away" at District HQ. As my squadron commander moaned: "I already have one man detailed permanently at the Signals Theatre for a reason quite unknown to me..." Actors and journalists were obviously kindred useless spirits.

Taffy was demobbed the following February, and thanks to his expert grounding, I was now able to put my own stamp on the make-up and content of the Express.

Charlie Childs's task, as editor, was to keep a wary eye on the excesses of budding Press barons, and to ensure that Army policy and discipline were not challenged. It is to his credit that, as far as I know, he never interfered in the choice or presentation of news or features except on the rarest of occasions when he wanted to fly a kite on some pet project of his own.

Though a civilian, ex-Captain Charlie was still subject to most Army disciplines and pressures. His immediate boss was the General Officer Commanding the Catterick District, General C.E.M. White, to whom he was linked directly by intercom. When the General wanted a meeting, the box on Charlie's desk in the tiny office we shared would come to life with the words.... "GOC here on one, Childs. Come up and see me please."

Only once do I recall General White expressing any concern about the *Catterick Express* during my tenure of responsibility, though Charlie himself occasionally expressed his horror over the sensitivities of some of my published news items. This time it was his turn to miss the significance of one news story.

From a friend I learned on a rare visit to my own regimental stores that recruits were having to scrub new webbing because of a shortage of Blanco. The water soluble paste (usually khaki coloured and rarely white in Army use in spite of its trade name) was normally applied to uniform belts and straps for decorative effect. I reported the shortage under a two-column head treating the story seriously and "straight," though I was well aware that it might cause a minor sensation.

For 75 years 'Blanco' was Pickering's major product, sold to the Military in over sixty countries.

BLANCO INGREDIENTS

China Clay
Zinc Sulphate
Borax, Gypsum
Oxalic Acid
Pigments

So I wasn't exactly surprised when the Nationals picked up the item the next day. The *Daily Mirror*, for one, led a page on what as far as I can recall, they saw as:

Halt to Army Bull - *Blanco Shortage hits Trainees*

Charlie apparently hadn't read the papers that morning. But someone had. The intercom came to life. "GOC here on one, Childs..."

I never did hear the full story. But the general wasn't too pleased. Someone at the War Office, he indicated to Charlie, didn't like the way the Army was being portrayed. If it could allow its regiments to run out of Blanco, it wasn't saying very much for forward planning. Strangely, no one thought to charge *me* with lack of judgement.

Blanco Shortage hits RAC Regiments

Shortage of skilled labour and raw materials is one of the reasons according to the manufacturers, for the serious shortage of BLANCO that exists throughout the country. Until the position improves, though it shows no sign of doing so, both Units and individuals are being asked to conserve supplies and economise whenever possible.

Worst hit by the shortage are Units using the Khaki Buff 'No. 61' which is due, it is believed to the increasing popularity of this shade. Some RAC Regiments have been unable to obtain supplies for over three weeks, and hundreds of trainee National Servicemen are having to scrub their equipment until more supplies are available.

One Regimental P.R.I., told an 'Express' correspondent last night, "We have written to private firms all over England but in vain. Our consumption in normal times is often as much as twelve dozen blocks a month. We managed to get a small supply, 350 blocks last week, our first for more than a month, but that issue is already exhausted.

Catterick Express
September 9 1949

These few paragraphs caught the eye of the *Daily Mirror*.

Newspapers throughout northern England had long regarded the *Catterick Express* office as an unofficial Army press office, particularly when additional background was sought on some previously published report which had caught their interest. This was even truer in January 1950, when the 18-years-old Yorkshire and England cricketer Brian Close was confined to hospital with a thigh injury.

For Brian was a patient in the military hospital at Catterick, where he had recently started his national service with the Royal Signals, and the newspapers were unable to contact him. Brian had sustained his injury while playing football for Leeds United Reserves the previous November, but had failed to report a problem to his unit M.O.

He was to remain in hospital for almost five months and for much of that time I was the only reporter able to see him, so I was able to provide occasional bulletins on his progress.

But those reports in the Nationals didn't earn me a penny. All I had to show for my regular checks were some quotes for a final story in March 1950 when he was able to play again successfully for Leeds reserves, his personal test for his fitness for the coming cricket season.

Those few months on the *Express* gave me invaluable experience in meeting deadlines, in filling blank pages with just the barest of news copy, in writing features. Regular columns such as the weekly film review had to be reinforced with a local history guide and a humour section, as well as frequently-requested series on Catterick regiments and services such as the Catering Corps, the Royal Army Service Corps, the NAAFI and others.

As a believer in the personal touch, I introduced a number of new writers to the columns of the *Express*, or rather a number of new *noms-de-plume.* "Alan Fraser" already existed as the paper's film critic. Among other guest writers I added Chris Logan and Bernard Rickmond, to mention just two partial derivations of my own name. "David Howard" too had a style very similar to my own in his weekly chat column. I can't even remember where the name of my latter *alter ego* originated, but curiously it became better known than my certificated original, and generated the paper's only fan correspondence.

Personal appreciation came later. The *Catterick Express* sponsored a number of local events during the year, most of them originating in the District Entertainments Office, such as the annual Catterick Fair and Catterick Ball. Inevitably the staff of the paper was heavily involved. That meant me.

At my first Ball, I had been checking that Captain Childs's efforts and instructions were being followed to the letter. After ensuring that the band was in place, that the compere's mike and the spot lighting was functioning, I walked back to the waiting throng at the main doors, and turned the latch. I was almost thrown to the floor in the rush. But I still had to unlock the inner doors which had slammed shut at the end of the corridor.

As I pushed and barged my way through, I turned at a tug on my sleeve, and looked into the eyes of a pretty brunette. She pointed to the sign above our heads. "That's a bloody lie for a start," she said.

The sign simply read: "BALLROOM."

Minutes later the dance was under way. Near the stage I ran into the brunette again. "Are you with the *Catterick Express*?" she asked. Then as I nodded:

"Would you do something for me? Would you point out David Howard? I adore his column, and I'd like to meet him more than anything. Could you do that?"

I'm ashamed to say I ducked out. "If I see him I'll let him know," I stammered. "I know he's here somewhere." Preserving his, my, anonymity was more important. That was my excuse at the time.

The *Express* was published fortnightly and sold in unit NAAFI canteens and corporals' and sergeants' messes for a pre-decimal twopence. The first week after publication I spent reporting and writing, the second on "make-up" and printing. Like my predecessors, I found it necessary to spend at least two days at the printers' in nearby Darlington, leaning over the stone as a compositor juggled with the slugs of hot metal typeface from the Linotype operator.

There were dire warnings from the father of the chapel – the printers' shop steward – about the terrible consequences if I as much as breathed on the type face as a non-member

My privileged exclusives: the stories they all wanted...

BRIAN CLOSE INJURED

Catterick Express Jan 5 1950

Impatient Patient

MEDICAL history sheet of a certain patient in Catterick Military Hospital is being very closely watched by the British National Press. During the last few weeks our telephone has rung three times with the query "How is HE?"

It isn't often so much attention is given to the progress of one patient — especially in Catterick—so why the interest? I'll give you a clue. The cricket season is fast approaching.

Got it now? Yes, centre of attraction is 19-years-old Yorkshire and England cricketer, Brian Close.

* * *

Brian hasn't yet seen much of Army life. Remember when he arrived in Catterick? As long ago as October, 1949—I know because I've just discovered it in our cuttings book. But after only 10 weeks in the army he was taken to hospital with an injury to his thigh, which he received in a football match—and he's been there ever since.

Back to Whites

RUMOUR started the wires buzzing again this week. It had reached the ears of one paper that Brian had been allowed a week-end home. After checking with the Medical authorities, though, it was discovered that the "week-end home" was in fact two hours out of bed.

The "Yorkshire Post" says this week that a long process of treatment will be necessary before he can use his leg freely again. Meanwhile, Brian, like the newspapers, is waiting anxiously for the day when he can get into white flannels.

As one of the hospital officials told a colleague, "He's one of the most impatient patients we've got."

Catterick Express Feb 16 1950 (by my alter ego, David Howard, for his column)

BRIAN CLOSE BACK IN HARNESS

Catterick Express April 4 1950

of the relevant privileged trade union. But somehow my headlines and captions survived countless theoretical arguments and discussions, while I absorbed the wonders of the printers' limited range of newspaper typefaces and sizes.

My experiences in trying to find the right fonts for the size and shape of our five-columned "tabloid" (even that was a misnomer) led me down strange routes. I might mix Cheltenham Bold with a Futura Medium because no bold sans serif was available, or fall back on Cooper Black italics to give weight to one item in five. And unfortunately, my typographical design instincts were far from reliable.

Somehow I did manage to boost the circulation of the paper slightly during my term, though in our efforts to raise advertising revenue we found it prudent not to be precise about actual circulation figures. We preferred to talk about "readership," something that has a familiar ring in some newspaper market reports today.

Nevertheless, circulation of the *Express* was ever close to my heart, if only because the job of door-to-door distribution throughout Catterick was also down to the News Editor, personally. The only transport available to me for a time was the General's Humber car. And there were few things more satisfying than sitting, huddled low in the back seat, quietly returning salutes as we sped through the unit lines, even though the owner's rank badge on the front bumper was covered.

When my own demob loomed, I had to hand over to a temporary replacement from the Royal Signals regiment who wasn't really Charlie's first choice, or mine. My natural successor would have been my pal "Nick" Nicholson, who still had several months ahead of him. But the 8th RTR stuck their heels in a second time and refused to let him go, at least until they had exhausted all the arguments.

For my part, freedom couldn't come quickly enough. As it was, I had just learned with dismay of a recent Government decision that 18 months' National Service wasn't long enough. It meant that we would now have to complete an additional 4 years "active" Reserve with the Territorial Army, a national, but until then a purely voluntary part-time service.

My intake, now due for demobilisation, would be the first to transfer to this new "N" Reserve, and we would be required to attend regular evening "parades" with our new units for the next four years. We would also have to report for at least four weekends and one summer camp a year in that time.

Then, to add irritation to injustice, I discovered the regimental adjutant had nominated me for a public relations exercise to represent the first national serviceman in the British Army to suffer this further indignity. Not that I had distinguished myself in any way during the previous 18 months. Indeed I had even been obliged to hide away in the barrack latrines on the day of our "passing-out" parade. My squadron warrant officer had decided in his wisdom that my personal style of parade ground presentation might let the side down. Somehow, I don't believe he had advised the adjutant of his drastic action.

Demob day dawned. I had made my farewells at District HQ. Now I had to report back to my own regimental lines at the other side of Catterick to be signed off. But there was one thing I had to do. I made my way through the 8th RTR's Waitwith Lines and up to the regimental tank park at the edge of the moor, where I had once stood my only, lonely, night guard duty. At last I found what I was looking for – a young second lieutenant with a group of trainee gunners.

I called out to him. "I'm getting demobbed today, sir," I said, "And this is the closest I've ever been to a tank. Would it be possible to have a look inside?"

The 2nd Lewie wasn't the slightest bit surprised. He hauled me up and showed me how to lower myself into the tank commander's seat. After a few moments I climbed out again.

"Thanks," I said. "That's all I needed to complete my tour of duty."

The War Office thought the occasion of my demob and my transfer to the Terriers of such public relations' significance they had arranged for a photographer from the Fleet Street agency of *Keystone Press* to record the departure of myself and two fellow reservists from Catterick. When we reported to the adjutant's office I discovered that (by one of those strange coincidences) the photographer, Chris Ware, was an old acquaintance from my Heathrow days. He had been among a handful of Fleet Street photographers with regular assignments at the airport.

DEMOBBED: 'DAVID HOWARD' ALIAS . . .

TODAY we remove the cloak of anonymity from David Howard, "Express" columnist, whose "Chatterbox" has found wide popularity in the Garrison.

Yes, readers, "David Howard" is a non-de-plume which has hidden the identity of none other than News-Editor Ray Berry, National Service corporal, who leaves Catterick this morning with Group 49.01.

Sorry to disappoint those who know Ray personally, but that's how it is! Seriously speaking, however, "Scoop," as he has come to be known throughout District Headquarters, has done a grand job on the "Express."

A member of the 8th RTR, he joined the staff last October, and took over the news-editorship at the beginning of this year. Since then he has been responsible for a brighter, crisper, "Catterick Express." It has taken much energy and no small number of disappointments and set-backs, but he has the satisfaction of leaving the Army having done a worthwhile job.

Ray started his journalistic career in the London office of the "Manchester Guardian," and later went on the staff of Brenard Air News Service, an agency covering London's airports.

He is returning there, but although he'll be spending most of his time looking sky-wards with note-book and pencil at the ready, he is not severing his connections with the "Express" and has promised to send a regular London column back under the familiar by-line: "David Howard." As his job brings him in contact with the people who make news, readers can look forward to a bright fortnightly contribution.

Catterick Express
June 22 1950

How many reels of film Chris used on his latest assignment I would hesitate to guess. His pictorial saga began with those shots at Catterick then followed my train journey from Darlington. It only ended hours later with me "trying on" my new cap badge and City of London Yeomanry shoulder flash at the TA unit's HQ near King's Cross. The shoulder flash read "Rough Riders," and the picture was put up as a frontispiece for *Soldier* magazine. (Apparently, it didn't make it.)

The cavalry had captured me after all.

*

Just six days into my terminal leave from National Service I was back in civilian harness, reporting again from Northolt. It could have been even less, but I had to have some new clothes, which meant several shopping expeditions. In eighteen months I had "filled out."

Otherwise, it was almost as if I'd never been away. No one had taken my place in any permanent sense. A number of reporters had helped out with Harry's coverage of the airport, but few had stayed long. They preferred the prestige and glamour of London's official Number 1 airport, Heathrow. I was grateful to them. It was as if they knew they were only keeping my personal manor warm.

Author's collection

June 1950: A Public Relations 'event' for the Army as the 8th Tanks adjutant dismisses a couple of 'demobs.'

Nothing had changed. I was immediately plunged back into the world of front-page news. On my first day, Mrs Eleanor Roosevelt, widow of the late, great US. Democrat President, and a respected stateswoman in her own right, flew in. When I asked her if her husband would have acted the same way as his successor, President Truman, in pledging US. assistance to South Korea, which had just been invaded by the Communist North, she replied, diplomatically:

"Ah, I never answer 'if' questions. But I know that all the people of the United States are behind President Truman."

Mrs Eleanor Roosevelt, widow of the late, great U.S. President, speaks at Northolt on a rare UK visit.

NO to IF

WOULD President Roosevelt have taken the same action over Korea as President Truman?

Mrs. Eleanor Roosevelt ponders this question before microphones at Northolt Airport.

Her reply? "Ah, I never answer *if* questions. But I know that all the people of the United States are behind President Truman."

She flew in from Paris after a visit to Norway, wore a grey flannel suit, lace blouse and a blue straw hat.

Brenard Press picture
Daily Herald
June 29 1950

Mrs Roosevelt was just one of a long list of British, American and Commonwealth political and military figures flying to and from London that summer. The Americans ranged from US Chief of Staff General Omar Bradley to General Alfred M.Gruenther, Number 2 to General Eisenhower, and his eventual successor as Supreme Commander in Europe. All of these talked freely to me, but only one, Admiral William Fechteler, controversial US Chief of Naval Operations, struck a sour note when he admitted to having "differences" with Britain over the role of the Royal Navy in the Mediterranean.

The Cold War between East and West continued unabated too, given added strength by the ideological clash in Korea. A majority decision by the United Nations to respond to the Communist aggression with a multi-national armed force was strongly opposed by two of the "Big Five," China and the Soviet Union, who promptly signed a new friendship pact.

At a more domestic level, Customs men at Northolt ceremoniously set fire to a stack of Communist propaganda posters left behind on a plane from Bucharest. And Britain's "Red Dean" of Canterbury, Dr Hewlett Johnson, set out on one of his much-ridiculed and hopeless solitary friendship missions behind the Iron Curtain.

Diplomats and other Britons were still being deported from Prague, and despite all the difficulties, refugees were still succeeding in fleeing the country. Two teenage brothers whose father had successfully reached Canada from Romania were detained at Northolt on their arrival from Prague, even though they had cut through a tangle of red tape to try to join him. British Immigration men said they would have to go back to Prague because they had no Canadian visas.

Staff of British European Airways at Northolt took up their case and clubbed together to pay for their keep while the boys, Johan, 16, and 14-years-old Alex Leeb, were held in detention. They discovered after three days that the boys' visas had been forwarded to Paris by mistake. With a final night spent in the comparative luxury of a Kensington hotel the boys were finally able to fly on to Saskatchewan to join their father.

Their story had kept me busy for three days. But my promotion of the good deed by the BEA staff won them recognition in a *Daily Express* editorial. The airline's press relations' office phoned to thank me: "That's the kind of publicity we really welcome." *(See over)*

JOHAN AND ALEX IN WUNDER LAND

HERALD REPORTER

SIXTEEN-YEAR-OLD Johan Leeb and 14-year-old brother Alexander, from Prague, looked at an egg-and-bacon meal at Northolt Airport, yesterday. "Wunderbar!" they said.

British European Airways officials showed them how to use a knife and fork. They'd never seen any before.

"*WUNDERBAR!*" chorused Johan and Alexander.

Then came icecream. Their eyes goggled. The icecream vanished.

"*WUNDERBAR!*" they exclaimed. "Just like heaven, it is here," they declared in halting German.

Johan and Alexander come from Rumanian peasant stock. Their one-way air tickets to Vancouver, costing over £200 had been paid for by their father out of his two years' savings as a farm worker at Saskatchewan.

Daily Herald *Aug 14 1950*

Iron Curtain boys freed

Johan and Alexander Leeb, Rumanian boys who were held at Northolt Airport over the week-end after arriving from Prague, slept last night in a feather bed at a Kensington hotel.

They spent two nights in the airport's detention room. Yesterday they said goodbye to B.E.A. officials who looked after them, and were driven to London.

Visas authorising them to join their father on a farm in Saskatchewan were waiting at Canada House. The papers had been sent to Paris by mistake.

The boys fly to Canada tomorrow.

Daily Express *Aug 15 1950*

(below) Editorial, Daily Express

Shining light

TWO little boys fly into Northolt Airport from Prague. They are on their way to Canada to join their farm-labourer father who has saved for years to bring them to safety.

But tragedy at Northolt. The boys have no Canadian visa. They must return to Prague and danger..

Into the picture steps a British European Airways official. He promises to get the necessary visas and to look after the boys until their papers arrive.

A little thing, this good deed of his? Maybe so. But it shines in a world where bureaucracy is more common than humanity.

Impressed by the editorial, British European Airways commented to me afterwards: "That's the kind of publicity we really welcome".

TWO CZECH BOY REFUGEES DETAINED

NO CANADIAN VISAS

DAILY TELEGRAPH REPORTER

Two young refugees from behind the Iron Curtain who think England is "just like heaven" were detained by Home Office officials at Northolt Airport yesterday. They spent two nights in the airport's detention room.

Clutching one handbag between them and two through air tickets from Czechoslovakia to Canada Johan Leeb, 16, and his brother Alexander, 14, stepped from an air liner from Prague on Saturday night. They spoke no English; they had no money: they wore peasant clothes.

They produced passports, but had no Canadian visas. They were told they could go no farther; that they would have to go back to Prague.

A British European Airways official said: "We will try to obtain the necessary visas. We can do nothing until Monday when the High Commissioner's office opens. We do not expect any difficulty. In the meantime we will care for the boys."

An interpreter said: "Apparently they come from peasant stock. Their one-way air tickets to Vancouver, over £200 each, have been paid for by their father. He emigrated to Canada two years ago and has been saving from his wages as a farm labourer in Lancer, Saskatchewan to bring his sons over."

Daily Telegraph (above) *Aug 14 1950*

CZECH BOYS GET CANADIAN VISAS

LEAVING TO-MORROW

Daily Telegraph Reporter

Two Czech refugees detained by Home Office officials when they arrived at Northolt Airport from Prague on Saturday night were yesterday given visas to join their father in Canada. They are booked to leave to-morrow.

The boys are Johan Leeb, 16, and his brother Alexander, 14. As reported in THE DAILY TELEGRAPH yesterday, they arrived via Paris with two air tickets from Czechoslovakia to Canada and with passports, but no Canadian visas.

Money for their tickets to Vancouver, over £200 each, was paid by their father. He emigrated to Canada two years ago and is a farm labourer in Saskatchewan.

A Canadian emigration official in London said: "Their documents for entry to Canada were sent to our Paris office, which we telephoned on Saturday, and arrived from there at mid-day to-day. The boys have now passed their required medical examinations and visas have been issued"

Daily Telegraph *Aug 15 1950*

There was, too, the case of "The Family Nobody Wanted," as the *Sunday Dispatch* headlined the page lead they gave Harry's story. The family was that of a 29-years-old American Communist, Arden Perin, his wife Lilyan, 23, and their six-months-old baby Dolores, all of whom had been detained at Northolt on arrival from Helsinki after being refused entry to the Soviet Union.

From his contacts in the Immigration service, Harry had learnt that Perin and his family had flown to Finland after selling up their home in America. They had approached Soviet and Hungarian Embassies in Helsinki for permission to settle in either country. Perin told the Embassies that he was a Communist, and sympathised with the way of life in the Cominform countries. But he admitted to them that he had been expelled from the US Communist Party as a "deviationist." As a result, neither Russia nor Hungary would grant the family visas.

After two months of trying, the family then tried to "gatecrash" the Iron Curtain by flying on to Prague, where Perin again sought entry. The Czechs promptly arrested them. Eventually the family was told they could go, but they would have to pay their own fares to the West. Perin decided they would head for London.

At Northolt Perin admitted he was homeless and penniless as he told immigration officers the story. Home Office officials decided to pass the problem to the US Embassy in London, putting the family under detention in the meantime. For the moment no one, other than Embassy officials and immigration staff could contact the family. And that certainly ruled out access by the Press.

Harry broke his story after the family had been held for three days with no sign of a solution. The American view clearly was: "The family has rejected their homeland and chosen an ideology which is totally alien to the American way of life. They can't expect us to be sympathetic." The British seemed to be saying: "They are not our responsibility and they still hold American passports."

But when he was shown the headlines in the Sunday papers Perin himself asked to be allowed to talk to the Press. Surprisingly, and almost certainly at the request of the Embassy, the Home Office agreed. It was the only occasion I can recall such a facility being offered by the Immigration Service until the ground-breaking "warts and all" BBC TV first *Airport* series of the 'nineties.

I was pleased to be on duty on the Sunday when Immigration left a message for Harry inviting him to talk to the Perins, so I was able to stand in for him. My interview confirmed all the facts Harry had spelt out in his copy, and provided me with some additional quotes direct from the American.

"The Russians told me they didn't want me because I had disagreed with the American Communist Party," he said. "They called me a deviationist and said my personal views as a Leninist were not sufficient grounds for an application for entry to the Soviet Union."

In Prague, he said, he and his wife were treated "like enemies" and were arrested at once. "We were imprisoned in a hotel after hours of questioning and were guarded day and night for five weeks. It was a brutal shock to be treated like that, but my wife and baby suffered most. For days we secretly had to send out for food for the baby. At times she was half-starved"

He said the Czechs decided he was an American agent. "I told them that was ridiculous," he said, and he insisted: "I am still a Communist. But under the Communist ideal you have to be a member of a Communist organisation, and I have no organisation."

The interview was splashed in Monday's papers, together with a picture of the family taken by the resident *PA-Reuter* photographer at Heathrow, Rex Standerwick, who had driven over in response to a call from his office. The *Daily Telegraph* gave the story some nine column inches on Page One, and the *Daily Herald* used it under the heading:

Lenin's disciple turned back by Russians

Daily Herald *Jan 22 1951*

The tabloid *Daily Graphic* ran it, completely in bold typeface, under a 3-column sans serif headline, but inexplicably and mistakenly switched the scene to "London Airport":

UNWANTED FAMILY STARVED IN 'RED HEAVEN'

MR. ARDEN PERIN, father of a family that nobody wants, described in the detention room at London Airport last night how his dream of a Communist heaven was broken.

be a Communist without being a member of the Communist organisation. I have no organisation."

The U.S. Embassy told him last night that reservations had been made for the family on a ship sailing for New York tomorrow.

Daily Graphic *Jan 22 1951*

The *New York Herald Tribune* gave their more sombre interpretation of my piece through the agency *Associated Press* in two columns on Page One, and made it clear that the American Embassy had still not made a decision.

U.S. Red Is Stranded in Britain After Failing to Get Into Russia

By the Associated Press

LONDON, Jan. 22.—Arden Perin, 29, who says he has been expelled from the American Communist party but is still a Communist, was stranded with his wife and baby at Northolt Airport today after a vain attempt to go to Russia to live.

The Perins were detained by British immigration officials when they arrived from Prague by plane last Friday. They had only $28, and lacked proper entry papers. Mr. Perin told reporters he had cabled friends in New York for money to get his family home.

Mr. Perin said he used to live at 345 West Fourth Street, New York. His wife, Lilyan, is 25, and their baby, Dolores, is aged six months. Mr. Perin told reporters this story:

Last year he was expelled from the American Communist party as a "deviationist"—that is, one whose views stray from the official party line.

Two months ago, still regarding himself as a good Communist, he decided he would take his family to Russia. He sold his home, and they flew to Helsinki, where they tried in vain to get permission to enter the Soviet Union.

"Our application for Russian visas was refused," Mr. Perin said. "The reasons given was my criticisms of the American Communist party."

The Perins then took off for Prague by air. Upon arrival, they were arrested for not having proper papers.

"The Czech authorities, after hours of questioning, imprisoned us in a hotel," Mr. Perin related. "Six security officers guarded us night and day for five weeks. It was a shock to be treated as we were. I am still a Communist, ideally."

Finally the Czech authorities agreed to let the Perins buy plane tickets for London.

The Home Office, which handles immigration matters in Britain, would say only that the Perins "arrived without means and without a booking for further travel."

A spokesman for the American Embassy said the American government provides travel aid for its citizens only in cases where they have no resources of their own. He indicated the embassy will wait to see whether the Perins' New York friends come through with ticket money before taking any action.

Meanwhile, the father, mother and baby are living in the Northolt customs lounge and sleeping in a small detention room.

International (New York) Herald Tribune, Jan 23 1951

STRANDED U.S. FAMILY HELD AT NORTHOLT

COMMUNIST FAILED TO ENTER RUSSIA

DAILY TELEGRAPH REPORTER

Officials of the Home Office and of the United States Embassy conferred at the week-end about an American family of three who were detained, penniless, at Northolt. The family arrived from Prague on Friday in a Czech airliner.

They are Mr. Arden Perin, 29, a Communist, his 25-year-old wife, Lilyan, and six - months - old daughter Dolores. Since arriving, without visas or permits, they have been under guard by Home Office immigration officials or airport staff.

Late last night they were informed by the American Embassy that a reservation had been made for them in the liner Washington, due to sail for New York on Tuesday.

While detained at Northolt, the family have remained during the day in the Customs section of the incoming passengers' lounge. At night they have slept in a small room in detention quarters

Officially they were "held pending inquiries." They have been given meals in the lounge and allowed out under escort twice a day for exercise round the airfield.

SOLD HOME IN U.S.

According to information given by Mr. Perin, the family has been trying for two months to enter Russia or one of the Cominform countries. Mr. Perin sold his home in America and flew to Helsinki with his wife and child.

There he tried, without success, to obtain entry visas to Russia and Hungary. He was confronted with the position that a short time ago he was expelled from the Communist party in the United States as a "deviationist."

Next, the family arrived by air in Czechoslovakia without papers, only to be arrested and held for five weeks. When offered an air passage to Britain, Mr. Perin spent his remaining money on the fares. British immigration officials found that he possessed an American passport but no other entry papers.

APPLICATION REJECTED

In the airport detention room Mr. Perin stated last night: "In Helsinki our application for Russian visas was refused. The reason given was that my criticisms of the American Communist party and my own personal views as a Leninist were not sufficient grounds for the application.

"On arrival in Prague we were treated as enemies. We were immediately arrested. The Czech authorities, after hours of questioning, imprisoned us in an hotel. Six security officers guarded us night and day.

"It was a shock to be treated as we were. I am still a Communist ideally but I have no organisation."

Daily Telegraph *Jan 22 1951*

This column, from top;
Daily Mail
Daily Herald
News Chronicle
Daily Telegraph
(all) Jan 22 1951

But the following day the Perins were suddenly shipped out. An Embassy hire-car was dispatched to Northolt to drive the family to the dockside at Southampton. There they were unceremoniously bundled aboard a New York-bound ocean liner to sail back to the country they had rejected only a few weeks earlier. The name of the liner: the SS Washington.

Many of Northolt's news stories of those days were lighter, but in their own way generated just as much interest. Like my story of the reindeer meat, one which was particularly memorable because it was a classic "scoop" in the way it was discovered, even if, at the end of the day, it made only a few inches of newsprint.

A newspaper propped beside me, I was lunching in the staff canteen at Northolt when my ears pricked up at a conversation between two airline workers seated alongside. They were wondering what was going to happen to a consignment of fresh meat which was waiting unclaimed in a cargo shed. It seemed it wasn't likely to be fresh much longer.

"No one wants to know 'cos it's reindeer meat" concluded one, "Whoever heard of anyone eating reindeers, anyway?"

I excused myself for breaking into their conversation, and in a roundabout way asked for more information. They were not very forthcoming but, they said, they knew what they were talking about. It was definitely reindeer meat… not venison.

My enquiries took me to BEA's import cargo unit. Officials there were more helpful. They too were worried the meat might go off before it could be collected. It had been held up at the airport because no veterinary health certificate had arrived. The importers, I learnt, were the Swedish Chamber of Commerce in London. I went back to the press room and telephoned them.

The 75lb consignment was a sample, destined for one of

Reindeer on menu soon

By Daily Mail Reporter

SWEDISH reindeer meat may be in the shops soon to supplement the tenpenny ration.

A 75lb. sample—half a reindeer—was flown to Northolt from Stockholm yesterday.

The Swedish Chamber of Commerce, London, has arranged to import supplies of the meat.

Three large Smithfield firms have agreed to buy it for wholesale distribution ; a fourth is negotiating. The sample is expected to help their decision.

It was detained at Northolt last night because no veterinary health certificate had arrived. It is expected to be issued today.

A Chamber of Commerce official said : "Reindeer meat is very popular and something of a delicacy in Sweden at this time of the year."

REINDEER on menu

Reindeer meat is here

BUTCHERS TO TRY REINDEER MEAT

Reindeer meat will be on the menu

AFTER whale meat and snoek comes —reindeer meat. A sample was flown to Northolt from Stockholm yesterday.

The sample, weighing 75lb., will be sent to Smithfield, after it has been cleared by Customs, to decide whether reindeer meat is suitable to eke out the meat ration.

It is expected that portions will be sent to different parts of Britain so that housewives can sample it and see if they like it.

But already three large Smithfield firms have agreed to buy for wholesale distribution and a fourth is negotiating.

Arrangements have been made by the Swedish Chamber of Commerce in London to import large quantities.

What does reindeer taste like? It is a cross between mutton and beef, a little tougher than venison, but not so strong tasting.

The price? Uncertain.

Suggestions to give Britain reindeer meat from Canada were made in 1948 and 1949.

(above) Daily Graphic Jan 22 1951

BRITAIN'S butchers may soon be selling reindeer meat from Sweden to help out the 10d. ration. A 75lb. sample consignment was flown into Northolt Airport over the week-end to help Smithfield men decide whether to place large orders. Three wholesale firms have already agreed to buy the meat.

A Swedish trade official said: "Reindeer meat is very popular. It has quite an agreeable taste."

Daily Mirror (above) 22 Jan 1951

Rudolph is now redmeat

(above) Daily Graphic Jan 26 1951

"More nails, boy, and STOP WHISTLING THAT DASHED SONG!"

"I GAVE him a piece of reindeer meat!"

Evening News (above): London Laughs - by Lee, and (right) sports section - by Styx Jan 26 1951

5s.-a-lb. reindeer may help ration

Daily Express Jan 22 1951

Hippothesis

I HEARD yesterday that a keeper at the Zoo asked a hippopotamus why he was looking so worried.

"Worried!" said the hippo. "So would you be. You've eaten whale and snoek. You're starting on reindeer. There's no knowing where it will end."

PETERBOROUGH

Daily Telegraph Jan 26 1951

On the list

POOR Rudolph the Red-nosed Reindeer. I read we are going to eat him now. What worries me is : Has Mr. Webb heard of the popular "Puddy Tat," and is that the next delicacy ?

(Mrs.) Winifred Brown.

Reader's letter, Daily Mail Jan 27 1951

three Smithfield meat wholesalers. Said a Chamber of Commerce official: "The three companies have agreed to buy a quantity of the meat to distribute throughout Britain on a trial basis." The two other samples were yet to be delivered. He described reindeer meat as "slightly tougher, but not as strong-tasting as venison." He thought the meat might be welcomed as a supplement to the more familiar beef and lamb of weekend roasts – still rationed in the Britain of 1951.

Strangely, it was the national reaction to the story which became the real news, overshadowing an average of a mere three column inches awarded to the piece in the nationals. In a country where, five years after the end of the war, several basic foods were still officially rationed or in very short supply, the idea of eating reindeer just a couple of weeks after Christmas (with the notes of "Rudolph the Red-nosed Reindeer" still echoing) touched a nerve, albeit a humorous one.

Every popular cartoonist of the day, it seemed, had to comment on the story. Lee, of the London *Evening News*, had a butcher replacing a bull's head trophy with a reindeer's antlers. And in the same newspaper's sports section, pocket cartoonist Styx visualised a greyhound fed on reindeer meat sprouting antlers. Yet another sketch, by the *Daily Worker's* Gabriel, showed a butcher with a shotgun at the zoo, asking which animals were next available for the "chop."

Stand-up music hall comedians and radio comics were not to be outdone, many of them offering one-liners or building part of their acts around thoughts of roast reindeer. And correspondence columns in the newspapers carried the inevitable protests from "Disgusted" of Surbiton *et al.* One *Daily Mail* reader blamed the Labour Government and suggested that the animated cartoon character "Puddy Tat" might be the next delicacy offered to the starving millions.

Most satisfying was overhearing two people discussing the story on the tube as I travelled home from work. I wanted to say: "That was my story you're talking about." But of course they would have been as unimpressed by my intervention in their private conversation as the two cargo workers in the canteen who started it all.

It's an irony of journalism that often the merest snippets of news can attract the most attention. Items tucked away in a column of "briefs" or at the foot of a page often inspire more comment and discussion than the lengthy and detailed page lead upon which hours of effort and man-hours has been expended.

Such was the case of the unsuspecting airline official who turned to a microphone to make a paging announcement in the passenger buildings at Northolt. He could hardly have known that his ten-word announcement would be heard over the air on coast-to-coast radio networks in America, not in its original form of a simple paging call but as a news item.

The announcement: "Will the lost property officer please contact his office immediately?" tickled me enough to make it a humorous paragraph (though I had to explain it to the lad at Brenards who took down my copy). I was in good company. It also tickled the *Daily Telegraph's "Peterborough"* diaryist.

Quis Custodiet . . .?

PASSENGERS waiting in the lounge at Northolt Airport late at night raised tired eyebrows when they heard the following announcement from a loudspeaker:

"Attention, please! Here is a staff announcement. Will the lost property officer please return to his office immediately?"

PETERBOROUGH

Daily Telegraph ***May 1948***

It also made passengers in a crowded departure lounge laugh so much that similar calls were later banned from the air waves, presenting me with a just-as-funny follow-up. Then, sixmonths on, I was able to report:

Then, In August 1950...

PAGE ONE ENDPIECE ***LOST AND FOUND***

A LOUD-SPEAKER call at Northolt Airport—"Will the *Lost* Property Officer please contact his office immediately"—was banned yesterday. Only his name will be called now. The reason: The old announcement caused too much laughter among passengers.

(above) Daily Express... ***Aug 14 1950***

PAGE ONE ENDPIECE ***LOST PROPERTY***

THE lost property office at Northolt Airport was closed for 15 minutes last night. The officer in charge had lost his keys. A duplicate key opened the office and the missing key was found inside.

...and (left) Jan 3 1951

And, as reported in the *Daily Herald* and the *News Chronicle*, both now sadly defunct:

HOW ODD **BICYCLE ON THE ROOF**

THE lost property man at Northolt Airport yesterday took details of a passenger's mislaid baggage, then noticed his bicycle was gone. He found it—on a roof.

(above) News Chronicle September 19 1952

...and some twenty-one months later.

Lost bicycle belonged to the lost property man

The lost property officer at Northolt Airport lost his bicycle last night.

After a two-hour search it was found on the 14ft.-high roof of a passenger building. How it got there is a mystery.

Daily Herald September 19 1952

Of some reporters it has been suggested: "If they don't have a story, they just make one up." Perhaps I was fortunate, I never had to. And I did learn that the missing bicycle didn't fly on to the roof of its own volition. Percy Price, a London Transport official who was responsible for the airline town terminal coach services took great delight in asking me daily: "What's news?" and always sympathised with a negative response.

Now he told me with a twinkle in his eye that he was glad I hadn't found the missing bicycle. "They might have suspected you," he grinned. I don't believe I told him of *my* suspicions.

There was the odd occasion, however, when I "engineered" a story by accidentally or deliberately creating a newsworthy situation which I could then report with a clear conscience. On one such occasion a paging microphone was again involved.

In the early 'fifties a science fiction series on BBC Radio, "Journey into Space" was holding millions of listeners enthralled every week. (The series was repeated in the 'nineties). So when I discovered a microphone point in a deserted departure lounge had been inadvertently left switched on, I couldn't resist the temptation. Holding the mike close to my lips, I breathed into it, with what I considered to be full dramatic effect: *"Hello Earth! This is Rocketship Luna calling from outer space....."*

FAR-AWAY VOICE FROM FAR-AWAY SPACE

A TERSE voice boomed over London Airport's loudspeaker system : "Hullo, Earth, this is rocket-ship Luna calling from outer space."

Airport officials were still trying last night to lay the ghost voice. Their only theory : A Christmas reveller at an unguarded microphone. Rocket - ship Luna is the name of the space-ship in the B.B.C.'s "Journey Into Space" serial.

Daily Mail

The ghost voice at the airport

THE "ghost" voice was terse, dramatic. It interrupted a loud-speaker announcement at London Airport last night with: "Hello Earth. This is rocketship Luna calling from outer space." Only airline staff and a few passengers heard the voice. Lounges were almost empty at the time.

Airport officials believe that a late Christmas reveller was responsible; several microphone points are unguarded. "Rocketship Luna" is the name of the spaceship in the B.B.C. serial, "Journey Into Space."

Daily Mirror
(both) Dec 29 1953

Fortunately for me the broadcast was confined to relatively few areas, and only a handful of passengers and staff would have been aware of it. Nevertheless, I called the airport press office to ask if anyone had reported hearing the announcement, and asking what they made of it. Next day at least two newspapers, the *Mirror* and the *Mail*, the latter with an artist's impression of "Rocketship Luna," carried my story of the "voice from outer space," and the airport spokesperson's comment that a "...Christmas reveller was probably responsible." It was the nearest this Christmas non-reveller ever came to making up a news story.

No such inventive input was required from me on another occasion in the same area when I was able to report:

"Someone hit the jackpot in an airport departure lounge last night when he dropped a coin into a liquid refreshment dispenser..."

The "someone" was again me, waiting, with a group of photographers in an empty lounge for a certain Hollywood actress (who it was completely escapes me), about to fly off to Switzerland. "Anyone like to join me?" I asked, turning to the fresh orange-juice dispensing machine standing nearby. My coin dropped, a paper cup fell into place, and was quickly filled. I took the cup and moved away – but as I did so, a second cup dropped and began to fill.

"Ha!" I said. "Now someone will *have* to join me." I waited for the cup to fill then lifted it out and passed it to one of the cameramen. Then I heard the unmistakeable "plop." Another cup had dropped and was filling up fast.

"I don't believe this," I said unnecessarily, as the photographers began to gather around me. I took the cup and passed it on. Another cup fell into place...and another, and another, and another. Soon all six of us had our hands full with cups of orange juice. And still the well was gushing. We pulled up a coffee table. One by one, cup after cup was placed brim-full on the table until there wasn't an inch of space remaining. We started to do the same on an adjoining window ledge. "We could open a shop," I said, half seriously, wondering which would run out first, paper cups or orange juice. At that moment neither seemed to be abating.

At last one of the photographers had an idea. He dived down behind the dispenser – and pulled out the power plug. With a last gasp of bubbles, the flow of orange juice finally dried up. We counted nearly fifty brimming paper cups before we all decided that discretion was the better part of decorum, and we moved hastily away from the vicinity. As I put it, a little unkindly: "You might all be charged with theft, or receiving. I did at least pay for mine." And of course, I had only passed on the free samples to avoid spillages.

This time I did my public duty. I insisted that the cameraman who had switched off the dispenser reported his actions to an airport duty manager, pointing out that he and his colleagues had saved as much of the orange juice as possible. All I could do was report the facts. And that was all that was recorded in several "news in brief" columns of the nationals and, pleasingly, as DJ chatter on at least one radio station...in Australia.

As for our intended target, the Hollywood actress, she failed to show. Perhaps she didn't like the idea of being upstaged by an orange drink dispenser. When we passed the machine again after passengers had boarded their flight, most of the cups were empty. And none of us had savoured the pleasure of shouting: "Drinks all round!"

Toys From Heaven

Trap door of the luggage compartment of a B.E.A. Viking from Berlin flew open over Hayes, Middlesex, and a canvas bag containing toys and other articles fell at the feet of Peter Heffron, who "thought it was a body."

Sunday Dispatch

Surprise packet

The trap door of the luggage compartment of a B.E.A. Viking flying from Berlin to Northolt flew open over Hayes (Middx.), and a canvas bag fell 1,000ft. It landed at the feet of Mr. Peter Heffron, of Shakespeare-avenue, Hayes.

Sunday Express

Earlier in these pages I told the story of the passenger who lay full length on the floor and held on to a door which had opened just after take-off. Not something that happened too often to aircraft, you might think. But in September 1950 the Sunday papers carried my story:

Peter meets a foreign body

Peter Heffron was walking in Hayes, Middlesex, yesterday when a "body" fell out of the sky at his feet.

The "body" was a canvas bag—luggage of a passenger in a B.E.A. Viking, which fell out as the plane, from Berlin, was nearing London.

Sunday Pictorial

BAG FROM SKY FELL BESIDE HIM

PETER HEFFRON was walking to his fiancee's home yesterday when a canvas bag thudded to the ground at his feet.

It had fallen 1,000 feet from a B.E.A. airliner flying to Northolt from Berlin, when a trap door in the luggage compartment opened when the plane was over Hayes, Middlesex.

"I thought it was a body," said Mr Heffron, of Shakespeare-ave., Hayes.

The bag was returned at the airport to its owner, Mr. Leslie Westlake, of Sheen-lane, London, S.W.

The People

Parcel From The Skies

SOMETHING crashed at the feet of Peter Heffron as he was on his way from Shakespeare-avenue, Hayes, Middlesex, yesterday to visit his fiancee. He "thought it was a body."

In fact, the door of the luggage compartment of a passing airliner had come unfastened and "the body" was a canvas bag which fell 1,000 feet.

The bag was ripped, but the only thing broken in it was a child's game which its owner, Mr. Westlake, was taking to his home in Sheen-lane, S.W.

Police rushed the bag to London Airport, where Mr. Westlake was waiting, hoping it would turn up.

News of the World (right)
(all) Sep 17 1950

"Peter Heffron was walking to his fiancée's home in Hayes, Middlesex, yesterday when a canvas bag thudded to the ground at his feet. It had fallen 1,000 feet from a BEA airliner flying from Berlin to Northolt, when a trapdoor in the luggage compartment opened..."

I'd tracked Mr Heffron down to his home in Hayes after I'd learnt that he had phoned the airport to protest. "I thought at first it was a body," he told me.

And in December of the same year, when I heard that a 25lb parcel of lipsticks had fallen from a Nice-bound freighter in a Maidenhead street, I dictated:

" Kisses from the sky fell on Maidenhead last night..."

PAGE ONE ENDPIECE

LIP SERVICE

LIPSTICKS in a sealed packet—believed to have dropped from an air freighter bound for Nice—fell in a Maidenhead street last night.

Daily Express

THE LAST WORD

Kisses from the sky fell in a Maidenhead, Berks, street last night.

They were lipsticks — in a sealed packet—believed to have fallen from a Nice-bound air freighter.

Daily Graphic

Lipsticks fall out of the sky

Daily Mail

A little bit of heaven

Kisses fell from the sky last night at Maidenhead. They were two parcels of lipstick weighing 25lb.

One fell through the roof of Mr. H. Forwood's prefab in Blenheim road, and the other crashed on a garden shed owned by Mr. T. Badnell, of Alwyn-road. The parcels were part of air mail from Northolt to Malta.

Daily Herald (all) December 21 1950

Some of today's regular travellers may still remember when airlines would hand out barley-sugar or boiled sweets to passengers on take-off. They were intended to counteract air sickness and reduce the effects of pressurisation changes on the ears. (A few airlines still provide them).

Not so well known is that a number of airlines, among them BOAC, later amalgamated with BEA into British Airways, offered chewing gum as an alternative. BOAC stopped the issue in 1950 when it found that passengers were complaining about the terrors of getting "gummed-up" by hastily parked or discarded chews. The cost of removing the wads of gum from seats and carpets was also becoming prohibitive. There was also the apocryphal little old lady, who on being told the stick of Wrigleys' was for her ears, had to seek help from a stewardess when her hearing became unaccountably gummed up.

For similar reasons chewing gum was later barred from sale in many airport shops. That didn't stop one ten-years-old American boy taking a supply with him when he boarded a BOAC airliner to fly to London with his parents. His passion for gum forced the pilot to turn back to New York when the aircraft was 250 miles out over the Atlantic

I can't take the credit for the original story. We had been asked by at least one Sunday news desk to check out a report they'd had from New York that a BOAC Stratocruiser had turned back. No one seemed to know the reason; it was left to us to find out.

That wasn't to prove too difficult. Every passenger on the flight seemed to know why they were three-and-a-half hours late arriving at Heathrow. All 86 on board were American hire-purchase credit agents who had chartered the airliner to fly to London with their families for a convention, and were only too pleased to tell the story. It would obviously become a convention classic for years to come.

They delightedly pointed me in the direction of the Rand family of Long Island. Ten-years-old Johnny Rand, I learnt, loved chewing gum. He boarded the airliner clutching 13 sticks of gum in his hand. In just over an hour he was popping the final piece in his mouth when he idly turned the packet over. His eyes alighted on the words: "Laxative: take one at a time."

Johnny decided he'd better tell his mother, who told her husband. Mr Rand called a steward, who told the Captain, who radioed Idlewild Airport, who called a doctor. Back came the radio message: "Keep the boy busy and bring him back for treatment."

For nearly an hour Johnny was kept active as a cabin assistant. Stewardess Anne Jenkins told me: "I gave him a tray and sent him out with drinks for the passengers."

When the airliner touched down back at New York, Johnny was rushed to a surgery for an injection. But at Heathrow, half-a-day later, he was ready to talk to me of his ordeal.

"Someone gave me the gum at the airport," he insisted, "It tasted okay until I read the label on the packet. It said the pieces had to be taken sparingly. I was real scared."

His mother, Mrs Ingrid Rand, said: "We thought there might be some drug in the gum. But he didn't show any ill effects, apart from fright. His sister had one piece, but Johnny had to be greedy..."

After a couple of calls to BOAC to check details of the turn-back, I was able to dictate the story in good time for the Sunday papers. It was given a good spread the next day with a 5-column page lead in *The People* and three columns in the *Sunday Express* among others.

13 Sticks of Chewing Gum

Laxative Upsets Air Trip

By United Press International

LONDON, Aug. 9. — A trans-Atlantic airliner arrived here three hours late from New York last night because a ten-year-old passenger ate 13 sticks of chewing gum—all laxative.

The British Overseas Airways Corp. Stratocruiser had to speedily return to New York's Idlewild Airport when Johhny Rand discovered that it doesn't pay "to be greedy."

Johnny was given an injection at the New York airport and then reboarded the plane for an uneventful and gumless flight to London.

Mrs. Rand said she had no idea who gave Johnny the laxative gum before they boarded the 60-ton, four-engined airliner.

When Johnny read the laxative warning on the gum package he told his mother, who told his father, who told stewardess Ann Jenkins, who told pilot Donald Simco. Mr. Simco called Idlewild Airport, which called a doctor.

"Keep the boy busy and bring him back for treatment," ordered the doctor.

Pilot Simco nosed the airliner around and flew at top speed nearly 300 miles back to New York.

International Herald Tribune ***Aug 10 1959***

THE PEOPLE, SUNDAY, AUGUST 9, 1959

The gum Johnny chewed turns back plane

LITTLE Johnny Rand loves chewing gum . . . and that forced a giant airliner to turn back 250 miles out in the Atlantic yesterday and race back to New York.

It happened like this. Johnny chewed ...

(left) The People (below) Sunday Express and headlines (far left) (all) Aug 9 1959

BY GUM! *Boy turns back plane*

Sunday Dispatch

John gums up BOAC timetable

Sunday Pictorial

Chewing gum scare turns back airliner

Sunday Express Reporter

On Monday the story was carried in American papers, or at least their European editions. I never did learn what Johnny did with his chewed-out sticks of gum. He wouldn't say, but no, he hadn't swallowed them.

Even younger and greedier was the six-years-old from West Berlin who was changing flights at Heathrow in 1954 on his way to Australia. A bemused restaurant manager called me in after he watched young Siegfried Reiman munch his way through seven full-sized mixed sandwiches, four cakes and two cups of tea.

"I thought he must have missed at least a day's meals. He was starving" he said, "But the stewardess who came to collect him told me he had eaten non-stop on the three-hours' flight from Berlin." He had consumed most of the aircraft's supply of chocolates, sweets, biscuits and fruit.

I walked with Siegfried to his Australian airliner. He was off alone to join his father in Sydney. At the steps he asked the stewardess: "What time is supper served?"

Human flyers, the airlines appear to believe, have to be plied with food and drink at regular intervals to give them the impression they are getting something in return for the cost of their tickets. Animal air travellers are usually less demanding.

With a few exceptions, such as rare zoo specimens which have to be pampered with a carefully selected diet, most flying animals (and there are a surprising number of them) get by with basic nourishment and a supply of water. Probably the most frequent animal flyers today are horses, en route to race meetings or destined for stud farms. They invariably travel in their own specially adapted cargo aircraft, accompanied by their own stable lads or veterinary attendants.

Wild animals, especially valuable specimens, will often be escorted by keepers, but security can still pose problems. The three crew members of a Danish Airlines Dakota, pilot, radio officer and engineer, all carried revolvers in their belts when they accompanied a "ferocious" baby gorilla, an over-playful chimpanzee, several poisonous snakes and a number of monkeys on a flight to Frankfurt.

The special freighter was one of a number of "flying menageries" of the era as zoos throughout Europe were trying to build up their exhibits. But only a fragile wire bulkhead separated the unarmed crew of a similar BOAC aircraft from a snarling leopard when it crashed free from its crate and tried to tear down the wire on a journey from India. A cryptic message: *"Leopard loose on Plane,"* was flashed to London; then nothing more was heard for two tense hours.

LEOPARD LOOSE IN A PLANE

A SIGNAL was flashed to London Airport last night from Castel Benito, Tripoli — "Leopard loose on plane."

B.O.A.C. officials waited impatiently for further news. Hours later came the sequel — "Leopard shot."

The animal, which was being flown from India on a York freighter, escaped when the aircraft landed at Tripoli to refuel.

Police, armed with rifles, hunted it down.

Sunday Pictorial

At last it was reported from Castel Benito, Tripoli, that when the York freighter touched down to re-fuel, the leopard escaped. Armed police, alerted by the airport, chased it. Teleprinters at Heathrow concluded their messages with a terse: *"Leopard shot."*

Fortunately for air crews and airport ground staff, to say nothing of the animals, such incidents are rare. But over the years hundreds of exotic birds have escaped from aircraft in Britain alone. Dogs have also frequently slipped their leashes, confounding the strict quarantine regulations, like the three beagles who headed straight for an airport lounge after being led from an aircraft, dodging several taxi-ing airliners on the way.

Even royal corgis, too, have been known to dash away at airports at the slightest chance, giving the run-around to dignified Household staff while the attention of their mistress has been otherwise engaged. And there was the case of the valuable Irish greyhound, Rochan, who was only caught after 12 hours of freedom in the grassy wastes around the Heathrow runways when his last owner was brought over from Belfast and called his name.

Rochan spent his freedom chasing rabbits, ignoring all attempts to capture him, when he should have been chasing a hare at London's Walthamstow Stadium. Said his owner: "His night out won't have done any harm and may make him a better runner than ever. Every time he sees a hare now he'll be thinking of the rabbits."

A LEOPARD LOOSE IN ZOO PLANE

A TOP priority message flashed last night from Castel Benito, Tripoli, to London Airport: "Leopard loose on plane."

The leopard broke out of its crate in a B.O.A.C. "zoo" plane flying wild animals from India. It hurled itself, snarling and growling, against a wire netting barrier erected to protect the crew.

When the plane landed at Tripoli the leopard escaped. Armed police went after it.

Then the teleprinters at Tripoli tapped out another message to London: "Leopard shot."

Its dispatch gave the North African town an hour's thrill—and immense relief to the crew of the aircraft.

Leopard Loose In Plane

Leopard loose in airliner

Leopard escapes in plane

(from top)
The People, News of the World, Sunday Graphic, Sunday Express
(all) Dec 16 1951

Pigs fly regularly and since the early days of aviation so have elephants, though not always on Jumbo jets, and usually before they have grown 'ear-wings' to any great size. Unfortunately, one of a pair of three-years-old elephants from Siam died before their aircraft touched down at Heathrow, just a few weeks after the leopard incident. But a nine-months-old baby elephant, a gift to the zoo at Boston, US, crossed the Atlantic safely a few days later, as did an eleven-months-old which arrived for London Zoo in 1953.

Other exotic animals I was able to see safely on to firm ground included Mohini, a half-ton rhinoceros, the first to arrive by air in London. A few hours after her arrival she was penned up near her future mate Mohan at Whipsnade Zoo. With her on the flight were an orang-utan, snakes, panthers, a tiger cub and 12,000 crated jungle birds.

The carriage of beautiful orca killer whales had also been successfully accomplished on several occasions, a challenging responsibility because of the essential requirement to keep them constantly sprayed with temperature-controlled water. As with dolphins, these have to be slung in specially designed hammocks and watched throughout the flight for signs of distress. Happily in more recent times the necessity for transporting these huge sea mammals has been in their interest, not simply for public exhibition or exploitation.

London Zoo was again the destination for an echidna, or Australian anteater, replacing the zoo's only other one, which had died ten years earlier. But the three-years-old kiwi presented by the government of New Zealand, was to be the first of its kind when it was flown in for the same zoo.

I reported too the gift of an Arab stallion by the Sheikh of Bahrein to his representative in Britain, the departure of fifteen English foxhounds for a Pakistan hunting club, the arrival of 80 chinchillas, worth £8,000 back in 1959, imported from Canada by Mr Alfred Moss, father of the racing driver, Stirling.

When I discovered that 5,000 goldfish were aboard the same airliner from Italy as 1,000lbs of fresh, if lifeless salmon, I couldn't resist reporting it as one news item. An end-of-page piece about ten giant turtles arriving for an exhibition at the Food and Allied Trades Fair at Olympia, London, concluded authoritatively with:

"The smallest will later go to a zoo. The others will probably go into soup."

BENJAMIN BEAR MEETS ROBERT

David Attenborough with his young son – and a bear.

Brenard Press picture *Evening Standard, September 6 1956*

Bears – black, brown and polar white – featured frequently over the years, and usually as bad-tempered, growling and snappy beasts far removed from their cuddly teddy image. One, a four-feet tall Mazanderan bear, a gift from the government of what was then Persia, tore the uniform coat of an RAF officer escorting him.

Two polar bears who stopped over at Northolt en route from Norway to the US., snarled and snapped even as they were offered food; and a tiny, six-weeks-old Malayan bear called Benjamin succeeded in nipping the nose of Television presenter David Attenborough when he tried to introduce it to his then five-years-old son Robert on his return from filming for the BBC's *Zoo Quest*. Some ten years later, flying bears were still winning headlines for their bad tempers. From Prestwick Airport, where I was by then managing Brenards' Scottish office, my colleague Chris Bramwell was to report;

"Boo-boo, the baby black bear presented to the children of Scotland by American school-children... snatched at a hand that slipped into its cage a bowl of bread, milk and honey specially prepared in the airport restaurant. BOAC officials hurriedly abandoned their plans to free Boo-boo at the airport, and handed him over immediately to a keeper from Edinburgh zoo."

When Whipsnade Zoo acquired a 14-weeks-old polar bear from Frankfurt zoo in the mid-fifties, it was hoped it might become as big an attraction as Brumas, the last baby bear in Britain. The new arrival had no name, but it threw the now familiar fit of temperament, snapping and snarling for twenty minutes as it "posed" for photographs with a Pan American receptionist. I promptly named it "Spitfire" for my story.

Of the dailies which ran the story, all but one used the name the next day with explanation: "...as named by airport staff."

But the *Daily Express,* reducing my story to a mere caption for their picture, ignored my suggested name of "Spitfire" and launched their own readers' competition to find a new name for the polar bear cub, offering a £25 prize.

After a few days, the *Express* announced a winner. The £25 prize, they said, had gone to a woman reader for being "the first of many" to suggest the name of...you've guessed – "Spitfire".

The name became official at London Zoo when the *Daily Express* later adopted the cub. But whether it was the choice of name or the lack of novelty, Spitfire never did become a second Brumas.

Why did I not claim the prize? As I wrote in my weekly column for a local newspaper at the time: "Professional discretion, you know. We just don't claim credit for these things." Now, if it had been a win on the pools... (Oh, and if my friends on the *Express* want to dispute this little tale, I can only suggest they take a look at the cuttings from other newspapers on the day. They can't all be wrong.)

Although apparently reluctant to advertise it, airlines do occasionally permit family pets in the cabins of passenger aircraft, if they are properly contained in a cage or crate. But I doubt if they would be happy about the creepy crawlies some children delight in calling pets, and which they were for ever bringing back to Britain from overseas holidays until existing regulations were enforced or strengthened.

When 12-years-old Tim Brain was asked by Customs men if he had anything to declare on his return from a visit to Canada, he presented them with a jam-jar stuffed with an assortment of dead grasshoppers, leaves and dry grass.

A CUB FLIES IN

Zoo wants name for Brumas II

Daily Express picture *Mar 23 1956*

Pan American ground hostess Norah Standerwick keeps a wary eye on her feeding charge, the bad tempered Polar bear-cub with no name.

"Only my *Mantis Religiosa*," he said brightly, "I've brought it back for my collection."

Patiently he explained to the suspicious Customs officers that he'd given the scientific name for a praying mantis, a two-inch-long insect so called because of the way it holds its two front legs. And he had to remain patient while the officers thumbed through their books of regulations. After 15 minutes it was decided that the mantis was not an "undesirable alien," and Tim was allowed to take it home to Staffordshire to join his collection of butterflies, moths and other insects.

"I plan to keep this one alive as long as possible," he told me, "It only eats other insects, so it shouldn't be difficult."

None of these childish trophies achieved the notoriety of *Megazopheus Chiliensis*, the two-inch beetle which, in March 1963, flew into Prestwick Airport. For "Mexican Meg," as she came to be known, travelled literally *harnessed to the lapel* of a South

Glasgow Evening Citizen (below)
Glasgow ©Evening Times (right)
(both) Mar 21 1963

'Live brooch' problem flies in to Prestwick . . .

A Mexican woman who passed through Prestwick Airport wearing a live beetle as a brooch has left the Ministry of Agriculture with a gnawing problem which has baffled even their top entomologists.

A few months ago Megazopheus Chiliensis—better known in its native Mexico as the "grey beetle"—was unheard of and unwanted.

It spent its life span of four months happily scratching around—until a Mexican in Yucatan, out for a quick peso, thought of "live" brooches.

The beetles, just two inches long, were fitted with saddles encrusted with imitation jewels and a chain to fasten them to lapels.

Real jewels

The idea caught on, a craze start[illegible]

THE BROOCH THAT WALKS SETS POSER AT AIRPORT

A MEXICAN woman who passed through Prestwick airport on her way to London wearing a live beetle "brooch" has set the Ministry of Agriculture a gnawing problem which has even their top insect experts baffled.

She told startled airline officials, as the "brooch" walked round her shoulder: "I feed and water it three times a day. It eats decayed wood."

BEETLE GAVE CUSTOMS MEN THE CREEPS

HERALD REPORTER

WOMAN who flew into Prestwick from Mexico [ye]sterday had a beetle [br]ooch to declare.

[O]h! what a fuss it caused [to] the Customs men—for the [two-]inch beetle was live. And [it w]as walking around her [shoul]ders.

[Som]e after a quick peso down [Mex]ico way has been rounding up the grey beetles and fitting them with tiny, jewel-encrusted saddles.

Brooch is live

AIRLINE officials' eye-brows shot up when they saw a jewelled brooch WALK ROUND a woman passenger's shoulder.

The brooch was a two-ich- [illegible]

feed and water it three times a day. It lives off decayed wood."

Banned

American customs men have been told not to admit the beetle Megazopheus [illegible]

Daily Record (above),
Daily Herald (right) both Mar 22 1963

American tourist.

Meg was alive and well and fitted with a jewelled saddle as she walked around the shoulder of her hostess to the full extent of her six-inch silver chain. Startled officials gaped in astonishment as they watched the woman passenger offer a snack to her living brooch. "It lives on decayed wood," she said, "And I have to feed and water it three times a day."

I was starting my reporting stint later that particular day, and by the time I arrived at our tiny airport office, my colleague Chris Bramwell, who had picked up the story a few hours earlier, had already done all his ground work. He had only learnt of the incident a full day after passengers on the transatlantic flight had cleared passport and Customs controls at the Scottish airport on their way to London. But that didn't deter him.

He talked with airline staff and to Customs officers who had dealt with the traveller. He had set the wires humming by tackling Government departments and he had checked with experts at the Natural History Museum to learn more about the giant beetle. He had discovered, through further digging, that similar live brooches were on sale to tourists in Yucatan, Mexico, where an enterprising trader thought of "harnessing" them and fitting the beetles with bejewelled saddles.

He learnt that the beetle-brooches were banned in the United States after agricultural experts became concerned about possible infestation, and he had asked Britain's Ministry of Agriculture for a ruling. They finally confirmed that checks had been made and it had been decided that the beetle (its Latin name simply meant "from Mexico") was harmless, and its owner was allowed to keep it.

Chris had already filed a story to the Scottish evening newspapers in Glasgow and Edinburgh, and was in the middle of ringing round the daily papers when I arrived. So I could only help him and congratulate him on what had to be a first class light news story. And so it was to prove – with every newspaper on both sides of the border giving it full coverage. This was in spite of the absence of "names, ages and addresses" normally and understandably paramount in all such stories.

It was, I suspected, because he felt aggrieved about not having these finer details, (quite unjustly I felt), that Chris gamely persisted with his enquiries in the hope of a follow-up whenever he found time over the next two weeks. His persistence paid-off. Now at last he had a name, and he managed finally to track down the beetle's owner to a London hotel. And it was there that he then learnt...that Mexican Meg was dead.

Magnanimously, Chris allowed me to give him a hand with this new development as I suggested a changed word here, a new phrase there. My input certainly wasn't necessary, but I was as enthusiastic about the update as he was, and wanted to be involved. Once again, more than three weeks after the original story, the copy did well.

As the *Daily Herald* ran it, barely changing a word:

"Megazopheus Chiliensis, otherwise known as Mexican Meg, is dead. She died of loneliness and a broken heart in a London hotel room, thousands of miles from her home, despite a two-day battle by the Ministry of Agriculture, the Home Office and HM Customs to grant her insectal asylum. A horrified chambermaid found Meg, still wearing her jewellery, gasping on the floor of a bedroom......."

Meg, it seemed, had slipped her chain when left overnight on a dressing table, and scuttled off –**"abandoning her life on the lapel of luxury."** She was found dead after

her owner, one Senora Salidad Montellano, had left the hotel to resume her travels. As the story continued in the *Daily Herald*:

"The maid called for the housekeeper. The housekeeper called the manager. The manager called for – a matchbox, because Meg, a two-inch-long beetle, had by then expired."

Telling how Meg had arrived at Prestwick, chained as a victim of the tourist trade to the lapel of her owner, our report went on:

"...The craze for live brooches had swept across Mexico into America. But Britain had never heard of Megazopheus Chiliensis until Senora Montellano arrived in Scotland. And it presented a problem; a gnawing problem. Meg lived off decayed wood – so was she a desirable insect?

After a two-day investigation, top entomologists managed to track down Meg's ancestry for the Ministry of Agriculture.

The beetle, they decided, could stay."

The decision came too late to save Meg. After discovering her loss, the Senora had to continue her package tour of Europe without her favourite brooch. Passing through Prestwick on her way home again she told Chris: "It was a lovely little thing. I called it 'Mayavech' and had grown quite fond of it. I was so sad when I lost it in the hotel room and hunted everywhere before I had to leave."

Two newspapers called us back on the story. The *Scottish Daily Mail* news desk told Chris: "Just got your beetle story; like it very much. Thought it very funny...thank you."

Praise from the *Daily Herald* in Manchester was even more overstated.

"This is the Assistant Editor.... want to thank you for the best story we've had here today. The Editor picked it out and said: 'I wish to hell some of our chaps could write like that.' Thank you very much." The credit, of course was down to Chris. But I was pleased to claim my two pennyworth.

It was in Scotland, too, that I found myself "interviewing" another domestic pet hoping to overcome national health restrictions – this time in the shape of US Government regulations. Sese the parrot was travelling on a first-class ticket (cost £6. 7s. 6d) and all the legal documentation he, or rather his owner, could muster.

My story to the dailies and American agencies ran:

"A wily bird is Sese the parrot. Who better to talk his way round the tough regulations of the US Public Health Department than a four-years-old African parrot who can argue and plead in four languages?..."

Sese's owner, English-born geologist, explorer and author Penha Sumner-Tait, who was travelling with him, was as unperturbed as Sese when the regulations were pointed out to her at the BOAC check-in desk. As I unashamedly eavesdropped, she readily signed a document absolving the airline from any responsibility. She told me: "Sese can speak Spanish, Norwegian and Swahili as well as English, and has a tremendous vocabulary, so he should gain a sympathetic hearing with someone."

Mrs Sumner-Tait was planning to make a lecture tour of America to promote her newly-published autobiography. Sese, she said, was an essential visual (and vocal?) aid to her presentation. I never did see, or hear of Sese or his mentor again after filing my copy. So I have to assume that someone in America listened to at least one of his languages and gave him his work permit.

Recalling these animal stories has meant spanning almost two decades in just a few pages. There were also many other cargoes which continued to make news in the early years, however, not least among them the occasional consignments of gold bullion. It was only after I realised that over some five weeks in 1951, more than ten separate loads of between two and four tons each, a total value of some £10m (or £160m in today's terms) had been flown into Northolt from Warsaw, that I made a serious attempt to discover the

The tragic death of Mexican Meg

HERALD REPORTER

MEGAZOPHEUS CHILIENSIS, otherwise known as Mexican Meg, is dead.

She died of loneliness and a broken heart in a London hotel room thousands of miles from her home in Yucaton, Mexico, despite a two-day battle by the Ministry of Agriculture, the Home Office and Customs officials to grant her insectal asylum.

A horrified chambermaid found Meg, still wearing her jewellery, gasping on the floor of a bedroom.

The maid called for the housekeeper. The housekeeper called for the manager.

The manager called for — a matchbox because Meg, a two inch long beetle, had by then expired.

Probe

Meg, a victim of the tourist trade, flew into Prestwick Airport from New York two weeks ago, chained to the lapel of her owner, Senora Salidad Montellano.

On her back was a jewel encrusted saddle and on her head were other precious stones.

The craze for "live brooches" has swept across Mexico into America, but Britain had not heard of Megazopheus Chiliensis

Here Meg presented a problem—a gnawing problem. She lived off decayed wood. Was she a desirable insect?

Entomologists tracked down Meg's ancestry at the request of the Ministry of Agriculture.

The beetle, they decided, could stay.

Escape

But Meg had already found freedom.

Left on a dressing-table overnight, she slipped her lead and scuttled, abandoning her life on the lapel of luxury.

Senora Montellano, on a European trip, continued her journey

And Meg now lies in an hotel vault—oblivious of the blow she struck for beetle freedom.

Daily Herald *Apr 16 1963*

"The best story today". But it wasn't mine!

MILLIONS NOBODY TALKS ABOUT

Mystery Gold Flown Here From Poland

By Sunday Dispatch Reporter

TONS of gold are being flown from Poland to Britain in great secrecy. The traffic has been in progress for five weeks. Total value of the consignments runs into millions of pounds.

The reason for this unprecedented transport of bullion from a Soviet satellite to a Western Power is being kept a mystery by all the British authorities concerned.

Worth £297,600 A Ton

Packed in plain, sealed wooden boxes, more than ten separate loads of between two and four tons each have been stacked aboard airliners at Okecie Airport, Warsaw, and flown via Copenhagen to London. Each ton is worth £297,600.

Sunday Dispatch
January 1951

reason behind this steady traffic.

Over several days I put questions to the Polish Embassy, the Bank of England and Government departments. Documents sent with each consignment not only failed to indicate the gold's destination, but the place of origin had also been left blank, contrary to normal practice. And though scores of airline and airport employees in Britain and abroad were involved in handling the shipments, not one of the agencies responsible during the 1,000-mile journey would admit to knowing the gold's final destination. The sealed wooden crates bore the address of the Bank of England. But as one cargo officer told me: "That doesn't mean the gold stops there."

A Bank spokesman would only say: "We are not admitting that any consignments have reached us. But if we should have a private consignment we would be obliged to maintain strict secrecy." And the Economic Information Office of the Treasury strongly refuted a suggestion that the gold was in payment of some outstanding international debt.

The Polish Embassy said: "We know nothing. It's a mistake – or a mystery."

Like me, the Sunday Papers plumped for the second suggestion. The *Sunday Dispatch* gave it the best treatment: a two-column second lead on Page 1 which ran to twelve column inches.

The "mystery" was never cleared up. As far as I am aware, there were no follow-up stories in the dailies, and even the city didn't appear to be interested. So I simply moved on to other matters. As to be expected, the principal news makers continued to be people. Stories over the next few months were to range through a spectrum of emotive hues from the sombre indigo of despair to the sunny highlights of good living.

Whether it was the three tragic mothers flying to Cairo in 1950 clinging desperately to the hope that the lives of their sons might yet be saved, or the Aga Khan giving tips for winners – and losers – for the Gold Cup, or "two-ton" Tessie O'Shea proudly announcing she had lost weight, every day brought a new situation, a new experience to be fully recorded and reported.

Platinum blonde Tessie, a popular ukelele-playing Lancashire comedienne of the music halls, was as much a household name for her "comfortable" figure as she was for her entertaining, and was happy to exploit the image. But she knew a good story, even if it conflicted with that familiar image. She had left her show at Blackpool's Opera House to make an air dash to London, she told me, to see her tailor (her word, not mine).

"I've lost 49 pounds since the show opened, love," she said. "I'm down to fourteen and a half stone."

Two-ton Tess loses 49 lb.

Herald Reporter

TWO-TON Tessie O'Shea is losing weight. She is down now from 18 stone to 14½, and she just doesn't know why.

Yesterday she flew from Blackpool, where she is appearing in "Out of this World" at the Opera House, to give her London tailor reducing orders.

She has lost seven inches from her 56-inch hips, eight inches from her 46-inch bust, and ten inches from her 44-inch waist.

Daily Herald

Tessie slims

"TWO-TON" Tessie O'Shea, from the Blackpool Opera House show "Out of This World," made an air dash to London yesterday—to see her tailor.

Since the show opened Tessie has lost seven inches from her 56-inch hips, eight inches from her 46-inch bust, and nine inches from her 44-inch waistline, and, with her weight down from 18 stone to 14½ stone, her tailor starts work today altering all her dresses and suits.

* * *

"It is the result of months of hard work and semi-dieting," said Tessie, "but I'm not worried. I said I'd be picked for a leading lady one day—it won't be long now the way I'm going."

Daily Mail ***(both) Aug 14 1950***

Seven inches had fallen from her 56-inch hips, eight inches from a 46-inch bust and her waist line had shrunk nine inches to a mere 35 inches "It's the result of months of hard work and semi-dieting, darlin'," she said, "But I'm not worried. It won't be long now before I'm picked as a leading lady."

The idea of a slim-line Tessie O'Shea fascinated *Star Man's Diary* in the London evening newspaper even after the dailies had run the story, and they gave it special treatment with their own artist's caricature and a poetic comment *(see opposite),* which concluded:

"...so hip-hip-hurray
for Miss Tessie O'Shea
Now she's 'One-and-Threequarter-Ton Tessie'."

The Aga Khan, grandfather of the present spiritual head of the Ishmaeli community, could always be relied upon to say something about horse racing, his favourite pastime, even to tipping a loser. I was there to bear witness to this when on arrival from Paris on one occasion, he slipped a 1,000-franc note into the hand of a porter and said: "Put that on *Fraise du Bois* if you want to lose in the Gold Cup on Thursday"

Then he pulled out another 1,000-franc note (then about £1) and whispered: "Put that on *Scratch* if you want to win." Average tip of the day to porters was 2s (or 10p). Scratch II, owned by M.Marcel Boussac, was favourite for the Ascot race at 7-2. *Fraise du Bois* was one of the Aga's own string of racehorses. He explained to me: "He's a funny horse. If he starts all right he will win. If not, he's an also-ran."

Albert Pierrepoint was a fresh-faced, friendly little Yorkshireman who might have been a farmer, or a publican, which he was. But he had another occupation. Like his father and uncle before him, Albert Pierrepoint was also Britain's official executioner, the public hangman. I had first met him with Harry when he was still travelling regularly to Germany to carry out sentences against Nazi war criminals and traitors such as William Joyce, better known to the British public as Lord Haw-Haw.

He was happy to talk about anything other that his work, even though once I had the temerity to resurrect a rumoured family skeleton that my siblings and I had a nineteenth-century public hangman as an ancestor. James Berry had hailed from Bradford, just a few miles from Albert's birthplace. Naturally Britain's last executioner knew all about his predecessor.

But he still declined to share with me details of his flight to Cairo when I spotted him in an airport lounge one day, carrying the familiar little attaché case which was purported to contain the tools of his trade – the hangman's noose.

A moment's thought should have given me the answer. British newspapers had given full coverage to the trial by military court of three young British soldiers accused of the murder of an Egyptian civilian, a night watchman in a garage. The three accused, part of the British military force still in Egypt, had been found guilty and sentenced to death.

I remembered Albert Pierrepoint's departure when a few days later three distraught middle-aged women were helped out to a Cairo-bound Constellation airliner. Three despairing mothers who were flying to visit their condemned sons, prepared to make their last poignant farewells, while still praying for a last minute miracle.

As they sat quietly together in an airport departure lounge apart from other passengers, the women, none of whom had met before, shared their distress. I struggled with my conscience. Would it be "intrusion into private grief" if I approached them?

A phalanx of photographers had been clicking and flashing away without any obvious concern about the feelings of the women, who for their part seemed to be quite unaware of the attention. I needed to know if anything had changed, if they had been given any further hope of a last minute reprieve. I waited patiently for the photographers to finish, then, as gently and sympathetically as I knew how, I approached the mothers.

In fact they seemed anxious to talk to me. One told me how her fare had been paid by her local MP. Another asked me to contact relatives who had brought her to the airport. The third told me of a last-minute telephone call from the girlfriend of her son. As we talked, with me crouching in front of them seated in their armchairs, I suddenly felt my arm tweaked. I turned to find the *Daily Mirror's* airport photographer Arthur Greated glaring at me.

"Why don't you leave 'em alone?" he demanded, "Can't you see how upset they are? How would you like to be hounded…?"

I got to my feet and pulled him away, excusing myself with the three travellers. But with Arthur, for a moment, I was speechless.

"Don't ever do that to me" I said at last. "I had their confidence. You were the one being offensive." And I added: "I didn't see you being sensitive when you were taking their picture. You didn't even ask them."

We were still arguing, fortunately out of range, when the women were finally escorted out to their aircraft. As far as I know we never did agree which was more intrusive, the camera or the reporter. In the circumstances it was a petty, an inconsequential and insensitive disagreement, even if it was one forced upon me.

This was just one of a number of stories I was now covering at Heathrow. Although

Cheer Up

[Miss Tessie O'Shea ("Two Ton Tessie") proudly announced today that she had lost 49 lbs and now weighed a mere 14 stones 7 lbs.]

Police Lose Track of Desperate Thugs
Doctor Loses Dangerous Drugs
England Loses Grip on Test
Punter Loses Shirt—and Vest
Little Girl is Lost at Play
MPs Lose Some Holiday
South Korea Loses Face
Secrets Lost in Atom Case—
Is there naught to gladden eyes on
Round this dreary Lost Horizon?

Raise a glad cheer
An example is here
Miss Would-be-Slim make joyful sounds
For our Two-Ton Tess
Is now pleased to confess
She has lost just on 49 pounds.
Such loss is a gain
That will rank and remain
With old glories like Blenheim and and Crecy
So hip-hip-hurray
For Miss Tessie O'Shea
Now she's "One-and-Threequarter Ton Tessie."

The Star ***Aug 15 1950***
Sketch by Joss

still based at Northolt, I was periodically filling in for absent colleagues at the "home base." I found the experience useful, in any event, as within a few months Northolt was due to revert to its former role as an RAF airfield, with BEA and half-a dozen foreign European airlines transferring their services. Even the preparations for the big move gave me a 3-column page lead in *The Star*.

Northolt's biggest operator, BEA, I was able to reveal, would be moving to Heathrow by the late Spring of 1951, and the 30-strong advance guard of some 7,000 employees would be handling the new 40-seater Ambassador airliner, later to be renamed the Elizabethan by the airline. By the end of the year, when the move would be complete, I forecast that London Airport would be second only to New York airport as the world's busiest air terminal.

Northolt Ready For BigSwitch

RAF GOING BACK

The Star ***December 13 1950***

In the meantime I was reporting the return of Britain's deputy foreign minister Ernest Davies from the 4-power talks in Paris the day after Herbert Morrison succeeded the ailing Ernest Bevin as Foreign Secretary. He was apparently unsure who to report to and said: "I expect I shall see both." He would be telling them of the difficulties he and other Western ministers were experiencing in dealing with their Soviet opposite number.

"But I refused to allow the meeting to be drowned in a sea of propaganda," he said.

The Cold War had its echoes outside the Governmental conference rooms too. Just a few weeks earlier British authorities had condemned an international "peace conference" planned to be held in Sheffield because they believed it was inspired by Communist front organisations rather than by sincere pacifists. Delegates arriving at Northolt to attend the conference were turned back by Immigration officers. They included two women and a man from Switzerland, a Dane and a group of 16 Hungarians.

At Northolt and London Airports would-be delegates were still being turned back yesterday. Sixteen Hungarians, returning to Budapest, listened to a speech by Mr. Alf Salisbury, there to welcome them and raised clenched fists when he gave the Communist salute.

He shouted: "There will come a day when we shall be able to welcome you to this country without hindrance." Then he was asked to leave by a Customs officer.

Daily Express

Four delegates were refused permission to enter Britain at Northolt and sent back to Geneva and Oslo. They were two men and a woman of Swiss nationality and one Dane. Their names were not revealed.

At Northolt 16 Hungarian delegates left for Prague a few hours after arrival.

Mr. Alf Salisbury, of the "welcoming committee" was there to see them off. He raised a clenched fist and shouted: "We shall continue to fight. There will come a day when we shall be able to welcome you to this country without hindrance."

A Customs officer and an airport official asked him to leave the airport buildings.

The delegates gave three cheers, their arms raised in the clenched-fist salute, and boarded the airliner, humming and singing "The Internationale."

An airport official said: "The delegates' attitude was becoming very warlike—and the service would have been delayed if we had not separated them."

Daily Mail (both extracts) Nov 11 1950

As I reported exclusively, the Hungarians re-boarded their Czech airliner singing *"The Internationale"* and raising their arms in the clenched-fist salute, while the leader of a welcoming delegation shouted to them:

"There will come a day when we shall be able to welcome you to this country without hindrance."

The entire scene, including the returning delegates and a solitary reporter scribbling in a notebook (though I can't say it was a true likeness of me) was recaptured by cartoonist Low for the London *Evening Standard*, even down to a key quote from the Hungarians which only the *Daily Worker* had used:

"Your government would not allow our important delegates into the country," said the woman leader of the Hungarians.

Low translated this as:

" ...they wouldn't allow our travelling majority in. There was a risk of things turning into a genuine conference."

chapter three

Evening Standard LOW cartoon reproduced by kind permission of Express Newspapers Ltd © in all countries

*

I was standing with Russian Embassy officials at Northolt when America's newest bomber, the giant B36, on a maiden flight to Europe, made a flypast for the benefit of the USAF base at nearby South Ruislip. If they were at all concerned about the world's biggest military aircraft of its day, none of the Russians showed it. When I asked what he thought, one of them turned to me and said: "It's big, and so beautiful."

My frequent sorties to Heathrow kept me in touch and involved in international affairs such as the Abadan oil crisis and the meeting of the UN Security Council in New York, with all the to-ing and fro-ing of its attendant delegates. It also meant an opportunity for me to increase my freelance output.

Aged 17, I was still living with my parents in North London and my journey time to either Northolt or Heathrow was taking me between an hour and 90 minutes, depending on connections. I was able to speed up and break the Northolt journey by making changes at King's Cross and Baker Street or at Holborn, to alternate between the Metropolitan or Central Lines. But for Heathrow I was still restricted to a long, winding journey on the Piccadilly Line. Somewhere along either route I was frequently able to report tube delays and other problems for commuters, supplementing my income with almost regular newspaper cheques.

But my strangest experience in freelance activity occurred on my weekly day off, and in the end earned me nothing but months of bewildered and unfulfilled anticipation.

My sister Joyce had recently left college and was working as a health visitor for the pharmaceutical company British Drug Houses, in Islington. My mother had asked me to telephone her during the day with a message. I had tried several times, but there seemed to be a fault on the line, as I was unable to obtain a ringing tone. I tried again – and this time unwittingly broke into a conversation on a crossed line.

Instead of hanging up and trying again, I found myself listening, totally fascinated by the exchange. The speakers appeared to be two scientists, or at least two executives of a drug manufacturing company which I could only assume was BDH. And after a few seconds I found myself reaching for a pencil and scribbling notes on a pad I always kept by the phone.

The conversation was unreal, barely credible. It had all the clichés of a Hollywood 'B' movie script. I no longer have those notes, but partly because of their sheer banality and partly because I'd kept them for years, I can remember some of the phrases as vividly as if I'd heard them yesterday.

"...You realise what we have here, don't you Doctor? This is not something we can hide away. A discovery of this magnitude will have to be shared with the industry....
(The Doctor:) ***"I agree absolutely. But we will have to launch, and we'll need Government funds for that. We'll have to meet to discuss finance if we go ahead on our own initially. And we must do that if we're going to stop the Americans getting their hands on this..."***
(The first speaker interrupts:)
" I simply can't believe what we've got here. It's sensational. It will rock the medical world....it's what we've all been looking for, for so long. But it's going to cost millions. There's no way we could carry this on our own....."

There was much more of the same. I filled page after page of the pad with more notes in my own personal shorthand, a mixture of evening class Pitman's, army class Duttons and my own short forms. The speakers continued to talk finance and production techniques. At one stage I even broke in and asked, intently: "Yes, Doctor. But what does it *do*? What will it cure?" But there was no response. The conversation didn't even falter. They obviously couldn't hear me.

At last the exchange tailed off. Then, in the midst of a technical discussion on laboratory equipment which was way above my head (and beyond my note-taking) I caught the fateful phrase: *"...Cancer cure."*

I bit my lip. After a moment's hesitation, I tried once more to break in. In a momentary gap I suddenly announced, loudly and clearly:

"*Doctor!* You don't know me. But I've been listening to your conversation about your discovery ...a cancer cure...?" I broke off. It was pointless to continue. They were speaking again and hadn't heard my interruption.

Out of sheer frustration I replaced the handset. I felt confused and frustrated. What had I stumbled on? What could I do about it? I calculated I'd spent at least 20 minutes listening to a conversation, much of which was beyond me. What I did understand sounded pure fantasy. I spent some minutes going over my notes, experiencing again those excited voices, the enthusiasm of the speakers. But that broken phrase worried me.

If I could convince a newspaper of what I'd heard, enough to make them want to investigate further, I might have to do it without mentioning that phrase. All newspapers of that time were wary of so-called "cancer cures" without documentary evidence, which of course at that time didn't exist. I decided to 'phone Harry at work for advice.

When I'd finished explaining the background to him, he asked a few questions. Then he said:

"Let me talk to Bernard Murphy and see how he feels about this. In the meantime, why don't you type up your notes? If he's interested he'll want those.

"But you can't keep quiet about the cancer bit, even though I understand your concern. It might be the very clue they need."

Bernard Murphy was News Editor of *The Star*, the London evening newspaper, and a good friend of Brenard Press. I'd never had any direct contact with him, but of course he knew Harry, and I could see the value of this approach. I hung up and hurried off to my typewriter. I could see it would be useful to have a readable, typed version of my notes available.

About an hour later Bernard called me. For a few minutes we talked about the crossed line. In answer to his question, I confirmed that I had tried to repeat the process again, without success. He asked me if my sister would know if any cancer research was being carried out at BDH. I replied that at this stage I didn't want to ask her as she had only recently started working there and I didn't want to compromise her. It seemed unnecessary to add that she would probably think the way I'd picked up the story highly immoral and expect me to drop it.

At last, as Harry had indicated, Bernard asked me to dictate my notes to a copy-taker.

"I'm going to put one of my feature writers, Roy Nash on to this."

Another of those "small world" coincidences. Nash was the feature writer who shared that *Star* Jubilee page with Harry back in the 'thirties. He was also one of the few *Star* "names" Harry had pointed out to me when I lunched with him in the Bouverie-street office canteen. And finally, my reporter chum in the army, Pat Nicholson, had once told me of a cousin who worked for *The Star*. It was, of course, Roy Nash.

I wish I could relate a fitting conclusion to this telephone tale, but I cannot. I heard nothing from Nash, or from Bernard Murphy, until I tackled the news editor myself some eighteen months later. "Did we not call you?" he asked. "We should have done. Roy Nash spent ages trying to make the tip stand up. As far as I know he still pours through medical journals without success. Did you never hear anything yourself?"

I knew what he meant, and was able to tell him that Joy had made some enquiries at BDH (surprisingly she seemed quite excited at the idea) but was never able to substantiate the suggestion of cancer research. For months, even years afterwards, I did a mental double-take whenever newspapers reported a "medical breakthrough," "new wonder drug" or "miracle cure." Finally I concluded that my two scientists must have been at least as disappointed as I. My story, like their "discovery," was a non-starter. One for the "spike"– the news editor's waste disposal tool. Ironically, and tragically, my sister herself died of cancer some years later.

There were other occasions when I found that stories had been "spiked" (not by my own news desk, thankfully), but by news desks of national or regional newspapers. Fortunately, the chances of every one of our clients rejecting the same story on the same day were pretty remote, unless it was a very weak one on an otherwise very busy or "big news" day. And sometimes the reason behind the rejection seemed insupportable and unjustified.

More of that later. There was certainly no chance of the newspapers ignoring the return to flying duties of BEA Stewardess Sue Cramsie in November 1950, after her recovery from the serious injuries she had received eight months earlier.

I was still in the army when in April of that year Harry broke the story of the explosion aboard a BEA Viking flying from Northolt to Paris. A huge hole had been torn in the tail of the aircraft, shattering the galley, the adjoining toilet and the linking companionway. And the aircraft's stewardess, Sue Cramsie, who had just returned to the galley, had taken the full force of the blast, with her body virtually shielding the passengers in the cabin behind her.

At first it was thought by some that the explosion had been caused by lightning. The aircraft had been flying through an electric storm at the time. But the pilot, Captain Ian Harvey, who was awarded the George Medal for bringing the crippled airliner safely back to London, was convinced a bomb was responsible. A later investigation proved him right, though it was never discovered who had planted the device.

Now, after months of plastic surgery, 27-years-old Sue was back and ready to fly again. BEA made an occasion of her return, with a full press call, and a number of photographers turned up to join our own cameraman to picture her on the steps of an aircraft. As I was the only reporter present, however, my copy provided most of the captions for the other agencies' pictures as well as ours. Although we had never met, Sue greeted me warmly. The reason, I realised, was not my personal charm, but that she knew of me as Harry's kid brother, and had known Bill Brenard from her own service days.

I ran into Sue frequently after that, on the Northolt tarmac or in the passenger buildings. Even so, I felt privileged when some months later she called me over to give me an "exclusive." British European Airways, she said, had decided to make an award to her of £2,500 (worth about £50,000 in 2005).

"When they told me of the award I thought they were talking about a few hundreds," she said, "So it was a very pleasant surprise."

I asked her jokingly if she was now planning to retire. "Not on your life," she said. "I even asked if I could stay on the same route to Paris. The only time I'm not happy about flying is on the 13th." Her accident had occurred on Thursday 13 April.

I phoned BEA to confirm the details of the award. There a spokesman asked me to emphasise that it was an"ex-gratia payment," as the airline was not legally responsible.

Air hostess injured by plane bomb gets £2,500 'gift'

Express Staff Reporter

AIR hostess Sue Cramsie, who was injured last year when a bomb exploded in a Viking airliner, is to get £2,500 from British European Airways.

The award was recommended by a committee on the advice of doctors and insurance experts. B.E.A. call it an "ex-gratia payment."

An official said last night: "It is not legally compensation, since there was no negligence by B.E.A."

"But it was considered an award should be granted in view of the injuries received by Miss Cramsie in the service of the corporation."

Tall, fair-haired, 27-year-old Sue was blown off her feet by the bomb. She spent several months in hospital.

Back to work

She reported back to duty last November, and asked to go back on her old route, London-Paris.

The bomb exploded while the Viking was over the Channel flying from Northolt to Paris. No trace of the bomb was found, but an official report said that an explosive object was "almost certainly" placed in the toilet compartment.

None of the 28 passengers was injured.

The date was April 13. And now Sue says: "I still love flying—any day except the 13th of the month."

Last night she was aboard another plane bound for Paris. "When I was told about the award I expected no more than a few hundred pounds," she said.

"This is a very pleasant surprise."

Daily Express *Nov 11 1950*

AIR 'COVER GIRL' GETS £2,500

MISS SUE CRAMSIE, 27-year-old British European Airways "cover girl" stewardess, has been awarded £2,500.

It is an "ex-gratia" payment for injuries she received in the bomb explosion aboard a Viking airliner on April 13 last year.

The award was recommended on the advice of doctors and insurance experts.

OFF TO PARIS

A B.E.A. official said: "The payment is not legally compensation since there was no negligence on the part of B.E.A.

"But it was considered that an award should be granted in view of the injuries received in the service of the corporation."

Daily Graphic *Nov 11 1950*

But they said the payment had been recommended by doctors and insurance experts.

The story was given full coverage the next day with a four-column heading in the *Daily Express* and single or double-column pieces elsewhere.

British photo agencies benefited again with the reprinting of stock pictures of Sue from the previous November. I began to wonder why Brenards were always being pipped at the photographic post. But at least, as reporters, we held our own with frequent exclusives and the occasional front page lead, such as my 1958 clue to Winston Churchill's health problems:

Macmillan gets an 'optimistic' telegram, then—

CHURCHILL—No 10 OXYGEN MYSTERY

Daily Sketch (page 1 lead) *Feb 21 1958*

Daily Sketch Reporter

A MYSTERIOUS consignment of oxygen equipment was flown from London Airport to Nice early to-day.

Were they sent for Sir Winston Churchill, ill with pneumonia at his holiday villa at Roquebrune?

No one would confirm it. But a representative of the manufacturers said:

"We are under orders from Downing-street. We cannot say more.

He added: "This publicity is putting me in a terrible spot.

"I cannot resort to lying by giving a denial that this equipment is consigned to Lord Moran. All that I am prepared to say is that it was not ordered by him."

A TENT

The oxygen, which included a tent and other equipment, was flown out in a twin-engined Dakota.

It had been driven in a sealed van into the airport and given immediate clearance by the Customs.

Sir Winston sent a "very optimistic" telegram to Mr. Macmillan at 10, Downing-street, yesterday.

It was in reply to a message of good wishes sent by the Prime Minister to Sir Winston at his holiday villa on the French Riviera.

Members of Sir Winston's family in London also received good news.

His daughter Diana, wife of Mr. Duncan Sandys, the Defence Minister, said her father's progress was encouraging.

Mr. Randolph Churchill, his son, who is in America, is flying to Nassau in the Bahamas to-day.

Sir Winston Churchill's health was of some national concern in his later years, and my discovery of a consignment of medical equipment on its way to his holiday home in the South of France gave me an unexpected page 1 lead in the *Daily Sketch*.

CHAPTER FOUR

Prominently displayed behind an information desk at Heathrow's Terminal 3 is a sign reading: "Passenger lists are not available at this counter."

Although it implies that they may well be available elsewhere, the disclaimer merely echoes the airlines' avowal that passenger lists simply do not exist. As far as the world and his wife are concerned, they have not existed for half a century. That's when the airlines decided that answering an inquiry from an anxious Mrs Robinson was a luxury they couldn't afford if all she wanted to know was whether young Johnny had arrived.

Yet Mrs Robinson still calls. And if she comes to the airport in person her inquiries are directed not only at the airline she thinks Johnny is travelling with, but also at anyone within range of a Customs barrier. Arrivals Information, provided in the passenger terminals by the management of most major airports rather than the airlines, do not consider it part of their function to explain the unavailability of lists.

The delusion exists because the majority of air travellers on scheduled services are still first time flyers and not as sophisticated as sometimes believed, at least in Europe. Their contacts, such as friends and family, are similarly inexperienced.

They base their assumptions perhaps on vague impressions of ocean travel in fiction and the purser's information on cabin occupancy. They may have memories of cinema films about air travel, depicting hostesses with a clipboard manifest, on references in the media to a celebrity being or not being "on the passenger list." Or, more likely, on the knowledge that airline reservations are booked for named individuals; that tickets the size and shape of cheque books are often still made out to those names and are non-transferable.

And it's not too difficult for them to understand that named reservations and individual tickets must mean a list. They know that manifests are necessary for security checks, for marrying passengers with their luggage. They are also only too well aware that the non-existent passenger list always quickly appears after an aircraft disaster.

Technically it would be easier for airlines today to check for one name on the passenger manifests of an entire fleet of 400-seater jumbo jets than it would from among fewer than a hundred passengers aboard the early jets of the 1960s. Computer technology could search thousands of such flights for a single name in less time than it takes to pick up a telephone.

It might well be possible for Mrs Robinson to do the same from her home in the future. In the meantime airlines would undoubtedly plead the prohibitive cost of the extra manpower required to provide a who's-on-board-what internet or telephone service for the contacts of the millions using the world's airports every day of the year. And there could be the problem of data protection laws…

As airport newsmen we believed the withdrawal of passenger manifests would be disastrous for us. Many of our bigger stories, as I've already shown, were based on a chance discovery of a newsworthy name. At the check-in desks we could establish if a missing passenger had failed to show up. With unofficial assistance we could discover if someone was booked under another name. And perusal of an arriving flight's passenger list (in a few cases in advance of the aircraft's arrival) often saved us from the tedium of checking the identity of every passenger at the barrier.

All this was in an era when every airline insisted that passenger lists were private, confidential information. We soon found however that this information we were unofficially privy to was not such a great loss. We simply had to work harder to seek out those newsworthy travellers we had been alerted to...and we avoided the drawback of over-reliance on a not-always-accurate printed manifest. (Finding John Robinson among 400-plus passengers on a transatlantic jumbo jet even with a passenger list is a daunting task in any event.)

Some regular newsworthy passengers continued to use aliases many years into the new age of airline anonymity. Swedish film star Greta Garbo regularly travelled to and from the U.K., inexplicably, as "Harriet Brown," refusing to acknowledge any other form of

KEEPING PACE WITH GARBO AND HER HOST

Miss Garbo

Cecil Beaton

AND NOW IN PARIS

CECIL BEATON, "world's best-dressed photographer," flew from Northolt to Paris yesterday in bowler hat, fur-collared black coat, drainpipe trousers, and spats.

With him, in flat-heeled fur boots, rubberised macintosh of dull blue, her rat-tail-cut hair half-hidden by a high collar, and eyes screened by dark-green glasses, went Miss Harriet Brown.

Or as one over-enthusiastic airport official addressed her . . . "Miss Garbo." He got a look that could only mean one thing.

Later she sat sipping coffee in a distant corner of the airport lounge as she waited for the plane to depart. When this was delayed because of engine trouble she strode up and down in the rain, umbrella up.

Daily Express
November 19 1951

spoken address. As I wrote for the *Daily Express*, the *Daily Mail* and the *Daily Graphic* on one occasion when she was accompanied on a flight to Paris by her long-time friend and companion, Cecil Beaton:

One over-enthusiastic airline official had the temerity to address her as "Miss Garbo." He earned a look that could mean only one thing, but was then totally ignored. When the official conversationally asked Mr Beaton how long the couple would be away, however, the photographer replied: "Ask Miss Garbo."

So much for anonymity.

If intended to avoid interest from the news media, the use of a pseudonym rarely succeeded. It frequently invited attention from airline staff who needed to know the true identity of the celebrity for aircraft documentation. They were only too ready to share with the Press their sneaking suspicion that the passenger must have something to hide.

In most instances, of course, the explanation was more mundane. An aide might be required to book a seat on a particular flight without being informed of the identity of the intending passenger. An agent or secretary making several reservations on different flights might use his or her own name to save the passenger embarrassment when the unwanted alternative bookings were eventually cancelled.

Why else would Winston Churchill, hardly a shrinking violet, add "Mr Hyde" to the many aliases demanded by security ("Colonel Warden" and "Mr Bullfinch" among them)? When I asked about the listing at the time I was informed by British European Airways: "He particularly asked not to appear on the passenger list. We were trying to keep it secret." The choice of Dr Jekyll's evil *alter ego* clearly suggested impish Churchillian humour to me.

At the height of his romance with Princess Margaret, Group Captain Peter Townsend travelled as "Mr Carter" so frequently that the pseudonym became pointless. And Princess Marina, mother of the present Duke of Kent, often, and again inexplicably, used the name "Mrs Green."

Sir William Penney, Britain's leading atomic scientist in the years when national possession of The Bomb was an essential tool of power politics, simply chose the name of a close colleague when he travelled to the Woomera testing site in Australia as "Mr Elmhurst." Perhaps he was far-sightedly hoping to remove himself from the backfire of anti-nuclear Aussies in later years. The real Sir Thomas Elmhurst, more wisely stayed behind, presumably to look after the "pound" at Aldermaston, while Professor Penney looked after himself.

The Professor, of course, might have described himself simply as "Mr. A. Bomb." He could then have turned up to reclaim a package addressed that way and left behind at an airline ticket desk. Security services were considering calling out the bomb squad when the real Mr Bombe with an "e" stepped forward. He said it really was his name, and almost exploded with frustration trying to prove it.

I was not so convinced of the reliability of the report of the American tourist Gordon Gosch who was said to have responded to a paging announcement by crying out:

Penney Off By Air To Woomera

SIR WILLIAM PENNEY, Director of Britain's atom research establishment at Harwell, left by air today for Sydney to attend the second British atom test at the Woomera range.

He carried a pair of binoculars, and in his pocket was a green paper backed novel entitled "A Pin for a Peep Show."

"I'm hoping it's a detective story," said Sir William. "I enjoy a thrill." He was down on the passenger list as "Mr Elmhurst."

The seat had been booked in that name—"borrowed" from a colleague, Sir Thomas Elmhurst—six months ago.

He was accompanied by a staff officer, Captain F. B. Lloyd. Sir William, who was hurried through Customs and Immigration by airline officials, said: "I expect to be back sometime in November. But I don't know exactly when."

Asked if he would mind being photographed, Sir William said: "If it is published today I shall be in trouble all the way to Sydney. There will be hundreds of people looking out for me."

There was a last minute hitch before the airliner took off on the first lap of its journey to Rome. A heavy mail bag being loaded into the nose of the BOAC Constellation became jammed in the door.

Passengers were taken off again while engineers removed the door to release the mail bag. Only Sir William and Captain Lloyd stayed aboard. The hold-up caused the airliner to be delayed 40 minutes.

The Star, Sept 19 1953

NO HAT, A CRUMPLED RAINCOAT, JAM-PACKED HANDBAG . . .
Mr. ELMHURST

LAST man in a line at London Airport yesterday. . . . The Sunday Express catches a picture of one of Britain's best-protected Hush-Hush celebrities—

MR. ELMHURST

That is the name atom-scientist Sir William Penney—Ministry of Supply Chief Superintendent of Armament Research—is using on a flight to Australia for the Big Bangs at Woomera.

Members of his family were there to see him off.

He was hurried through Customs; sat for several minutes in a private lounge.

Before boarding the airliner he said: "I expect to be back some time in November."

There was a 40-minute delay—caused by the jamming of a mailbag in loading.

Mr. Elmhurst stayed on board.

Sunday Express (right) Sept 20 1953

"G. Gosch! That's me! And I was prepared to believe that the longest name I ever came across should have been blamed on that well-known teleprinter stammer. The honour apparently went to a Greek gentleman listed as Mr Papadistrinopopoppoulos (if I have correctly remembered the number of 'pops'.) And I can personally vouch for the time when staff at an information desk drew lots to avoid having to page "Mr Mustapha Fahti."

One airline was presented with a minor identification problem back in 1952. As I reported at the time for the Daily Herald:

Ten Burmese sailors on their way home after a course with the Royal Navy gave their names as Khin, Lin, Win, Khin, Win, Tu, Myint, Khin, Sutherland and Fischer. Only Lin and the first Win were kin. They were twins.

English speaker Sutherland (who claimed Scottish descent) explained: "In Burma we have no first names or surnames as you know them..."

MUCH IN LITTLE

ENTER 10 BURMESE PUZZLES

TEN Burmese sailors on their way home after a four-year course with the Royal Navy set London Airport girls a puzzle last night.

They gave their names as: Khin, Lin, Win, Khin, Win, Tu, Myint, Khin, Sutherland and Fischer.

Only Lin and Win were related. They are twins.

The 10 explained: "It's no puzzle to us. In Burma we have no first names or surnames as you know them."

Daily Herald *March 22 1952*

MRS OH AND SON FLY IN

Brenard Press picture

The Star August 12 1953

Mrs Audrey Oh, a young Chinese mother, didn't mind one bit being photographed with her six-months-old baby Adrian when we approached her. They were changing 'planes on a flight home to Malaya after a visit to Mrs Oh's husband, a doctor working in New York, and she clearly enjoyed the interest her name was generating.

Dr Oh seems quite acceptable now, particularly as the Ian Fleming villain with a similar name is now part of fiction and cinema history. But I was a little wary when an air-girl pointed out to me the passenger with an even shorter variant. A 50-years-old Belgian businessman flying from Brussels to Dublin via Heathrow gave his name as "Anton O." When they asked: "Mr O what, sir?" he replied: "O nothing. Just O."

Silence, then: "Oh", they said. "O," he echoed.

Wearily he repeated the story to me when I caught up with him. "Nobody believes it," he said. "In France they spell it 'Haut' or even 'Eau.' In Holland they write it 'Van O.' and in England they think I'm an Irishman who's lost or forgotten part of his name."

In Ireland itself, where he again insisted: "My name is 'O, really,'" a Dublin airline booking clerk carefully and deliberately typed: "Mr Anton O'Rearly."

He had tried to trace the origin of the name but gave up when he had gone back as far as 1723 with nought to show for an explanation. He concluded nothing other than that the name may have originated with Lake O in the South of France.

At least four newspapers printed my initial report the next day, though perhaps understandably in truncated form.

Nothing is his name

THE man with the shortest name in the world passed through London last night. He is Mr. O, a 51-year-old Belgian businessman who flew from Brussels to Dublin.

At both the London and Northolt Airports, staffs were surprised when he gave his name as Anton O.

"Mr. O what, sir?" they asked.

"The only disadvantage about my name is that nobody will believe it," said Mr. O. "In France they insist on spelling it 'Haut' or 'Eau.' In Holland they write 'Van O.' In England people think that I'm an Irishman who has lost half his name."

MISTER O

THE man with the shortest name in the world, Mr. O, passed through London last night.

Mr. O, a 51-year-old Belgian business man, was flying from Brussels to Dublin. At London Airport ticket staff blinked when he gave his name as Anton O.

"Mr. O what, sir?" they asked.

Disadvantages of the name: In **FRANCE** they spell it "Haut" or "Eau." In **HOLLAND** they write "Van O." In **ENGLAND** people think he is an Irishman who has lost half his name.

Advantage: As a business man he finds people always remember him.

IN BRIEF

O—That's His Name

THE man with the shortest name in the world passed through London last night. He is Mr. O, 51-year-old Belgian business man flying from Brussels to Dublin.

At London and Northolt, airport officials asked, "Mr. O what, sir?" He replied: "O nothing, just Anton O."

Later he said: "Nobody will believe my name. In France they spell it 'Haut' or 'Eau.' In Holland they write 'Van O.' In England they think I'm an Irishman who has lost part of his name."

O

THE man with the shortest surname in the world passed through London last night on his way to Dublin. He is Mr. O, Belgian businessman.

At London Airport, when he arrived, he gave his name as Mr. Anton O—and spelt it. The ticket staff said, "O what, sir?" He repeated, "Just O." The staff said, "Oh."

Mr. O, who is fifty-one, traced his name back in his family to 1723, then gave it up. It was still O. He thinks the name may have originated from Lake O in the South of France.

(l to r) Reynolds News, Sunday Express, Sunday Dispatch, Sunday Pictorial

(all) November 25 1951

* THE woes of Mr O. Stephen O — that's his real name — fails to fit any computer profile. Computers cannot come to terms with a single-letter surname. He's been turned down for credit cards, hassled by insurance companies and ignored by banks. O gets a big No everywhere, so last week the South Korean immigrant gave up and changed his name by deed poll to Oh. Soh there.

Sunday Express ***September 1991***

Then, nearly forty years on, in September, 1991, (see left) Tim Miles reported in his "Eye on America" column for the *Sunday Express* (which, as I show on the preceding page, had also carried my story).

*

Sixteen-years-old French student Bernard Dabezies, who arrived at Scotland's Prestwick Airport in 1963 from Paris, might have wished *his* host had been traceable, just by dialling "O."

The only hint he could give to the identity of his host, who had failed to meet him at the start of a four-week visit, was "Mr Brown of Ayr." Walking their fingers through 10 columns of Browns in the local telephone directory, BOAC staff dialled every one of 40 numbers in the nearby town of Ayr without success. In desperation they asked Bernard to turn out his pockets. There at last was the clue they needed: the English address of the students' organisation which had sponsored his visit.

A further telephone call, and an official was able to provide the address of Bernard's host. It was discovered he lived just five minutes from the airport. But Mr Brown had spent all day at the Glasgow city airport 30 miles away waiting for Bernard, probably demanding to be allowed to check passenger lists for his missing guest.

As with any business organisation dealing with repetitive situations, the airlines have developed a number of codes and symbols over the years, which by usage or design have become internationally standard. Among the more obvious of these are the destination codes which appear on tickets and baggage labels, some of which can be read like supermarket bar codes by baggage-sorting equipment.

Just as familiar is the significance of *VIP* alongside the name of a passenger on a reservations checklist. Its close cousin *CIP*, probably a prominent businessman and a regular traveller who is regarded as commercially important to the airline, is not so widely known. *INF*ant and *MIN*or, whether with an adult or *UNACC*, (which, believe me, translates as "unaccompanied" rather than "unacceptable") are standard symbols. Others, such as *FTJ* when written as "Failed to Join" are understandable. And if an expected passenger is then "Not On Board" he or she is unlikely to challenge the mnemonic *NOB*.

Inevitably some abbreviations have been misunderstood or misinterpreted by alert or over-wrought travellers. Such as the occasion when one woman complainant waiting impatiently for information berated a BEA receptionist for gossiping to her boy friend "Ken" on the telephone. She was less than convinced by the assurance that the conversation was with an anonymous colleague at the Kensington air terminal in London.

In those distant days before security checks made it more difficult to accommodate late-comers for departing flights, borderline cases were sometimes given the opportunity to hurry out to the gate after others had boarded. Such was the situation I reported when two middle-aged women pleaded successfully to be allowed to sprint to Departures with their single item of joint luggage slung between their hands.

The problem arose only because the check-in clerk was late advising her colleagues at the departure gate to expect two more passengers. Her message rang loud and clear over the intercom just as the two women staggered up, completely out of breath.

"Just to let you know...we have two middle-aged hags for you. We told them they'd have to run all the way."

It was left to a stewardess on the flight to explain to the two women that "hag" was not what it seemed. In airline jargon it simply meant a passenger who was prepared to "Have A Go…"

Two little, older, ladies ("*Women* are only ladies, old boy, when they're titled, little, or old..." as an early mentor put it to me) unwittingly became listed as "FTJ" after their over-enthusiastic cab driver gave them an unplanned mystery tour of Scotland back in 1962. The two visitors, Miss Elizabeth Happersett and Miss Irene Sailer, both elderly school teachers from Philadelphia, had flown from Dublin to Glasgow after "doing" the Emerald Isle in two days. At Renfrew, then the city airport, they boarded a waiting hired car for the 30 mile drive to Prestwick Airport to catch an onward flight to Norway. More than two hours later, as other passengers waited to board the Bergen-bound airliner, officials at

Prestwick decided they could wait no longer. Reluctantly they scored through the two names on their list, scribbling the explanatory symbol beside them.

Then suddenly the missing tourists appeared – 50 minutes later than the deadline for the flight. Their airliner was already standing, its engines running, at the end of the runway, awaiting take-off clearance. Agitatedly, little Miss Happersett explained to me: "Our driver told us he would take us on the picturesque route to Prestwick. We thought we'd never get here."

Said her companion: "We kept asking him to hurry but he wanted us to admire the scenery."

I had been alerted to their absence by the repeated paging calls. And as I commiserated with them, airline officials hastily consulted in whispers. For once, they decided, the airlines' golden rule of no turning back could be bent. Out to the pilot of the airliner flashed the message: "Please return for two more passengers."

As the two grateful visitors were bustled out, the airline manager told me: "This was an exceptional case. If they'd missed this flight, the two passengers would have lost their bookings for a sea cruise from Bergen." The cab driver was given the benefit of any doubt over his motives and ticked off by the airline for being too patriotic. I suppose I could have thanked him for providing me with nearly 30 inches of column space in the Scottish dailies, at a cost to the airline of thousands of gallons of wasted aviation fuel.

PLANE TURNS BACK FOR 2 OLD LADIES

Daily Sketch (left)

AIR LINE BREAKS ITS GOLDEN RULE TO HELP TWO

Scottish Daily Mail (below)

TAXI TO TROUBLE FOR 2

AN airline broke its golden rule yesterday—by holding back a plane for two passengers.

Elderly school teachers Miss Elizabeth Happersett and Miss Irene Sailer, from Philadelphia, arrived at Renfrew from Dublin.

With two hours to spare, they took a taxi the 35 miles to Prestwick, for their plane to Bergen, Norway.

The driver thought he'd give them the chance to see a bit of Scotland, and took them by a more picturesque route.

When the ladies failed to arrive at Prestwick they were crossed off the Scandinavian Airways flight list.

But, two minutes before take-off time, the missing passengers arrived. Hurried consultations—and the pilot was told to come back for them.

Daily Record

Plane recalled for two little old ladies

Daily Herald

Two old ladies have airport in tizzy

Scottish Daily Express

(all) June 11 1962

When a flight has been chartered by a travel club or group the unfortunate passenger who misses it loses more than a cancellation fee. The original cost of the flight, albeit at a bargain price, is sacrificed by that passenger. And invariably an alternative booking can only be made on a scheduled service, often at twice the cost.

Canadian Barbara Anderson of Toronto was one of 90 members of the city's Thistle Club due to return home after a three-weeks' visit to relatives in Britain. Before her chartered Trans-Canada jet was due to leave, Miss Anderson telephoned the airline to confirm her reservation. Only then did she discover that the flight was taking off in forty-five minutes and that other passengers were already in the airport departure lounge.

"I thought it wasn't leaving for another twelve hours," she told airline staff. Calling a taxi, she drove 40 miles on country roads to the airport in just over an hour, only to be told: "We closed the flight 30 minutes ago." But once again airline officials took pity, even though they could have insisted she transfer to their own scheduled flight leaving an hour or two later. The Canadian jet turned back to the tarmac, steps were wheeled out and Miss Anderson was hustled aboard.

Not so fortunate was a frail, silver-haired widow who found herself stranded at Prestwick Airport on her 75th birthday when her Canada-bound jet touched down to refuel on a flight from London to Ottawa. Along with other passengers Mrs Myrtle Stubley had left to stretch her legs during the forty-minute stopover but then missed the re-boarding announcement.

Widow, 75, 'stranded' as jetliner leaves without her

By Daily Mail Reporter

FRAIL, silver-haired Mrs. Myrtle Stubley—75 today—rummaged through her handbag at Prestwick Airport yesterday as she searched for an air mail letter from Canada.

'My son will be so worried," she said. "But I just can't remember his address."

Widowed emigrant Mrs. Stubley had suddenly found herself "stranded" at Prestwick yesterday when the jet airliner flying her from London to Ottawa had taken off again without her after refuelling for its Transatlantic crossing.

Scottish Daily Mail May 29 1964

AIRCRAFT STOPPED—BY ORDER

A man waving an umbrella hailed a four-engined Israeli airliner on the tarmac at London Airport on Wednesday, and brought it to a halt like a 'bus at a request stop.

The passenger failed to hear the departure announcement for the flight to Lydda. He dashed from a toilet in the North Terminal lounge as the giant Constellation taxied away, and running alongside, waved his gamp at the pilot until the aircraft stopped. Steps were pushed out, and the passenger was taken aboard.

Said airport officials: "It has never happened before in the history of the Airport.

There must have been a miscount when the passengers went aboard."

Airport Post *July 24 1957*

Author's note: Although I recall this incident clearly (it was long-talked about by airport staff) this is the only cutting, printed a week later, I have been able to trace.

I came across her seated in an otherwise-deserted departure lounge. She only suspected something was wrong when I asked her if her 'plane had taken off without her. At last she admitted: "I did hear an announcement but I thought it was for some other flight. I'd forgotten my flight number."

Airline staff were horrified and apologetic when I took their passenger back to them with the news. Said one: "We can't understand how it happened. We always do a head count on board. And we don't know how we missed her in the lounge."

This time there was no question of bringing the airliner back. It had already crossed the Mull of Kintyre on its way to the North Atlantic. But after a number of telephone calls the airline gave Mrs Stubley the news that they had been able to book a seat for her on another flight leaving four hours later.

Another absent-minded traveller gave the same reason for missing the final call for his flight to Lydda back in 1957, but took more drastic action. Emerging from a washroom into a deserted lounge he was seen to grab his umbrella, rush on to the Heathrow tarmac and hail the four-engined Constellation airliner as if it were a London 'bus.

He told bemused Israeli airline officials: "The noise of the taps in the washroom must have drowned out the Tannoy. I wasn't going to let that 'plane go without me."

The airliner's pilot spotted him waving his umbrella when his sprint took him out ahead of the slowly taxiing Constellation. The airliner slid to a halt and steps were pushed out for the umbrella man to be taken aboard.

A Heathrow Airport spokesman was stunned when told the story. "That's something that's never happened before," he gasped. Forty years on he might have added: "...or since." After all, El Al officials might have told their passenger: "Don't worry. There'll be another along shortly."

It was a different story for an elderly passenger on another Lydda flight. The 80-years-old German-born woman had disembarked with other passengers when the Israeli airliner from New York touched down at Heathrow to re-fuel. When the time came to re-board, the woman refused to leave, screaming: "I won't go! This is my home."

Other passengers helped airline staff to carry the woman, still struggling, on to the aircraft. Then, after the engines had been started, the captain appeared at the doorway. He said he couldn't take the woman as she refused to remain in her seat. But after fifteen minutes an air hostess on the flight called out to me: "She is safe now. We have strapped her in."

After the airline had safely left, an Israeli airline official said: "Sadly the woman was a little confused. She thought she was back in her childhood home of Bucharest. But we had been asked by her family in Lydda to look after her. It was our duty to get her back on board."

THE ONLY WAY TO KEEP UP WITH THESE JONESES

Brenard Press picture

IF you want to keep up with the Joneses, just sell everything and board a jet aircraft for New Zealand.

For that is just what the Joneses—all 14 of them—did yesterday. Probably the largest single family ever to emigrate by air, they scorned the easy way of assisted Government passages. It cost them nearly £3,000 to make the trip.

News of the World, Sept 6 1959

Any airline would have been just as anxious to ensure that passengers like the Jones family didn't wander away from them. For the Joneses had sold all their possessions to emigrate from the UK to New Zealand, all 14 of them at once.

Scorning Government-assisted passages and paying their own way on BOAC were: Grandad John Jones and his wife Jessie; their eldest son Philip, his wife Thena and their five children aged from 18 years to five months. Then came Philip's sister Hilda, her husband Harry Barber and their three children, aged 16, 12 and 7.

The family was pictured on a flight of aircraft steps they commandeered to wave from for the front page of a broadsheet *News of the World* in 1959. As John Jones told me proudly when I'd spotted them in the departure lounge: "We had to plan the whole thing like an Army manoeuvre."

Just as well organised, and with an even greater responsibility, was young Kathleen Rowse, who took charge of her young brother, aged 2, and three sisters, aged 9, 4 and fourteen months, on a 6,000-mile flight from Johannesburg to London. For Kathleen herself was only eleven.

She had cared for the four younger children since her mother entered hospital seven months earlier in Nyasaland (now Malawi), where their father was a Government contractor. The London *Star* carried Brenards' picture of the family on Monday, after my story appeared in several Sunday newspapers.

Alerted in advance to their arrival by their airline, we had found them trooping from the 'plane shortly before they were welcomed at the barrier by their grandparents. The couple had driven to Heathrow from their farm in Cornwall to meet them. The children's parents planned to join them in Britain soon after Mrs Rowse's discharge from hospital.

But it was a Sussex grandmother who became Britain's first licensed flying baby-minder, earning the soubriquet "Mrs Stork" when she accompanied two babies to Northern Ireland. She was taking them to a new home with her own son and his wife who had just adopted them. Now she was on a second such trip, and the London *Star* and the *Evening News* had asked us to cover her departure.

I tracked down Mrs Stork (real name Mrs Ruth Townsend-Green) to the Heathrow departure lounge just before she boarded a flight for East Africa. She was carrying a baby in each arm, due to be delivered to childless couples 5,000 miles away in Bulawayo.

"This seems to be becoming something of a habit. Hence my nickname," she said. "I expect to get dozens of inquiries when I get back as I did last time. And it's such a rewarding job."

Mrs Townsend-Green herself put the parents and the adopters in touch with each other, and was granted a licence by Bow-street magistrates to act as go-between. One of them described her as a "veritable fairy godmother." As Mrs Stork told me: "I just love babies."

*

In March 1960 the front page of the *News of the World* gave over 14 inches of column space to my story of a New-York-bound jet airliner from Paris which suddenly turned back over the Atlantic. The pilot of the American Boeing 707 decided to head for London, his nearest major airport, after an unborn baby on board announced an

THE 'LITTLE MOTHER'

Girl of eleven who has been a little mother to her brother and sisters while her mother was in hospital in Johannesburg, flew into London Airport with her "family." She is Kathleen Rowse, and with Valerie, 9; Margaret, 4; David, 2, and 14-months-old baby Sylvia, she is to spend a holiday with grandparents on a farm in Cornwall. Their father, a Nyasaland Government contractor, will join them with their mother when she is well enough to travel.

The Star (all) June 14 1962

LITTLE MOTHER

LITTLE mother Kathleen Rowse stepped off a plane at **LONDON AIRPORT** with her not-so-little family—David, 2; Valerie, 9; Margaret, 4, and, in a hostess's arms, Sylvia, fourteen months.

Kathleen is really their sister. Her age? Eleven.

Sunday Pictorial

Kathleen (11) flies family

Reynolds News

Brenard Press picture

"MRS STORK" FLIES WITH MORE ADOPTED BABIES

Grandmother Mrs Ruth Townsend-Green—"Mrs Stork" to her neighbours at Blackboys, Sussex—left London Airport today for Bulawayo, East Africa, with two babies being adopted by childless couples. This is the second baby delivery service she has carried out. A few months ago she took two babies to her own daughter-in-law in Northern Ireland. To make the necessary contacts between the parents and adoptors, she is licensed under an Act of Parliament.

The Star, Sep 2 1955 *Brenard Press picture*

'Mrs. Stork' Takes Off With 2 More Babies

WITH a baby boy in each arm, a silver-haired grandmother —"Mrs. Stork" to her neighbours and friends—left London Airport to-day on a 6,000-mile flight to Bulawayo, Rhodesia, to deliver her sleepy-eyed charges to their new homes.

"Mrs. Stork" is Mrs. Ruth Townsend-Green, Malls Bank, Blackboys, Sussex. The babies are going out to be adopted.

This is the second baby deli...

Evening News *Sept 2 1955*

ATLANTIC JET DRAMA

SOS—a baby is expected

NEWS OF THE WORLD REPORTER

A GIANT jet airliner over the Atlantic on its way from Paris to New York sent a radio SOS to London last night asking if it could make a priority landing.

Inside the jet, a Boeing 707, the pilot, Captain Jake Marcum, hastily broadcast: "Is there a doctor on board?"

For among the 119 passengers was a 30-year-old expectant mother whose baby just couldn't wait till they reached New York.

Two doctors, one French, the other American, stepped forward as the airliner turned for London.

When it touched down a convoy of duty cars and refuelling tankers was followed by an ambulance called in from Hillingdon Hospital.

A hydraulic freight truck was manoeuvred into position alongside the cabin door and the woman, Mme. Lucienne Vignali, was taken off in a stretcher.

Mme. Vignali was driven to hospital with her husband—and gave birth to an 8lb. 4oz. boy an hour and a half later. Both are doing well.

Her two children and her sister went on to New York.

Said the pilot: "Both doctors on board believed the baby was due at any moment. With a full load of passengers there were no facilities on board. So I was given full priority to land at London."

News of the World (Page One lead) Mar 20 1960

imminent ETA – estimated time of arrival.

Inside the jet, the pilot, Captain Jake Marcum, had made the time-honoured appeal: "Is there a doctor aboard?" when one of his 119 passengers, a 30-years-old expectant mother, was taken ill. Two doctors, one French, the other American, responded and examined Mme Lucienne Vignali behind a hastily erected screen. Together they agreed there was no time to waste and advised the Captain to land as soon as possible. He radioed Heathrow for permission to make an emergency landing.

A small convoy of duty cars and a medical team met the Boeing jet on the tarmac. A scissor-lift truck was wheeled up to the aircraft door and the patient was taken off in a stretcher and rushed by ambulance to nearby Hillingdon Hospital. Her husband, M Marcel Vignali, went with her as the airliner was re-fuelled.

The couple's other two children later flew on to New York with an aunt who was travelling with the family. An hour and a half after her arrival at the hospital, Mme Vignali successfully gave birth to an 8lb 4oz baby boy. His bedside portrait with proud parents duly appeared next day in the *Express* alongside a follow-up story from the hospital.

*

Minutes before an airliner bound for South America from Stockholm touched down at Heathrow late one night I learnt from the airline that they too had been warned by radio: "Please expect one extra passenger."

From the edge of the tarmac a photographer and I watched as an ambulance raced to the foot of the aircraft steps with a doctor, a midwife and a nurse. Shortly afterwards, while her fellow passengers cleared passport controls, Italian-born Signora Norma Moldini gave birth to a 6lb son, also at London's Hillingdon Hospital. She and her husband, neither of whom spoke English, were rushed to the hospital after the doctor confirmed the birth was imminent.

The stewardess on the Pan American Clipper, 27-years-old Leonora George, from Missouri, told me: "We were all ready to deal with the birth on board if necessary. When I noticed Mrs Moldini was ill I called the purser and we made up a bed for her at the rear of the cabin, moving other passengers forward.

"I told the Captain what had happened and he radioed ahead for the doctor. As a trained nurse I could have dealt with the delivery. But a 'plane is not exactly the best maternity ward."

ALL FOR A BABY

- **Plane radios Help**
- **Doctor stands by**
- **Visa law waived**

AN airliner nearing London Airport last night radioed: "Expect one extra passenger."

An ambulance, a doctor, a midwife, and a nurse were called, arriving two minutes before the plane landed, and one of the passengers, Mrs. Norma Moldini, was taken to Hillingdon Hospital, Middlesex.

Half an hour later a 6lb. boy was born.

Mrs. Moldini, and her husband, flying from Stockholm to San Salvador, South America, on Italian passports, do not speak English, nor had they British visas.

Daily Express Oct 3 1952

The birth announcement appeared the next day free of charge in the news columns of the English national newspapers. And the Home Office gave the Moldinis special permission to stay in Britain until mother and baby were fit to travel on to their destination. Although the parents were Italian and were only "passing through" the UK by accident, baby Moldini became British by birth.

The *Daily Express* ran the story on page one immediately alongside the lead story – also mine – of a prominent trade union leader at Heathrow criticising left-wing Labour MP Aneurin Bevan *(see Chapter 13).*

Even quicker on the airport scene was another 6lb arrival, a brown-eyed daughter born to a passenger from Paris just ten minutes after she was helped from an Air France Viscount airliner. Mrs Anna Saleh felt faint as she stepped on to the tarmac and an airport porter rushed her to the nearby Port Health office, normally just an administration centre.

Almost before she could examine her, Ministry of Health Sister Colette Cooke was delivering Mrs Saleh's baby, with her husband waiting outside in passport controls with the couple's three other children.

"The baby arrived in record time, just three minutes after her mother came into the office," said Sister Colette. "There wasn't even time to call the doctor." And as his wife was being taken to hospital for a medical check, Mr Saleh told me proudly: "The baby's name will have to be 'Ariel.' What else is appropriate?"

Flying babies, whether in being, incoming, or in transit, are not always as welcome. A simple request from a passenger for a travel sickness pill caused an airline to ground an entire family for 24 hours in August 1964, as they set off for a new life in Canada.

Sunday Post (below)

EMIGRATING MUM-TO-BE TAKEN FROM PLANE AT PRESTWICK

Baby on way—so jet Mum grounded

Scottish Sunday Express

'Banned' mother told: You can fly Atlantic

News of the World

STORK STOPS FLYING MUM

A FAMILY emigrating to Canada were left stranded last night after the first leg of their flight ... because Mum had asked for a travel-sickness pill.

The steward of the B.O.A.C. transatlantic jet making a 30-minute hop from Manchester to Prestwick, in Scotland, viewed 31-year-old Mrs. Josephine Dunn with alarm when she made the request.

It was obvious to him that she is expecting another baby —soon.

He hurried off to report to the captain that there was a chance of landing in Canada with one more passenger than they should have.

As the jet fuelled up at Prestwick for its ocean leg, the captain went to see Mrs. Dunn —armed with a B.O.A.C. regulation stating that *"expectant mothers must not fly within 35 days of the expected date of birth."*

She told him the baby isn't due till the middle of next month, but he ordered her off the plane for an examination by the airport doctor.

The airport doctor said he couldn't give a precise date . . .

A frantic phone call was put in to Mrs. Dunn's doctor in Manchester. He was away on holiday. And his partner refused to give any information without her authority.

The captain of the jet said he couldn't wait to argue. And away he flew, leaving a tearful Mrs. Dunn behind him, stranded with her husband, John, and their two youngsters, Alistair, 5, and Jacqueline, 4.

'In the papers'

Mrs. Dunn—"I'm a terrible traveller and I just wanted a pill in case I felt sick"—was moved into the tiny airport hotel with her family.

Her husband said: "The ironic thing is that our neighbours in Dickenson Road, Longsight, were joking about Jo being in the papers if she had the baby during the flight."

But as the family disconsolately unpacked for the night at the hotel, Mrs. Dunn's authority to reveal the information B.O.A.C. wanted was passed to her doctor's partner.

He was able to tell B.O.A.C. that a jet liner leaving Prestwick early today direct for Toronto would outpace the stork, and B.O.A.C. booked the family on it.

Said the airline's manager at Prestwick: "We had to be sure as we do not have the facilities on board our aircraft for handling a maternity."

The People (all) August 9 1964

The Dunn family, mother-to-be Josephine, 31, her husband John, 32, and their two children were obliged to leave the Toronto-bound airliner they'd boarded at Manchester airport less than an hour earlier after saying goodbye to relatives and friends. During the 30-minute flight to Prestwick, where the airliner was due to pick up more passengers, Mrs Dunn felt unwell and complained to a steward of airsickness.

The steward reported to the Captain and he ordered Mrs Dunn to see a doctor at Prestwick. After examining her, the airport medical officer suggested that Mrs Dunn's own doctor be consulted. But a call to his surgery revealed that he was himself away, on holiday in Spain. A colleague refused any information about Mrs Dunn without her authority. The Dunn's waiting BOAC airliner finally had to take off without them.

When I heard of the drama I approached the airline for an explanation. There I was told: "We have a regulation that expectant mothers must not fly within 35 days of the expected birth. This is as much for their sake as it is ours. Unfortunately Mrs Dunn doesn't seem to know the date, so we must have the information from her doctor."

A harassed and bewildered Mr Dunn, from Longsight, Manchester, told me: "No one asked if Jo was pregnant when we booked our seats, even when we had our emigration medical."

He and his family waited for several hours in an airport hotel room, the children playing with hastily unpacked toys. "I don't know what we will do if we can't travel," said Mrs Dunn, "We have sold up and we have no home to go to."

But at last the airline was able to tell the family they were being re-booked on a flight the next day. With Mrs Dunn's authority given on the telephone, the doctor's partner was able to confirm her fitness to travel.

"We weren't too happy about the symptoms Mrs Dunn showed on the flight," said BOAC later. "We were led to believe that the baby was expected within two or three weeks. But we were prepared to finance the family's stay at Prestwick if medical opinion had required it."

Expectant mum flies out at last

HERALD REPORTER

MRS. Josephine Dunn, the 30 - year - old expectant mother who was taken off a transatlantic plane at Prestwick on Saturday because it was feared her baby might arrive during the flight, boarded a second jet yesterday.

She and her family—husband John, an electronics engineer, five - year - old Alistair and Jacqueline, four — were given VIP treatment after their 20-hour delay in Scotland.

A B O A C officer fetched them from their hotel and took them out to the waiting airliner ahead of other passengers after they had signed autographs for people also emigrating to Canada.

Daily Herald *Aug 10 1964*

The Dunns were cleared to continue their interrupted journey the next day with a guarantee from BOAC that their jet would beat the stork on the transatlantic crossing. They were able to take with them a set of Sunday's newspapers carrying the headlines which shouted my story of their flight that almost wasn't. And we were happy to forward on to them the follow-up report of their departure carried in most of Monday's dailies.

Six months earlier in another incident, also at Prestwick, Customs officers barred 79 passengers on an incoming Copenhagen flight from disembarking – because of a baby's cold. For nearly 30 minutes the passengers, 55 of whom were in transit to New York, had to remain in their seats when the Customs men, who had boarded the airliner for a routine check, discovered that 18-months-old Birthe Svendsen, travelling with her mother to the US, had a fever.

The airline officials found a doctor was among passengers due to board the flight, and at check-in they asked his help. He examined the tiny patient, then pronounced: "It's nothing contagious, just a throat infection. Or, in other words, a chill."

After that, the passengers were allowed to disembark from the parked airliner. And an airport official explained: "At Prestwick, Customs officers have the responsibility for aircraft health declarations. Normally, in cases like this, the local medical officer would be notified, but he wasn't immediately available. Passengers were saved from further delay when a doctor was found to be travelling."

● CUSTOMS MEN BAN 79 PASSENGERS IN GIANT JET

BABY HOLDS UP A PLANE

THE passengers in a giant jet airliner were banned from landing at Prestwick yesterday . . . because of a baby's cold.

And the plane was ...
at the airport f...

Baby's chill holds up 79 on jet liner

Sunday Mail (above)
Scottish Sunday Express (right)

BABY BIRTHE'S COLD HOLDS UP AIRLINER

Sunday Post *(all) Jan 5 1964*

Dual nationality may have its advantages for some. But that certainly wasn't the case for baby Elizabeth Scott who was stopped by red tape from flying to America with her mother.

Mrs Beryl Scott was British. She was returning to her temporary home in America to rejoin her husband, a British doctor studying at the Mayo Clinic. But 12-months-old Elizabeth, who had been meeting her grandparents for the first time, was born in the US, so was both British and American. Yet when Mrs Scott handed in the return half of her ticket to New York with her passport also carrying Elizabeth's name and photograph, airline officials checked her American visa, then demanded one for Elizabeth.

"But she's an American subject," protested Mrs Scott. "She has an American birth certificate and doesn't need a visa."

Replied the check-in clerk: "Sorry, but she can't fly. Your daughter is on your passport. That makes her British. She will need a visa."

My attention was drawn to the situation as Mrs Scott pleaded and argued for 45 minutes at the desk, backed by her father and other relatives

RED TAPE BANS BERYL AND HER AMERICAN BABY

Daily Express, March 1962

seeing her off. But officials were adamant. They pointed out that the airline would be fined if Mrs Scott were stopped by US Immigration. As arrangements were made to book her and Elizabeth on another flight the next day, Mrs Scott turned to me and said: "This is ridiculous. This is an innocent baby we're talking about.

"Now I have to try to get an American passport for Elizabeth in less than 24 hours. I will have to be at the Embassy when they open up. And they will have to cable our home in Minnesota for her birth documents."

The story had a speedy conclusion after I'd alerted the Embassy press office to the problem. Someone must have pulled out all the stops. By the time I checked in for duty the next day Mrs Scott and Elizabeth, plus either an American passport or a British-national visa, were already on their way safely to New York.

MOTHER, SON IN AIRPORT DRAMA

Daily Sketch

The sad case of Mrs Robinson and her son (no relation to the Robinsons who inspired this chapter) was quite different. She too was stopped from leaving Britain with 3-years-old Michael. But she had neither passport nor visa for him. Earlier that day she had flown in from Paris to claim Michael from a local authority nursery in London where he had lived for the previous eighteen months.

She drove back to Heathrow with him to catch the last Paris-bound flight of the day. Four officials from the nursery accompanied the pair. But at the airport, Home Office officials stepped in and told her: "You can't travel without a passport for Michael."

For over an hour she pleaded in vain with the Home Office to be allowed to take her son with her on her passport. Then as she left the passport desk almost in tears to 'phone a solicitor, Michael was suddenly whisked away, half-carried and half-led to a waiting car by the nursery officers. Said a spokesman for the local authority later: "It had become very late. The child had to be allowed to sleep the night. The mother is not well and we might regard her as being unable to look after her son." But he then added inexplicably: "If the passport had been available we would have allowed him to travel with her."

To me, Mrs Robinson would only say: "Michael's father is an official at the British Admiralty. But I don't know what these people have done to my child. He doesn't know me and he looks ill.

"I have a job in Paris and I have to get back. But I won't go without Michael."

The *Daily Sketch* and *Daily Mail* carried similar stories.

NO PASSPORT STOPS FLIGHT TO PARIS

Mother at airport pleads to take son

By Daily Mail Reporter

A FAIR-HAIRED American woman pleaded with Home Office officials at London Airport last night for permission to take her three-year-old son back with her to Paris.

The woman, a Mrs. Robinson, pleaded for more than an hour—in vain.

She had claimed her son, Michael, who has been at an L.C.C. nursery home for the past 18 months, earlier in the day.

Almost in tears

With four officials from the nursery she had driven with the child to London Airport to board the last Paris-bound airliner of the night.

But at the airport she was told her son could not leave. He had no passport. Almost in tears, Mrs. Robinson begged that he might leave on her passport.

This, it was explained, was not possible. Mrs. Robinson went to telephone her solicitor.

Meanwhile officials hurried the boy from the airport lounge down the escalator to a waiting car which took him back to the nursery.

Work in Paris

An L.C.C. official: "The child must be allowed to sleep the night. It is true the mother is not well, and we might regard her as being unable to look after her son.

"But if the passport had been available we would have allowed him to travel with her."

***Daily Mail* (both) Oct 25 1955**

"Tug-of-Love" is one of those useful journalistic phrases which through over-familiarity have robbed many marital adversaries of public sympathy. Which is unfortunate because at one time it evoked an accurate image of two parents in conflict, trying to move in opposing directions with the best of motives, their child or children at the centre of the dispute.

The cliché was relatively short-lived after critics complained that it described nothing more than an emotive display of parental selfishness. The view was often misleading. Most of the parents I came across in such situations seemed totally caring and concerned for the child involved. It was because they believed they were doing the right thing for the child that they could tug so hard. Selfishness and a desire for revenge against an estranged partner were not obvious typical incentives.

We were alerted to the sad tale of the naval officer and his small son by several newspapers. They would have been aware that the police would become involved as soon as he boarded a London-bound flight in Geneva with his two-years-old son, Shaun. For a High Court judge had issued a writ for contempt of court when Lieutenant Basil Duncan Abbott failed to obey an order to hand over the boy to his wife. Mrs Mary Abbott was seeking a judicial separation from her husband.

As the Lieutenant stepped from the Swiss airliner at Heathrow carrying Shaun in his arms, he was approached by police officers. "We would like to speak to you," I heard one say, then father and son were escorted to an airport office then on to Harlington police station adjoining the airport.

Shortly afterwards Lt. Abbott, wearing civilian clothes, a battered pork pie hat and belted raincoat, left the police station with a naval escort. Police told me that he was wanted by the Royal Navy for alleged absence from his depot in Malta, where he had originally been ordered to hand Shaun over. Airline officials then revealed that he and his son were in fact booked to fly onwards to Dublin after merely changing 'planes at Heathrow.

An hour later, as I waited and watched from Brenards' newsroom window, just a few yards from the police station, Mrs Abbott arrived by car with two friends. I hurried out as she ran excitedly into the interview room crying breathlessly: "Where's my baby?" Then, with police smilingly looking on, she was reunited with Shaun, who had been the subject of an international search covering Britain, Ireland and the Continent.

Returning with her companions to the car, with Shaun peering happily from under the hood of his red romper suit, Mrs Abbott told me: "This is a wonderful moment. Any mother would know how I feel to have him back."

The story, with its standard happy ending, at least from one viewpoint, was a natural for the *Daily Sketch*, who gave it a two-page centre spread with a huge oversize picture of Mrs Abbott and Shaun in the car under the 4-column heading:

POLICE DETAIN FLYING FATHER

Daily Sketch (reduced)

The *Daily Mirror* accorded it similar treatment with its own picture, seen here, among others, while the *Daily Mail* came up with the heading below.

Baby Shaun is back with mother again . . .

'DAILY MIRROR' REPORTER

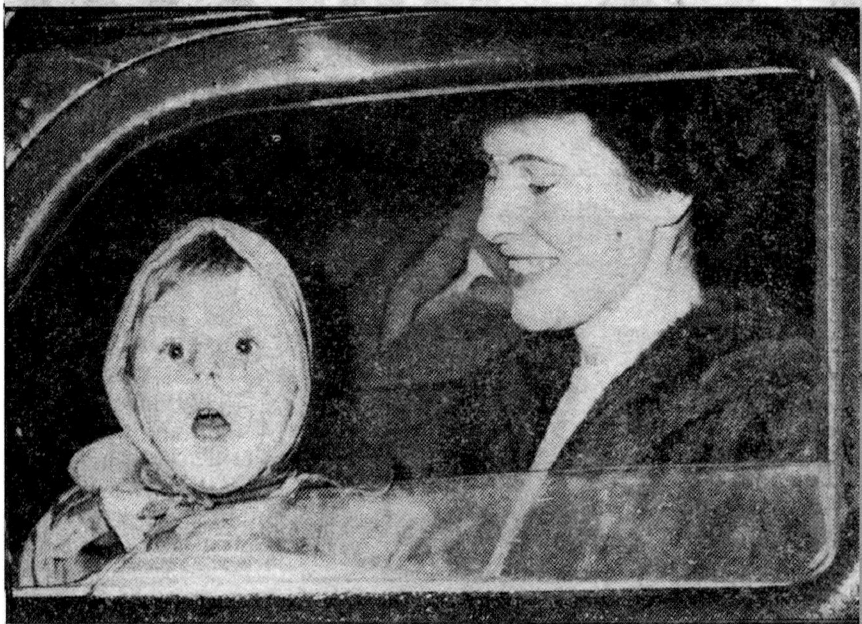

Together again . . . Mrs. Mary Abbott and baby Shaun last night.

Daily Mirror (above)...,

Missing officer seized with son at airport

—THEN MOTHER IS REUNITED

By Daily Mail Reporter

LIEUT. BASIL DUNCAN ABBOTT, of the Fleet Air Arm, was detained by police when he arrived at London Airport from Geneva last night with his two-year-old son, Shaun.

A warrant for contem

...Daily Mail (right), both reduced (both) February 18 1954

Another father's action could be seen as even more drastic. Mr Hannan Har-Shefi, a 37-years-old engineer, had taken his baby daughter Adina from her pram as she lay asleep at a council nursery and flown with her to Paris. After the alarm was raised, father and daughter rushed from hotel to hotel in a hide-and-seek chase until Scotland Yard officers, co-operating with local police, finally tracked them down.

When Mrs Har-Shefi learnt of their whereabouts two days after their disappearance, she followed. It took the couple just thirty minutes together with Adina to settle their differences, then the runaway father told me: "We have made it up and we are going home to Hampstead. And it's all down to Adina, whom we both love."

There was no sign however of an early reunion for 20-years-old medical student Jamshid Hashemi and his estranged wife when he flew home to Teheran to seek legal and diplomatic advice over the custody of the couple's nine-months-old baby, Karim. Earlier, Hashemi, who said he was a cousin of the Iranian Foreign Minister, had lost his claim for custody of the baby by taking him out of the jurisdiction of the British courts against the wishes of his mother. He had returned when he learnt of the international search for him.

"I thought it would be better for everyone concerned if I brought Karim back," he said, "Now I've lost him and I think the court has given me a very raw deal."

He claimed his wife wanted to stay with him. "And I know if I could have just five minutes with her I could persuade her to come back to Teheran," he said. "There are tickets awaiting her at the airline office any time she wishes to join me. And I have left £2,000 with a solicitor to assist her."

But he added: "I have to get started on my case for guardianship in Teheran as soon as possible."

*

It was Christmas Eve at the airport. News was very slack. Which in its way was a blessing, for the next two days were then the only consecutive days in the year when no national newspaper would be published. So those of us on duty assumed that ours was just a watching brief. There should be no major situation to interfere with our responsibility to join the variety of staff celebrations throughout the airport. It was the one time of the year when we might almost say that no news was good news.

Almost. For there was still radio and TV. Hardly our daily bread in terms of income; indeed, as gluttons for news agency output, the audio and visual media interests were frequently in conflict with ours. Everything they consumed over the holiday would mean only left-overs for the printed pages of December 27, unless it could be served up again as some re-hashed or warmed-up dish.

My story of the Little Girl Lost was ideal for Christmas. It had a touch of Dickensian pathos, warmth and kindness... the "aah" factor in abundance. It did not demand immediate release and might even benefit from the delay before publication with no harm to the participants. It was not a national radio story, and television coverage would need more visual impact. And it could remain in my exclusive domain for just as long as I needed to explore its potential.

Marieanne Gabriel was a receptionist for British European Airways at Heathrow I had known since Northolt days. When I spotted her behind the BEA desk in Heathrow's Terminal 2, I hurried over to wish her a happy Christmas and found her sitting with a small, blue-eyed girl in a check pinafore dress. "Hello, Marieanne," I said, adding jokingly: "Is this 'Adopt a young traveller' week?"

"You might just say that," she replied, "The way things are looking for this little lady, it may come to it."

I wasn't sure at that stage how serious she was, but I asked her to tell me more. It emerged that six-years-old Caroline Dalzell-Payne had arrived alone at Heathrow an hour or two earlier, a "U/M," (unaccompanied minor) on a flight from Stuttgart, Germany. She spoke no English and carried only a small attaché case containing some sandwiches and a chocolate Santa Claus. She had been despatched by the children's home where she had spent most of her life to join her mother in England.

A telegram had been sent from Stuttgart to advise Caroline's mother of the flight and her time of arrival, and a nurse from the home saw her off. But no one was at Heathrow to meet the young traveller and Caroline had no address for her mother, and no papers to give any other information. Just a tattered photograph with the words: "To Caroline, from her mother," written on the back.

Airport officials cabled the home in Stuttgart for the address. Then Scotland Yard checked at Somerset House and found that Caroline's mother had re-married and was now Mrs Tatiana Gardiner. They sent a car to a London address and found the unopened telegram behind the front door. They learnt that Mrs Gardiner had gone away for Christmas and no one knew where.

For six hours their inquiries continued, while Caroline played happily with Marieanne and other new-found friends in BEA, several of whom went out to buy her toys and sweets. When it grew dark, Marieanne, who spoke fluent German, offered to take Caroline home with her to Iver Heath, Bucks, some seven miles from the airport.

Then came a breakthrough. The Yard's search led them to the village of Redmarley in Gloucestershire, and there the village bobby traced Mrs Gardiner to a house where she had taken a job as housekeeper. She explained that she hadn't expected to see Caroline until after Christmas. "Now there are no trains. I can't collect her for two days," she said.

She was put in touch with Marieanne and her husband, who had cancelled their plans to visit relatives for the holiday to look after the little girl. "Don't worry," they told Mrs Gardiner, "She's contented and happy and is watching television for the first time. We're happy to look after her until you can travel."

With the agreement of Marieanne and her husband, Brenard photographer Pete Ward and I drove over to Iver Heath to get some pictures of them at home with Caroline, to add to those he had already taken at the airport. And on Boxing Day I was finally able to round off my story before circulation with a joyful mother-daughter reunion. Only one difficulty remained. Mrs Gardiner could not be persuaded to pose for a picture with Caroline and was too embarrassed to talk about the slip-up.

So, 48 hours "late," the longest I could remember holding a story by choice, I was finally able to release it for the Sunday papers appearing on December 27, 1959.

It was well worth the wait. Because time was on our side, Pete was able to produce a variety of photos for the picture desks to choose from. And I was able to get the story circulated early and in good time for the newspapers' news conferences when space is allocated for "known" stories of the day. And more than one news desk telephoned to express their thanks for brightening a dull day.

The headlines on the Sundays' front pages, and the columns of print echoed my "little girl lost" theme. The *Sunday Express* devoted more than twelve inches to it with a picture of her in the arms of Marieanne, and holding a new doll (opposite). The *Sunday Pictorial* offered the following:

It's a happy Boxing Day for Caroline after all

THE LITTLE GIRL LOST FINDS MUM

Caroline flies in all alone

A happy reunion for Little Girl Lost

Sunday Pictorial *Brenard Press picture*

The People (above), Reynolds News (all) Dec 27 1959

A GIRL LOST AT CHRISTMAS

But then Caroline finds a home

THE SNAPSHOT
Caroline carried it

Sunday Express Reporter

SIX - YEAR - OLD, blue-eyed Caroline Dalzell-Payne flew from Germany on Christmas Eve to spend Christmas with her mother. But her mother did not turn up at London Airport to meet her. And Caroline spent Christmas as a little girl lost.

It was not until last night that she found her mother.

Caroline, who speaks no English, lives in a children's home in Stuttgart. Her German-born mother lives in North End-road, Walham Green, London.

On Christmas Eve a telegram was sent from Stuttgart to tell her mother that Caroline was on the way

A nurse put Caroline on the plane, and she travelled alone. She carried only a little case.

She had no papers that would give her mother's address. Only a tattered photograph of a blonde woman, on the back of which was written: "To Caroline, from her mother."

Then, big, bustling London Airport. No one to meet her.

Married again

Where was her mother? The airport officials cabled the children's home for her address. Police who checked at Somerset House found she had married again and was now Mrs. Tatiana Gardiner.

They called at her home—and the telegram lay unopened behind the front door. Mrs. Gardiner had gone away for Christmas. But where?

Scotland Yard and county police launched a full-scale search.

Back at the airport girls looked after Caroline while arrangements were made to send her to a Red Cross home for Christmas.

But a B.E.A. receptionist, Mrs. Marieanne Gabriel, who speaks German, volunteered to take her home to Iver Heath, Buckinghamshire.

The airport staff hurriedly bought toys and sweets. Caroline spent Christmas Day with Mrs. Gabriel and her husband, Charles.

The hunt went on for Mrs. Gardiner. Scotland Yard finally traced her yesterday to the Gloucestershire village of Redmarley. A message was flashed to the village constable who began a house-by-house search.

In Redmarley Mrs. Gardiner was found

Would it be possible, she later asked London Airport over the telephone, for Caroline to be put on a train to Gloucester?

But Mrs. Gardiner finally agreed to travel to London for a reunion.

Caroline—she has a sister but does not know where she is—said in German: "If my mother comes I will say hello. But I want to stay with Marieanne tonight."

Mrs. Gabriel said: "Caroline seems happy and settled. I think she believes she is home."

Mr Gabriel said: "She is a wonderful kiddie. We haven't any children and I would be happy to adopt Caroline."

Sunday Express

The People *(both) Brenard Press pictures*

On Monday came the icing on the cake. British European Airways press office telephoned just to say: "Thank you." As the spokesman put it: "That heart-warming story probably earned us several thousands with the kind of good publicity we'd love to achieve ourselves." I refrained from commenting "You could. My brother, your colleague in the BEA press office has frequently done just that for your airline without getting any credit for it!"

Some weeks later Marieanne Gabriel's role was also recognised by the airline. She proudly became the first winner of a "customer service" award, presented from then on annually, in recognition of staff services beyond the range of normal duties.

To move directly from minors to honeymooners may seem cynical even with the current vogue for open relationships. But the airport has rarely been a significant setting for the theatre of a wedding or the drama of a marriage ceremony. The church, the register office, the reception venue, all offer a preferable scenic backcloth for an audience, even for a participating audience.

By the time the newly-weds reach the airport, the die has been cast, the knot tied. For that audience, the guests, the curtain has fallen. For the principal players the drama may be only just beginning.

In the 1950s, long before a hard-hearted Chancellor decided he was being too generous with a national wedding present to the happy couples, there was a huge upsurge in the springtime rush to the altar. Signing the register before 5 April meant that one income earner in each partnership could claim a whole year's rebate in income tax as he or she would henceforth qualify for paying less tax as a married person.

First to benefit, apart from the couples themselves, were the seaside hotels in Britain that cater particularly for honeymooners. And in no time, holiday spots outside Britain's miserable Spring beaches came into their own. Tops among these in popularity were the Channel Islands, which of course could claim the status of being both British and "abroad." That essential element, the holiday privilege of duty-free shopping with cheap cigarettes, liquor and perfume no doubt helped, even if it also went some way towards cancelling out any saving on income tax.

It became essential for the airport news watcher to check for a potential record number of honeymooners on all Channel Island flights, and indeed other services on romantic routes such as Paris, Amsterdam, Rome and Florence. As early as 1950 I was pleased to see that on board a twin-engined Dakota flying to Jersey all but six of the passengers were "just marrieds." And on the last day of March seven years later I was able to report that British European Airways had put on no fewer than fourteen "Cupid Specials" to the Channel Islands. The airline announced that it was carrying nearly a thousand newly married couples over the weekend.

As far as I could confirm, the entire operation went without a hitch – of the other kind, that is. Yet only three years earlier a similar exodus had gone sadly wrong when a fleet of honeymoon aircraft from Northolt Airport was forced back to Britain by bad weather. On the last day of the financial year 1953-54, up to 75% of all the passengers on flights to Dublin, Paris, the South of France and other Mediterranean resorts were newly-weds with no travel problems. But for 150 passengers heading across the Channel it was a different matter. The *Sunday Pictorial* gave my two-column story a 5-column banner (*opposite*) and went on to talk of "sixty beat-the-income-tax honeymooners...", under a 'LAST NIGHT'S NEWS' strapline, an unfamiliar claim of topicality for a national Sunday newspaper which normally would have gone to press by the previous early evening.

Apart from the unexplained adjustment to the figures, the story was as I had dictated. I had watched as my total of 75 *couples* boarded five separate twin-engined BEA airliners a few hours earlier. Bound for the Channel Islands, many had been seen off by family and friends in a flurry of cheers and confetti. But as the aircraft neared Jersey and Guernsey they were met by an impenetrable wall of fog, and were forced back to Britain.

The "*Pic*" corrected their figures later, re-running the story in final editions (curiously without the "last night" strapline this time) under an amended headline, though as the story revealed, only two couples out of the total were so honoured. The remainder were left to fend for themselves after I reported BEA as saying: "Accommodation arrangements as

LAST NIGHT'S NEWS

THIRTY BRIDES FLY TO—NOWHERE

SIXTY beat-the-income-tax honeymooners were beaten by bad weather yesterday when they flew out from Northolt Airport for the Channel Islands.

Fog and low cloud drove the air liners, "Cupid Specials," back to the airport.

The newly-weds were faced with the prospect of spending their first nights in armchairs in the reception lounges.

But a B.E.A. official said: "This is embarrassing us as well as the couples. We must do our best for them."

A fleet of coaches drew up on the tarmac and the honeymooners were driven back to the London Air Terminal at Waterloo. Hasty plans were made to accommodate them in nearby hotels.

"We hope to fly them on their delayed honeymoons in the morning," the official said. "But we shan't make it too early."

Last Day

Yesterday, the last Saturday in the financial year, was also the last day on which newly-weds could claim the full income tax rebate for 1953-54.

Although British European Airways made every effort to find hotel rooms for the couples, an official

Sunday Pictorial

A DAY OF UNUSUAL WEDDINGS

75 Couples Faced Armchair Honeymoon

TWO hours after leaving Northolt for the Channel Islands last night scores of "beat the taxman" honeymooners were back in London.

Sunday Dispatch (above)

Honeymoons delayed

BAD flying weather delayed the honeymoons of 75 newly-married couples yesterday.

Low cloud made landing impossible at Jersey, so five planes from Northolt with the honeymoon couples aboard had to turn back.

The couples were faced with the prospect of spending the night in the airport lounge.

But a fleet of coaches took them to London Air Terminal at Waterloo, and officials phoned hotels to find rooms for the honeymooners. They expect to fly today.

People

HONEYMOONERS STRANDED AT MIDNIGHT IN LONDON

SO THEY SPEND FIRST NIGHT AS GUESTS OF THE 'PIC'

Sunday Pictorial (right) late edition

THE FOG CLIPPED CUPID'S WINGS IN HONEYMOON RUSH

75 Couples Went To The Channel Isles—And Then Came Back Again

SEVENTY-FIVE honeymoon couples trooped disconsolately into the otherwise deserted lounges at Northolt Airport, Middlesex, last night after bad weather had clipped Cupid's wings and forced their airliners to turn back from the Channel Islands.

One after another only an hour or two earlier they had boarded their "Honeymoon Specials" amid the customary cheers and confetti from friends—part of the "beat-the-taxman" rush which had given airport officials the busiest honeymoon day ever known.

As they neared their destination fog and low cloud descended on both Jersey and Guernsey Airports. Two of the "Honeymoon Specials," carrying 30 newly-weds, were forced to turn round and fly back to Northolt.

Three other services circled the Channel Islands waiting for the weather to clear. Then they, too, turned back.

So one after another—their friends and well-wishers gone—the honeymooners found themselves back in the airport lounges.

This was the greatest challenge yet to the efficiency—and tact—of British European Airways.

Said a B.E.A. official: "This is embarrassing for us as well as the couples. We must do our best for them."

So while the honeymooners were still reflecting that the path of true love never did run smoothly, or perhaps dreaming of those far-off Channel Islands, a fleet of coaches drew up on the tarmac.

The word went round and the newly-weds and their piles of luggage went aboard to be taken to the London Air Terminal at Waterloo.

There a B.E.A. duty officer said that every effort would be made to accommodate them in local or easily reached hotels.

"But the arrangements are really up to the passengers themselves," he said. "We cannot be responsible since the delay was caused by bad weather, and not by any mechanical failure."

And the bridegrooms, he added, would have to pay for the night's board and lodging themselves.

"We hope to fly them on their delayed honeymoon in the morning."

NoW reporters continued the story with interviews from the couples' hotels... and they asked me to "let the story run," as my colleagues at Heathrow added their contributions.

Last night's headache was the biggest of a day that had been one long "honeymoon headache" for officials both at Northolt and London Airports.

In addition to the normal three evening services to the Channel Islands there were four special flights, all fully booked.

On one of the special flights were 15 couples and the only other passenger was middle-aged Mrs. Stella Johnson, of West Malling, Kent, who was flying to visit her sister in St. Helier.

"It is really quite embarrassing," she said, "but there just wasn't a seat available on the normal service."

It was the same at London Airport. On aircraft leaving for Paris, the South of France, Dublin and even the Mediterranean, as many as 75 per cent. of the seats were occupied by honeymooners.

The rush grew last night as dozens of couples arrived to board late-night flights after their wedding receptions.

At one stage there was almost a riot when guests broke the barriers and invaded the strictly-controlled Customs Hall to see off couples.

Officials who pleaded with them were booed down—until a policeman was called in.

By 10 p.m. all was quiet at both airports. Only the confetti and a few discarded buttonholes remained.

News of the World (Page 1 Lead) (all) April 4 1954 and all reduced

a result of this delay are really up to the passengers. We can't be held responsible for the weather, however sorry we may feel for the couples."

The *Sunday Dispatch* and the *People* both ran Page One single column pieces and the then broadsheet *News of the World* gave the new story a front page lead *(previous page)*.

It allowed the story to run a full nineteen column inches after their news desk had twice called asking me to "keep it going."

I had little opportunity to get the reaction of the newly-weds themselves to the huge about-turn. Most were picked up on the tarmac at Northolt and transferred directly to waiting coaches to be driven to London. But with the few quotes I included I was able to tell the Sunday news desks that the delayed honeymooners were being driven to an air terminal where a choice of hotel accommodation would be offered them.

Both the *Pic* and the *NoW* took advantage of this information to follow up the story with interviews at several small London hotels. And BEA told me: "We hope to fly all the passengers out again in the morning," adding feelingly: "We won't make it too early."

The story was ready made, of course, for my own follow-up on Sunday for Monday's dailies. And when BEA's "not too early" became an alarm call for most couples of 4.30 am, a completely new angle provided me with even more column inches, and in one case even larger headlines.

HONEYMOON CALL —AT 4.30 a.m.

SEVENTY-FIVE honeymoon couples were called at 4.30 a.m. in London yesterday after their first night of married life.

They were given cups of tea in bed and told "Your planes are waiting."

The newlyweds planned to spend the first night of their honeymoon in the Channel Islands, but their fleet of Cupid Specials was turned back by fog and low cloud.

Most of them stayed at the same London hotel, where airline officials found them accommodation.

But 4.30 a.m. . . . "It was rather early to call them," said a B.E.A. spokesman, "but if planes leave early the passengers have to get up early."

An hour later they were on their way by coach to Northolt Airport, where five airliners flew them to their honeymoon destination.

It cost £3

The one-night stay in London depleted honeymoon funds. Said one couple: "B.E.A. told us that since it was a weather delay they could not be held responsible. Our night's accommodation cost us nearly £3."

The honeymoon rush to the Continent, an airline record, went on all yesterday.

All the couples married on Saturday, the last day to qualify for a 12-month husband and wife income-tax rebate.

Daily Sketch (all) April 5 1954

FORTY HONEYMOONERS WERE ROUSED AT 4.30 am

FORTY couples were wakened at 4.30 a.m. in London hotels yesterday to continue their interrupted honeymcon journey to the Channel Islands

They were passengers in three BEA "honeymoon special" planes which took off from Northolt for Jersey and Guernsey on Saturday evening. Heavy sea mist clcsed the island airports, and the planes turned back over mid-Channel.

hotel accommodation, but they had to pay hotel bills themselves.

Roused at 4.30, they were taken by coaches to Northolt, where their planes took off at 7.15, 7.30, and 7.45 a.m. By noon all the honeymooners were in their Channel Island hctels.

A BEA official said: "We had to put on the three extra flights to deal with the rush of people

Daily Mail

CALLED AT 4.45 a.m. —ON HONEYMOON

Daily Mirror

4.30 CALL FOR NEWLY-WEDS

Seventy-five couples reached their honeymoon hotels yesterday —a day late. Fog had prevented their planes landing on the

arranged rooms for them in London hotels. They were called yesterday at 4.30 a.m. to catch their planes

Daily Express

"It was rather early," BEA agreed sheepishly when unmercifully I reminded them of their earlier promise. And they added, tactlessly and unhelpfully: "If planes leave early passengers have to get up early."

I wasn't about to complain. The early start gave me the opportunity to wrap up the story before the daily news desks could chase round to the hotels for more interviews with bleary-eyed honeymooners. By noon three of the delayed five "Cupid Specials" had touched down safely in the Channel Islands. The remainder tagged on behind an hour or two later.

It wasn't just a honeymoon but the nuptials themselves which were disrupted when British law halted a Hollywood film director's romantic plan to fly with his oil heiress bride-to-be 6,000-miles to the UK for the wedding. Former US Air Force bombardier Vince Evans was one of the crew of the first Flying Fortress bomber to complete an operational tour of duty in World War 2. He remembered his period of service in England as "the happiest time of my life" and wanted to marry Margery McDonald of Los Angeles at the village of Bassingbourne, Cambridge, near his former base.

But when the couple arrived at Heathrow they were told: "The wedding is off. You need 15 days' residence to wed in England."

Said Vince: "We can't stay that long. And neither can my best man. He has to leave for the US within a few days, and I can't do without him. Now we'll have to try to get married

COUPLE FLY 6,000 MILES, TOLD: YOU CAN'T MARRY

Daily Sketch

on the Continent." His sister Peggy, who accompanied the couple, told me: "Now I'm a bridesmaid without a bride." She added: "I don't mind where they get married. I'll still try to be there. But I know Vince always wanted his wedding here."

Sadly for the couple and their two attendants, even next day's headlines, with six-columns in the *Daily Sketch*, two columns and a picture in the *Daily Herald* among them, failed to change the law. After an unsuccessful appeal to the American Embassy for help, Vince and his bride-to-be were last seen heading for Dover.

For attractive brunette Joyce Fuller marriage was even more elusive. After nine years as a receptionist and air hostess with BOAC, she handed in her uniform and her notice in 1956 and checked in to board a flight to Accra, West Africa. There she planned to marry Captain Colin Gray, her Royal Engineers fiancé.

As an ex-BOAC employee she was entitled to a 75% rebate on the normal one-way fare – but only if she was prepared to stand down for any late-booking passenger paying the full fare. And over the next three days she had to do just that ...on three different flights. Each time she sent off a cable to her fiancé explaining the delay.

"Every flight has been fully booked," she told me ruefully.

Bride's trip stopped for fourth time

FOR the fourth time in four days, attractive brunette Joyce Fuller said goodbye to her family and friends and drove to London Airport yesterday.

And for … fourth time, by a margin of only 20 minutes … on the BOAC plane that was … wedding

Wedding trip off four times

For the fourth time in four days, Miss Joyce Fuller, former B.O.A.C. hostess, said goodbye to her family in Radlett, Herts, and drove to London Airport yester- … miles to her

People (above), Sunday Express, (both) Feb 7 1956

On the day fixed for the wedding she learnt shortly before the departure of yet another flight that one seat appeared to be vacant. At last she had her luggage weighed and checked in. Then, just 20 minutes before take-off was due, the missing passenger turned up. June, from Radlett, Herts, lost her seat again.

The unfinished story made at least two Sunday newspapers for me.

Then I lost Joyce Fuller. The next day she failed to appear for the Accra flight. And it was several days before I was able to discover she had switched routes and flown south-east to Nairobi, East Africa, instead of south-west. She had been assured, it seems, that there were plenty of seats available on trans-African flights. Her two-and-a-half-thousand-mile diversion swallowed up a sizeable portion of her fare rebate.

Vince Evans and his bride-to-be.

RULE BEATS ROMANCE

THEY flew 6,000 miles to London last night just to be married here. And then they had to call it off.

"You need 15 days' residence to wed in England," they were told.

Said Vince Evans, Hollywood film director: "It's a great disappointment. We can't wait that long. We'll have to marry on the Continent."

He and his bride-to-be, oil heiress Margery McDonald, have come from Los Angeles. They had hoped to wed at Bassingbourn, near Cambridge, where Evans served with the U.S. Air Force.

"Those days with the U S A F were the happiest of my life," he said. "I've often told Margery about them, and because of that I wanted to be married there."

His sister Peggy who flew in with them interposed: "Now I'm a bridesmaid without a bride."

And in a London hotel last night auburn-haired Margery looked at her trousseau—white satin wedding dress, 12 dresses, two suits, eight pairs of shoes and a whole trunkful of lingerie—and said: "Lovely, yes. But when do I wear them?"

Today, Vince and Margery are going to call at the American Embassy to see if it can get round the 15-day rule.

Daily Herald, Nov 7 1955 ***Brenard Press picture***

GI Brides, journalese composite for the UK wives of US servicemen from land, sea and air forces, provided all of us with hundreds of inches of column space over the years. They had, after all, helped in their thousands to reinforce a transatlantic special relationship by renewing family links between Britain and America first forged by the Pilgrim Fathers.

Though that historical foundation is unlikely to have had any significant influence on the marital migration, many of the new wave of adventurers must have had a similar pioneering spirit. GI Bride associations and clubs sprang up across the length and breadth of America, from Alabama to Oregon, from Arizona to Vermont. And when group charter flights, with their cut-rate membership fares, became fashionable, the GI Brides were in the forefront of transatlantic reunions.

Some of those women were little more than schoolgirls when the lure of a candyfloss-neon society or a living Disney world first snatched them away from the drab streets, cold houses and coal fires, smog and rain of Britain. But these too grew up to have families of their own as the 'fifties produced their successors, the GI Brides of the Cold War. And the new generation of brides seemed to be even younger.

JANET (15) FLIES OFF TO JOIN HER SAILOR SWEETHEART

Sunday Post *May 20 1962*

JANET'S SCHOOL PROBLEM

A 15-YEAR-OLD Scots girl flew out of Prestwick Airport yesterday to visit her American sweetheart's family

Daily Record *May 21 1962*

Scots schoolgirl Janet Smith from Dunoon was only 15 when she gave up her gymslip and exercise books and flew to join her American sailor sweetheart in the United States. But she and Raymond "Sonny" Parsons from Oxford, Maine, had met a year earlier while he was serving at Scotland's Holy Loch on the American depot ship Proteus. And they had been unofficially engaged for several months, with the full agreement of both families.

Then, after breaking his leg at the nearby nuclear submarine base, the young American was unexpectedly flown to a Boston, Massachusetts, hospital and it was thought unlikely he would be returning to Scotland. His family agreed that Janet could join them until Sonny's discharge in three years' time. As she boarded a transatlantic airliner at Prestwick Airport, clutching an envelope containing her visa and other documents for her entry into the US, Janet told me:

"I was so excited when I thought I'd finished with school for good. Then I found out that under American law I had to complete at least two more years' education."

Hardly an eyebrow was raised in the Scottish papers at the tender age of the reluctant schoolgirl, even though she referred to Sonny as her "fiancé." And in their follow-up story on Monday, the *Scottish Daily Express* and the *Scottish Daily Mail* seemed more interested in their angle of another Proteus sailor's American wife travelling with Janet. She had given up her first-class return seat just to escort her in economy class.

WIFE at 14 WISHES...

PIC NEWS SNACK BAR

THE bride, AGED 14, wants two babies—a boy and a girl.

SHE is Barbara Scruggs, married in North Carolina in August, who flew into London yesterday.

HE is U.S. Navy electrician Norman Scruggs, aged twenty-one, stationed here, who has a five-room flat waiting for the wife he first met at her grandmother's.

Said Barbara, a pony-tailed blonde 4ft. 3in. tall: "I want to be a housewife—not a schoolgirl.

"Sure, I've had dance dates since I was thirteen.

"But it was love at first sight for Norman and me . . . no need for a proposal."

PS. — Norman is on week-end leave.

On week-end leave . . . Barbara and Norman Scruggs.

Sunday Pictorial, Nov 1958 *Brenard Press picture*

In November 1958 the *Sunday Pictorial* ran my story with a Brenards' picture of US Navy electrician Norman Scruggs and his pretty blonde and pig-tailed wife who told me she was hoping for a family of two – a boy and a girl. The couple had been married in North Carolina three months earlier. Mrs Barbara Scruggs was *14*; her husband was 21.

They had met at her grandmother's while Norman, who was stationed in England, was on leave. Now they were returning from the US to the five-roomed flat he had rented near his base. "It was love at first sight for me," said Barbara, "Norman didn't have to propose.

"Now I want to be treated like a married woman, not a schoolgirl. I've had dates since I was thirteen. And it's not unusual for girls of my age to marry in America. So Norman's family weren't surprised when he took me home."

As in the case of the fifteen-years-old bride of the Egyptian student "barred" from his side in America[1] the news desks seemed to treat these romances with something akin to amused indulgence. The national press was however less philosophical when it splashed the arrival of another young wife at Heathrow. This time my description of the "Child Bride" of a rock singer was front page news. It led to a concerted national campaign, an outcry in Parliament and virtual banishment of a star

[1] *See Chapter 6, p.142*

performer, his career shattered...

We were alerted on the morning of Thursday, 22 May, 1958, to the expected arrival of Jerry Lee Lewis via a couple of London news desks, advised by the promoters of his proposed British tour. With hindsight, I suppose I should have been more enthusiastic about the entertainer some rock'n'roll enthusiasts were describing as the contender for Elvis Presley's title as "the King of Rock'n'Roll ."

The simple truth was that at 28 I was no student of the new popular wave of wild music, though I had no strong feelings about it. My taste, such as it was, embraced what is now usually described as "easy listening." I was aware of Lewis's big country and rock hits and enjoyed some of his sensational piano playing techniques, but that was about the extent of my knowledge. So I was unlikely to have a meaningful interview with him.

Without any specific questions to ask, I knew I could only expect the standard responses of any visiting American entertainer..."It's wunnerful to be in England... I've always loved this country... you have such great audiences... I wanna see Bucking Ham palace, the Houses of Parliament, British Bobbies..."

So I had to fall back on a standard tactic: looking for the "different" angle. I wasn't aware of any other reporters being present, though I did think I glimpsed a familiar face from one of the music periodicals. And there were two or three photographers at the Arrivals barrier who, I knew, would be joined at the last minute by airport resident cameramen and others returning from their vantage points at the aircraft steps and on the tarmac.

It was late evening and the tiny arrivals area at London Airport's prefabricated north terminal was now crammed with friends and relatives of passengers on several different flights. Jerry Lee Lewis's transatlantic service was a few hours behind schedule after a touch-down for a minor emergency at Shannon Airport. Its arrival at Heathrow now coincided with the arrival of several peak-time long-distance flights.

When the pianist finally emerged from the screened-off Customs hall he was almost completely surrounded, so it was difficult visually to separate his entourage from other emerging passengers.

I had moved ahead of any photographers who might have been lining the barrier to wait almost out-of-sight in a virtual "no-man's-land." I knew from experience that some passengers, by accident or design, occasionally slipped out from here through a "baggage only" exit, just to avoid the throng of meeters and greeters or the questionably more disciplined news media representatives. My colleagues and I also knew that this area could provide the only opportunity to buttonhole the newsworthy traveller before he or she was claimed by relatives, friends or minders – or protectors, as we called them then.

On this occasion the move gave me no great advantage. It was too crowded. But I was able to see that there were at least four or five adults in the party sticking close to Lewis, as well as two or three youngsters, a small boy and two girls, who were bringing up the rear. As they moved past me I tackled one of the men in the group.

"Who's the little lady?" I asked, quickly introducing myself as I nodded in the direction of the two girls. I remember thinking that perhaps Jerry Lee had brought along some young members of his fan club with him. We had come across such an arrangement before, when young fans, rarely with a parent, were politely described as "friends." (We more cynically thought of them privately as "camp followers." Today they might be called "groupies.") The musician I assumed him to be glanced back over his shoulder. "Why, that's Myra," he replied. "That's Jerry's wife."

For a moment I thought he must be referring to a young woman in the party, one who seemed close to Jerry's age (he was then 22). Then I realised he was looking beyond her towards the youngsters.

"His wife?" I echoed incredulously. One of the girls looked to be in her teens. The other was smaller, possibly less than five feet tall; a schoolchild who might have been no more than twelve. There was no reply. The speaker had moved past me. Now the two girls were level with me. "Mrs Lewis?" I asked the taller of the two, but glancing at both.

"I'm Myra Lewis." The confident response came, not from the teenager, but from the child, smiling back at me from under a pert little white fur hat. "I'm Jerry's wife."

"But... but," I stammered. Then, in desperation: "How old are you? How long have you been married?"

"About two months ago. And I'm fifteen."

We had reached the exit doors. Somewhere in this throng, a few feet to my right, Jerry Lee was posing for the photographers. But now someone was holding Myra's arm, half-guiding, half-leading her to the open door of a limousine. "That's enough. No more," he said, either to me or to the two girls as he bundled them into the car. "We have to go."

Now he was reaching back for Jerry Lee, who was being swept to the doors. "Jerry!" I cried out over another shoulder. "How old is Myra?"

"She's fifteen," he shouted back... and was gone.

His protector followed, pausing just long enough to call out as the car door was slammed behind him: "Come and see us at the Westbury Hotel. We'll have a press conference..."

That was the sum total of my story. What could I do with it? I wasn't even sure that the two items of information I'd gleaned were news, though I believed that even I would have heard of such a young bride of a rock 'n' roll star. Perhaps there was a way I could check.

*

Hurrying back to my 'phone, I asked for a line and called the *Daily Sketch*, whose diarist, Simon Ward, was among those who had ordered coverage of the Lewis arrival. Briefly I explained the situation, advised them of the hotel press call, and learnt that they too were unaware of a recent marriage for the rock star.

"Let us have everything you've got," I was told. I dictated my two brief paragraphs directly to one of their own copy-takers, and to cover myself, added a "Note to news desk," excusing the lack of detail. I repeated the procedure with my own news desk, instructing: "Full circulation." I remember adding ruefully: "That won't take long."

Coverage next day was disappointing. The *Daily Sketch* led their front page with nothing more than a huge picture of Jerry Lee and Myra, taken in their hotel room, and giant 84-point headline which screamed: "Mrs Rock 'n Roll, AGED 15!"*(opposite)*.

As far as I could recall, few of the specific words that followed on an inside page were mine. The *Sketch*, the paper I'd called for advice, simply stated the facts of the arrival, echoing my description of the scene and quoting Jerry Lee's confirmation that Myra was his fifteen-years-old wife of just two months. As another rock'n'roller put it so succinctly, I could get no satisfaction...

Inside information

by Simon Ward

JERRY FLIES IN WITH A GAL CALLED MYRA

For the rock king—a bride (AGE 15)

ROCK 'n roll singer Jerry Lee Lewis arrived in from America yesterday with his wife, AGED 15.

Then hastened to tell me that although he's only 22 he's already been married three times.

Which I must say was an improvement on the usual publicity story....

The 15-year-old, Myra, sat on an unmade bed at the Westbury and burbled: "It feels kinda nice to be married. I guess the other schoolgirls were enviable, but they were happy for me."

Flaxen-haired Jerry, here for a variety tour, butted in: "Yes sairr, this is my third. But this time it's the real thing."

What went wrong before? I asked. "I was 15 when I married. I guess I was too young to wed. Goils are different. They're ready to wed as soon as they wanna be."

Jerry married Myra in a chapel in Louisiana "around two months ago."

For Myra last night when we met there was no make-up or wedding ring. You see, she's a simple, homely gal, everyone told me.

She said: "I left school to get married Of course, I know all about Jerry's other wives. But they don't matter."

I pressed Jerry to tell me more details about them. He murmured: "Sure, foist there was Dorothy . . . er, Barton. She was old, 17. That lasted a year. I guess we didn't see eye to eye.

" My second was Jane Mitchell. Both of us 17. That's right. Lasted four years. Jane gave me a little boy who's three."

Too young

HE shook his sleek fair locks philosophically. "Yes sirr. I was too young."

Myra, her hair in a pony tail, snuggled up to him.

As I walked out Jerry's manager, Oscar Davis, said to me: "I keep telling Jerry not to talk about his private life. It might worry his fans."

Daily Sketch (page 4) reconstructed from damaged microfiche record ***23 May 1958***

Quickly the Lewis sensation became more visibly documented. Within hours the *Daily Mirror* discovered that the wedding had been four months earlier than Myra had claimed to me, that her parents (who were in the Lewis entourage) hadn't known of the wedding; that it had taken place before Jerry's divorce from his second wife;[1] that the new Mrs Lewis was Jerry's second cousin... and that she was not 15 *but still only 13 years old.*

Over the next few days the revelations became a public scandal which built up to a crescendo. Newspapers faithfully reported the opinions and comments of a shocked

[1] *Jerry always insisted he wasn't legally married to his second "wife."*

DAILY SKETCH 2½d

FRIDAY, MAY 23, 1958

© 1958, by the Daily Sketch

SHE KEPT WEDDING A SECRET

MRS ROCK 'N ROLL, AGED 15!

JERRY LEE LEWIS, the American rock 'n roll singer, flew into London yesterdaywith a shock for his fans. For the girl around whom he put a protective arm when they arrived at their hotel (above) turned out to be his wife.

And wife Myra –his third– turned out to be only 15. Said Myra: "I guess we've been married about two months. I don't remember really. Age doesn't matter back home; you can marry at ten if you can find a husband."

And this picture is unique. They have never before been photographed together. –See Simon Ward, Page 4.

May 23 1958 (Page One lead, reduced) Reproduced by kind permission of the Daily Sketch and Associated Newspapers Ltd. Caption reconstructed from damaged microfiche record.

citizenry, then launched into their own editorials to echo the outcry of popular condemnation of the rock star's morals and life-style.

Even Parliament became involved. Police officers called at the Westbury Hotel to check the passports of the visitors after questions were asked of the Home Secretary. Then, only three days into what had been planned as a five-week's concert tour of Britain, Jerry Lee Lewis's promoters pulled out. The bookings cancelled, the pianist, his child-bride and his entourage were forced to fly home.

Jerry Lee Lewis's career nose-dived as a moral America then reacted to the storm in Britain. His record sales dropped to the bottom of the charts; radio stations banned the airing of his music. Even his live concert bookings became few and far between, with his fees falling to a fraction of the thousands of dollars he could have demanded at his peak.

Although by determination and persistence, to say nothing of an unquestioned talent, he was able to climb back eventually, it was never really the same for Jerry Lee. If he really was the King of Rock as he and some of his faithful fans believed, he was a King in exile, his throne a broken piano stool.

Great Balls of Fire, the movie, was released in 1989. I wasn't asked to the British premiere, perhaps because by then I had taken early retirement. When I did see a video of the film a few years later, I was gratified to note that the Northolt location chosen for the airport scenes as I'd suggested, was an acceptable reproduction of the original Heathrow setting.

The arrivals' barrier scene followed Myra Lewis's description, which was a fair interpretation under dramatic licence. But an added exchange between two waiting reporters, contributed presumably by her co-writer, Murray Silver, was entirely fictional. I felt my real-life role was over-dramatised in the film and over-played by the "British actor" referred to by Brad Ricker, who turned out to be the late comedian and writer Peter Cook. He made me far too cynical. But then, you might suppose I would say that.

Myra Lewis later told of an approach at the airport by a reporter blocked from access to the star. She believed it was Paul Tanfield, the *Daily Mail* reporter[1] she had met shortly afterwards at the hotel. The man who hustled both Myra and Jerry Lee into their waiting car and away from my eager notebook that day, I learnt, was Oscar Davis, Jerry's manager.

The other two children accompanying Myra were her three-years-old brother Rusty and Jerry's 15-years-old sister, Frankie Jean. The young woman I had first thought to be Mrs Jerry Lee Lewis was, I discovered, Lois Brown, Myra's own mother, wife to Jay… and Jerry Lee's mother-in-law.

The member of the party I first approached was Jerry's drummer Russ Smith. If it had been Jay Brown, Jerry Lee's cousin and the band's guitarist, he would have been more likely to say: "That's Myra, my daughter." Almost certainly he would have added: "..and Jerry's wife."

[1] *Paul Tanfield was also the name (or pen-name) of the Mail's diarist/gossip columnist of the day.*

CHAPTER FIVE

The sudden November shower had passed and the drifting charcoal thunderclouds were crumbling away to the south. Silver puddles shimmering with oily iridescence, patchily reflected the polished aluminium of the graceful Constellation airliner as it waited on the London Airport tarmac

A flight of steps was already in place at the passenger door of the four-engined airliner, the arching curve of a delicately balanced fuselage giving it the appearance of some slumbering winged serpent. Baggage hatches were being clamped into place. An engineer was making his final exterior checks.

At any moment a brief boarding announcement for "Passengers to New York" would break the spell of the slightly nervous tension of the departure lounge, and interrupt the hubbub of impatient self-conscious conversation.

A famous Hollywood screen actress, the easily-recognised Jane Russell, stood just a few yards from the exit doors, a little apart from other passengers. It was as if she expected to be whisked aboard the transatlantic airliner along some magical red carpet, instead of tip-toeing through those scattered pools to cross a couple of hundred yards of unadorned concrete.

Best remembered as the pouting, sultry sex symbol of Howard Hughes's aptly-named and long-banned "The Outlaw," *Jane Russell had since become "legitimate" and respectable in light comedy. In recent years she had played opposite Bob Hope in* "The Paleface." *She was about to be seen as the brunette to Marilyn Monroe's blonde in* "Gentlemen Prefer Blondes."

She had just been in London attending a Royal Film premiere. Now, as she defensively clutched a tightly rolled, long-handled umbrella, she was waiting to fly home, no doubt hoping she would not have to unfurl it in those angry, if intermittent gusts still sweeping across the airfield.

We had met several times, and now chatted together for some minutes, the star and the news reporter, but our small talk had dried up. There was one subject remaining for me, and she had failed to voice it. That meant Jane Russell had no intention of willingly sharing her secret. She was no longer seeking publicity for what had become, in recent months, a dedicated mission. I would have to make my challenge. Purposefully I put to her the one question I had been holding back.

My tone was merely conversational, but the silence that followed was thunderous. It was as if everyone in the airport lounge had heard the question and was awaiting the answer.

Author's collection

Jane Russell.
Would she share her secret?

*

My generation has seen the last of the contemporary movie buff. A cinema-going habit of once, twice, even three times-a-week, which began with Saturday morning matinees in our tens, continued with the gangster films and back-row necking of the tender teens, then faded fast with the impact of television on our adult leisure hours.

But the giant black-and-white images of those massive silver screens remained vivid and unfading. The Hollywood stars of the thirties and forties, and to a lesser extent those of wartime and early post-war British cinema, really were stars to us. Twinkling only in some distant firmament, unattainable, unreachable, and like their screen images, so much larger than real life.

If some fortune teller had told me that one day I would meet, talk and exchange pleasantries (mostly) with, and question some of my teenage idols... Orson Welles, Ronald Colman, Tyrone Power, Gary Cooper, Cary Grant, Charles Laughton, George Raft, Edward G.Robinson, Peter Lorre, even Boris Karloff, I would have dismissed the idea as unlikely at least, and at most as sheer fiction.

To suggest I would have the opportunity, if I so desired, to confess my adolescent but undying devotion to Pier Angeli, Jean Simmons, Virginia Mayo, Rita Hayworth, or to receive and accept personal invitations from admired favourites such as Maureen O'Hara and Kenneth More to watch them working with their peers at nearby Pinewood, would

Author's collection
Lovely Italian star Pier Angeli let down her hair for a two months' visit to Britain, in June 1953. She came to complete studio scenes for her film "The Flame and the Flesh."

JOHN ROLLS
LIFE IN THE MIRROR

MRS. HILL IS OH SO HAPPY...

THE tall chestnut-haired beauty who arrived at London Airport yesterday was looking happier and more vivacious than I have ever seen her.

She said "Call me Mrs. Hill. I prefer it that way."

Her smile was a stunner. Her complexion had an open-air glow.

I thought she looked just as young as when she was called Mrs. Edward Judson (1937-1942); Mrs. Orson Welles (1943-1948); Princess Aly Khan (1949-1951), or Mrs. Dick Haymes (1953-1955).

Yet Mrs. (Rita Hayworth) Hill is thirty-eight and on her fifth honeymoon

Lovey-Dovey

SHE flew in from New York clinging to the arm of film producer **JAMES HILL**, whom she married six weeks ago. She said then "I never thought I could be so happy."

Yesterday she was still emphatically lovey-dovey towards Mr. Hill.

She hung on his words. She didn't answer a question without looking to him for the answer.

Said Mr. Hill: "We have a lot of friends to look up, but we hope to spend most of our evenings in the theatre."

Then he took her off by car

★

to the luxury of Claridges Hotel . . . *just the place for first, second, third, fourth, or fifth honeymoon*

Mrs (Rita Hayworth) Hill and her husband at London Airport.

Daily Mirror March 17 1958 *Daily Mirror picture*

Rita Hayworth arrives at London Airport on honeymoon with her fifth husband, film producer James Hill.

RITA HERE WITH FIFTH HUSBAND

RITA HAYWORTH, with chestnut hair cut short, a willowy figure, tanned look, slight limp, diadem mink and her fifth husband, flew into London yesterday.

"I'm on my honeymoon," 39-year-old Rita, told me, "so call me Mrs. Hill."

News Chronicle March 17 1958

Author's collection
Irish red-head Maureen O'Hara invited me to watch her at Pinewood Studios during the filming of "Malaga" (re-titled "Fire over Africa" in the U.S.)

have added fantasy to the fiction. But it was all to be.

The first cinema film I remember seeing starred Mae West. I can't recall its title, if I was ever aware of it or its story, or if it had one. But I do remember Miss West repeating a scripted invitation to "Come up and see me some time." It made a considerable impact on me, one I insisted on sharing for weeks afterwards with the rest of the family, pleased but slightly bewildered by the giggles my impression of the phrase seemed to generate. I can think of no reason why I should have been taken to see such a picture (I must have been about six or seven at the time) unless the alternative was to leave me at home alone.

A Shirley Temple 'weepy' I found distressing and disquieting at such a tender age, perhaps because the child star was only a year or two older than me and was experiencing all the childhood nightmares possible up there on that screen (and for all I know, off-screen as well). With the magnificent Paul Robeson of "*Sanders of the River*," and "*King Solomon's Mines*," I was delighted and thrilled. For years afterwards I dreamt of becoming such a powerful *basso profundo.*

Author's collection
Once the world's most popular and successful child star, Shirley Temple gave up films in adulthood to become a career diplomat for the United Nations. She is seen above, age 22, in one of her last films, "Adventure in Baltimore", re-titled (a very non-PC) "Bachelor Bait" in Britain.

Author's collection
Shirley Temple

Miss West in person I never had the pleasure of coming up to see. Shirley Temple Black, as she became after her second marriage, I talked with on two or three occasions. But that was after her retirement from Hollywood, in her new role travelling Europe and the world as a roving Ambassador for the United Nations. I was disappointed that she only provided me with a few inches for a news diary column on one occasion, and a five-line picture caption on another.

Paul Robeson, opera singer, actor and black activist constantly pilloried in America for his radical politics, returned to Britain in 1959 to play Othello again for the first time since 1930. His arrival at Heathrow gave me an impressive spread on the diary and entertainment pages. The *News Chronicle* story led both a page and its ***John London*** column with the story, while the *Daily Herald* competed with twelve inches across 3 columns.

Robeson's jealous Othello will not be so zealous

I FEAR that **Paul Robeson's** "Othello" at Stratford will not be the vibrant, energetic performance he had hoped to crown his great career. I could see that when, white-whiskered and weary, the Negro singer-actor flew back to London yesterday from Moscow, where he has lain ill for more than two months.

He looked older than his 60 years. And his thin American suit hung slackly on what was an 18-stone frame.

He admitted his performance at the Shakespeare Memorial Theatre next month would now have to be a very muted one.

"I'm still taking things quite slowly," he said. *"And I don't think my Othello will be quite so energetic. I won't do a fall down the stairs—and I won't creep like a panther on Iago."*

For my money, even a muted Robeson will be worth seeing in the role of the jealous Moor.

ROBESON LAST NIGHT
Stubble on his chin

Daily Herald picture

NEWS CHRONICLE, TUESDAY, MARCH 10, 1959

John London

The Robeson mystery cleared up at last

STUBBLY PAUL TELLS OF RUSSIAN ILLNESS

THE mystery of Paul Robeson's illness—first it caused him to withdraw from the role of Othello at Stratford, then a few days later he decided he was fit enough—was solved last night.

Robeson arrived in London from Russia yesterday ready for next week's rehearsals. He explained: "The doctors thought I had heart trouble. They advised me to cancel all future bookings."

For ten agonising days Robeson lay in bed, thinking his career had come to an end. Then the Soviet doctors revised their verdic[illegible]

Daily Herald ***News Chronicle*** ***(both) March 10 1959***

The reason was that a month or two earlier he had announced that he would have to cancel his Stratford stage commitment because of poor health. A few days on he changed his mind and decided he was fit enough to travel after all. He arrived aboard a Russian TU104 jet from Moscow, where he had been undergoing treatment in hospital as a guest of the Soviet Government.

"They thought I had heart trouble," a 60-years-old Robeson told me, "I began to think my career was at an end."

"But they changed their diagnosis and decided I was suffering from 'flu!"

His wife Eslanda had also been seriously ill, and she was staying on in Moscow for a couple of weeks. Robeson himself had lost a great deal of weight and he was still very weak. I reported his thin American suit hanging slackly on his former 18-stone frame. But he thought it very amusing that "so many people seemed more worried about the effect on my voice than about me."

And he chuckled: "Some of them wouldn't have minded if I'd had to crawl back from Moscow on crutches just as long as I can still sing."

Anyone who has ever revealed working at a major international airport will know that admitting such an experience usually prompts the impressed response: "*Really*? Then you must meet so many interesting people."

For "interesting" read "famous." And an acknowledgement will inevitably produce the supplementary question: What film stars have you met?"

In the "'noughties" the response might be Tom Cruise, Brad Pitt, Bruce Willis, Demi Moore, Hugh Grant, Meg Ryan, Sharon Stone... just for a start. But even against current competition from DVDs and videos, and an ever-growing new audience for cinema and made-for-TV films, the answer in the 'fifties, 'sixties and 'seventies could be more impressive.

Former colleague Chris Bramwell and I once discussed this very question. "Whenever anyone asks me who I've met I have to say, 'Give me a name,'" he said, "Otherwise, where do you start? It's much easier for me to say who I *haven't* met."

With the aid of a cinema reference book, I once took his point a further stage. I discovered I had talked with more than 400 screen actors and actresses, all of them household names, and all stars at one time or another. Some, it is true, I approached simply for the personal pleasure of meeting, with often only the forlorn hope of a story. In practice, over some thirty years, almost half that number provided me with copy, ranging from a simple diary page item to a front page scoop.

Together with other show business personalities in the theatre and more recently in television, the cinema star has always been newsworthy. It has to be a major achievement of Hollywood specifically, and the film industry at large, that the success or failure of films can be due as much to the amount of publicity it receives as it can to the stature of its cast or the quality of the product.

No other workers in a single industry have had so much time, money and effort devoted to making them famous above and beyond their individual contribution or achievement. And with the exception of a few individuals, no one in history has been given so much media exposure, a merging of their personal and professional lives so completely, if sometimes inaccurately. Yet the public appetite for more information is hardly assuaged.

For obvious reasons, the airports, especially the busier international terminals, have always been popular location settings for film or television drama, as they have so often for real-life drama. Heathrow saw the making of its first feature film in the mid-fifties; "*The Runaway Bus*," featured a split-level BOAC town terminal transport link. It was literally a vehicle for the comedy talents of the then radio comic Frankie Howerd, teamed up with a young Petula Clark, already established as a singer. A host of big screen names was dropped into the airport's newly-opened central terminal area with "*Out of the Clouds*." And one of the most recognisable Heathrow settings was the then brand-new Terminal 3 for the 1960s film "*The VIPs*," starring the even more recognisable Richard Burton and Elizabeth Taylor.

The airport, its staff and its activities were the real stars of each of these feature films, just as they became in several series of BBC television documentaries from the 'eighties onwards. But Heathrow and other British airports have continued to provide major location backcloths in the scripts of dozens of television and cinema dramas for nearly fifty years, as the railway station did in an earlier era.

After an initial interest in these activities, we would find little to whet our news appetites further. However much attention the famous actors on location at an airport may attract from the travelling public, they are simply carrying on their trade at an alternative film studio. And to the casual observer, few places can be more boring than a film set once the novelty has worn off. We were far more interested in the real-life traveller than the celluloid imitation. But when the two roles were combined...

Plane waited for Paulette's manicure

A TWENTY-FOUR-SEATER Viking aircraft bound for Paris waited five minutes after take-off time at Northolt yesterday, said a B.E.A. official . . . because film star Paulette Goddard was finishing painting her finger nails.

While twenty-three other passengers sat in the plane, waiting, Miss Goddard sat at a table with her toilet accessories laid out before her.

She Ignored It

The loud-speaker announced the plane's departure—but Miss Goddard went on painting her nails.

A traffic clerk made a similar announcement—but she ignored it.

A senior airport official delivered an ultimatum: "The plane is leaving."

"I know. I have been told that before," replied Miss Goddard who collected her make-up and strolled out.

Daily Mirror *Sep 9 1947*

Nails

From "DISGUSTED," Clapham Common, London.

What do you think of Paulette Goddard's nails holding up an air-liner?

We think she should have used her nails to scratch her silly head.

Daily Mirror *Sep 11 1947*
A reader's letter

QANTAS Airways picture
Paulette Goddard

I interviewed my first film star within my first few weeks as a cub reporter. The name of Paulette Goddard, who was waiting to board a flight to Paris when I approached her, was of course known to me. I knew too that she had been married to Charlie Chaplin, and that she had starred in two of his major films, the silent "*Modern Times*," and his wartime satire, "*The Great Dictator*." And that was all I knew of her.

When I introduced myself, she invited me to join her at her coffee table. Then as we chatted, she emptied the contents of her handbag on the table, and proceeded to make up her nails from a collection of toiletries. A loudspeaker call came for her flight departure. She ignored it. Concerned, I rose from my seat, mumbling: "I think perhaps you should go, Miss Goddard." She impatiently waved me back to my seat.

A uniformed receptionist who approached her was also waved away. It was only when a senior airline official announced: "The flight is leaving now, Miss Goddard," that she swept her toiletries back into her bag and snapped: "I know, I've been told that already." She marched out with a simple: "'Bye!" to me.

Only the *Daily Mirror*, as far as I could see, deigned to use the story the next day, using my line that Miss Goddard's nails had held up the departure of an airliner and its 24 other passengers for a full five minutes. And the item earned me my first reader's comment on the paper's letter page, from "Disgusted" of Clapham Common, no less.

Very soon afterwards I faced a whole 'plane-load of British stars, among them Stewart Granger, Mervyn Johns, Joan Greenwood, Valerie Hobson, Greta Gynt, Kathleen Ryan and Hazel Court. They were returning from the Dublin premiere of "*Captain Boycott*" on a chartered aircraft, seven hours late on what should have been a two-hours' flight.

I chose to ask Hazel Court, youngest and prettiest of the group, what had gone wrong. She told me that because of a radio fault on the aircraft they had returned to Dublin three times for repairs. Doug Shillito, on my Heathrow news desk, asked me why I hadn't spoken to the "public idol" Stewart Granger. I had to tell him that Mr Granger was in no fit state to talk. He was... under the weather. Not something for the libel-fearing reporter to describe in print in those days.

Brenard Press picture
Richard Greene and Myrna Loy at Northolt

Stars Touch Down

FANS and autograph hunters had a busy time over the week-end when a "film star special" flew in to Northolt from Rome.

Out of the plane stepped Myrna Loy, Ursula Jeans, Peggy Cummings, Richard Greene and Roger Livesey; all had been on location work in Italy for the film "The Strange Case of Lady Brooke."

My picture shows Myrna Loy and Richard Greene shortly after their arrival at the airport.

Evening News Oct 25 1948

Strangely, because film companies were usually sensitive to the insurance implications of so much of their "merchandise" being contained together in one aircraft, it wasn't long before a second large group was giving autograph hunters a busy time at Northolt. From one Rome airliner stepped Myrna Loy, Ursula Jeans, Peggy Cummins, Richard Greene and Roger Livesey. Not such familiar names today, except perhaps on afternoon TV, but all had been on location for "The Strange Case of Lady Brooke."

Film company publicists were among the first to appreciate the value of free newspaper space offered them by an airport departure or arrival. So we were advised of most of these well in advance, to enter in our daily news diary. Others were the result of casual contact in an airport lounge. It's debateable which of these forms of close encounter offered the better prospect of column inches.

Such contacts with film stars and other show business personalities certainly provided me with a series of cameos over the years. But not all could be translated directly into news items. Some could only be filed away in my memory banks as too contentious, too personal or too irrelevant to publish at the time.

How could I reveal in the early 1950s for example, that someone even as outrageous as Tallulah Bankhead, star of that early Hitchcock masterpiece "Lifeboat," would proposition me and try to abduct me? Or tell how Gracie Fields had invited me into her taxi to sing me a solo? That the Beverley Sisters and Eartha Kitt had also personally serenaded me?

How would I explain Bing Crosby's letter to me criticising my handwriting? Or tell how I irritated Bob Hope when I asked him to return a valued borrowed pen? How could I insensitively report that Carole Landis had proudly unwrapped and shown me the "new blue dress" she was said to be wearing when she tragically committed suicide later, supposedly because of rejection of her love for Rex Harrison?

Could I argue or complain when Valerie Hobson denied my story of her missing gems, apparently because of her fear of "loaded" insurance premiums?

Carole Landis

Author's collection

Joan Home To Take Lilli's Part

Today's "Star" picture of Joan Greenwood on arrival.

"Star" Reporter

JOAN GREENWOOD flew into London today from the United States to take over Lilli Palmer's part in the play "Bell, Book and Candle" at the Phoenix Theatre.

Miss Palmer has left the cast of the play.

Mr Martin Case, manager of the company, said today: "She has gone to make two films in Germany. It was a prior commitment. We had known for some time that she would be leaving. It cropped up sooner than expected, but we knew last week that she would be leaving on Saturday.

Rex Harrison, Miss Palmer's husband, who starred with her in the play, has been on holiday in Portofino, where he has a villa with his brother-in-law and sister, Lord and Lady Kilmuir.

"Mr Harrison originally intended to take a fortnight's holiday, but his doctor ordered him to take three weeks," said Mr Case, "otherwise he and Miss Palmer would have played the last week together."

Today Mr Harrison, who also produces the play, was meeting iss GreenMwood to discuss her part.

At the airport a copy of the play was handed to her. "It will take a week or two to learn it," she said.

The understudy, Miss Shirley Cain, 20, of Birmingham, will continue in the role for the time being.

Brenard Press picture
The Star, Sep 2 1955
Joan Greenwood flies in.

And could I tell the true story behind my conspiracy with Trevor Howard, and my call to his wife to tell her he was leaving England for good?

I did find a way of disclosing that I was the only man in the life of Brigitte Bardot at a time when every red-blooded male in the country would have aspired to such a claim. I was pleased to record too that Greta Garbo, on the other hand, really did "Vont to be alone." She told me so herself on more than one occasion. The ever-glamourous Marlene Dietrich I was surprised to catch out wearing odd shoes… but only, she insisted, because she'd suffered a strained ankle. But it needed the picture alongside my brief paragraph or two of copy to provide verification.

Tough guy George Raft I was able to report literally polishing off his Hollywood career and making a start on his last film. He was giving it all up, he told me, to go into business, making furniture polish. Within a few years he was to be barred from visiting Britain again because of suspected links with the Mafia.

There was certainly nothing so original about my early encounter with Frank Sinatra. His: "Do you want a punch on the nose, fellah?" before I had even uttered a word, was something of a Press cliché. And it was some months after the event that I learned I'd played a fully supporting role in a Charlie Chaplin film. News to me, perhaps, but hardly of interest to your average newspaper reader, even if it happened to be an experience shared with another non-actor, the late Lord Mountbatten.

The honeymoon flight of Elizabeth Taylor and her second husband, the "golden boy" of British films, Michael Wilding, I did report. This was no extravagant excursion to the romantic South Seas, the West Indies or even the South of France. Instead the couple had chosen to follow the example of day-trippers to London Airport and take a "round-the-houses" joy-flight. They took off from the airport's public ground enclosure in a twin-engined biplane, the de Havilland Dragon owned and operated by husband and wife pilots Monique and Ray Randell. After the official and more formal honeymoon trip, I hasten to add.

MARLENE —IN ODD SHOES

THE woman who always looks so smart, Marlene Dietrich the glamorous, left London yesterday wearing ODD SHOES. Miss Dietrich, who flew to Paris, explained: "I broke two toes on my left foot when I was visiting an orphanage. While playing with some of the children on the lawn I tripped over a wire."

Daily Express picture August 3 1954

NOTE THAT HAND, DEEP IN HIS POCKET

IT could well be the George Raft of 20 years ago. *(Remember Scarface, Under Cover Man?).*

But Raft changes as little as his screen parts—and this is the perpetual tough-guy arriving in London last night to make his 102nd film.

Only his greying hair gives a hint of his 56 years.

The new film is based on the disappearances of British and American scientists. Raft could not say much more about it: "I haven't even seen the script."

One thing is definite: a British actress will play opposite him.

Note the real-life "hangovers" from many George Raft gangster roles: the snap-brim hat at just the right angle, the turned-up collar, and the hand thrust deep in the coat pocket.

Daily Express picture May 5 1952

George Raft arrives...

Polished Off

FILM STAR George Raft is retiring from films to make furniture polish.

Flying home to Hollywood last night after filming in Britain, fifty-six-year-old Raft said:

"I have two more films to finish and then I finish."

Raft said he was vice-president of a firm making a new kind of polish which repels stains and cigarette burns.

Sunday Pictorial July 27 1952

...George Raft leaves.

HIS baggage loaded with Christmas presents for Ava Gardner, his wife, and in a "desperate hurry," Frank Sinatra made a surprise dash from New York to London by air today on his way to Madrid.

Little more than an hour after stepping from a BOAC Stratocruiser at London Airport, Sinatra hired a taxi to Croydon where a special plane, chartered at a cost of £160, set off for Madrid.

"I am going to spend Christmas with my wife," he said. "A reconciliation? I never comment on my personal affairs."

Asked if Miss Gardner, who recently announced her intention to divorce Sinatra, was expecting him, he replied, "She is."

Sinatra spent nearly 45 minutes in the Customs Hall while airline officials tried to find him a booking on a normal passenger flight to Spain. He told Customs officers: "I've just got to get to Madrid—even if I have to stand all the way."

The Star Dec 24 1953

The Star, Brenard Press picture Dec 24 1953

The photographer was granted a half smile. All I was offered was: "Do you want a punch on the nose?"

The twin-engined de Havilland Dragon Rapide which became a bridal chariot for Elizabeth Taylor and her groom, Michael Wilding on their honeymoon. The aircraft, owned by Island Air Services, normally operated joy flights for sightseers from the London Airport public enclosure in the '50s.

Author's collection

British actress Valerie Hobson, later to be admired as the deceived and forgiving wife of sex spy scandal Minister John Profumo, denied my story in the *Daily Mail* that she had left £7,000-worth of jewels behind at Northolt. She couldn't have known that a Customs officer had specifically described the contents of her red leather case to me, saying they included a diamond necklace, bracelet and brooches. Neither could she know that they had made a formal valuation of the gems, normal practice when such items are left behind in a Customs hall.

But the following day Miss Hobson spoke to the London Evening News diary, "Talk of the Day," and apparently told them that the dressing case had contained merely make-up and some personal papers. She was quoted as saying that the case was locked and that Customs evidently thought it contained jewellery. Hardly the kind of assumption the Customs officers I knew were likely to make.

Significantly, I thought, Miss Hobson then told the News diary: "I've had to write to my insurance brokers to assure them that all is well and I haven't been a careless girl." Miss Hobson and I were to meet on numerous occasions in the future, and the atmosphere remained cordial. I never held the *Evening News* story against her.

Bob Hope had borrowed a favourite blue gold-nibbed fountain pen from me when autograph hunters, with familiar ill-manners, constantly interrupted our chat in a departures lounge. He failed to return it to me before boarding his 'plane. I didn't miss it until some hours later, and light-heartedly asked for it back when I saw him again on his return journey, assuming he would make a joke of it and provide me with a humorous comment. Instead, with an unexpected flash of impatient temper, he turned to a minion and snapped: "Give the guy a pen. I've got a million of 'em," and stalked off...

Hope's partner in those Hollywood "Road" films, Bing Crosby, was however, always charm itself, and regularly requested any news cuttings on his visits to the UK to be sent on to him for his scrapbooks. Following one of his golfing holidays in Scotland, I was happy to forward a number of news items to his Hollywood home. His brief "thankyou" note complained that my signature was indecipherable.

"Your penmanship requires a refresher course," suggested Bing. I should have explained to him; it was all due to the fact that his regular golfing partner still had my best handwriting pen.

Miss Hobson forgets

A red leather jewel-case containing a diamond necklace, bracelet, and brooches, valued at £7,000, was left behind at Northolt Airport Customs hall yesterday by a passenger from Nice.

Twenty minutes later a telephone call was received from the forgetful owner—film star Valerie Hobson. The jewels were sent to her home off Berkeley-square.

Daily Mail Aug 14 1950

Valerie Hobson circa 1950

Wishful Thinking

VALERIE HOBSON was laughing to-day over the news that a dressing-case left behind in Northolt Airport Customs Hall on her return yesterday from Nice, contained £7,000 worth of jewellery.

"I would very much like to have so much," she said. In fact, the red dressing-case contained make-up and some papers. The porter who handled her luggage left it, and officials sent it on after her.

Not So Careless

"This case was locked, and Customs evidently thought it contained jewellery. Actually the only jewellery I had with me was a bracelet. So I've had to write to my insurance brokers to assure them that all is well and that I haven't been a careless girl," she told me.

Evening News Aug 15 1950

The Star, Sept 1947 Brenard Press picture

Stars under contract to J.Arthur Rank studios were sometimes required to meet or see off other celebrities at the airports as part of their own promotional publicity. Here the British star Valerie Hobson was at Northolt to greet a 14-yr-old French music prodigy.

English-born American comedian Bob Hope pictured entertaining American forces in 1987.

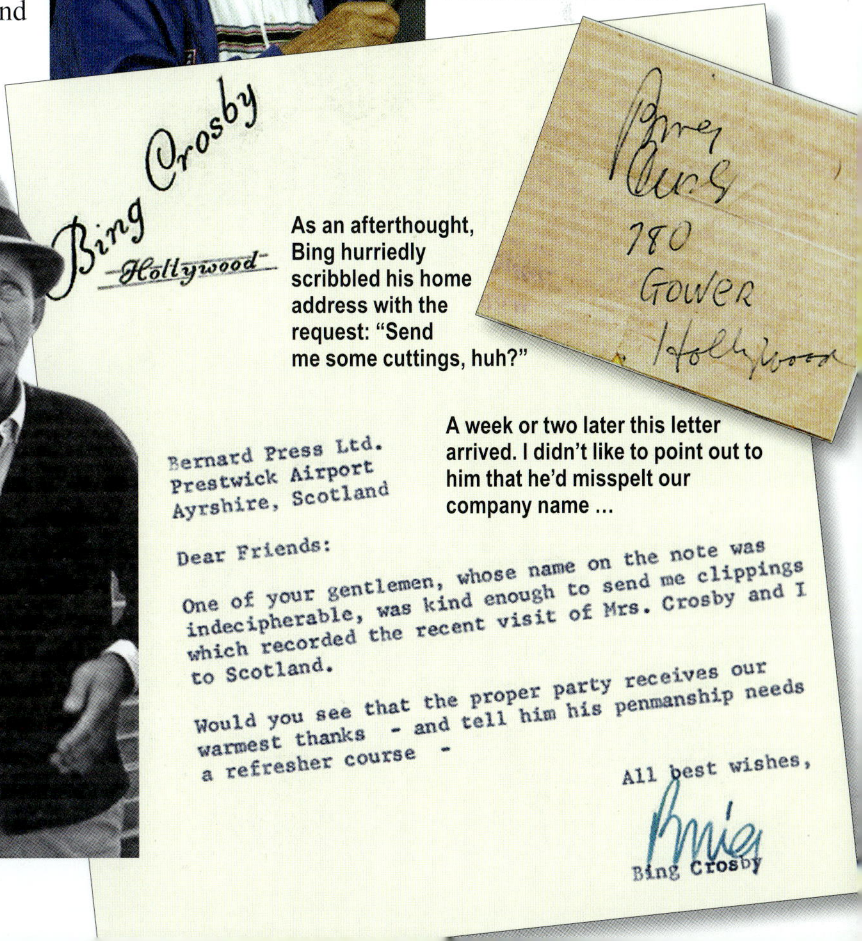

Bing Crosby
Hollywood

Bing
780
Gower
Hollywood

Bernard Press Ltd.
Prestwick Airport
Ayrshire, Scotland

Dear Friends:

One of your gentlemen, whose name on the note was indecipherable, was kind enough to send me clippings which recorded the recent visit of Mrs. Crosby and I to Scotland.

Would you see that the proper party receives our warmest thanks - and tell him his penmanship needs a refresher course -

All best wishes,

Bing

Bing Crosby

As an afterthought, Bing hurriedly scribbled his home address with the request: "Send me some cuttings, huh?"

A week or two later this letter arrived. I didn't like to point out to him that he'd misspelt our company name ...

"Then I hit it , straight down the middle..." Bing Crosby recounts an animated golfing anecdote as he waits to board a transatlantic flight at Prestwick Airport, Scotland. He was on his way home after a playing tour of the Scottish courses in the mid-sixties.

Brenard Press picture

Frank Sinatra, I am convinced, had a sixth sense that warned him of the presence of Press men, even when there were no photographers snapping at his heels, so I shouldn't have been surprised at his aggressive reaction to my approach. Indeed I felt somewhat honoured to have joined the ranks of those who had been similarly threatened.

It might be that he simply remembered my meeting with him and his wife, Ava Gardner, the previous year when I reported their reaction to rumours of a rift in their three-years-old marriage ("Everything between us is fine. It generally is"). Or he may have recalled the headlines on my story of a public row between the couple and BEA of just a few months earlier.

The Sinatras had turned up to fly to Milan only seven minutes before the aircraft was due to take off. With them they had eleven pieces of luggage, and an airline official reluctantly told them: "Sorry, you're too late. We can't delay 32 other passengers on the flight."

Frank's reaction was to lose his temper. "I'll never fly BEA again." he snapped. Not to be outdone, Ava chipped in: "I'd rather swim the Channel." As I reported, it didn't help when someone standing nearby (not me, on this occasion) remarked loudly: "Maybe they would have held the 'plane for Bing Crosby." Frank whipped round to glare at bystanders: "Who said that?" he demanded, angrily but pointlessly.

Finally, subdued but still quietly fuming, the Sinatras had to wait in a crowded departures lounge for an hour for an alternative flight to Rome. The *Star* and the *Evening Standard* ran my story in later editions. The *Express* tied it in with an unsmiling shot of the couple eventually boarding another airliner and revealed that the singer then scuffled with a photographer on their arrival in Rome.

But now the couple were living apart, with Ava in Spain said to be talking of divorce, and Frank back in the US. He had flown to London from New York, his arms loaded with Christmas presents, and was hurrying on to Croydon Airport where a private aircraft waited to fly him to Madrid.

As he seemed unwilling to put his burden down and he was smaller than I anyway, I bravely ignored his offer of a bloody nose and persisted with my questions. At last he confirmed the obvious; yes, he was on his way to spend the holiday with Ava, and yes, though I felt, not so positively this time, she was expecting him. But he was adamant about not discussing the possibility of a reconciliation, a stance reinforced and repeated by Miss Gardner herself when she flew to London to film "*The Little Hut*" four years and more rumours later.

The legendary glamour of Garbo, like that of Deitrich, was an unacquired taste as far as my researches were concerned. Perhaps the generation gap was too wide to be bridged by the changing face of fashion. Perhaps, with Garbo at least, my lack of appreciation was due to the

So Frankie And Ava Are Still Sweethearts

AVA GARDNER and Frank Sinatra, married a year, flew into London Airport to-day from their Hollywood home, and to questions on the recent rumours of a rift their answer was just "Everything's fine."

As they stepped from the T.W.A. airliner, which flew them from New York, Mr. and Mrs. Sinatra posed together for photographers and stood side by side and smiling. But they declined an invitation to "say a few words" into a newsreel microphone.

Ava wore a silver grey sapphire mink stole over her grey tailored costume and wore uncut emerald ear-rings.

The couple are spending a day in London before flying off to Kenya, where Ava will make a film.

Said her husband: "I have to have one or two business talks in regard to a singing tour of London and the provinces which I hope to make next year."

And those rumours? Both seemed too shy to talk about them, but, said Frank: "I often read about things that startle me. I can assure you everything between us is fine—it generally is."

Evening News *November 6 1952*

FRANK AND AVA MISS THE PLANE

"Star" Reporter

FRANK SINATRA and his wife, Ava Gardner, arrived at London Airport to-day seven minutes before their plane was due to take off for Milan.

The Star *May 8 1953*

Sinatra was too late

SEVEN minutes before their airliner was due to take off for Milan to-day, Frank Sinatra and his wife, Ava Gardner, arrived at London Airport with 11 pieces of luggage.

They were told: "You are too late. Passengers are already aboard."

For several minutes Mr. Sinatra argued with airline officials. Then he shouted: "This is the last time I ever fly by this line." Said his wife: "I'd rather swim the Channel."

Car broke down

Sinatra said his car had broken down at Shepherd's Bush.

Evening Standard *May 8 1953*

Channel swimmer Ava

AVA GARDNER says that she would "sooner swim the Channel" than travel by BEA again. Personally, I think it a pity they didn't tell her to try. —*F. W. Hamilton, King's Cross Road, St. Pancras.*

Reader's letter, Daily Express, May 11 1953

It was such an angry day for Sinatra

FRANK SINATRA got angry in two capitals yesterday. *In London* he had a row with airport officials. *In Rome* he had a fight with a photographer.

THE BAD TEMPER started in London. He arrived at London Airport seven minutes before his plane was due to leave for Milan.

With him was his wife Ava Gardner. And they had 11 pieces of luggage.

"Sorry," said airport officials, "you are too late to fly." One of them pointed out that all passengers are warned to be at the airport at least 30 minutes before the time of departure.

Frankie shouted angrily: "This is the last time I ever fly B.E.A."

Ava chipped in: "I'd rather swim the Channel." Someone remarked: "Maybe they would have held the plane for Bing Crosby."

And that didn't help, either. Later the Sinatras were put on a Rome-bound plane.

Said a B.E.A. spokesman: "It is not our policy to inconvenience a plane-load of 32 passengers just because two people are late."

THE BAD TEMPER was still there when Frankie and Ava got off the plane at Rome instead of Milan.

A photographer raised his camera. Frankie charged. There was a scuffle—a brief, indecisive sort of fight.

Police intervened. The Sinatras bustled off, indignant.

The photographer smiled—he had two pictures.

Daily Express, May 9 1953 *Daily Express picture*

Here before dawn

SEVERAL hours before dawn today, film actress Ava Gardner arrived in London. She flew from Paris, where she had been having some dress fittings.

Miss Gardner is here to begin work with Stewart Granger and David Niven, in a film made from the play The Little Hut.

For her night flight, she wore a dress of minutely patterned French brocade and matching summer coat. "It is my wedding dress," she said. "Not my wedding, but Grace Kelly's. That is when I last wore it."

When she was asked about rumours of a possible reconciliation with her husband Frank Sinatra, Miss Gardner was a long time replying. Then she said: "To that question—no answer."

Evening Standard *June 30 1956*

Ava Gardner circa 1950

simple fact that I never once gazed upon that face, masked as it always was with the combination of dark glasses, head-scarf or wide-brimmed hat.

After two or three attempts and subsequent rebuffs, I gave up trying to talk to Garbo. She would tonelessly repeat those familiar words, turn her head away and draw silk over her mouth and nose as if veiling some embarrassing blemish. She always avoided contact or conversation in public, even if with her long-time friend and occasional travelling companion, society photographer Cecil Beaton.

Her obsession for hiding from public gaze gave her trouble on at least one occasion. An American friend accompanying her on a trip to Paris screened both of them so well with an umbrella they failed to see where they were going and climbed the wrong flight of steps to a waiting aircraft, only to find there was no aircraft door at the top. They were engineers' inspection steps, appropriately perhaps, leading nowhere.

Many years later I had the opportunity to visit Garbo's grave in a Stockholm cemetery. Though in a tastefully designed setting, her simple headstone, unlike the hundreds of others surrounding it, stood completely alone.

Author's collection
My Swedish-born wife, Angela (seated above), shares in the serenity of Garbo's final resting place.

Tallulah Bankhead, on the other hand, hated being alone. It was, she once said, one of the three phobias of her life. Provocative, controversial, always outrageous, Tallulah lived ahead of her time. If she'd been a man, she would have been a hell-raiser, a Richard Harris or a Peter O'Toole. As it was, she came pretty close to elevating the underworld whilst remaining extremely feminine and sober.

Courtesy of Carl Van Vechten Estate
Tallulah Bankhead – a talking tornado with two new friends.

Daughter of a lawyer and a Southern beauty who died soon after giving birth to her at the turn of the century, Tallulah was named after her grandmother, who in turn was said to be named after Tallulah Falls, Georgia. As a stage presence, screen star and society belle, she was as well known in London in the 1940s and '50s as she was in New York and Hollywood. She was also some 25 years older than me, which became significant in what was to follow.

Leaving London for Switzerland, she swept through Heathrow like a talking tornado. There was no question of interviewing her; even throwing questions at her was almost impossible. From the first introduction as she stepped from her car, through check-in and departure formalities, she talked incessantly, not just to me but to anyone within range, which, with her stage-trained voice projection, meant a radius of at least fifty yards.

Surrounded by autograph hunters, she talked about her childhood, about her happiness at seeing her "wonderful Britain" again, about a ten-years-old American fan who had written to her. She was still talking and wildly gesticulating as she changed a book of travellers' cheques into cash. Suddenly realising that her secretary was missing from her side she cried out: "Where is he? He has deserted me!" And with a sob: "I get so frightened when I am alone. He is supposed to be looking after me."

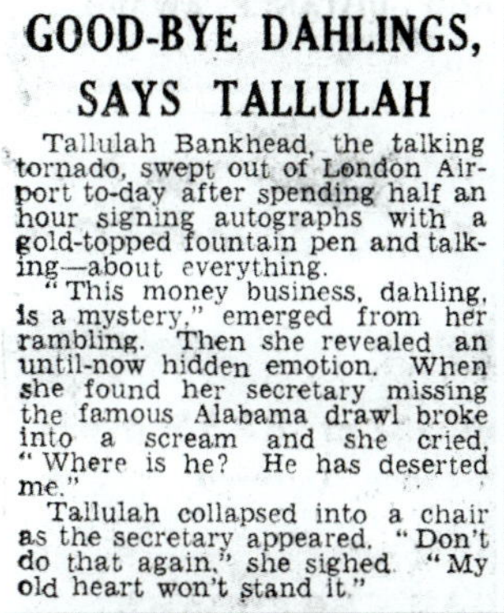

GOOD-BYE DAHLINGS, SAYS TALLULAH

Tallulah Bankhead, the talking tornado, swept out of London Airport to-day after spending half an hour signing autographs with a gold-topped fountain pen and talking—about everything.

"This money business, dahling, is a mystery," emerged from her rambling. Then she revealed an until-now hidden emotion. When she found her secretary missing the famous Alabama drawl broke into a scream and she cried, "Where is he? He has deserted me."

Tallulah collapsed into a chair as the secretary appeared. "Don't do that again," she sighed. "My old heart won't stand it."

Evening News *Sept 19 1951*

She collapsed into a chair when at last the missing secretary appeared at her shoulder. "Don't do that to me again," she admonished the hapless fellow with a sigh that might have been heard across the tarmac.

Tallulah Went Out Talking...

"Star" Reporter

TALLULAH BANKHEAD left London Airport for Paris today—still talking.

When she arrived at the airport she was surrounded by autograph hunters and signed book after book—talking all the time.

She talked about her childhood; about her happiness at seeing "my wonderful Britain again"; about a ten-year-old fan who wrote to his "favourite American."

She was still talking and wildly gesticulating as she turned a book of travellers cheques back into dollars.

As she went through customs she found that her secretary was missing. She called, "Where is he? He has deserted me." And with a sob: "I get so frightened when I am alone. He is supposed to be looking after me."

Tallulah collapsed into a chair as the missing secretary appeared at her shoulder. "Don't do that again," she sighed.

With officials surrounding her she went out to the waiting airliner. All the other passengers were aboard.

The Star, Sept 19 1951

And as she finally boarded the 'plane, joining other passengers already on board, I realised I didn't need the answers to any questions. I had it all; a descriptive piece that apparently said it all about Tallulah, a piece which was published in the *Star* and the *Evening News* almost word for word as it appears here.

But it wasn't quite all. Between the going and the returning of her secretary, Tallulah decided that I would do nicely as a replacement. "I have fallen in love with you," she announced, "So you will be even better. Come with me... now. No arguments." The command was reinforced by a steely grip round my forearm as she dragged me through the departures Customs area. Protesting every known commitment I could muster, I made my get-away only when her attention was distracted by the return of the attempted escapee secretary.

In the time-honoured cliché of the Sunday sensationals I quietly made my excuses and left, breathing heavily, but with relief. That was the part of the story I didn't file, although for hours I lived in embarrassed dread of a threat from colleague Ray Watts to dictate an "add" to my story. He promised it would be the "ultimate exposé of the white slave traffic" at Heathrow. For some time after this I was known to my jealous colleagues as "Tallulah's Toy." And this was forty years before "toy-boy" came into the English language.

Brenard Press picture

Not Nelly's hat – but Gracie's.

Kiss for Gracie

GRACIE FIELDS and her husband Boris flew back to Naples and their villa in Capri today after their visit to England.

"We came for the week-end on May 5 and stayed for six weeks" said Gracie at London Airport.

A little girl was at London Airport to see them off and she kissed Gracie goodbye. "Her mother has been one of my fans for years," said Gracie. "She used to stand outside my stage door. Now she is bringing her daughter up to it too."

The Star *April 1957*

My taxi-cab assignation with "Our Gracie" was on a more aesthetic level. Some months earlier I had been wearied by my then wife's constant singing of a snatch of a song which always ended: "...said the saucy little bird on Nellie's hat." It was, I was informed, a song that Gracie Fields had made famous.

"It just doesn't scan," I complained haughtily, "I can't believe you've got it right. And to prove it, next time I see Gracie I'll ask her." I did just that. Gracie, back in London from her home in Capri, was making her way to way to the Heathrow taxi rank when I explained the problem. "Ee lad, That's reet," she said, "It's a song of mine. Jump into t'taxi with me and I'll sing it to thee. I don't want to lose this cab."

And with the window wound down so that her driver, her porter and two passing policemen could listen in, she gave me a complete, highly musical rendering of "*Nellie's Hat,*" and several verses at that, as I sat in my front stalls seat. I jotted down the relevant chorus when she came to it and it scanned perfectly. But when I got home, I realised couldn't remember how the tune or the key changed at that point to accommodate the words, so the rendition was wasted on me.

Brenard Press picture

A rare shot of only two of the three harmonious Beverley Sisters, twins Teddy and Babs – or was it Babs and Teddy? And wherever was big sister Joy?

Some years later Eartha Kitt, one of my favourite entertainers, also sang me a solo verse or two as she waited to fly home to the US. after a highly successful tour here. "Someone came to my dressing room in London with this new song for me," she said. "It's called '*An Englishman Takes His Time*' and it's just perfect for me. I'm going to record it when I get home. But you can hear it first and tell me what you think...."

This time I was the audience for a premiere in an otherwise deserted departures lounge. I'm glad I was able to agree with her about the song. It became one of Eartha's best known hits.

That everlasting trio, the Beverley Sisters, still harmonising in the new millenium after nearly fifty years, would happily and very professionally launch into song at the least excuse. So I cannot claim any mesmeric power in persuading them to give me a brief run-through of some of the music they had prepared for an American tour as we sat in the relative privacy of the restaurant foyer at London Airport's old northside.

With the connivance of the restaurant manager, I frequently recommended this hideaway for departing personalities before they were called out to passport controls. My motives were mostly selfish; it meant avoiding onlookers and autograph hunters, and enabled my victims to relax and perhaps be more forthcoming.

It was from here that a very young but self-assured Julie Andrews first left for America with her parents Ted and Barbara, themselves former artistes, soon after her big London success in the musical "*Starlight Roof,*" at the ripe old age of 12. It was here too I met again the ever-delightful Petula Clark with her manager father Ted, who had guided her career from about the same tender age.

I chose the same hideaway for Nadia Gray, a former Romanian princess turned actress, to have some urgent fittings for her London role in the Mario Zampi film "*Top Secret.*" Nadia had planned to leave her home in Paris to fly to Canada on the very day she was being called to the studios for the costume fittings. She couldn't postpone the transatlantic trip, so asked if the dresser could meet her at London Airport. She appealed to me to find her somewhere relatively private where her dresser could take measurements. "Relatively private" to me also meant somewhere where my photographer could take some "action" pictures.

We were rewarded with a page lead and oversize picture in the *Daily Graphic* the next day. Nadia, who had only entered films at the instigation of her husband, Prince

Cantacazino, was already in Canada by the time the paper appeared. After two hours at London Airport, she had flown back to Paris still clutching her film script. Stopping only to pick up her packed bags, she left for Montreal immediately. A film publicity stunt? Almost certainly. But it worked, and it was a story. And very smartly, Leslie Frewin, publicist for the picture, didn't even put in an appearance.

None of us had any doubts that from time to time we were "used" unashamedly by film and show-business publicists, among others. But as long as the story they were trying to put across was true and credible, we were usually happy to go along. Newspapers didn't often see it like that. In those far-off days they felt, with some justification, that advertising should be paid for.

Theatrical agents were in many cases their own publicists. We had examples of occasions when, for the cost of an air ticket to Paris, potential stars of the future were able to get their pictures on the front pages of three London newspapers with a total readership of up to eight millions. The agents had discovered that any photo-worthy female client only had to appear in a departure lounge of London or Northolt airports at a reasonable time of day to stand a good chance of being picked out by roaming Brenards' photographers.

Among those who had already "made it" there were of course a number of stars who generated their own publicity, for themselves, for their latest picture, or both, though it's fair to say sometimes unwittingly, and sometimes to the initial horror of the studio bosses.

The girl who looks in on Page 8

FILM STAR NADIA PAYS LONDON PETER PAN CALL

Brenard Press picture

—And her business? Top Secret

By Daily Graphic Reporter

NADIA GRAY, Rumanian princess who turned film star, paid one of her briefest visits to London yesterday. So brief that London did not have time to see her. . . .

Two hours after arriving at London airport and without leaving the passenger building, red-haired Nadia was on her way back—still clutching a newly-typed film script.

The 100-page script was her part in the British film "Top Secret" and the reason for her brief visit—to be fitted for costumes for the film.

☆

Back in Paris at 9 p.m., Miss Gray boarded another plane for Canada.

She explained: "I had arranged to go to Canada and could not put that off, but the fittings were too urgent to miss."

Twenty-seven-year-old Miss Gray, who speaks six languages because she likes to be understood in the countries she visits, became a film star four years ago at the instigation of her husband, Prince Cantacazino.

Nadia came to Britain over two years ago to make one film—"The Spider and the Fly." It was such a success that other bookings quickly followed.

☆

During the war she lived in Bucharest under German occupation and claims to have been in a concentration camp for some time.

Her name? She decided that Gray (after Dorian) was the right name for a film career after reading Oscar Wilde.

Her dressmaker had top priority . . . and here is Nadia Gray being measured yesterday at London Airport for the clothes she will wear in the film "Top Secret." The fittings were urgent, and meant a busy two hours for Nadia.

Daily Graphic *April 14 1952*

In the late 'fifties, Victor Mature was known as the "Baron of Beefcake" after a string of movies as the bare-chested, all-action costume-drama hero. His visit to London was interesting to British fans because of his new romance with a 23-years-old English society girl who had been on location with him in North Africa. It became even more significant when, as I reported at the time, he stepped straight into a row with the producers of the film, a wartime story entitled "No time to Die."

As he and his companion, Miss Joy Urwick, of Knightsbridge, West London, cleared Customs at Heathrow he cheerfully informed me he'd given her a part in the film.

"Oh no he hasn't," said an official for Warwick Films who was at my shoulder to meet the couple at the barrier.

"Oh yes I have," rejoined Mature immaturely.

And he claimed that Miss Urwick had already made part of the scene on location in Tripoli. "It's a small part, but an important one," she told me proudly. And Mature chipped in to add: "It's only four lines at the moment. But by the time I've finished it will be four pages. I always get my way, even if I don't get any money for it."

The Warwick official drew me to one side. "I'm speaking for the producer, Irving

Allen," he told me. "You can take it from me Miss Urwick will not be in the picture. There is only one girl in the film, and that is not Miss Urwick."

Mr Mature heard this last remark. "I say she *will* have a part in the film," he retorted, "Allen is not the only producer. Cubby Broccoli is co-producing, and he's just as powerful as Mr Allen. He also says she will have a part."

After 'phoning Warwick Films myself to confirm the "official," and Irving Allen view, I filed the story for the three London evenings, and followed up with similar piece of two or three hundred words for the dailies. I was able to follow up with an "add" when Mature's co-star, Italian actress Luciana Paoluzzi flew in an hour or so later from Rome. She was magnanimous when I asked her about her potential rival.

"There is plenty of room for another woman in the film," she said, "I don't mind in the least if Miss Urwick appears." I was rewarded with a page lead in the London "*Star*" diary.

The *Daily Sketch*, successor to the *Daily Graphic*, followed up by calling on Mature in his London flat, but stuck with my story, adding just a few later quotes from Irving Allen. They gave it a full double-page spread with their own more informal oversize pictures.

Mr Mature insists

But his film bosses say it's 'No Joy'

STAR DIARY

VICTOR MATURE flew into London Airport today from North Africa with his London deb "discovery" Joy Urwick—and stepped into the centre of a storm with top officials of his film company.

The dispute rages around blonde Miss Urwick of Knightsbridge. Mature, starring in the wartime tank story No Time To Die, has promised her a part in the film.

But film company officials in London say emphatically: "There is only one girl in the film—and that is not Miss Urwick."

Retorted crimson-coated Mr Mature: "I say she will have a part in the film."

And Miss Urwick? "I have already made part of the scene on location in Tripoli," she said. "It's a small part but an important one."

Doesn't mind

Mature broke in: "It's only four lines at the moment, but by the time I've finished it will be four pages. I always get my way even if I don't get any more for it."

The company have six more weeks to make up their minds. That is the time allowed for the studio shots.

Mature also heard that his Italian co-star Luciana Paoluzzi had expressed her disappointment at Miss Urwick's part. He said: "She should not be so selfish. There is room for more than one girl in this picture."

But auburn-haired Miss Paoluzzi had changed her mind about Miss Urwick when she flew into London later today.

She explains

She said magnanimously: "There is plenty of room for other women in the film. I do not mind in the least if Miss Urwick appears."

About her earlier remark in Rome that she wanted Mr

The Star

I'll Get My Own Way...

VICTOR MATURE arrived at London Airport to-day from North Africa with his debutante "discovery" Joy Urwick — and stepped right into a storm between top officials of his film company.

Mature, starring in the war story "No Time To Die," with Italian star Luciana Paoluzzi, has promised Miss Urwick, of Knightsbridge a part in the film. But the film company says: "There is only one girl in the film and that is not Miss Urwick."

The company, Warwick Films, was quoting producer Irving Allen. Retorted crimson-coated Mr. Mature: "He is not the only producer. Cubby Broccoli is co-producing and his word is just as powerful as Mr. Allen's.

"I say she will have a part in the film and he says she will."

Mr. Mature added: "It's only four lines at the moment but by the time I've finished it it will be four pages. I always get my own way, even if I don't get any money for it."

Evening News (right)

Victor Mature is greeted at Heathrow

HOLLYWOOD actor Victor Mature flew into London today from Africa with Miss Joy Urwick, 23-year-old London ex-debutante. And he found himself in the middle of a row raging over Miss Urwick's blonde head.

Mature took her to Africa, where he is shooting scenes for the film No Time to Die, and promised her a part in the picture. But the film company in London, quoting producer Irving Allen, said: "There is only one girl in the film, and that is not Miss Urwick."

Retorted Mature today: "Allen is not the only producer. Cubby Broccoli is co-producing, and his word is just as powerful as Mr. Allen's.

"I say she will have a part in the film, and he says she will."

Four-line part

Miss Urwick has already made part of her scene on location in Tripoli. "It is a small part, but an important one," she said.

Mr. Mature broke in to add: "It is only four lines at the moment, but by the time I have finished it will be four pages. I always get my way, even if I don't get any money for it.

Star is magnanimous

Later the woman star of the picture arrived: the auburn-haired Italian Luciana Paoluzzi.

Miss Paoluzzi was magnanimous about Miss Urwick. "There is plenty of room for other women in the film," she said.

Last word from the film company officials who met Miss Paoluzzi: "You can take it from us. Miss Urwick will not be in the picture when it is finished."

Evening Standard (all cuttings) Oct 28 1957

'NO JOY (HIS EX-DEB FRIEND) IN THIS FILM' STARTS VIC MATURE ROW

Daily Graphic, October 29 1957

'I'll get a part for her, or else—'

Hardly any other paper used the story. They may have decided it was purely a publicity stunt. If Irving Allen, if his representative at the airport, if Miss Urwick or indeed Mr Mature had been convincing actors, I might have had my suspicions as well. But the studios bosses' horror that an actor would have the nerve to dictate to the producers was too genuine. In either event, it was still a good story.

And what did happen? Miss Urwick got her part, though I believe it was only a fleeting appearance. I have to assume she and Mr Mature were happy.

The Gabor sisters, particularly Zsa Zsa, who might be seen as a natural successor to Tallulah Bankhead in her outspokenness, were particularly successful self-publicists. Everyone knows of Zsa Zsa and Eva; how many of their admirers could name the films they have made? Of the eldest sister, Magda, little is known this side of the Atlantic, though in the US she appeared regularly as an actress in films and on television.

Over the years Zsa Zsa was the most frequent visitor of the three to Britain. In spite of a number of audiences with her (you didn't talk to Zsa Zsa, you listened) her personal appearances have perversely not featured in my own news cuttings. But inevitably her name had to come up either indirectly or indelicately in conversation with her sisters (to the undisguised pique of Eva) and with her mother, Mrs Joli Gabor.

"Why does everyone have to ask me about Zsa Zsa?" complained Eva to me on one occasion. "I'm Eva. Talk to me about me."

Was she perhaps being a little jealous of her sister? I ventured.

A flash of temper. "No, no. We are very close. But we do different things. No wants to know what I do. You only want to hear about Zsa Zsa. And she can look after herself."

With Magda I tried to be a little more subtle. I asked her what she thought of Englishmen (Zsa Zsa was at that time married to the Hollywood version of the archetypal Englishman. pipe-smoking, smooth-talking George Sanders).

"A perfect menace," was how she summed up what she had described as the "pipe-smoking Englishman, with his smooth ways, condescending manner and heavy flattery." And as the *Daily Herald* reported me, she contended: "The English can beat anyone at being wolves."

How did she know? "Personal experience," she replied, with a look that said: "Don't ask!"

Almost a year later, the aptly named Mrs Joli Gabor, was firmly denying to me rumours of a rift in the Zsa Zsa-Sanders union. She had been invited by Zsa Zsa to join her daughter in Deauville, and telephoned her from Heathrow when she changed 'planes on her flight from Mexico. "Divorce?" she repeated to my question, "Ridiculous. They are too much in love."

ZSA'S MOTHER CALLS HERE

When Mrs Jolie Gabor. Hungarian-born mother of the three lovely Gabor girls. flew in to London Airport today on her way from Mexico to France, she at once put in a telephone call to her favourite, Zsa Zsa, who is at Deauville and cabled her mother to go to her. (See Star Man's Diary.)

Zsa Zsa's Mother

THE mother of three well-known daughters called in at London Airport today on her way from Mexico to Deauville to see middle daughter Zsa Zsa Gabor.

The mother: Mrs Jolie Gabor, who eight years ago was a refugee from Hungary and is now one of the leading jewellers in the U.S. "I had a cable from Zsa Zsa so I hopped over," she said.

Of her three daughters, Magda, Zsa Zsa and Eva, Mrs Gabor had this to say: "Their success has made me proud. But I, too, am a success."

Brenard Press picture
The Star, August 22 1953
Mrs Jolie Gabor

The girl who cried 'wolf'

A PERFECT menace, that's what Magda Gabor thinks of the "pipe-smoking Englishman with his smooth ways, condescending manner and heavy flattery."

Miss Gabor, eldest of the three Hollywood sisters, contends that "as wolves the English beat anyone."

How does she know? "Personal experience," she said at London Airport yesterday before flying to America after a three-month holiday in Europe.

Miss Gabor—back home she's a T V and screen actress—added: "I'll take a Frenchman any time.

"But the English. I've learnt more about them on this trip than I ever thought possible."

In Miss Gabor's family there is a well-known pipe-smoking Englishman—actor George Sanders, who married Zsa Zsa the middle Gabor sister.

Brenard Press picture
Daily Herald
September 18 1952
Magda Gabor – the eldest sister.

Zsa-zsa loves George

AN attractive mother of three daughters arrived at London Airport yesterday after an almost non-stop flight from Mexico.

Immediately she put through a telephone call to her favourite daughter—Zsa-zsa Gabor, in Deauville.

Mrs. Jolie Gabor, eight years ago a near-penniless refugee from Hungary, is now one of the leading jewellers in the U.S.

. . . But No Divorce

Of rumours that Zsa-zsa, now filming in Paris, may soon be divorcing her English husband, George Sanders, Mrs. Gabor said:

"That is ridiculous. Separate, yes. But divorce, no never, they are too much in love."

"Zsa-zsa phones George every day. He phones her every other day. It is only being apart that makes them unhappy."

Mother denies Zsa Zsa divorce

Mrs. Jollie Gabor, passing through London...

Empire News (above), Sunday Chronicle (right) both Aug 23 1953

The Third Gabor

HUSH-HUSH visitor to London who slipped in from New York unannounced and today found herself grounded for another day by fog was Eva Gabor, youngest of the three Gabor Girls — the others are Zsa Zsa and Magda.

She came to discuss a stage play in the New Year. She drove to London Airport today to fly to Paris and joined hundreds of travellers in a waiting lounge when all flights were held up by thick fog. She waited for nearly two hours then cancelled her booking.

She had planned to buy evening gowns and cocktail dresses in Paris to join suits and coats she bought here.

It is her first visit to Britain since she appeared in London cabaret two years ago.

About that play: "I've decided I like the part," she said, "but I don't want to talk about it. I'm always very superstitious before everything has been signed."

Author's collection
December 19 1956
Eva Gabor

Then she added, with typical Gabor illogicality: "Separate, yes. Divorce never. Zsa Zsa 'phones George every day. He 'phones her every other day. It's only being apart makes them unhappy."

There was almost an echo of Eva when I asked Joli about the success of her daughters. "They have made me very proud," she said. Then she added quickly: "But I am a success, too."

However hard they try, there will always be those who just don't hit it off with the press. Sweden's Anita ("The Iceberg") Ekberg was one Scandinavian import who failed to impress anyone with anything but her blonde Viking looks. Except apparently Anthony Steel, another golden boy of British films.

When the couple, originators of the 'fifties phrase "just good friends," broke a joint appointment to open a new cocktail lounge in London's Piccadilly to fly instead to Stockholm, the press just had to believe they were eloping, however unlikely it seemed. The decision was so last-minute they couldn't even book seats on a direct flight, but had to change 'planes in Copenhagen. They checked in at London Airport only minutes before the flight closed.

"Are you eloping?" I asked Steel. "Definitely not," he insisted. And he added: "I'm going to spend a few days with Anita's family in Malmo."

Anita herself would only say: "If anything develops I'll let you know."

Of the broken appointment, nightclub owner Al Burnett was apparently too upset to talk. But his wife told me: "This has been quite a shock. It came as a complete surprise to us when we heard about their departure. We were with them both last night and neither of them said anything." Ironically Al, who was known to the gossip writers as a pretty good self-publicist as well, probably won more free advertising for his club by the absence of his guests of honour than if they'd been there to cut the tape. Pictures and stories in all the evenings and most of the dailies...perhaps he was a *very* good publicist.

'Just Good Friends' Fly Out From London

Anita and Anthony: Romance in the Air?

"Evening News" Reporter

BRITISH screen star Anthony Steel and Sweden's Anita ("The Iceberg") Ekberg dashed aboard a Scandinavian airliner at London Airport to-day after half denying a report that they intended to wed in Stockholm.

Steel, wearing a fur-lined leather jerkin and carrying another one on his arm, helped Miss Ekberg from the car which brought them to the airport only a few minutes before their airliner was due to take off.

As tall, slim Miss Ekberg, her hair in a bun, checked in at the ticket desk with their luggage, Steel said: "Definitely not," to the question: "Are you eloping?"

A FEW DAYS

With the Family

He added: "I'm going to spend a few days with Miss Ekberg's family before she flies back to Hollywood. We have been good friends for some weeks."

Twenty-four-year-old Anita — she was Miss Universe in 1951— and Anthony Steel—he is 37— were due to appear as host and hostess at the opening to-night of a new cocktail lounge in Piccadilly.

Mrs. Al Burnett, whose husband is opening the new bar, told me: "The news that they had gone to Copenhagen came as a complete surprise to us. I was with them both last night and neither said anything to me."

Miss Ekberg came to England in December to finish making her latest film, "Zarak Khan," in which she appears as a dancing girl, at Elstree Studios.

Anthony Steel began his career in repertory at Worthing and Aldershot at the end of the war.

He was in the escape film "The Wooden Horse." One of his latest films was "Drums Along the Nile."

Just over two years ago Mr. Steel's artist wife, Juanita Forbes, divorced him.

Evening News
Feb 15 1956

Daily Express picture

Some three months later the couple were married in Florence and soon afterwards they were on their way from Heathrow again to visit Anthony's new Swedish in-laws. They posed happily enough for photographers, then Anita decided I was a handy target for a bitter attack on the British press as a whole. For 15 minutes she harangued me about the way her wedding was received in Britain.

"I've never felt so angry in my life," she said, "In Britain our wedding was made a joke. I wouldn't have minded if I'd been married several times before. But it was my first wedding and something very sacred."

As I wrote, her husband broke in repeatedly to back up her remarks.

"My wife is very bitter about the way we have been received and treated in Britain, and rightly so," he said. "I only hope we get some peace and respect in Sweden."

In fact the London *Evening News* was the only paper to use this follow-up to the wedding, and even tucked it away in the diary column as just one item in a whole series of my contributions from the airport that day.

If Ekberg was the Iceberg, Marilyn Monroe was a hothouse flower, a child of the desert, exuding warmth and passion. Her talent for creating an image of genuine unaffected innocence, and her self-projected sensitivity was unique. I only met her once – at a hectic press conference on the completion of her film "*The Sleeping Prince*" (later re-titled "*The Prince and the Showgirl* ") with Sir Laurence Olivier, who was at London Airport to see her off.

Not for me this time the cosy one-to-one chat I preferred and was used to, but merely a typed, formal statement which Marilyn read out to the assembled throng. A stiff, diplomatic "thank-you" to the British public who had been "so warm." To my one question, about rumoured rows on set between her and her leading man, she would only say: "There were no more differences than usual in the making of a movie."

The occasion was more of a "photo opportunity" than a press conference. But Marilyn's undeniable appeal – the dreamer's eyes, the transluscent complexion, the sylph-like figure and her natural child-like exuberance – left me with a lasting impression which has never been equalled. I was not alone. Several hard-bitten Fleet Street reporters confessed later to having been just as bewitched, a rare experience in itself.

There have been several attempts over the years to emulate this Monroe magic, in the 'nineties, quite incredibly, by the pop-singer Madonna, and even in the 'fifties by contemporaries Jayne Mansfield in Hollywood and Diana Dors in London, who were each compared favourably but unrealistically with the "fairy goddess."

Jayne Mansfield's own death in 1967 was even more violent than that of Monroe when she was involved in a fatal road accident. In my own brief meeting with her she had told me excitedly in that little-girl breathlessness she tried to make her own, of the Hollywood bathroom she had just redecorated. As her muscle-man husband Mickey Hargitay alternately grinned and grunted beside her, she enthused over the "solid gold faucets and mink-lined walls and floor" she had installed.

If that was all I could get her to talk about, my colleague Chris Bramwell at Prestwick Airport later in the 'sixties, discovered that all she knew of Scotland was that the men there all wore "skirts." Diana Dors at least succeeded in breaking out of the blonde bombshell mode when a talent for acting was

Marilyn Monroe says goodbye...

MARILYN kisses Sir Laurence goodbye at London Airport. Vivien Leigh and Arthur Miller look on.

...TO SIR LARRY AND ALL

MARILYN MONROE, mink coated and smiling, said goodbye last night.

GOODBYE to Britain and to English food including Yorkshire pudding.

GOODBYE to Sir Laurence Olivier and Vivien Leigh who were at London Airport to see her off.

But before she went she denied that her making of the film "The Sleeping Prince" had been punctuated by rows with Sir Lawrence.

There had been no more differences than usual in the making of a movie, she said.

What had she bought in Britain? Well, there were woollens and sweaters and such—and an Oxford Dictionary about four inches thick. This was for her dramatist husband Arthur Miller who was with her.

Certainly they had an abundance of baggage, and before they flew out Mr. Miller had to pay £80 to cover their excess luggage.

Sir Laurence? He added his comment: "Miss Monroe was wonderful person," he said "She's been really poorly since she's been here, but I'd make a film with her again."

Extra police

Seventy-one extra policemen were drafted to the airport for the star's departure. "We don't want any trouble," said one "but we're prepared for the worst."

But the "worst" didn't happen. Miss Monroe's car drove in alosmt unnoticed. The star stepped out and went inside to face a V I P Press conference.

STAND-IN

★ Mystery girl who mingled with the fans and film company officials at the London Airport send-off for **MARILYN MONROE** was London-born actress **PEARL HANCOCK.**

Her appearance, 30 minutes before the arrival of Miss Monroe and her playwright husband, Mr. **ARTHUR MILLER**, set heads turning and prompted the question: "Who is she?"

The interest was under-

IN LONDON LAST NIGHT

standable. Miss Hancock—professional name Una Pearl—has been filming with Miss Monroe in The Sleeping Princess as her double and stand-in.

She was chosen from three auditions for the part, mainly because her hair and height are similar.

'Wonderful'

Said Miss Hancock: "It was wonderful working with Marilyn. She's a very warm person. Temperamental ?—I don't think so, though she was very nervous."

Miss Hancock, whose home is in Croydon, is training to be an opera singer. "But I have to earn my living while I'm studying," she explained.

Despite her wait at the airport, Miss Hancock, like the fans, was able only to glimpse Miss Monroe from a distance as she was hustled through the Customs.

Arrangements had been made to take the star from the Press conference room direct to the Customs Hall, dodging the crowd of sight-seers waiting in the airport lounge.

Daily Herald picture
Daily Herald (above)
Evening Standard (left)
(both) December 1956

Marilyn saying goodbye to her co-star Lawrence Olivier and his wife, Vivien Leigh, at the London Airport press conference.

Jayne Mansfield

A new HAIR-DO
ACCENT
COMPLEXION
and NAME

QUOTE . . .

. . . from 19-year-old British actress Jackie Collins, sister of film star Joan, at London Airport, yesterday, after a spell in Hollywood: "I haven't changed a bit. I'm as English as when I left these shores 11 months ago."

Jackie turned up with a new

JACKIE COLLINS
A CHANGE

hair-do, an accent, wore American-styled clothes, and a new name—Jackie Douglas.

Daily Express (top)
News Chronicle (above)
both Oct 10 1956
Jackie Collins, who soon discarded her 'new name'.

Brenard Press picture
Diana Dors home from US.

DIANA DORS HOME

DIANA DORS arrives back in Britain. At her side as she flew into London Airport from New York yesterday: 22-year-old piano-playing Peter Garlick.

Miss Dors has been appearing on American TV. Mr. Garlick? He has been a popular escort of debutantes this year.

Why? "I suppose they like me because I talk about music, art, and the theatre instead of horses," he says.

★

Garlick, who wants to be a concert pianist, sipped a gin at his home near Ascot, Berks, last night, and said: "Quite a jump from debs to film stars, isn't it?

"Diana and I have seen a lot of each other these past two weeks. I was on holiday in New York when she phoned me there.

"A romance? I must say no comment. I don't want to complicate things."

Daily Express summer 1957

Joan Collins - a 1950s studio portrait, and (above left) even more glamorous in the '80s
(both) Author's collection

eventually allowed to show through. For years her comings and goings through Heathrow, whether with her erstwhile husbands or with other escorts, were as frequent and eventful as those of Joan Collins, then a Rank starlet, and even her younger sister Jackie, who became a prolific author, were to become in the 'eighties. She finally won the respect and admiration of the British Press for her acting talents when she gave up trying to beg space in the tabloids with her wild life activities.

Mass hysteria at airports among showbiz star-gazers had its first blush in the 'fifties with the arrival of Frank Sinatra for his British stage debut. It peaked with Beatlemania in the 'sixties, but was still evident in the 'seventies and 'eighties, spotlighting the travels of pop singers and groups from David Cassidy to the Osmonds, the Bay City Rollers and others whose names have either faded from memory or passed into record-making history.

As a human phenomenon, such hero worship is of course much older. Rudolph Valentino broke a few hearts and stretched a few bra straps as bosoms heaved during his brief career in the 1920s. For all I know Helen of Troy may have launched a thousand shipbuilders. And how many snakes did Cleopatra charm before she aspirated finally for love of Mark Anthony?

When American "cry-crooner" Johnny Ray came to Town, as he did with almost annual regularity in the mid-'fifties, a season of mayhem for Heathrow was guaranteed. Scores of fans, some as ancient as eighteen, but most in their early teens or younger, invaded the passenger buildings days in advance of the expected arrival, alerted by the singer's fan club or by advance theatre publicity.

They were rarely advised of the actual date or time of arrival, quite deliberately, it was suggested unkindly, to ensure that they spent as long as possible at the airport drawing attention to the big event. Day by day the fans grew more impatient, and more frustrated. They honestly believed that everyone, from the press to the police, airline staff, Customs, indeed anyone who seemed likely to have any information, was conspiring to ensure they would miss their idol.

But they were determined to persist with their vigil. As I reported in my column for a local paper at the time, they told one airport worker who dared to ask why the fans waited so long:

"We don't mind coming as long as we're paid our five shillings a day. And we get double time on Sundays."

When I challenged the fans on this claim, they were in a rush to deny it. But one group finally claimed they were paid by a prominent London publicist. She herself ridiculed the idea. She certainly seemed to have little influence over the teenagers, who swarmed everywhere. Airport police, then part of the inexperienced Ministry of Civil Aviation constabulary, were untrained in crowd control and knew even less about dealing with juveniles. When one group "escaped" from the public enclosure above Terminal 2 over a parapet and on to adjoining roofs to make their way down to the strictly forbidden tarmac area, they were detained by Customs officers, only to be let off by police without even an admonition.

Years later a number of young fans were injured when part of that same parapet collapsed as they waited with hundreds of others in the roof gardens to see the Beatles. It was my day off. But that was one airport incident I wasn't sorry to miss.

Johnny Ray himself talked about this hysterical adulation in NewYork a few days after a London Palladium performance. I was visiting Manhattan as a guest of BOAC, a passenger on an inaugural transatlantic flight. With me at the time was Percy Banyard of the *Daily Telegraph,* the only non-Brenard reporter based at Heathrow. On his departure from London earlier that week the singer had invited us to look him up, and gave us his number to call. We 'phoned his calling service from our hotel soon after our arrival, and finally found ourselves at his apartment door.

Ray expressed what he called his reservations about the kind of emotions unleashed in impressionable adolescents by such hero worship. But like Liberace, laughing before him, he was honest enough to admit that he was continuing to cry all the way to the bank. Any conviction he might have carried was put further in doubt, however, by something else that occurred that evening.

As we chatted, Ray's live-in partner watched television on a large-screen colour receiver, the first I had ever seen. He called our attention to fellow singer Perry Como, whose live show was at that moment coming from Radio City, just a block away.

Como was apologising to his audience for the absence of a guest. "As you know," he said, "We had hoped to have Johnny Ray with us to-night. But we've learnt that he's indisposed. "I hope you'll join me in wishing him a quick recovery."

Ray sat staring at the screen, his face deadpan. He said nothing. And he seemed perfectly well to us. It was as though Perry Como was talking about someone else. But when, a few minutes later, American comedian and TV host Milton Berle and his wife called at the apartment to commiserate on his "indisposition," Ray explained with a grin: "It's my hearing aid. It's not working properly."

Milton Berle, the man Bob Hope once referred to as "the comedian's comedian," laughed. "Did it ever?" he asked, "How long have you got away with that one?"

Ray's response was from behind a cupped hand as he indicated an obvious concern about how Percy and I were reacting to his disclosure. All I caught was: "...it's served me for a long time. Might be time for a change."

Author's collection

(l to r) **Milton Berle, me, Johnny Ray, in Ray's Manhattan apartment, just a block from Radio City.**

We tried to keep the conversation open by asking Ray how bad his hearing was, but he quickly changed the subject by asking Berle to tell some amusing, if long-winded tale about a radio show. At the same time Ray's partner irritably turned up the volume of the TV, making it difficult for even us to hear anything else. Val (he preferred this short-form to 'Percy') later agreed with me that we had no story. The half-heard comment was ambiguous, so any revelation about the validity of Johnny Ray's hearing-aid trade mark would have been difficult to substantiate.

Thirty years on, during his last tour of Britain before his death, my wife Angela and I went back stage to say hello to Johnny Ray after watching him perform at the Beck

Knock Blue back on fur wrap

Elizabeth Taylor

Theatre in Hayes, west London. As a reminder, I took along a Polaroid snapshot Ray had himself taken during that visit to his apartment. He greeted first Angela, then me with a bear hug, but obviously didn't remember me, or my US visit. He was no longer wearing a visible hearing aid.

There are many show business stars who rarely need to manipulate the news media. They are news because their talent or their public, and sometimes both, have made them so. Elizabeth Taylor has been called the last and greatest surviving star of the Hollywood film industry. Since her childhood here she has regularly returned to visit Britain. Curiously my records show little evidence of her as a page filler in my reporter's notebook. However, she was always a target of the airport cameramen.

My abiding memory of Miss Taylor, whose marital state, like her career, spans more than fifty years (though not with the same devotion to singularity) has been her ability in either competing with or complementing the personality of her husband of the day.

Of Husband No.1, Conrad Hilton Jnr, I have no personal knowledge. But with Michael Wilding, who epitomised the upright, decent and well-bred Englishman, Miss Taylor was all charm itself. Mike Todd, the All-American showman, however, was a total contrast. He brought out a startling vulgarity in Elizabeth. They appeared to enjoy nothing so much as shocking by-standers with public slanging matches at the top of their voices.

On one occasion at Heathrow while waiting to board an aircraft, they appeared to be about to come to blows with Todd half-seriously calling her a "bitch" and Liz rejoining with "stupid bastard," both shouted across an otherwise deserted departure lounge, while still remaining on perfectly good terms.

Singer Eddie Fisher, husband of Elizabeth Taylor's best friend, Debbie Reynolds, left his wife for her after the sudden death of Todd. He was unashamedly dominated by his new partner, who adopted a matronly and school-marmish attitude to him in public. She would scold him like a child, as she did once when they left London to complaints by tradesmen that they hadn't settled their bills. Before repeating it out loud, Elizabeth clearly indicated to me behind Eddie's back that it was all his fault.

Richard Burton adjusted the balance again. And here Elizabeth competed and complemented simultaneously; to say they were a perfect match would be to understate a relationship which was both fire and water and thunder and lightning. They were two Roman candles which flared and burst out in sparkling profusion together, then flickered and glowed as one.

All the elements of Elizabeth's previous marriages seemed to be brought together in her union with Burton; the clash of two strong personalities, the barbed exchanges as well as the softness and tenderness, so like the inter-play between the screen characters they developed together. To have the courage to try to re-light the touch-paper after the glow had faded was to fuel a fiery passion a second time. Her marriages after the death of Burton never seemed to compensate her for the loss of what had gone before. But there is yet time...

A similar relationship to that of Burton and Taylor, embracing a healthy respect for each other's professional abilities, though perhaps at a calmer level, seemed to be the basis of an earlier cinema union, that between Charles Laughton and Elsa Lanchester. At one time, when meeting his wife at Heathrow, Laughton was asked by photographers to kiss her on the cheek.

"On the cheek, indeed!" snorted Laughton to me, "What sort of marriage do they think I have?" Whereupon he completely enveloped Elsa in his arms as he kissed her fully on

Angry Liz and Eddie fly out

UNPAID BILLS? RIDICULOUS

Express Staff Reporter

EDDIE FISHER and Elizabeth Taylor flew from London Airport yesterday still fuming about reports of their unpaid household bills.

The fact that they missed their plane to Paris by seconds—and had to wait two hours for the next flight—did not help.

"As far as we are concerned we know nothing about debts outstanding," said Eddie.

"The system in my country is that tradesmen send in their bills and a detailed list of things we've bought. We haven't had any bills."

Said Liz: "I always sign the household cheques myself. But I don't sign cheques for bills I have not received."

Back to Eddie: "The whole thing is quite ridiculous. Was I expected to go round to the milkman with my hand in my pocket and say, 'What do I owe you?' Anyway, our credit is good."

The Fishers flew to Paris, on their way home to America, with four-year-old Christopher and six-year-old Michael—the children of Miss Taylor's marriage to Michael Wilding.

Daily Express
November 11 1959

the lips. Trouble was, the cameras couldn't see either of them. Laughton and Lanchester had to do a re-take for a photographic peck … on the cheek.

The Laughton-Lanchester union lasted more than thirty years until Laughton's death. And there were and are, many similar "solid" marriages in showbusiness in spite of rumours to the contrary. Britain's Michael Denison and Dulcie Gray worked individually and together on stage and screen for a lifetime.

In more recent times, John Alderton and Pauline Collins have emulated their successful partnership. And of course there were the long-surviving, if challenged Redgraves, and the ever-loved Sir John Mills and his playwright wife Mary Hayley Bell.

Trevor Howard and his wife Helen Cherry first met when they co-starred in the stage play "The Recruiting Officer" after he was invalided out of the Army in the early 1940s. They were both already friends with the Denisons, who were already married, though Trevor and Helen's shared professional appearances were not to be as frequent. I met them as a married couple on a few occasions and was impressed by how well they seemed suited.

Trevor had the reputation of being something of a hell-raiser. He certainly loved to play to the gallery and more than once caused a few eyebrows to be raised at Heathrow when something upset him. But his impatience and apparent bad temper was, as far as I saw, only directed at the "system," and I never witnessed him being rude to anyone, however put out he was. Helen endured his whims with fortitude.

There was the time when he and Helen stepped from a flight, tired after a long journey and "Dying for a drink," only to find the bars closed. Trevor blew his top.

"Damn stupid country," he fumed, "When are they going to stop telling us how to run our lives?" Then, suddenly lifting his hold-all on to a table, he pulled out a bottle of Scotch, turned to me and said, "I want a drink, and I'm going to have one. If you want to join me, could you rustle up some glasses?"

In true wifely style, Helen protested with a not too convincing: "Oh, Trevor," but took a seat beside her husband. One of several photographers who had been busily but politely goading Trevor into grimacing for their lenses, had already hurried away to collect some paper cups from a dispenser, and in no time at all, Trevor was pouring out nips all round. He didn't stop there, but proceeded at the top of his voice to invite all and sundry in the busy airport lounge to join him, still protesting about "crazy licensing laws."

I don't believe anyone other than the press, who would never pass up a free drink, took up the invitation. They no doubt thought he was drunk and found the idea too embarrassing. Trevor wasn't drunk, of course. And I don't believe he was all that angry.

All-embracing

CHARLES LAUGHTON greeted his actress wife Elsa Lanchester with a real kiss when she flew into London today from New York to join him for a brief visit.

Photographers protested that they could not see the faces of either.

Laughton, in the best of humour, retorted vigorously: "I refuse to kiss my wife on the cheek. What kind of relationship do you think we have."

Miss Lanchester wore two coats, a black one on top of a rust-coloured one to match her hair—"It is to keep out the London fog."

She will visit her mother. "But don't ask me how long I am staying," she said. "I only made up my mind to come at the last minute after Charles had left."

She was last here five years ago.

The Star *May 1957*

Courtesy of Carl Van Vechten Estate
Charles Laughton

DULCIE GRAY FLIES HOME

Actor Michael Denison greets his wife, actress Dulcie Gray, as she arrives at London Airport today from Australia. Their work has kept them apart for the last six months. Miss Gray has been touring in South Sea Bubble.

The couple will have only six weeks together before Miss Gray leaves for South Africa to continue the tour. Mr. Denison has television commitments in London.

Brenard Press picture
Evening Standard
February 27 1957

Elsa Lanchester in costume as Madame d'Annard in the 1935 production "Naughty Marietta".

Helen, as ever, took it all in her stride. Just as she did when, on another occasion he asked me to 'phone her and warn her he was leaving England for good.

I had come across the actor sitting morosely in a bar in the departure lounge at Heathrow late one evening. His transatlantic flight was delayed. He invited me to join him for a drink, but would only confirm he was on his way to Hollywood, not tell me why he was going.

Not anxious to press the point, actors often being superstitious about offered roles until they've signed a contract, I continued cautiously. "I can understand it if you don't want to talk about some new film part you're being offered, Trevor," (he was one of the few actors ever to invite me to call him by his first name), "But I have to say something about your trip. Can I at least say you're going to discuss a new film? And will you give me some idea of how long you'll be away? Perhaps you'll be able to say more when you return....?"

But he wouldn't be pressurised. For the next few minutes he teased around the subject, never giving me a straight answer when I tried to steer him back. Then suddenly he announced: "Oh, to hell with it. Tell 'em I'm going, and I won't be back. Tell 'em I'm off for good. I've had enough." And at that moment his flight was called.

Trevor wasn't going to be rushed, but picking up his bag, he slowly made his way across to the exit ramp. I walked at his side and, as I scribbled furiously, he warmed to his theme. "And you can tell them that as much as I like working in England there just hasn't been enough to keep me busy. In the US I have hundreds of friends and contacts and there are several offers open to me. My visa allows me to stay for two years...and I know it can be extended."

Some months earlier there had been rumours of a problem with his tax payments. "Will the Chancellor of the Exchequer be upset if you leave now?" I asked innocently. Replied Trevor: "I'm sure he'll be interested to hear that I don't expect to be back.."

At last I looked up from my notebook. Trevor was finishing the drink he still carried. He placed the empty glass on a table. Then he turned back to me, a half-smile on his face. I began to be worried. "Are you sure about all this?" I asked. "It's going to cause one hellava'n upset." I waited for his reply. I certainly didn't want him to change his mind now. But he stuck to his guns.

"I've said it. Go print it. But..." a sudden thought, "...you'd better give Helen a ring and warn her. I don't want her taken unawares when the 'phone calls start. No need to go into any detail. Just tell her what I've said. Tell her I'll call her." He quickly scribbled his 'phone number down on the top of my pad. Then he was off to board his 'plane, turning just to give me a brief salute.

To say I had my doubts about the story would be putting it mildly. Trevor had said it. He might have meant it. But I wasn't convinced. It was obviously said on impulse, or Helen wouldn't have to be "warned." Unless of course she did know and they'd agreed he wouldn't say anything about the plan.

Did it matter what I thought? I decided it didn't. I would only be quoting his words, and he hadn't given me time to question him. But I would reserve final judgement until I'd spoken to Helen. At least if she didn't buy the story, I could quote her comments.

When she answered my call she sounded sleepy. I apologised though it was still early in the evening. I gave her the message from Trevor, but I didn't voice my suspicions. "He said he'll call you to explain," I added, a little lamely.

"Thank you for letting me know," said Helen, as if I'd just called her to say her husband was working late at the office. "Did he leave a number?" The next day was Sunday.

Trevor Howard For U.S.—'Not Coming Back'

***Sunday Dispatch* February 2 1955**

...ran the Page One two-column headline in the *Sunday Dispatch* .....

Now Trevor Howard's off —for good

Sunday Pictorial Feb 2 1955

...said the tabloid *Sunday Pictorial.*

Twelve days later the *Daily Express* films writer David Lewin reported that Trevor hadn't meant it that way. And he was planning to return from the film capital.

Sure enough, within twelve hours he was stepping from a plane on to the Heathrow tarmac, only to run a gauntlet of photographers. "No, and be damned," he shouted at them when they asked him to pose by the aircraft. And he hurried into the terminal, screening his face with a huge envelope. I met him at the Customs barrier and hustled him, protectively and possessively, to the darkness of a nearby bar.

TREVOR HOWARD IS COMING BACK

by DAVID LEWIN

TREVOR HOWARD, the film star, is flying back to London from Hollywood on Thursday, just 12 days after he left London Airport saying he would not be returning.

On that night, when he suddenly took a plane to California, he said: "I'm not coming back. Much as I like working at home, there is not enough to keep me going here."

But now, it turns out, that is not quite what he meant. For Trevor Howard went to Hollywood to discuss a starring part in a film about the Royal Marine Commandos, called "The Cockleshell Heroes," which is to be made in London in the spring.

WIFE *Helen Cherry*

HUSBAND *Trevor Howard*

Daily Express Feb 17 1955
(David Lewin report)

Three weeks later, David Lewin, the *Daily Express* film critic filed this report of his own.

Thrusting a gin and tonic into his hand, I hung on every word as questions were thrown at him by Fleet Street reporters dispatched to the airport to cover his ignominious homecoming and perhaps uncover the truth of his about-turn. Was he denying that he ever intended to leave? What did he say that had been misunderstood? All the questions I would have been asking myself if I didn't know or couldn't have guessed the answers.

But I held my tongue, wondering if Trevor was about to deny the whole thing. Would he say he'd made it all up simply because he wouldn't give me a story? Or that I had – for the same reason? Without even a glance at me, Trevor parried every probe. Hamming up the scene for all it was worth, his response to most questions was simply a dismissive gesture, implying they were unworthy of response.

The *Daily Sketch* gave it the best spread the next day with a giant close-up of an anxious looking Trevor Howard at the bar, g & t glass at his lips, with a second picture of him entering the terminal with his face screened. *Sketch* reporter Alison Sutherland played the story straight, quoting his limited comments, just as I noted them: "No, I've not come back because of the income-tax merchants. I'm paid up. Me paid up! Does that surprise you? No, Helen knew I was returning. She's no fool."

And what about the Chancellor of the Exchequer? "Don't bring that up against me. I was joking..."

So he didn't try to back out or put the blame on me. If he'd been at all embarrassed, he didn't show it. Neither did he give the slightest indication that he and I had met before. So I felt I could forgive him for implying that I might be more foolish than Helen for believing him in the first place. But he and Helen did have a slightly different recollection of the incident, according to a biography of Trevor published in 1986.

Helen's reaction to my news that her husband was leaving was to ask if she could rely on that. Trevor, it was claimed, enjoyed teasing the Press, who would have found the truth dull. He was, after all, only going to Hollywood to discuss the offer of a part in the war film "Cockleshell Heroes."

Which was where I came in…

*

In the opening italicised paragraphs of this chapter, I left a certain Miss Jane Russell reeling from a question as she waited to go aboard her TWA airliner to fly back to Hollywood.

Two weeks before that encounter, on her arrival in London, Miss Russell had announced that she and her husband, American footballer Bob Waterfield, were seeking to adopt a second baby as a brother for their adopted daughter. And they were looking to European orphanages to help them. British newspapers weren't overly impressed. The story had the familiar ring of a Hollywood publicity stunt, and perhaps a distasteful one. Apart from a paragraph here and there, or a caption to a more acceptable photograph of her arrival, the mission received little attention.

Co-incidentally, it fell to me on each occasion to pursue the theme, with little linage success as the intending parent slipped out on hurried sorties to Germany and Holland

TREVOR OF NO RETURN IS BACK

By ALISON SUTHERLAND

FILM star Trevor Howard, who said he was "going for good" when he left Britain 12 days ago, jumped down from a plane at London Airport yesterday and went into hiding—behind that outsize envelope, right.

"No and be damned," he shouted to photographers who asked him to pose beside the plane.

Off he went for a drink, carrying his envelope. Inside it was his new film script.

One gin and tonic later—see above—the 5ft. 11in. ex-paratrooper captain who captivated screen audiences in Brief Encounter, dropped the temperament.

"No, I've not come back because of the income-tax merchants," he insisted, unbuttoning his camel-hair greatcoat. "I'm paid up. Me, paid up! Does that surprise you?"

'SHE'S NO FOOL'

Did he come back because of the wife he left behind—Helen Cherry, of TV fame? He wouldn't say. "Well, Helen is no fool," he grinned. She knew he was returning and would probably be waiting at their home, Rowley Green, Arkley, near Barnet.

I reminded him of what he said when he left for Hollywood—"I don't doubt that the Chancellor of the Exchequer will be pleased to learn that I won't be back."

"Don't bring that up against me," he begged, grasping my hand. "It was just a joke."

Daily Sketch's own report

Daily Sketch reporter Alison Sutherland apparently asked all the right questions as I stood at Trevor Howard's side on his return to London. But he didn't let me down by denying a thing.

over the next few days. The only thing that would revive newspaper interest would be positive news that some fortunate child (or unfortunate, depending on one's viewpoint) had been selected. When the day came for her planned return to the States, the Jane Russell "adoption" story was no more. The mission, it seemed, had failed.

I was about to start a late evening shift with photographer Tony Hewson and my predecessor as chief reporter, Ray Watts. We were sharing out the evening's likely duties between us, and agreed to toss for the pleasure of seeing Miss Russell.

I lost.... so it was down to me yet again to salvage something from the story. Possibly, I mused, I could get her to admit that the whole idea of the adoption was a stunt… publicity for her latest picture? No that was unlikely, but even a forceful denial might make a paragraph or two. Impatiently, I waited near the high-fronted counter which served as the Trans World Airlines check-in desk. This was 1951, when flights to and from Heathrow still used the single-storey northside terminal opposite the Bath-road.

TWA Receptionist Margaret Rowlands was the solitary figure on duty at the American airline's desk to greet Miss Russell in November 1951.

Both pictures, Author's collection

The airline check-in desks in London Airport's original "Northside" long-haul departures (circa 1950). At the far end, alongside the half-obscured indicator to "Customs and Departures" was the desk of Trans World Airlines, where Hollywood star Jane Russell was to check-in for her flight home.

A handful of passengers were checking-in for the one remaining transatlantic departure. As they moved away, I took advantage of a lull to pass the time of day with Margaret Rowlands, the one receptionist at the desk, her small frame almost hidden behind it. In front of her was a column of names and initials, and all the excessive personal detail which in those days illuminated every passenger list. I quickly eye-scanned the inverted list. The name I was looking for was easily spotted. Heading the list was "Miss Russell, Jane."

A tap on the shoulder and I swung round to find a TWA senior management official, looking furtive. With the air of a conspirator, he leaned forward and whispered in my ear: "Don't ask me any questions. Just ask Jane Russell about Tommy Kavanagh..." He turned away... and was gone, not to appear again that evening.

I said something inconsequential to Margaret, and quickly scanned the remaining entries. And there, added at the end of the teleprinted list was one handwritten name; "Kavanagh, Thomas." Alongside it was the symbol "INF," for a passenger under five years of age. And in the final column was the passenger ticket number, some five or six figures ending with "...611."

All this I absorbed in a matter of seconds as I chatted to Margaret, thanks perhaps to my familiarity with inverted "hot lead," the metal slugs of reversed type-face on a printer's stone. My eyes switched back to the top of the list. Alongside the name of Jane Russell was the consecutive number ending "...610."

The sequence of allocated numbers could have been co-incidence. But that would mean that Tommy was travelling with another passenger with a totally unrelated reservation number. Or he was unaccompanied; even more unlikely, and there was no "u/m" for "unaccompanied minor" against his name. There appeared to be no listing for ticket "...612."

Within minutes the film star herself swept into the terminal, briefly reporting to the desk as each item of her baggage was weighed. I moved out of the way, and stood by as RKO Pictures publicist David Jones and other film company officials bid her goodbye at the Customs door adjoining the airline desk. For a few minutes I waited to see the mysterious "Tommy" arrive, but to delay too long could mean missing the actress in the final departures lounge, as she might be boarding early.

I had already briefed Tony and Ray Watts, aware that I would need back-up. Now, with a wave to Tony to say, "I'm going through," I hurried across the Customs hall to the departures lounge. As "resident" Press at Heathrow we were permitted into the controlled departure areas to which only passengers and essential staff normally had access. It was the one advantage we had over visiting reporters and photographers from Fleet Street, and gave us the additional facility of joining passengers while they relaxed before boarding.

Brenard Press picture
The late Ray Watts, Brenards' chief reporter for more than 25 years, seen here working from his favourite "office" in Heathrow's Terminal 3.

Now, as I faced Jane Russell, awaiting an answer, a TWA hostess began opening and securing the doors which led out to the tarmac. It was now or never. I asked my question. I had to repeat it:

"Tommy... Thomas Kavanagh, Miss Russell," I persisted, "How old is he?"

The actress was aghast. Her face fell, the smile vanished. There was a look of horror, fury and anxiety as she struggled to find words.

"How did you...? You mustn't... he's only a baby," she stammered. "You must leave him alone. You can't say anything about this."

She was not pleading... but telling me. As if to emphasise her words, her grip tightened on the umbrella as she raised it menacingly. Then came abuse, threats. She was deaf to anything I said as I tried to reason with her. I pointed out that she could never have kept such a secret, that even if she wasn't spotted at New York airport with Tommy, the news would leak out from Hollywood. I reminded her of the number of times she had talked about adoption, and I argued that I was giving her the opportunity to put everything into perspective... she would only make a bigger mystery by refusing to confirm the obvious.

All this, and my questions about Tommy, who he was, how she had found him, who his parents were, all were ignored and rejected. Relief came for her in the shape of a hostess who stepped in to lead the way, just ahead of the other passengers, to the aircraft, a mere 200 yards away. I walked at her shoulder for some yards, still pressing for answers. She relented only to the extent of finally saying: "All right. Tommy is going with me, but only for a visit. You must emphasise that..." Now she was pleading: "I swear I'm not adopting him. Be sure not to say that I am..."

She stopped at the aircraft steps just long enough to pose for Tony, who had been hovering nearby, flashing the standard Hollywood smile and momentarily switching off her anxiety. I returned quickly to the lounge as Tony followed discreetly at a distance.

Several minutes went by, but eventually, as passengers began to file out, a slight figure in a belted green coat, her hair hidden under a woollen headscarf, appeared from the passport control area, carrying a small, wide-eyed baby boy. Casually I moved towards her, then, as if an interested bystander, I spoke to the woman.

"That's a bonny lad," I said, reaching out and taking his hand. "What's his name?" She replied that it was "Tommy," and when I spoke to him, volunteered that he was fifteen months old. She spoke unselfconsciously in a soft Irish brogue, and seemed pleased that someone was prepared to talk to her. She appeared to be feeling out of place among all the fur coats and finery of the transatlantic travellers as she paced the thick carpets in her down-trodden shoes, apparently waiting for someone to come for her.

Carefully I tried to draw her out, but the questions became too personal, too obvious. Suddenly she suspected this was not a stranger's casual interest. I quickly introduced myself and told her I had spoken to Jane Russell, who had confirmed she was taking Tommy to America on a visit. But Mrs Kavanagh was not prepared to listen; it was as though she believed she had been deceived. Nothing I could say would draw another word from her.

When I tried to regain her confidence, she repeatedly turned her back on me, forcing the little boy's head to swivel as he watched me innocently. But now the tears were welling in her eyes. I apologised and left her. I could do no more without upsetting her further and inviting the attention of other passengers. One or two were already curious about someone

Brenard Press picture

After her outraged protests, Jane Russell flashes a disciplined familiar smile for Tony at her aircraft steps, blissfully unaware that a few minutes later he would also be capturing her future adoptee son on film.

who had switched suddenly from talking to a glamourous film star to an apparent nobody, neither of whom seemed to relish his attention!

Moving back to an adjoining ante-room at the entrance to the lounge I found Tony standing by for information. He had deliberately kept his distance, while keeping an eye on the situation. A hurried consultation and we agreed that the only way he was likely to get a picture of Tommy was to "snatch" it. He could always try for a posed shot afterwards. Ray Watts had joined us, and he and I together sauntered back to the lounge, shoulder to shoulder, with the shorter figure of Tony behind us.

Four yards from our target, Wattie and I stepped aside, he to the left, I to the right. Up came Tony's Speed Graphic camera. There was a blinding flash of his Sasha gun, and the picture of Mrs Florence Kavanagh and baby Tommy which in a few hours was to appear on the front page of every national newspaper in Britain and round the world, was in the can.

It was too much for Mrs Kavanagh's peace of mind. Blindly, she dashed for the door. Sympathetic airline staff stepped in to help. A car was rustled up from nowhere and she and Tommy were bundled in. Tony had slipped out and rushed to the 'plane ahead of them, changing slides as he ran. More pictures on the steps as Mrs Kavanagh hurried aboard to hand Tommy into the care of his benefactor...

Only now did Tony abandon the scene, his attempt to picture Jane Russell and Tommy together on board thwarted by the airliner's cabin crew when he was only a few feet from his goal, his last slide exposed. Not for him the automatic multi-exposure of present day motor-driven cameras. The number of pictures a photographer could get depended entirely on the size and number of his pockets to hold the 7x5-inch slide sheet-film holders, each of which weighed a quarter of a pound. Before he returned to the building, I was already on the telephone, dictating an introductory story "cold" from my brief notes.

JANE RUSSELL FLIES HOME WITH A BABY BOY FROM BATTERSEA . .

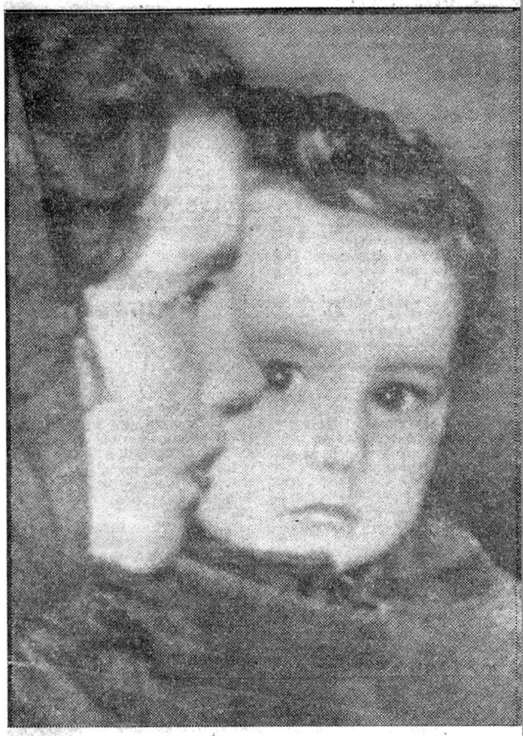

THOMAS KAVANAGH, 15 MONTHS OLD, WITH HIS MOTHER
She stood on the tarmac, red-eyed, as he left.

Brenard Press picture

Mrs Florence Kavanagh, who offered her son Tommy to Jane Russell for adoption, moved quickly away when she saw Tony raise his camera, unwittingly turning the toddler's face towards the lens.

Then I joined Wattie as he tried to pump airline staff for snippets of additional information. Jane Russell's film company representatives seemed resigned to the discovery that their subterfuge, carefully prepared at a preliminary meeting between them and Mrs Kavanagh at the Savoy Hotel before driving to the airport, had been to little avail. Their plan, to keep the mother and her baby apart from the film star until the plane's departure, was poorly conceived. We would have learnt the truth as soon as we began making enquiries about the shabbily dressed lonely woman in the departure lounge, who stood out so obviously from the crowd.

My TWA contact never once referred to the story, though I talked to him often in the following months. So I deliberately let the matter rest, deciding that was what he wanted. In a way I understood. He and Jane Russell worked for the same man, the fabulously wealthy, eccentric and reclusive Howard Hughes, who owned both RKO Pictures and TWA.

Almost before Mrs Kavanagh, had been safely returned to her tiny home in London's Lambeth, now sobbing desperately over the child she had given up, the national newspapers were on the streets. all telling the front-page story. Shortly afterwards, newspapers in New York and California, and American wire services, alerted by my transatlantic flashes, were picking up the trail as Jane Russell and Tommy, now openly together, tried to change planes to fly on to Hollywood.

Miss Russell later told of her arrival in New York, where, she said the news had preceded her by about eight hours. She told of a horde of television camera crews and photographers awaiting her as they shouted and fought to get pictures and a story.

There was not a mention of my earlier role. Just a passing reference to a Heathrow photographer. And for me it was the close of a chapter anyway. For news at Heathrow is as transient as the traveller, and I was not likely to have a direct concern with the story again.

For the news media, politicians and lawyers, it was by no means over. Day after day the story grew as Hollywood correspondents and gossip writer sought news of baby Thomas's new life. In London, other newspapers slowly but surely broke down resistance by the Kavanaghs as they pictured the family's terraced home and their two other children.

Questions were asked in the House of Commons about a possible breach of the law.

LONDON BABY GOES WITH JANE RUSSELL

JANE RUSSELL, the Hollywood film star, left London Airport last night for New York with a London baby. Miss Russell arrived at the airport with her mother by one route. The baby, Thomas Kavanagh, fifteen months, arrived by another route with his mother, whose home is in Battersea.

At first Miss Russell denied that the baby was travelling with her.

But as she walked across the tarmac to the plane she said: "Thomas is going with me, but only for a visit. You must emphasise that. I swear that I am not adopting him."

Mrs. Kavanagh went to the aircraft with Thomas to say goodbye.

An official of R.K.O. Radio Pictures said: "The baby is officially going for a three months' holiday. I can tell you no more. But Miss Russell is hoping that her husband, Bob Waterfield, will get to like the baby as much as she does. I cannot say that the baby will be adopted."

Adopted a Girl

When Miss Russell arrived in Britain for the Royal Film Performance she said that she was seeking to adopt another child.

She has already adopted a four-month-old girl.

She saw three children in Italy and also made inquiries in Ireland before continuing her search in Britain.

Daily Mirror

Mother goes to plane

Express Staff Reporter

JANE RUSSELL of Hollywood, who searched Europe for a second baby to adopt, flew out of London last night bound for America with a 15-month-old Battersea boy called Thomas Kavanagh.

Daily Express (left)

News Chronicle (below)

Baby flies with Jane Russell

THOMAS KAVANAGH flew from London to Hollywood last night.

Thomas Kavanagh is from Battersea, S.W. He is 15 months old. And above he is seen in the arms of his mother.

Boarding the same plane (as you see above) was Jane Russell, the film actress who has been seeking a baby boy to adopt. She has already an adopted girl, Tracey, aged four months.

Thomas Kavanagh is fair and curly haired.

Miss Russell came to the airport with her mother and film studio officials. Thomas and his mother came separately.

Going towards her plane Miss Russell said: "Thomas is going with me, but only for a visit. I am not adopting him."

Thomas Kavanagh's mother went on the plane to say goodbye. She watched the plane depart. She had a cup of tea. And she went back, without saying a word, to Battersea.

There were tears from the women concerned . . . but a spokesman of R.K.O. Pictures sized up the situation like this: "The baby is going for a three months holiday. Miss Russell is hoping that her husband will get to like the baby as much as she does."

The star who smiled: Jane Russell at the airport last night.

JANE FLIES HOME WITH A BABY

SCREEN star Jane Russell, who said recently she wanted to adopt a baby, flew from London Airport with one last night.

The baby was curly-haired, 15-month-old Thomas Kavanagh, from London, and he was "smuggled" out to the plane to avoid sightseers.

Miss Russell, who is bound for her Hollywood home, drove to the airport with her mother and officials of her film studio.

The baby, whose passage was booked only three hours before the take-off, arrived by another route with his mother, a small, dark-haired woman whose home is at Battersea, S.W.

Brenard Press picture

Daily Graphic

BABY GOES WITH JANE RUSSELL

Jane Russell, the film actress, left London Airport last night for Hollywood, taking with her a 15-month-old fair-headed Battersea baby, Thomas Kavanagh. He was smuggled to the plane to avoid sightseers. His mother, in a lime green coat and head scarf, went aboard to say goodbye.

Miss Russell, who was accompanied by her mother, said: "Thomas is going with me, but only for a visit."

An official of R.K.O. Radio Pictures, Miss Russell's studios, said: "The baby is officially going for a three months' holiday. I cannot say whether he will eventually be adopted." Miss Russell, wife of Bob Waterfield, an American footballer, has already adopted a baby girl, Tracy, aged four months.

Daily Telegraph

Calm before the tears

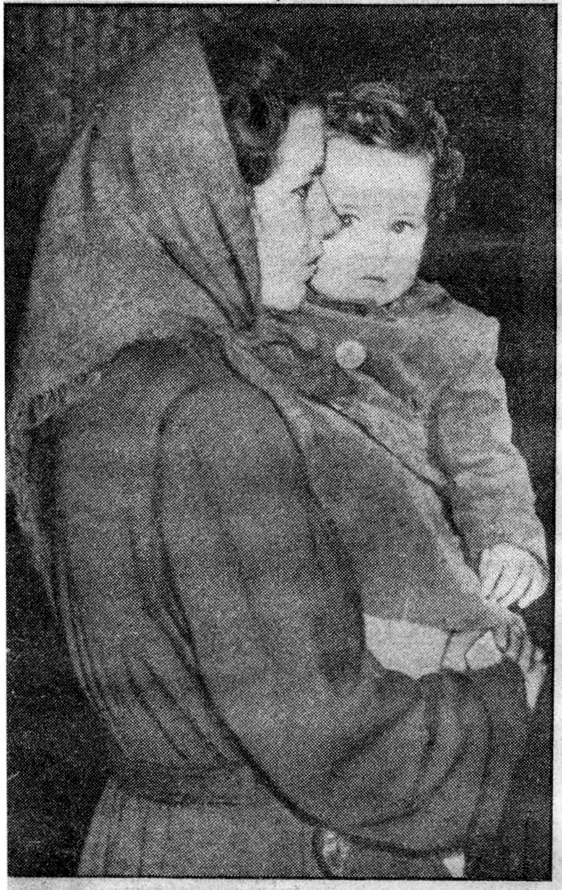

BABY TOMMY AND HIS MOTHER

He cried when he left her.

Brenard Press picture

Jane Russell takes London baby to U.S.

HERALD REPORTER

FILM star Jane Russell flew back to Hollywood from London last night, taking with her a 15-month-old, fair-haired baby "just for a visit."

Said Jane, who has already adopted a four-month-old girl: "I swear I am not adopting him—on my honour."

She had driven to the airport with her mother and studio executives.

The baby, blue-eyed Thomas Kavanagh and his small, dark-haired mother came from Battersea by another route.

Thomas was smuggled out to the plane to avoid the sightseers. His mother, in a lime green coat and headscarf, went aboard the plane to say goodbye to him.

'Held up by red tape'

At first Miss Russell said: "I am still planning to take home a German boy. But regulations and red tape have held me up. I shall have to write to the United States authorities again."

As she walked to the plane she said: "You must emphasise that Thomas is going only for a visit."

A close friend of Miss Russell's family said: "Officially, the baby is going for a short stay. If the United States immigration authorities thought she was adopting him there would be trouble. It would take months through the usual channels."

Baby Thomas, in a brown corduroy coat and bootees, took it all calmly—until the goodbye. Then he cried. Mrs. Kavanagh sobbed, too.

Star was sad, too

An airline official told me that Miss Russell "murmured something about not being able to part him from his mother."

But the airliner took off with Jane and baby, leaving Mrs. Kavanagh a lonely figure on the tarmac.

She had a cup of tea, then went home.

Star Jane Russell takes baby

Daily Graphic (above)

Daily Herald (left)

(all) November 7 1951

Miss Russell Takes a Baby Back to U.S.

THOMAS CAVANAGH LEAVES BATTERSEA

By Daily Mail Reporter

MISS JANE RUSSELL, the film star, who said last week that she wanted to adopt a boy, left London last night with 15-month-old Thomas Cavanagh, of Battersea.

Earlier Thomas' parents had visited London's American Embassy and signed a document. Mrs. Cavanagh was at the

Daily Mail

Newspapers called in feature writers to look into the whole business of international adoption procedures. Editorial opinion discussed the moral issues of parents giving away children, and, of course, once again cartoonists and radio comedians had a field day. (Low of the *Evening Standard*, for example, substituted Winston Churchill for Mrs Kavanagh, and a fur-coated Miss Russell appeared as "Washington." The baby being thrust into Washington's hands was labelled "British financial pickle.")

Cartoon by Low. By kind permission of Express Newspapers Ltd. ©All countries

"Take the baby? Who do you think I am – Jane Russell?"
(Vic Oliver at baby show in "Oliver Again")

"...All the men dressing up in schoolboy caps and blazers. They heard Jane Russell was adopting!"
(Ted Ray in "Ray's a Laugh")

"Jane Russell's worried. They made a mistake at London Airport - she got wee Georgie Wood!"
(Ted Ray in "Ray's a Laugh")

"You're acting like a fifteen-month-old child!"
"I know. I want to be adopted by Jane Russell too!"
(Derek Roy's "Happy-go-lucky")

...and from a cartoon featuring two squaddies passing a huge "frontal" poster of the film star: "Oo look - Jane Russell, the girl with the... er ...adopted baby."

(BBC Radio programmes, Nov 1951)
Extracts from comedians' scripted comments on my Jane Russell exclusive.

Scotland Yard interviewed the Kavanaghs at length, and eventually they were summonsed under the Adoption Act. In America, too, there was uproar when it was revealed that Tommy had been issued with immigration papers at the US Embassy in London, not the usual three-months' visitor's visa. There was even talk of an "international incident."

In April 1952, five months later, Mrs Florence Kavanagh and her husband appeared at Bow Street Magistrates Court in London, charged with permitting the care of a child to be transferred to a person not a British subject. They were given a conditional discharge. At the same time, from Hollywood came the news that Jane Russell and her husband were arranging formally to adopt Thomas.

Eventually interest in Tommy and his prospects waned. Little more was heard of him other than the occasional "progress" photograph with his new parents whenever they were seen in public together. In the late 'sixties Jane Russell's "ideal marriage" to Bob Waterfield broke up. The baby from Lambeth, now Tommy Waterfield, was pictured again, leading his own pop group.

Now his real mother, photographed with Tommy's elder brother and sister, and, ironically, a younger daughter born a year after Tommy's flight, was quoted as saying; "I don't really know why we let him go." Mother and son were briefly re-united in 1968 when he flew with Jane to London to visit her.

I met up with Jane Russell just twice more. In the late 'fifties she performed a classic double-take as our eyes met in an arrival lounge at Heathrow, so I had to say with a grin, if only to break the ice: "I hope you've forgiven me, Miss Russell."

She snapped back: "No, I have not." But then she flashed that familiar smile. "But it's a long time...." In no time at all she was telling me all about Tommy, his schooling, his music, just as any proud parent might. But a year later, in 1959, I was with a colleague in that original departures lounge when we met yet again. She greeted me with the words: "Ah, my old enemy!"

On January 11, 1980, it was reported that Mrs Florence Kavanagh had been found dead after a fire in a bed-sitter in Clapham, London. An investigation by Scotland Yard established that she had died of asphyxiation, and that her death was being treated as suspected murder.

The investigation was however later dropped and at an inquest, a verdict of accidental death was recorded. Florence Kavanagh's marriage had broken down and she was living alone. Her son Tommy, now in his late forties, was reported to be still recovering from drink and drugs addiction in the US. He has three children of his own.

Although like others of her generation, she was later re-discovered through the revival of her films on TV, the name of Jane Russell now belongs to Hollywood history. For me the Tommy Kavanagh story was one of my most satisfying, a scoop which saw not only world-wide coverage on the day, but also had its echoes for months, even years later, in newspaper stories and pictures. The impact the event itself had on moral and legal arguments on child adoption procedures was substantial.

Brenard Press picture

"No, I haven't forgiven you. But it's a long time..." (Jane and me seven years after she left with Tommy).

Few other encounters I had with film stars have been quite so dramatic. Neither have they been so rewarding or productive in column inches. Some, like my interview with Marlon Brando, in professional terms simply never happened.

There was a hint of deja-vu about this meeting in the transit lounge of Terminal 1 in the early 1970s. We had been advised that Brando was changing 'planes at Heathrow on his way to Paris or Geneva. I wasn't convinced. I had been asked once before to look out for Brando on a flight from New York. He had made a booking at London's Dorchester Hotel, I was told. He had, but "he" was Marlon Brando Senior, the actor's father, a film company executive. That was some ten years earlier. So I was a little taken aback when I learnt that this time it really was the son, not the father. And I found myself suddenly and quite unwittingly becoming a confidant, a repository for the actor's pent-up political and social disaffections, displeasures, aggravations and irritations.

At my initial approach he was unresponsive. That didn't surprise me; Brando was not known for his willingness to be interviewed. But I took the opportunity to point out that my photographic colleagues had already taken pictures at the aircraft ramp, and surely he wouldn't want the captions to be inaccurate. Surprisingly, since this is the most obvious and over-used line in the world, he relented after I had pressed him for some minutes. But he had at least an hour to wait for his onward flight, and he may have thought he could quickly rid himself of me.

"Look here," he said, "I don't give interviews. But I don't mind talking a bit if you promise not to publish anything.."

I think I laughed. At any rate I pointed out how ridiculous his request was. "With respect, Mr Brando," I said, "that's rather like you agreeing to make a film provided you're neither seen nor heard on camera."

The analogy, weak as it was, must have appealed to him. Or he just wanted someone to talk to. Anyway, he motioned me to an empty seat beside him. "Okay," he said, "Let's talk. But put that notebook away or check with me first if I say anything worth publishing."

I could have said that almost anything he had to say would be worth publishing, for rarity value if nothing else. But I thought better of it. His offer, if unfair, was better than nothing, which would have been the alternative if I'd rejected it. In the time I had before his flight was due I didn't really expect any revelations, but I might learn something about what made him tick.

Authors collection

The young Marlon Brando

Authors collection
Marlon Brando, older, but no less opinionated.

The useable quotes just didn't happen. He wouldn't agree to me using any of his pearls of wisdom. On the other hand I certainly did learn what made him "tick", though not in the sense I had hoped for. In a slang popular in my Army days, Brando's "tick," or grouse, was mainly against the American press, and the American way of life as he saw it.

For some twenty minutes we talked, or rather I listened while he talked, about politics, American and British, about the film business, about the news media and his less than complimentary views of the US media in particular. Of American newspapers he was most vehement in his criticism. He spelt out several brushes he'd had over what he claimed were inaccuracies and distortions.

I ventured that perhaps the popular American Press was no worse than the mass-circulation British tabloids, that distortions were rarely deliberate, that mistakes were always possible.

"The failings of the British newspapers are nothing compared with ours in America," he insisted, "I hope for your sake they never become as corrupted." Sometimes recently I have wondered how close we may have come towards realising that fear.

Soon afterwards we parted as he gathered up his young son, who had been playing nearby, teasing the waiting photographers. One of those photographers, from a big circulation magazine, came over as the pair boarded their 'plane. "You must have had one of the longest interviews Brando has ever given," he said, adding patronisingly: "you could sell that round the world."

I tapped my nose knowingly. "No go," I said, "It was all off the record." The photographer was understandably lost for words. His face was a picture.

My notebook stayed secure in my pocket too, at the last of several meetings I'd had with Charlie Chaplin at Heathrow's Terminal 2, also in the seventies. At the time he was no more aware than I that we'd played a scene together in a television film, though I doubt if he would have been as impressed.

Brenard Press pictures
Two pictures, almost four years apart, but the same destination each time. Charlie Chaplin, his wife Oona and their daughters Josephine and Geraldine, then only 7 and 12 respectively, leaving London Airport in the mid-50s for Switzerland. It was soon to become their home country.

On an earlier visit, Charlie and I had walked from the Northside terminal to his waiting car, as I scribbled in my notebook, unaware we were being filmed for a newsreel. Months, or even years later, friends told me BBC television had used some footage of that newsreel in a documentary about sinistrality (left-handedness) to demonstrate that Chaplin, among other famous figures similarly selected, was left-handed. It showed him walking towards camera in animated conversation with me, constantly using his left-hand to emphasise a point. I never did see the newsreel, or the documentary, and I doubt if Charlie did. In any event I always found him very even-handed.

On this occasion, he and his wife Oona, together with their children, were returning home to Switzerland after a short visit to London. Their flight was delayed. I had already talked briefly with them and filed a "diary piece," a few paragraphs for the gossip pages of the London evening papers. Now, as the delay was announced, I returned to commiserate with the family. Charlie was as philosophical as ever, and invited me to join him and Oona in a cup of coffee.

For a while we talked about airports, airlines and the perils of "technical hitches" to aircraft. Then somehow the conversation turned to international affairs, and I was impressed to find just how well informed both Oona and Charlie still were. I was well aware, of course, of Charlie's radical views, but I was fascinated to find that even in his eighties, he still agonised about the problems of the world's poorer countries.

No undertaking had been requested or

given about not reporting the conversation. I knew that properly structured and edited, our chat could have made a highly readable magazine feature. But at one point Charlie's face fell and he stopped in mid-sentence as I pulled my notebook from my pocket. I hurriedly reassured him. I was merely checking my information on his flight number in response to a flight announcement. I had no wish to be responsible for him and his family missing his departure. As the family finally left, Charlie, as charming as ever he could be in his films, shook me vigorously by the hand and said: "Goodbye again. I have so enjoyed our chat. I can't remember when I last talked so freely to a journalist and felt so safe!"

I have to admit his parting comment left me wondering, just a little, whether I was doing my job properly.

Claire Bloom, one of Charlie's last leading ladies, posed prettily for a photographer when she flew back to London after making two films in Hollywood, then sulkily refused to speak to me. As I introduced myself, she inexplicably turned her back on me with the words: "I don't want to speak to you. Go away."

My reaction was instinctively dismissive. "Very well, Miss Bloom," I replied with a shrug, "If that's how you feel...I'm not the one who needs publicity." And I walked away. In a moment she was calling me back. "Please," she said, "I'm sorry. I didn't mean that. How can I help?"

As far as I could recall, we had never met before, so I like to think she must have mistaken me for someone else. Or it may have been just a bit of temperament after a bad flight. Ironically, I didn't need to speak to her; the picture said everything. Hollywood had given Claire Bloom a new image, a softer, more feminine look and a new hair style. This formed the essence of the very brief story the *Daily Express* used the very next day, with their own addition of an inset showing a severe former Claire Bloom for comparison.

Authors collection

Claire Bloom is reported to have said: "My face has always been my fortune anyway, not my body."

Later I remembered I had used a similar response just as successfully before, not for a film star, but for that great jazz singer Ella Fitzgerald. When I spotted her outside Terminal 2 Arrivals at Heathrow, I wasn't even aware she was expected in Britain. So as I greeted her with: "Hello Miss Fitzgerald, what brings you to London?" she was, perhaps understandably, annoyed.

"If you don't know, I'm not telling you," was her less understandable answer. And she snapped: "Go and do your homework before you come to me asking stupid questions."

It was my turn to be annoyed. No agent had thought to advise us that she was due here for a series of concerts, and I resented her assumption that I had been sent along just to meet her. "I wasn't even aware you were arriving until I saw you a moment ago, I said, peevishly, "But it doesn't worry me a bit if you want to be rude. I've nothing to lose."

I was halfway up an escalator to the first floor of the building when I felt a tap on the arm as a panting voice said: "Miss Fitzgerald would like to apologise to you. She was very rude." Gallantly, I returned to speak with her. She apologised again and made no excuses. In no time at all we were chatting away as if nothing had happened.

Brenard Press picture

"Now see here..." Edward G. Robinson emphasises a point to me – but unthreateningly – on his arrival in London in November, 1959

My list of favourite people is happily a longer one. Some have already featured elsewhere, like Robeson, Chaplin, Crosby and Trevor Howard. I drew immense pleasure, too, from interviewing the likes of Edward G. Robinson and Boris Karloff, both so different from their familiar screen images. I must make special mention of the ever-pleasant, ever-gentlemanly David Niven, Number One in the popularity stakes of airport and airline staff. There was the always delightful Deborah Kerr, the cordial Douglas Fairbanks Jnr., the invigorating Sir John Mills, self-effacing Roger Moore and his devil-may-care near-namesake, Kenneth More.

There was too the lovely and unforgettable Ingrid Bergman. I first encountered her with her daughter Pia Lindstrom, then ten, and was to meet her again and again during her "exile"

Authors collection

Everybody's favourite at Heathrow – the late David Niven.

Same address

FOR Deborah Kerr, her film executive husband Anthony Bartley, and their children, Melanie, nine, and Francesca, five, it was "Hello again London" today when they arrived at Waterloo from America.

They came back for a two weeks holiday before going to France. Miss Kerr is to make a film for Otto Preminger, "Bonjour Tristesse," which will be shot in Paris and the South of France.

At Waterloo to meet Miss Kerr and get her autograph was Anita Philmere, 14, who lives in Onslow-gardens, Muswell Hill — the road where Deborah Kerr used to live.

Mr Bartley, who handles distribution for the Columbia Broadcasting System has business in France, Germany, Sweden and Switzerland, while his wife is film-making. He will make his headquarters in Paris. "I expect to be with Deborah and the children most weekends," he said.

He and his wife were in London last Summer when Miss Kerr wrote a series of articles in "The Star" telling the story of her life in America and her rise to stardom.

The Star *April 1957*

Authors collection

Another favourite who regularly flew with one or more of her children whenever she returned to the UK from Hollywood, was Deborah Kerr.

Authors collection

Ingrid Bergman

from Hollywood. I had learnt at first hand from her husband Petter of his agony when she deserted him for Roberto Rosselini.

Some big names were harder to categorise, other than to say they could be "difficult" to interview. Gary Cooper, true to image, rarely volunteered anything, invariably answering simply "Yup," or "Nope," to questions; Robert Mitchum was also totally non-committal. Cary Grant simply was off-hand and uninterested, while John Wayne was mostly abrupt. Gregory Peck, though polite and friendly, appeared withdrawn, and, in spite of his image as a tough guy, Lee Marvin was reticent, almost shy. He took almost childish pleasure from my accurate prophecy that his recording of "*Wanderin' Star*" from "*Paint your Wagon,*" would be a Number 1 hit.

Of the legendary women stars, Bette Davis was bossy and autocratic, so like many of her film roles, Katherine Hepburn wary and unforthcoming. (She would happily pose for still photographs, but curiously, for a film actress, would run from TV movie cameras, screaming: "That's my enemy!" A familiar phrase.)

Brenard Press picture

Gregory Peck

Authors collection

Judy Garland

Among the most memorable has to be the great Judy Garland, who looked so ill and thin when I last met her shortly before her death, but was emotionally still as bubbly and as enthusiastic as ever; the awe-inspiring Orson Welles, who always seemed to find any interest in his activities faintly amusing, in spite of his reputation for being egocentric.

Harry Secombe, gentle, ever clowning, and still able to make his wife Myra as well as fascinated bystanders roar with laughter at his public antics; the brilliant and highly entertaining raconteur Peter Ustinov, the inspired fiendish fun of Peter Sellers, and of course, the unequalled Danny Kaye – all held the promise of classic entertainment.

In this category of favourite personalities, because of our "personal" relationship, I must include the idolised Brigitte Bardot, Europe's answer to Marilyn Monroe. I met her and literally fell at her feet when she arrived in

Brigitte Bardot arrives in London today to shoot scenes for her new film Babette Goes to War. Here she is at London Airport after flying in from Paris. Her outfit: a kingfisher blue suit with a fur collar.—Page TEN.

BARDOT AGAIN?

Brigitte Bardot is on the front page. Is this her again? No. It is Maguy Mortini arriving at London Airport today. Who is she? Brigitte Bardot's stand-in.

Brigitte makes a change

Brigitte Bardot, highest paid actress in the history of the French cinema, flew into London Airport today. She is here to film with the boys of the RAF in her first dramatic role — not the strip-tease which has entertained cinema-goers for the past six years.

Miss Bardot goes to the RAF station at Abingdon tomorrow for location work for her new film Babette Goes to War. The RAF will see not the Brigitte they know but a girl in battledress tunic and trousers.

She plays a Free-French resistance worker who parachutes into France.

Disappointing?

"Of course, I would not have accepted this role two years ago" she said. "Then I preferred my sexy parts. Now I want to become known as a dramatic actress."

Miss Bardot faced question after question.

"Would her friends be disappointed by this change of part?"

"Of course they will if all they want to see is strip-tease," she said.

"Who is the man in your life?" A flutter of eyelids and back came the answer "At the moment—you."

Did she intend to get married again?—"That all depends on the weather."

Miss Bardot twitched down the knee length skirt of her kingfisher blue tweed suit and was hustled out to her waiting car.

Evening Standard pictures (both) April 9 1959

Authors collection

Brigitte Bardot, Europe's answer to Marilyn Monroe. A favourite studio shot from the 1950s – before I became "the man in her life."

London to make her first "serious" film, playing a French resistance fighter in "*Babette Goes to War.*".

As with Monroe, I had to share her for a while with scores of Fleet Street reporters and photographers making a rare excursion to Heathrow. We all crowded into a stifling Queens Building press conference room, scene of so many world news events. I found myself kneeling on a carpeted floor at Brigitte's feet as she sat in a wicker armchair with her rumoured boy friend, actor Jacques Charrier beside her.

With one eye on Charrier, I asked Brigitte innocently: "Who is the man in your life at the moment, Miss Bardot?" For just a second she hesitated. Then, with a flutter of eyelashes, she fixedly returned my gaze. "At the moment – you are," she replied.[1]

I remember nothing of the rest of that press conference interview. But I made certain of recording that one line for posterity by including it in my copy, once again employing that useful introductory phrase, "...someone asked." It was dutifully reported that day by the London *Evening Standard.* I don't think they gave it the prominence it deserved.

Two months later Jacques Charrier and my Brigitte were married.

[1] *Forty-five years later Miss Bardot stated in an interview: "…I was always the man in my life." As Virgil put it: "A fickle thing, and changeful, is woman always!"*

CHAPTER SIX

The prospect of a news Klondike at Heathrow tempted a number of freelance press photographers in the 1950s. For most of them it was a short-odds gamble which quickly paid off thanks to a lack of competitive effort by the "home" team, our own half-hearted photographic department. Not that the newcomers made a fortune in the early stages; the opportunities were there, but the pickings were small and the hours long. Among those in the second wave of newcomers was one John Kennedy.

Until then, apart from Brenards, only one newspaper and one Fleet Street photo agency had thought it worthwhile to provide cover at Heathrow with full-time cameramen. *PA-Reuter Photos*, the news picture branch of *Reuters* and the national home news agency jointly owned by Britain's major newspaper groups, offered a regular flow of pictures to its clients in London and beyond. It was a thoroughly reliable, if somewhat unadventurous service. There were, predictably, few nuggets in its repetitive output of gracious or ungrateful royalty, earnest statesmen, pompous politicians, posturing film stars and grinning footballers.

As the newspaper pioneer, the *Daily Mirror's* coverage was soon emulated by the *Daily Express*. The two prospectors concerned were both staff men of long experience. It may have been significant that both were approaching retirement, and both lived to the west of London, within easy driving distance of the airport.

From time to time since then, most nationals and at least one London evening newspaper have been directly represented by staff men or retained photographers on exclusive contracts, but few of them stayed the course. In most cases the newspaper picture desks wouldn't, or weren't allowed to bear the costs. And there were very few Fleet Street-based photographers keen to spend every day camping out in airport terminals, even though the returns in publications in those early years were probably higher than they would find elsewhere.

Newspapers have always looked for choice in the photo market. With the written word it is only necessary to move a paragraph or two, or change a word here and there to suggest an exclusive or dedicated contribution. By adding a staff reporter's by-line above a re-written, syndicated and otherwise unedited story it is a simple matter to add to this impression. Intended or not, it's a practice which has been experienced by every newspaper "stringer" or freelance (sometimes compounded by innocent non-payment for the original!).

No such originality can be claimed for an agency photograph, which appears simultaneously on a dozen rival front pages. Some picture desks may occasionally reverse an image to make a picture appear different, suggesting that this is for aesthetic reasons or artistic "balance"on the page, sometimes understandably. In the days of plate cameras and subsequently fewer available negatives, no agency could afford to offer that ideal choice by distributing more than a couple of alternative prints of the same subject. Thus a number of freelance photographers realised that they could make individual agreements with other photo-agencies to provide a competitive service to rival *PA-Reuters*. As freelances, they could boost their income by retaining the copyright of their pictures and selling them on to other (mainly overseas) markets.

There were dangers, not the least being the periodic clash of interest between the parties to the agreement. But these were overcome sufficiently well by the late '50s to result in the long-term establishment of a corps of freelance news photographers at Heathrow. Today they and their successors supply between them, directly and indirectly, virtually every newspaper, magazine or photo-agency in the world. As reporters we believed, as did some of the freelances themselves, that Brenards' own photographic service could and should have attained such a role.

When John Kennedy made his first appearance at Heathrow, it was to join four other freelances, their feet already firmly under the Press room table. Unlike them, he wasn't to stay long on the airport scene.

It was just after seven one morning when he put his head round the door of our telephone booth in the old Heathrow departures terminal. I looked up from the morning papers I had just collected from the adjoining Smith's bookstall.

"Hi," he said, introducing himself in a slightly nasal accent I couldn't place. "I'm with the *Daily Sketch*."

I responded without any enthusiasm, and possibly rudely. I hadn't really time for pleasantries. I had only just arrived at work myself and had to get through the papers before a junior from Brenards' newsroom claimed them from me. And I still had to check the early morning flights and make the first routine calls of the day. The first editions of the London evening newspapers went to press at 8.30 a.m., so if there was to be anything to report from the early hours, there was no time to waste.

But from Kennedy's next few comments I did discover that he wasn't on a single assignment at the airport, usually the case with Fleet Street visitors. He was looking for something more permanent... a future at Heathrow as yet another independent news photographer and competitor for us. With that realisation my irritation must have become obvious. He shrugged off the slight and left me to my own problems.

Over the next week or two all we learnt about John Kennedy was from the snippets his fellow freelances dropped when they were communicative. He was, he apparently said, a New Zealander who had followed a number of careers in the most recent of his twenty-five-or-so years. But his apparent brashness failed to impress anyone, and indeed we felt he was becoming something of an embarrassment to the clique because of an infuriating habit.

Whenever the *Daily Sketch* published a picture taken at Heathrow, Kennedy would take the first opportunity to sidle up to a group of us, casually open a copy of the newspaper under our noses, and with a stab of his finger, would gleefully proclaim: "That's mine!"

Sometimes it was, but not always. He knew it. We suspected it. And he knew we suspected. But that was irrelevant. It seemed he was claiming, publicly, almost every airport picture in "his" paper. And as we realised he could not have been serious, we quickly gave up denying him, even though a quick 'phone call would have settled each such claim. I don't believe he was being serious, but in any event, his initial enthusiasm for covering the airport steadily dropped from seven days a week to one or two.

Kennedy's "That's mine!" became a byword for months whenever photographers argued about the quality of their efforts. Just as legendary, though more acceptable, were the colourful stories its originator continued to tell of his varied experiences around the world. So when he cheerfully announced one day that he would soon be saying goodbye to Heathrow, no one was over concerned. But he had, he said, made a discovery which was going to make his fortune, and it was right here in London.

In a London basement coffee bar he'd found "Britain's answer to Elvis Presley" in a young cockney performer he saw as a major pop star in the making. And John Kennedy was going to make him that. His name: Tommy Hicks.

Within days Kennedy had negotiated a recording contract, signed business deals and opened a publicity campaign. Tommy Hicks was launched on the British pop scene with a new guitar and a new name: Tommy Steele. He was an instant success. Rock'n'roll had come to Britain. John Kennedy had confounded us all.

I never ran across Kennedy again, though for some reason, colleagues met up with him several times. One, Chris Bramwell, joined him for a while in his promotions company. He became a frequent visitor to Heathrow, as a passenger on his way to his millionaire's retreat in the West Indies. With his new partner, Larry Parnes, he had gone on to sign up a string of performers, among them Billy Fury and Marty Wilde. Later still came the book on how it all started.

picture courtesy of www.internationalartistes.com

I always felt it should have been entitled: "That's mine!" At the time of course, I didn't believe a word of it. But it did become another good story that for me, at least, got away.

Our relations with the freelance newcomers, particularly those retained by the photo agencies rather than individual newspapers, were never very happy. As reporters we resented the idea that any photographer from a rival agency might win publications on the back of our stories, as was often the case. We saw little evidence that any of the freelances we had endured to date were capable of achieving this on their own initiative. Our stories were even providing free captions for their pictures.

We were jealous too, because we felt that Brenards had missed its chance to develop the photographic side of its agency services. And we believed we had demonstrably failed to seek retainer and contractual agreements with picture desks and agencies like those pioneered and won from the news desks. With limited resources of print production and, more importantly distribution, we could only try to offer an alternative service by providing back-up pictures to our hard-won exclusive stories.

Bill Brenard recognised our frustration; we talked about it often enough. At times it must have sounded as if we were censuring him. But he readily admitted he wasn't a "pictures man" and had enough on his plate negotiating with news desks. In the early years he brought in a succession of picture managers in a vain attempt to break the stalemate. He even opened a Fleet Street office to overcome the difficulties of photographic print distribution, a briefly lived venture which was financially prohibitive.

Mike Richardson

When Mike Richardson, a former RAF comrade of Bill's finally came in to join him as a junior partner, he brought with him some muscle in the form of a dark room manager and a couple of additional photographers from his own specialist aerial photography company.

But Mike, who, in his turn, also readily admitted *he* was not a "news man," believed that the only future for a Brenard photographic company lay in its unique ability to offer a round-the-clock *commercial* service to the dozens of airlines and a range of private businesses based at Heathrow. News would become a second string only to be plucked when there was a good chance of an unopposed "hit" on our favourite targets, the news pages. As news men, we were never convinced this was the only route to success, but now we had to accept that there would no longer be any encouragement for trying to compete directly with *PA-Reuters* or the other established picture agencies.

The challenge offered by the introduction of independent television in Britain and an opportunity for Brenards to provide news cine-film from the airports was still a year or two away. It was to involve both *ITN* and *BBC* television in months of negotiations with the powerful film unions before they could openly discuss the possibilities with Mike. (The issue was eventually resolved, we learnt, because the union members themselves couldn't accept the prospect of being permanently based at Heathrow, the probable alternative suggested to them.)

An early "overnight" picture from the Brenard darkroom, though few subjects were such celebrities. Princess Achraf Pahlevi was the twin sister of the last Shah of Persia, now Iran. Leaving for Paris on her way home, she was reunited at Northolt Airport with her pet Pomeranian, Tutti Fruiti, which stayed in quarantine during her visit to London.

The Star October 15 1947 Brenard Press picture

One other news market was open to the Brenard team of photographers. The first editions of London's three evening newspapers, most of which were made up during the news-starved hours between midnight and dawn, were desperately short of both copy and pictures. Anything which could be offered an hour or two ahead of this time stood an almost certain chance of publication and was understandably known as "overnight" material.

So the pressure was on the photographers to occupy their spare moments between "commercials" by finding picture-worthy subjects to photograph, caption, process, print and deliver to Fleet Street well in time for the next day's presses. This was the one area where the Brenard cameramen had an advantage over their opposition. Those few who didn't have a natural nose for news could call on the experience of their reporter colleagues to find a news angle in their chosen subjects.

Looking for overnights, the story or the picture, was rarely an exercise we relished. It usually meant we were experiencing a dearth of hard news. It could also be frustrating and under-rewarding. But as "picture-worthy" invariably meant "pretty" and "female" in that order (this was an openly male-orientated era) it did offer reporters as well as photographers the opportunity of a legitimate chat-up line. And, of course, engaging the subject's attention elsewhere often provided a more natural picture.

Our offer to any lusted-after victim came with a built-in promise of instant fame. It was also a promise, that was more often fulfilled than the standard Hollywood seduction technique of: "Let me get you into pictures!"

London publicity agents, anxious to win a few column inches for a client, like the aspiring young model or the starry-eyed actress just out of drama school, soon caught on to this opportunity for low-cost publicity. In no time at all we were finding subjects who openly admitted they were not flying anywhere. They had simply been sent down to the airport "to have my picture taken for the papers." The more successful agents, of course, splashed out on an air ticket to Paris and back, and carefully rehearsed their clients with a cover story.

Now and again there were real compensations for us. My photographer colleague Tony Hewson and I had no reason to question the story one very pretty young "actress" told us. Twenty-one-years-old Penny Austin had been sitting alone sipping a cup of coffee when we spotted her in the Arrivals area, her eyes glued to the indicator board. At first she appeared reluctant to talk. When she admitted to me she was not travelling but meeting her boy friend, a Canadian crew-member, I asked her how they had met.

"He bought a poppy from me when I shook a collection tin at him in Leicester Square," she said. "Then he bought another. Then he bought the whole tray. Then he asked me for a date."

The episode apparently took no longer in the doing than it did in the telling. But there was more to come. Six hours later, on Remembrance Sunday, the poppy-lover, an airline purser, had asked Penny to marry him. "And," she told me, "I said 'Yes'."

No, she had no objection to us taking a picture of her. And, after posing for Tony's close-up and full-length "leggy," Penny insisted on going to find her fiancé. We, in turn insisted on accompanying her, anxious for another picture, of the happy couple together. We were too late. Fatefully they had somehow missed each other at the barrier. The Canadian had apparently given up and departed for London, alone.

The story had to be one for the dailies. As Tony dashed away to process his negatives and arrange for the delivery of prints, I dictated my story to a young Brenard copy-taker.

Marking it: "Dailies, full circulation," I added satisfyingly: "Attention picture desks: pictures available."

Within minutes of its telephoned circulation, orders for pictures had

DAILY SKETCH 2d

AND DAILY GRAPHIC

TUESDAY, NOVEMBER 17, 1953

Poppy Penny says Yes

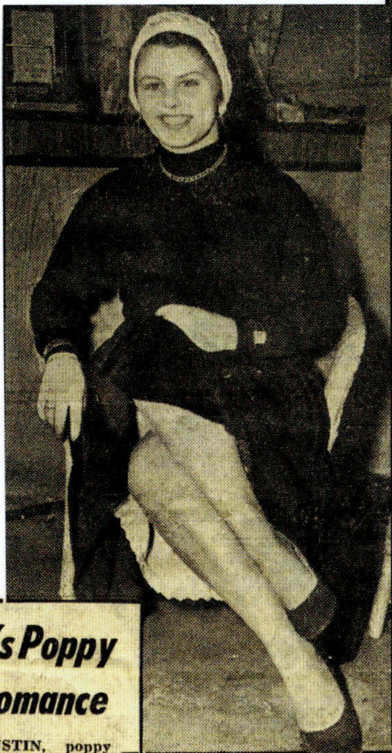

He bought a poppy from her as he went to the cinema. He bought another as he came away.

He asked her for a date, too. And a few hours later on Remembrance Day airline steward Adam Steinbach, aged 28, proposed to the poppy seller he met in Leicester-square — 21-year-old Penny Austin, above, of Oxford-road, Putney.

Penny said "Yes" just before Adam's plane was due to leave for Canada.

Last night she went to London Airport to meet him from his return flight. But Adam had arrived early, and left to look for her. "I hope he doesn't think I've forgotten him," said Penny as she went off to find him. "We have only two days to discuss plans. Then Adam flies to Canada again."

Daily Sketch (all) 17 November 1953

Brenard Press picture

Penny's Poppy Day romance

PENNY AUSTIN, poppy selling in London on Remembrance Sunday, collected a tinful of silver—and a marriage proposal. Less than six hours later she had said "Yes" and "Au revoir" to Adam Steinbach, a man who bought two poppies from her.

Yesterday, Penny, a 21-year-old actress *(above)* went to London Airport to meet Adam again. He is an airline purser. But he had arrived an hour earlier and had gone off to look for her. Penny's last word: "I hope he doesn't think I've forgotten Remembrance Sunday."

Daily Herald

JUST 6 HOURS . . .

● Meet Penny Austin, aged 21. Nine days ago she was selling poppies in Leicester-square. Canadian airline purser Adam Steinbach bought one, dated her, then proposed. Six hours after their meeting Penny said "Yes." Adam flew back to Canada. Yesterday Penny was at London Airport waiting to meet him again.

Daily Express

come in from five daily papers. Next day, the story and Tony's pictures were carried prominently on four front pages (with one print reversed in the *Daily Sketch*) under headlines like: "Penny's Poppy Day Romance" and "Penny finds Romance."

That should have been the end of the story, apart perhaps for the follow-up I was already visualising for the wedding day. For Penny it was indeed the end… the end of a romance. Before the day was out we had heard from Steve Anderson, the airline's public relations manager in London, that much of the story was the invention of a theatrical press agent. He had persuaded his client Penny to embellish a casual fling with the crewman if the Press spotted her at the airport when she drove out to meet him.

But what neither the agent nor Penny knew was that the misguided "fiancé" was already married back home in Canada. Not surprisingly, his wife was upset when Canadian papers picked up the news of the poppy romance that day. Steve, whose immediate concern was for his airline's image, could only admonish Penny. Civil airline crews were expected to be purer than pure.

The crewman was sent home to face the domestic music. And I was pledged to secrecy. Steve would never have told me the truth without my undertaking to allow the poppy tale to die.

As a newspaperman himself (he was a former *Express* reporter) he probably recognised the potential follow-up story: "Lovesick poppy-seller hoodwinked by Atlantic Romeo..." (I didn't care to think of the other possibility: "Press conned by smartass publicity man.") And there was always the chance the newspapers might think we had dreamt up the whole idea ourselves...

Married, Divorced—

Brenard Press picture

She married a 'ghost'

MISS ROSEMARY JANSA, 25-year-old Czech, revealed yesterday how she escaped the Communists by marrying a "ghost."

It was, she said in London, "a real marriage of convenience." She wanted to leave Prague ; the Reds refused a passport. So friends in Amsterdam arranged for Miss Jansa to marry a businessman by proxy.

—BUT SHE'S NEVER SEEN HUSBAND

A MARRIAGE was arranged between Rosemary Jansa (above) and a middle-aged Dutch businessman, 300 miles away on the other side of the Iron Curtain.

The couple had never met. In less than three days they were married—and divorced. That was four years ago. But to this day THEY HAVE NEVER SEEN EACH OTHER.

As she left London after a holiday yesterday, golden-haired, green-eyed Rosemary, a Czech, who lives in Frankfurt (Germany) now, told the story of the strange romance that began when she was a fashion-designer in Prague

"When the Communists took over the country they would allow only foreigners to leave," she said. "But friends in Amsterdam found a man who agreed to marry me by proxy.

"After the ceremony, in which another friend stood in for me, the news was telephoned to the Dutch Embassy in Prague. In less than forty-eight hours I was stepping from an airliner in Amsterdam with a Dutch passport in my handbag."

'I Wonder'

The same day Rosemary applied for and was granted a divorce. "Sometimes I wonder what my Dutch benefactor looks like," she said yesterday.

Rosemary, who speaks six languages, had used her savings for her holiday, which was a trip round the world.

DIVORCED -YET SHE NEVER MET HIM

Express Staff Reporter

A BEAUTIFUL 25-year-old Czech girl married a Dutch business man, divorced him three days later . . . *and they have never met.*

Daily Express (above)
Daily Mail (inset left)

She wed and divorced in 2 days

MARRIED to a man she has never seen and divorced two days later. . . .

That is the strange romance revealed yesterday by Rosemary Jansa, pictured above as she boarded a plane at London Airport for Frankfurt.

It happened four years ago when Rosemary was a 25-year-old Czech fashion designer.

BY PROXY

"The new regime was allowing only foreigners to leave the country and my passport was taken from me," she explained.

"But friends in Amsterdam found a middle-aged Dutch business man who agreed to marry me by proxy.

"After the ceremony in which another friend stood in for me, the news was telephoned to the Dutch Embassy in Prague.

"In less than 48 hours I was stepping from an airliner in Amsterdam with a Dutch passport.

"The same day I applied for and was granted a divorce. It was a real marriage of convenience."

Daily Mirror (above)
Daily Sketch (right)
(all) Feb 7 1953

Marriage was also in the mind of a Czech-born fashion designer, Rosemary Jansa, 25, whom a photographer and I found in a departure lounge waiting for a flight to Frankfurt. She told us of her "romance" too, a deliberate charade which led her to marriage and divorce in just three days... with a man she had never met. I'd spotted the unusual carved gold ring on the third finger of a left hand. "No," she said to my question, "I'm not married. That's a gift from a Spanish bullfighter friend. But I *was* married. For three days."

The story she told in the next few minutes gave me a total of fifteen column inches in four nationals. Pete Ward's picture highlighted the headlines.

Rosemary was the first of a number of proxy brides I came across around that time. Like the others, she had tried unsuccessfully to leave her native Prague. But when she contacted friends in Amsterdam they came up with a solution. They found a Dutch businessman willing to marry her, by proxy. Another girl deputised for her at a civil ceremony in Holland, and the wedding made Rosemary a Dutch citizen. The Dutch Embassy in Prague was thus able to issue a new passport to Rosemary as soon as the news was telephoned to them.

"In less than 48 hours I was stepping from an airliner in Amsterdam, my Dutch passport in my hand," Rosemary told me, "And the first thing I did in Holland was to apply for a divorce. It was granted immediately."

Had she any regrets at not meeting her unknown husband? For a moment Rosemary was wistful. "It was a real marriage of convenience," she said, "Everyone was happy. But I have wondered sometimes what he looked like. I only know he was middle-aged."

Another "pretty-as-a-picture" visitor en route this time between Texas and Turkey was 22-years-old brunette June Martin from Houston. She was taking a £300 gamble on love by buying a one-way ticket to visit her Turkish boyfriend "on approval." The couple had met when the boyfriend was a student engineer in Texas. "We had an understanding that we might get married someday," she said. "A few days ago he 'phoned me and asked me to come over. But I'm not rushing into things. I may change my mind when I see him again, or he may change his. We haven't seen each other for nine months."

June gave up her job in an insurance office and spent her savings on the air fare. "I shall insist he buys my ticket home if it doesn't work out," she said. I desisted from voicing the obvious "what if" question. As was so often the case, the final chapter of that fairy-tale romance never came to light. The moving finger having writ, moves on...

Each of these stories, as with many others, started out as a simple target for an overnight picture either a photographer or I had plucked out from the crowd. But one such potential subject for the *Star-News-Standard* front pages did challenge our powers of persuasion. Three weeks after leaving for America, a reward for winning a "beautiful swimmer" contest, Marilyn Davies, a 17-years-old blonde from Stockport in Cheshire, was flying back to Britain, disappointed and disillusioned. The US immigration authorities had told her she was four months too young to take up the major part of her prize, a role in a big water gala in Florida. She was refused the work permit that was essential for her participation.

Too upset to talk about her misfortune, Marilyn had tried to slip home unnoticed, in complete contrast to the previous month when her departure had been highlighted in her local press. But she too was spotted by a Brenard photographer as a possible picture as she stepped from her transatlantic 'plane. He came looking for me when he realised she was trying to avoid him. It was only when I pressed her for information on her US visit that Marilyn finally told me the whole story for the daily papers.

But my favourite example of a simple overnight picture becoming a national news story, clearly validating Bill Brenard's oft-repeated maxim: "There's a story on every

June goes to meet him— 'on approval'

DARK-HAIRED June Martin, 22, posted five postcard views of London yesterday before

June Takes a £300 Gamble on Romance

PRETTY dark - haired June Martin, 22-year-old Texan, stepped from a Transatlantic airliner at London airport to-day clutching her one-way air ticket to Istanbul—a £300 gamble on romance and the future.

June, who has thrown up her job as underwriter for an insurance company, was flying to Turkey to take a prospective husband "on approval" for two weeks.

He is 27-year-old Turkish engineer, Ozcan Turer. They met while students at a Houston, Texas, college.

"We had an understanding that we might get married one day," said June, as she changed planes. "John—that's my name for him—rang me last week and asked me to come over.

'Not Rushing'

"But I am not rushing things. I may change my mind when I see him again." She and John have not met since he returned to Turkey nine months ago. "I've almost forgotten what he looks like."

June has saved her £300 fare from her salary. "If I decided not to marry John," she smiled, "I shall insist on his paying my fare home."

As she boarded her Istanbul airliner she posted five postcard views of London addressed to boy friends in America.

She joked: "I don't want to burn all my bridges."

Brenard Press picture
Evening News
(all) August 4 1954

Too young to work for £18 a week

"Daily Mirror" Reporter

A SEVENTEEN-YEAR-OLD beauty queen who won a six months' trip to America, arrived back in London last night—three weeks after she left.

The dream holiday of pretty Marilyn Davies, of Stockport, Cheshire was over. . . .

And all because she was four months too young.

When Marilyn won the beauty contest it meant two weeks lazing in the Florida sunshine at Cypress Gardens and the offer of six months' work in a water show there at £18 a week.

Marilyn enjoyed her holiday. Then she started training for the show.

And then the American authorities stepped in. The law said Marilyn was four months too young to take a job.

But the offer of the water show job still stands — when she is eighteen.

Daily Mirror

AT 17–'TOO YOUNG TO WORK'

SEVENTEEN - YEAR - OLD Marilyn Davies—she left for Florida with a fanfare of publicity 24 days ago—was back last night . . . back with her mother in Didsbury-road, Stockport.

She had hoped she was going to stay in America six months at least. After all, they called her "Britain's Esther Williams," as winner of a big film competition.

The prize: A fortnight in Florida.

But long before Marilyn left for the United States there had been talk of a six-month job in a Florida water ski-ing show.

THE LAW

What went wrong? Marilyn is four months too young to be given a permit to work in Florida. That is the law there. . . . No labour permits under 18.

And Marilyn had been frolicking about Florida lakes for 10 days before she was told she couldn't stay on.

Said Marilyn: "I've had a lovely time—mostly water ski-ing and having my picture taken—but it was disappointing having to cut it short.

"I did meet one film star—Barry Sullivan. Well, I didn't meet him properly. He was with other people."

Brenard Press picture
Daily Express (above)
(both) Nov 5 1954

aircraft", was the fifteen-years-old bride of a student in America sent home to Egypt because her presence at his side "emotionally disturbed" him.

Brenard Press picture
Tony Hewson

Tony Hewson and I had been kicking our heels for some hours with little to do but talk to the occasional passenger in the vain hope of picking up a story or a picture. He suggested we looked at an incoming Air India flight from New York. My response was hardly enthusiastic. London was really only a staging post for the flight, which after refuelling, was due to continue on to India via the Continent and the Middle East. So it was unlikely there would be many passengers disembarking at Heathrow.

"That'll make it easier to spot a story," Tony pointed out. And as I could think of no answer to that, I went along with him.

We watched from the edge of the northside tarmac as passengers disembarked. This was January 1962, shortly before the opening of Terminal 3, and the old prefabricated terminal was still in use for long distance flights. We dismissed the handful of passengers heading for the Arrivals building. They were clearly businessmen and "socials" (our word for family and friendship visitors). We quickly turned our attention to the "transits", those passengers who were staying with the flight and were merely leaving the aircraft to stretch their legs during refuelling.

There were about a dozen of them, a mixed bunch which included a number of Indians, possibly diplomatic staff on their way home on leave, one or two Americans, possibly technicians or engineers, and a few assorted Brits, including one obvious former colonial family.

Then we spotted Wayla. She was a ravishingly beautiful teenager with the pout of a Bardot and coal-black eyes set in a light tan complexion which offset her flowing honey-coloured, shoulder-length hair. She dressed like a model, in a white leather jacket over a figure-hugging knee-length green dress.

Walking into the transit lounge, escorted by an airline stewardess, she was shown to a bench seat. She was apparently travelling alone; only one other passenger joined her on the blue leather bench, and he took a seat about six feet away. With Tony at my side, I introduced myself, and without any preamble, told her: "We would like to take your picture."

I suspect it wasn't the first time she had experienced such an approach. She was un-awed and unconcerned, and responded unsmilingly, in broken English: "How you wish me to sit?"

Glancing at Tony for his nod of agreement, I told her: "Don't worry about that. We'll take some pictures as we talk." Pulling out my notebook, I crouched down beside her and asked her to tell me about herself. After a few moments I realised this was not going to be so easy. Her English was somewhat limited. She appeared to understand my questions, but found it difficult to put her answers into words.

But I had to persist. I had her name: Wayla Khalifati from Cairo. Now I had her age: fifteen. And that was a shock, because she repeatedly referred to her husband, a student in America. I asked her to repeat her age and checked by holding up the fingers of my free hand three times.

And gradually, her story emerged. But language difficulties meant that my questions and her replies had to be repeated several times before we were both sure of what we were saying or hearing. Wayla's fellow passenger, an Englishman, still seated nearby, appeared to be following the conversation step by step. Suddenly, during one phonetic hiccough, he broke in. "Excuse me," he said, "Perhaps I can help? I speak Arabic...so if you're having problems...?"

I looked back at Wayla. "If the young lady doesn't mind, I'd welcome your help," I said, "But tell me if I've got it right so far..."

Consulting my notebook, I read: married four months to a 24-years-old Egyptian student reading engineering at a university in Austin, Texas (echoes here of my previously-reported love-gamble romance?); travelled with him there, but found it difficult to settle down. Says she doesn't like America and can't understand the way they talk in Texas. Didn't want to leave her husband, but was made to return home when he complained she was a "disturbing" influence on his studies.

I reminded him how I had tried to get Wayla to explain what she meant by this, and commented that she appeared reluctant to talk about it. At my prompting, my volunteer interpreter asked Wayla if she meant "emotionally" or "sexually" disturbing.

She thought about this for a moment, then replied: "Emotional." I thought she was going to explain. Then shyly she shook her head and said something that obviously meant she didn't want to elaborate further.

"Have you been a bad girl?" I asked.

Neither the interpreter nor Wayla had a problem with that one. Wayla shook her head vigorously as she replied, and with a grin he told me: "She says no, she hasn't. And there's not going to be a divorce. She is going home to her family in Cairo, and her husband will join her there when he's finished his studies." Was she being sent home by her husband, or by the American authorities? Wayla would only repeat: "I don't like America."

At that point the Air India stewardess appeared again, and taking Wayla by the arm, gently escorted her away, back to the waiting aircraft. I thanked my interpreter, making a note of his name and his destination address in Alexandria, as he too returned to the 'plane.

Leaving the lounge, Tony and I were buttonholed by Alan Seed, the airline's Heathrow manager. "How in heaven's name did you get on to that story?" he asked in barely disguised wonder, "I've only just heard about her myself – from New York."

"What have you heard?" I responded, ignoring his question.

"Why, that she's a potential runaway," he replied. "I've just received this message." He handed me a telexed signal from the US.

"This passenger is being returned to her family against her will. University officials feel strongly she will attempt by any means to disembark en route," it ran.

Happily disclaiming any inside knowledge, I told him the background and asked him if that was why the young passenger had been accompanied to the transit lounge by the aircraft's stewardess, an unusual duty for an air crew member. "Yes," he replied. "The stewardess was given the responsibility of keeping an eye on her. She was being watched all the time you were with her." And he added: "That's why I was called in. To watch you!"

It was early afternoon. With two or three hours to go before the last editions, we could have run the story for the evening papers and still have covered the national dailies (it had, after all, started out as an overnight for the next day's evenings). But that would mean taking some of the impact off the story for the dailies, and it might reduce their interest in pictures. By holding back, the extra couple of hours would enable Tony to run off a selection of prints, have them properly captioned, addressed and wrapped for delivery by the Brenards' motorcycle dispatch rider even before the orders which were certain to follow came in.

We both hurried away, Tony to the darkroom, I to our private telephone booth. The story was already writing itself in my head. By the time the copy-taker had fitted his headphones I was ready to go, referring to my notes only for the "quotes," most of which I could have remembered word for word anyway, thanks to the constant repetition at the time.

Then came what could have been a serious hitch. Making a routine check that the flight had actually left to continue on to Paris, Geneva and Cairo, I discovered with concern that the aircraft was still at Heathrow. It had been delayed first with an engineering fault, then by bad weather en route. The transiting passengers had disembarked again and were being taken to a late lunch in the airport restaurant.

My story was already being telephoned to the nationals. I recalled that I had only referred to Wayla's arrival, not her departure from Heathrow, so no amendment to the copy was needed. But I knew that once it dropped on the news desks, our opposition, the contracted freelances and national photographers at the airport would all be alerted to get their own pictures.

We could hardly expect airline staff on duty to protect our interests, even if they understood the commercial rivalry among the airport press corps. After all, they frequently saw us working together, amicably enough, on the same assignments. But if I could persuade the airline it was in their interest to get their young passenger out of sight... I quickly 'phoned an Air India contact. Within minutes he was able to join me.

"Mike," I said, outlining the situation to him, "Don't think I'm interfering, but now the flight's been delayed, do you think it's a good idea for the young lady in question to come back through passport controls to the restaurant? It would be so easy for her to give her escorts the slip in such a public place."

Mike Richardson was the airline's part-time public relations adviser at the airport. And he also still performed another, full-time role, as Brenards' photographic director, and Tony's boss. But of course, for the moment that had no bearing on the matter.

Firmly wearing his PR man's hat, he took my point. "I'm thinking exactly the same," he said. "I think I'll suggest she has lunch on board the aircraft on the tarmac." Then he added helpfully: "I don't think our friends will be able to get to her there."

I hurried back to the departures lounge, just in time to see a group of our "friends" the opposition tackling an Air India official about one of his passengers, someone they said was held up somewhere. They were obviously having little success, and when he broke away, they turned to me.

Frank Apthorp, the *Associated Press* agency photographer, spoke up. "My office called me about some girl you've been talking to," he said. "They've asked me to get a picture. Any idea where she is?"

"I'm sorry, fellahs, "I replied, probably unconvincingly, "But you're too late. She's already gone." I could have added the words, "to the aircraft," but didn't think it necessary.

I was pretty sure none of them would have been told the full story by their picture desks, and all may have assumed the girl was disembarking in London. I certainly wasn't about to enlighten them. And I couldn't resist adding, wickedly: "You're welcome to tell your office we have pictures if they want them." I suspect they didn't get around to it.

The nationals loved the story. The *Daily Mail* gave it a page lead:

Student banishes child bride

Daily Mail

'Disturbing' bride of 15 sent home by husband

A 15-YEAR-OLD girl, who has been married four months, flew 7,300 miles home to her mother yesterday.

Reason: Her husband, a 24-year-old Egyptian engineering student, said she was an "emotional disturbance" to his studies.

The bride, Wayla Khalifati, also an Egyptian, is pictured at London Airport on her way from Austin, Texas, to Cairo.

She said: "I didn't like America. I couldn't understand the way people speak there. But it is true my husband thought I was a disturbing influence. I don't want to talk about that.

"I haven't been a bad girl, and I expect my husband to come back to me in Cairo when he finishes his studies.

"I'm going back to my father and mother. There is not going to be a divorce."

Wayla went to Austin, Texas, after her wedding because her husband attends university there.

Before she arrived in London yesterday, airport officials got this message from New York:

"This passenger is upset and may try to leave the plane at any transit point."

HE SAYS SHE'S TOO DISTURBING AT EXAM TIME

Daily Sketch (r)

STUDENT'S 15-YEAR-OLD WIFE TAKES HIS MIND OFF BOOKS SO HE SENDS HER HOME TO MOTHER

Child bride sent home

A 15-YEAR-OLD wife —being sent home to

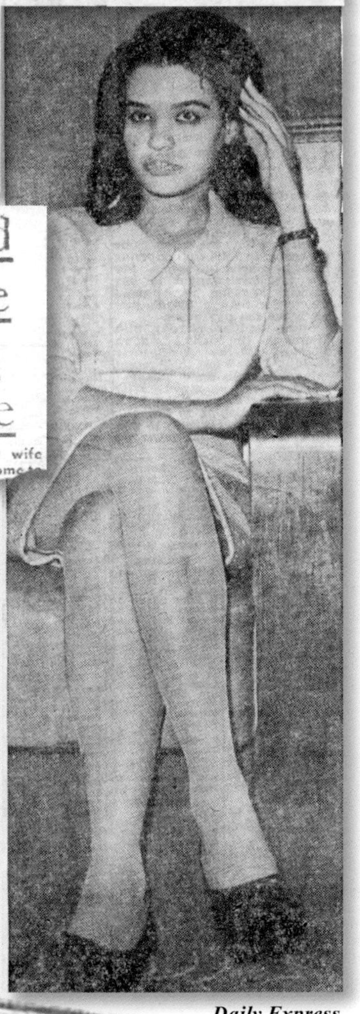

Daily Express

The 'DISTURBING' BRIDE, AGED 15

Daily Mirror, (all) Jan 9 1962 *Brenard Press pictures* *Daily Herald*

...with a "blown-up" head-and-shoulders' crop of Tony's picture. My self-satisfaction was dented, however, when I saw that one of their staff reporters, Hugh Moran, was given the credit in a by-line for merely subbing my story. The copy ran to an average of seven column inches everywhere.

Alongside the story were two or three-column oversize reproductions of the same picture in the *Daily Herald*, the *Daily Mirror* and the *Daily Sketch*, with the *Daily Express* choosing Tony's alternative full length picture of the teenage bride.

The American papers ran the story from our copy filed to the American wire services, and I learnt later that reports had been carried as far afield as Egypt, India and Australia. Not that we made a fortune from either the story or the pictures. Our only payment was the standard linage (payment per line) from the dailies and agencies and four or five pounds for each picture published. Other than our wire service fees, we would earn nothing from the overseas publications. But the income to Brenards was still considerably more than the picture alone would have earned if it had been held simply for circulation as an overnight to the evenings.

Very few potential overnight pictures, however, became national events. And as reporters, we found it somewhat humbling and time-consuming acting as mere caption writers. While constantly proclaiming to our photographer colleagues that a news picture was worth nothing without a good caption, we did our best to build on the basic details whenever possible. This usually required us to "sell" the subject for the diary pages or gossip columns of the newspapers (the word today would be "spinning").

It might mean the unknown bit-player becoming a "starlet," the amateur singer becoming a "budding pop star" (or "promising soprano"), the part-time photographic assistant becoming a "model." Non-working girls under twenty were "debs," "socialites" or "students;" office workers became "business secretaries." Their home towns and travel destinations became important too; either could guide the "interview" towards the kind of quotes needed to give some credibility or justification for the diary offering.

It must be obvious to most readers that no single reporter could be in so many different places or talk to so many different people day after day as a news diary sometimes suggests. Yet every newspaper with such a column likes to perpetrate the myth of their all-seeing, all-hearing individual "diarist." They may even have invented his name to ensure continuity as insurance against the day when a principal diary contributor has his final disagreement with the editor and departs in mid-event or is brazenly headhunted by a competitor.

In reality, most newspaper diaries are put together by a team, headed by an editor who may or may not inject something of his persona into individual contributions. Otherwise, all newspaper diaries are a hotchpotch, a collection of interesting views and anecdotes of, and by, well-known people, They can include often unsubstantiated but rarely malicious rumours about those same people from a variety of sources. These will be distinguished by such phrases as: "I learn," "revealed to me," or "it is whispered" or "reported." Even more familiar in recent years has been the oft-reported: "...as I told you here first." The diarist would also be allowed considerably more comment and self-expression than would normally be acceptable in the hard news columns.

The *Evening Standard's* ***Londoner's Diary***, the ***Star Man's Diary*** and ***Talk of the Day*** in the *Evening News*, were all useful sources of Brenards' income for what was really little more than tittle tattle about both the famous and the unknowns hoping to be famous. They were also columns which the three London evenings often found hard to fill, particularly early in the day, so they paid above the standard rate for contributions.

The daily diaries too were important customers, even though they were aware that our offerings could rarely be to the exclusive benefit of one client, so often the jealous requirement of a diary column. Brenards' one-to-one policy on exclusives was straightforward, but required a level of trust on both sides.

We always maintained that we would honour a request from a news desk for an exclusive story on an ordered item. But we made two essential provisos: that we were not already aware of the subject and were unlikely to learn of it in the normal course of events, and that no other client subsequently ordered the same story.

Bill Brenard felt that the road to such an exclusive service, though potentially paved with gold, was also strewn with the stumbling blocks of customers who were all paying us retainers to look after their interests, not side with one individual client or another.

In the long term the policy undoubtedly paid off. We might have denied ourselves the chance to scoop up the benefits of an exclusive big 'un, the one story that might have paid the equivalent of a year's linage from just one newspaper. But our major stories, invariably scoops in their own right, frequently earned valuable payment bonuses even when the news was shared by rival newspapers.

Just occasionally our policy raised doubts, particularly when we would have to call a client back to say another news desk had ordered their same "exclusive" story, or perhaps even less convincingly, that we had learnt of the subject from our own airport sources. But on the whole the news desks themselves trusted us and would still pay over the odds for an ordered story.

Newspaper diary columns are about people and particularly about people in the public eye. Airports and airlines have a surfeit of people in the public eye as their customers. Consequently our contact with the leading diarists was on a daily basis, and airport comings and goings regularly dominated the columns of ***William Hickey*** in the *Express*, the *Mail's* ***Paul Tanfield***, the *Daily Herald's* ***Henry Fielding, Simon Ward*** in the *Sketch*, ***John London*** in the *News Chronicle*. Even the *Daily Telegraph's* more restrained ***Peterborough*** was known to give way on occasions.

On one momentous day, all but two of the twelve items covered in one prominent diary were contributed by Brenards, just one of the many records we established for a freelance agency.

One of my most pleasing contributions over the years had to be my interview with the eccentric and reputedly irascible Sir Thomas Beecham, when he brought his new bride back to London after the couple's secret wedding in Switzerland. While I can't claim any credit for breaking the original news of the union, I was the first and sole reporter to talk to the couple during a 24-hour flying visit to Britain. This did not deter one diarist from claiming to have talked with the 80-years-old conductor at his hotel, reporting my quotes as proof of contact.

Sir Thomas, famed for his mock temper and his biting sarcasm on the competence or otherwise of musicians under his baton, had married his 27-years-old orchestra manager-secretary Shirley Hudson in Zurich two weeks earlier. The couple had broken their honeymoon so that she could join the Royal Philharmonic at the Edinburgh Festival. The conductor had travelled with her to London and was now at Heathrow seeing her off to Edinburgh before returning to Switzerland himself.

His reputation included an ambivalent attitude to reporters, of which I'd already had personal experience, and I was aware he was a difficult man to talk to. But I was convinced his manifest impatience in answering questions was part of his carefully considered image building and that he would respond to the direct approach, if it were open and inoffensive.

I dived in, nose first. "How did you pop the question, Sir Thomas?" I asked with what I thought was a conspiratorial grin, but which probably came out like a leer.

His response I reported verbatim. As if addressing a concert-hall audience, he said: "I approached the problem in all trepidation. With inward terror and a quaking heart. When I finally asked her, she received the question with equal dismay."

To further probing, he insisted: "It was no snap decision. I have known Lady Beecham for nine years. I thought about asking her to marry me for a long time."

Why the secrecy? "We had no intention of telling anyone," he snorted. "Marriage is largely the concern of two people only. There is no reason why the world should know. I cannot think of anything quite so ridiculous."

He co-operatively answered several more questions in similar vein, and I finally turned to the new Lady Beecham who had been hanging on his words indulgently and his arm supportively. "Of course I shall continue to work with the orchestra," she said, implying that the idea was unworthy of an answer. "I have no intention of giving up."

At which Sir Thomas commented, typically: "Someone has to look after my interests with that Philharmonic crowd. They're such an undisciplined, unruly mob."

There was more of the same banter, particularly when a well-meaning airline official brought up a wheelchair for Sir Thomas, his usual conveyance across the tarmac on previous visits. The conductor gave him the kind of withering stare usually reserved for the second fiddles. "You should know by now that I ignore those things," he growled.

I decided I was going to let the story run and not trim the interview. It was the silly season anyway, that time of year when news is reputedly scarce, and it was all amusing stuff. The decision was justified. With the back-up of pictures, this time mainly from the photo-agencies, who like us had been advised in advance, all the daily diaries ran the story, with ***Henry Fielding*** in particular giving it a full page-width spread:

2 DAILY HERALD August 24 1959

HENRY FIELDING

—in Edinburgh where the world gathers . . .

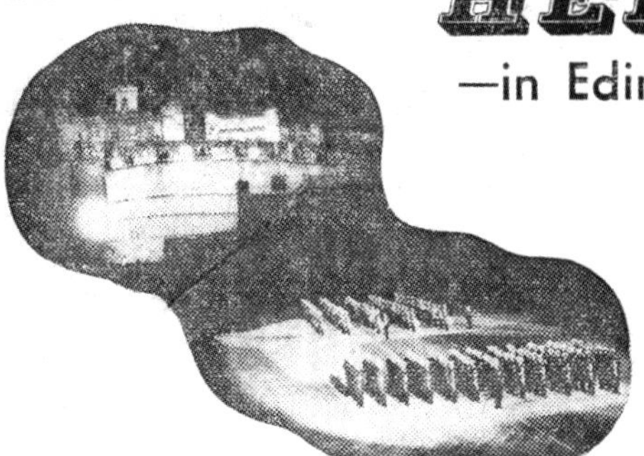

Look who's here–the new Lady Beecham back at work

SUNDAY

SHE wasn't expected among the quarter of a million visitors who will pour into this city for the Festival. She wasn't on the programme as a celebrity.

But **Lady Beecham**, 27-year-old bride of conductor **Sir Thomas Beecham**, flew into Edinburgh tonight.

And I could have sworn the piper on the castle ramparts threw in a few bars of the wedding march.

The girl, who as Shirley Hudson married 80-year-old Sir Thomas secretly in Switzerland a fortnight ago, has broken her honeymoon to manage the Royal Philharmonic Orchestra here at the Festival.

Business - as - usual Lady Beecham, brilliant in royal blue silk, looked surprised that I was surprised.

"*Of course* I shall continue to work with the orchestra as manager indefinitely. I have no intention of giving up," she said at the airport.

Or, as Sir Thomas characteristically put it when they parted at London Airport (he to fly back to Switzerland; she to leave for Edinburgh): "Someone has to look after my interests with that Philharmonic crowd. They are such an undisciplined, unruly mob."

"I have known Lady Beecham for nine years," he said there. "I thought about asking her to marry me for a long time. It was no snap decision.

"I approached the problem with all trepidation. With inward terror and a breaking heart. When I finally asked her she received the question with equal dismay."

Self-exiled

This was typical Sir Thomas. "We had no intention of telling anyone," he snorted. "Marriage is very largely the concern of two people only. There is no reason why the world should know. I cannot think of anything quite so ridiculous."

Lady Beecham, the girl from Southgate, will join her husband in Switzerland next week.

Daily Herald

How I proposed—by Sir Thomas

SIR THOMAS BEECHAM talked happily about his surprise wedding to his 27-year-old orchestra manager, Miss Shirley Hudson, when he flew back to Switzerland last night after a 24-hour business visit to London.

Lady Beecham, radiant in a royal blue silk suit, travelled with him to London Airport to see him board his plane. She too was flying off — but in the opposite direction, to join the Royal Philharmonic Orchestra at the Edinburgh Festival.

News Chronicle

Beecham back with his bride

SIR THOMAS BEECHAM, the 80-year-old conductor, flew back to London

Daily Mail

No snap decision

SIR THOMAS BEECHAM talked last night about his secret marriage to his 27-year-old orchestra secretary, **Miss Shirley Hudson.**

"It was no snap decision," he said. "I have known Lady Beecham nine years—and I have thought about asking her to marry me for a long time."

Sir Thomas, 80, and his bride —very smart in a silk suit— arrived together at London Airport and then split up.

Sir Thomas flew out to his home in Switzerland. His wife went north to join the Royal Philharmonic Orchestra at the Edinburgh Festival.

"Someone has to look after my interests with that crowd, said Sir Thomas. "They're such an undisciplined mob."

Marriage is obviously good for the maestro. When an airport official arrived at his car with a wheel-chair — his usual conveyance across the tarmac— he brushed him away and said: "You should know by now I ignore those things."

Sir Thomas turned to the problem of marriage. "I approached it with all trepidation," he said. "With inward terror and quaking heart. When I finally asked her, she received the question with equal dismay."

Daily Express

Sir Thomas says

★ **I TALKED to 80-year-old conductor Sir Thomas Beecham yesterday for the first time since his marriage in Zurich two weeks ago to his 27-year-old secretary Shirley Hudson.**

"The older I get the more I appreciate the state of matrimony," twinkled Sir Thomas. "Age doesn't count. One is never too old, young fellow. . . ."

Sir Thomas and his bride were on a brief 24-hour-visit to London when I saw them at the Grosvenor House Hotel.

"I had thought of marrying Lady Beecham for a long time—it was no snap decision," he said. "I approached the problem with all trepidation. With inward terror and quaking. When I finally asked her she received the question with equal dismay. . . ."

Then the couple went off—Lady Beecham to join the Royal Philharmonic Orchestra, which she manages, at the Edinburgh Festival.

And Sir Thomas back to Switzerland. They plan to meet in the South of France in a week's time.

Daily Sketch
(all) August 24 1959

The cinema cartoon character Mr Magoo, a short-sighted, bumbling but well-meaning senior citizen, was well known around the world. Not so well known was his creator, Stephen Bosustrow. Canadian-born Bosustrow set up his own company in 1945, two years after being fired by Walt Disney under wartime economy cuts.

His first big cartoon, Gerald McBoing-Boing, won him Academy Awards on both sides of the Atlantic. A series of popular Magoo cartoons followed. He wasn't difficult to spot when he flew in with his actress wife Audrey and their two sons to provide me with a simple diary piece for the evening papers. At six-feet-three, he towered over most of his fellow transatlantic passengers. But height apart, he was also the double of his former employer Disney. "It's true – people tell me that all the time," he said, "I could never see it. But I think Walt did. And as I'm taller maybe that's why he didn't want me around."

I might have asked Walt Disney himself that, when curiously, I found myself talking

Mr. STEPHEN BOSUSTOW
With his wife in London to-day.

McBoing-Boing here

IN London to-day on a three-day "jaunt" with his wife and two sons is 40-year-old Stephen Bosustow, Canadian-born creator of McBoing-Boing and Magoo, and Hollywood's principal pretender to the Walt Disney throne.

Bosustow, a towering 6ft. 3in., but otherwise a perfect double of the cartoon king himself, set up his own company in 1945, four years after being fired by Disney in the early war-time economy cuts. His first big cartoon, Gerald McBoing-Boing, earned academy awards on both sides of the Atlantic.

For his wife, former actress Audrey Stevenson, his sons, Stephen junior, 14, and Nicky, 11, the three-day stay in London will be a first visit to Europe, a vacation. But for dark-haired Stephen senior it includes a business venture.

Brenard Press picture
Evening Standard
June 19 1952

to the cartoon king a few weeks later. But I didn't get the chance. Disney was all excited about a new project he was planning. He called it "Epcot," his vision for a city of the future. It finally became the centre piece of his "countries of the world" theme park at Disney World in Florida. He told me of his plans in considerable detail, and said I was the first this side of the Atlantic to hear of it.

This time the newspapers were not impressed. As far as I was aware, very little was printed of his revelations. Perhaps they'd already heard it all. As I tried to tell Walt, we do occasionally get news from America, rather more than the Americans hear of us. I wished later I'd insisted on asking him what he thought of Mr Magoo.

My first meeting with another tycoon, newspaper and publishing boss and financial fraudster the late Robert Maxwell was in the early 'fifties. Harry had met him several times, and it was he who introduced me to Maxwell in the departures lounge at Northolt when he was making one of his frequent trips to the Continent. Like Harry, I found him a fascinating and larger-than-life character, in more senses than one.

He seemed to find it highly amusing to play the mystery man, constantly dropping hints about his service and background in British Intelligence, without giving anything away. I remember on one occasion a snapshot fell from his wallet as he went to buy a drink at the bar. I bent to pick it up (as I suspect he intended) only to see that it was an informal picture of him chatting with Pandit Nehru, the Indian Prime Minister. It was a first hint of his elevated connections.

Even then Maxwell was keenly interested in newspapers and was constantly asking questions such as where we obtained our information, and how we circulated news stories. I am consoled by the thought that I wouldn't have been able to tell him anything about pension schemes...but perhaps he already knew all there was to know on the subject.

He was however abnormally forthcoming when in January 1954 he flew to Moscow in his capacity as a publisher and head of Simkin Marshall, the book wholesalers. As the first of 30 British businessmen to win visas for trade visits to the Soviet Union, he told me he was hoping to persuade the Russians to lift their ban on English language publications.

He said he would also speak to them in their own language (one of nine he spoke) and appeal to them to pay royalties to original authors of Western books they had republished in Russian. Ironically, with hindsight of his own chicanery and the prophetic representation of a satirical "Captain Bob the Pirate" more than thirty years on, the ***William Hickey*** diary in the *Express (below)* chose to give my eight-paragraph story the only possible heading:

EXPRESS DIARY

William Hickey

OFF TO SEE THE PIRATES

IAN MAXWELL, the bookseller, who flew to Moscow yesterday to try to do some business, is one of the most remarkable men in his trade. At 30 he is managing director of Lange, Maxwell and Springer and runs Simpkin Marshall's, the big book wholesalers.

His real name is Jan Ludwig Hoch. He came over here in 1940 as a boy soldier in the Czech Army. He was transferred to Intelligence, acquired the name of Maxwell and did excellent work.

At the end of the war he served in Western Germany, realised that there was money to be made in the export and import of books.

Nine languages

He started up his firm in one room—and did so well that Hambros Bank gave him the financial backing to run Simpkin Marshall.

Not bad going.

He will be able to speak to the Russians in their own language. It is one of the nine he knows.

He wants to get the Russians to lift their ban on English publications. The Soviet has also been publishing English books and not paying royalties to the author.

Said Maxwell yesterday: "I want to stop the piracy."

Note Maxwell's use, at the time, of the first name "Ian" rather than "Robert".

Daily Express
Jan 18 1954

...or as he told me : "I want to stop the piracy."

Russian translation of 'Efficient Electricity Use' published by Maxwell's *Pergamon Press* in '78. Despite, or perhaps *because* of, his efforts in '54, the Russians never did pay any royalties for it.

Courtesy of Craig B. Smith, the original editor of "Efficient Energy Use".

It's not often a reporter knows, with absolute certainty, that the personality he's about to interview or simply buttonhole will provide him with a story. But in every era there are a handful of names guaranteed to make copy, sometimes without even opening their mouths, though a "quote" or two wouldn't go amiss. They may or may not be in the entertainment business; they will usually be rich and eccentric, or at least nonconformist in achievement or ambition, lifestyle, opinions or dress.

Everything about oil millionairess Olga Deterding also seemed overstated, though not disagreeably so. Two separate confrontations among many I had with her stand out clearly. Some diarists used one of the stories. As far as I know only one used the other.

It all started when oil-heiress Miss Deterding, who later became a close confidante of travel writer and TV broadcaster Alan Whicker, checked in at Heathrow for her flight to Nairobi on the arm, and in the arms of, Italian writer Alfredo Pieroni, there to see her off. They stayed close at the ticket desk as Miss Deterding's baggage was being weighed, clasping hands and cuddling. They snuggled up close on a red leather couch, whispering sweet nothings. And Signor Pieroni's arms crept round her waist as they parted at the entrance to the departures area.

Said the 38-years-old writer wistfully, as Olga turned to give him a final wave: "Anything is possible with Olga, but I don't think we shall be marrying. Once, some time ago...perhaps, yes. But not now."

What had changed the situation? The Signor would only say: "So much time has passed. Olga has been in Africa since we first met. I have not seen her very often." She had indeed spent some months assisting humanitarian Dr Albert Schweitzer at his African leper hospital.

And the heiress herself? When I joined her in the departures lounge she would only say: "Everyone wants me to get married. But I shan't begin to think seriously about marriage yet." And she brought the conversation firmly to an end by adding mysteriously: "As for the gentleman who saw me off … he just didn't exist."

Holding hands with Olga . . .

HEIRESS **Olga Deterding** was seen off to Paris last night by a 38-year-old Italian journalist **Alfredo Pieroni.** And their behaviour in London Airport lounge was very friendly indeed. . .

They held hands . . . they clasped arms . . . they snuggled together on a red leather bench.

Mr. Pieroni put his arm round Miss Deterding's waist as he saw her through Customs hall to say goodbye.

Afterwards he said wistfully: "Anything is possible with Olga—but I don't think we shall be marrying now. Once, some time ago perhaps, yes. But not now."

What had changed the situation? Mr. Pieroni would only say "So much time has passed. Olga has been to Kenya since we first met. I have not seen her very often."

Said Miss Deterding: "Everyone wants me to get married. But I shan't begin to think seriously about marriage just yet."

And she added mysteriously: "As for the gentleman who saw me off—he just didn't exist. . . ."

Daily Mail

☆ Fooled

☆ AN Italian writer, 38-year-old **Alfredo Pieroni**, was at London Airport last night seeing off heiress **Olga Deterding.**

Olga, who once worked at Dr. Schweitzer's hospital in the African jungle, held Alfredo's hand, clasped his arm, cuddled him in the waiting lounge.

And indeed Alfredo confessed: "Marriage? A long time ago perhaps it might have been possible—but not now, I think."

Said Olga as she left: "Marriage? I don't think I shall get married till all my friends have That gentleman? He just doesn't exist."

Well, he had us fooled.

Daily Sketch

At that point I bowed out. I had my story, indeed it made several news-column inches and one diary piece. Olga was a popular and well-known figure of the day.

On another occasion, Olga asked me to stay and keep her company until her flight was called. Moments passed and a BOAC girl approached. "Miss Deterding," she said, "I'm sorry, but there's a slight delay. One of the crew members for your flight has failed to turn up...."

Olga immediately jumped up. "I'm a pilot," she cried. "Won't I do?"

Mildly I suggested it might be a stewardess who was missing. She had her answer ready. "That's all right," she said brightly. "I'm a trained nurse. And I'm the right build and weight. I've only my age against me."

Courtesy: The Albert Schweitzer Fellowship

Albert Schweitzer at his African hospital, where Olga worked while Alfredo pined.

She was only 33, hardly ancient for a stewardess, but no one had the chance to point that out. She had moved on and was still talking. Now she was telling me that the wad of papers she was carrying was her latest batch of begging letters, invaluable aids to airborne millionairesses, she said, because they would be "something to read on the 'plane." During her stay in England she had employed a secretary to deal with her mail. "But she's out of a job now," she sighed, "I couldn't possibly afford permanent servants. Why, good heavens, I'm almost broke."

My story concluded:

And with that, Miss Deterding tipped a porter £1 (equal to an average day's total tips), complained about having to pay £27 excess luggage charges and said she would probably charter a 'plane to fly her the 300-miles from Nairobi to Malindi, where she was having a holiday.

Million-pound footnote: ***Miss Deterding's offer to fly her 'plane was graciously declined. A standby arrived, and the flight left 20 minutes late.***

SKETCH DIARY •••• SKETCH DIARY •••• SK

OLGA TO THE RESCUE

MILLIONAIRESSES are entitled to be eccentric. Expected to be a little odd. And at times, just to keep up appearances, of course, to behave a little strangely.

Let no one accuse **Miss Olga Deterding**, who inherited an oil fortune from her father but chose to spend her time at **Dr. Albert Schweitzer's** African leper hospital, of not conforming with the rules.

Consider what happened when she left London last night for Nairobi.

'I'm a pilot'

THE departure of the BOAC Comet was delayed. A crew member had not turned up.

Miss Deterding jumped forward.

"I'm a pilot," she cried. "Won't I do?"

But perhaps it was a stewardess who was missing?

"That's all right, I'm a trained nurse," said Miss Deterding. "And the right build and weight—I've only my age against me."

Mail

SHE is only 33, but no one had a chance to point that out as Miss D. was still talking.

She explained that the wad of papers she carried were "mostly begging letters."

These are invaluable aids to air-borne millionairesses because "it will be something to read on the plane."

During her stay in England Miss Deterding has had to employ a secretary to deal with her mail.

"But she's out of a job now," sighed Miss Deterding. "I couldn't possibly afford permanent servants—Why, good heavens, I'm almost broke."

And with that, Miss Deterding tipped a porter £1, complained about having to pay £27 excess luggage and said she would probably charter a plane to fly her the 300 miles from Nairobi to Malindi, where she will have a holiday.

Million-pound footnote: Miss D's offer to fly the plane was graciously declined. A stand-in arrived and the plane left 20 minutes late.

Daily Sketch
Nov 10 1960

I filed the story exactly as it happened. The *Daily Sketch* diary used every word, as a page lead (left).

*

Alongside the alliteratively rich, Ruritanian royalty and newly republic-redundant rulers of Europe featured strongly in the national and London evenings' diaries more than once throughout the 'fifties and 'sixties. As a literally dying breed, few of them remain as household names forty-five years on, and are only remembered, in most cases by their "pretender" successors or by family links with British Royals.

Heathrow's paparazzi invariably came into their own with the comings and goings of the Windsor "Royal Firm" on its national business. Within the British Isles this usually meant the use of an aircraft of the RAF Queen's Flight from a selected piece of hallowed tarmac adjoining an available but infrequently-accessed VIP suite, the Royal Lounge.

Depending on the numbers present and whether their identities were familiar to the airport police, the photographers might be permitted to within a few feet of the royal aircraft steps, or corralled behind metal barriers up to fifty yards distant. Whether on close-up or telescopic extension lens, however, the cameramen's combined objective was ever the same: to achieve that definitive "different" shot of the most photographed people in the world.

It may well have been a photographer who first proclaimed, "Every picture is worth a thousand words." It is just as likely to have been reluctantly uttered by a reporter out on the same assignment. Though he may have demurred on the quantity of column inches being sacrificed, he would have seen the picture as a simple and sometimes essential aid to his writing.

From the safety of elapsed years I can grudgingly admit there were times when I was silently grateful to the airport's freelance cameramen for providing a desirable pictorial back-up to my words. I can even recall (shock, horror) occasions when, in the absence of support from otherwise-engaged Brenard photographic colleagues, I found myself treasonably telling a selected opposition snapper of my exclusive "angle" on a story to ensure that it was embellished with an apt illustration!

In defence I have to say that a form of negative co-operation has always existed between commercial rivals on major news stories where everyone has an equal stake and the opportunities for scoops or even exclusive angles are few and far between. My "co-operation" was however far from altruistic.

For similar reasons we had to be thankful for the devotion of photographers to their Royal coverage. Reporters can be easily missed in a crowd, with nothing to distinguish them but their notebooks. But you only need to bring a photographer within fifteen yards to animate some Royals and provide something more to write about than the shape of a hat or the colour of a coat. The subject might even be persuaded to offer a deliberate snub to the cameras by turning to face unnaturally in the opposite direction. Not much use to the photographer, but a useful point for exploitation by the hungry seeker-after-copy in the days before it became a standard reaction.

Any professional "snapper" of Royals will tell you that every member of the family has his or her own way of acknowledging photographers when they can be expected to be present, and usually they are consistent. The Queen is aware yet unaware, usually prepared to present herself to the cameras without appearing to do so, but sometimes displaying signs of apparent irritation, by putting on her renowned "Miss Piggy" face.

Prince Philip, temperamentally irascible, makes his dislike of the photographers obvious with both vocal and body language. The objects of his scorn generally return the sentiment.

The Queen's younger sister, the late Princess Margaret, was something of an enigma in those early days. She could swing between a sweeping disdain, demonstrated by keeping an aide or a policeman between her and the cameras, to a blatant coyness with both reporters and photographers quite at odds with her reputed imperious nature. Diana,

Princess of Wales, was by no means the first to flirt with the camera lens, and I swear the Queen's sister returned the wink I was dared by photographers to give her on one occasion before her ill-fated marriage. Presumably it was too fast for a 250th at f8.

The Princess Royal and the Prince of Wales have in their time shown the same sparks as their father's short fuse, though the former has more often committed the cardinal insult of totally ignoring the photographers. The heir to the throne, on the other hand, can be variously chummy and sympathetic or clearly irritable, on edge and impatient.

The late Queen Mother was always the airport photographers' favourite Royal. A frequent flyer well into her 'nineties, she was ever alert to the needs of the camera and became very adroit at moving to the side of a less sympathetic official to ensure there was a clear line between her and the lenses, however close or distant.

More than once I was aware of her deliberately getting out of an official limousine on the "wrong" side, moving across the seat to do so, when she realised, as she unfailingly did, that the vehicle was blocking the view of the photographers. I have seen her pointedly walking away from a direct route from car to aircraft steps, only to place herself immediately before the press "pen." While talking animatedly to an aide she would suddenly turn and flash a natural smile or give a regal wave as if she has only just become aware of the lenses.

As reporters, our presence on these occasions, however much we hoped otherwise, was mostly obligatory, a form of insurance that nothing sensational or even mildly newsworthy would illuminate the Royal departure or arrival.

An irritated Prince Philip at one time gave the then airport management strict instructions that his numerous flights to and from London Airport's relatively deserted south side were to be omitted from the airport's daily but restricted list of VIP movements, even though RAF helicopters were sometimes used. He argued that many of these journeys were routine and therefore not newsworthy. The press nevertheless heard of most of the trips, and wondered at times of their purpose. But the Prince was right. No one was really much interested.

Source: Wikimedia Commons, Library and Archives Canada

Princess Margaret, Oct 1967

Source: Wikimedia Commons, photographer unknown

Queen Mother, 1985

There were, however, the major Royal events which, unlike the shuttle-like regularity of the round-Britain journeys or the seasonal holiday flights to Sandringham, Balmoral or Dyce, attracted the attention of Fleet Street's finest, and, in later years, the outside broadcasts of radio and TV news units.

As monarch and a visitor rather than a passenger, the Queen herself inaugurated most of the major developments at Heathrow, opening in turn, the central terminal passenger buildings as they were completed, the subways linking them and the extension of the London Underground into the airport some 30 years after it was first proposed.

Some years later the Prince and Princess of Wales opened Terminal 4, the former commenting on the point that although a regular user of the airport, he had never before followed the route taken by most passengers through the terminal, and obviously had no idea of some of the distances involved.

The Queen, of course, has some poignant memories of the original northside terminal. It was here that she first stepped on British soil as monarch in February 1952, following the sudden death of her father, King George VI. She and the Duke of Edinburgh were visiting Kenya as part of a Commonwealth tour when the news reached them. They flew home immediately.

Many years later the original management of the airport hotel, which stands on that very spot alongside the Bath-road, wanted to commemorate the Queen's accession with a plaque, and sought the approval of Buckingham Palace. They were advised that the Queen would prefer not to have the occasion remembered in such a way, as it provoked sad and painful memories for her, something I believe has never before been recorded. Such a plaque is however now displayed in the hotel's adjoining restaurant.

Along with scores of other press, reporters and photographers from British and overseas newspapers and agencies, radio reporters and TV commentators, cameramen and sound and lighting technicians, I was also present when the new Queen descended the steps of her BOAC airliner, dressed, unfamiliarly, entirely in black.

Pale and drawn, she looked a calm, if fragile and slightly uncertain figure as she was quietly greeted by the Prime Minister, Winston Churchill, and the Leader of the Opposition, Clement Attlee. In an eerie silence, broken only by the clicking of camera

Author's collection

Prime Minister Winston Churchill waits with head bowed to greet the new Queen Elizabeth II, dignified but sad, as she steps onto British soil as monarch for the first time.

shutters, we looked on from a huge pen set up at the edge of the tarmac as the Queen climbed into her waiting car, the Duke close behind her.

With many of those same colleagues I had been there too just eight days earlier, when the King, together with Queen Elizabeth and Princess Margaret, had driven out to Heathrow with other members of the royal family to see off the Princess Elizabeth and her husband. King George himself was to have made the same Commonwealth tour, but had been forced to hand over to his daughter because of illness. He too looked fragile on what was to be his last public appearance. He was only just recovering from a recent operation to remove one of his lungs.

A similar Press enclosure had also been set up then alongside a lawned veranda to the airport's public restaurant. Conscious that every newspaper had between one and three reporters present to cover the occasion, I had accepted that there was little linage potential for me unless I could come across some completely different aspect of the story, an exclusive angle.

So I chose to hover close to the Royal Lounge, a single storey annexe to the sprawling, prefabricated huts which formed the temporary North Terminal passenger buildings. Although about a hundred yards away from the edge of the tarmac, I had the advantage of a solitary, unhindered close-hand view of the doorway of the Lounge from the adjoining arrivals' building entrance.

Almost directly facing me, behind another barrier on the other side of the access road, was a small group of photographers, a representative rota privileged to wait within camera range of the VIP exit. Beyond them, alongside an aircraft taxiway, was London Airport's temporary public enclosure, now crowded with scores of sightseers. They watched in silence as the King and Queen, with other members of the royal family and Mr and Mrs Churchill walked past to board the aircraft to say their farewells.

While they were gone, I took the opportunity to move closer to the Lounge, now empty except for other officials and members of the royal household. I positioned myself at the foot of a flight of concrete steps which led up to the roof of the annexe. Here I would have an ideal vantage point if, on their return from the tarmac, the royal party decided to watch the airliner's take-off from the doorstep of the lounge, just a few feet to my right.

A few minutes later the King, with the Queen at his side, slowly began to walk back from the tarmac. It was bitterly cold, and the King constantly brushed his hair back with his hand in the strong breeze which had blown up. Princess Margaret followed her parents, with Lord and Lady Mountbatten, Commonwealth diplomats and others. I broke off a conversation with Superintendent Goldsack, head of the airport police, as he suddenly sprang to attention with a salute. The royal party had changed direction and was heading straight for us. The Superintendent stepped backwards and I in turn was forced to move on to a grass verge at the side of the steps. The King and Queen wanted to pass, and I was in the way.

At the last moment the airport commandant, Sir John D'Albiac, had suggested to the King that he might wish to see the take-off from the roof, and the King had led the way up the external steps. For nearly fifteen minutes, as his Prime Minister peered through the glass door of the warm lounge below him, the King stood hatless in the wind, one of a group lining the waist-high stone parapet just a few feet above my head. He remained there until the BOAC Argonaut airliner taxied off to the distant runway, finally took off and disappeared from view in the distant cloudy sky.

A week later the King was dead. He suffered a coronary thrombosis at Sandringham, his Norfolk country estate. Princess Elizabeth heard the news at Treetops Hotel in Kenya from an equerry. He had heard it first from a journalist accompanying the royal couple.

Hotel Treetops, Kenya, where Princess Elizabeth learned of her father's death.

Courtesy of Treetops Hotel, Aberdare National Park

Author's collection. From an original BAA archive picture by Arthur Kemsley

On the parapet *(from l. to r.)*: **the present Queen's uncle, Earl Mountbatten; Sir Miles Thomas, chairman of BOAC; Lady Mountbatten; an unnamed official; Sir John D'Albiac, the London Airport commandant** *(turning to his left);* **another unknown; Queen Elizabeth,** *(later the Queen Mother)*; **King George; Princess Margaret; Whitney Straight, BOAC managing director. At the doors of the lounge, peering through the glass, the then Prime Minister, Sir Winston Churchill. Looking on at the entrance to the Royal Lounge: Major Ronnie, Chief Constable of the Ministry of Aviation constabulary** *(left)* **and Superintendent Goldsack, commander of the Heathrow police force** *(right).*

A rare, and previously unpublished picture of the last public appearance of King George VI with other members of the Royal Family on the roof of the old Royal Lounge at London Airport's Northside terminal.
The King, the Queen and others climbed an outside staircase to watch the departure for Africa of the airliner carrying the then Princess Elizabeth on the start of a royal tour. Just a week later in the Treetops hotel in Kenya, the Princess and Prince Philip learnt of her succession to the throne after the King's sudden death.

European Royals, both incumbent and "retired," were regular visitors to Northolt and Heathrow throughout the 'fifties. Prince Bernhard of the Netherlands frequently piloted his own aircraft on private trips and on at least one occasion was accompanied by the then heir-apparent, Princess Beatrix, as a passenger. A Dutch officer then flew the royal Dakota aircraft back to Holland, only to return a few hours later with Queen Juliana and her second daughter, Princess Irene. Avoiding travelling together by air was a safety procedure followed by most royal families.

Ex-King Michael of Romania made a less auspicious appearance at Heathrow when he drove from London to meet his mother, ex-Queen Helen. His small saloon car caused a traffic jam when he tried to find a parking space adjoining the terminal. An airport policeman lost his patience and told the king what he thought of "wheel-happy" drivers.

"I told him off good and proper," said the policeman later when I told him who his victim was, and he added: "He seemed very contrite and apologetic."

Ex-Queen Anne of Romania, like her husband, was also unrecognised, at least by fellow passengers, when she flew from London to Lausanne. A member of her household,

General Constantin Lazar, told me she was expecting her third child and was on her way to a private hospital for the confinement. The news was reduced to two or three paragraphs tucked away in the middle of the three London evening diaries.

It was the younger British Royals, together with their European cousins, who most often featured in the news columns – just as another generation did a few decades on. When two cars screeched to a halt outside the passenger terminal, a hair's breadth separated them from a head-on collision. Airline official Joe Chamberlain dashed forward, and realising no one was hurt, he slapped the nearest driver on the back.

Nice work chum, he told Duke

COCKNEY JOE CHAMBERLAIN patted the 17-year-old car driver benevolently on the shoulder and said: "Smart bit of driving that, chum."

Two cars had screeched to a bumper-to-bumper halt to avoid a broadside collision at London Airport yesterday.

"I was pretty lucky, wasn't I?" agreed the young man, who had an attractive young lady at his side.

Curious, Joe followed the car, a brown station wagon. It pulled up at the Royal lounge.

"It gave me quite a turn when I discovered who it was I had called chum," said Joe later.

It was the Duke of Kent. At his side was his cousin, Princess Elizabeth of Yugoslavia. In the back, the Duke's young brother, Prince Michael and the chauffeur.

The Duke was driving down to see the Princess off to Paris

Daily Sketch
(both) Aug 1 1953

—H.R.H.—
'Chum' to him

FIFTY - SEVEN - YEAR - OLD Mr. Joe Chamberlain darted forward yesterday as two cars braked at London Airport to avoid a collision.

Joe, who has worked at this airport for years, patted the young driver of one car on the shoulder and said: "Smart bit of driving that, chum."

The young driver, a young, attractive girl at his side, replied: "Yes, I was pretty lucky, wasn't I?"

The driver? The 17-year-old Duke of Kent. The passenger? His cousin, Princess Elizabeth of Yugoslavia. In the back were the Duke's young brother, Prince Michael, and a chauffeur.

Daily Mail

"Smart bit of driving, that, chum," he said. Pleased, the driver, with an attractive girl at his side, looked up and replied: "Yes, I was pretty lucky, wasn't I?"

Curious, Joe watched as the car, a brown station wagon, moved off. It pulled up outside a VIP lounge. The driver was the 17-years-old Duke of Kent. His passenger was his 20-years-old cousin, Princess Elisabeth of Yugoslavia, and in the back travelled Prince Michael, his younger brother, with the car's chauffeur.

Two or three years later it was the same Princess Elisabeth who played a leading role in another Heathrow cameo. VIP greeters and senior airline officials had been waiting outside Terminal 2 for a Kensington Palace limousine. They had been warned that the young Princess was joining a flight to Paris after a week's visit to her aunt, the Duchess of Kent.

Then a scruffy, hand-painted baker's delivery van pulled in at the kerbside. The baker's name had been smudged out from a dented side panel. Airport police looked on in disfavour, and were about to move the van on when someone recognised the young passenger easing herself from the back as none other than the Princess. As one official hurriedly called up the reception committee, the Princess made a dash for the check-in desks. Two male companions followed her from the front seats of the van, dutifully taking charge of her luggage.

Witnessing the scene, I had little chance to talk to the Princess, who was already late for her flight, so I tackled the friends. But they became agitated when I mentioned the van. They were, they said, students at Oxford, and had not been given permission to drive the Princess to the airport. It would be better, they insisted, if their names were left out.

Too late. Now the police wanted the same information. One of them approached as I tried to persuade the students to tell me more. The van, he said, was in a no-parking area, was causing an obstruction, and was holding up a score of passengers trying to leave a bus.

"Oh dear, what a frightful bore," groaned one of the two young men as he told the police his name was Peter Zinovieff, and said that he was studying at University College, Oxford. His companion took the opportunity to return to the van and Mr Zinovieff carefully placed the policeman between us, moving away as he did so. He was not going to be more forthcoming.

Tanfield, the *Daily Mail* diarist, gave the story a page lead together with a posed picture of the Princess, captured at the aircraft by a photographer *(see opposite)*.

The *Express* carried a shorter, similar piece. But it was the *Mail* who made the effort to tie up any loose ends of the story. The diary provided some background on Zinovieff, describing him as a high-spirited and brilliant 24-years-old. His van was well-known in the Oxford streets, but had not been seen for some days. They also contacted his mother, Lady Jean Zinovieff, who told the *Mail*: "He's always getting up to some sort of madcap stunt. He's known Princess Elisabeth for about two years and I think they are quite good friends".

When, in 1959 we learnt that Prince Michael of Kent was flying to Paris we were puzzled because, although his name was on Heathrow's privately-circulated VIP list for the day, no VIP lounge had been allocated for his use. When I asked why, I was told that he was being escorted through passport controls as an ordinary passenger. Yet his sister, Princess Alexandria (incidentally another great favourite of the photographers) had travelled as a VIP only a few hours earlier, and Prince Michael had been permitted the VIP privilege of seeing her off on the tarmac.

As with his cousin Princess Elisabeth three years earlier, I decided to wait for the 18-years-old Prince on the forecourt of Heathrow's Terminal 2. There appeared to be no one waiting to receive him, and for a moment I wondered if he might have been driven directly to a VIP area after all. Then suddenly I spotted a familiar young man striding through the doorway, apparently alone.

I positioned myself within hearing range as he marched confidently up to a check-in desk, placed his small suitcase on a weighing machine and handed over a ticket. "Air France Flight 849," he announced. A senior passenger officer for the airline immediately stepped over to him and offered his services, then, after a word from the Prince, quietly backed away, simply pointing the Royal passenger in the right direction for proceeding. As I followed at a discreet distance, not wishing to take him unawares, he finally joined a queue of other passengers at a passport control point. He was quite certainly alone and unaccompanied. I moved in.

To the mass audiences of the 'nineties, the sight and sound of reporters and photographers calling out questions to members of the Royal Family, and sometimes getting a response (even if only "Naff off!") was not unfamiliar. The Queen, because of her unique position, has remained relatively immune, at least until recently. Her husband, though perhaps for different reasons, has also generally avoided similar targeting. The Prince of Wales, Princess Anne, Prince Andrew and Prince Edward have each used or been used by the modern media.

But this is a comparatively rare phenomenon. Before the 'sixties it was almost unthinkable that members of the Royal Family might suffer the indignity of press questions. Indeed their voices were rarely heard outside formal speechmaking or inauguration ceremonies. There was almost an unwritten rule among journalists that the Royals were unapproachable under any circumstances.

All this ran through my mind as Prince Michael moved forward, almost meekly, in the passport queue, unnoticed by his fellow passengers. Then I thought: "In a moment he will be addressed by a passport officer who will read his passport. Other passengers on the flight will be able to talk to him, even if they recognise him. Any one of them could be a reporter..." I knew I needed no further justification for approaching him.

Moving alongside, I introduced myself.

"Would you mind telling me why you are visiting Paris?" I asked, and almost immediately wished I'd put that another way. After all, he was eighteen years old and entitled to a life of his own...

But Prince Michael wasn't the least bit concerned at my breach of protocol, if that is what it was. He was polite and pleasant. "I'm going to spend four months in France," he told me, "Trying to learn the language, you know"

And to my further questions he said: "I shall be staying with a family…friends of ours… and not at a school. So I shall be learning the hard way."

We exchanged a few more pleasantries. I wished him a good trip and luck with his lessons, and he in turn asked me some questions about my work, and how I knew he was on the flight. Then we were interrupted. Another airline official stepped up to ask if he would like to board his 'plane ahead of other passengers.

"Thanks, but no thanks," said the Prince, "And I don't want any fuss. I'd like to go out to the 'plane on the coach like everyone else."

TO AND FRO

OUT: **Princess Elizabeth of Yugoslavia**, 20-year-old niece of the **Duchess of Kent**; to Paris, after a week at Kensington Palace.

The princess arrived at

PRINCESS ELIZABETH

London Airport in a delivery van with two Oxford students 15 minutes before take-off. She dashed from the van with the students sprinting at her heels carrying her two suitcases. . . .

Lord and Lady Astor, to Lisbon, travelling with **Lord Douglas of Kirtleside**, B.E.A. chairman (Said Lord Douglas: "I hope to persuade the Portuguese airline to allow us to step up services from London"). . . .

Daily Express

How Elisabeth went by van

IT was a dirty, hand-painted baker's delivery van. The name of the Oxford baker had been smudged out from a dented side panel.

It slithered to a stop yesterday outside London Airport's main terminal building. Airport policemen looked on in disfavour.

Then out stepped the Princess. Behind her, her two gentlemen attendants, carrying the cases.

Airport high-ups and BEA officials had been expecting **Princess Elisabeth** of Yugoslavia, who is 20.

NOT AS EXPECTED

They had been warned that she had completed a week's unofficial visit to her aunt, the **Duchess of Kent**, at Kensington Palace, and was expected to join a flight for Paris.

But things had not been expected to turn out like this.

The startled bigwigs hurried forward as the Princess, in a loose-fitting cherry-red coat, sprinted for the ticket desk.

Dutifully the two young men sprinted behind.

When the Princess was safely aboard her plane I asked the young men to explain the van and they turned a little angry.

They were, they said, Oxford students. They had not had permission from their college to bring the Princess to the airport. It would therefore be better if names were left out.

But outside, the airport policemen were eyeing the baker's van aberration with renewed disfavour. It was blocking the path of an airport bus.

"Oh dear, what a frightful bore," muttered the young man with spectacles.

He told the police his name was **Peter Zinovieff**, that the van was his and that he was studying at University College, Oxford.

Mr. Zinovieff, who is 24, is a high-spirited and brilliant young man who took a scholarship in geology and is doing a post-graduate course at University College.

JUST LIKE PETER

His van, well known in the Oxford streets, has been missing all week-end.

Last night, at her home in Rusper, Sussex, his stepmother, **Lady Jean Zinovieff**, told me: "I'd no idea that Peter was getting up to pranks like this.

"But I'm not surprised. He's always up to some sort of madcap stunt with his Oxford friends.

"He's known Princess Elisabeth for about a couple of years. I think they are quite good friends. If I remember, they met at a party or something in London."

Daily Mail (both) Feb 26 1957

He did just that. And there was no one on the tarmac waiting to see him off with a kiss the way he'd seen off his sister just six hours earlier. Most of the newspapers carried the *PA-Reuter* photo of that kiss, Princess Alexandra's hand resting on her brother's shoulder. The *Daily Express* suggested that perhaps she was giving him some "sound sisterly advice" on the occasion of his first trip to Paris – alone. But all of them carried my "interview," the *Mail* again heading a *Paul Tanfield* diary lead with the words, in an even larger type-face.

PAUL TANFIELD

A long French lesson for Prince Michael

HE WILL STAY WITH FRIENDS OF THE FAMILY

THE young man with one small suitcase strolled up to the check-in desk at London Airport, obligingly placed his case on the weighing-machine, and handed over his ticket. "Air France, flight 849," he said.

Prince Michael of Kent was off on his summer holiday — without any of the commotion which usually attends the departure of a member of the Royal Family.

No officials tripping over themselves. No posse of policemen. No porters.

That—as you might expect of a young man who chose to play the bassoon in the cadet band at Eton—was the way the 18-year-old Prince wanted it.

The hard way

And, as you might expect of a young man who likes to borrow a bassoon to practise on during his school holidays, this vacation isn't going to be all fun.

"I'm going to spend four months in France," he said. "Trying to learn the language, you know.

"I shall be staying with a family—friends of ours—and not at a school. So I shall be learning the hard way."

Then he went off to join the queue of holiday travellers waiting to pass through the Customs.

An airline official inquired anxiously if he would care for some V.I.P. treatment that would allow him to be first aboard the plane.

"Thanks very much," said the Prince who, after his holiday, intends to follow his brother, the **Duke of Kent** into the Army, "but I don't want any fuss.

Two kisses

"I'd like to go out to the aircraft on the coach like everyone else.'

A refreshing note of informality.

It was the Prince's second visit to London Airport in one day. Six hours earlier he had dutifully accompanied his sister, **Princess Alexandra**, when she flew off to Italy to join the **Duchess of Kent**.

And, as his reward, collected a sisterly kiss on each cheek.

Daily Mail* *Oct-Nov 1960

One news desk 'phoned back to congratulate me on the story with the words: "That's the first time we've ever had direct interview quotes from a Royal. You may have started something." He was wrong. In reality, the honour would probably go to my brother Harry, who, I learnt much later, had once had a similarly brief conversation with the Duke of Windsor at Northolt when he was making one of his rare visits to London. But perhaps a non-serving member of "The Firm" didn't count, even if he was an ex-King.

Prince Michael had flown BEA. But the Kents usually favoured the French airline for their crossings. Some weeks later, Prince Michael's mother, Princess Marina (still the Duchess at the time, as her son the Duke had not yet married), featured in another London Airport picture story. As she too was about to board a flight to Paris, on her way to visit her son at the home of her niece, Countess Kyburg, the stiletto heel of her shoe sank in a melted tar expansion joint in the concrete, and almost threw her over.

Momentarily she lost her balance, and her shoe. The Air France Manager at Heathrow, Jean Freullet, dashed forward to offer a supporting Gallic arm, and the Duchess quickly regained her poise *(See opposite).*

Over the years some Royal household staff became familiar figures through our regular contact with them at the airport. It was from one household driver I learnt why the Duke of Kent's bride, the former Miss Katharine Worsley, carried her arm bandaged and in a strap sling during one official flight on a Royal aircraft in the early seventies.

"That's down to me," he said, matter-of-factly, "I slammed the door on her fingers."

My involuntary wince became a shudder when he went on: "She was reaching into the car to pick something up from the seat, I think, and she held the door column just above the hinge. I didn't even see her hand there.

"Oh yes, she yelled all right. Wouldn't you? It must have been very painful. Her fingers were badly bruised and it's a wonder the bones weren't crushed. All I could say was, 'I'm so sorry, Your Royal Highness,' but although she was near to tears, she kept assuring me it wasn't my fault. She could have bawled my head off."

The story only made a few lines partly, I suspect, because the bandages didn't show in photographs. And of course I couldn't use any of the quotes from the driver, which would have given strength to the story. His job might have been at stake.

From the very early days of post-war civil aviation, the mother of Prince Philip, Princess Alice of Greece, or Princess Andrew, after her late husband, as she preferred to be known, was a familiar traveller to and from London. On occasions, although she was widely known for wearing the grey headress and habit of a Mother Superior in a Greek religious order, she almost passed unrecognised.

After attending her daughter-in-law's Coronation, she mingled with holidaymakers in

Oops! But Duchess of Kent stays as cool as her daughter receiving a child's bouquet

COOL in a tricky situation at London Airport yesterday was the Duchess of Kent.

COOL in the sticky heat of Lagos was her daughter, Princess Alexandra.

The Duchess was off to Paris to see her niece, Countess Kyburg. As she stepped from her car she lost a shoe. It stuck in a patch of soft tar.

She stumbled slightly but quickly regained her poise. An Air France official hurried over to give the Duchess his arm. Gracefully, she slipped her foot back into the shoe.

Daily Express

Displaying legendary French gallantry, Air France Manager Jean Freullet dashes forward to offer a supporting arm to the then Duchess of Kent, as she stumbles on the Heathrow tarmac.

Freullet was later awarded the prestigious French order of chivalry as a Chevalier de la Légion d'honneur, though the two events were not thought to be related.

The Duchess steps OUT!

The Duchess of Kent holds on to a car door to steady herself as she steps into her right shoe at London Airport yesterday. The shoe stuck in a patch of wet tar like this (pictured left) as the Duchess got out of the car.

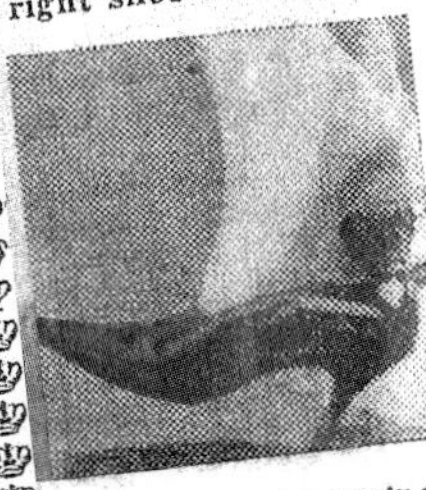

She was flying to Paris to visit her niece, Countess Kyburg, and her younger son, Prince Michael.

The eighteen-year-old Prince is staying with friends there to learn the French language.

Daily Sketch

Tar hitch

THE **Duchess of Kent** overcame a classic embarrassing situation with commendable good grace at London Airport yesterday.

She lost her shoe as she stepped from a car onto the tarmac before boarding a Paris-bound airliner. The stiletto heel became wedged in soft tar and was left behind for a moment as the Duchess regained her balance.

With true Gallic gallantry an Air France airline official gave her his arm as she reached out for the car door. The Duchess slipped her foot into her shoe again and went off joking about the problems of high fashion.

She was off to stay with her niece, **Countess Kyburg.** Her younger son, **Prince Michael,** is now in France brushing up his French.

Daily Express *circa July 1959*

the London Airport check-in hall, supervising the weighing and labelling of her own luggage under the attentive eye of the Greek Minister in London. Before being whisked away to a VIP lounge I looked on as she even found time to buy an armful of magazines carrying photographs of the Coronation.

The Princess may, of course, have decided after an earlier experience, prior to the Queen's wedding, that she was safer looking after herself than relying on official help. The existence until 1954 of Northolt as the principal London airport for European services continued to confound many, even in Royal circles. Like airport officials there, I began making my own enquiries when the personal limousine of the then Princess Elizabeth turned up to meet her future mother-

Brenard Press picture

Flying Home

PRINCESS ALICE of Greece, mother of the Duke of Edinburgh, flew from London Airport to-day back to Athens after attending the Coronation.

Though wearing the now familiar grey headdress of a Mother Superior in a Greek religious order, Princess Alice mingled unrecognised among travellers in the main passenger lounge at the airport, supervising the labelling and weighing of her own luggage.

Then an airline official spotted her and conducted her to the Royal V.I.P. lounge. She bought an armful of magazines, carrying Coronation photographs of her daughter-in-law—the Queen.

The Greek Minister in London saw her off at the airport.

Evening News and Evening Standard (both) June 12 1953

Princess Alice of Greece

in-law. No one at Northolt knew of her expected arrival.

We all discovered pretty quickly that Princess Andrew had already arrived – at Heathrow – and was looking for the car. Someone had sent it to the wrong airport. The limo was despatched to London, empty. The Princess left in the Greek Ambassador's car. He at least had got it right.

Her son was even less lucky. When bad weather forced the Royal Flight Viking airliner bringing him home from a tour of Germany to divert to its base at RAF Benson, Oxfordshire, Prince Philip was obliged to wait more than an hour for his car to pick him up. An RAF officer at Benson told me: "We simply don't have any suitable transport for him here."

There were red faces too when, only a month after the Coronation, the young Queen arrived at London Airport with Prince Philip nearly 20 minutes early for their flight to Belfast. Officials and onlookers, including the press corps, were taken by surprise.

No route-progress radio messages were available in those days, just an out-posted policeman to yell: "Here she comes!" in time to alert the Heathrow commandant, Air Marshal Sir John D'Albiac in the VIP lounge. He had to make an undignified dash for more than 100 yards to greet the non-stop Royal couple at the steps of the aircraft.

Normally unflustered Air Commodore Sir Edward "Mousey" Fielden, Captain of the Queen's Flight, also arrived at the aircraft just in time to salute. Another officer tried in vain to remove his gloves to shake hands with last-minute passenger Sir David Maxwell Fyfe, the Home Secretary, holding up the departure as he struggled. He finally shook hands with the gloves on... the engines roared and the Royal aircraft took off well ahead of time.

In the early days of her sister's reign, Princess Margaret was one of the busiest members of the Royal Family, and a regular user of the London airports on her official duties. In later years she was more frequently seen as a passenger on scheduled British Airways services travelling alone or with friends.

Press interest in mid-1953 however, centred on one special friend, Group Captain Peter Townsend, a former equerry to the late King, and strongly tipped as the future husband of the Princess. In temporary "exile" as Britain's air attaché in Brussels, the much-photographed RAF ace flew frequently between the two capitals, and should have been instantly recognisable, even out of uniform.

So it was surprising that on one occasion a good-looking, dark-haired man in a grey suit and an RAF blue shirt was "recognised" and approached separately by three airport press photographers who independently asked: "Aren't you Group Captain Townsend?"

Wearily, he denied it each time. Then the passengers for Brussels were called. The Townsend double didn't move. He was flying to Paris.

The mere fact that the photographers had to ask proved something. And if I'd been there I would have known better... wouldn't I? Well, I *did* find him some months later when he again slipped back to London, the collar of his raincoat turned up and a trilby hat pulled low over his eyes – even though he travelled, inexplicably, as "Mr Carter."

Peter Townsend —secret London trip

GROUP CAPTAIN Peter Townsend, 39-year-old former royal equerry and friend of Princess Margaret, flew back to Belgium last night after a secret visit to London.

His ticket from London Airport was booked in the name of Carter.

The B.E.A. airliner was delayed an hour, and "Mr. Carter" in a raincoat and low pulled trilby, spent the time in a private office.

Townsend is air attaché at the British Embassy in Brussels.

Daily Express July 2 1954

It was not until October 1955 that the Princess finally announced her decision not to marry the much-decorated former fighter pilot on the grounds that he was a divorcee. For some months it had been reported that she had consulted with a number of church leaders.

Indeed back in May, the Archbishop of Canterbury, Dr Geoffrey Fisher, had been quoted as saying that the couple would wed – a statement he vehemently denied making when I asked him about the report.

"My answer to questions at the time was simply 'No comment'," he told me, "I made no such comment then and I make no comment now. That is all there ever was to it."

Not all that glisters in the lenses of the news photographer is gold for Fleet Street, sometimes for obvious reasons. The contact prints and eight-by-sixes that have dropped on national picture desks hourly may have been simply unfit to print, legally, morally, tastefully or aesthetically. And as I've indicated elsewhere, similar restraints are now and again also placed on the written picture. It might have been difficult to sell one little Royal scenario in the national news market, but it found a stage in my column in the airport edition of the local weekly newspaper. It ran:

Resident Press membership was well represented, otherwise the moral might not have been so conclusive. The occasion: the return to London of the Queen Mother after her holiday in Scotland. The resident photographers were in place early behind the mesh fencing of the "press pen" bordering the North terminal apron. In the caption writers' idiom they were, left to right: 1, 2, 3... and finally Arthur Greated of the ***Daily Mirror****. The door of the Royal Viking airliner opened and out rushed the first passenger – one of the Queen Mother's pet corgis. Hardly pausing even to acknowledge the RAF ground staff milling round the aircraft, the Royal pooch made a beeline for the press pen, some 20 yards away. Disdainfully it sniffed at every pair of feet in turn, singled out the* ***Daily Mirror****, and with an air of sudden decision, promptly mistook him for a Clarence House lamppost...*

As I reported, the Queen Mother may have heard the laughter of bystanders, or noticed the sly grins of officials. But she missed the incident itself. She stepped out of the 'plane seconds after a footman snatched up the relieved corgi and placed it in the Royal car.

Rarely have the Royals had to suffer the indignities of delays and diversions experienced by the ordinary fare-paying traveller. But just occasionally bad weather or even mechanical breakdowns can upset the most carefully structured official programme.

When in 1958 the Queen Mother left for home after an exhausting tour of Australia and New Zealand, it was planned she would stop off in Kenya to open a new airport at Nairobi. My exclusive of a sudden rethink of those plans won for me a front page lead in the *Daily Sketch* two days running – an achievement never before equalled by a Brenard reporter, or, I suspect except in national disasters or emergencies by many newspaper staffmen.

After reports reached London that the British Colonial government had smashed a plot by Mau Mau terrorists to assassinate her during the ceremony (a plot denied by Kenya), I learnt that the Queen Mother's route to London had been changed. Her return had been delayed for 48 hours in Mauritius when her special Qantas Australian airliner was grounded there with engine trouble. The airline confirmed to me that after consultations with the respective governments and Buckingham Palace, the aircraft would now call at Entebbe in Uganda and Malta, missing Kenya altogether.

The reason, according to London Airport officials for the Australian airline, was nothing at all to do with rumoured assassination plots but because "Nairobi is much higher above sea-level than Entebbe, and that would mean a greater load of fuel." They claimed that changing the route would also eliminate two night-stops on the final leg of the journey.

"We haven't been given any details" Julia Bradbury, the airline's spokeswoman in London told me. "We only know that the aircraft's inner starboard engine was being changed at Mauritius. A spare engine was standing-by there in case of any trouble."

The *Sketch* added a tailpiece to my story which was headed:

DAILY SKETCH ★★★

MONDAY, MARCH 10, 1958

QUEEN MOTHER SURPRISE—KENYA NOW CUT OUT OF TOUR

ROYAL PLANE RIDDLE

Daily Sketch Reporter

THE Queen Mother made another surprise change yesterday in her plans for the final stages of her return flight from Australia.

It came after rumours that the Kenya Government had smashed a Mau Mau plot to assassinate her at the opening of Nairobi's new airport.

Kenya denied the plot report.

Then came an announcement that the Queen Mother, delayed 48 hours in Mauritius, will MISS KENYA ALTOGETHER.

Instead, her plane will call at Entebbe, in Uganda, and Malta.

Why? Airline officials explained:

"Nairobi is much higher above sea level than Entebbe, and that would mean a greater load of fuel.

"By changing the route, we eliminated two night stops on the final leg of the journey."

It was stated that engine trouble delayed the Royal plane at Mauritius.

What went wrong?

London officials of the Australian airline Qantas which owns the 'plane, were unable to say.

"We haven't been given any details," said Mrs. Julia Bradbury, the company's spokeswoman in London.

DAY LATE

"We only know that the aircraft's inner starboard engine was being changed at Mauritius.

"A spare engine was standing-by there in case of any trouble."

On the Queen Mother's new route the nearest point to Nairobi will be 400 miles away.

She has sent Nairobi a message saying she was "greatly distressed" that she could not open the new £2,500,000 airport.

Instead, the opening was performed yesterday by the Governor of Kenya, Sir Evelyn Baring, who read her message.

Daily Sketch March 10 1958
– a Page One lead

The Queen Mother, they said, had sent Nairobi a message saying she was "greatly distressed" she had been unable to visit the Kenyan capital. The airport opening was performed instead by the Governor of Kenya, Sir Evelyn Baring.

The following day I was able to break the news that after high level talks between BOAC and Government officials, a British Britannia airliner had taken off to "rescue" the Royal traveller after she had been further delayed in Mauritius by bad weather. And the Britannia was heading for Nairobi.

In the meantime, Qantas had flown out another airliner carrying additional engine parts and to act as a relief aircraft if necessary. But both Australian aircraft had then been grounded in Mauritius by a cyclone.

The dispatch of the Britannia was confirmed by BOAC chairman Sir Gerard d'Erlanger following a meeting with the Minister of Transport, Harold Watkinson. Crew members, I was able reveal, were given only an hour's notice of their special flight, and the Kenyan Government was advised that the Queen Mother would be arriving in Nairobi after all – if only to change 'planes. In fact the Britannia wasn't needed. The Qantas Super-Constellation airliner was finally able to take off on its way to London, just over three days late and routed to by-pass Nairobi.

My *Daily Sketch* Page One lead, this time basically in 102-point upper-case, ran:

DAILY SKETCH 2½d

TUESDAY, MARCH 11, 1958

© 1958, by the Daily Sketch

Daily Sketch
March 11 1958
Just a day later – a second Page One lead

BRITANNIA SOS FOR QUEEN MOTHER

Daily Sketch Reporter

A STAND-BY Britannia airliner was flown out to Nairobi last night in case it is needed to rescue the Queen Mother.

It left London Airport at an hour's notice after talks between high-level Government and BOAC officials.

The decision to fly out the Britannia was taken because of the continued delays to the Queen Mother, still stranded in Mauritius.

She should have returned yesterday from her Australasia tour. Twice she has been held up by engine trouble in a Qantas Airline's Superconstellation.

Another flight hold-up

...and covered almost a third of the page, occupying more space than my copy. But as we so frequently disclaimed (usually in some other context) reporters aren't responsible for the headlines…

CHAPTER SEVEN

Mike Richardson came on the line as I finished dictating copy to the office, my last story on a busy day.

"Glad I caught you," he said, "I've just taken a call from Brian Hitchen at the *Express*. He has some appointment out this way later this evening, and says he'd like to take the opportunity to pop in and buy everyone a drink. And he insists...'everyone.'"

I waited, expecting more. It didn't come. "Everyone?" I asked lamely, "What did he mean? Why emphasise everyone? Sounds a bit strange. What does he want?"

This was early 1974. Brian Hitchen had recently been appointed news editor of the *Daily Express* and was an important client of ours... if not the most important. Traditionally since the early years of Lord Beaverbrook, the *Express* had enjoyed the reputation of being leaders in the encouragement of fresh journalistic talent. It almost certainly had the widest network of stringers (retained local correspondents) in the country. It was also generally thought to pay over the odds for an exclusive or even just a "beat" (advance warning or tip-off) on a story. Where the *Express* led others followed, it was said.

Much of this was well-earned. My later years of responsibility as Brenards' news manager, battling with news desks in general for appropriate compensation for our contributions, proved the *Express* reputation to be fully justified. Other newspapers, in particular the *Daily Mirror* and even the old *Daily Herald*, were also as ready as Beaverbrook's crusading flagship to recognise the value of those contributions, and to recompense us adequately without the need for constant reminders.

Nevertheless, the *Express* had been the first national newspaper to back Bill Brenard in his plans for coverage of the airports in the late 'forties (and the first to support a return to Scotland in the 'sixties). Other newspapers followed suit by paying up front for a service. They could not afford to miss out, even if it was officially against avowed policy to pay a retainer for anything less than exclusive coverage.

My initial reaction to Brian Hitchen's invitation was still, perhaps a little uncertain. We had occasionally seen executives and editorial representatives of national newspapers at the airports as travellers. And of course Bill Brenard, Ray Watts and I made occasional visits to the offices of our Fleet Street clients to maintain contact (and to beg for more money!). But I couldn't remember anyone ever deliberately asking to meet us on our ground.

Mike simply couldn't answer my question. "I honestly don't know what he wants," he said. "Maybe he doesn't want anything. But he did say he hoped to meet as many of the Brenard staff as possible. And I think he was being genuine".

He added: "I think we should take up his invitation. If he does want something from us we'll find out what it is and we don't have to commit ourselves to an answer immediately. If he doesn't want anything and it is purely a goodwill visit, then we should take advantage of the goodwill and pressurise him over payments."

I couldn't fault that argument, and I said that I'd discuss a battle plan with Ray Watts. In any event, I said, I'd be there. And I would pass on the invitation to the late duty reporter who would be relieving me. Said Mike: "Good. I'll come too and I'll bring along some photographers. I'm not sure if Brian meant to include them, but it will help to boost our numbers."

Wattie and I talked about the invitation a few minutes later when he called from Terminal 3. He too had his suspicions about the visit, but asked: "What have we to lose?" Bren himself was away on holiday at the time, and we were short-staffed through other holidays and sickness, but we could probably gather together up to eight people. Wattie said that he would join us as soon as possible in the airline staff's Vanguard Club where we'd agreed to meet Brian. If the meeting went our way, the *Express* man could be late for his other appointment. It was likely to be a long session.

Brenards' reputation with Fleet Street news desks had grown steadily from the early 1950s. The quantity and quality of stories from the airports was high, amply justifying the monthly retainers paid by most newspapers and news agencies for our virtual round-the-clock service. Accuracy and reliability were also rarely questioned. The few problems that occurred from time to time usually proved to be due to misunderstanding or poor communications.

At one level, between certain newspaper copy-takers (or telephone reporters as some liked to be called) and Brenard copyreaders there was constant friction. Fault lay on both sides. Used to dealing with staff reporters and experienced correspondents, a few newspaper typists were impatient and aggressive with youthful callers who were unversed in the techniques of dictation, with its essential emphasis on phonetic spelling and vocalised punctuation.

They apparently assumed that these teenagers, mostly school-leavers looking for a future in journalism, were also the authors of the copy they were dictating. Hence the deprecative and derogatory suggestions that "Brenards employ school kids as reporters." They might more justly have been admiring the standard of work of those "school kids."

For their part, the Brenard editorial assistants also had a somewhat inflated idea of their own importance, as I well remember guiltily. To some extent this was understandable. They were usually the first point of contact between the agency and its newspaper clients. In the frequent absence of someone with experience to man the news desk, and with no immediate telephone access to a senior, these would-be cub reporters were sometimes tempted to overreach themselves.

Fortunately, there was nothing to suggest that this mutual antagonism on the part of a handful did any lasting damage. In one case particularly, the system threw up a natural desk-man for Brenards who could have held down a similar Fleet-Street job with ease. David "Willie" Wenlock was also the fastest, most accurate self-taught touch-typist I've come across, as well as being adept at scanning copy, subbing and correcting where necessary, speedily and reliably. We once secretly tested his typing speed against one of the best copy-takers at the *Press Association*. He left his rival standing.

An imaginative writer himself, he knew a good story instinctively, and though he wouldn't push it, he was ever ready to discuss and advise junior reporters on an "angle" if requested. But Willie never sought formal training as a reporter, and had no ambitions in that direction. He also frustrated our well-intentioned attempts to persuade him to develop his natural writing skills in some allied direction. We last heard of him holding down a copy-taker's job in Fleet Street, where he appeared to be perfectly happy, even if we all felt he was unfulfilled. His new employer told us with regret: "His skills are wasted here. But we can't persuade him to do anything else."

Even if economics hadn't dictated that productive staff should be out producing, we could defend our "in-at-the-deep-end" policy of training junior reporters. From the early part of that first decade and for many years to follow, some ninety per cent of the Brenard reporting team was successfully recruited from the company's own intake of editorial assistants. This policy in no way detracted from the quality of the reporting staff, so many of whom made successful career moves later.

Among those who served an apprenticeship at Brenards', either as editorial assistants, as "cubs," or as full reporters, or both, were Gill Martin, who went on to become a reporter and feature writer for both the *Daily Express* and the *Mail* in turn. Alan Garrott progressed first to features editor of *Reveille*, then of the *Daily Mirror*. His near namesake, Alan Gallop, became years later a prolific author with a string of books to his credit, including one on the 60-year history of Heathrow. Annie Barr, another reporter, progressed to deputy editor of *Harpers & Queen* and was co-originator of the popular and memorable "*Sloane Ranger*" books before moving to the *Weekend Telegraph*.

Peter Game, a "hard news" man at Brenards, had a long stint on the news desk of the *Sun*. Charles "Chic" Henn left Brenards Manchester Airport office to pursue a related job as aviation correspondent for the northern edition of the *Daily Telegraph*, moving on to the paper's news desk. His airport colleague, Bernard Spilsbury, followed him later to a similar aircorr post with the *Manchester Evening News* – my own first employer in Fleet Street.

Chris Bramwell, my valued erstwhile colleague for several years at Heathrow and Scotland's Prestwick Airport, earned a niche on the night news desk of the *Daily Telegraph* in London. And Bob McKenzie, whom I employed direct from school and later became my final and valued promising junior at the Scottish base was, by the nineties, a motor rally co-driver to Martin Blundell, and travelled the world as *Daily Express* Formula 1

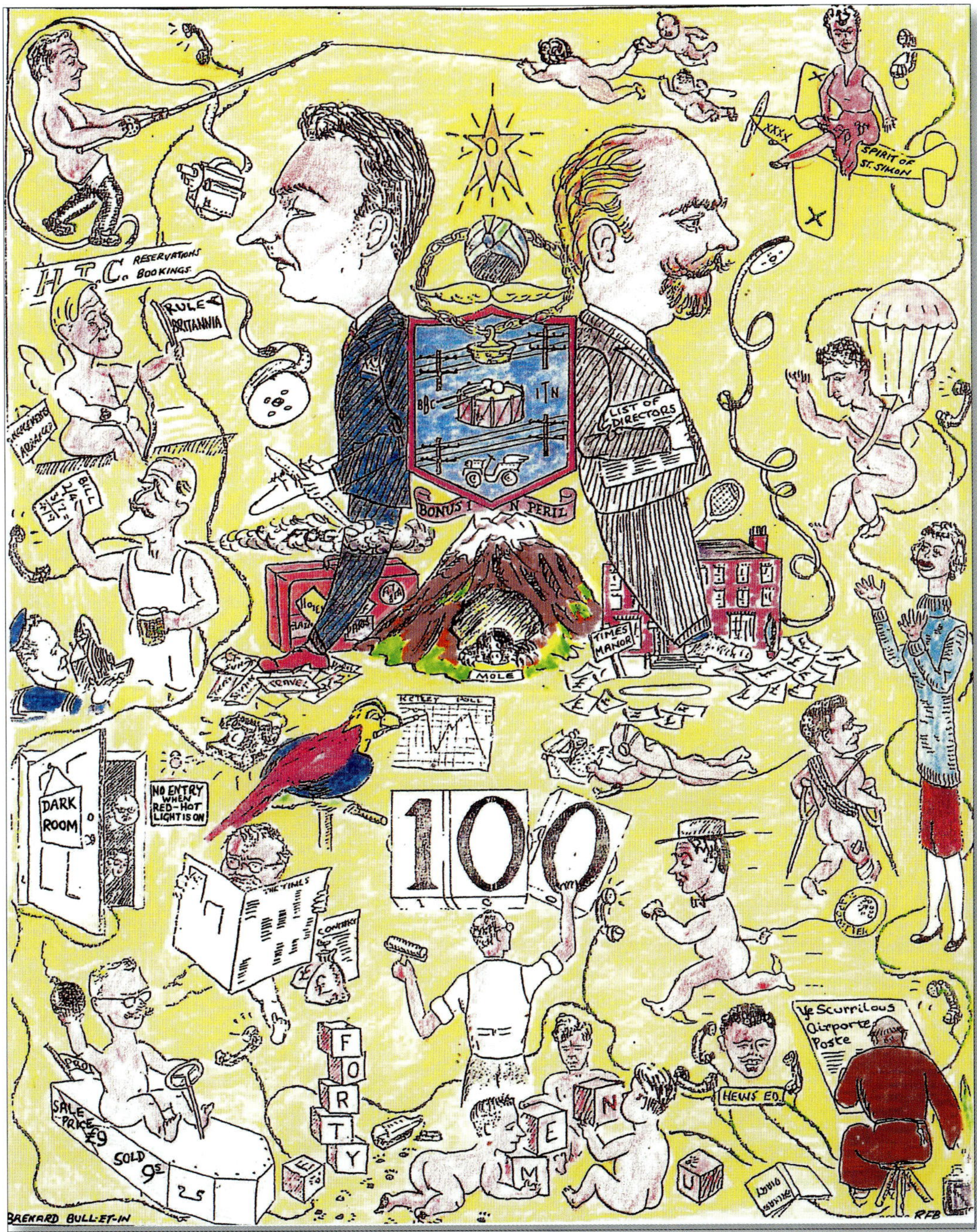

Author's collection.

My offered representation of a 'coat of arms' for Brenard Press featuring some of its early reporters, photographers, news room and print-shop staff, which became the back cover of the 100th issue of the monthly staff magazine 'The Bulletin' in the 1950s. Though the activities feature in-house jokes impossible to interpret here, some of the participants might still recognise themselves. The two supporters of the shield at the centre should be even more recognisable as Bill Brenard *(right)* and Mike Richardson, while the significance of the plug, the big drum, the vintage motor and a mole emerging from a mountain all had their part to play.

motor racing correspondent and as a specialist in other sports such as world class tennis.

There were others. David Cass, who had changed his name from something hardly pronounceable to English ears and certainly not memorably spellable, turned first to radio then to television to become sports and news reporter at home and overseas for the *BBC* and later for *ITN*. John Hambley moved into another area of television to become controller of children's programmes for a London TV company, then an *ITV* executive producer and an executive of *Euston Films*.

Ken Dunjohn's voice became familiar on radio as a chief spokesman for the brewing industry. Peter Dobbie left the *London Evening Standard* to promote and defend the Channel Tunnel, then went on to become first, political editor, then executive editor of the *Mail on Sunday*. Arnold "Tammy" Thomson returned to journalism as a freelance travel writer after some years as a successful businessman. My brother Harry became widely respected as Public Relations Manager at Heathrow for British European Airways, later to be merged with BOAC under the British Airways banner, with whom Alan Solloway also served as a Public Relations Officer.

There may well be other career improvers (that word again) I have forgotten about and if so I beg their pardon. There were certainly many Brenard stalwarts who prospered with provincial and local newspapers, to say nothing of specialist publications. Nigel Tomkins started his own *Air Cargo News* after several years as the first editor of *Skyport* for Bill Brenard. An independent newspaper for Heathrow staff had been Bill's dream for twenty years.

Chris Wright became news editor of the *Ealing Gazette*, moving on to a motoring magazine before setting up his own specialist motoring news agency, while his schooldays chum Dave Parker became a *Daily Mail* resident photographer at Heathrow. He took a "Photographer of the Year" award for his pictures of the Iranian Embassy siege in London whilst on a stand-in stint away from the airport. I had given them both their first jobs as school-leavers in the early 1970s. Their contemporary, Steve Meller, stayed on at Heathrow as a reporter to run his own news agency when Brenards' folded in the '80s soon after the death of its founder. Steve could still be seen interviewing the famous well into the 2000s, featured as one of the "stars" of "***Airport***," a popular *BBC* television fly-on-the-wall documentary series on Heathrow from 1997.

Our commitment to our clients and the increasing news tempo at the airports back in the 1950s meant that we were beginning to face a dilemma familiar to so many small companies: how to cope with growing demands without adding to costs by increasing staff. Our story output was already considerably higher than any other freelance agency in the country. On some days we could be filing as many as twenty different news stories, though not always to the same markets.

The *News Chronicle* acknowledged this surfeit of news by once devoting an entire page to our airport stories under the banner and strapline which read, if I remember correctly:

Glamour, Drama, Joy... Tears - It all happens at London Airport

AFTER WASHINGTON - the WORLD'S No.1 NEWS CENTRE

On one occasion, when I told a visiting Fleet Street reporter that I'd just filed my tenth story that day (a record for me) he was dumbfounded. "I'd think myself lucky if I had that number of stories in a week," he said. I didn't tell him that at least one other Brenard reporter had well exceeded that figure but then neither did I tell of the countless times when I'd had a completely blank day.

On the subject of quality, how many Fleet Street staff reporters could claim the number of front-page lead stories directly attributable to Brenards? I alone totalled 73 Page One leads in the between the late 'forties and mid-sixties, (some of them are illustrated in these pages). Twenty-seven of them were in English national dailies or Sundays and twenty-one of these were original exclusives, mainly with no further input from newspaper staff reporters. Some might ask: "Who's counting?" *I* certainly was.

Only rarely did Fleet Street cover airport stories with their own staff men. A couple of attempts by freelances to set up a rival news service to Brenards faded away after only weeks. Even the *Press Association* withdrew their area correspondent back to the airport boundary. Only the *Daily Telegraph* persisted in retaining a Heathrow staff reporter until they too finally threw in the towel and agreed to take our all-airports service in the 'sixties.

When reporters for the nationals did appear at the airport, it was for situations in which one or more of those newspapers might have a financial stake. Or it might be to have their own cover for the occasional major national news event or incident, or for a story where they judged significant interest of their own readers already existed. The range of subjects here was inevitably wide... from the UK debut of a leading pop singer to the homecoming of British ex-pat refugees from some third world revolution, or victims of an overseas disaster, down to the departure of a British sports team… or the players' disappointed about-face return following a "non-result."

Our job at the airport could have been made more difficult by the discovery that sometimes newspapermen had secured themselves seats on the same London-bound airliner as the newsworthy passengers. But inside the cabin of a crowded airliner is not always the ideal setting for pictures, interviews or even the odd uplifting quote. And the chances of pursuer and quarry reaching the sanctuary of the airport baggage hall simultaneously are slim.

As anyone will know who has had to queue inside an aircraft in order to leave it, then has had to walk hundreds of yards to join another queue at passport controls, only to hover at a carousel to claim what has to be the very last bag on a conveyor belt, one passenger can be in a taxi on the way to town while another is still avoiding the eyes of the Customs man in the green channel. Which means that the reporter who can only stand and wait at a barrier for his interview is also served – theoretically.

Such was the situation with the escaped convict, Dennis Stafford, who in 1957 walked from a BOAC airliner handcuffed to a Scotland Yard detective sergeant. At least two popular newspapers had booked seats on the flight from Port of Spain, Trinidad, which, sice his escape from Wormwood Scrubs seven months earlier had been the bolt-hole of the dapper, 23-years-old criminal.

Stafford had served only a few months of a seven-year sentence for housebreaking, for receiving stolen property and for possessing a loaded pistol, when he escaped from jail and succeeded in boarding a ship for the West Indies. His criminal career had started much earlier. And even as a sixteen year-old he was a prosecution witness against the notorious Kray Twins when they were convicted and sent to Borstal for grievous bodily harm during a street fight in Hackney. Later he was jointly convicted for murder, but returned to his role of a confidence trickster after finally being paroled.

As far as I could tell from their reports carried in the London papers the next day, the two staff men might have been on another flight altogether. Neither of them could add anything to the little I had learnt from a stewardess on board – that Stafford and his two escorts had travelled in a sectioned-off area of the first-class cabin of the four-engined Stratocruiser, and that few of the other passengers would have been aware of him.

The travelling reporters also apparently failed to make any direct contact in the old Customs hall or baggage reclaim at Heathrow. There wasn't a word of descriptive writing from that inner sanctum either. My own first view of Stafford cheekily waving to photographers as he disembarked from the aircraft alongside the north side terminal building was shared only with the photographers and the Telegraph's Percy Banyard.

From that point I played my familiar lone role. By chance I'd spotted a police car with its driver standing by at a Customs emergency doors, normally used for baggage deliveries only. The car was facing the airport exit route. Some twenty photographers and reporters were however waiting at the other end of the building, crowding the arrivals barrier alongside the terminal's main exit.

Author's collection

An aerial view *(circa.1955)* of the original London Airport 'Northside' terminal area adjoining the Bath Road. A number of aircraft can be clearly seen on the parking apron, some with passengers disembarking or boarding from the adjoining waiting lounges. The arrows indicate (1) where I positioned myself outside the arrivals exit and (2) the baggage reclaim emergency exit, fewer than 100 yards away, to 'catch' the arrival back in the UK of prison escapee Dennis Stafford.

The two doors were more than a hundred yards apart. But I could watch both areas from 15 yards away outside the building. I would be able to see if there was any activity alongside the distant police car by whilst watching the normal exit adjoining the arrivals barrier from the roadway. Two Brenard photographers had joined their Fleet-street colleagues at the barrier on their return from the tarmac, and I contacted them to tell them quietly of my plan. The flashes of the cameras would alert me to Stafford emerging from the Customs hall, but the photographers would have to watch for my signal to join me if my hunch was correct.

Some fifteen minutes passed while the prisoner and his escorts waited for their baggage, and I became steadily drenched in a sudden downpour of rain. Then I realised that another, unmarked car was pulling in front of the police car, which had moved back to make way for it and was now out of sight round the corner of the building. And baggage was being loaded from the emergency exit into the second car....

Frantically I gave the agreed signal, a beckoning wave, to the photographers as I looked the opposite way. Then praying silently that he and no one else had noticed our exchange,

I sprinted along the side of the arrivals building to the emergency exit. I was just in time to see Stafford emerge, still handcuffed. And as he was guided into the back seat of the car I shouted:

"How do you like being back, Dennis?"

He deliberately paused, lifted his handcuffed hand in acknowledgement and replied cheerfully:

"It's quite nice. But I don't like this rain."

That was the sum total of my exclusive "interview" with Stafford. But I did manage to talk briefly with his escort's boss, Detective Inspector George Mullins, who readily gave me his name and that of Detective Sergeant Jack Huntley.

Had Stafford given any trouble on the flight? "Not a bit," he replied. "Everything was quite straightforward. We had a good flight back despite a twenty-two hour delay in Bermuda with an engine fault." And, said the Inspector, the airliner had overflown scheduled stops at Gander, Newfoundland and Shannon, Ireland to make up some time.

A Heathrow Special Branch officer who, out of courtesy, had met the group in the Customs hall and escorted them to his office, told me Stafford was being taken directly to Cannon Row police station in London, and he was expected to appear before Bow Street magistrates the next day charged with absconding from prison. As the car and its passengers sped away, I moved round to the boot of the second car. There were two or three suitcases, a briefcase and several paper-wrapped packages addressed to "The Commissioner of Police."

Neither of my photographer colleagues had appeared. They hadn't seen my signal. But then neither had anyone else, and as I walked back into the building on my way to a telephone, everyone was still waiting at the barrier. I did the right thing, naturally. I told as many as I could that Stafford had gone. Only because, of course, I was anxious that they shouldn't have to hang around for nothing.

Most of the papers carried my story the next day, the *Express* and the *News Chronicle* both gave it a page lead. The *Chron* splashed it with part of the "quote" (*see opposite*).

Stafford home in handcuffs

TWO DETECTIVES BRING HIM 'FIRST CLASS'

It is nice to be back but I don't like rain, he says at the airport

Express Staff Reporter

WITH a wave and a grin, 23-year-old Dennis Stafford flew home from the Trinidad sunshine to Britain yesterday—in handcuffs.

As he waved his handcuffed hand Stafford—in a smart grey suit and white patterned tie—said to the bystanders at London Airport: "It's quite nice to be back—but I don't like the rain."

With Stafford, who escaped from Wormwood Scrubs last November, were the two detectives who flew out to Port of Spain to bring him back.

The airliner was 22 hours late because of an engine fault at Bermuda.

Said Detective Inspector George Mullins—he was accompanied by Detective Sergeant Jack Huntley: "We had no trouble coming back. Everything was quite straightforward, and it was a good trip, despite the delays."

Special cabin

Few of the other passengers on board the flight even glimpsed Stafford or his escort. They travelled in a sectioned-off first-class part of the cabin at the rear of the Stratocruiser.

Special Branch officers who met the plane took him and his escort to a private office adjoining a passenger lounge.

Stafford and his escort were met in the Customs Hall by

detectives who drove to the air port in two police cars.

Stafford, still confident and breezy, climbed into one of the cars and was driven to Cannon row police station.

Non-stop flight

Inspector Mullins said that the airliner did not stop either at Gander, Newfoundland, or at Shannon, Ireland, as expected.

"We came straight across from Bermuda," he said.

Among their personal luggage the two Scotland Yard men brought back a number of large paper-wrapped packages addressed to the "Commissioner of Police." They were carried in a separate car.

Daily Express June 11 1957

The *Daily Express* repeated it in full… but in a sub-head (*left*).

Full size photographs showed Stafford, handcuffed to Det.Sgt. Huntley, leaving the 'plane earlier, ahead of other passengers. A *News Chronicle* picture suitably caught sight of me over the policeman's shoulder, at the edge of the parking apron. Another paper carried my same story, almost word for word, but with a by-line, the name of one of its staff reporters on board the aircraft. Someone obviously had to justify the expense of it all.

*

Seven of us, including Mike and three photographers, were waiting in the bar of the Vanguard Club when Brian Hitchen arrived shortly after six pm. Gill Martin, Alan Gallop and I represented the reporters, and Ray Watts had promised he'd be there. We all had drinks in our hands, but Brian insisted on calling up another round immediately.

IT'S NICE TO BE BACK, GRINS STAFFORD

First class all the way from Trinidad—and a cheery wave at the end

NEWS CHRONICLE REPORTER

GRINNING broadly and wearing a smart grey suit, 23-year-old escaped prisoner Dennis Stafford stepped from an airliner at London Airport handcuffed to a Scotland Yard officer yesterday and said : " It's quite nice to be back. But I don't like this rain."

He had been flown back to Britain on an extradition order from Port of Spain, Trinidad, after vanishing from Wormwood Scrubs last November.

Stafford was driven to Cannon Row police station and charged with escaping from prison. He will appear at Bow Street today.

Det.-Insp. George Mullins who, with Det.-Sgt. Jack Huntley, flew to Trinidad last Tuesday, said : " We had no trouble coming back.

" Everything was quite straightforward and it was a good trip despite a 22-hour delay due to an engine fault at Bermuda."

He waves to the public

Few passengers in the B.O.A.C. Stratocruiser glimpsed Stafford. He and the detectives travelled in a sectioned-off first-class cabin at the rear (single fare : £176). The plane did not stop at Gander or Shannon, as had been scheduled.

As he was led from the plane, Stafford waved jauntily to onlookers.

Special Branch officers took him to a private office adjoining the airport passenger lounge.

Then plain-clothes men, who had driven to the airport in two police cars, took him and his escort to a waiting car.

The two Scotland Yard men brought back several large paper - wrapped packages addressed to " The Commissioner of Police." These left the airport in a separate car.

News Chronicle
June 11 1957

Creative Commons license, courtesy of photographer P Glenwright

Stanhope Castle, Weardale in Co. Durham, which Dennis Stafford made his home after a spell at Wormwood scrubs and a lifetime of dramatic breakouts and years on the run. This region has one of the UK's highest rainfalls!

Brian Hitchen was a short, stocky Northerner, ruddy-complexioned, bald and shiny-pated, with something approaching a paunch concealed beneath his belted camel-hair coat. He was easy-going and friendly, but far from patronising. As if addressing an editorial meeting he began by asking: "Is everybody here?" but didn't seem too concerned when we admitted that at least three reporters hadn't been able to make it. Mike apologised for the absence of Bill Brenard, and I said that Wattie would be along shortly...

For a few minutes we talked in general terms about our service, about current news stories and about mutual acquaintances. Then Mike, who was no newspaperman, and seemed uncomfortable by the shop talk, steered the chat round to the subject of retainers and constantly-increasing costs. As Brenards' financial director, this was much more familiar ground to him.

Although the days when Bill Brenard had to send a messenger to Fleet Street to collect a few due newspaper cheques to pay his staff were long past, salaries along with telephones were still the company's highest costs. In the years of mounting inflation it was essential to keep our clients aware of their responsibilities to us.

As far as the freelance correspondent is concerned, the newspaper business is the original buyers' market. In how many businesses does the customer decide how much to pay his supplier or whether to pay him at all? Even an agreed minimum linage rate, it seems, is negotiable when a newspaper tells its stringer at the end of the month how much his copy is worth or which one of the alternative "suppliers" of the same news item is likely to be reimbursed in that month.

Though unable to pay Fleet Street rates, Brenards was proud to claim it had always paid its staff the maximum it could afford, and, in practice, the agency's reporters were paid above non-Fleet Street scaled rates worked out with the journalists' union for what was a unique service. It was one way of ensuring a continuity of quality staff, and of maintaining high standards. But it also meant that we had to be sure of a good income during the troughs as well as during the peaks of productiveness.

Our office accommodation costs had always been relatively low. Brenards' newsroom and photographic departments had progressed from the caravan of the 'forties and early 'fifties to a builder's site hut and finally to a Victorian cottage on the Bath Road. Only when that lay in the way of expanding airport development did the newsroom move again, first to the administrative offices of the Queens Building, in the airport's centre, and later to a long-term home on the airport's perimeter. So we could never be accused of indulging ourselves.

As news manager I had introduced the use of telex in place of telephones to speed up copy circulation, resulting in long-term savings, even though some newspapers were unhappy about the system. Brian saw the sense of the move from our viewpoint though he too seemed a little reluctant to approve it. Possibly the copy-takers' union was worried about us setting a trend among stringers. My argument was that the national news agencies, *PA, Ex Tel, Reuters* and the American wire services, *UP* and *AP*, had been using their own teleprinters for circulating their copy for years, and no one was suggesting they should use telephones.

Brian agreed to look at the possibility of adding a percentage to our retainers as a contribution towards communications' costs, now rising again in spite of the savings. And we assured him we would be looking for the same sort of help from our other clients. He also agreed to look at the *Express* monthly retainer, suggesting that we submit regular legitimate expenses which might be more acceptable to the new breed of Fleet Street accountants.

The time slipped rapidly by until at last Brian announced that he would have to be on his way. He had been with us for about an hour and a half. Ray Watts had failed to show up. I was unhappy about that because I felt that it was for him as news director to lead the negotiations, particularly as he'd indicated that he wanted to raise a number of ideas himself. I said as much to Brian without spelling out my displeasure. But he said he'd be happy to see Wattie and myself at the *Express* at any time to follow up our talks.

Then he was gone. Mike and the rest of us stood around a few minutes holding a post-mortem. We felt rather pleased with ourselves. We thought we'd put a good case for a bigger retainer. Then someone (I think it was Gill) put all our unspoken thoughts into words.

"I don't understand," she said, "What was all that about? What did he really want to see us for?"

We thought we knew the answer three days later.

On Saturday, 2 February, 1974, the *Daily Express* front page screamed:

TRAIN ROBBER BIGGS CAPTURED IN RIO
Our Men are There

Exclusively, the newspaper revealed that Detective Chief Superintendent John Slipper of Scotland Yard had arrested 44-years-old Ronald Biggs in a Rio de Janeiro hotel. And it wasn't necessary to read between the lines to realise that it was the *Daily Express* that had tracked Biggs down, and that Slipper and his deputy, Detective Inspector Peter Jones, had been called in and escorted to Rio by the *Express*. Patently clear, in fact, in spite of the *Express* claims that they just happened to be there when the Flying Squad burst in. A likely story, but part of the deal to win the Yard's co-operation, it emerged later.

Biggs, fugitive extraordinary, had been on the run since 1965 after a spectacular escape from Wandsworth prison, where he was serving a thirty-year sentence for his part in the Great Train Robbery of two years earlier. Now, more than eight years on, an English ex-pat in Rio, a man calling himself Michael Haynes had apparently confessed to an acquaintance that his real name was Ronnie Biggs and that he wanted to come home. He believed he could win a new trial and a lighter sentence by making a deal with the police over "new information" about the train robbery. On a visit to London, that acquaintance had passed on his snippet of news to an *Express* reporter, Colin MacKenzie.

The puzzling get-together with Brian Hitchen coincided with the eve of a ten-days' winter break I had booked. But I couldn't resist 'phoning Ray Watts at the airport the day after the *Express* revelations to voice my suspicions that there must have been a connection between the two events. Wattie confirmed it.

"I called Brian today," he said, "I told him I wanted to apologise for missing him.

I'd been unavoidably detained. Then I congratulated him on the *Express* scoop and for pulling the wool over our eyes."

His intended association of events worked. Brian admitted his ruse immediately, assuming we knew the truth. "I'm sorry," he said, "But we couldn't take the chance that one of you might spot Slipper or one of our team at the airport when they left for Rio. It wouldn't have taken much to work out what we were up to."

What Ray Watts didn't say was that he was in the Terminal 3 departures lounge bar for most of the evening anyway, drinking with two of his Special Branch contacts. As Scotland Yard officers at the airport they should have known of the departure of one of their own senior officers, and would have if they hadn't been drinking with Ray Watts at the time. And Wattie almost certainly would have learnt of the Yard man's departure very soon afterwards.

The full story of Brian's duplicity and our gullibility was told shortly afterwards, albeit somewhat patronisingly, by another prominent journalist and author, Anthony Delano, in a very funny tale of the tracking of Biggs and the vain bid to bring him back to serve his sentence. Thankfully our embarrassment was spared in the later BBC television adaptation of the *Express*-Biggs saga.[1]

Dealano confirms what we now knew of Brian's plans to keep us out of the way, though we might have taken some exception to his interpretation of our reasons for welcoming the attention of the *Express* news editor, which we believed was a little removed from reality. As was also the conclusion that as we all aspired to working in Fleet Street we would have welcomed the opportunity to meet up with someone who might one day be influential in our career futures. Of that little gathering I don't believe there was a single one of us who considered Brian Hitchen's visit in that light. Perhaps we should have. But we were too proud of our own heritage (or too convinced of our own abilities) to need that kind of condescending sponsorship, though perhaps Wattie took his objections a bit far.

Only rarely does the news desk of a national newspaper ask for the name of the author of a news agency report. It could be in the context of follow-up enquiries or, in extreme circumstances, for legal reasons following a denial or contradiction (though here again the agency could be legally responsible). So it was particularly pleasing when any of us were approached directly by a national newspaper with the offer of a job. I know that Ray Watts was headhunted several times this way to no avail.

I too had my moments. Brian Park, news director of *Associated Newspapers*, wanted me to join the *Daily Mail* or London *Evening News* (he implied the choice would be mine). I had known him slightly during his days as an *Evening News* reporter a few years earlier. And I had once been tempted by the *Sunday Express* with the carrot of an expense account which alone equalled two thirds of my total pay at the time. That offer came from the news editor… but as he happened to be Arthur Brenard, Bill's brother, perhaps it wasn't so significant.

Neither was dismissed out of hand. But I told myself I dreaded a daily journey to town from my home in Iver, Bucks. And I was very comfortable in my job. I had grown up with London Airport and felt I was part of it, or it was part of me.

Later, I had to admit to myself there was also a fear of the unknown, probably a lack of confidence in holding my own in Fleet Street. At best I would be a small fish in a big pond, at worst a fish out of water. And I liked to see my stories given widespread coverage. I liked wagering my knowledge of the airport against the best of Fleet Street. I drew immense satisfaction from trying to come out on top, finding that little bit extra in a news story; that different slant, that fresh angle which could secure Brenards a stake in the coverage given to an airport news event even if the whole was attributed on publication solely to a "staff reporter."

One such occasion was the disaster at Heathrow in October, 1956, involving an RAF Vulcan bomber. The aircraft was returning to Britain after completing a 26,000-mile record-breaking trip to Australia and New Zealand, and tragically crashed on landing, killing four of its six-man crew. On board, flying as one of that crew, was the Chief of Bomber Command, Air Marshal Sir Harry Broadhurst.

[1] *"Slip-up" by Anthony Delano, pub. GB1977 by Andre Deutsch Ltd.*

Waiting in a central terminal VIP lounge for the aircraft, which normally would have flown to an RAF airfield, were Lady Broadhurst with her four-years-old daughter Clare and a number of service chiefs. And nearby also waited air defence correspondents, photographers and TV crews, a few of whom, I learnt later, had ascended to the roof of the passenger building to see the touchdown from a distance… but also a long way from telephones.

Less than a mile away, but separated from that central terminal by an expanse of grass and the concrete of the landing runway, I should not even have been involved. Ray Watts was covering the centre of the airport that day, while I was propping up an arrivals' Customs barrier in the northside terminal. My diary entry was the return to Britain, from self-imposed overseas exile, of a former popular ballad singer. She was coming home, said her publicists, to make her big theatrical comeback.

Paula Green

Tommy Handley

Her name, if my memory serves me correctly, was Paula Green. She had featured in that hugely popular radio show ITMA until the untimely death of its star, Tommy Handley, seven years earlier. I don't know if Miss Green ever made her 'comeback.' But she wasn't afforded the courtesy of a Press welcome at the airport that first day in October.

I had just greeted her at the barrier when through the window to my left, a brilliant flash of flame, a distant billowing cloud of smoke, suddenly caught my eye. A muffled roar, rumbled and echoed like thunder in the split second that followed. Mumbling something like: "I'm so sorry, Miss Green..." I bolted for a staff access door and out to the edge of the airfield a hundred yards away.

Visibility was poor and it was raining, but a horrific sight confronted me. Right across my field of vision a snaking line of fire was racing along Heathrow's Number One runway, spewing out great chunks of twisted, charred or still blazing metal. A huge, unrecognisable shape slithered and scraped, enveloped in a pall of dense, acrid smoke, at more than a hundred miles an hour as the scream of dying jet aircraft engines coughed and spluttered into the distance.

Already slowly drifting away from that smouldering trail of detritus, which only seconds earlier had been a beautiful, if monstrous and slightly-menacing delta-winged bird, was a mourning legacy of black smoke, as though some huge non-stop express train had sped past, trackless, but as straight as a dart, on a final journey into oblivion.

I had reached the grass verge, anxious to penetrate the heart of the blackness at the end of that trail, but wondering how long it would take me to cover the many hundred yards. A car pulled up beside me and the assistant airport manager Jack Goodyear leaned out. "Jump in, quickly," he said, opening the passenger door behind him. We bounced and bumped over the grass alongside the runway for a few hundred yards at a breakneck speed. Then we were halted by a police car which waved us down. "There's likely to be more explosions," shouted the driver, "The tanks haven't gone up yet."

As I reported at the time:

"Even as he spoke, another muffled roar sent up great pieces of twisted metal..."

We turned back as Jack gave me the first eyewitness account of the disaster. He had been watching for the arrival of the Vulcan jet out of professional interest, and had spotted it in the distance as it approached Heathrow from the west, almost directly over Windsor Castle. I scribbled down his vivid comments, jumped from the car with a brief acknowledgement and ran back to the terminal and my nearby telephone. Less than five minutes had passed since the bomber had struck the ground. A few minutes more and my opening paragraphs were being 'phoned through to the London *Star*, as I added my own description of the scene as from a legitimate bystander.

I'd learnt from the office that Wattie hadn't been in touch from the central terminal, so there was a good chance I had won a "beat" over the opposition, the Fleet Street reporters on the scene. I had to get some back-up copy fast. Then I would have to 'phone the Air Ministry...

Back outside again, I found another eyewitness, an airline man who had been in his car on the perimeter road, almost opposite the touch down point. He told me:

> ***"The 'plane bounced as its wheels hit the runway and it seemed to leap back into the air. The engines revved up – then there was this violent explosion which shook the buildings nearby. I felt the shock-wave myself. The bomber dived back to the ground enveloped in flame and smoke and hurtled along the runway."***

Then from a senior police officer I heard that Sir Harry Broadhurst had miraculously survived. He and the Vulcan's pilot had safely ejected after touchdown, and had been picked up near the runway. (Later Jack Goodyear admitted to me that he thought he'd seen a parachute against the grey clouds, but wasn't sure. He didn't mention it because he "didn't want to mislead me.")

Again I hurried back to the 'phone. This time I had to wait on the line. Wattie was now dictating copy. The Brenards' copy-taker patched me into his call through the mini-switchboard. He too was quoting eyewitnesses. Most of the visiting press had been waiting in the conference room near the VIP suite, and were not immediately aware of the situation.

Wattie had been standing at the door of the suite, and was probably the first among them to discover something was wrong. After I'd told him about Sir Harry's escape, he confirmed we were well ahead with the story. But the Fleet Street people were rapidly catching up, and as there was plenty of time for the daily papers, the staff-men's stories would take priority, unless we had something different.

The Air Ministry was expected to put out a statement shortly, and Wattie thought it unlikely we would come up with anything more on an exclusive basis, and might have to be satisfied with our coverage in the evening papers and the credit for our "early alert." We agreed I would now leave the rest of any coverage to him in the central area except in the unlikely event of something new cropping up on my side of the airport.

All this had happened in a matter of minutes. We had to wait a couple of hours for the three London evenings to reach us. All three gave over their full front pages to the story. *The Star* and the *Standard* carried the Brenard quotes fully and some of the descriptive paragraphs with huge page-wide pictures from the scene of devastation:

The Star ***October 1 1956***

THE STAR

No 21,255 Twopence

V-BOMBER BLOWS UP

4 DIE IN LONDON AIRPORT CRASH

Air Chief And Pilot In Miracle London Escapes

A VULCAN four-jet bomber crashed, exploded and burst into flames at London Airport today at the end of a 26,000-mile tour of Australia and New Zealand.

Six people were on board. Two—Air Marshal Sir Harry Broadhurst, Chief of Bomber Command, and Squadron Leader Donald R. Howard, the captain and pilot, escaped by using their ejector seats.

The other four were killed.

They were:

The navigator, Squadron Leader Edward J. Eames, of Ashford, Kent; second navigator, Squadron Leader James G. W. Stroud, of Waddington, Lincolnshire; air electronics officer, Squadron Leader Albert E. Gamble, of London; and Mr Frederick Bassett, of the Air Ministry.

'Two Bangs'

An Air Ministry spokesman said the Vulcan was making a ground control approach to the main runway.

"At 400 to 500ft the canopy came off the aircraft and the plane then banked to starboard in a slightly nose down attitude," he said.

"There were two loud bangs, which I presume were the successful ejections.

"The aircraft continued in its nose - down attitude, getting steeper and steeper until it hit the ground and burst into flames."

As the bomber crashed there was a booming roar of an explosion and a huge sheet of flame surrounded by thick black smoke swirled upwards.

Cordoned Off

Fire engines and ambulances drove out to the runway.

The crash area was quickly cornoned off and apart from fire-fightilng and medical services no-one was allowed near the wreckage.

Despite heavy rain the wreckage blazed for more than half an hour.

For nearly 200 yards burning metal snaked along the runway.

The main hulk of the giant delta-winged Avro Vulcan lay in a blazing jumped mass of twisted metal, engine parts and fabric.

Parts of the bomber were blown 500 yards away by the shattering explosion.

Muffled Roar

A senior official said "There is a danger of further explosions when the fire reaches the fuel tanks."

Even as he spoke a muffled roar sent up giant twisted pieces of metal.

Sir Harry Broadhurst was ~~later stated to havei njured a~~ foot.

Lady Broadhurst, who was in the VIP lounge, went to the scene of the crash. Her ofur-years-old daughter, Clare, waited on the steps of the lounge.

Sir Harry was taken to hospital for examination.

Squadron - Leader Howard escaped injury except for a bruised forehead.

He met his wife at the VIP lounge. They embraced wordlessly. Then they drove away to their Cheltenham home.

An airline official said the plane bounced as its wheels touched down on the main runway.

400-Yard Skid

"The aircraft seemed to leap into the air. The engines revved up their power and there was then a tremendous explosion that shook the airport building," he said.

Another eye-witness said: "The plane exploded as soon as it touch down on the centre of the airport in pouring rain.

"It left a huge patch of name where is exploded which could be seen from the main airport buildings and then it skidded on its belly for 400 yards leaving a trail of burning wreckage behind it.

The RAF Vulcan bomber pictured taking off from Boscombe Down at the start of her 26,000-mile flight to Australasia and back.

Evening Standard picture, October 1 1956

Evening Standard
41,153 MONDAY, OCTOBER 1, 1956 Twopence

VULCAN CRASHES AT LONDON AIRPORT

Bomber chief and pilot escape

Smoke pours from the crashed Vulcan as firemen pump foam on to the wreckage at London Airport today.

FOUR OF CREW DIE

Evening Standard Reporter

The Vulcan four-jet bomber returning from a 26,000-mile flight to Australia and New Zealand crashed and blew up on landing at London Airport today. Four of the crew were killed.

Two of the crew are known to have survived. They are Air Marshal Sir Harry Broadhurst, C-in-C Bomber Command, who was acting as second pilot, and the captain, Squadron Leader Donald R. Howard.

An Air Ministry spokesman said that Sir Harry and Squadron Leader Howard used their ejector seats.

The spokesman said the Vulcan was making a ground control approach to the main runway.

"At 400 to 500ft. the canopy came off the aircraft

Back Page, Col. Two

Air Marshal Sir Harry Broadhurst (centre) with the Vulcan's crew, left to right, Squadron Leader Stroud, Squadron Leader Gamble, Squadron Leader Howard, captain of the aircraft, and Squadron Leader Eames. This picture was taken three weeks ago at the RAF station, Boscombe Down, Wilts, at the time of the Vulcan's departure for Australia.

VULCAN BOMBER CRASHES IN FLAMES AT END OF 26,000-MILE FLIGHT

From Page One

and the airplane then banked to starboard in a slightly nose down attitude," he said.

"There were two loud bangs, which I presume were the successful ejection.

NOSE DOWN

"The aircraft continued in its nose down attitude getting steeper and steeper until it hit the ground and burst into flames."

The crash occurred just south of the main runway, about 100 yards from the crowded central passenger terminal.

People waiting in the VIP lounge saw the great airplane go up in a sheet of flame. A party of Russians awaiting arrival of Bolshoi ballet—whose airliner had been diverted to Manston because of bad weather—watched as a sheet of flame from blazing fuel snaked along runway.

FOUR BODIES

When the blaze was put out, rescue workers found four bodies in the wreckage.

It was foggy and raining hard as the Vulcan made its approach run to the airport.

Nobody was quite sure what happened in the last few seconds before the bomber hit the ground.

But people in many parts of the airport saw it touch down and slew round on one wing, plunging the wing into the runway.

ONE WHEEL

Flames shot from the Vulcan as it slithered along on one wing and one wheel. Blazing fuel flowed in all directions as rescue teams raced through the fog and rain.

Within second engines were beside the blazing wreckage, pouring on jets of foam.

From a distance all that could be seen was a long line of leaping flames across main No. 7 runway and a 50ft. pall of smoke.

For nearly 200 yards the red-hot metal and rubber wiring snaked along the runway. The main hull of the giant delta-wing bomber lay in a jumbled mass of twisted metal engine parts and fabric, glowing with a bright white magnesium glare.

Parts of the bomber were blown up to 500 yards away by the explosion. One engine cowling lay on a deserted taxi track. A piece of the tailplane, jagged and razor-edged, lay half-buried in the muddy grass.

Ground staff racing out to help were held back by the police. Said a senior official: "There is a danger of further explosions when the fire reaches the fuel tanks."

Even as he spoke a muffled roar sent up great pieces of twisted metal.

Squadron Leader Howard's wife had seen it all from the VIP lounge. She was still there when her husband appeared.

They fell into each other's arms without saying a word. Squadron Leader Howard's only injury was a bruised cheek.

(continued opposite)

The *Evening Standard* devoted some 35 column inches to the copy alone on both the front and back pages (*previous page and right*).

Only the *Evening News* gave both coverage and credit entirely to their man on the spot, as did the nationals the next day, even though we had been as fast as or faster than the staff men. Nevertheless, at the end of the month we were amply compensated for our efforts. Even our unused contributions to the nationals were recognised by bonus payments. But this was exceptional. National newspapers were often notoriously lax in paying correspondents, particularly if the story had also come in from another source, or a staff reporter had been handed the story to sub or rewrite to fit a particular space or presentation.

When I became responsible for checking payments for our services, I soon discovered that some leading popular newspapers were failing to credit us with up to 25 per cent of our published stories each month. That meant, over the years we might have lost hundreds of pounds which could have boosted our reporters' pay.

I was determined to do something about it, at least in the coming months. It became a daunting task. Every piece of copy had to be checked against the line-by-line statements of the newspapers' own accounts department. And since each newspaper headed its correspondents' telephoned copy with its own catch line (a short phrase or a single word describing the content-matter) some contributions were difficult to pin down. How could I be certain that a newspaper had paid for an ordered human-interest story when their copy-taker has decided that "Airport" was the only catch line necessary?

The problem was compounded when a newspaper client failed to pay us for a few paragraphs used within a story from another source, however significant or important those paragraphs might be to the whole as in the Vulcan disaster.

Bill Brenard was initially shocked, then mildly philosophical about my revelations when we had our next company finance meeting. "The simple answer is to get the newspapers to increase their retainers," he concluded, "Otherwise we'll be chasing them for ever."

After some discussion, Mike and Wattie agreed with him. I wasn't happy, because I saw it as a cop out for the newspapers, who, I was convinced, would be horrified when the matter was pointed out to them. I also felt that we shouldn't need to argue a case for increased retainers in this way. But I agreed to sort out a number of watertight examples for our next round of visits to Fleet Street offices. That meant hunting out our original copy with its list of circulated clients and the time it was 'phoned or telexed. Ideally too we should have cuttings from the relevant newspapers if possible, at the very least those early editions we saw at Heathrow, which were reasonably the only ones we could discuss.

At the first opportunity Ray Watts and I raised the subject with one of the three national news editors or their deputies we had arranged to call on. Or at least, Wattie raised it, casually and simply as if only an afterthought. I stood by, nodding agreement and clutching my evidence, hoping the challenge would be taken up.

The reaction was predictable and understandable. Oh no, the newspaper's administrative system wouldn't permit correspondents to be forgotten in such a way. The names of contributors were automatically marked on copy however many times it was transferred from one piece of paper to another. Or so we were assured. And when at his request I produced one example, the news editor, anxious to prove his point, picked up a telephone and called for the original copy file to be brought to him.

It said something for his newspaper's records that the file, though some three months old, appeared within minutes. But it didn't say enough. At the top of the newspaper's

(from facing page)

Lady Broadhurst, who was also in the VIP lounge, went to the scene of the crash to join Sir Harry. Her four-year-old daughter, Clare, waited in the lounge.

Sir Harry had an injured foot. He was taken by ambulance to the RAF Station, Uxbridge, for a check-up.

TERRIFIC BANG

Two stewards, Mr. Thomas Stanley Buttress and Mr. A. V. Reid, who had just landed at London Airport from Rome, gave this eye-witness description of the crash.

"We were in Customs when we heard a terrific bang. We dashed out and saw the Vulcan approaching the runway at great speed. She was about 200ft. up and seemed to be out of control, but there was so sign of any fire then.

"She was travelling at an angle of 45 degrees, hit the main runway with her nose well down and immediately burst into flames. She tore along the runway blazing like an inferno for about a quarter of a mile before stopping.

An airline official said the Vulcan bounced as its wheels touched down on the main runway.

"The aircraft seemed to leap into the air," he said. "The engines revved up their power, then there was a tremendous explosion that shook the airport building."

RECORD TRIP

The Vulcan reached Melbourne on September 11 after doing the 11,475-mile flight from Britain in 47 hours 26 minutes—an average speed of more than 500 m.p.h.

Evening Standard *October 1 1956*

Vulcan crash man keeps job

MR. JOHN MANNING is to stay at London Airport as Traffic Control Officer.

Arrangements to transfer him to a desk job at the London headquarters of the Transport Ministry have been cancelled.

Mr. Manning was the officer in charge of ground control approach at London Airport when the giant Vulcan jet bomber crashed last October. He was held partly responsible for the disaster in a Commons statement.

But the findings of Dr. A. G. Touch, the electronics expert who held a one-man inquiry into the crash did not agree completely with the statement by former Air Minister, Mr. Nigel Birch.

The name of the mystery girl assistant, who helped Mr. Manning when the Vulcan was "talked down," was also revealed last night.

She is Miss Ann Maley, an Air Force traffic control assistant. After the crash —four crew were killed— Miss Maley was taken ill and was off duty for nearly three months.

Daily Sketch (above)

Vulcan control man keeps airport job

By Daily Mail Reporter

ARRANGEMENTS to transfer the controller who talked-down the ill-fated Vulcan bomber at London Airport last October have been cancelled. It had been proposed to post him to a desk job at the Ministry of Transport and Civil Aviation.

Members of the air-traffic control branch said yesterday: "The posting decision was cancelled a week or two ago. Mr. Manning is very happy that he is remaining at the airport."

Mr. Manning, officer in charge of the Ground Control Approach caravan at the airport, was held partly responsible for the disaster in a statement in the House of Commons by the former Air Minister Mr. Nigel Birch.

Yesterday it was disclosed that an independent report by Dr. A. G. Touch, electronics expert, did not wholly agree with Mr. Birch's statement.

Daily Mail (both) Jan 21 1957

The official inquiry into the loss of lives in the bomber lasted more than three months, and the Government rejected some of its conclusions. It was agreed that a number of factors may have contributed to the accident.

version of our story appeared the well-known name of one of their staff reporters. To it was appended "*PA*." Probing further, he picked out an original *Press Association* standard teleprinter transmission.

"There," he exclaimed triumphantly, "It's not even your story, I'm afraid, lads. We used the *PA* piece. Now you wouldn't expect us to pay twice, would you?"

His final words indicated he anticipated our response. He was well aware that the *Press Association*, whilst a rival to us when we were covering the same story, was also a major client of ours. He would have known that we gave virtually the same copy to *PA* as that we circulated to everyone else, though it was always later. What he didn't know was that we could usually tell the difference because we deliberately used alternative phrases or omitted occasional words, even moving sentences or paragraphs around when repeating a story to the news agency.

I quietly produced from my file a copy of the version we had sent to *PA*, and suggested he compare it to my sample he had in front of him. "If you read this carefully, you'll see that your published story is identical in several respects with our original, but not with the *PA* version, even though that was also ours," I said gently, "I think you'll agree that someone must have attributed the copy wrongly. You apparently paid the wrong agency."

A moment's study and he was contrite and obviously irritated, not with us, but with his apparently infallible system. "I'm sorry," he admitted, "It seems something's gone wrong. Your original copy's not on file. Obviously we'll have to make it up to you.

"You'll have to give me the details of any other non-payments you're claiming."

A similar situation occurred with another national newspaper an hour or two later. This time a staff reporter was responsible for the major part of a published story. But he had failed to mark a credit to Brenards for some important additional paragraphs he had used. The error was acknowledged as soon as the records were checked and, fortunately in this case, our original copy was on file.

Over the next few visits we had to further embarrass news desks with claims of this kind. But for a while our income was boosted, in some cases by bonus payments by way of compensation, from the *Express* and *Mirror* particularly. I don't recall a single newspaper being completely blameless, though every incident was obviously due to human error and from their standpoint the sums involved were insignificant. Happily, most news desks appreciated how much more significant such debts were to us, and presumably any other freelances who experienced the same problem.

Finally Bren said enough was enough. We had made our point, he said, and if we continued to embarrass our clients the campaign might prove counter-productive and lose us the goodwill we had built up over the years. Our future tactics would return to periodic pleas for an increase in retainers and perhaps new allowances for expenses, which would go a long way towards easing the pains of searching out account discrepancies.

The mid-'fifties had, in any case, brought a new source of revenue for the company which was to grow steadily. The arrival of commercial television meant a big increase in the demand for filmed news, by the brash newcomer, *ITN*, and the more staid and gentlemanly *BBC*. Mike's photographic team, used to wielding cumbersome Speed Graphic quarter-plate cameras, half-a-dozen spare film slides and huge flash guns, now found themselves also operating small virtually silent 16mm Bell and Howell cine-cameras.

It didn't happen all at once. Contracts with both *BBC* television news and *ITN* had to be negotiated and union fears overcome as I've already described. But eventually almost every major story at Heathrow was covered for the two organisations by Brenard cine-cameramen on an "ordered" basis. It became a daily priority for the agency to advise each TV news organisation of likely stories in advance, and to ask them if they wanted cine coverage.

The financial separation of Brenards' news and photographic departments, which as the news gatherers we reporters resented, inevitably led to frequent clashes over who was in fact generating the overall revenue. It was the Brenard news desk, in the main, which supplied information to the Brenard picture desk, which in turn took the TV orders, just as they took picture orders from the newspapers.

Unlike the newspapers, neither *BBC* television nor *ITN* took copy directly from Brenards or any other freelance agency as a matter of policy. Instead they relied for domestic news on their own correspondents or the teleprinter tapes of the *Press*

Association (which of course supplied them with our stories nonetheless). When they felt it necessary to provide their own reporter as back-up to a filmed story, these would be part of a full camera-sound crew, though normally Brenards' 16mm cine-film (and in later years, video) would still be a principal element of the TV broadcast material.

Our reporting staff suffered even more now from the lack of photographic back-up with the cameramen constantly "engaged elsewhere." Ever more frequently we found ourselves unwittingly aligning our copy to the photographic activities of the "opposition" freelances. This did nothing to help morale in an area where the news side had historically felt unsupported.

Many of the television newsmen (the new *ITN* called them newscasters, because they played an active journalistic role as well as simply reading the news) partly learnt their techniques in the press conference rooms at Heathrow. Robin Day, Ludovic Kennedy, Alistair Burnet, Peter Snow and Reggie Bosanquet were all to become household names as well as familiar figures and part colleagues to us, though our attitude to the novelty was ambivalent.

Their questions to statesmen, prepared as they were in advance from research sources, could on occasions be a considerable boon to us as mere scribblers with no ready access to the latest library cuttings and news tapes. But as often as not we were irritated by their presence. The setting up of television cameras, with their yards of cabling, ponderous equipment, special lighting and teams of technicians usually over-formalised an interview. It reduced the chances of an off-the-cuff and sometimes unguarded newsworthy comment.

Repeated "takes" invariably worked against our tighter deadlines. So did the TV editing technique of cut-away shots of the reporter nodding his head in mock reaction to his subject's remarks for later editing into the filmed interview (hence the highly technical terminology "noddies"). This interlude unintentionally gave the subject the opportunity to amend an earlier answer if he so desired. So we couldn't afford to leave.

TV involvement meant that the average press conference at Heathrow would last at least an hour, with very little to show for it in our news column inches other than a few platitudes. Whether television gave the subject more impact is arguable. But a change of scene from the static newsreader in the studio to an outside location at least provided the viewer with some variety in what otherwise might have been a very dull item.

Heathrow's first press conference room was a wartime Nissen hut, a survivor from the Second World War, some sixty feet in length by fifteen feet wide. It was situated on the north side of the airport about a hundred yards from the original VIP suite, which had been the setting for the last public appearance of the late King. Its hooped, corrugated iron roof painted a matt green, it had boasted a recent existence as a staff canteen under the predictable name of the Green Dragon, which stuck with it.

When the central terminal area came into use in 1955, another, purpose-built conference room with radio studio alongside was opened in the Queens Building, close to two Government-nominated VIP suites. Floor-to-ceiling drapes on two walls and suspended banks of powerful arc-lamps to provide the high levels of illumination required for the huge TV cameras of the day, were installed by the television organisations themselves.

Specially designed cavity walls and surface soundproofing muffled all but the most intrusive noises from outside. Unfortunately the effect was spoilt by the pervasive hum of an air-exchange ventilation system which the puristic broadcasting sound engineers insisted had to be turned off during interviews. On the comparatively rare occasions of a major news event attracting scores of media reporters and cameramen from around the world, any facility lasting more than an hour became sheer torture for the participants. No longer were the politicians solely responsible for the hot air which frequently typified the airport press conference.

Later, other press conference facilities were provided, alongside other VIP suites, then at the prestigious Royal Lounge on the south side of Heathrow. None of them has been without its faults or drawbacks, due to constantly changing needs, different priorities and financial cutbacks.

Facilities for VIPs, those privileged individuals whose rank or standing on the world stage is recognised by Government as warranting some special attention, have also been expanded and refined over the years. An eligibility guide drawn up by the Foreign and Commonwealth Office covers some 40 categories, ranging from British and foreign royal families through heads of state and prime ministers to a comprehensive diplomatic list and leaders of international alliances, civil and military, as well as national church leaders.

For many years, the three passenger terminals at Heathrow Central each boasted at least one VIP room or suite of rooms. In the 1980s a new combined suite was provided for Terminals 1 and 2, and a new complex was provided at Terminal 4. The facility is just a few hundred yards from the Royal Lounge, normally only available to the Royal Family and heads of state or prime ministers travelling on non-scheduled private or military aircraft.

In spite of the Government limitations, the number of VIPs taking advantage of the facilities at Heathrow grew from a few hundreds in the 1950s to some 15,000 annually 40 years on. Set against a current total airport throughput of more than 62 million a year, the number of passengers who sit in comfort while their passports are taken away to be checked, who have their baggage collected for them, and to whom Her Majesty's Customs give a touch of the forelock is still relatively small.

At the same time, the newsworthiness of the average VIP has also proportionately declined. Until the mid-'sixties, Brenard reporters could be seen door-stepping at the suites regularly. The restricted daily VIP list issued by the airport primarily to alert Customs, Immigration and police, was an essential tool of our trade. Then these reliable cameos of interest faded as air travel itself began to reach out to the common man who has to queue at ticket check-in and push his own baggage trolley.

There are still a number among this remaining 60-million-plus who believe they are "important" enough to warrant this special recognition, even when they appear aware of the necessary qualifications. Some of course are confused by such phrases as "pop star given VIP treatment," or "actress waits in an airline VIP lounge," which occur from time to time in the news and gossip columns, phrases I have used myself. They are descriptions, which while not inaccurate in themselves, can be misinterpreted.

It can be difficult explaining the difference between the assistance provided by or on behalf of the Government hospitality office and the services offered by most airlines for those passengers they consider to be commercially important (or those who simply pay for privilege by travelling first class). As one airport management official once put it, though I suspect only half-seriously: "From the classified ads. can you tell the difference between a health clinic and a massage parlour?"

British screen producer Michael Winner, known for his crime and rough justice films, and not a retiring nature, is one who over a period persistently demanded VIP status, insisting on speaking to the "top man" when he was politely but firmly rejected. Furiously, he more than once complained: "If I'm not a VIP, who is? I've earned this country millions of dollars with my pictures."

Labour MP Keith Vaz,[1] much admired for his constituency work, once threatened to pull strings to win similar recognition for an Indian holy man and religious sect leader who was due to visit Britain. He had to be advised that the only religious leaders recognised as VIPs at Heathrow were the Primates of the Anglican and Roman Catholic churches in England and the Chief Rabbi of the UK. (Though the Pope would also qualify as Sovereign Pontiff of the Vatican and head of state).

When he angrily indicated he was going to "take the matter higher," the MP was referred to the Foreign Office, which finances the major part of the cost of the VIP suites. Nothing more was heard of the demand.

Ironically, the group heading the list of qualifiers, the Royal Family, rarely enter the suites, even the Royal Lounge. In most instances they drive directly to and from their aircraft, unless they are passengers on a scheduled flight. Prince Philip rejected Terminal 2's Brabazon[2] suite on his first visit.

He was totally scathing of its siting, which he found depressing and dismal. He complained that it looked out on dustbins; that it was overshadowed by and overlooked by a walkway used (perish the thought) by ordinary mortals. He refused ever again to use it, but the suite, luxuriously and comfortably furnished as it was and extremely convenient for the aircraft stands, remained in constant use for less demanding VIPs for nearly thirty years.

Military men and Cold War diplomats were inevitably the most frequent users of the VIP facilities in the early 1950s. General Eisenhower, Supreme Commander of the victorious Western Allies, was a regular visitor before his return from Heathrow to Washington to run

[1] *Later a Labour Government Minister* [2] *See p.178 (Brabazon suite)*

successfully for the American Presidency. Yet I have no particular memories of those visits and no cuttings to indicate that he made any great news impact.

When his successor in Europe, General Matthew Ridgway, flew in from Paris for a dinner date he unexpectedly found himself surrounded by 170 uniformed foot police and a motorcycle escort. They were to see him safely to the north terminal VIP lounge just 100 yards away. (I had time to count them as they lined up on the tarmac – though any plainclothes security men must have escaped my calculations.) A senior police officer explained to me: "There was a big demonstration last time he flew in. We wanted to make sure it didn't happen again."

The Daily Mirror's columnist, Cassandra, took up my story:

"The security arrangements were ten times as stringent as when Royalty arrives. Who asked for it? The Home Office? The US Embassy? Surely the genial and amiable General Ridgway isn't hated as much as that and surely the British public is not given to bomb-tossing on any hair-trigger excuse?"

A year later, yet another Supreme Commander, General Alfred Gruenther, appeared to be less welcome. He found the VIP lounge locked against him and had to wait on the doorstep while an official ran to get the key. As I reported at the time for the *Standard* diary, thc Gcncral was quite unperturbed. "If I have any trouble leaving again, we'll shoot our way out," he told me, "I have a bodyguard of Tommies with me."

The General had given a lift in his special USAF aircraft to the "Tommies," nine British squaddies from his NATO headquarters. I didn't like to point out to him that the soldiers had already deserted him. They'd gone the way of all other ranks, through the standard passport and Customs controls. The general would have been on his own if he'd had to fight his way out of the VIP lounge.

General Gruenther was in good company. The Government's constitutional commissioner in Cyprus, Lord Radcliffe, was similarly locked out on another occasion, and Britain's former top soldier Sir John Harding, (yet another General), was also barred from the lounge, though that was because another VIP took precedence at the time. William Draper, a roving ambassador in Europe for President Eisenhower, was already in situ when Sir John turned up to fly to Kenya.

Diplomatic niceties meant that the two VIPs had to be separated, I was informed, so Sir John was "demoted" to an adjoining lounge normally used by ordinary passengers.

In another incident, a Soviet Ambassador to Britain, M.Jacob Malik, complained bitterly about regulations at Heathrow, which restricted the number of people, permitted on the tarmac to see off VIPs. Mr Malik had entered the lounge with his wife and fifteen officials from the Embassy who had driven in a fleet of cars to the airport with them. They were there to see the Maliks off to Moscow on what he said was a "short private visit."

But only three of them were allowed on the tarmac. An airport official stopped the others at the VIP doors. "I'm afraid you can't go any further," he said firmly.

Mr Malik was pulled up short. "Don't you make any concessions,

170 guard Ridgway for a dinner-date

MORE than 170, police and security men guarded London Airport last night when General Ridgway, Atlantic Pact Commander in Europe, flew in from Paris for a dinner-date.

A police officer explained: "There was a big demonstration last time he came. We were just making sure it didn't happen again."

General Ridgway's date was with the Anglo-American Pilgrims' Society at the Savoy.

He told them that the forces

Daily Herald Oct 25 1952

Who Goes There?

YESTERDAY General Matthew Ridgway, the Supreme Commander of NATO, arrived at London Airport.

Nobody got hurt.

And to see that nobody got hurt there were 100 Metropolitan Policemen, seventy Airport Policemen and an unknown quantity of plain clothes detectives. Every approach to the airport was lined and look-out posts were manned inside the gates and throughout the terminal buildings.

When his plane touched down a motor-cycle escort roared out on to the runway to meet him.

The security arrangements were ten times as stringent as when Royalty arrives

The General "**appeared to be puzzled by his reception.**"

I don't blame him. It is true that there have been disturbances organised by Communist roughs before, but on nothing more than the scale of a public house brawl. This sort of costly jitteryness, however, is pure lunacy.

Who asked for it? The Home Office? The U.S. Embassy?

✦ ✦ ✦

These spectacular precautions were almost on the same fantastic scale as those taken by Adolf Hitler and were not unlike the anti-assassination screens that surround Joe Stalin whenever he leaves the Kremlin.

Surely the genial and amiable General Ridgway isn't hated as much as that, and surely the British public is not given to bomb-tossing on any hair-trigger excuse.

Daily Mirror Oct 25 1952

A typical reaction to my story from the *Mirror's* outspoken columnist, 'Cassandra' *(above)*

General surprise

GENERAL ALFRED GRUENTHER, Supreme Commander of the North Atlantic Treaty Forces, flew into London Airport to-day and took everyone by surprise. Ministry of Civil Aviation officials had no warning that he was expected. The VIP lounge was locked.

The General was unperturbed. He told an apologetic official after the lounge had been unlocked for him. "I am perfectly happy." He added jokingly, "If I have any trouble I have got a bodyguard of Tommies. We'll shoot our way out."

The "Tommies" were nine British soldiers from NATO headquarters to whom General Gruenther had given a lift in his aircraft.

General Gruenther is speaking at the Imperial Defence College to-day. He returns to Paris to-night.

Evening Standard Oct 15 1953

VIP shuts out Sir John

Express Staff Reporter

THE Royal Lounge at London Airport—reserved for "super - V.I.P.s" — was not available for General Sir John Harding, Chief of the Imperial General Staff, when he waited to board his special airliner for Kenya last night.

The lounge had already been booked for President Eisenhower's "Roving Ambassador," Mr. William Draper, U.S. Special Representative in Europe, who was flying back to his Paris headquarters after a routine visit to London.

So General Harding had to leave from the West Lounge next door.

Mr. Draper watched him walk out to his aircraft from a window of the Royal Lounge.

The C.I.G.S. was starting a week's visit to the troops called in to assist in quelling the Mau Mau activities.

Daily Express, Feb 18 1953

Angry Malik

RUSSIAN Ambassador Jacob Malik got mighty angry at London Airport last night—with RED tape.

It ended with this bitter remark to the airport officials:

"*Perhaps soon we shall have a direct jet service to London. WE are ready but YOU are reluctant.*

"*Our T Us are no noisier than the Boeing or the Comet.*"

What started the outburst? Fifteen Russian Embassy officials arrived to say au revoir to Malik and his wife as they flew off for Moscow.

Three of the farewell party were allowed to walk part of the way to the tarmac. But an official told them: "You can't go any farther."

Second time

Malik at first smiled bleakly. "Don't you make any concessions—even for ambassadors?" The Airport man shook his head sadly.

Then Malik's smile faded. "Your rules are much too strict," he snapped.

I'm sorry for Mr. Malik. It is the second time he has been upset by our airport arrangements.

I remember how angry he got last May when the T U jet bringing the Moscow Arts Theatre group was diverted to bleak Stansted Airport in Essex. "This is no way to welcome visitors," he told me.

Rules stump Mr. Malik

REGULATIONS at London Airport stumped the Russian Ambassador, **Mr. Malik**, when he flew home yesterday for a "short private visit."

He arrived at the airport with a seeing-off party of 15 Russian officials. But 12 of them were stopped at the V.I.P. suite. The remaining three were allowed to walk part of the way along the gallery leading to the tarmac. Then they, too, were stopped.

"I am afraid you cannot come any further," said an airport official.

Mr. Malik pulled up short, and said with a wry half-smile: "Don't you make any concessions, even for ambassadors?" The official shook his head.

The ambassador grunted, and said. "Your rules are much too strict."

Daily Express (above)
Daily Herald (left)
(both) Nov 11 1958

even for ambassadors?" he asked with a bleak half-smile.

The official shook his head sadly. The Russian's smile faded. "Your rules are much too strict," he snapped.

The airport press office tried to explain. "We have to draw the line somewhere," they told me, "The numbers have to be limited on safety grounds." But Mr Malik was still angry when he reached his turbo-prop Aeroflot aircraft. Out of the blue he turned to his airport escort and commented bitterly and bewilderingly: "Perhaps soon we shall have a direct jet service to London. We are ready but you are reluctant. "Our Tupolevs are no noisier than the Boeing or the Comet."

Britain's genial Lord "Pug" Ismay, secretary-general of NATO, wouldn't have been worried by the controversial introduction of jet airliners. He flew from Paris in an American B17 bomber, the original Flying Fortress, and had to lower his burly, six-foot frame through a four-foot wide hatch. Lady Ismay and a woman secretary followed. Seats had been fitted for them behind the bomb bay.

The bomber had been lent by General Eisenhower's headquarters. "I'm not used to luxury air travel," said Lord Ismay as he waited at the VIP lounge for airport officials who were expecting him aboard a scheduled flight. "Flying by bomber is the most comfortable way I know."

I turned to Lady Ismay for a comment. She diplomatically shook her head and just smiled.

A pose for the photographers ...before Miss Landis turned her back on Britain to come down safely to earth, backwards.

Film star leaves plane by ladder

ACTRESS Jessie Royce Landis had to make a big climb-down—at London Airport yesterday.

She flew in with her husband, Major-General John Seitz, in his special U.S. Air Force aircraft. Only to find that the airport had temporarily run out of steps.

Gently down the ladder comes the General's wife, holding on to the rope handrail. She is actress Jessie Royce Landis.

The general, who heads the U.S. military commission to Persia, grew tired of waiting.

He called for the wooden ladder which is carried in the plane for just such an emergency as this.

The ladder was lowered to the ground. The general climbed down.

He took down with him a knotted rope handrail, fixed to the plane.

The rope was held taut and Miss Landis was persuaded to climb down.

"Very embarrassing," she said as she touched down.

And then, of course, the proper steps arrived.

How high was the plane off the ground? "Seven to 10ft." said the general

"Nonsense, it was at least 20ft." said his wife.

She is here to see her film "My Man Godfrey." The general is here on a routine NATO call.

Daily Sketch

THE HARD WAY

JESSIE ROYCE LANDIS, the American actress, made a spectacular and unrehearsed entrance into England last night.

She flew into London Airport from Paris with her husband, **Major-General John Seitz**, in his U.S. Air Force plane.

She had to climb out of the cabin backwards down a wooden ladder, hanging tightly to a knotted rope.

Miss Landis said: "It's the first time I have landed backwards in Britain. Most undignified. And, of course, as soon as we were off they turned up with some very comfortable steps."

Daily Express (both) Nov 1 1957

American actress Jesse Royce Landis almost certainly would have disagreed with the noble lord. She too flew to London in a USAF aircraft, in this case piloted by her husband, an air force major general. As this was a four-engined Douglas C54, the military version of the civil Skymaster, it was at least designed to carry passengers rather than bombs.

But Miss Landis too found the leaving of her aircraft slightly undignified. When her husband learnt that the airport had temporarily run out of suitable steps, he decided to lower a basic wooden ladder kept aboard for just such an emergency. Clambering down himself, he took with him a knotted rope handrail, attached at one end to the aircraft. A crew member held the rope taut and Miss Landis was persuaded to follow her husband down. "Most embarrassing," she told me. "It's the first time I've arrived somewhere backwards."

How high was the drop? "Oh, only about seven feet," said her flyer husband. Replied Miss Landis: "Nonsense, it was at least twenty feet."

It was appropriate it should be the Minister of Civil Aviation himself who chose to make the first "air taxi" flight from the House of Commons to Heathrow to join another aircraft. Mr Alan Lennox-Boyd's special Bell helicopter covered the distance in just 13 minutes.

Not for him the VIP lounge on that occasion. The helicopter dropped him off at the edge of the tarmac and he walked a mere hundred yards to board a Government twin-engined de Havilland Dove. "We made pretty good time, didn't we?" he called out as he recognised me observing from the edge of that tarmac. Then he was off, to attend the commemoration of an earlier transport innovation: the 100th anniversary of the opening of the Swansea and Mumbles railway.

Twenty minutes later I took pity on the solitary airport official, one of the Minister's own staff, who was still waiting at the door of the lounge to receive him. When I told him of the Minister's arrival (and departure) he didn't appear to believe me. I left him talking heatedly on a telephone.

Although, as a former Prime Minister, Lord Attlee was still entitled to the privilege, he spurned VIP facilities on several occasions. Just sixteen months after his resignation as

Source: US Library of Congress, photographer unknown, 1 Aug 1945

From the 'Big Three' conference at Potsdam in 1945, with US President Harry S.Truman and Soviet Leader Marshall Joseph Stalin, to a ride for Clem Attlee on a descending escalator in a London tube station a mere six years later.

Labour leader and his elevation to the House of Lords – when he was pictured on a London Underground escalator carrying a suitcase after clearing his desk – I was expecting him at Heathrow on his return from a trip to New York. I had to track him down as he cleared Customs, as self-effacing as ever among other Transatlantic passengers.

Several newspapers had asked us for his comments on statements by Dame Florence Bevin about the retirement of her late husband, the former Labour Foreign Secretary, some five years earlier. Dame Florence had alleged in a *BBC* radio portrait of her husband that he had been sacked by the Prime Minister in a 'phone call on his 70th birthday in March 1951. His former secretary supported the claim. Ernest Bevin had died just a month later.

Earl Attlee said he had heard of the broadcast in New York, at the end of a lecture tour. "It's quite extraordinary," he told me, "I really cannot understand why they should say such a thing.

"It's all very strange. Mr Bevin and I talked about his resignation over a period of a week. He was not a well man. There was never any question of a 'phone call. I chatted with him practically every day."

When, on another occasion "Clem's" name appeared on the VIP list, I dutifully waited for him at the lounge until the last minute. Then thinking he might have checked in at his airline ticket desk, I hurried there. Finally an airline man told me: "We've just had a cancellation of his reservation. We're leaving without him."

After the Australia-bound flight had taken off I made my way to the 'phone to advise my desk of the apparent cancellation. Then I suddenly remembered… I had Earl Attlee's private number in my book of contacts. The former Premier had given me the 'phone number of his home in Great Missenden, Buckinghamshire, on some previous occasion. I called him. Once again he appeared bewildered.

"I know nothing about a booking today," he said, "I was supposed to fly out last Friday, but the 'plane wouldn't start or something.

"Nobody told me about a flight today. I am now flying out on Monday via India."

I have no explanation for the coincidental vagueness. Despite his diffident manner, and the physical frailties which marked his final years, Clem Attlee wasn't known for appearing vague. He had a reputation for political astuteness, a fact grudgingly conceded even by his opponents after his retirement. Perhaps it was something to do with me....

I'd spotted Lord Brabazon of Tara in a crowded departure lounge. He was seated alone in a wicker armchair, reading a newspaper, a cup of coffee beside him on a small table. As one of Britain's best-known aviation pioneers, his was a very familiar face. I had seen him several times in the past at various aviation functions; I may even have talked to him, though I couldn't be sure.

PAUL TANFIELD

Lord B, it seems, is not a VIP

A LESSER man than **Lord Brabazon of Tara,** the aviation pioneer, who was flying before London Airport was ever dreamed of, would perhaps feel slighted by the treatment he got there last night. Waiting for a flight to Zurich he sat in the crowded departure lounge for 15 minutes.

Not for him a VIP lounge . . . *not even the one that is named after him* !

That is reserved for royalty, Heads of State, Government Ministers, Ambassadors, and their guests.

"Lord Brabazon is not important enough to be entitled to use the Brabazon Lounge," said a London Airport spokesman last night. "He just doesn't qualify."

Lord Brabazon, 77-year-old first holder of an English commercial pilot's licence, seldom flies these days. Last night, however, he was quite philosophical.

"It does seem a pity not to be able to make use of the lounge," he said. "But, unlike the other pioneers who have suites named after them, I was at least able to see over mine before giving my name to it."

'NO DIFFERENCE'

Lord Brabazon is the only survivor of the pioneer pilots who were honoured in this way. Cody, Kingsford-Smith, and Alcock and Brown all died before the suites were named.

But London Airport, which prides itself on being flexible about giving VIP treatment to those below Ambassador level, if informed in advance, would have ignored them too, it seems.

"We did not know that Lord Brabazon was here," said a spokesman. "But even if we had it would have made no difference."

Film stars who are given special treatment, by the way, are always put in the *private* lounges maintained by each airline. Although this is called VIP treatment, it is not officially recognised by the airport as such.

Daily Mail **Feb 3 1962**

BRABAZON BARRED FROM V.I.P. LOUNGE

IT WAS TOUGH on Lord Brabazon, the bluff old pioneer of British aviation.

There he was yesterday at London Airport (where they have just gone to great trouble to name a V.I.P. lounge after him), sitting for 15 minutes in the throng of the departure hall.

Why on earth could he not use his own lounge? He is the only survivor of the four aviation pioneers whose names have been given to the luxury suites.

"It seems a pity," said Lord Brabazon, 78 next week. "But I don't qualify."

Who does? Royalty, heads of State, Government Ministers, ambassadors, and their guests.

Daily Express **Feb 3 1962**

But this was February 1962, just a few months after Heathrow's VIP suites had been renamed. And the suite at the Europa Building, itself soon to be re-designated as Terminal 2, had been named after the holder of the first English commercial pilot's licence, Lord Brabazon. Here, I thought, was an opportunity for a little bit of harmless fun. I approached him, and when I introduced myself he asked me to take a seat. As I asked him, conversationally, where he was travelling and why, I added lightly: "I wouldn't have expected to see you here. You should be waiting in comfort in your own lounge."

He glanced at me to see if I was teasing. Then he smiled and conceded: "I suppose it does seem a pity. But I don't qualify, you know. It's reserved for real VIPs, not people like me." He didn't sound particularly concerned, but I commiserated with him anyway. "Oh, it's all right," he said, "Unlike the other aviators who have suites named after them I was at least able to see all of them, and had the privilege of choosing the one I wanted."

Lord Brabazon, by now just a few days away from his 78th birthday, was the only survivor of the flyers honoured in this way. The others, Cody, Kingsford-Smith and Alcock and Brown all died before the suites named after them were opened. Terminal 1 had not yet been built and its de Havilland suite was some years into the future.[1] We shook hands as Lord Brabazon cheerfully boarded his airliner for Zurich. Then I slipped away to telephone the Ministry of Aviation press office. I needed quotable formal confirmation that his Lordship did not feature in the official list of VIPs, even though I was already aware of the fact. I took the opportunity to ask if the airport management was aware that he was travelling that day.

"Lord Brabazon is just not important enough to qualify," said the spokesman. "And no, we were not aware he was travelling. But even if we had been, it would have made no difference." Now I had my story. And even if it was argued that I had inspired the story by inviting a reaction, I had no qualms. I was only reporting what had happened, and reporting the comments of the people involved. I wasn't deliberately being mischievous; I wasn't taking sides. I had no view of my own, unless it was to highlight an apparent

[1] *The names were dropped in the '80s on the opening of the combined Hounslow Suite for Terminals 1& 2. At Terminal 3, the Alcock and Brown Suite was renamed after the London Borough of Hillingdon and the new Terminal 4 facility became the Spelthorne Suite after the third Heathrow neighbouring borough.*

injustice... as I was vehemently to insist later.

The newspapers, of course, loved it. The story screamed of bureaucracy gone mad. The *Daily Mail's* diarist *Paul Tanfield* gave it a 4-column lead. The *Express* was more straightforward, its succinct headline was placed over a double-column box.

The published story brought an immediate stable-door response from the naïve and now contrite airport press office. "It was a misunderstanding," said the spokesman. "We will, of course, make an exception for Lord Brabazon in future."

And he went on: "It followed quite naturally that when Lord Brabazon allowed his name to be used for the lounge he would be given full use of it whenever he requested it. We have now asked his secretary to inform us whenever he is travelling through the airport so that he can be offered the facilities of the suite."

That promise was put embarrassingly to the test just a few days later when Lord Brabazon returned from Switzerland. Unaware of the fuss. Bowled over by the reception. Ushered into "his" suite by airline customer relations' staff and an airport management representative, as I reported for *William Hickey* in the *Express* (but not by the airport's general manager, Robert Edwards, as the diary mysteriously and mistakenly added). And all in the unfeeling presence of the photographers. I just happened to be there too.

It was Lord Brabazon himself who rightly had the last words on the day. And I faithfully reported them, to accompany the pictures of him at the door of the suite published the next day with a re-vamp of my original story printed alongside as a reminder. The story served to compound the sensitivity of the issue the next day for the unhappy airport management.

THE RELUCTANT VIP

The William Hickey Page

BRABAZON ASKS: WHY ALL THIS FUSS?

HERE is the last chapter in the London Airport legend of Lord Brabazon, our air pioneer.

Denied, you will recall, the use of the V.I.P. lounge they have named after him. Then official recriminations. An announcement that henceforward he would be welcomed inside the hallowed doors.

★

Yesterday he came back from Switzerland. Unaware of the fuss. Bowled over by the warmth of the official reception. Mr. Robert Edwards, general manager of the airport, there to usher him into his suite. Everyone effusive.

Lord Brabazon embarrassed. "All this fuss isn't for me," he said. "Ordinary people like me should not use the lounge. I won't use it again. I don't want V.I.P. treatment. I would rather be the same as everyone else."

Sober words from a fine old man.

An embarrassed Lord Brabazon is shown into the VIP lounge.

Daily Express picture Feb 9 1962

"All this fuss isn't for me," Lord Brabazon protested to me, "Ordinary people like me shouldn't use the lounge. I won't use it again. I don't want VIP treatment. I would rather be the same as everyone else."

As *William Hickey* added to my story:

"Sober words from a fine old man..."

CHAPTER EIGHT

John Foster Dulles, soon to become one of America's most formidable Secretaries of State was, in 1951, President Truman's special envoy to the Japanese Peace Treaty negotiations. The war with Japan which, following victory in Europe, had threatened to continue for at least another year, had ended suddenly in August 1945 with the enemy's total surrender after the dropping of atomic bombs on Hiroshima and Nagasaki.

It would be some years before the signatures of the Allied Powers on a piece of paper launched the Japanese economic miracle. Meanwhile, the talks struggled on.

Early that June I had been advised that the PA wanted coverage on Dulles when he stopped off at Northolt on his way from Washington to Paris. I'd learnt that his special USAF aircraft was to make an early morning refuelling halt at the civil air terminal. Without even knowing if he would leave the 'plane, I made my way directly to the airport's departure and transit lounge after my long tube journey from north London. There were no exclusive VIP suites available at Northolt then, other than at the RAF station on the far side of the runway.

It was not yet seven thirty, but the C54 aircraft had already touched down. There, half-leaning on a buffet counter, in an otherwise deserted lounge, was the American diplomat, sipping black coffee.

*

Almost every reporter faces, at some time in his working life, the disquieting experience of having a story or part of a story contradicted, denied, even ridiculed. In some cases the denial may be a defensive reaction to a personal embarrassment, such as the incident of Valerie Hobson and her jewels.[1]

When the complaint is from an independent witness to some situation or event, it is likely to take the form of: *"That didn't happen. It just wasn't like that. I know, I was there."* Or, as the bystander who suddenly becomes newsworthy may protest, on seeing himself in print: *"I didn't say that."*

Sometimes the critics are right… or partly so. Every collector of evidence will confirm that no two people remember seeing exactly the same thing at the same time. Their recall and re-telling is coloured by their emotions, their judgement and, of course, their memory.

The reporter is expected to be among the more accurate of eyewitnesses. But he's there to report a situation or an incident not only as he sees it. If he is the sole witness, his report will obviously be his own interpretation of an event. Though just as valid, his interpretation may be simply different from that of others. On occasions, it has to be said, any witnesses' impressions may be inaccurate, for a variety of reasons. Though he does have a notebook to record his impressions at the time, the reporter, obviously, has to rely on what his senses tell him, just as any other witness does.

A report of someone's words or "quotes" should be straightforward and unequivocal. But what if the sole reporter's impressions of a situation are false? I learned the dangers early on in my training as a cub.

Arriving at Northolt one morning to start my duty, my bus from Ruislip was held up at lights which halt the traffic on West End Road (the A4180) where it cuts across the eastern landing approach to the airport's main runway. It was a wild day, and I was already thinking in terms of a weather story for the first editions of the evenings as I watched a Swissair Dakota descend across the road in front of me on its final touchdown approach.

The aircraft's wheels touched the ground two or three hundred yards to my right, beyond the hatched lines of the runway threshold. The approach was at an angle because of the severe crosswinds, and a sudden gust made the aircraft swing violently as if in a drunken stagger. The port wing dropped, and its extreme tip appeared to touch the ground. My bus was on the move again and now almost at right angles with the runway threshold. I believed I saw a spray of mist or dust as the wing tip dipped towards the asphalt surface.

I reported the sighting merely as part of my weather story, talking of the severe

[1] *See Chapter 5, p109*

crosswinds. And I used the phrase: *"...the wing tip of a Swissair Dakota scraped the ground as it was blown sideways by one gust."*

Of course, it wasn't so. And if I had used the words *"appeared to brush"* or had dictated *"almost scraped,"* it's unlikely I would have heard any more of it. But when later that day the *Star* appeared carrying my so-brief reference to the aircraft incident, Swissair's station manager at Northolt, Bert Unholz, took it as a personal affront. He stormed into the tiny Press Room Harry and I had made our base.

His command of colloquial English was superb, even if his accent left something to be desired. For some minutes he harangued me about my alleged damage to his aircraft and what he saw as horrendous damage to his airline's reputation. I tried desperately to defend myself in the face of his threats to sue me, sue Brenards, sue *The Star* "for every penny" he could.

"But I saw it..." I pleaded at last. "I saw the wing touch the ground...er... brush the ground. Or appear to brush the ground...."

He knew he had won the day. "Now, then," he said, "You come with me." And he marched me out to the tarmac, ignoring my defensive protests that I wasn't allowed out there. We stood beneath the wing of his aircraft, due to take off shortly on its return flight to Switzerland. "There," he said triumphantly, "Show me the damage. Show me where we scraped the ground."

Not a graze. Not a scratch. The wing tip just above my head was clean and clear, the aluminium burnished and shining. I could only mumble my apologies. "I could have sworn…" I began and stopped. "You're right. I'm wrong. I was mistaken. I'm sorry…"

Lawyers for Bill Brenard and the *Star* would no doubt have been horrified at my admission. Fortunately my apology was accepted. Bert became more conciliatory. But he did ask: "You realise the damage this sort of thing could do to our reputation? You realise you were suggesting our pilot couldn't handle the aircraft?" I accepted that possible interpretation, and said so.

At last, suitably mollified, Bert said: "OK. This time we'll forget it." I remembered the lesson.

Home from home

LONDON'S longest serving foreign airline manager — he has spent nearly 17 years at Croydon, Northolt and London Airports — said goodbye to the hundreds of friends he has made in Britain and flew home to Switzerland last week.

Swissair's Station Manager, W. "Bert" Unholz, was the first foreign airline representative in Britain immediately after the last war, and was appointed manager London stations, soon afterwards.

Now he has been promoted to Station Controller at Zurich, Swissair's base airport.

With him when he flew home last week travelled his wife and their two children, both born in Britain. "The happiest days of my life have been spent in London" said Bert. "In all the years I've been here, I've never had a rough deal from the English. I feel as if I'm leaving home."

Airport Post *Nov 16 1960*

Some ten years later I found myself reporting the departure from Heathrow of a longtime friend.

The reporter's notebook is even more important in recording the views and opinions of the newsworthy. And, as I've implied, even harder to understand than the mistaken impression is the challenged "direct quote." Or, as some would have us believe, the misquote.

No one likes words put into his or her mouth, particularly when they're not representative of the speaker's views or emotions. But the newspaper reader expects the storytelling to be brief and concise. Few of us are as articulate as we like to think. Consequently few of us would like to see our words and sentences printed exactly the way we construct them. President Nixon's "expletives deleted" is not the only example of a cover-up.

Those hard-won quotes may have to be tidied up, even paraphrased. And the reporter has to ensure that if he can't use the actual words, for whatever reason, then his interpretation, in indirect speech, must accurately reflect the sense of what was being said.

There may be times when published quotes are little more than wishful thinking on the part of the reporter. At worst they may employ phrases or words straight out of the reporter's vocabulary, and not even recognised by the speaker.[1] At best they may have originated in the form of a reporter's leading question, with which the hapless victim has simply concurred. (The question that began innocently: "I suppose you think that…?" or "Wouldn't you agree that...?" may beg the answer the reporter wants to hear.)

There are also those occasions when the reader's intelligence is challenged by "quotes" attributed to a child. A three-years-old could become a prodigy sensation if endowed with the lucidity imagined by reporters in some newsworthy situations.

Statesmen, politicians, leaders of industry and trade unions, indeed all who have

[1] *In my later life on the other side of the fence as spokesman for Heathrow, I was once quoted by a national newspaper reporter as having said that a proposed activity by her colleague might "exacerbate" a difficult situation. The word is not in my vocabulary and with other phrases, made my response appear pompous and bureaucratic. A few days earlier the word had become fashionable when it was attributed to former Premier Edward Heath. Perhaps the reporter had borrowed his dictionary.*

achieved some status by arguing a case; these are made of stronger stuff. Every word they utter is carefully considered. It could be as a measured pronouncement, a rehearsed statement designed to support or excuse, attack and criticise, arouse sympathy, admiration or understanding, or instil distaste or distrust for an organisation, a policy, cause or a view they either espouse or oppose. Or so you, and they, might believe. The reporter who gets it wrong has a problem. The politician who gets it wrong has the solution.

A denial. He was misunderstood. Or he was "misquoted"...*or not even present.*

*

Foster Dulles was not alone at the buffet. With him was one of Northolt's three chief preventive officers of Her Majesty's Customs and Excise, Harry Lane. The two seemed to be having an animated conversation, and I hovered within earshot for a few moments to establish that Mr Dulles was not being relieved of contraband. Harry Lane, I believe, was telling some rambling anecdote about fishing.

Interrupting during a pause, I quickly introduced myself. Answering my question, Dulles confirmed that he was on his way to Paris to confer with the French Foreign Minister. I asked him how the talks over Japan were progressing.

Without hesitating he replied: "So far they've not been at all satisfactory. We have a lot of areas of disagreement."

This seemed promising, I thought. Would he be more precise? I asked. Who was disagreeing with whom, and what about? Nothing, I said, had been reported about difficulties, as far as I was aware.

As if sensing he had said too much, he paused before answering. Then choosing his words, he added slowly: "It would not be helpful if I went into detail. It's not something that can't be sorted out. I would hope that we can settle our difference by next week."

With that he gave a dismissive gesture and turned back to the buffet. "Thank you," he said, and with a final glance in my direction picked up his conversation with the Customs man, who had stayed nearby, an indulgent smile on his face.

British newspapers showed little enthusiasm for such a negative story. At the time I saw only one cutting, a "brief" from the *Evening News*. A peace treaty six years after the end of the war seemed little more than a technicality. The Americans were more interested. We had filed the item to their wire services after *PA* as a matter of routine, and *United Press International* decided to follow-up the "differences" with Dulles later that day in Paris. A few hours on I learnt the result of their inquiries.

The US envoy, their London desk reported, had strongly denied the attributed quotes, describing them as "a complete fabrication."

Foster Dulles apparently told *UPI's* Paris correspondent that he had met no Press representatives in London and had made no statement to anyone about the talks... indeed, he stated, he had not even left his seat when his aircraft stopped at Northolt to refuel. He was, he insisted, still fast asleep on board.

This was all relayed to me by my own news desk. *UPI* in London, they said, wanted a statement from me. "You bet they can have a statement," I snapped, demanding an outside telephone line from the Brenard switchboard to call them myself. I simply couldn't believe my office had taken the message correctly.

But when I spoke to the American agency's general desk, they repeated everything I'd just heard. For a moment I was lost for words. Then patiently the American correspondent at the other end of the line listened as I related the sequence of events while he, nonchalantly, broke in once or twice with a question. Finally, I added, as if I considered it unimportant to substantiate the story: "Oh, and by the way, I do have an independent witness."

Even as I said it I wondered if a public servant would be free to verify a conversation in which he'd not been involved. But the *UPI* man was still apparently unconcerned anyway. "Okay, fine," he said. "Just give me all that in copy, will you? I'll put you over."

I dictated the account once more, this time to a typist, and signed off. Then for our own records, I repeated it to a Brenard copytaker. This time, though, I made no mention of a witness. For one thing it sounded too defensive. For another...well, I would have to talk to Harry Lane first.

This wasn't possible until the next day. The Customs officer's reaction was one of amusement. But his grin irritated me. My youthful ethics were in question. I was unjustly and quite ridiculously being accused of making up a news story and all he could do was smile. Petulantly, I pointed this out to him, and he sympathised. "But I don't see what I can do about it," he said, "I couldn't hear everything he told you. I wasn't paying that much attention."

I said that I wasn't asking him to verify the detail of the American statesman's comments, only to agree, if it should be necessary, that Dulles had left the 'plane, that he and I had met and had spoken, and that Dulles had made references to the Japanese peace treaty talks. I told him that I didn't think I would ever need to call on him, but I would like to know he was there if needed.

At last he saw the point of this and agreed, although reluctantly. He confirmed my concern that as a senior Customs officer he might not be allowed to take part in a public debate, but said he would go along with me as far as possible. This I had to accept. In fact, it was never necessary to call on his support. In spite of the hesitant inquiries I made with the American wire service later, I heard nothing more. Dulles, I was told, refused to discuss the matter further.

A little over two years later, the new White House incumbent, President Eisenhower, appointed John Foster Dulles as his Secretary of State. Never again did I have the opportunity of an exclusive from him. I wasn't sorry.

Dwight Eisenhower and John Foster Dulles, Aug 8 1956
Source: Wikimedia Commons
After winning the US presidency, Dwight Eisenhower, the former World War 2 supreme commander appointed John Foster Dulles as his Secretary of State.

*

Sir Anthony Eden succeeded Sir Winston Churchill as Prime Minister in April 1955; the cynics saw it as the bridesmaid following the bride. The name of Eden had been synonymous with Britain's overseas policies since the early 1930s. He first became Foreign Secretary in 1935, and later held the office for two more periods, serving a total of ten years.

With the rise of Naziism, he stood shoulder to shoulder with Churchill in opposing appeasement while out of cabinet office, but as a statesman he was nevertheless overshadowed by the future war leader. Eden himself described this period as his " long era as crown prince."

Imperial War Museum Collection
Source: Wikimedia Commons
The young diplomat Anthony Eden, later Sir Anthony, then Lord Avon.

Similarly, when a few months after his eventual succession, Eden promoted the little-known Selwyn Lloyd, then Minister of State, to Foreign Secretary, it was widely assumed that the new Prime Minister wanted to keep the reins of foreign affairs very much in his own hands. It wasn't long before Lloyd found himself at odds with his American contemporary, Dulles, particularly over the Eden Government's gunboat attitude over control of the Suez Canal. The republican uprising in Egypt and a surge of nationalism had led the revolutionary government there to seize the canal from its Anglo-French operators. The press conference rooms at Heathrow became the setting for constant tub-thumping by diplomats on all sides in what was to become a major international crisis, leading directly to Eden's eventual downfall.

The Egyptian President, Colonel Nasser despatched an envoy, Wing Commander

Nasser's right-hand man, Ali Sabri, attracted more press attention than any of the Suez Conference delegates when he arrived at London Airport. He insisted that he was here only as an observer.

Sabri wants the lot

WING COMMANDER ALI SABRI, chief political adviser to President Nasser, arrived from Cairo in London Airport last night.

"We insist," he said, "that we shall have the sole right of control of the Canal and its economy. If force is applied then we shall defend ourselves."

Other nations, he said, could not take part in control. They were like customers coming into a shop.

IN CAIRO LAST NGHT, Egyptian Government officials said the Dulles proposals were not acceptable.

Daily Herald picture *August 24 1956*

Invitations for 15 'user' nations

The text of the invitation sent on behalf of Britain, the United States and France to the remaining 15 countries who supported the 18-nation plan for the Suez Canal was released by the Foreign Office today.

It said: "The governments of France, the United Kingdom and United States of America have proposed that a meeting should take place of representatives of the 18 governments who supported the proposals to be put to the government of Egypt by the mission headed by Mr. Menzies.

"The agenda for this meeting would be:

(a) **THE REPORT** of the committee of five and the action to be taken thereon;

(b) **THE MEMORANDUM** from the Egyptian Government delivered after the Cairo talks;

(c) **THE PLAN** for a Canal Users' Association.

"HM Government in the United Kingdom accordingly have the honour thereby to invite the government to take part in a conference to be convened in London on Wednesday, September 19, at 11 a.m."

The conference will again take place in Lancaster House, where the original conference was held.

The 15 nations are.—Italy, The Netherlands, Spain, Turkey, Australia, Denmark, Ethiopia, Western Germany, Iran, Japan, New Zealand, Norway, Pakistan, Portugal and Sweden.

Mr. Selwyn Lloyd, British Foreign Secretary, arrived in Paris today for Suez crisis talks with the French Foreign Minister, M. Pineau.

Mr. Lloyd said they would discuss the latest arrangements for the first meeting of the new Suez Canal Users' Association, to be held in London next Wednesday.

Asked if he had any comment on a suggestion that the canal users should buy the Canal from Colonel Nasser, Mr. Lloyd said: "It is an interesting suggestion, but there would have to be a seller as well as a buyer."

Evening Standard *August 17 1956*

Sabry flies with report for Nasser

Wing Commander Ali Sabry, Colonel Nasser's political adviser, left London Airport for Geneva today on his way to Cairo. When he was asked about the London conference on Suez, he shrugged his shoulders.

"I don't know whether Colonel Nasser will agree to meet the five-man committee," he said. "There is nothing more I can say."

He expected to report to Colonel Nasser as soon as he reached Cairo.

Optimistic

Dr. Ardalan, the Persian Foreign Minister, and a member of the "canal committee," also flew home today. He said he did not think Colonel Nasser would reject the 18-nation proposals.

"We are very optimistic," he said. "There is no reason why it should not be acceptable."

Evening Standard *Aug 25 1956*

Ali Sabri, to attend, as an observer, talks in London between the 18 Canal user-nations. I reported his press reception at Heathrow as bigger than any similar reception for actual delegates to the talks. Sabri told us that Egypt was insisting on the sole right to control of the canal and its economy. "The users of the canal are customers," he said, "They have the rights of a man going into a shop and no more."

Shortly afterwards, Selwyn Lloyd flew to Paris to discuss the developing situation with his French opposite number. I asked him if he had any comment on a suggestion that the users should *buy* the Canal from Colonel Nasser. The Foreign Secretary looked nonplussed and turned to an adviser.

"No one has come up with that idea," he said. Then after a whispered consultation he added: "It is an interesting suggestion. But there would have to be a seller as well as a buyer."

I didn't tell him that the proposition had originated as a simple family aside over my domestic toast and marmalade conversations that morning. The *Evening Standard* used it as a tailpiece to a general report about the talks but spoiled it for me by claiming the comment had been made in Paris. What they and others failed to spot was that he was making it quite clear that the Government was entertaining no thoughts of recognising Egypt's right to nationalise and become the legal owner of the Canal.

I was next to meet Selwyn Lloyd for a more serious confrontation some three years later. He was flying to New York for a meeting of the UN General Assembly. Coincidentally, (or intentionally) that same evening in September 1959, the Russians were aiming for the moon. They were making at least their second attempt to hit a relatively tiny target in space, 235,000 miles from Earth. If successful, Lunik 2, the Soviet rocket, would be the first man-made object to reach the moon. It was due to crash land about midnight GMT, just minutes before the British Foreign Secretary was to board his BOAC airliner at Heathrow.

The time was critical for us. It was almost edition time for the dailies. I was determined to get Selwyn Lloyd's comments on the moon shot to tie in with any story the papers would certainly run on what could be the most sensational space shot to date. If the Russians were able to hit the moon with a rocket, it would be man's first non-terrestrial contact. A "soft" landing, possibly a manned landing, could easily follow.

Officially I was off duty at 11 pm. A colleague, Bob Leigh, who had been covering the Central Terminal earlier in the evening, was also about to leave. But I asked him to join me at the north side terminal, still in use at that time for long-haul flights. I explained the problem.

"Selwyn Lloyd may well want to make some statement about the General Assembly meeting," I said, "But by the time we get whatever he says dictated and filed out to the dailies, its likely to be well-past midnight. Unless it's really significant it won't see the light of day. But we still need to cover him."

I said I thought we had a far better chance of publication if we could get a quick reaction from the Foreign Secretary on the moon shot, which we could file before he took off. I asked Bob if he would look after the routine statement to enable me to concentrate on what could only be a couple of sentences at most and which, with any luck I could win from Lloyd first. "If I can get my question in quickly, I can dash away to the telephone and leave you to pick up the other pieces," I requested, shamelessly.

We made our way round to the VIP Lounge through the quick-access side door in the old Arrivals area. (the same exit I had used to witness the Vulcan bomber disaster.) There we discovered, already waiting at the entrance to the VIP suite, *BBC* radio reporter Leonard Parkin, later to become a familiar and popular ITN newscaster. "Hello," he said. And nodding towards the door: "He's just arrived."

Leonard was carrying, from a strap over his shoulder, a portable but bulky Ewer reel-to-reel tape recorder, its mike in his hand. But the ambient sound of an airport, with its constant wind, its whine of aircraft engines, is rarely conducive to *outside* broadcast interviews. "I've asked him to come over to the conference room," he added.

That was a minor blow. The Green Dragon press conference room (a war-time Nissen hut so called after its previous function as a staff snack-bar) was only a hundred yards away, but every minute was precious to us. Leonard's radio deadline was obviously not as pressing as ours. I would have to "door-step" my target, putting my questions to him on the hoof as he left the lounge to cross to the conference room. Deliberately peering through the glass door of the lounge, I caught the eye of Peter Hope, head of the news department of the Foreign Office. He nodded in response, as if to say, "Yes, we're coming now."

Moments later Mr Lloyd emerged, Peter Hope at his heels, and we moved briskly towards the press conference room. I fell in beside the Foreign Secretary on his left. Leonard Parkin took up his right, mike held at his chest. Bob followed , one pace behind, at Peter's shoulder.

"Mr Lloyd," I said quickly, "The Russians are just about to hit the moon with their rocketship.

"We should get confirmation at any moment now. Would you like to make a comment? How do you feel about their achievement?"

His response stunned me. "***Rockets***?" he questioned. Then, grunting irritably, he made a dismissive gesture with his hand and snorted:

"Oh,* that *rocket! I don't think many people are worried about rockets. They're not terribly interested in rockets."

I was so taken aback I could only gasp in astonishment at his reaction for a second or two. Before I could reply or perhaps rephrase the question, Leonard broke in. Thrusting his microphone forward he followed up the reply by prompting: "Journalistically speaking they are, sir."

Mr Lloyd wouldn't be swayed. "I'm not here to talk about rockets," he said firmly. By now we had reached the Green Dragon. Leonard and I stepped to one side to allow the Foreign Secretary to enter. As Peter Hope followed his leader, he glanced at me and raising his eyebrows, shook his head. It appeared to be the nearest he could get to a sympathetic shrug.

Turning to Bob I said: "I'm dashing off to the 'phone. See you in a minute." And I added, half to myself: "I wonder if he realises what he's done?"

Hurriedly I dictated my one-and-a-half paragraphs. "All round. Dailies and agencies," I said, "As fast as you can." Then I suddenly remembered. "Hang on," I asked quickly. "What did the radio say about the Russian rocket?"

Replied my copy-taker: "Oh, I thought you must have heard. They were spot on. A bull's-eye. It's just been confirmed."

One more try, I thought. I must pass the news on. I dashed back to the conference room. Leonard Parkin was just running his tape through for Selwyn Lloyd to hear. Bob was taking the opportunity to check his notes against the recording. They all looked up as I hurried in. "Thought you'd like to know, sir," I said, "The *BBC* says the Russians have pulled it off...."

Before I could finish, the Foreign Secretary broke in. "I don't intend to say this again," he snapped, "I won't talk about the Russian rocket. I don't want to hear any more of this." Even as he was speaking, Peter Hope had moved towards a telephone on a side table and picked up the receiver. "It *would* be interesting to find out if it reached its target..." he began, but Mr Lloyd forestalled him. Again he angrily interrupted. "Put that down," he ordered. "Don't worry about rockets. There are far more important things."

Bob and I returned to our telephone booth, and he quickly dictated Mr Lloyd's formal statement on the UN Assembly meeting. I grew more and more restless. Finally I broke in and said, "Bob, I'm going back. I can't leave it like this. I have to give him another chance, even if we're too late for the editions. I simply can't accept that he could be so short-sighted."

Mr Lloyd and Peter Hope were now back in the VIP lounge, preparing to board their aircraft. A mere twenty minutes had passed since I'd first spoken to the Foreign Secretary. Now I stood again in the glare of the light cast by the French windows so that I could be seen. After a moment Peter Hope came to the door. "I had to try once more," I said. "Does he realise how silly he will look?"

The FO newsman ignored my comment. Politely, but, I thought, resignedly, he said: "He won't change his mind. He just refuses to discuss the moon shot."[1]

Returning to the 'phone, I asked the office if there had been any reaction from the national news desks. Then I stood down the copy taker. "Thanks for staying on," I said. "I just hope we get something out of it." And after a final cup of coffee at the nearby buffet, and a quick check to ascertain the flight's departure, Bob and I mutually signed off for the night.

My hopes of the previous night were dashed when I saw the papers for the next morning, September 14, 1959. As far as I could see from the editions of the nationals available at Heathrow (we were once told they were in fact the early, South Wales, editions), only the *Daily Express* carried Selwyn Lloyd's gaffe. At least *they* saw the significance of it, placing it centrally and directly beneath their front-page lead on the Russian moon success. It appeared as a small box at the foot of the page under the heading:

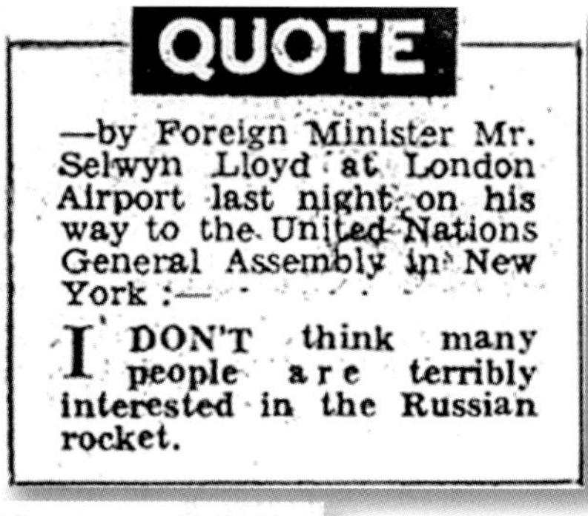

QUOTE

—by Foreign Minister Mr. Selwyn Lloyd at London Airport last night on his way to the United Nations General Assembly in New York :—

I DON'T think many people are terribly interested in the Russian rocket.

Daily Express (enlarged)
September 14 1959

LONDONER'S DIARY

"Never mind Ike, Mr. Selwyn Lloyd says he doesn't think many people are terribly interested in it . . .

Courtesy of Express Newspapers ©All countries ***Evening Standard Sep 14 1959***

It wasn't until Vicky's quarter-page cartoon appeared in the London *Evening Standard* later that day that the British Foreign Secretary's considered view of space exploration began to be examined. Vicky depicted an anguished President Eisenhower and Vice-President Nixon in front of the Capitol watching a flypast by a Russian rocket. At a port-hole, peering through the visor of a space helmet, was the face of Soviet chairman Nikita Kruschev. And scrawled on the side of the spaceship was the poignant inscription: "Moscow-Washington via Moon."

Tuesday's dailies gallantly tried to make up for lost ground. Almost without exception the Soviet achievement was recognised and acclaimed, while Mr Lloyd's remarks were condemned and ridiculed. Alongside a cartoon by Waite showing a shaded crescent

[1] *Of Peter Hope, Lloyds biographer said that when the Foreign Secretary was disappointed with Press coverage he blamed himself and apologised for briefing Hope poorly.*

The Sketch says— SO SILLY, SELWYN LLOYD

FOR the silliest remark of the hour, listen to Selwyn Lloyd as he touches down at London Airport and comments on the Russian moon-shot.

Says he: "I don't think many people are terribly interested in the rocket."

Right now we don't think many people are terribly interested in Mr. Lloyd. But this attempt of his to pooh-pooh a brilliant scientific achievement by the Soviets is plain daft.

OF COURSE people are interested in the race into space. OF COURSE they care who gets there first. OF COURSE they don't hold back their excitement at an epoch-making success by the Russians.

Mr. Lloyd's unworthy remark finds echoes in Washington, where Vice-President Nixon says sourly that the Russians have already failed three times to get a rocket to the moon. So what? They've got one there now—and how!

Cut out the sour grapes, you big-shot politicians. The Russian rocket is a sign that Mr. K, when he arrives in America to-morrow, comes as the leader of a powerful, space-age state. He will sit down with Ike as an equal.

That's fine by us. The fewer chips Mr. K has on his shoulder during these crucial talks, the better for us all.

... THIS IS WHAT MAC SAYS

Mr. Macmillan sent this message to Mr. Kruschev last night: "Allow me to send my congratulations and those of British scientists on the accomplishment of a notable step in man's exploration of outer space and on a further fine achievement of Soviet technology."

Courtesy of the Daily Sketch and Associated Newspapers ©All countries

Daily Sketch cartoon
Daily Sketch Editorial
September 15 1959

moon with a black eye, the *Daily Sketch* splashed an editorial.

They went on to refer to the "not terribly interested" quote and sniped back:

> ***" For the silliest remark of the hour, listen to Selwyn Lloyd...***
> ***Right now we don't think many people are terribly interested in Mr Lloyd. This attempt of his to pooh-pooh a brilliant scientific achievement by the Soviets is plain daft."***

A *Daily Mirror* editorial was even more critical (*see over*). They described the remarks as a "niggardly comment" and claimed:

> ***"The truth is 2,690,000,000 people - the whole population of the world - are FASCINATED by the Russian rocket."***

Writing in the same paper, Labour Member of Parliament and columnist *Richard Crossman* said Mr Lloyd had put the Russians in their place to his (own) satisfaction and achieved immortality for one of the "**most imbecile remarks**" ever uttered by a British Foreign Secretary.

Meanwhile, the Foreign Office news department was engaged in a huge damage limitation exercise, or as the *Daily Mirror* news desk told me over the 'phone: "They're running around like a headless chicken." Which I suppose was understandable, with their Head, Peter Hope, at Selwyn Lloyd's shoulder in New York. The *Express* called to ask for a statement on the events leading up to my story. And they asked me to rush them a copy of my notebook with the incriminating quotes, even after I'd explained that we were only talking of a few words. We despatched a motor-cycle messenger post-haste with a photographic print of the notebook page.

Cables and telephone calls passed rapidly between London and the US. Initially, the Foreign Office news department strongly denied that the Foreign Secretary had made any statement about the Soviet moon shot before leaving London. In New York, Mr Lloyd himself was reported as saying: "I have no recollection of saying anything of the sort. It does not represent my views. I gave these on my arrival in New York when I said to correspondents that it was a remarkable achievement."

When later the *Daily Mirror* asked one of Mr Lloyd's team if the Minister was saying he had been misquoted, a spokesman repeated: "Oh dear no. He just said he had no recollection of using those words."

Then, by Tuesday, the F.O. had changed their tune, we were told. But the tune seemed

DAILY MIRROR

FIRST ON THE MOON

(Knocking the Knockers)

MAN'S race to reach the moon is the most thrilling and wonderful drama of our time.

How supremely stupid was Mr. Selwyn Lloyd's niggardly comment—"I don't think many people are terribly interested in the Russian rocket."

Richard Crossman (see Page 8) is right when he describes this as **one of the most imbecile remarks** ever uttered by a British Foreign Secretary.

The truth is that 2,690,000,000 people—the whole population of the world—are FASCINATED by the Russian rocket.

And how supremely petty was the statement by Mr. Richard Nixon, the American Vice-President, who tried to belittle Russia's grand achievement by saying that the Russians had three times before tried to hit the moon.

Triumph

Who cares about past failures? It is success that counts.

And the Russians have splendidly succeeded.

The Mirror agrees with Professor Lovell, the famous scientist who has given Britain at least **one** achievement in Space Science—the Jodrell Bank radio-telescope.

Professor Lovell is neither mean nor jealous in his judgment of Russia's triumph.

He says that no praise is too high for it.

He is right. The only pity is that Britain cannot afford to join in the race for the moon

More Important

Knocking the Russians only makes the knockers look silly

Whether the first man on the moon travels there by Russian "Lunik" or American "Pioneer" is a minor matter.

Mankind's 20th century conquest of Space is far more important than Mankind's 19th century frontiers.

CROSSMAN SAYS...

SELWYN LLOYD PINPOINTS THE BIG TORY DECEPTION

FOR a brief moment Mr. Selwyn Lloyd has seized the limelight from Mr. Macmillan.

At London Airport on Sunday night he gave his verdict on the Russian moon rocket—and achieved immortality for one of the most imbecile remarks ever uttered by a British Foreign Secretary.

"I don't think many people are terribly interested in the Russian rocket," he observed.

and we are warned that a change of Government would ruin this cosy existence.

Whenever any unpleasant fact turns up which contradicts this success story, a Minister is there to soothe us by saying that it is quite irrelevant and anyway "I don't think many people are terribly interested."

long time ago the importance of education.

Industrial development depends first and foremost on the quality of your scientists and technologists.

This in turn depends on the quality and number of your

Daily Mirror (left and above) (both) September 15 1959

to have different melodies for different audiences. One news desk (I believe it was the *Express*) told us they had spoken directly to Peter Hope in New York. "Mr Lloyd did not deny using the words," Hope told them, "But he says they were not intended for publication. They were used in the context of a discussion prior to recording a statement for the BBC.

"He was simply telling the BBC that he was not prepared to speak about the Russian rocket until its success had been confirmed."

On Wednesday – two days after my encounter – the *Daily Mirror's* foreign editor Michael King wrote:

> ***Last night in London... a spokesman denied that Mr Selwyn Lloyd had said on Sunday night that he did not think many people were "terribly interested in the Russian rocket."***
>
> ***The spokesman declared: "As far as we can discover, in the course***

WORLD NEWS SPOTLIGHT

THE GREAT SELWYN LLOYD ROCKET MYSTERY

By MICHAEL KING, Mirror Foreign Editor

WHAT DID Mr. Selwyn Lloyd, the Foreign Secretary, say about the Russian moon-rocket?

Did he drop a big brick? Or didn't he? This simple question has thrown the Foreign Office into a mighty and embarrassing "flap."

Transatlantic phone calls have been made, cables have buzzed between Whitehall and New York, where Mr. Lloyd is attending the United Nations

But the mystery remains.

Here is the timetable of this curious episode:

SUNDAY NIGHT, London Airport. Mr. Lloyd was waiting in the VIP lounge before boarding his New York-bound plane.

He was approached by two reporters of the Brenard news agency about the Russian moon-rocket.

They reported that Mr. Lloyd replied to questions: "Oh, that rocket. I don't think many people worry about that rocket. They're not terribly interested in rockets."

'Interesting'

Mr. Peter Hope, the head of the Foreign Office news department, who was with Mr. Lloyd, said it would be interesting to find out officially if the rocket had reached its target. He moved towards a telephone, according to the Brenard reporters.

But, they say, Mr. Lloyd forestalled him and said: "Don't worry about rockets. There are much more important things."

And as he sat down before a microphone, he waved a hand and said firmly: "No questions about rockets."

MONDAY MORNING—Mr. Lloyd's alleged remark was prominently printed in the British Press.

The scene shifted to New York where Mr. Lloyd said: "I have no recollection of saying anything of the sort. It does not represent my views.

"I gave these on my arrival at New York today when I said to correspondents that it was a remarkable achievement."

Later, in New York's Waldorf Astoria hotel, the Mirror asked one of Mr. Lloyd's team if the Minister was saying he had been misquoted.

The spokesman said: "Oh dear no. He just said he had no recollection of those words."

LAST NIGHT—In London, the Foreign Office was undergoing an agonising reappraisal of the situation.

A spokesman denied that Mr. Selwyn Lloyd had said on Sunday night that he did not think many people were "terribly interested in the Russian rocket."

'Private'

The spokesman declared: "As far as we can discover, in the course of a private discussion on questions that the Press might be likely to ask before Mr. Lloyd left London, somebody mentioned the Russian moon-rocket.

"Mr. Lloyd said: 'I don't think the people are interested in **MY** views on that.'"

What will be the next dramatic step in the puzzle of Mr. Lloyd and the moon-rocket?

Daily Mirror *September 16 1959*

of a private discussion on questions that the Press might be likely to ask before Mr Lloyd left London, somebody mentioned the Russian moon-rocket. Mr Lloyd said: 'I don't think many people are interested in MY views on that.'"

And King asked:

'What will be the next dramatic step in the puzzle of Mr Lloyd and the moon rocket?'

BEADS FOR THE NATIVES

Courtesy of Express Newspapers © All countries — *Daily Express (above and right) (both) Sept 16 1959*

On the same day, *Express* cartoonist ***Cummings***, apparently somewhat slower off the mark than usual, saw President Eisenhower on the moon as a near-naked Red Indian chief surrounded by his braves, being greeted by a beaming Pilgrim Father Kruschev handing out "Lunik" pennants. The Russian rocket is named "Mayflower 2" – and in the foreground under a bush (playing gooseberry?) lies a snoozing Selwyn Lloyd. He holds a sign which reads: "Sh! Not interested!"

The *Express* also gave a potted background to the story on its letters' page, in response to a reader's query under the heading: What did Selwyn Lloyd really say?" It repeated his opposing statements – the first as reported by me from Heathrow, and the second in New York describing the Russian effort as "remarkable." It referred to two news agency reporters at London Airport "…who last night confirmed the original words from their notes taken at the time."

Another politician and journalist, Michael Foot, MP, who became leader of the Labour Party from 1980 to 1983, gave the background to the story again in his column in *Tribune* the following Friday, writing under his pen name of ***John Marullus***.

"The Press agency which sent out the first quote are not happy about Mr Lloyd's denial. I called them up – they are Brenard Press at London Airport – and I was informed they have photostat copies of the pages in the reporters' notebooks to prove they were right. Two senior reporters of the agency – one was the chief reporter – approached Mr Selwyn Lloyd and Mr Peter Hope, the Foreign Office press officer. It was suggested that the Foreign Secretary might like to say something about the rocket. Selwyn Lloyd then made the statement."

He gave a few more details, then added:

"Mr Lloyd...had given an answer which reflected the mentality of real Toryism. His gun-boat mentality...cannot really grapple with the ramifications of Russia's moon-shot. His mental processes have not graduated from the level of Suez."

Michael Foot MP, leader of the Labour Party 1980-1983

WHAT DID SELWYN LLOYD REALLY SAY?

SELWYN LLOYD is quoted as saying he did not think many people are interested in the Russian moon rocket (**Page One, Monday**). Has the Foreign Minister no understanding of people? This event in world history, impossible to ignore, is of tremendous fascination to the ordinary person.

● ON MONDAY Mr. Selwyn Lloyd was reported to have said, commenting on Russia's moon rocket: "I don't think many people are terribly interested in it."

YESTERDAY he was reported in New York to have said: "I have no recollection of saying anything of the sort." The original quotation was, in fact, recorded by two reporters working for a news agency at London Airport the night that Mr. Lloyd left for America.

LAST NIGHT these reporters confirmed the original words from their notes taken at the time. Later, in America, Mr. Lloyd said the Russian effort was "a remarkable technical achievement."

Daily Express Reader's letter and editorial reply

Speaking for myself

A rocket for Selwyn

WHAT does Mr. Selwyn Lloyd really think about the Russian rocket? He gave us his opinion the other day at London Airport:

"I don't think many people worry about that rocket. They're not terribly interested in rockets."

Ah, you say but he denied he ever said that. Indeed he said in New York: "I have no recollection of saying anything of the sort. It does not represent my views. I gave these on my arrival at New York today when I said to correspondents that it was a remarkable technical achievement."

But the press agency which sent out the first quote are not happy about Mr. Lloyd's denial. I called them up—they are Brenard Press at London Airport—and I was informed that they had available photostat copies of the pages in the reporters' notebooks to prove that they were right.

This is what happened. Two senior reporters of the agency—one was the chief reporter—approached Mr. Selwyn Lloyd and Mr. Peter Hope, the Foreign Office press officer. It was suggested to Mr. Hope that the Foreign Secretary might like to say something about the rocket. Selwyn Lloyd then made the statement.

Mr. Hope then remarked that it might be interesting to find out if the rocket had hit the moon. But Mr. Lloyd stopped him, saying: "Don't worry about rockets. There are much more important things."

Why did Mr. Lloyd go out of his way to deny the report which was made by two reputable reporters? The answer is obvious. He had given an answer which reflected the mentality of real Toryism.

His master was much more adept. He quickly sent congratulations to Mr. Khrushchev on his country's achievement.

But what does Mr. Lloyd know or care about this fantastic achievement? His gunboat mentality which has only just struggled into the 20th century cannot really grapple with the ramifications of Russia's moon shot. His mental processes have not graduated from the level of Suez.

SELWYN LLOYD
Still at Suez

★ JOHN MARULLUS

Courtesy of Tribune magazine September 18 1959

This is how, five days later, journalist MP Michael Foot summed up for *Tribune* magazine the now notorious "quote" by Britain's Foreign Secretary. Mr Foot was writing under the pen name John Marullus, after a Roman tribune.

I wasn't on duty when the Foreign Secretary returned from the General Assembly, and I didn't ask my colleagues if he had chosen to meet them or other news media. The optimum nine days of wonder passed all too rapidly. Bill Brenard told me with great delight that he had been visited by a mysterious gentleman in a trenchcoat who introduced himself as "just a civil servant, from the Ministry of Defence" (a familiar euphemism for MI5). He wanted to know if I was "a card-carrying member" (of the Communist Party, rather than my trade union, presumably) and if he thought I would like to see the Government "brought down."

Bill's response (he told me) was: "The answer to the first question is 'None of your business, and certainly not mine.' The answer to the second is: 'Almost certainly. Wouldn't we all?'" Bit of a reactionary Liberal, Bren.

At the height of the issue, Leonard Parkin, who sadly lost a long fight against spinal cancer in 1993, six years after his early retirement from ITN, telephoned me. "I'd just like you to know you can rely on me to back you up if you have any serious trouble with the Foreign Office or the papers over your story," he said, "I'll be happy to confirm everything."

As with the earlier confrontation with Foster Dulles, the need for witness verification was never required, though of course I thanked him for the offer and for taking the trouble to call. I was pleased to have an opportunity to remind him of his thoughtfulness again before his death.

Courtesy of Dave Poole
www.sporting-reliants.com
Leonard Parkin

There was a sequel many years later. Selwyn Lloyd had moved on to become a respected Speaker of the House of Commons. He and I met up once more when he made a rare visit to Europe in the mid-seventies to speak on behalf of the Inter-Parliamentary Union. As a "special category" the Speaker was entitled to use the Heathrow VIP facilities, and I learnt that he was departing from the de Havilland suite in Terminal 1. As I made my way there, I couldn't help wondering if he remembered the incident back in 1959. I was certainly not expecting him to remember me. It was all of fifteen years earlier.

At the suite, I asked the attendant airport management official to tell Mr Lloyd I would like to see him for a moment. When he returned, it was to invite me in. As I stepped through the door from the lobby, Mr Lloyd came towards me, his hand extended. And before I could say a word, he announced with a beaming grin:

"You can't make me say anything I don't want to, you know. I'm the Speaker now, but I'm not allowed to speak even if I want to."

And he chuckled at his little joke, which at least thirty Speakers before him must have made at some time. I stammered: "I'm surprised you remember," but wondered if we were talking about the same thing. His next words proved however that he did remember, and only too clearly.

"Oh, a great deal of water has passed under the bridge. But I haven't forgotten anything," he said, still good-humouredly, "That's why I'm warning you that you can't make me say anything. Let's talk about the weather, shall we? I'm not allowed any political opinions any more."

I took that as my cue to ask him to confirm the reason for his trip, avoiding the temptation to rake up the ashes. I believe I dictated one paragraph to the *Press Association.* It hardly warranted that much. People just wouldn't have been terribly interested.

*

On October 21, 1963, headlines in the European editions of the *New York Times*, the *International Herald Tribune* and the *Guardian* in London ran:

GROMYKO DENIES REPORT OF GLOOM

New York Times

Mr Gromyko denies he is pessimistic

The Guardian

Gromyko Story From Prestwick Was Erroneous

New York (International) Herald Tribune (all) Oct 21 1963

Veteran Soviet Foreign Minister Andrei Gromyko was accusing me of "plain distortion" in my account of an exclusive interview he had given me two days earlier at the Scottish transatlantic airport. And according to one of those newspapers, he suggested that Brenards had "tendentious motives" for circulating the story. (Whatever would MI5 say now about my allegiances?)

I had previously talked to Andrei Gromyko at Heathrow and Prestwick on several occasions. It was mostly to seek his comments on some international situation. But that was usually in the formal atmosphere of an airport VIP lounge. He spoke good English, with the extensive vocabulary befitting a career diplomat, but as with many English-speaking Russian politicians, he invariably called on the additional services of an accompanying official interpreter.

By the 1960s, Scotland's Prestwick Airport had become a major staging post for non-scheduled flights by the Soviet airline, Aeroflot, between Moscow and New York, and indeed other points in the Americas, as I make clear elsewhere. How I came to be in Scotland seeking out news stories on these flights I will recount later.

Glasgow Evening Times © picture
Mr Andrei Gromyko and his wife stop off at Prestwick on their way to the UN Assembly in New York– on another of his many visits to the Scottish airport.

Relatively isolated as it was from the diplomatic pressures of Whitehall and Kensington Gardens, the airport became a regular informal setting for contacts between Ministers or other Soviet government delegates and their London ambassador and his staff, who had to seek Foreign Office permission to venture that far from the embassy.

Gromyko was one of the most frequent Soviet visitors. He even left the airport on one occasion to visit the birthplace of Scottish bard Robert Burns in nearby Alloway; a personal pilgrimage to honour such a man of the people was almost obligatory to all such privileged Russians. But for Gromyko it was an exception. There were no separate VIP facilities at Prestwick. So while his official Ilyushin turbo-prop airliner took on extra fuel for the second leg of its 4,700-mile flight from Moscow on his bi-annual visits to the UN General Assembly or Security Council in New York, he rarely ventured beyond the comparatively under-used departure lounge

He always seemed cheerful and pleased to talk as he waited in the lounge, occasionally asking me to join him for coffee. Always on such occasions, his likeable interpreter Viktor Sukhodrev would suddenly appear at his master's shoulder, ready to break in with a word of advice or, quite unnecessarily, to interpret my questions. Viktor, I discovered from our earlier chats, had learned his English as a child attending school in London, where his father had been based as a Soviet diplomat. Further tutoring in Washington gave him an enviable command of basic Anglo-American colloquialisms, which he frequently expressed in a curious transatlantic mixture of accents.

More than once Gromyko's son Anatoly, first secretary at the Soviet Embassy in London, travelled to Scotland to spend an hour or two with his father. When they had strolled together in the autumn sunshine after one such reunion in 1963, the Foreign Minister was again in a good mood. I'd asked him the simplest of introductory questions: how long did he plan to spend at the General Assembly?

He replied: "That depends on the situation." he said, "If it's good I shall stay. If it's bad I shall hurry home. Whether the situation's good or bad depends on Britain." Then he added hastily, in response to my questioning look, "I am not thinking of any specific issues. I am only generalising in that Britain is one of the great powers that can influence policy."

The "Britain is great" phrase went down well with the English papers. The Scots were more impressed by his

A little praise from Gromyko

RUSSIA'S Foreign Minister, Mr. Andrei Gromyko, thinks of Britain as an influential voice in the United Nations. He described her as "one of the Great Powers" when he passed through Prestwick Airport yesterday on his way to the General Assembly in New York.

Mr. Gromyko, in good humour, spent nearly two hours at Prestwick when a special Russian airliner carrying the 75-strong Soviet delegation touched down to refuel.

Asked how long he planned to stay at the Assembly, he said wryly: "That depends on the situation. If it's good I shall stay. If it's bad I shall hurry home. Whether the situation's good or bad depends on Britain."

But he added hastily: "I am not thinking of any specific issue. I am only generalising in that Britain is one of the Powers that can influence policy. One of the Great Powers."

Did Mr. Kruschev propose to visit the Assembly this year? "He has no such plan," said Mr. Gromyko.

Reunion

The Foreign Minister and his wife had a surprise reunion at the airport with their son Anatoly, first secretary at the Soviet Embassy in London. He flew to Scotland to greet them, and they walked in the sunshine after breakfast at the airport.

Said the Foreign Minister: "I like calling at Prestwick. You always provide us with perfect weather."

Scottish Daily Mail *Setember 16 1963*

Kruschev Not Going to U.N.

GROMYKO STOPS AT PRESTWICK

Mr Kruschev does not intend visiting the General Assembly of the United Nations this year, it was stated yesterday at Prestwick Airport by Mr Gromyko, the Russian Foreign Minister, who was on his way to New York.

Mr Gromyko, jovial, and in a good humour, spent nearly two hours at Prestwick when a Russian air liner from Moscow landed to refuel.

Asked how long he planned to stay at the General Assembly, Mr Gromyko said:—"That depends on the situation. If it's good I shall stay. If it's bad I shall hurry home. Whether the situation is good or bad depends on Britain.

"I am not thinking of any specific issue," he added. "I am only generalising in that Britain is one of the Powers that can influence policy. One of the Great Powers.

Reunion With Son

The Foreign Minister and his wife, who accompanied him, had an unexpected reunion at the airport with their son, Anatoly, First Secretary at the Russian Embassy in London, who had flown to Scotland to greet them.

They walked in the sunshine after breakfast in the airport's V.I.P. room.

"I like calling at Prestwick," Mr Gromyko said. "You always provide us with perfect weather."

© Glasgow Herald (all) Sep 16 1963

Britain is still great, says Gromyko

RUSSIA'S Foreign Minister, Andrei Gromyko, still thinks of Britain as an influential voice at the United Nations.

Daily Herald

Happy landings for the Gromykos

Scottish Daily Express

departing comment. "I like calling at Prestwick," he said, "You always provide us with perfect weather."

The transit stop provided another bonus for the Russians in the opportunity it gave them to patronise the "colonised" Scots, and to sympathise with what they naively saw as their second-class citizenship status. Local airport management happily exploited this situation by honouring every Aeroflot flight with a piper's greeting. *"Scotland the Brave"* welcomed each arrival. *"Will ye no' come back again?"* heralded their departure.

The visitors were always delighted by the bagpipe reception, and after a year or two, Prestwick's resident piper Jimmy MacCallum was greeted as an old friend by the Russians. One distinguished visitor, Marshal Vasily Chuikov, hero of the battle of Berlin in the last few days of World War II, showed his appreciation by presenting Jimmy with a bottle of brandy.

Then, six months later, an aide to the Foreign Minister handed Jimmy a bottle of vodka. This time Customs officers called the tune and said the piper must pay. They demanded that Jimmy hand over the thirty shillings (£1.50) duty they said was due on the bottle before he could take his gift home. When he declined, they confiscated the vodka.

Jimmy told me of his sad loss as he waited dutifully in the wings, or rather under a wing, for the Russians to depart. "Leave it to me," I promised rashly, and in a moment I was telling all to my friend Viktor. "We'll see about this," he responded ominously.

As Jimmy piped: *"I'm nae awa' tae bide awa,"* there was a hurried consultation in Russian on the tarmac. Said Viktor to me: "Yes, you could say we are angry." And an Embassy official approached Jimmy and proffered bottle number two. Tactfully Jimmy declined the gift. "I don't want to insult Mr Gromyko by refusing it," he told the aide, "But Customs might not understand." Just as tactfully he turned down my suggestion that he might play *"The De'il's awa' wi' the Exciseman."*

I telephoned Customs House in London for an official explanation. But their Press Office seemed embarrassed. "We'll have to look into this," a spokesman told me, "Where diplomatic privilege is involved, we have to tread very warily."

Their formal reply never came, so I had to file my copy with this as the only comment from Customs. The story ran well in both English and Scottish nationals the next day. A follow-up was obviously called for. Again I called Customs House. And at last I was able to call "time" on the story as I reported:

Prestwick Airport piper Jimmy MacCallum will be able to drink the health of the Russians – and Her Majesty's Board of Customs – in a large glass of vodka after all. For in an unexpected spirit of concession, Customs and Excise officials yesterday reversed an earlier decision. They were no longer imposing duty on a bottle gifted to the airport piper by a Russian diplomat. The change of mind was "in the interest of international comity," said a spokesman.

Brenard Press picture

Resident piper Jimmy MacCallum greets travellers at Prestwick Airport. He was almost caught up in a diplomatic incident involving the Soviet Foreign Minister.

I was able to break the news to Jimmy myself after filing the story. He didn't seem as pleased as I expected. He confessed: "I can't stand vodka." And he added with laudable Scottish generosity: "I'll have to give it to my wife, and buy her a bottle of orange to go with it."

The bottle of vodka was, of course, a gift from Andrei Gromyko. But Viktor had asked me not to reveal this to the Scottish media. I made the point as obvious as I could without breaking my promise.

After his description of Britain as "one of the great powers," and indicating that he would remain at the General Assembly if the situation there was "good," the Foreign Minister spent just one month in New York. Now, on his return trip in October, I buttonholed him again as he sat in the Prestwick lounge chatting with members of his delegation. Gromyko's month was a long time in international negotiations; so the news should therefore be "good" in his terms.

In reality I was not expecting more than a few platitudes. The UN Assembly hadn't attracted much media attention. Behind-the-scenes discussions between the Russians and the West to further reduce world tensions after the recent nuclear test-ban treaty were being looked upon with some scepticism.

Viktor Sukhodrev; chief Soviet government interpreter

However I was aware that the pundits of international politics would seize upon any top-level comment at this stage of the talks. It would be sifted, analysed, re-analysed and turned upside down for any hidden significance, any hinted change of emphasis or apparent deviation from avowed policy. Such indeed was to be the case, but for all the wrong reasons. But because of it I was happy to report even the most basic of responses to my admittedly uninspired questions. I would mark my copy for transmission not only to Glasgow and Edinburgh-based Scottish daily newspapers, but also to the English nationals in Manchester and London, and to the London offices of the international news agencies and wire services. Almost anything the Soviet statesman had to say would be flashed to newspapers and radio stations around the world within minutes of my telephone dictation.

I could not have foreseen the full outcome of the next few moments, however, as Gromyko motioned me to a chair at the side of his coffee table. On the third side, opposite me, sat Viktor, a grin on his face which seemed to grow broader as the Foreign Minister spoke, a grin which seemed to say: "You were not expecting this...."

Disarmament, more than anything, was still the one aspect of East-West relations to which most people could relate. So my opening question had to be: "How are the disarmament talks going, Mr Gromyko?"

He answered without hesitation. "They are not going very well," he said, "To be frank, the state of affairs in our discussions is bad. We are making no progress whatsoever. It could not be worse...."

He then went on to talk of "carrying the whole burden of disarmament on our shoulders," and of Soviet determination to reach a general disarmament agreement similar to the Moscow Treaty. Then he passed from disarmament to repeating familiar Russian views on the status of Berlin. Finally, he diplomatically side-stepped a closing question from me on the appointment of his British opposite number, Foreign Secretary Lord Home, to succeed Harold Macmillan as Prime Minister.

"That is an internal matter," he said briefly. "It would be wrong for me to comment."

All this I noted accurately, and in context, thinking afterwards that if this was the good news, I wasn't sure I would want to hear the bad. Returning to my office two hundred yards away in a service corridor of Prestwick's terminal, I hurriedly typed up my notes.

In Scotland, with no editorial back-up to take dictated copy direct from notes, the reporter, in this case me, was his own sub-editor, typist, editorial assistant and telephonist. So for the sake of standardisation, accuracy and future reference, it was essential to spend a few minutes putting a full story on to a typewriter. Only that way could we ensure that identical copy was dictated to newspapers in Glasgow, Edinburgh and Manchester as well as to our own head office at Heathrow for transmission to any remaining national and international clients.

My intro read:

> **Soviet Foreign Minister Andrei Gromyko said last night at Prestwick that progress of the Big Three talks on international disarmament "could not be worse."**
>
> **"To be frank," he said, "the state of affairs in our discussions is bad..."**

The report continued, and nothing was left out. It wasn't world shattering news as far as I was concerned, although I was comfortably aware that it would be widely and routinely used. It took me the better part of an hour to telephone the story, repeating the same phraseology eight times in separate calls. Because of busy lines, it took me a little longer to get through to my Heathrow office. When I did, the line was poor, and I had to repeat some phrases before the copy-taker was happy with them.

The next day saw the story as a mere four-column inches in *The Scotsman* with a little more in the *Glasgow Herald* and the *Scottish Daily Mail.* The wording sequence was changed slightly, but the essence remained. Indeed the *Glasgow Herald's* single-column headline and sub-head was succinctly accurate (*left*).

But south of the border it was, so to speak, a different story. There was a significant change of emphasis. The *Daily Herald* in Manchester, for example, ran the story under a four-column heading:

"NO PROGRESS" IN TALKS ON DISARMAMENT

Mr Gromyko is Pessimistic

©Glasgow Herald

BIG THREE TALKS GETTING NOWHERE: GROMYKO

By Daily Mail Reporter

SOVIET Foreign Minister, Mr. Andrei Gromyko said last night that the progress of the Big Three's talks on disarmament "could not be worse."

Scottish Daily Mail

'No progress' shock from Gromyko

By W. N. EWER

SOVIET Foreign Minister Mr. Andrei Gromyko shattered a lot of hopes last night. He said that the progress of Soviet-American-British talks "could not be worse."

Then he added: "To be frank, the state of affairs in our discussions is bad. We are making no progress whatsoever."

The Foreign Minister was speaking at Prestwick Airport during a 90-minute stop to refuel the Russian airliner taking him home from the U N.

He made the usual claim that the Soviet Government had been "carrying the whole burden of disarmament on their shoulders."

They had been doing their best to reach agreement.

But could they convince their partners in negotiation? That was another matter, he said.

'FREE STATE'

Then, ominously, Mr. Gromyko pushed the Berlin question to the front.

"The status of West Berlin should be abolished, and a free State established."

The Soviet Government would continue to stress the importance of this, in spite of the fact that some Western statesmen underrated the significance of the issue.

This is the first tough utterance by a Soviet Minister since the signing of the test-ban treaty.

It now looks as if they were deliberate "probing" operations in preparation for a new bid to turn on the heat on the Berlin issue.

● Mr. Gromyko would not comment on the appointment of Lord Home, his former partner in the New York talks. "This is, of course, an internal matter. It would be wrong for me to comment," he said.

Gromyko: Big 3 Talks Going Badly

By United Press International

PRESTWICK, Scotland, Oct. 18.—Soviet Foreign Minister Andrei A. Gromyko said tonight the progress of the Big Three talks on international developments "could not be worse."

"To be frank," he said, "the state of affairs in our discussions is bad. We are making no progress whatsoever."

Mr. Gromyko spoke to newsmen at Prestwick Airport durlng a 19-minute stopover en route home from the United Nations meeting in New York.

He said the Soviet Union would continue to press for the abolishment of the status of West Berlin and the establishment of a "free state." A German peace treaty was "one of the most crucial problems of European security," he said.

Mr. Gromyko said the Russians "have been carrying the whole burden of disarmament on our shoulders and we have been doing our best to reach agreement.

"But whether we shall be able to convince our partners in negotiations or not is another matter."

Mr. Gromyko met in Washington with President Kennedy and held talks in New York with former British Foreign Secretary Lord Home, named Prime Minister today. and Secretary of State Dean Rusk.

"We have proposed certain steps toward the lessening of tension. steps similar to the (partial) Moscow treaty" on nuclear tests.

Daily Herald (above)
New York (International) Herald Tribune (right)
(all) October 19 1963

GROMYKO GLOOMY ON 3-POWER TALKS

In Scotland, en Route Home, He Says State of Parleys 'Could Not Be Worse'

By The Associated Press

PRESTWICK, Scotland, Oct. 18—Foreign Minister Andrei A. Gromyko said here tonight that Big Three talks on further lessening of tensions were making no progress and "could not be worse."

He spoke to newsmen during a refueling stop for the Soviet airliner carrying him home from the United Nations and conversations with President Kennedy in Washington. He said of Soviet-United States-British talks:

"To be frank, the state of affairs in our discussions is bad. We are making no progress whatsoever."

Mr. Gomyko contended that the Soviet Union was showing goodwill by taking the initiative on disarmament.

"We have been carrying the whole burden of disarmament on our shoulders and we have been doing our best to reach agreement," he said.

"But whether we shall be able to convince our partners in negotiation or not is another matter. We have proposed certain steps toward the lessening of tension, steps similar to the Moscow (nuclear test) treaty. But I would like to stress the importance of a German treaty—one of the most crucial problems of European security."

"The status of West Berlin," he added, "should be abolished and a free state established. We shall continue to stress the importance of this despite the fact that some Western statesmen underestimate the importance of this issue."

New York Times

The story ran:

Soviet Foreign Minister Andrei Gromyko shattered a lot of hopes last night. He said the progress of Soviet-American-British talks 'could not be worse.'

Under the by-line of their staff correspondent, **W.N.Ewer**, the *Daily Herald* continued with Gromyko's statement on the "burden" of disarmament, the failure of Britain and America to see the need to reach agreement, the repeated Soviet call for a German treaty, the abolition of West Berlin and the establishment of a German free state.

But Ewer then added his own expert observations. This was, he said, the first tough utterance by a Soviet Minister since the signing of the test-ban treaty.. And he concluded that Gromyko's words could be "... **deliberate probing operations in preparation for a new bid to turn up the heat on the Berlin issue."**

The significance of this interpretation did not strike me until I saw the international editions of the *New York Times* and the *International Herald Tribune* later. In the meantime I was to learn from Heathrow on Sunday, the day after my report appeared, that the East German news agency *ADN* had circulated a story quoting Mr Gromyko's rejection of my account as **"a total distortion."**

The American wire service *UPI* called to tell us that my story had been followed up by *ADN*, who had questioned the Soviet Minister after his arrival in East Berlin from Prestwick. Gromyko had flown there for talks with East German leaders on his way home to Moscow.

The Communist agency reported that Mr Gromyko "...denied...that he had voiced pessimism over the state of East-West negotiations." Tass, the Soviet news agency, then circulated a similar denial from Moscow. Once again, *UPI* asked me to dictate a memo to their general desk "just for the record." Soon afterwards their American rivals, *Associated Press* and our own *Press Association* asked for similar background notes.

The official denials had come too late for the Sunday newspapers, whose political commentators also tried to read significance into Gromyko's words. The *Sunday Telegraph's* diplomatic correspondent **Gordon Brook-Shepherd** thought the remarks heralded a new phase of Soviet toughness.

Soviet Toughness Is Challenge to Lord Home

By GORDON BROOK-SHEPHERD
Sunday Telegraph Diplomatic Correspondent

A NEW phase of Soviet toughness over Berlin is heralded by the verdict passed by Mr. Gromyko, Soviet Foreign Minister, that the prospects of a settlement on major East-West disputes " could not be worse."

Mr. Gromyko made this comment in Prestwick on Friday, on his way home from the United States. He also made a surprise landing in East Berlin for talks with Herr Ulbricht, the East German Communist leader.

After these talks, sources close to Mr. Gromyko stated that the two had reached " complete agreement " on the conclusion of a German peace treaty and the West Berlin question.

Clearly premeditated

As for the " interview " at Prestwick, this is a sour statement even from a sour spokesman, and was clearly premeditated. It is likely to produce the first foreign policy challenge Earl of Home will have to face as Prime Minister.

Western experts are hoping that this renewed Russian aggressiveness over Germany will be only temporary. It may indeed be a purely tactical move to give a background of Russian strength to next month's Party Congress and international Communist gathering in Moscow.

But it makes the gallant attempts of Western spokesmen to pass off the recent Russian holdups of Berlin convoys as " a misunderstanding " appear even more inadequate. There now seems to be a direct link between these actions and Mr. Gromyko's gloom, with both part of a set pattern.

This indeed has been admitted in private by Soviet officials in London during the past few days.

Sunday Telegraph

No signs in Moscow yet

from MARK FRANKLAND

Moscow, October 19

THERE is no sign here yet of any public follow-up to Mr. Gromyko's gloomy remarks about the progress of East-West talks.

It is still too early to forecast if there will be a serious change in the Soviet approach to East-West relations. But disenchantment over Britain and America's inability or unwillingness—as some Russians put it—to control West Germany could account for some of the drop in temperature

Shadow of China behind Soviet toughness to West

By Stuart Novins, Moscow, Saturday

Authoritative Western observers here see the shadow of Communist China behind yesterday's statement at Prestwick by Mr Gromyko, Soviet Foreign Minister, that progress in the Big Three talks " could not be worse."

During a brief stop he said: " To be frank, the state of affairs in our discussions is bad. We are making no progress whatsoever."

No appeasement

His observations came as a harsh contradiction to the generally held view that the signing of the nuclear test ban treaty had brought a new thaw in Soviet-Western relations.

The estimate here is that the Gromyko comments and the recent halting of Allied armed convoys en route to West Berlin through East Germany are both part of a new Soviet propaganda line, induced by Russia's conflict with China.

Russia, it is believed, apparently now feels it necessary to prove to China and her adherents that Moscow has now appeased the West in signing the nuclear test ban agreement or in its projected, but still uncompleted, purchase of American wheat. The need to appear tough, it is said, derives from the urgency to ensure the loyalty of the world's Communist parties in any intramural showdown.

Among professional diplomats and observers from the West, there has been little expectation that genuine progress would be made quickly on the German question, disarmament, Berlin or any other outstanding East-West issues.

But Russia sees her immediate problem as China, not the West. From this premise it is thought, the new tougher propaganda line emerges. The expectation in some Western circles is that this new line will not change, in any dramatic way, the present basic Soviet policies. Russia, it is said, will talk tougher, but not so tough that further East-West explorations would be inhibited.

Sunday Times (above)
Observer (left) *(all) October 20 1963*

The interview at Prestwick he described as a clearly premeditated sour statement from a sour statesman. It was likely to produce the first foreign policy challenge for the new British Prime Minister, he forecast.

The *Observer's* Berlin correspondent, **Mark Frankland**, talked of a "drop in temperature" though he admitted there was no public reaction in the former capital. But the *Sunday Times* reporter in Moscow, **Stuart Novins**, claimed the shadow of Communist China lay behind the Gromyko remarks, according to his authoritative Western observers. Russia, it was believed, now needed to demonstrate to China that it could get tough with the West.

The more I read of these follow-ups, the more puzzled I became. Some of them seemed to be bordering on hysteria. Then it suddenly became clear when I saw copies of the two American papers carrying my original story... or what appeared to be my story. In neither of them was there a direct reference to the "progress of international disarmament talks." The *New York Times*, which attributed its story to the *Associated Press*, referred to "talks …making no progress," while the *Herald Tribune,* whose report was by-lined *United Press International*, read: "…talks on international developments could not be worse."

Where had this word "***developments***" come from? It was not in my copy. I reached for the telephone and called Brenards at Heathrow, "Look out the original Gromyko copy I dictated to you on Friday," I said, "And read it back to me please."

In a moment the lad, the same junior who had taken my dictation two days earlier, was reading the opening sentences:

> **Soviet Foreign Minister Andrei Gromyko said last night at Prestwick that progress of the Big Three talks on international developments "could not be worse."**
>
> **"To be frank," he said, "the state of affairs in our discussions is bad..."**

"Developments" instead of "disarmament." One word had made all the difference. The Soviet Foreign Minister had in fact expressed concern not about the East-West talks as a whole, but about just one aspect of them…the one aspect I had asked about.

The Scottish newspapers had got it right because I had dictated the story myself directly to them. The London offices of wire services and other newspapers had got it wrong because of the change of word. And the Manchester edition of the *Daily Herald* had also got it wrong because they used the version wired to them by their London-based diplomatic correspondent, who had picked up the *Press Association* version of my story, in spite of the fact that they had the correct story directly from me.

How did the error occur? Was it simply poor dictation on my part? Carelessness on the part of the young Brenard copy-taker? Or was it down to a poor telephone connection? I had no way of knowing. And now wasn't the time for recriminations. Hurriedly, I asked the typist to take a memo from me for circulation explaining the error that had occurred. This time I asked him to read it back, and to warn Ray Watts of what he was doing before calling the various news desks.

I looked forward to Monday's papers. As I thought, the Scottish papers decided they had nothing to apologise for. But the *Glasgow Herald* fell into the trap of running an editorial echoing the Sunday "heavies." And it was basing its comments on the London version of the story rather than its own correct one of two days earlier!

Curiously, the London *Times*, in reaching much the same conclusion that all was "gloomy," nevertheless accepted that this pessimism was not borne out by the Soviet Press. And it apparently ignored both Gromyko's denial and the explanation for the error that had led to its conclusion.

The *Daily Herald* gamely continued on the original theme, only grudgingly admitting that the Prestwick remarks had been "partly explained away." But the *Guardian* and the two American newspapers gave both Gromyko's denial and our explanation of the transmission error full coverage.

At the end of its news story headed: "Gromyko Denies Report of Gloom," the *New York Times* carried three paragraphs, datelined *London, Oct.20*, which explained:

"…Mr Gromyko used the phrase 'could not be worse' in reference only to Big Three talks on disarmament."

The *Herald Tribune,* quoting the *Press Association*, said: "...the error arose in telephonic transmission between a news agency reporter at Prestwick Airport and his head office on London."

But the *Guardian,* for their part, went a stage further. Quoting the Soviet press, it reported:

> **Mr Gromyko says that he was asked by a reporter how he assessed the disarmament talks and that he replied that they were proceeding badly.**
>
> **He adds that he did not speak in pessimistic terms about the outcome of the talks between the big powers on all other international issues.**
>
> **This was a "plain distortion," which he attributed to the "tendentious motives" of the news agency that circulated the report.**

The *Guardian* continued:

> **Brenards news agency, whose reporter interviewed Mr Gromyko at the airport, maintained last night that its reporting of his remarks was accurate except for one error, which occurred during transmission....**

The newspaper concluded their correct explanation of the events by adding a view from their own expert on international affairs, Victor Sorza. He wrote that Mr Gromyko probably knew that any misrepresentation of his remarks was more likely to be the "unintended result of a language misunderstanding than of any deliberate and politically-motivated distortion."

I called Ray Watts and discussed the saga at some length with him. He said the *Press Association* had taken the matter very well considering they felt they had to accept

Red Puzzles

KREMLINOLOGISTS, by no means for the first time, are beginning to have doubts about the accuracy of their interpretation of what is going on in the higher reaches of international Communism. Until very recently they were agreed, in fact, that the higher they reached the less international Communism was. It seemed at one moment that the frontier disputes between imperial Russia and imperial China were being replayed in Central Asia. It is still unclear whether the fraternal parties will be summoned to Moscow for the forty-sixth anniversary of the revolution, on November 7, to pronounce the excommunication of the heretic Chinese. This melodramatic event may yet take place, but there have been a few signs recently that we may be wrong after all, and the Soviet-Chinese rift may not be permanent.

First of all there were the incidents on the Berlin autobahn, which were only explicable by a hardening of the Russian attitude towards the German problem and possibly towards other things as well. Then there was Mr Gromyko, the Russian Foreign Minister, who is reported as saying at Prestwick that the East-West talks at New York had been making no progress. Most important of all is the evidence of the dog in the night: since the vituperations of last September the Chinese have said nothing at all. Where once the Chinese press was all corrosive calligraphy there is now a discreet silence, and Mr Chou En-lai has even made a point of reaffirming his faith in the Russian alliance.

The Chinese Parliament is due to hold a session shortly, and it will be interesting to see what, if anything, it has to say on the subject of Russo-Chinese relations. There is the possibility that it will say nothing. There are rumours in China that a new series of discussions between the two Communist parties will be held shortly. The last meetings, in July, were quite fruitless. Apart from the public polemics of last month nothing has happened since. The Chinese candidature for membership of the U.N. was proposed this year by Albania, not the U.S.S.R., and seconded by Cambodia. The Russians showed no interest in the debate. Mr Gromyko may be disappointed with the progress of talks in America, but they achieved a success last week by banning nuclear weapons in space. But Russia and China have still a great deal in common, despite all their disagreements, and it would not be too surprising if some sort of a reconciliation were achieved. If, at the same time, Russo-American relations continue to improve it will be a triumph for Mr Kruschev. If not, there is still the test ban to be remembered with gratitude as a souvenir of the temporary split in the Soviet bloc.

© Glasgow Herald editorial

CIA reference photo of Soviet ballistic missile, Moscow.

GROMYKO DENIES REPORT OF GLOOM

Says Comment on Status of Talks Was Distorted

Special to The New York Times.

BERLIN, Oct. 20—Andrei A. Gromyko, the Soviet Foreign Minister, denied yesterday Western news reports that he had voiced pessimism over the state of East-West negotiations.

He charged that reporters had "distorted" a statement he made Friday night at Prestwick, Scotland, during his return from the United Nations General Assembly meeting in New York.

The Soviet diplomat left for Moscow at noon yesterday, after secret talks with East German leaders.

Western reports had quoted Mr. Gromyko as having stated that disarmament talks between the Soviet Union, the United States and Britain were at a standstill and that "the state of our talks could not be worse."

The East German press agency, ADN, said that Mr. Gromyko had rejected these reports as untrue. It said that he had merely expressed dissatisfaction with the present state of the talks.

Diplomats in East and West Berlin, including representatives of Communist-bloc countries, regarded Mr. Gromyko's stopover, and recent Soviet harassment of Allied access routes, as portending new Communist pressure on West Berlin.

The sources noted the new emphasis that Mr. Gormyko had placed on settling the Berlin issue and on concluding a German peace treaty, both at Prestwick and during his talks here.

"The Russians know they cannot get us out of Berlin short of a war," one American official said, "but they seem to entertain the hope they can bring pressure to bear on us to make the West accept international agreements along Soviet terms."

For the Communist regime of East Germany, Mr. Gormyko's visit came as a welcome assurance of continued Soviet assistance on the eve of the country's general elections, the first in five years.

Word Distorted in Transmission

LONDON, Oct. 20 (AP) — The Soviet press agency, Tass quoted Foreign Minister Andrei A. Gromyko yesterday as having said it was a distortion to write that he had spoken in pessimistic terms of talks among the United States, Britain and the Soviet Union on all international subjects.

The British Press Association, rechecking its report, distributed to The Associated Press and other news agencies, said Mr. Gromyko used the phrase "could not be worse" in reference only to Big Three talks on disarmament.

New York Times

Mr Gromyko denies he is pessimistic

The Soviet press yesterday carried a denial by Mr Gromyko, the Foreign Minister, of the pessimistic remarks he was said to have made when passing through Prestwick Airport on Friday.

Mr Gromyko says that he was asked by a reporter how he assessed the disarmament talks and that he replied that they were proceeding badly. He adds that he did not speak in pessimistic terms about the outcome of the talks between the big Powers on all other international issues. This was a "plain distortion," which he attributed to the "tendentious motives" of the news agency that circulated the report.

Brenards new agency, whose reporter interviewed Mr Gromyko at the airport, maintained last night that its reporting of his remarks was accurate except for one error, which occurred during transmission. The agency reported Mr Gromyko as saying that progress on international developmenst "could not be worse." This comment was meant to refer to international disarmament.

Anxiety apparent

Victor Zorza writes: Mr Gromyko probably knew that if there was any "misrepresentation" of his remarks, it was more likely to be the unintended result of a language misunderstanding than of any deliberate and politically motivated distortion. But his imputation of "motives" to the news agency serves to emphasise his anxiety that he should not be taken as being too pessimistic.

Whatever was said at Prestwick, it cannot be taken as a reliable guide to the official Soviet line at this moment. It must be viewed as a casual response to the kind of questions fired at Foreign Ministers whenever their planes touch down at airports.

The considered Soviet view would be conveyed by a more formal statement when the results of the recent talks had been fully evaluated, and would be carried in the Soviet press. Mr Gromyko's remarks at Prestwick were not reported in Russia, apparently because they were not regarded as being of any importance.

The Guardian *(all) Oct 21 1963*

Gromyko Story From Prestwick Was Erroneous

LONDON, Oct. 20 (AP).—The British Press Association said yesterday that it had erred in reporting Soviet Foreign Minister Andrei Gromyko's comments on East-West discussions during a stopover at Prestwick, Scotland, Friday.

Mr. Gromyko said during a stopover that progress in the Big Three's talks on disarmament "could not be worse," the BPA said He had erroneously been reported as saying that the talks in general are making no progress and "could not be worse."

A spokesman explained that the error arose in telephonic communication between a news agency reporter at Prestwick Airport and his head office in London. The erroneous report was then passed on to the British Press Association, which relayed it to its subscribers, including the Associated Press.

The Soviet Tass news agency yesterday quoted its Berlin correspondent as reporting that Mr. Gromyko described reports of his Prestwick remarks carried by another news agency as having distorted their meaning.

New York (International) Herald Tribune

RUSSIA MARKS TIME IN NEGOTIATIONS

FROM OUR DIPLOMATIC CORRESPONDENT

The surprisingly gloomy remarks about the "bad state" of east-west talks which were reported to have been made by Mr. Gromyko, the Soviet Foreign Minister, at Prestwick on Friday night on his way home from the United Nations to Moscow have not been borne out by the Soviet press; and Mr. Gromyko himself was later reported to have said in east Berlin that he had been misinterpreted and had merely said that negotiations with the western powers had proved "difficult."

POSSIBLE TOUGHNESS

The fact is that after the test ban treaty in Moscow and the agreement in the United States to ban nuclear weapons in outer space it has always seemed likely that the Soviet Government would wait for a time before the next advance. This pause is all the more to be expected if, as seems increasingly probable, a meeting of Communist Party leaders is to be held in Moscow after the anniversary celebrations of the Soviet Revolution on November 7.

Indeed a tougher tone may be expected, but in spite of some emphasis on the obstacles which the west is accused of placing in the way of east-west progress there is no real evidence that the Soviet Government's desire for ultimate progress towards a *détente* may have changed.

The Times

responsibility for the error. They and the newspapers who suffered were philosophical and shrugged it all off as the kind of accident that will happen from time to time.

But I had to agree that in future I would make sure that any possibly contentious copy was read back to me before circulation by Brenards, something none of us had been in the habit of doing. And as no one thought to draw teasing parallels with John Foster Dulles or Selwyn Lloyd, or to talk of my "foreign affairs hat-trick," the matter rested. Or so I thought.

The Soviet Foreign Minister was not so forgiving. Nothing was said about the disarmament statement the next time we met. Indeed nothing was said about anything, and we barely "met." Before I could approach him at Prestwick on his next trip to New York, Viktor stepped forward to intercept me. "The Minister has asked me to say that he has no statement to make today," he said, pleasantly enough, "This is just a routine trip."

Naturally, I took the opportunity to ask Viktor if I could talk to the Minister about the previous October's incident and explain what had happened. "Oh, I wouldn't do that," advised the interpreter. "He has probably forgotten the whole thing. He wouldn't want to be reminded."

When the same situation persisted for the next two years, with Mr Gromyko repeatedly refusing to see me, I decided something had to be done to end the private Cold War. I had already asked Viktor to intervene on my behalf, at one stage producing cuttings of the Scottish papers with the correct reports of his statement. He appeared very interested in these, and asked if he could keep them. It apparently changed nothing.

I had sufficient confidence in Viktor to believe he had tried to intercede on my behalf. By now he at least was talking freely and totally frankly to me about Soviet foreign policy, historical and current, which as an avowed Communist, he nevertheless defended vigorously. But it took a chat with my local MP finally to resolve the issue with Gromyko. The late Emrys Hughes, a one-time Welsh firebrand and Labour left-winger who frequently rebelled against party policy, was the member for South Ayrshire. He lived in his constituency, in Cumnock, birthplace of the founder of the Labour Party, Keir Hardie, whose daughter he had married.

© Evening Time picture Dec 16 1963
Emrys Hughes, Labour 'rebel' and my local MP in Scotland.

He was a near neighbour of mine. My home in Scotland for eight years was a village just four miles from his home and I was one of his constituents. We met occasionally at Prestwick on his trips to London, and he was the source of several news stories for both my colleague, Chris Bramwell and me. In the mid-'sixties I mentioned my problems with Gromyko. He invited me to tell him the whole story.

When I'd finished, he said: "Let me know when you next expect Gromyko through the airport. I can't promise anything, but I'll try talking to him. Gromyko knows me and I speak Russian, so he may be more sympathetic to me."

I was lucky that Emrys was at home in the constituency later that year when the Soviet Foreign Minister next appeared, again on his way to the UN. The MP hurried out to the airport when I called him, and Emrys asked to be allowed to greet Gromyko in the departure lounge. They chatted animatedly for almost an hour, as I watched furtively from a distance. At last, after the Russian had re-boarded his airliner, the MP returned to join me.

"I think you'll find everything will be all right from now on," he said, "I'm afraid he's been playing games with you. I don't think there was anything personal in it. In fact he assured me he knew the truth about the telephone mix-up some time ago.

"He wouldn't admit it to me, but I think he simply wanted to get back at the Western Press generally. He still feels it is very biased against the Soviet Union." And added the rebel left-winger, in character: "I must say I don't blame him for thinking that."

I next saw Gromyko on his return from New York a few weeks later. This time he greeted me as if we'd never been estranged. He even spoke briefly to me about the Soviet view of world affairs, as he did at other times over the next few years. But never again did he choose to make newsworthy pronouncements for me. Neither his heart nor the headlines were in his words.

CHAPTER NINE

"Why not ask the girls what they think about the Calderon cartoons?"

If the suggestion had come from anyone but my brother Harry, I might not have taken it so seriously. But he obviously had a good reason for making it. Always the newspaperman, he was telling me there was a story there.

This was January, 1955. Some two years earlier Harry had been headhunted by British European Airways (now part of British Airways) to become the airline's press relations manager at its London base, Northolt Airport. He was the natural choice for the post once held by Humphrey Downes (of "I'm here and here I stay" fame.[1])

He was, first and foremost, a journalist, when few PR men in the fledgling aviation industry had anything other than a war service or civil service background. With his Fleet Street and Brenards experience he could relate directly to other journalists. Secondly, he had built up a huge number of friends and contacts in BEA who trusted him. And because he was all things to all men instinctively, he put on no false airs or graces, and was able to relate comfortably with senior management and junior staff at all levels.

Brenard Press picture

My brother Harry hosting a BEA reception for the British Press who were guests of the airline on a visit to Hamburg, Germany.

He was to take his job seriously and conscientiously, winning a sympathetic public image for his airline among the many media representatives he had to serve. But he was rarely serious about life, and was ever ready to look for the lighter moment, the funny, the whimsical, the ridiculous.

He was ever alert to the possibilities of news stories in the day-by-day operations of the airline, its human face – something that would have been derided by the "no-comment" mentality of much of the airline and aviation hierarchy of the time. He was seated at his desk when he gave his response to my familiar opener: "Harry, I'm looking for a story…" But I didn't react to his responding challenge immediately. I knew there'd be more to come.

He slid a copy of the BEA staff magazine across the desk to me. Without even the hint of a twinkle he pointed to the reproduction of a cartoon. "Don't you think the girls might be very upset by that?" he asked guilelessly. "It's very unkind… pretty insulting, you might say."

I knew of course that he wasn't expressing an opinion – well certainly not a PR man's opinion. But I looked at him questioningly, still not quite sure if he was joking. "Why don't you ask them?" he repeated. "You might get some interesting comments."

The "girls" he was referring to were of course the traffic clerks and stewardesses of BEA – popularly referred to by the media and public alike as ground receptionists and air hostesses. They were constantly featured in the airline's monthly magazine and its other publications as the butt of artist Roy Calderon. A 33-years-old traffic officer with the airline himself, he saw the girls, his own colleagues, as St.Trinian-like characters, all shapeless and bowlegged, with unkempt hair and ill-fitting uniforms. "I can't believe anyone would be that sensitive," I ventured, "It's only a bit of fun. Surely no one's going to mind?"

"You don't know that," he replied, "You might find they are fed up with it."

I still wasn't convinced. And I wasn't too happy about the idea of going round asking the girls if the cartoons upset them, and said so. "You'll just have to make sure you find some who *are* upset," he replied enigmatically.

With a photographer I made my way over to the terminal to talk to the girls. I had armed myself with a couple of recent issues of the BEA magazine. And, as I'd suspected, the first two or three girls I spoke to saw nothing objectionable in the sketches. One of them said: "I would hope anyone could see we're not like that."

Another suggested, perhaps more wisely: "With some of us the characters are not so far from the truth. As a matter of fact that's just the way I feel at the end of a hard day...."

This wasn't going at all well. "We'll just have to find the prettiest girl on duty, and see what we can do to get the right reaction from her," I said to the photographer. And that's when I spotted Sue.

*

[1] *See Ch.2, p.20.*

The second most frequent comment to any Heathrow-employed young male, red-blooded bachelor or otherwise, has to be: "How do you manage to do a day's work with all those pretty girls around you every day?"

This of course would be from his peers. Other generations might stick with the less contentious but equally envious comment about "meeting all those interesting people," which helps to establish the theme of at least one of my earlier chapters. In my time I'd like to think that I would have given some succinct and witty response to the implied idea of a male worker's heaven – or harem. Instead I probably resorted to a sly wink, an embarrassed grin which was supposed to suggest that I wasn't about to give away any secrets. Not a small number of my colleagues might have answered: "We marry 'em."

There were a few uniformed goddesses I admired from afar, of course. There were also one or two I'd had a brief fling with, perfectly innocently in those pre-permissive days, only to discover, very sadly at the time, that I hadn't the financial solvency to keep them entertained in the manner to which they were accustomed.... I'm not sure if Sue came into that category; but I believe she would still have been among those beyond the reach of a mere penniless mortal.

Sue Grimshaw was 21, blue-eyed and very pretty. She was also very photogenic – and very bright. When I asked her what she thought of the cartoons she smiled sweetly and replied: "What would you like me to say?" It was almost as if Harry had planted her for us to find. I never did ask him; his answer might have taken the gloss from the story.

"I'd imagine you to be very hurt…indignant," I replied, once I'd recovered from the shock of finding such a willing victim. "After all," I added, "Almost all the women in the drawing are grotesque. I don't know any of you like that. Do you?"

"Oh no, I don't," she said. Then, warming to the theme: "A joke's a joke. But these drawings are cruel, undignified." And she added: "What if some of our foreign passengers saw these drawings? They wouldn't understand they are meant to be funny...." Sue paused, then asked helpfully: "Is that the sort of thing you want?"

Her astuteness stunned me. "Er, yes," I stammered, "That's just what I want…er, what I thought you might feel, that is." Then, feeling a little guilty, I added: "Aren't you worried that someone might say you can't take a joke if we print all this?"

"Not a bit," replied Sue. "I'd just tell them they're talking nonsense. Everyone knows that in this job a sense of humour is a must."

At my pressing, Sue insisted that she knew of several of her colleagues who would privately agree with her that the cartoon caricatures went just a bit too far. "But they wouldn't want to say so out loud," she said.

Sue's flawless features duly appeared the next day alongside my story in at least the *Daily Sketch* and the *Daily Herald*, both giving it an inside spread across four columns. The *Sketch* countered with: ***"'Cruel' cartoons make girls mad".***

Harry reinforced his management of the story by arranging for the BEA magazine to waive it's copyright on the cartoonist's work, so our portrait of Sue was accompanied by a sample Calderon cartoon in each newspaper. And to wind up the story, at my request Harry tracked down the artist himself who told me: "I'd no idea anyone was worried. And I'd be terrified to admit any similarity between the cartoons and the real thing.

*

CARTOONS START ROW AT AIRPORT

DAILY HERALD 3 Monday January 7 1955

Brenard Press picture
Not amused...! Sue Grimshaw

The girls are not amused

HERALD REPORTER

GIRL receptionists at London Airport are indignant about the way they have been portrayed by a cartoonist in the British European Airways magazine.

Cartoons show them as the girls of St. Trinian's might look when grown-up—in fact, rather worse, for the St. Trinian's girls have a horrible charm. The air girls in the cartoons are just horrible.

What worries the receptionists is that the magazine can often be obtained by passengers. Foreigners to whom the British sense of humour is a mystery might be misled.

'GOING TOO FAR'

In the vanguard of the attack on the cartoons is 21-year-old Sue Grimshaw, who is as pretty as a picture, and that picture on the left proves it.

When Sue is accused of having no sense of humour she replies: "That's nonsense. In this job it's a must. But these cartoons take the joke too far."

The cartoonist, 33-year-old station officer Roy Calderon, a bachelor, doesn't agree with all this.

"I'd no idea anyone was worried," he said last night. "But I'd be terrified to admit any similarity between the cartoons and the real thing."

This is one of the cartoons showing the air girls as cartoonist Roy Calderon sees them.

'Cruel' cartoons make girls mad

B.E.A.'s grey-uniformed receptionists at London Airport are angry.

Cause of the trouble is a series of cartoons which are appearing in the airline magazine.

Daily Herald (left and above)
Cartoon by Roy Calderon
Daily Sketch (headline)
(all) Feb 7 1955

chapter nine

As an intro to a news story, ***"Four smart girls flew swiftly to Paris today"*** should, even in a politically correct climate, invite you to read on and find out more. Back in the 1950s' world of male-orientated and mainly male-controlled newspapers, those eight words almost could have stood alone, particularly if backed by an appropriate photograph. With just that phrase, Bill Brenard was able to demonstrate convincingly his long-held claim that the essential requirement for a Page One second lead was minimal. For "smart" read: pretty and photogenic. For "girls" read girls.

The second world war, it has been suggested, was the dawn of the final emancipation of women. For the first time they were thought to be capable of carrying out some of the functions truly supportive of their warrior menfolk, like driving trucks as well as ambulances; like plotting movements of bombers and fighters – even piloting the same aircraft, in a non-combative virgin state, on delivery flights to their war bases.

Some of those women, like the young Princess Elizabeth, heiress to the throne, were even permitted to get their finger nails dirty as they poked among the spark-plugs and carburettors of the military combustion engine. But they were generally seen only as a kind of desirable accessory to the fighting soldier, even if they did "man" a few ack-ack guns around the country. Of the three main women's services, only the WRNS recognised them as a force in their own right, at least in name. Women in khaki or air force blue were simply "auxiliaries."

Source: Wikimedia, author unknown

A young Princess Elizabeth gets her hands dirty as she changes a tyre during her spell of training with the Auxiliary Territorial Service, the women's army.

Nevertheless the Great British Public, encouraged by a patriotic press, looked upon this emergence of "our girls" in uniform with a kind of proud if patronising indulgence, particularly when the subjects of that interest were young ladies from middle and upper-class families who in normal times simply wouldn't act that way.

The post-war growth of civil airlines with their demand for predominantly female aircraft cabin staff and a high ratio of women in passenger reception roles on the ground fostered the trend. The concept of girls in uniform in peacetime became a glamourised one when their duties, though almost menial in some respects, called for rigid employment qualifications.

Applicants needed to be of a "smart, attractive and tidy" appearance, articulate and at ease with people and have a good standard of education. For many airlines, cabin staff applicants would be expected to have nursing experience and at least one other language.

Many of these requirements were highly subjective and their levels decided by a mainly-male selection board. They were more often met by young women with a public school or at least a grammar school background. Despite this, a high turnover in female staff through marriage and a steady increase in traffic meant constant recruiting drives by all the major airlines and a huge response from girls, often little more than schoolchildren.

Within a period of six months, Pan American Airways alone had more than 5,000 British applicants for fewer than 50 vacancies on its transatlantic and European routes. These included applications from 20 experienced BEA stewardesses, attracted by apparently higher pay rates. All but four of these, I learnt, withdrew their applications when they discovered that a higher cost of living in the US meant that in practice they would be worse off financially. They also found that they would be expected to buy their own uniforms from the American airline, at a cost equivalent to a month's pay – and that wearing glasses would win no passes.

Brenard Press picture

The first six German girls to be recruited by BEA show off their new uniforms as they fly to London to train with the airline to fly as stewardesses.

When I challenged them on this ruling the company claimed: "This is not a matter of appearance, but of safety." The company also insisted that it was recruiting in Britain because: "…American passengers love to hear the sound of an English accent." But only 19 of the 5,000 applicants were successful, and like Britain's flag carriers, the American airline was also advertising for cabin staff in many other parts of the world.

British European Airways set the pattern when it recruited a number of German girls for its internal German routes early in 1951. And by 1958 BOAC was flying young women from India and Pakistan, Japan and Taiwan to train in London as stewardesses for the

Brenard Press picture
Sixteen-years-old Patricia Cameron *(right)*, a secretary in the Heathrow Press Office, looks skyward with a colleague after she was crowned the first-ever "Miss London Airport"

airline's Far Eastern services.

To Bill Brenard, all women under 30 were "popsies." The standard RAF flyers' slang was not intended to be offensive. It was a term of endearment, unlike the more dismissive "floosie" or even the later, derogatory "bimbo." Not that I was ever aware of any women objecting to his attitude, though today he would certainly be castigated for sexism. It may well be that women in the 'fifties were not encouraged to protest at such male flippancy.

Nevertheless, Bill was always comfortable with both male and female airline staff, a core of whom were, anyway, also ex-RAF or ex-WAAF. And Coral, his wife, was herself a former BOAC stewardess who had moved in similar circles. It was Bill who reintroduced the annual Miss London Airport contest, first launched as a one-off staff event by the Ministry of Civil Aviation in 1951.

That original title was won by a very pretty 16-years-old brunette, Patricia Cameron, who then went on to win the heart of a 21-years-old reporter. My proposal some months later was, however, turned down. Patricia was persuaded by colleagues in the Ministry's press relations' office, where she worked as a secretary, that newspaper men were very poor husband material. She also believed she was too young for marriage. That at least was probably true for both of us.

Some ten years on, a by-now married Patricia, her husband, who also worked at Heathrow, and their three small children emigrated to Australia. She went on to carve out successful careers and businesses for herself, first in public relations, then in real estate.

Bill's idea was to reserve the Miss London Airport title for uniformed staff. He invited British and foreign airlines using Heathrow to enter. In later years uniformed women of other organisations based at the airport – travel agents, airport shops, hotels – also competed.

The first winner of the new contest, which was judged on both looks and personality, was appropriately, Miss BOAC. Miss Sonia Simpson was a delightful girl who charmingly belied the general airport view that staff of the British overseas airline were stand-offish, even snobbish. In successive years most of the major world airlines gained the title in turn, earning some valuable publicity at minimal cost with coverage of the event thrown open to the news media at large by Brenards.

Staged mainly in the roof gardens of the Queens Building and adjoining Terminal 2 at Heathrow, the annual contest continued to be sponsored and organised by Brenards for more than thirty years. Its appeal as a national or even a London-only news event gradually waned, as did its big sister, the international Miss World contest. But it continued to be the one day in the year when competing British and foreign airlines got together for a "fun" day. It also helped to ensure that the news service offered by Brenards, together with the company's commercial photography and later, its cine and video, printing and promotional businesses were remembered on the airport.

The event was always attended by large numbers of airline and airport staff anxious to cheer on their often shy colleagues and favourite contestants. It was a surprise bonus too for members of the public, sightseers and other visitors to the roof gardens who normally might have little contact with the airport. So it became a showcase for the airlines, proud of the turnout of their staff, and a minor fashion show for their latest uniforms.

In the early days of the mid-forties, the handful of domestic and international airlines favoured a naval-like styling for both male and female staff uniforms. BEA stewardesses and receptionists in their navy-blue tricorns and brass buttoned jackets were frequently mistaken for Wrens, and aircraft captains for Royal Navy officers. By the end of the decade, under strong influence of American trends, efforts were being made to break away from militaristic styling. New uniform designs were to become a regular feature of the news columns, if only because they were such an emotive issue for the potential wearers.

Brenard Press picture
...and, some years later, the first winner of a new, annual "Miss London Airport," contest now organised by Brenard Press, Miss Sonia Simpson, a receptionist with BOAC.

One of my earliest stories from Northolt in the late 'forties appeared in the dailies under such headings as:

UNIFORMS SHOWN IN SECRET

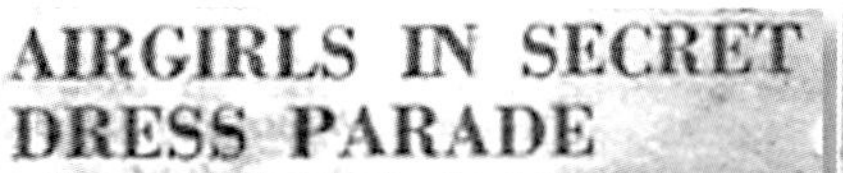
AIRGIRLS IN SECRET DRESS PARADE

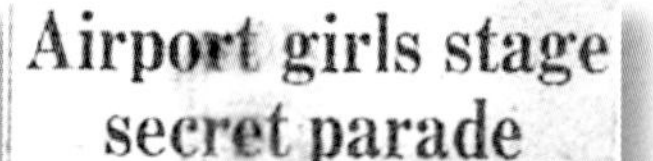
Airport girls stage secret parade

(l to r) Daily Mail, Daily Graphic, News Chronicle *(all) circa Summer 1948*

It told of a "mannequin" parade staged behind locked doors by BEA to answer staff criticisms of proposed new grey uniforms.

> ***Several girls paraded in the uniforms before a few male members of BEA staff and tailoring representatives. The girls had complained that the uniforms did not fit and were of poor material,*** I reported.

The criticisms were apparently accepted, for shortly afterwards the new designs, still slightly militaristic, but now well-tailored and provided with matching "cockaded" hats, were given a huge welcome both by the staff and the public. It was, unhappily, a muted welcome when the girls learnt, and passed on to me, the news that they would have to pay for the expensive new matching blouses themselves – and that they would have to sacrifice valuable personal coupons out of the Government's meagre national clothing ration allowance.

Whether it was the girls' employment qualifications or the Roy Calderon caricatures that influenced the thinking of one male airline duty officer never became clear. But his bold directive to forty BEA ground receptionist issued early in 1952 couldn't have been clearer. My story made a page lead in the *Daily Mirror* under a 5-column heading which ran:

HOW-TO-DRESS ORDERS SHOCK GIRLS WHO 'MUST BE ADVERTS FOR BRITAIN'

BRITAIN'S "shop window" girls—British European Airways ground receptionists who greet passengers arriving at London Airport—were ordered last night to smarten up and be a "100 per cent. advertisement for British Airlines."

And they were shocked. The forty grey-uniformed girls were told to trim their hair two inches above the collar, take off all jewellery except wedding and engagement rings, and come to work in plain black low-heeled shoes.

The instruction—signed by a B.E.A. duty officer, a man—ordered the girls to be keener at their work, told them not to lean against desks and radiators, and asked for more initiative and sympathy in handing passengers.

"An improvement is looked for immediately," said the notice. Later a B.E.A. official said: "Passengers say our receptionists are a pleasure to meet. I think so, too. They are so smart. But extra smartness is demanded by us—to put our receptionists ahead of other airlines. Maybe there have been lapses lately and, rather than tick off individuals, this instruction is reminding them all of the way to dress and act on duty."

'This Is Humiliating'

The girls were shocked because they claim to be the best groomed ground receptionists at London Airport. Their job is to meet more than fifty planes a day and then guide passengers through the Customs and Immigration departments to London-bound airline coaches.

One of the girls said last night: "This order is humiliating. We try so hard to be well turned out. Every night I press the skirt of my uniform. My cream blouse is clean every day. Look at my shoes—plain, two-inch heels, and shining."

Margot Eva, senior hostess of an American line, said: "The BEA girls are always smart. A very high standard is

Daily Mirror

Girls told how to dress—by a man

THE grey-uniformed airgirls of London Airport went up in the air last night—over a 100-word directive circulated to all departments by a zealous duty officer.

Daily Herald

and similarly caught the attention of the *Express*, the *Mail* and the *Daily Herald*. The intros used by each paper varied. But my phrase ***Britain's shop-window girls*** – one I was to use again in the future – was echoed by the *Mirror*.

The 100-word directive took the form of a letter to the girls. It listed five "do's" and "dont's" and gave hints on "How to dress and act while on duty." A copy was passed to me by several of the girls when I did my daily rounds one day in March. And one of them told me angrily: "It makes us look like a bunch of scruffy schoolgirls. We'll be told to go and wash our hands next."

The letter forbade ill-fitting uniforms, non-issue shoes and the wearing of jewellery other than wedding and engagement rings. It told the girls to trim their hair to two inches above the collar of their jackets and it required them to adopt what it called "a keener attitude" to their work. It prohibited "leaning against doors or radiators."

Another instruction set the girls guessing. It required them to "show more initiative and sympathy" towards passengers. "Sounds reasonable until you try to analyse it," said one girl, "How sympathetic do they want us to be when airliners are delayed?"

AIR GIRLS ANGRY AT DO-AND-DON'T LIST

MAKES US LOOK LIKE A BUNCH OF CHILDREN, SAYS ONE

AIR girls at London Airport were angry last night because of a 100-word letter circulated by a zealous duty officer. The directive listed five-point "Do and don't" instructions and hints on "How to dress and act while on duty."

It forbade the wearing of jewellery, wearing "too long" hair—two inches above the collar is regulation length—dressing in ill-fitting uniforms, and the wearing of non-issue shoes.

It required the girls to adopt a "keener attitude" towards their work, and prohibited leaning against desks or radiators.

The girls' objection: The instructions were issued not by one of their own supervisors but by a male duty officer—with a rider that an improvement was looked for immediately.

'A reminder'

Said one girl: "It makes us look like a bunch of scruffy schoolgirls. We'll be told to go and wash our hands next."

Daily Express

Air girls told—NO LEANING

AIR girls at London Airport were yesterday discussing a 100-word circular letter sent to all departments giving a five-point plan on "How to dress and act while on duty." It forbade wearing of jewellery, "too long" hair (two inches above the collar is regulation length), and non-issue shoes, demanded a "keener attitude to work," and prohibited "leaning against radiators." The girls' objection? The instructions were issued not by one of their own supervisors but by a man duty officer.

Daily Mail

(all) March 17 1952

What upset them most was the fact that the list was not issued by one of their own women supervisors, but by a male, who added the rider: "An improvement is looked for immediately."

Before dictating the story, I called BEA for a comment on the directive. The PR department seemed to be unaware of it, but eventually a spokesman called back with a carefully considered response. "Passengers say that our receptionists are a pleasure to meet. I think so too. They are so smart. But extra smartness is demanded by us to put our receptionists ahead of other airlines.

"Maybe there have been lapses lately and rather than tick off individuals, this instruction reminding them all of the way to dress and act accordingly."

Interestingly, leaning on radiators may have been an abhorrence peculiar to airline managers. A couple of years on, BEA's sister airline, BOAC, came down heavily on one of their receptionists at Heathrow. They sacked 24-years-old Oonagh Redvers for doing just that – listing her offence of radiator-leaning under the umbrella of "slovenly conduct." The dismissal and the phrase were withdrawn after an appeal by her trade union (and a colleague's story in the nationals), but too late. I was able to follow up by reporting that Miss Redvers, who was shortly to be married anyway, had already given in her notice before the incident, and had made up her mind not to return to her job... or her favourite radiator.

British European Airways themselves seemed to be playing a different tune when they issued another internal memo a few months later telling staff: "Don't be too polite on the Tannoy."

Setting out the style and content of a list of standard loudspeaker announcements drawn up by heads of BEA's passenger section, the notice required all announcements to be "brief, precise and informative only." The words "Attention, please," were banned. And "thank you" and "please" were to be limited to paging calls, announcements of delays and the boarding call for the luxury Silver Wing service to Paris.

The airline staff gave a grudging welcome to this instruction. "It sounds impolite, but it should cut down on excessive use of the microphone," said one golden-voiced girl announcer. But Ministry of Civil Aviation public information desk staff who made more announcements daily than all the airlines put together said: "We have no plans to change." They were to continue to precede announcements with: "May we have your attention, please…"

It wasn't long before some of the girls were complaining about "glamorisation" of their jobs. In April 1953 I reported for the *Daily Sketch* that the smart blue or grey-uniformed stewardesses and passenger receptionists of both BOAC and BEA were tired of their public image. After being feted for seven years as model examples of young womanhood, I now revealed that the showcase girls were retorting: "It's a myth."

The girls' main objection to the popular concept of a much-travelled air-wise hostess was that it created the impression that they did little real work. And a ground-based BEA traffic clerk told me: "We'd rather be acknowledged as plain Janes with brains than dumb blondes with no attributes but sex appeal."

Both airlines agreed with their staff, and said they made it clear to all applicants that there was little "glamour" in the job. Said a BOAC spokesman: "We are besieged by girls who are only attracted by the so-called romance of flying." And his opposite number

Airport girl gets reprimand

Miss Oonagh Redvers, 24-year-old London Airport receptionist sacked for leaning on a radiator, was told yesterday that BOAC had decided to substitute a reprimand for the sack and to withdraw the phrase "slovenly conduct." Instead, they accepted Miss Redvers's resignation—which she handed in three days before the incident.

Daily Mail ***Mar 4 1955***

OONAGH CLEARED

MISS Oonagh Redvers, 24-year-old B.O.A.C. receptionist who was sacked last Monday for "slovenly conduct" has been reinstated. The words "slovenly conduct" have been withdrawn.

But Miss Redvers is not going back to B.O.A.C. She resigned three days before she was sacked.

Miss Redvers is to be married next month. She was sacked for leaning on a window-sill while talking to passengers.

Her dismissal was withdrawn after an appeal. Officials of the National Association of Clerical and Supervisory Staffs say "a reprimand" has been substituted.

Daily Sketch ***Mar 4 1955***

Too much politeness can waste so much time

GIRL announcers for British European Airways at London and Northolt Airports have been told: "Don't be *too* polite."

When making announcements the order is: "Be brief, precise and informative only."

"Attention please" is banned and "Thank you" and "please" are limited to paging calls and delay announcements.

This is laid down in a list of officially recognised calls drawn up by heads of B.E.A. passenger section.

But there is one exception—the all aboard call to passengers on B.E.A.'s luxury Silver Way service to Paris.

Most of the girls—officially known as traffic clerks and assistants—like the new rules.

"It cuts down announcements to the minimum without losing effectiveness," said one.

FOOTNOTE: The Ministry of Civil Aviation's inquiry girls who make most of the general announcements at London Airport, will still say: "May I have your attention, please."

Daily Graphic

'Please' becomes a luxury

BRITISH EUROPEAN AIRWAYS has banned "excessive courtesy" in loudspeaker announcements at London and Northolt airports.

Its grey-uniformed girl receptionists have been told to be "brief, precise, and informative only."

The "Attention, please" that preceded announcements is now out; so is the signing-off "Thank you." And "Please," with one exception, is limited to paging calls and delay information. The exception: the "All aboard" call for the luxury Silver Wing service to Paris.

Daily Express

FAR AND NEAR

BEA cut the cackle

AIRGIRLS making loud speaker announcements at London Airport and Northolt have been told by BEA to "be brief, precise and informative only."

Banned is "excessive courtesy" and with it all the "thank yous" and nearly all the "pleases."

Daily Mail

Girls told to cut out 'please'

GIRL receptionists of British European Airways at London and Northolt airports will cut down "Please" and "Thank you" in their loud-speaker announcements.

A list of briefer announcements has been drafted for them—to lessen the time the loud-speakers are blaring.

The "Attention, please" preceding general notices to passengers and the final "Thank you" are dropped.

The inquiry girls of the Ministry of Civil Aviation, who make most general announcements at London Airport, will retain: "May I have your attention, please?"

News Chronicle
(all) December 22 1952

in BEA claimed brashly: "The glamourisation began in America where air girls were originally little more than night club hostesses."

The complaints fell mostly on deaf ears. I don't believe a single newspaper, apart from the *Sketch*, ran the story. The glamour image remained. And, it seems the girls had no problem retaining their trim, glamourous figures. Two summers later I was able to report for the London *Star* that unions were being asked by the staff to add " loss of weight" to complaints about working conditions in the Central Terminal area. They were concerned over the walking distances they would have to cover in the newly-opened passenger buildings.

"It's the best slimming treatment yet," said one airgirl. "We are losing pounds every week escorting passengers through miles of corridors, halls and lounges. We're just a bit worried about when it will stop."

Their cabin staff colleagues had no such worries. Though often on the feet for thousands of air miles, they were limited to just the length of an aircraft cabin for their working exercise. And some airgirls on flights between Britain and the Mediterranean admitted to skipping meals to save... not their figures, but money.

From an official BEA publication, the cabin staff bulletin, I learnt that the company doctor was anxious about both the airgirls and their male colleagues who were saving their meal allowances by cutting down on what they spent on food whilst abroad. According to the bulletin, one stewardess had admitted that in three days away on duty all she'd had to eat was half a bread roll and a small portion of salmon. She reported sick on her return to London and told the doctor she felt exhausted. On closer questioning she had admitted that she preferred to save her meal allowance, and that in any case she wanted to stay slim.

The doctors were concerned about a number of gastro-enteritis cases among the crews, and the BEA medical director commented: "The present method of paying meal allowances does much to encourage eating in cheap restaurants and cafes where hygienic standards are deplorably absent." The general attitude of cabin staff, he said, appeared to be that the allowances were perks and not to be used for the purchase of proper meals.

BEA were obviously embarrassed by the report in one of their own publications, even though it was intended only for internal circulation. A spokesman told me: "Of the 50 stewardesses regularly on the Mediterranean routes, only five have been reported for not using their meal allowances to buy proper food."

He agreed that the cabin staff had been advised to be careful where and what they ate. But he denied a claim by some of the girls that there was a ban on some Continental dishes. The *Daily Express* and the *Daily Mail* gave equal prominence to the story – some eight inches of column

AIR GIRLS SAY CUT OUT THE GLAMOUR

Daily Sketch Reporter

BRITAIN'S show-case girls—the smart blue-and-grey uniformed stewardesses and passenger receptionists of B.O.A.C. and B.E.A. —are tired of their " glamour " tags.

For seven years they have been feted by air travellers and the stay-at-home public as model examples of young womanhood.

And the girls now retort: "It's a myth."

British Overseas Airways and British European Airways make it clear to young applicants for stewardess and receptionist vacancies that there is little " glamour " in the job.

Said a B.O.A.C. spokesman yesterday: "We are besieged by girls who are attracted only by the so-called romance of flying.

Janes with brains

"We have a very strict selection board, but we try strongly to disillusion successful applicants during their training "

Main objection of the air girls themselves to the popular conception of a much-travelled hostess is that it creates the impression that they do little real work.

Said a B.E.A. traffic clerk at London Airport yesterday: "We'd rather be acknowledged as Plain Janes with brains than dumb blondes with no attributes but sex appeal.

"Our reputation of being Britain's most beautiful girls is no help when trying to handle disappointed passengers."

An official of B.E.A. added: "The glamorisation began in America where air girls were little more than night club hostesses."

"Our girls have a highly responsible and practical job of work to do.

Daily Sketch April 6 1953

AIRGIRLS LOSE THEIR CURVES

THE smart girls of British European Airways are losing weight—because of all the walking they have to do in the new building at London Airport.

Their union representative will be asked to add "loss of weight" to their complaints about working conditions.

"The best slimming treatment yet," is how one girl described her job. "We are losing pounds every week, escorting passengers through miles of corridors, halls and lounges."

Another girl, a small, attractive blonde: "I've already lost seven pounds and I haven't stopped reducing yet. So few of us can afford to lose that amount."

"Working here has done more to waste the curves than any modern weight reducing methods or prescribed diet sheets," commented another girl.

Daily Herald June 22 1955

THE AIR GIRLS DIET TO MAKE PIN-MONEY

AIR girls flying between London and the Mediterranean have been starving themselves to keep their meal allowance.

This was revealed yesterday in a BEA medical bulletin warning the girls of the dangers of " poor eating habits."

Daily Mirror Nov 16 1955

BEA girls cut meals to save money

SOME air girls on flights between Britain and the Mediterranean are skimping food to save money.

One of them admits that in three days away on duty all she had to eat was half a roll and a small portion of salmon, say B.E.A. medical authorities.

The girl given as an example reported sick when she arrived back at London Airport. She told the corporation doctor she felt exhausted.

"On closer questioning," said a medical officer, "she admitted she preferred to save her meal allowance and that anyway she preferred to stay slim."

Air girls 'starve' to save cash

Express Staff Reporter

SOME of the air girls on flights between Britain and the Mediterranean have been starving themselves to save money.

One of them admits that in three days away on duty, all she had to eat was half a bread roll and a small piece of salmon.

This girl reported sick when she arrived back at London Airport.

She told a British European Airways doctor she felt exhausted.

The doctor says: "On closer questioning she admitted she preferred to save her meal allowance, and that anyway she preferred to stay slim."

The doctor's warning about not eating has been passed on to stewards and stewardesses through B.E.A.'s weekly bulletin Cabin Staff.

'Perks'

The doctors are concerned about a number of cases of gastro-enteritis among catering crews, and B.E.A.'s medical director comments :—

"The present method, paying meal allowances, does much to encourage eating in cheap restaurants and cafés where hygienic standards are deplorably absent.

"The general attitude of cabin staff appears to be that meal allowances are personal 'perks' not to be used for the purchase of proper meals."

One stewardess said yesterday: "We are repeatedly warned about so many Continental dishes that we are left little choice."

PAY NOTE: Meal allowances vary from 10s. to 18s. These are in addition to pay for stewardesses, which ranges from £10 a week to £14 10s. a week. On some routes full hotel accommodation is provided for crews.

Daily Mail (left)
Daily Express (above)
(both) Nov 16 1955

length in each.

But it was Harry again who provided me with one of the biggest BEA uniforms' "fashion" stories of 1959, less than a week into the new year. On my morning call at his office, Harry had mentioned that his chairman, Lord Douglas of Kirtleside was flying back to London from Paris that day with Lady Douglas. I'm not sure now if I did say "So what?" but I probably felt it.

The 64-years-old former RAF Air Vice Marshal was not an obvious seeker after publicity, either for himself or for his airline. With the typical wariness of the military man, he never really understood the news media, its needs or its purpose. But unlike many others of his ilk, he was prepared to allow those who did understand to carry out this function without very much interference. So I knew that if he was going to make the papers that day it would have to be for a reason dreamt up by his PR advisers.

Lord Douglas of Kirtleside in 1944, prior to his appointment as Chairman of BEA

"Has he been doing anything newsworthy?" I asked hopefully, after racking my memory for a moment to think of a subject for an airline chairman's comment. Some industrial dispute... a new aircraft order... new routes... future developments? Harry pondered as well for a moment. "Don't think so…" he mused. Then, as if he'd just thought of it: "Of course, you could ask *Lady* Douglas what she thinks of the length of the girls' skirts. As an ex-model she might have a view." Another brief pause and then he added: "In fact I know she does have a view. She expressed an opinion on the matter when they flew out. But don't say I told you."

Well, I remember thinking, it's different. And the idea of tackling the boss's wife rather than the boss himself on the subject of skirt lengths appealed to me. Paris fashion houses had been dictating the length of women's skirts for so long (this was before the Brits stunned the world with the mini) and the ponderous question "Are they up or down?" had become a regular annual issue for the papers.

The mid-fifties fashion trend had seen skirt lengths fall to below mid-calf, possibly their lowest for twenty years, but just a few months earlier they had risen to just below the knee. With their personal wardrobes, most women could choose for themselves by reaching for the scissors if bold enough or buying new if they could afford to. Uniforms were another matter. They needed uniformity, and change needed unanimity.

I approached Lady Douglas as she emerged from the Customs hall a few feet ahead of her husband, and with very little preamble asked her what she thought of the length of the grey skirts of the BEA girls and if it were true she had asked for them to be shortened. She must have assumed I had been told officially of her earlier comments. Without even a glance at her husband the 5ft 7ins ex-fashion model replied:

"I did say that I thought the skirts were a little too long," she said, "But I certainly didn't ask for them to be shortened. I wouldn't dare to interfere in my husband's affairs or those of BEA.

"I merely made a suggestion. I pointed out that some of the girls looked dowdy. My husband agreed, and he spoke to someone about it immediately – though I didn't know that until later."

Lady Douglas went on: "Personally, I like the new short length. I have shortened all my skirts."

As soon as I could, I broke away. If the BEA chairman had already acted, any orders he had given could be announced at any time. I hurried away to find a photographer... and a model of our own. I drew on my memory banks of favourite figures, and we sought out 24-years-old Eve White, a married receptionist and reservations clerk with a perfect turn of calf.

"Eve," I told her, "We want a picture of your legs." Hastily I explained that we needed "before and after" pictures of her hemline, first at normal length, then raised. "But we don't have time to get approval for the photograph," I added, "So we don't want to identify you. Only your legs will show."

Fortunately Eve agreed to go along with the stunt, because within hours we learnt that a notice from the airline's personnel branch was being circulated among 700 stewardesses and women ground staff requiring them to raise their uniform skirt lengths by 3 inches to some two to three inches below the knee.

Now I needed to hear the reaction of some of Eve's colleagues to the instruction. My first surprise was that some of the girls were relieved – they had taken the scissors to their skirts on their own initiative weeks and even months earlier. Most others welcomed the new order... but inevitably the liveliest comments came from those totally opposed to the cutbacks.

Said one: "I wouldn't raise my skirts for the Queen, let alone Lady Douglas." And a colleague: "Let's be honest about this. We're all shapes and sizes. Some of us would look ridiculous in short skirts." Even the BEA promise to cover the cost of alterations failed to meet all the objections. "Most of us now have two grey uniforms – the first one issued to us and a later version which has a modified shorter jacket," said one traffic clerk, "A shorter skirt would look all wrong with the long jacket."

The airline insisted on the final word, however. Their spokesman said the girls would have five weeks to meet the hemline deadline. And after that? An ominous pause. Then: "We'll have to look into it."

The story grabbed the headlines the next day. The *Daily Express* ran it as a page lead

Short-skirt girls revolt

BEA chief's wife prompts 'snip' order

Daily Express *Jan 5 1959*

under a six-column banner with sub-head *(above and left)*.

Also across six columns the *Daily Sketch* offered another page lead, with some fifteen inches of copy (below), and the *Daily Mirror* gave it twelve column-inches under an even larger heading *(see over)*.

The *Sketch* and the *Daily Herald* ***('Show more Leg,' says Lady Douglas)*** both used our pictures of Eve's anonymous

SHORTEN YOUR SKIRTS ORDER TO 700 AIR GIRLS

By MICHAEL KEMP

Daily Sketch *Jan 5 1959*

SEVEN HUNDRED BEA air girls are angry over a "shorten your skirts" order. Because their boss's wife, Lady Douglas of Kirtleside, who suggested it, thinks they "look dowdy."

But the order issued by BEA's thrice-married chairman, 64-year-old Lord Douglas, must be obeyed.

By February 15 hemlines must go up by at least three inches—so the skirts are "one to three inches below the knee."

Before her marriage, lovely, 5ft. 7in.-tall Lady Douglas modelled before Queen Elizabeth the Queen Mother and Princess Margaret.

THEN she boasted the smallest mannequin waist in London. Now—she is 39—her personal measurements are 33-19½-33.

Yesterday Lady Douglas told me at her Denham, Bucks, home: "I did not ASK for the skirt shortening. I just happened to mention it to my husband.

"I pointed out that so many of the girls looked dowdy — and suggested shorter skirts. It's as simple as that.

"But my husband acted on it. I did not even know he had. He just went ahead on his own. I never interfere with his business affairs."

SHOW A LITTLE MORE LEG

Lady Douglas paused, then said: "Frankly, I felt the girls were not showing themselves to best advantage.

"We have attractive girls and they were letting themselves down. Such long skirts—calf-length—make them look older. It's good to show a little more leg.

"I like short skirts. On the whole they are far more practical—especially for getting in and out of cars and helicopters and things.

"I have altered all my own skirts to 1½ inches below the knee.

"But for the girls the suggestion is one to three inches below — which is giving quite a lot.

"The Paris length is knee-level, which seems to be over-doing it. But there

It's smarter says the boss's wife

is no doubt that shorter skirts are more classical.

"Of course, the precise length depends largely on a girl's legs."

A handful of young BEA receptionists welcome the order. But a lot of others resent it.

One declared: "I shall not shorten my skirt for anyone, let alone Lady Douglas."

Another said: "Most of us have two uniforms.

WE'RE NOT ALL MONROES

"The newer has a shorter jacket, which would suit the new skirt-length. But the longer jacket of the older uniform will look out of balance."

A senior air girl said: **"It's ridiculous to assume we all have Monroe figures and nice legs. We're all shapes and sizes—short skirts will look ridiculous on some girls."**

Cost of alterations? BEA has offered to pay for tailoring.

● BEA is one of the last air lines to fall in with the new short skirt fashion set by Paris.

BEFORE: BEA girl shows the old length.

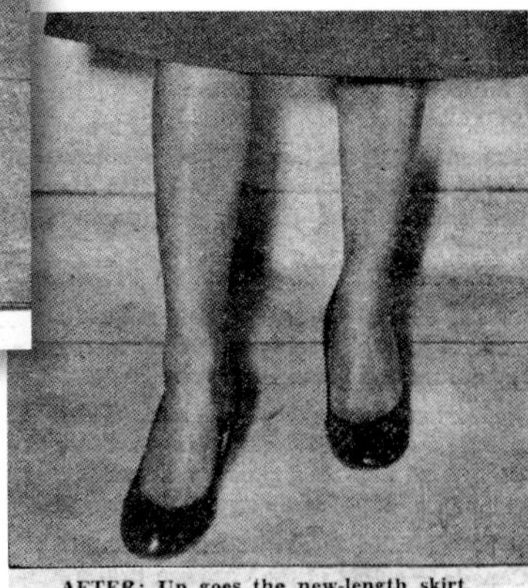

AFTER: Up goes the new-length skirt.

(above and right, Daily Sketch captions)

Brenard Press pictures

SHOW MORE LEG SAYS LADY DOUGLAS

HEMS-UP ORDER ANGERS AIR-GIRLS

Henry Fielding

AN order has gone out to 700 airgirls of British European Airways to SHOW A LEG.

It follows a suggestion from Lady Douglas of Kirtleside, 39-year-old wife of the B E A chairman and a former fashion model.

She told her husband that the girls' skirts, which are down to mid-calf, are too long.

"They look grotesque," she said last night. "They make me wince. I have shortened all my skirts.

"Lord Douglas agreed completely with me and had the instruction issued."

So all the grey-uniformed receptionists, ticket clerks, flight clerks and stewardesses got the order from personnel branch: *Slash those skirts to a couple of inches below the knee.*

RESENTED

February 15 is the deadline and B E A promises to pay for any tailoring involved.

Except for a handful of the younger girls most of the B E A staff resent the order.

One long-service girl said: "Let's be honest. We haven't all got Monroe figures and nice legs; we're all shapes and sizes. A short skirt will make some of us look ridiculous."

One brunette, a receptionist, said: "I wouldn't shorten my skirt for the Queen, let alone Lady Douglas."

Brenard Press pictures
Daily Herald (above)
Daily Mirror (right)
(all) Jan 5 1955

'PUT SKIRTS UP 3 INCHES'

—700 airline girls are told

SEVEN hundred girls employed by British European Airways are to hoist their skirts three inches next month—by order.

DAILY MIRROR REPORTER

The instruction, from the Corporation's personnel branch, follows a suggestion by Lady Douglas, wife of Lord Douglas of Kirtleside, chairman of B.E.A.

She noticed that the girls' skirts were well below the present fashionable length dictated by Paris—and mentioned it to her husband.

Ex-Model

Lord Douglas told me yesterday: "My wife used to be a model and, of course, she notices things like this."

He added: "Naturally we want our girls to be in fashion."

B.E.A. has told the girls in a typewritten instruction that uniform hemlines should be brought up from their present mid-calf length to two or three inches below the knee.

The Corporation will foot the bill for the alterations.

Over to the grey-uniformed stewardesses, traffic clerks and receptionists at London Airport—

Traffic clerk Mrs. Audrey Clifton, 32, of Hayes End, Middlesex, said yesterday: "Most of the girls welcome the new ruling—provided we can all have the new issue of shorter jackets which will go well with the shorter skirts.

"Many of us have the old-type uniform which has a long jacket. That would look awful with a short skirt."

Mrs. Rosemary Bowen, 22, of Colnbrook, another traffic clerk, said: "I'm all for the new line. It will look much smarter."

But a stewardess said: "Let's be honest. It's ridiculous to assume we all have Monroe figures and lovely legs. A short skirt would look frightful on some of us."

Now over to the chairman's wife—

Lady Douglas said yesterday: "Some of the girls wear the uniform skirt much too long. They look grotesque.

"Personally I like the new length. I have shortened all my skirts. After all, this order is a compromise. Two or three inches below the knee is not all that short."

★ **AILSA GARLAND, Mirror Woman's Editor,** writes: B.E.A.'s new skirt length is still longer than the current just-below-the-knee fashion.

Air girls rebel at Douglas hemline—

SEVEN hundred B.E.A. air girls were ordered this week to lift their hemlines three inches following a suggestion from an ex-model—Lady Douglas, wife of the airline's chairman And the order has led to a revolt.

A typed instruction from the airline's personnel branch to the grey-uniformed receptionists, clerks and stewardesses gives "two to three inches below the knee" as the desirable skirt length

News Chronicle

legs, and both the *Daily Mail* and the *Herald* carried an agency picture of the former model Lady Douglas, née Hazel Walker.

I later heard from Harry that Fleet Street interest in my early story led him to call up a BEA bus to ferry other reporters and photographers out to the Buckinghamshire home of Lord and Lady Douglas for a follow-up. But it was my original version of events which commanded the major share of attention.

For the *Airport Post*, my part-time interest with the Heathrow edition of the local *Weekly Post* series of newspapers, I was also able to provide two new angles on the story the very next day. In response to his wife's comments, I was told, Lord Douglas had consulted a senior BEA official who had accompanied him through the terminal to his aircraft. He was informed that the airline's staff uniforms committee had recommended a change to skirt lengths several months earlier but no instruction had been issued.

Confirming this, Harry, as BEA spokesman, told me: "These recommendations can occasionally take a long time to come into effect. If it had not been for a gentle push by Lady Douglas, the order might not be out now." When signed and published, the order required the grey-uniformed girls to raise their skirt hemlines to two to three inches below the knee "according to height."

I was also able to reveal that several girls had already been reprimanded for their unilateral cuts while the order was still in the pipeline. It was also now safe to identify Eve White as our anonymous hemlines model. The *Post* front-paged a Brenard picture showing Eve, this time in full length pose, as a male colleague took up the tape-measure and scissors on her behalf. The colleague was Eve's husband Arthur – a load control officer with BEA (*see opposite).*

Hemline lengths and the cut-or-not-to-cut controversy had in fact been a major issue for the female ground staff of the major transatlantic airlines for almost a year before Lady Douglas made her move, and was to continue for several more summers. As I had reported for the evenings and dailies in April 1958:

> **With one exception airlines...** *(at Heathrow)* **...are drawing the line at the latest fashion decree for hitching up women's skirts. The calf-length hemline of airgirls' uniforms is to stay – at least for the present...**

The one exception, I revealed, was BOAC, whose girls were to have the hems of planned new uniforms taken up by a whole inch. And the decision sent a wave of envy flooding round the desks of rival companies. Trans World Airlines and Pan American Airways both warned staff they faced disciplinary action if skirts were shortened without formal permission. As Pan Am's manager Jim Naylor put it: "Let's just say we've stopped trouble before it started. We've nipped it in the bud."

...AND OUT COME THE SCISSORS!

THE girl whose legs became national news — when they decorated the disclosures about the new skirt lengths on Monday—was identified accidentally by her colleagues. Though the photographs were cut off at knee level, girl colleagues of 24-years-old Eve White recognised her . . . by her legs alone.

Eve, a receptionist and reservations clerk for the past seven years was married in September, to BEA load control official Arthur White. They are seen together here measuring Eve's skirt before using the scissors. And Eve's own comments on the short-long issue? "I don't mind if we can shorten our long jackets. But I wear most of my own dresses and skirts long."

Brenard Press picture for Airport Post

From an unlikely source came yet another point of view. The Heathrow manager for Air India responded with: "With us it must be all or nothing." Hastily he added: "I mean of course that all the girls or none at all must shorten their skirts." Then he pondered: "On second thoughts I think we'll await a ruling from India."

The last word had to be with BOAC. Explaining their reluctance to boldly go still further than their competitors, they explained delicately: "We must consider the number of times our girls have to mount steps. Two inches off the hem or just below the knee would be a shade too high for that sort of thing...."

Uniform design was a recurring theme for the airport reporters (to say nothing of the photographers). In April 1957 BOAC released details of a "tunic and dress" outfit for stewardesses. A month later Aer Lingus, the Irish airline, shocked the civilised aviation world by abandoning its much-admired emerald green uniforms for a more casual style in Donegal tweed. With unashamed blarney, the change they said had been inspired by "meadows, sky, sunset and peat." Or as one cynic put it: "Ideal for growing potatoes in." No, it wasn't me.

Soaring temperatures and complaints about air circulation in the passenger terminals led to less than uniform agreement for BOAC management officers in early summer that same year. Male and female ground staff apparently found themselves facing contradictory orders not only about the wearing of jackets but also whether shirt sleeves should be rolled-up or buttoned down. When most of the staff decided to please themselves anyway, two opposing managers buttoned their lips instead and ignored the rebellion.

Other airport organisations and their staffs, male and female, continued to attract media attention over uniforms, justifiably or not, right through to the mid-1960's. Even the staid Ministry of Aviation, the airport landlords and operators, became involved in minor controversies over their staff uniforms, mainly over unimaginative styles. Interest only waned as the range of their designs, materials and colours became finally so diverse they also became instantly forgettable.

Issues of such direct interest to airport staff naturally provided me with a great deal of copy for the *Airport Post* as well as a constant supply of light-weight "inside page" news for the nationals. My "moonlighting" for the *Post* had begun in the mid-fifties, though it was neither night-work nor illegitimate. Up to that time a visiting reporter from the series' nearby Hayes branch office had produced the airport edition of the *Middlesex Weekly Post* on a part-time basis. He often found himself at a considerable disadvantage to resident reporters.

Co-owners Ronald Richards, a former Beaverbrook protégé, and his brother Derek wanted to transfer their airport reporter to another edition full-time. They needed another part-timer with airport "resident press" status to replace him. When they approached me, I agreed readily, and sought out Bren for his necessary approval. As Brenards' did not normally serve local newspapers, there would be no clash of interests. Or so I believed. Fortunately for me, so did Bren – at that time.

An intensive half-a-day's writing, plus the occasional picture begged or bought from my photographic colleagues provided me with just over a page of news. Used as a frontispiece, that page was sufficient to justify an Airport edition of the *Post* continuing in tandem with the Uxbridge, Hayes and Ruislip editions of the series, all published from the company's offices in West London. It also gave me an enviable opportunity to sound off to my heart's content in a personal gossip column on the back page of the paper, an indulgence I had enjoyed during my national service journalism.

As with most local newspapers of the day, the pay was minimal. In practical terms I was working for or representing the *Airport Post* at least five days a week for less than a day's money. I'm not sure my union would have approved, even if I could have convinced them that the alternative would have meant no airport newspaper and no job for any reporter. The Richards brothers benefited from my knowledge of the airport news scene for the cost of peanuts. But I doubt if they could have afforded more, while I had just taken on a mortgage and needed as many peanuts as possible.

I saw my role with the *Post* as one of finding a local angle on some of the stories I was producing for the nationals. If one wasn't obvious I could often introduce the "vox pop" element of comment from airport staff on a national airport news event. Many of those staff lived in the *Weekly Post* circulation area, so their newsworthy activities were also of interest to a wider local readership.

This laudable objective might have ended my new part-time career as soon as it had begun. My first by-lined front page lead in the *Post* for October 1955 "revealed" less than detailed plans for the Queen's forthcoming opening of London Airport's "diamond city" as the new Central Terminal area had already been dubbed.

What became significant was my elementary error of mixing comment with news, something I had been encouraged to do – against all my instincts – in my earlier tabloid, the Army's *Catterick Express*. I had spent the next few years learning never to comment or express a personal opinion in a news story, so I could not claim ignorance. Ironically, in the enlightened 21st century, such elementary teaching is apparently regarded as an old-fashioned ethic. Pick up any national newspaper today and you will find either the by-lined reporter's comments or the newspaper's own opinion shining like a spotlight in many a controversial news story.

Announcing that no fewer than 800 officials from the Royal Court, the Diplomatic Corps, the Government and its Ministries were attending the ceremony, I questioned what arrangements had been made to enable the Queen to meet the "little people" involved in running the airport. What opportunity, I demanded to know, would there be for the Queen to hear the views and opinions of the men and girls at the ticket desks, the Customs officer at his bench, the passport men, the shop attendants, the cleaners, the porters? And I wrote:

> **Cannot the formal nature of the visit be laced with a little more informality?**
>
> **Protocol says "impossible."**
>
> **But the *Post* says it *can* be done.**
>
> **It can be done by readjusting the time allowed for the strictly formal unveiling ceremony, by slashing the presentation of officials, by smoothing out the "procedure" barriers…**

This clarion call was backed up by my efforts to seek staff support for my views (rather than the other way round) through a hurried survey of some thirty airline and airport staff. Of these, predictably, 27 said: "Of course the Queen should be allowed to meet the ordinary staff." So I concluded:

> ***…the airport must carry on working. The airliners must continue to fly. Let the Queen see the buildings, by all means. But let her see them - in use.***

Derek Richards, as *Post* news editor, provided the headline – in heavy, 72-point sans serif typeface – for the Page 1 lead, with a strapline *(opposite):*

Wednesday, Oct. 26, 1955 THREEPENCE Vol. 2. No. 383

AIRPORT POST

An Independent Newspaper

REGISTERED AT THE GENERAL POST OFFICE AS A NEWSPAPER

AIRPORT STAFF SQUEEZED OUT OF ROYAL VISIT

Why not let the Queen meet the "little men"?

By RAY BERRY

OVER 800 members of the Diplomatic Corps, courtiers, Government Ministers and other officials are to attend the official opening of London Airport's "Diamond City" by the Queen on December 16.

The "chosen 800" will accompany Her Majesty on a tour of the Eastern Apex and South East Face buildings, joining her for tea in the main passenger restaurant. The entire tour is planned to take only 90 minutes—including possible hold-ups.

Even if the time permits it—and no-one would wish to make the Queen's first visit to the new buildings a tedious one—what opportunity will the planned programme give her to meet the staff who combine to make the new airport work?

FORMAL AFFAIR

What arrangements have been made to give her the opportunity to hear the views and opinions of the people who matter almost as much as the passengers—the men and girls at the ticket desks, the Customs officer at his bench, the passport men, yes, and the shop attendants and cleaners, the porters?

Details of the plans for the Royal visit, said to be a "formal affair ... National level," were revealed last week at a secret meeting of senior airport staff.

Airport Post* *Oct 25 1955

Immediately below was my first *Airport Post* by-line – so there was no doubt at all who was expressing these dangerous opinions.

Bill Brenard took it all very calmly considering that he was at the other end of the telephone when the newspaper landed on the desk of airport commandant Sir John D'Albiac. The Air Marshal was, said Bren, very unhappy. "I've told him it's nothing to do with me or the agency," he said, "So now it's over to you. It's your name on the story. You'd better call him and make your peace."

I'll draw a veil over my telephone conversation with Sir John. Not that I backed down, except to admit that I could have given him or his press office a chance to respond in more detail to my criticism. He said that many airport departments would be represented in the line-up, even though the purpose of the Royal visit was not to inspect the workings of the airport but formally to inaugurate the new buildings. And he insisted that trade unions and staff associations had been consulted throughout the planning for the visit.

In the end I think we came to an unspoken agreement to differ. But I did promise to try to redress the balance the following week if Sir John wanted to make a statement. He did; and it said a great deal for his personality that he neither contradicted nor made direct reference to my published opinions. And he never allowed the disagreement to interfere with our future relations. He remained courteous and helpful to me and to all my press colleagues until his retirement.

For the first few months my weekly chat column in the *Post* appeared under the by-line of ***David Howard***, the pen name I had adopted for my Army newspaper column. This was deliberate. The column was an echo of my personal views which on occasions might have compromised Brenards. I dropped it when it was suggested I was hiding my opinions behind a pseudonym. But a year or two later I voluntarily revived my alter ego once more. I had a suspicion that Bren's amused tolerance of my frequent outbursts in print might be wearing a bit thin...

*

It was inevitable, I suppose, that as reporters we would often find ourselves providing captions for "Airgirl to wed" pictures set up by our photographers. They had an ulterior motive, of course. A good picture of a potential bride in a London evening newspaper could often lead to an invitation to the same cameraman to provide the lucrative wedding photo coverage, a private perquisite above and beyond the call of the news service. It had to be purely coincidental that almost every one of the photographers I worked with over the years, as well as several of those "opposition" freelances I have referred to elsewhere, ended up marrying either stewardesses or airline ground hostesses themselves.

Although mere reporters we too had our special contacts among the airgirls as we did among all airline and airport staff – those who recognised a good story when they saw or heard one (and were neither asking for nor expecting payment) and were only too happy to pass it on. Sometimes this meant that our interests and those of the photographers were

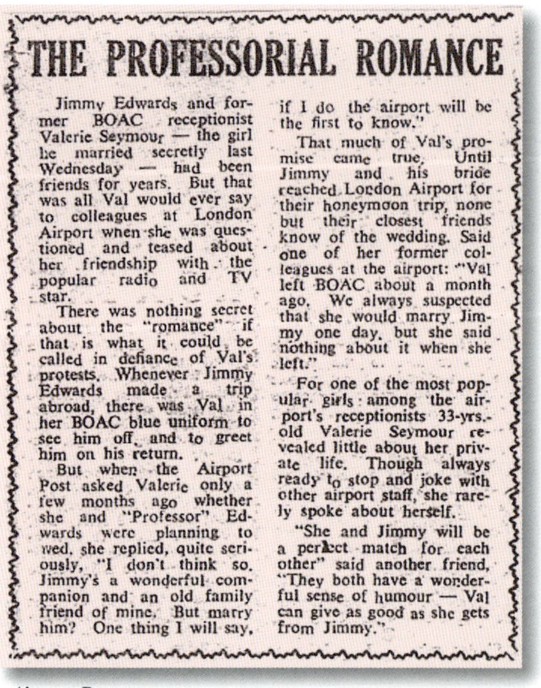

THE PROFESSORIAL ROMANCE

Jimmy Edwards and former BOAC receptionist Valerie Seymour — the girl he married secretly last Wednesday — had been friends for years. But that was all Val would ever say to colleagues at London Airport when she was questioned and teased about her friendship with the popular radio and TV star.

There was nothing secret about the "romance" if that is what it could be called in defiance of Val's protests. Whenever Jimmy Edwards made a trip abroad, there was Val in her BOAC blue uniform to see him off, and to greet him on his return.

But when the Airport Post asked Valerie only a few months ago whether she and "Professor" Edwards were planning to wed, she replied, quite seriously, "I don't think so. Jimmy's a wonderful companion and an old family friend of mine. But marry him? One thing I will say, if I do the airport will be the first to know."

That much of Val's promise came true. Until Jimmy and his bride reached London Airport for their honeymoon trip, none but their closest friends know of the wedding. Said one of her former colleagues at the airport: "Val left BOAC about a month ago. We always suspected that she would marry Jimmy one day, but she said nothing about it when she left."

For one of the most popular girls among the airport's receptionists 33-yrs.-old Valerie Seymour revealed little about her private life. Though always ready to stop and joke with other airport staff, she rarely spoke about herself.

"She and Jimmy will be a perfect match for each other" said another friend, "They both have a wonderful sense of humour — Val can give as good as she gets from Jimmy."

Airport Post

diametrically opposed to each other. We wanted to protect our sources. They might be obliged to expose them.

We did come together over the story that Valerie Seymour was hiding. Valerie was a BOAC receptionist and one of that rare and enviable breed who seem to be popular with everyone, friends, colleagues and acquaintances. In spite of an attractive, bubbly personality however, she rarely spoke of herself and revealed little of her private life.

We all knew that she was friendly with Britain's leading comedy actor of the day, Jimmy Edwards. When he travelled through the airport she would often meet him or see him off. But in the days when "just good friends," could still be a literal truth as well as an euphemism, Val dismissed all suggestions of a romance.

When I asked her if she and "Professor" Edwards were planning to marry, Val told me, quite seriously, "I don't think so. Jimmy's a wonderful companion and an old family friend. But marry him? That's another matter." Then she added: "One thing I will say. If I do marry him the airport and you boys will be among the first to know."

That part of her response was literally true. We learned of the wedding when she and Jimmy slipped out of Heathrow on honeymoon. I wasn't "in the know" or even there, and there were no perks for the photographers on this occasion. No one but the families and closest friends were aware of the wedding. Airport colleagues and those of the resident press on duty learnt of the departure only as the newlyweds checked in. Thirty-three-years-old Val had quietly left the airport scene and her job some two or three weeks earlier, and said a close colleague: "She said nothing about a wedding then – and that's typical."

Brenard Press picture
Pat Taylor
Candid Camera victim

Another airgirl always ready to pass the time of day with us was pretty, 24-years-old Pat Taylor, a receptionist with Air France. Early in 1962 she sought me out in Terminal 2 to tell me of a brush she'd had with TV practical joker Jonathan Routh. Like Jeremy Beadle, his successor of thirty years on, Routh hosted a public participation programme, the British version of the popular American show *Candid Camera.* Subjects of the programme, usually filmed on High-street locations, were members of the public who were secretly targeted as victims of some outrageous hoax or practical joke.

Pat, it seemed, had called in at a petrol station opposite the Bath-road entrance of Heathrow to fill up on her way in to work. As she paid for the petrol she turned suddenly to see her gleaming red Mini apparently being stripped down by a team of mechanics. The wheels were whipped off, the seats removed and a start made on taking out the engine – all part of a "free service," she was told when she protested.

Pat demanded to see the garage manager as first her pleas, then her anger were totally ignored. Then the "mechanics" suddenly and quietly slipped away for a tea break. They completely abandoned the little red car Pat called "Sylvester" on the forecourt, stripped, as it were, to the buff.

"It was only then I began to realise what was going on," said Pat, "But before I could recover my composure a form was thrust under my nose and I had signed, giving my permission for the film to be used.

"Then Jonathan Routh stepped forward and gave me my fee for the filming. He thrust a ten-bob note (50p) into my hand with the words: "That's for your trouble."

As far as Pat was concerned the fee – worth about £20 in today's terms – was the last straw. "I didn't tell my friends how much I was paid. And they all assumed it must be a small fortune for agreeing to look such a mug on television," she told me, "and I must say I also thought the television companies paid more than that to their victims."

Pat's sorry tale made several dailies, complete with a nevertheless cheerful picture of her perched on the bonnet of a restored Sylvester. The practical joke itself was comparatively insignificant and harmless. What made the story was the cavalier treatment of the victim by a peak programme which constantly insisted that it had the unreserved co-operation and permission of its subjects.

There was a happy sequel, as I was able to report the next day. When TV executives read the story they telephoned Air France to apologise to Pat, and promised to send someone along to see her. That "someone" turned out to be Jonathan Routh himself, who later appeared at Pat's desk with a huge bouquet of flowers. She called me immediately, and I hurried over, to arrive just in time to challenge him.

"Why does *Candid Camera* treat its victims so miserly?" was my provocative question. He had the perfect answer – off pat, you might say. "We always try to avoid giving the impression we have a set scale of fees, or in fact that we pay anything at all," he said, "If that idea became a widespread expectancy, our subjects might play to the camera when the penny drops. That would defeat the whole spontaneity of their reactions."

The moral of the story for the producers of such programmes has to be: if you insist on making a fool of someone without reasonable recompense for their participation, make sure they don't have friends in the news media.

Pat felt vindicated by her fifteen minutes of newspaper fame. Not so happy were a group of Scandinavian Airlines staff at Prestwick Airport. Their good-humoured and harmless tomfoolery gave me a splash in all the Scottish dailies which was picked up by wire services and radio stations round the world. But not everyone was laughing.

My attention had been caught by the sight of a small group of people gathered round the airline's ticket desk at a time when the departures area was normally devoid of any passenger activity – and well outside the normal operating times of SAS themselves. Curious, I approached to discover that the six or seven bystanders were chatting up…a set of baggage scales.

Of course there was a story there. And it was the kind of story that wrote itself. All but the most dour of the Scottish nationals revelled in it, gleefully passing it on to their London and Manchester offices. And most of them used my opening words without amendment:

> **The rasping metallic voice echoed above the hubbub at Prestwick Airport, constantly repeating its staccato invitation. 'I am a talking weighing machine' it said. 'Step…on…me.'**

Gingerly, my story continued, the bystanders took up the invitation. They were joined in no time by others, curious staff from other airport organisations, the odd passenger, greeter or sightseer. They all watched in amazement as first one, then another had their weight accurately read and repeated back to them by the speaking scales. For a time all went well as the machine – intended for passengers' baggage – reliably read more personal weights. Then everything began to go terribly wrong. The "robot" developed a bug, a mind of its own. It began to add comment to statistics.... caustic, sarcastic and aggressive insult to embarrassing injury.

A buxom teenager was told: "You are 126 pounds 12 ounces and overweight." A woman passenger was advised: "Your diet sheet is useless." And a solitary male who tried to test the machine with one foot as he looked around him apprehensively was informed curtly: "You weigh precisely one leg. Place a leg on another machine for an accurate reading."

The crowd grew. Questions were asked. Then somebody spotted movement behind a half-mirrored screen window at the rear of the airline baggage counter. The secret was guessed... and the scales fell from the eyes of the audience. The "robot" voice was being provided by an airline official, speaking into an intercom behind the screen, where the weight readings could be easily seen. The intercom was wired to an amplifier concealed near the baggage scales.

The joker turned out to be the Scandinavian Airlines senior passenger officer Hugh Armstrong. He confessed all when I challenged him. "It was all good clean fun and harmless," he said. "Only my victims could hear clearly what I was actually saying directly to them. I made sure I wasn't too rude – and I only picked on people who could obviously take a joke.

"The most amusing part was seeing the reaction of airport staff when the machine addressed them by name."

Said a colleague in the know: "We can see the public quite clearly through the mirrored screen, but they can't see us unless we move about. Their reactions were like a scene from *Candid Camera*. One woman actually called the scales a liar – and jumped when it answered her back."

At the time I deliberately withheld the name of Hugh's employer airline. My instinct told me it was not the kind of publicity the company would be enamoured of. Unfortunately

'STEP ON ME' THE VOICE SAID: THEN SHOCK

THE metallic voice echoed above the hubbub at Prestwick Airport yesterday—repeating its invitation: "I am a talking weighing machine . . . Step . . . on . . . me."

Daily Record *(all) October 26 1964*

Robot that had them weighed up

WHAT THE ROBOT SAW (and said)

Scottish Daily Mail (above)
Daily Mirror (left)

What a giggle when the airport robot weighs in

Express Staff Reporter

THE rasping, metallic voice echoed above the hubbub at Prestwick Airport, repeating its staccato invitation: *"I am a talking weighing machine. Step on me."*

They did. One after another, passengers, visitors, airport staff, paused, then hesitantly accepted the invitation to test the accuracy of the novel baggage-scale, at an airline counter.

Quite a crowd gathered. Some people amused, others annoyed. Questions were asked.

Then someone spotted an airline official hiding behind a glass panel, who seemed to take an unusual interest in the goings-on.

Joker

The secret was out. The "robot" was a practical joker, sitting at an office intercom set, wired to a loud-speaker alongside the scales.

A colleague said: "We can see the public and read their weights clearly through the glass panel. But the public can't see us."

For a time, all went well. The machine reliably, if publicly, reported the avoirdupois pounds and ounces of its victims.

THEN . . . sensation. The clipped voice began to add comments to its statistics, some caustic, some sarcastic, some strictly personal.

One buxom teenager was told: *"You are 126lb. 12oz.—and overweight."*

A middle-aged woman passenger was curtly advised: *"Your diet sheet is useless."*

Liar

And a solitary male, who gingerly tested the machine with one foot, as he glanced round apprehensively, was admonished: *"You weigh precisely one leg. Place a leg on another machine for an accurate reading."*

"Watching their reactions was like a scene from Candid Camera. One young woman called the machine a liar—and jumped into the air when it answered her back."

And "the voice," senior airline official, Hugh Armstrong of Coodham, Ayrshire, said:

"It was all good, clean fun. I made sure I wasn't too rude—and I only picked on people who could obviously take a joke.

"It was amusing to watch the faces of air-girls when I addressed them by name."

Scottish Daily Express

WEIGHING MACHINE PULLED A FEW LEGS

SUN REPORTER

THE voice of the airport robot rasped out to surprised passengers: "I am a talking weighing machine. Step . . . on . . . me."

Gingerly they tried it. Airport staff, who did not know the robot's secret, stood in amazement as it invited everyone to test the accuracy of the scales meant for baggage.

For a time all went well—as the machine reliably announced the weights of passengers and visitors.

Then it developed a mind of its own. Comments on vital statistics were offered. Advice followed. Replies were forthcoming when passengers expressed surprise.

One buxom teenager was informed: "You are 126 pounds 12 ounces — and overweight."

A middle-aged woman passenger was advised: "Your diet sheet is useless."

And one man, who tested the machine with one foot, was told sharply: "You weigh precisely one leg. Place a leg on another machine for an accurate reading."

In the small crowd that gathered at Prestwick airport, not all were amused—eyebrows and questions were raised.

Then someone found out about the airline official who was sitting behind a glass panel from which he could read the dial of the weighing machine. And his "robot" secret was out.

Clean fun

At his side was an office intercom wired to a loud-speaker concealed near the machine.

The joker was senior airline official Hugh Armstrong, of Coodham, Ayrshire.

Yesterday, he said: "It was all good clean fun. I made sure I wasn't too rude—and I only picked on people who could obviously take a joke.

"The most amusing thing was to see the reaction of airport staff when I addressed them by name."

The Sun

that same instinct failed to warn me of the response of Hugh or his colleagues to the day's headlines on his "clean, harmless fun." For some reason they were not too keen to pass the time of day with me.

Scotland's *Daily Record*, sister paper of the English *Daily Mirror*, carried the story under a three-line banner heading, the pre-tabloid *Sun*, successor to the *Daily Herald,* headed a nine-inch two-column piece while the Scottish *Daily Express* gave it almost a full column. The Scottish *Daily Mail* and Manchester edition of the *Daily Mirror* gave it similar treatment.

It was at least a couple of weeks before the air of resentment cleared. No one raised the matter with me directly, but finally I was "reliably informed" that the Airport Commandant, Wally Waldron, who was well aware of the identity of Hugh's employers, had called the Scandinavian airline's Prestwick manager to his office and read him the riot act over misuse of rented airport facilities. In his turn the manager, John Young, had been obliged to discipline his deputy, Hugh Armstrong.

I had similarly miscalculated the reaction of a number of airline staff at Prestwick a year or two earlier and discovered, much to my discomfort, that Coventry was as accessible to Scottish outcasts as it was to English ex-communicants. In July 1962 the British Open golf championship was being played at Troon, Ayrshire, just along the coast from the Scottish transatlantic airport. As regular visitors to Scotland, the home of golf, many of the international competitors were well known to airport staff.

So I didn't find it surprising when one airgirl told me that she and a number of friends from the airport, all golf fans, were thinking of holding a "consolation" get-together for the 70 prominent professional and amateur golfers who had failed to qualify that year. Honey-haired Liz Robertson said that she and her friends, like her, all ground staff with the five international airlines, had agreed that they would host the party at her home alongside the airport.

"We didn't want to make it too formal by holding it in a hotel," she said, "After all quite a lot of us will be strangers to each other, even though we are all fans."

Among the golfers they planned to invite were several big names who had failed to play under 154 in the two qualifying rounds of the championship. They included former Scottish champion Bobby Walker, Spanish champion Angel Miguel, Australian Alan Murray, American Richard Davies, holder of the British amateur crown, and England amateur champion Mike Bonnalleck.

My story on the airport's invitation to the golfers was front-paged by the Glasgow *Evening Times* under the headline:

FANS HOLD 'OPEN' HOUSE FOR UNLUCKY 70

AN "open house" invitation to 70 unlucky golfers to attend a consolation get-together went out at Troon to-day from a group of sympathetic fans.

The unlucky 70 are those who failed to qualify for the British Open Championship when they scored over 154 in the two rounds at Old Troon and Lochgreen.

Their fans — and hosts at to-morrow night's party—are air girls and staff of five international air lines at Prestwick Airport.

The party will be in the home of one of the girls, honey-haired Elizabeth Robertson, in Links Road, Prestwick.

BIG NAMES

"We didn't want to make it too formal by holding it in a hotel," said Elizabeth, an air line receptionist at the airport. "We hope it will make people feel more at ease—after all, quite a lot of us will be strangers to one another."

Among the 70 non-qualifiers are several big golf names . . . like former Scottish champion Bobby Walker, Spanish champion Angel Miguel, Australian Alan Murray, American Richard Davies who holds the British amateur crown, and English amateur champion Mike Bonallack.

"This get together wasn't really my idea," said Elizabeth. "It was suggested by a friend and all of us at the airport thought it would be nice to make a gesture of this kind to some of the disappointed players.

"We would have liked the qualifiers to come too — but they will certainly want to stay fit for the championships."

Glasgow © Evening Times *July 11 1962*

The *Evening Citizen* also gave the story a hesitant mention, and the *Evening Times* concluded with another quote from Liz. "The idea wasn't mine," she said, "But all of us at the airport thought it would be nice to make a gesture of this kind to some of the disappointed players.

"We *would* like some of the qualifiers to come too. But they would certainly want to stay fit for the championship."

All quite innocent, I thought. And so, apparently, did the Glasgow papers. But Liz was furious with me. "That wasn't for publication," she spluttered when the papers appeared later that day. "It wasn't a serious suggestion... I was just thinking aloud. None of us had thought it through.

"And people could take it the wrong way – particularly that bit about the qualifiers wanting to stay fit."

Other fans agreed with Liz. "It all sounds a bit sordid and sleazy," protested one. "It makes us sound like camp followers. My boy friend was very upset when he read about the party. He knows I'm a big fan of golf. He 'phoned me and said he hoped I wasn't involved."

Liz didn't deny using the words, and I had to admit that the key phrase was open to misinterpretation. Though I thought the girls were over-reacting, I said I'd try to help if Liz agreed to "cancel" the party. "But you'll have to come up with a valid reason; one that's believable," I added. And I meant believable to the news desks, as well as their readers.

The solution took the form of my follow-up story in the *Evening Times* the following day, under the considerably reduced heading:

"Open" door is closed

A double "Open" disappointment for 70 unlucky golfers. The 70 – who failed to qualify for the final rounds of the "Open" at Troon on Tuesday night – were to be the guests tonight of five sympathetic airline girls from Prestwick.

But today the girls, who planned to throw a party for them in a Prestwick flat, called it off.

"Our shifts at the airport have been switched round and now it will be impossible to go with our plan," said Elizabeth Robertson, one of the girls. "We can only hope that the boys hear the party is off. It would be embarrassing all round if they turned up and found their hostesses missing."

It was to be the first and last time I'd had to "withdraw" a story. Either following or before publication.

"Open" door is closed

A double "Open" disappointment for 70 unlucky golfers.

The 70—who failed to qualify for the final rounds of the "Open" at Troon on Tuesday night—were to be the guests to-night of five sympathetic air line girls from Prestwick.

But to-day the girls, who planned to throw a party for them in a Prestwick flat, called it off.

"Our shifts at the airport have been switched round—and now it will be impossible to go with our plans," said Elizabeth Robertson, one of the girls.

"We only hope the boys hear that the party is off. It would be embarrassing all round if they turned up and found the hostesses missing.

"This is very unfortunate. We had been looking forward to the patry. But it can't be helped. we have our jobs to do."

Glasgow © Evening Times
July 12 1962

*

My own embarrassment was fortunately short-lived – thanks mainly to the airgirls' bosses, managers of the major Prestwick airlines. Led by John Young of the Scandinavian Airlines System and Harry Pusey of BOAC, the managers decided they would like to sponsor an annual Miss Prestwick Airport contest, and they needed someone to run it for them.

Harry and I already had a very good working relationship. We had both been posted to Prestwick from Heathrow within weeks of each other, so we were both new boys seeking acceptance in a Scottish working environment. Although we had never met previously in London, Harry had been primed well by his own PR people on Brenards' activities at Heathrow and was quite happy to talk to me both on and off-the-record on a range of matters.

So when he asked me to take on the organisation of the contest on behalf of the airlines, presumably by drawing on Brenards' experience with Miss London Airport, I accepted the challenge readily. He appeared either unaware or indifferent to my dented reputation among airline staff. I was possibly more concerned at that time about boosting our standing with the airline managements. And there would be the small matter of earning some linage from inside knowledge of the contest and its participants.

In practice, it fell to my deputy, Chris Bramwell, who did most of the organising and administrative work, and there was far more organisation involved that either he or I had bargained for. But without any previous personal experience of running a beauty-personality contest, he performed the role admirably. Much to Harry Pusey's delight, it was BOAC's Hazel Coatsworth who took the first Miss Prestwick Airport title, just as it had done eight years earlier for Brenards' first Miss London Airport contest. News of the event won huge slabs of coverage throughout the Scottish nationals. We were able to break the story of the seven pretty contestants when they were chosen by their companies two or three days before the big day. And on the day most of the papers responded to the airlines' invitation (through us) to send along their own photographers to cover the contest.

Chris won additional column inches for us when he arranged for the winner and her runner-up to attend the Miss London Airport contest a few weeks later as Brenards' guests-of-honour. But the airline bosses' long-term hopes of making the contest an annual event came to nothing. Eleven months later we had to report:

This year's Miss Prestwick Airport contest may have to be cancelled – because of shyness among the airport's personality-plus girls. The competition, first held last year, was fixed to be repeated next month. But so far none of the girls has returned an entry form...

AIRPORT'S SHY HOSTESSES HOLD UP A BEAUTY CONTEST

By Daily Mail Reporter

THIS year's contest for the title of "Miss Prestwick Airport" may have to be cancelled — because of shyness among the airport's personality-plus girls.

The competition, held for the first time last year has been fixed for early next month. But so far none of the girls has returned an entry form.

"We are not beauty queens—just ordinary girls," said one slim and attractive hostess.

Another added: "We have to parade before three judges and however many passengers and sightseers there are on the airport. It's all very embarrassing."

A third girl commented: "I think it causes jealousy among friends. It wouldn't be so bad if there were more airlines—that would mean more competitors. But, at the most, only eight girls can enter.

Girls eligible for the contest are those employed by the eight airline companies as ground hostesses at the airport. They are judged on their personality, deportment and grooming.

Last year station managers chose the girl to represent their airline. But this year the choice is being left to the girls themselves.

"I don't see why they should be embarrassed about appearing in front of members of the public since they do it every day," said an airline manager.

"They will be in uniforms—not bikinis."

The winner—last year it was BOAC receptionist Hazel Coatsworth, from Bridge of Weir, Renfrewshire—will be given a free flight to London.

She will be a special guest at the "Miss London Airport" contest.

Scottish Daily Mail

BLUSHING BEAUTIES

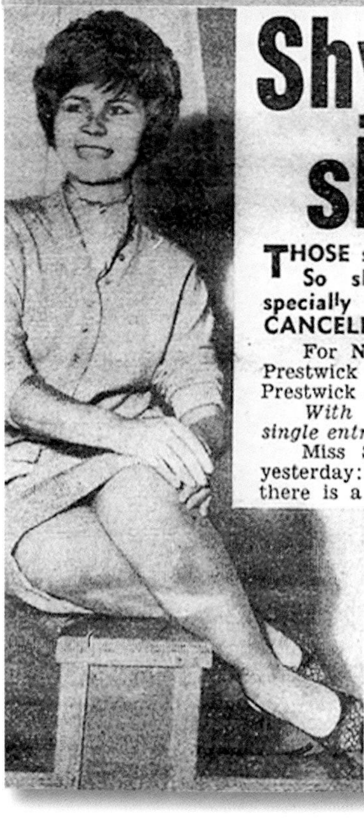

Shy air girls shun title

THOSE so-pretty air hostesses are shy, too. So shy that a beauty contest held specially for them may have to be CANCELLED.

For NOT ONE of the ground hostesses at Prestwick Airport seems to want the title "Miss Prestwick Airport."

With the contest two weeks away, not a single entry form has been handed in.

Miss S.A.S., 19-year-old Lynn Davies said yesterday: "We have discussed the matter and there is a definite reluctance to enter."

"We just don't want to do it. Most of the girls are shy."

SIGHTSEERS

Miss Caledonia Airways—24-year-old Elizabeth Ann Ross—said: "I was runner-up in the competition last year. But I will certainly not be entering this year."

A third girl said: "We have to parade before three judges and however many passengers and sightseers there are on the airport.

"It's all very embarrassing. We aren't beauty queens, just ordinary girls."

● *ELIZABETH ROSS: runner-up in last year's contest.*

Daily Record

SO-SHY AIR GIRLS CAUSE CONTEST HITCH

Scottish Daily Express

SHY GIRLS GROUND AIR CONTEST

Daily.Herald (all) Aug 17 1963

In reality, both Chris and I knew that the contest wouldn't work on an annual basis anyway. There simply weren't enough girls to take part. Only BOAC and SAS had more than one scheduled departure and arrival a day at Prestwick and even they had minimal staff. So the girls themselves were only too happy to admit, as the would-be Miss SAS did: "We have discussed the matter among ourselves and there is a definite reluctance to enter. We just don't want to do it. Most of the girls are shy."

The *Scottish Daily Express,* the *Scottish Daily Mail* and the *Daily Herald* all ran Chris's story, illustrated with pictures of the previous year's winner. The *Daily Record*, adding their own input and pictures, splashed it across a whole page, so we were able to salvage something from the saga.

It was fortunate for us, and a well-known television presenter, that another Scottish airgirl proved to be a little more adventurous and co-operative when we met up after a flight from London to Renfrew, at that time the city airport for Glasgow.

I was returning to Scotland after a brief visit to London and spotted the tall, pretty girl among my fellow passengers on the BEA flight. She was wearing the distinctive sky-blue uniform of Pan American Airways…and naturally my professional interest was aroused. The American airline had no staff in Scotland other than those at Prestwick, and I knew she was not one of those.

When I asked her what she was doing so far off base, the 5ft 8ins redhead replied in a Glasgow accent: "I'm coming home." She told me her name was Ella McCutcheon, she was a stewardess with Pan Am, one of a number recruited in the UK the previous year, and she was snatching a few days' leave between flights to visit her family in Scotland.

During the flight she had found herself sitting next to BBC television announcer and presenter Alex McIntosh, host of the long-running and popular ***"Come Dancing"*** programme, (revived by the BBC in a new, highly successful format in 2005). When she confessed to me that one of her ambitions was to watch the programme as a member of the studio audience, I told her rashly: "I'll see what I can do."

Quickly I sought out the TV host as he waited at a baggage belt and introduced myself. "That's very strange," he said. "During the flight we hardly exchanged a word. I wanted to ask her to join me on the show but it didn't seem right to ask a perfect stranger." Immediately he walked back with me – and invited 24-years-old Ella to be his guest on the show that evening.

I won their agreement to run the story and left them together as I hurried to a telephone. Prestwick was almost an hour's journey away by road and I didn't want to lose any time. I could only hope Chris was in the office so that I could dictate the story to him for circulation, something that would take too long from a call-box. But I'd also had an idea.

This was a story which cried out for pictures. What could I do about it? McIntosh and Ella were at that moment collecting their baggage from the flight. They both planned to take the airline 'bus into town, a journey time of about twenty minutes. Then they would part…until the show that evening. I decided I would have to break a golden Brenard rule. I telephoned the *Express* picture desk – with the offer of an exclusive.

The *Express* had to be my first choice. It would have been for almost any freelance, even if few of them could have said why. I gave them an outline of the story which I said would be coming to them shortly, then added: "If you hurry – you'll catch them both at the town terminal. And your pictures will be exclusive. No one else will know in time to do anything about it."

Then I called Chris, luckily found him in the Prestwick office and dictated my copy. I said I was on my way back – then told him what I'd done. "I even thought of offering them an exclusive on the story as well," I said, then, trying to justify myself added: "After all, this is a Renfrew story and we don't get a retainer for Renfrew.

"And anyway, as far as we're concerned, pictures are a bonus. There's no other way anyone could get pictures of the couple together in time for tomorrow's editions, so its better we sell the idea to one paper rather than none." Chris, I think, saw the sense of it, but in any case I was prepared to defend my decision if necessary. And as Brenards' Scottish manager, I told myself, I should be able to bend the rules if I thought it necessary.

When I arrived back at Prestwick, Chris had finished 'phoning round the nationals with the story. The *Daily Record* gave suitable prominence next day by making it the Page One

Air girl Ella gets a TV surprise

ALEX McINTOSH
invitation to the dance

A PRETTY air stewardess received an out-of-the-blue invitation yesterday to appear on television . . .

. . . a direct "please come dancing" from B.B.C. TV personality Alex McIntosh to be his guest in front of live cameras.

It happened because the girl, 24-year-old Ella McCutcheon, and Alex were sitting beside each other on the lunch-time B.E.A. flight from London to Renfrew.

Ella, who has been a Pan American stewardess since August, was going home to Viewpark, Uddingston, Lanarkshire, for a two-day "between flights" break.

'Courage'

Alex was bound for the Mecca Ballroom, Glasgow, to compere the Glasgow v. Amsterdam contest on "Come Dancing" last night.

They said hardly a word during the 70-minute flight, but at Renfrew Airport when mutual friends formally introduced them Alex said, a trifle shamefaced:

"I have been trying to pluck up courage to ask this young lady to join me on the show.

"We usually try to get a pretty girl to sit with me during the dancing. Ella semed the ideal choice—but somehow it didn't seem right to invite a complete stranger to sit out the dance with me."

Scots lose

Tall, willowy Ella, a former model, replied: "I'd love to appear on the show. I've never been on television before."

She saw Glasgow beaten by Amsterdam by 96 points to 103.

Among the ballroom dancers representing Glasgow were Bob Dewar and Maureen Alexander, Diana Kay and James Harper, and Andrew Cowan and Margaret Mathieson.

INVITATION

OUT of the blue yesterday came an invitation for 24-year-old Glasgow air-line stewardess **Ella McCutcheon** to star on TV—a direct and personal "please come dancing" request from B.B.C. screen personality **Alex McIntosh** to be his guest in front of the live cameras.

McIntosh and tall, willowy, former model Ella, of Viewpark, Uddingston, Glasgow, were fellow passengers in the lunch-time Vanguard flight from London.

'Come dancing' invitation in mid-air

AN invitation to "Come dancing" on TV came like a bolt out of the blue for an air hostess yesterday.

Former model Ella McCutcheon, of View Park, Uddingston, Glasgow, was on a flight from London—and sat next to BBC TV personality Alex Mackintosh.

They hardly exchanged a word. But as they waited to collect their luggage at Renfrew Airport they were introduced and Alex issued his invitation.

Taking their coach-seats to drive to Glasgow's Mecca Ballroom, the usually never-lost-for-the-right-words BBC man confessed a little shamefacedly:

"I had been trying to pluck up courage to ask the young lady to go on the show.

"But somehow it didn't seem right or proper to invite a complete stranger."

Scottish Daily Mail ***Daily Record*** ***(all) May 8 1962*** ***Daily Herald***

second lead story with a single-column portrait of McIntosh. The *Scottish Daily Mail* used it on their diary page; the *Daily Herald* a slightly shorter five column inches.

The *Express* gave the story the full, half-page treatment under their regular ***Photo News*** feature. Their heading, across six columns:

Ella keeps a TV date

Daily Express picture, May 8 1962

introduced their own two oversized pictures, one a full-length leggy pose by Ella, together with a street shot of McIntosh apparently "chatting-up" his pretty guest. It couldn't have looked more like an *Express* exclusive. They must have sent a reporter along to the air terminal as well as their photographer. Their ***Photo News*** story contained none of my copy, other than basic details.

The *Express* accountants obviously believed the story was the exclusive property of the paper. When the newspaper payments came in a month later, I eagerly ran my eye through the story credits to see what the "beat" had been worth to them. The story wasn't even shown in the statement. They hadn't paid us a single penny either for the exclusive advance tip-off or for the dictated story they shared with our other clients. In the end, it was to be weeks before the *Express* acknowledged a claim from me with a retrospective, and standard payment.

So much for exclusives… and bending the rules. But not a typical failing of the *Express*.

*

Although I had known the chief mourner for several years and was acquainted with the "family," the death of Fred came as a complete surprise to me. Indeed, I wasn't even aware of his existence until his death. For Fred was just a budgerigar – though a budgerigar with friends among airline ground staff and aircrews from around the world. Well, around Europe anyway. His home was a large British European Airways office in the Queens

Building at Heathrow, an office visited regularly by BEA flying staff and the crews of a number of foreign European airlines handled by the British company. which is why they were friends.

Fred had the free flight of that office for almost a year, only returning to his cage in the corner for refreshment. Until he made that fatal error of the feathered flyer, mistaking the clear glass pane of a closed door as open "skies." While flying a fast circuit, he tried frantically to pull out of his dive towards the glass at the last moment, only to crash headlong into an adjoining wall. Fred died instantly in a flurry of green feathers.

Telexed messages of sympathy poured in from French, German, Belgian, Greek and Spanish aircrews who had paused awhile to say "Hello" to Fred during their brief visits to Heathrow. Several posies of flowers too were delivered to the office. But no one thought to tell either me or my colleagues of the tragedy. I was alerted only by a plaintive lament on mouth-organ, guitar and drum as a gathering of mourners passed by the Queens Building press room to make their way to a grassy bank at the edge of the tarmac.

Following the slowly-moving throng, I found that more than sixty staff from the BEA offices in the building had given up their lunch breaks to attend Fred's funeral. Dozens more joined in from other offices and airport departments. And there at the head of the procession, was Fred, lying in state in a miniature coffin, covered in black silk and carried aloft by four bearers.

Traffic halted as the procession crossed an airside airport road to reach the grassy patch. The announcer in the public enclosure roof gardens, three stories above, described the scene to curious sightseers lining the parapets. And as Fred was laid to rest in a place prepared for him, top-hatted Dudley Foy, the chief mourner, gave a brief address and read out the "will."

Fred's keepers and owners, BEA clerks Peter and Arthur White, were appointed executors, with Fred's cage left for the use of a successor. Birdseed was scattered over the burial ground and a marble headstone, professionally engraved "In memory of a favourite budgie," was set up over the grave.

The funeral was all over in minutes. The mourners returned, some lunch-less, some tearfully, I was assured, to their desks. As far as I know, Fred was never replaced by a successor. Chief mourner Dudley Foy went on to become, some years later, a media relations manager for British Airways. The public announcer, Flo Kingdon, had a similar role in the public relations' office of the British Airports Authority (and became a member of my team when I switched jobs). Neither had thought to tell the press of the funeral plan. Dudley's response, when I chided him about this was: "I had no idea you'd be interested. It was a very private affair."

It was also a silly season story widely welcomed by the nationals, all of whom gave it prominent coverage the next day.

DEATH OF THE VIP BUDGIE

AIRPORT STOPS FOR FRED

FRED, London Airport's favourite budgie, was buried near a runway yesterday as hundreds of spectators stood in silence.

Fred, two years old, went on his last flight on Friday. He was doing a fast circuit round the huge BEA office where he lived when he crashed into a wall and was killed.

Messages of sympathy poured in from air crews from all over the world.

Yesterday 60 airline staff stood bareheaded as four pall-bearers carried Fred to his grave. Bird seed was sprinkled over the tiny coffin.

Spectators in the public enclosure — there to watch the planes — were given a running commentary over the loud-speakers.

Then a top-hatted mourner read out Fred's will leaving the cage to his successor—if any.

Daily Herald

A GUITAR PLAYS FAREWELL TO FRED

Express Staff Reporter

SIXTY British European Airways employees lined the tarmac at London Airport yesterday to say good-bye to Fred.

Messages of sympathy were still coming in from French, German, Spanish, and Greek airline crews.

For Fred, a two-year-old budgie, made many friends during the year he lived in the B.E.A. offices.

On Friday, while flying a fast circuit round the huge office, Fred crashed into a wall and was killed.

Surrounded by flowers he lay in state during the week-end.

Yesterday his tiny coffin was carried out by four bearers. Two mourners played a lament on a guitar and mouth-organ.

THE WILL

The bearers halted at a patch of grass near the tarmac. Seed was sprinkled over the grave as the airline staff stood bare-headed.

Then Mr. Dudley Foy, mourner-in-chief, in a black topper, produced Fred's will. Appointing as executors his joint-owners, B.E.A. clerks Peter and Arthur White, he left his cage to be used by his successors, if any.

A marble slab headstone professionally engraved "In memory of Fred, our favourite budgie," was set up over the grave.

Daily Express

Airport turns out to mourn budgie

Daily Sketch Reporter

SILENCE descended over the hundreds of spectators lining the parapet of London Airport yesterday . . . silence for the funeral of Fred the budgerigar.

All eyes turned down to the huge gathering of airport staff at the edge of the tarmac, 80 feet below.

A woman announcer gave a commentary over the loudspeakers on the last moments of the airport pet.

Fred lived in the BEA office for 11 months. On Friday, while flying a fast circuit round the huge office, he crashed into a wall and was killed.

Messages of sympathy poured in from French, German, Belgian, Greek and Spanish airline air-crews and ground staff.

Dozens more came from other airport departments —many of them with flowers.

Since his death, Fred, surrounded by flowers, "lay in state" in an airline office.

In silence

After a lament played on a guitar and a mouth organ, the tiny coffin was carried by four bearers to a patch of grass alongside the tarmac.

Seed was sprinkled over the grave. And then 60 airline staff stood bareheaded in silence.

Tears appeared in the eyes of at least one by-stander.

Mr. Dudley Foy, mourner in chief, in his black topper, produced Fred's will.

Appointing as executors his joint owners, BEA clerks Peter and Arthur White, he left his cage to be used by his successors, if any.

A marble slab headstone, professionally engraved "in memory of Fred, our favourite budgie," was set up over the grave.

Not even Cock Robin could have boasted such a fond farewell.

Daily Sketch (all) August 18 1958

60 MOURNERS FOR FRED THE BUDGIE

By ANNE LLOYD

SIGHTSEERS on the roof gardens of London Airport stared yesterday at a little group of people walking slowly along to the sound of mournful music. . . .

On a large board, carried by four airline workers in the centre of the group, lay a tiny coffin covered with black silk.

A woman announcer stopped announcing flights to explain solemnly: "The scene below is the funeral of Fred. . . ."

Fred was a BUDGERIGAR, the friend of aircrews and airline officials from all over the world. He lived in a British European Airways office at the airport.

He died there on Friday —trying to fly through a glass door panel.

Typed messages of sympathy began to pour in from French, German, Belgian, Greek and Spanish aircrews and ground staff who used to say "Hello" to Fred.

Posies of flowers arrived, too.

Yesterday, airport employees Arthur Searle and Dudley Foy played a plaintive lament on harmonica and drum as the funeral procession, sixty strong, marched out to a grass patch beside the tarmac.

Hats and caps were removed. Seed was sprinkled on the grave. A headstone engraved "In Memory of Fred" was set up.

His 'Will'

An address in praise of Fred said he was "A cheerful bird who brought something of sunshine and pleasure to a lot of people."

Then Dudley Fox produced Fred's "will," appointing his joint owners, B.E.A. clerks Peter and Arthur White, as his executors. He left his cage to his "successor" and his birdseed to be "scattered for the benefit of other birds."

His successor has not been found yet. But there will be one. . . .

Arthur Searle said: "His funeral started as a semi-humorous thing. But with all those messages and flowers and things, we were all quite overcome in the end."

***Daily Mirror* Aug 18 1958**

Poor Fred the budgie

AIR-CREWS, ground staff, and employees from 12 different airlines at London Airport yesterday attended the funeral of Fred, a two-year-old green budgerigar who found his home in the the BEA office.

Fred was killed when he flew into a wall. He was carried in a special coffin to a grave near the tarmac.

Messages of sympathy poured in from French, German, Greek, and Spanish air-crews, and some mourners wept.

Daily Mail (right) Aug 18 1958

"AIRPORT STOPS FOR FRED" said the *Daily Herald.* **"A GUITAR PLAYS FAREWELL TO FRED"** ran the *Daily Express.* The *Daily Sketch* gave the story over four columns, and the *Mirror* gave it a full ten-column inches.

More significantly, perhaps, it became one of those few stories which years later always seem to crop up in conversation whenever former airport colleagues come together. And, silly and sentimental as it is, it still pleases me to be able to say: "Yes. I reported that."

CHAPTER TEN

Parking in the yard to the rear of Brenards, I made my way through the back door into the news room. It was some twenty minutes after 11 pm on an early spring night in 1962. The solitary late-shift copy-roomer was seated at the news desk, his feet up, reading a paperback. Both of us had experienced a boring evening with no news for me to dictate or for him to circulate.

He looked up, then swung his feet to the floor guiltily. I slipped into the opposite chair. "Okay, off you go, old chap. I'll lock up," I said.

The teenager willingly wished me goodnight, and leaving by the front door, slammed it behind him. Instead of signing off by 'phone, I'd driven over to Brenards' Bath Road office from the Central Terminal area at Heathrow. I wanted to check the following day's diary and run through the final editions of the evening newspapers before driving home. As I was on early next day, I would still be on call overnight as duty reporter. But as the last editions of the dailies were already being put to bed, I expected to be doing the same shortly afterwards.

Reaching for the *Star*, *Standard* and *News*, I turned my attention to the mini-switchboard at the end of the long desk, flicking off lines routed through to extensions. Almost at that moment, one of the news desk telephones shattered the silence. Grudgingly, I looked at my watch. What could anyone want at this time? I lifted the receiver with my left hand, automatically reaching for a pencil with my right, but before I could speak, the caller whispered gruffly:

"Don't say anything. Just listen.

"There's a bomb aboard your service to Canada tonight

A pause. "Yes?" I said, prompting. "I understand. Which flight? The time, the flight number?" And, desperately: "Who is that?"

There was no response. The telephone was suddenly slammed down. I held the receiver to my ear for a moment as I glanced at the switchboard. Then I hung up. The call had come in on Brenards' main line – SKYport 1234 in the old letter/number style. But not for a moment did I believe it was meant for us. The number for Heathrow at the time was misleadingly similar... SKYport 4321.

The message was vague, too vague to mean anything, so it was almost certainly a hoax. But I could take no chances. Hoax or real wasn't a decision for me to make. I would have to act on it. Wearily I picked up the phone again. I was not going to be driving home just yet.

I was aware there was only one Canada-bound flight due out, the last service from Terminal 3 before Heathrow operations were halted for the night. The daily BOAC service to Montreal, via Manchester and Prestwick, was due off in less than an hour. Its passengers could already be in Departures. I called BOAC on an airport line and asked for the passenger duty officer. Not the most senior airline official available, but one who would probably know me.

He answered my call immediately. I was doubly lucky. The duty officer was someone I knew well. George August had been a passenger officer with the airline at Poole Marine Airport during my apprenticeship twenty years earlier, and we had renewed contact when he was later posted to Heathrow. He listened intently as I outlined exactly what had happened. There wasn't much to tell.

He asked me a couple of questions about the caller, which of course I was unable to answer. Then he asked: "Are you doing a story on this?"

I didn't hesitate. "I honestly can't answer that either, at the moment, George," I said, "It depends on what happens next. I'll have to stand by, but at the moment I think it's pretty unlikely."

There was nothing more I could do for the present. If I had to stay, I might as well be at the centre of the action. Switching off the news room lights, I abandoned the office, and locking up behind me, returned to my car parked at the rear. I drove as quickly as I dared back to Terminal 3 and parked in the almost empty car park alongside.

The terminal was a hive of activity. Passengers for the Canadian flight buzzed round the check-in desks seeking information.

Some who had already cleared through passport controls were being escorted back to the ticket desk area. Police were everywhere, though this was many years before the days of heightened security against terrorist threats. X-ray surveillance of baggage was undreamed of, and I knew that any searches would have to be manual, tedious and time-consuming.

I made my way to the BOAC duty-room and sought out George. He confirmed to me that all the baggage destined for the Canada flight was being assembled on the tarmac apron a safe distance from the aircraft. Some had already been loaded but every single piece would have to be identified and claimed by individual passengers, then checked and perhaps opened before being allowed into the hold.

"It could be hours before we're satisfied – if there isn't an explosion in the meantime" he told me. He asked me again about the 'phone call and told me he'd passed my name on to the police. Then he added: "The police wanted to know why *you* were called. Do you have any ideas? Do you think they did it to make sure they got publicity?"

I said I thought it unlikely. I pointed out that we were only known on the airport and within the newspaper world. If the caller had been a disgruntled member of the airport staff, he or she would have been more specific about the flight details. I said I thought it was far more likely it was a caller who confused our telephone number with that of the airport.

As I made my way back to the check-in area, a police sergeant called me over. "Phone call for you," he said from behind an empty desk, and added as he handed over the receiver: "It's the airport manager."

Leslie Green I had known for years too. He had been airport manager at Northolt Airport back in the fifties,[1] and was an old friend of ours. His opening, I think, was meant as a joke.

New airport manager

Mr. Leslie Green, 43, has been appointed airport manager at London Airport. Here he is in the control-tower. Mr. Green was an officer in the Royal Air Force during the war.

Evening Standard picture September 1956

"Making your own news now, Ray?"

So word had obviously got back to him, via BOAC and the police whom the airline had quickly alerted, that I had taken the "bomb" warning. He asked me to outline briefly what had happened. I repeated everything I had told George August. I also told him about the possible confusion over our telephone number. Then, echoing the BOAC duty officer's question, "Are you reporting this?" Leslie added: "You are aware of our agreement, aren't you?"

He was referring to an agreement the Civil Aviation Ministry said they had recently reached with the (then) Newspaper Proprietors' Association and with the *Press Association* over the non-publication of bomb warnings. (Many civil servants and others who should have known better always seemed to regard the latter as a representative body rather than the commercial news agency it is in reality. For all I know they probably still do).

In fact few of the news desks we talked to seemed to be aware of any agreement. *PA* themselves told us on more than one occasion that there was no such agreement, nor was one likely. They did concede that there had been discussions, arising from indications that publicity given to bomb warnings were frequently followed by a spate of copycat hoax calls. But there was concern on the part of the news media that any voluntary censorship of this kind would be difficult to guarantee. And as David Chipp, the *Press Association's* chief news editor put it: "Where does it leave us if we ignore a warning because someone decides it's a hoax and there really is a bomb after all?"

I wasn't going to get into a discussion on this occasion. I simply repeated to Leslie my earlier comments. "It's very late, and at the moment there doesn't seem to be a story for me," I said. But I added, "I'm sure you'll understand that like everyone else, I may have to wait for the all-clear before I can commit myself completely."

My wait was not as long as I believed it might be. BOAC and the police completed a thorough search of baggage in record time, and less than two hours after my telephone call the airline announced that the flight was about to leave. I stayed on until the airliner finally took off.

This was shortly before my posting to Scotland, where I was to spend the next eight years. Two or three months and a couple of other unrelated bomb hoaxes later I was passing the time of day with Harry Pusey, BOAC's newly appointed manager at Prestwick Airport. Somehow the subject of bomb warnings came up in conversation.

"There are few aircraft delays that worry passengers more," he mused, "I suppose it's

[1] *See Chapter 2, p.19*

because there is a lingering fear that something might have been missed in a search. And I can speak from personal experience. It happened to me not so long ago."

I looked at him, half convinced I knew what was coming. "It was the day I took up this post. My wife and I had checked in for the late night flight to Montreal, as it was the easiest way to get to Prestwick. Then some idiot apparently phoned to say there was a bomb on the flight..." I felt obliged to tell him who passed on the idiot's message.

There had been several international incidents earlier in the 1950s involving bombing attempts and some actual attacks on aircraft – most notably in Britain, that on a Paris-bound British European Airways Viking airliner.[1] But it was several years before the "bomb hoax" calls became common place, and of serious concern to the airlines and security authorities. It was widely believed that it was a Hollywood film, *"Cry Terror,"* starring Rod Steiger and featuring a telephone warning by an aircraft bomber, which set off the first of such patterns.

Shortly after the opening of the film in London, in June 1958, a scare call was received at Heathrow. It forced a Swissair flight back to London. A few days later a German airliner also had to turn back soon after take-off, and a BEA flight was delayed on the ground for a full search.

Six weeks later, after the film had gone on nation-wide release, a caller told a switchboard operator at Manchester Airport; "There's a bomb in one of your 'planes." Immediately, a Viscount airliner bound for Palma, Majorca, requested emergency landing facilities at London Airport. Other flights, heading for Jersey and Dublin, turned back. More aircraft were delayed at Birmingham and London for searches to be carried out.

SEVEN AIRLINERS IN 'BOMB' HUNT

Holiday planes are searched after hoax

Seven airliners were searched at London, Manchester and Birmingham today after someone telephoned Manchester's Ringway airport and said in a muffled voice: "There is a bomb on an airliner." No bomb was found and a British European Airways official at Birmingham said: "The report was a hoax."

A Viscount flying from Manchester to Majorca with seven passengers, including two schoolgirls and an elderly woman, was diverted to London Airport.

Fire engines and police cars raced out to meet the airplane as it landed.

It was isolated from the passenger building and other parked airliners at a runway junction. While the fire engines stood by, the passengers got off and were driven to a lounge. Their luggage was searched.

A second Viscount was being brought in to continue the journey.

50-minute hold-up

Another Viscount was searched at Elmdon Airport, Birminham. The aircraft was bound for Dusseldorf, via Birmingham. It left Manchester with only three passengers on board.

"The report that there was a bomb aboard appears to have been a hoax," said a British European Airways official.

Warning Halts Three Airports

PLANES STOPPED AFTER 'BOMB ABOARD' ALERT

AIRLINERS were searched at three airports in Britain to-day after someone telephoned Manchester Airport and said in a muffled voice: "There is a bomb on an airliner."

The man, who telephoned Ringway Airport, did not say which plane. He rang off after giving his warning.

Shortly before he made the call a BEA Viscount with seven passengers—they included two schoolgirls and an elderly woman—had set off for Palma, Majorca.

Another plane, belonging to AER Lingus, with 32 passengers, had also set out for Dublin. Signals were sent out to the pilots.

The Viscount was directed to London Airport and the Irish plane was ordered back.

Firemen, crash tendors and police, reinforced from forces nearby, stood by to search the planes.

Evening Standard Page One lead (above) Evening News (left) (both) Aug 19 1958

[1] *See Chapter 3, p. 77-78*

'BOMB ON PLANE' SCARE

AN anonymous telephone call to Ringway Airport, Manchester, today started a bomb scare there, at Birmingham and in London.

The caller said in a muffled voice: "There is a bomb on an airliner."

An Aer Lingus Manchester-to-Dublin plane was called back to **Ringway** and four other planes there were searched.

At **London** Airport fire engines and police cars raced to meet a four-engined Viscount airliner diverted following the warning.

Luggage check

The Viscount, flying the holiday route from Ringway to Palma, Majorca, was radioed by BEA.

Passengers disembarked and were driven to a lounge where their luggage was searched.

Experts boarded the Viscount to carry out a close search of the cabin and hold.

Star *Aug 19 1958*

Nothing was found. But as BEA told me: "We dare not ignore these calls. The amount of time and effort involved in carrying out searches is expensive and operationally disruptive, and passengers have been seriously inconvenienced. But most of them would rather be inconvenienced than dead or injured, however angry it makes them feel against the hoaxer."

The Government too, took the matter seriously enough to call in Scotland Yard for help, and it was suggested that it was on their advice that the co-operation of the news media was sought in not publicising the bomb warnings. But within a few days there came a break through. A young woman was arrested and charged with misuse of a telephone by making an anonymous malicious telephone call. The woman, it was discovered, worked for one of the major airlines at Heathrow.

In court, the woman, a ground receptionist, admitted making the call to a colleague "for a joke." Police said in evidence that about 40 such hoax calls had been made to Heathrow during the year. The woman was fined just £10, with £6 5s costs – but lost her job.

It wasn't only in Britain, of course, that such hoaxes were a problem. In the United States a series of incidents continued throughout the 1960s involving international airlines, and because of America's leading position in civil aviation, many of these frightening and malicious warnings had an echo in other parts of the world.

In the Spring of 1968 a domestic tiff between an American married couple in their Chicago home led to an international bomb alert as four major airports on two continents were put on an emergency standby. At an angry parting, the wife told her husband she was leaving him and taking a 'plane to London. In retaliation, the husband telephoned the Chicago Airport to claim: "I've put a bomb on the London-bound flight."

Several hours later the man repeated his warning to a local telephone operator, adding: "Now I'm shooting myself." The operator heard the double report of a gun, then silence.

The first alert had come just as BOAC Flight 568 was leaving Chicago Airport for Montreal en route to London, England. Unknown to other passengers, security men

AGAIN—'A bomb in plane'

POLICE HUNT HOAXER AFTER HIS FOURTH CALL IN SIX WEEKS

Express Air Reporter PETER WOON

A BOMB-HAPPY hoaxer who may also be a film fan put an airport into a panic yesterday—for the fourth time in six weeks.

He rang Manchester's Ringway at 10.15 a.m. and told the switchboard operator in a muffled voice: "There's a bomb in one of your planes."

[**COINCIDENCE**: In the film "Cry Terror," now showing at four Manchester cinemas, Rod Steiger phones an airline company: "There's a bomb on your plane—follow instructions or it will go off."]

Immediately crash, fire and ambulance services at Ringway were told to stand by.

A B.E.A. Viscount which had just taken off for Palma was diverted to London. Aircraft heading for Jersey and Dublin were turned back. And another Viscount flying to Dusseldorf was delayed at Birmingham.

Luggage searched

Passengers were asked to leave all the airliners. They and their luggage were searched outside any possible danger area.

At London, Palma-bound passengers were transferred to another aircraft and took off one and a half hours behind time. Birmingham passengers were delayed 50 minutes.

But nothing was found.

Said a B.E.A. spokesman at London Airport: "Nothing ever is. The trouble is, we dare not ignore these calls."

In the last six weeks the hoaxer has forced Swiss and German airline planes to turn back to London Airport and delayed a B.E.A. flight.

Yard called in

The B.E.A. spokesman said: "Perhaps things got too hot for him down here so he is now turning his attention to Manchester."

[**COINCIDENCE**: "Cry Terror" was being shown in London before the first of the scare calls.]

An order for a police hunt for the hoaxer has gone out from the Ministry of Transport and Civil Aviation.

A Ministry official said last night: "We regard this as a very serious and expensive business and have called in Scotland Yard.

"The difficulty is that all the calls are made from public phone boxes and are so short they are difficult to trace."

[**DIFFERENCE** between fact and fiction: in the film there *IS* a bomb on the plane.]

Daily Express *Aug 20 1958*

checked every piece of luggage, including that of the man's wife after she had been identified from the flight reservations list. Nothing was found and at last the British Super VC10 jet was allowed to take-off. The wife stayed aboard while police tried to trace her husband.

The second of his calls came when the airliner was already high over the Atlantic. This time the caller identified himself to the operator before saying he was turning the gun on himself. When she heard the shots, the operator contacted Montreal Airport, which the man named as the airliner's last port of call. Unaware of the earlier incident at Chicago, BOAC's Canadian staff flashed urgent coded signals ahead to London. And officials at Heathrow decided to divert the airliner to its nearest UK airport, Prestwick, on the Scottish coast.

There a full scale "explosives emergency" was called. Civil police, fire engines and ambulances raced in the join the airport emergency units and a local bomb disposal squad was asked to stand by.

When the airliner finally touched down in the early hours of the morning, it was chased along the runway by fire engines and directed to a little-used corner of the airport. More than a hundred passengers and the crew of ten were disembarked and taken to the terminal building. Called from my bed by an airport contact, I found them there after my 15-mile drive. More importantly – I learnt the details of the international alert from friends in BOAC.

Before another full-scale search could be initiated, further signals were flashed from Montreal. Police had traced the husband and found him unhurt. Only then had he admitted that his calls were a hoax. Passengers on the flight were almost all ignorant of the drama. Said one: "I only learned of the bomb warning when I enquired about the reasons for the delay."

After 90 minutes and yet another baggage search, which airline staff described as "routine and superficial," the airliner eventually left for London. There the woman passenger at the centre of the drama was told of her husband's confession. Said the BOAC man: "We don't know if she is planning to return to him."

In none of these cases, as far as I am aware, did we have any official assistance from the police in gathering information. We had to rely entirely on our own sources – which fortunately, of course, included personal contacts among individual police officers.

Up to the mid-seventies, policing of civil airports was the responsibility of the Ministry of Transport and Civil Aviation Constabulary, with its poor training, limited powers of arrest and authority, and unsuitable uniforms and equipment which failed to do anything to promote an image of competence and authority.

We suspected too that even the Ministry's Press Relations office had failed to win the confidence of their own police. We were regularly being told: "The police won't tell us.... For their part, individual police officers complained that neither the Press nor the public took them seriously. They were well aware of the "Keystone Cops" tag pinned on them by airport staff, and a frequently-heard taunt by public lawbreakers and wrongdoers when challenged was: "Who do you think you are? You're not a real policeman...."

In court defendants would regularly take the line: "I didn't realise he was a policeman, your honour." Questioned further it was usually a case of: "The uniform didn't look like a policeman's," or more vaguely: "He didn't have the authority of a policeman."

It wasn't until Parliament decreed that policing of the airports would in the future be the responsibility of local civil forces that official relations with the news media and recognition by the public began to improve, and even then it was a slow process. Until then, your average airport constable with his high collared tunic jacket and his basic peaked cap with its simplistic "MTCA" badge had to battle constantly for recognition.

In 1957 I was able to report that police constables at London Airport were requesting the issue of helmets to replace their "bus conductor" peaked caps. "Foreign visitors expect to see a bobby when they leave their planes," one of them told me. Fifteen years were to pass before they finally won their argument.

In addition to being the proverbial law unto themselves the police were often their own worst enemies in their naïvety over the need to maintain public credibility. In December 1955 I couldn't resist reporting – though merely for my local paper gossip column – the police "investigation" of an incident of petty theft of a colleague's personal property.

Learning that a raincoat and a pair of kid gloves had disappeared from the London Airport press room, the Ministry policeman, pencil poised over notebook, asked the owner: "Do you want to report this as a theft? It will mean so much paper-work."

Puzzled, my colleague, Ray Barnes, asked him to explain. "Well," replied the policeman, "If you don't know it was actually stolen..." he paused conspiratorially, "...we would only need to report a simple loss. I could record that as missing property."

When we'd all recovered our breath, I called our friendly neighbourhood inspector for an explanation. His comment: "It's true a bit more paper work is involved for stolen property than for careless loss. But I'm surprised at the officer's comment. Most of us prefer to deal with larceny than loss of property. It gives us something to work on."

Another detective certainly found something to work on when he looked into the same press room in response to another case of reported theft – or loss. While his colleague scribbled down a description of the missing items, he passed the time idly pressing the coin-return "Button B" of every one of a row of old-style public telephones provided for the use of visiting news media, in the apparent hope of finding the odd abandoned coin.

He'd almost reached the end of the line before he realised who he was supposed to be as he caught the questioning eye of the victim of the crime, still dutifully answering his colleague's questions. And my column pondered on what the policeman would have done with any unused coins the telephones might have coughed up for him.

Air bomb hoax: Woman gets summons

By ARTHUR TIETJEN

A WOMAN airline receptionist at London Airport has been served with a summons under the Post Office Act which is returnable at Feltham Magistrates' Court on September 25.

The summons is understood to relate to an anonymous telephone call received at the airport which spoke of a bomb being placed in an airliner.

Daily Mail, circa Aug 1958

Airport bomb hoax —girl accused

By Robert Traini

AN attractive young woman employed at London Airport is to appear in court over an anonymous phone call alleging that a bomb had been placed in an airliner.

She was interviewed by Ministry of Civil Aviation police who for months have been investigating "there is a bomb in a plane" calls to Scotland Yard and to the airport.

Telephone operators who took the calls reported that on at least one occasion a hoax call was made by a woman.

Every time one of the "bomb" calls was made planes were temporarily grounded and a careful inspection made. On one occasion recently four planes were held up.

The woman has been summoned under Section 66 of the Post Office Act, 1953, in connection with one anonymous call to the airport. The summons will be heard at Feltham, Middlesex, on September 25.

Daily Herald, circa Aug 1958

It was just a few weeks after this latest episode that my news desk passed on a message for me. Someone had called from the airport police station (in reality two or three offices in a block of single-storey 'pre-fab' accommodation) asking me to call in to see a detective superintendent.

That sounded very promising, and intriguing. On the rare occasions that senior police officers made contact with us it was during some newsworthy incident or an event involving a VIP arrival or departure. Usually it was just to pass the time of day or to require us to "move back there." And sometimes it was to pass on a morsel of information which, for their own reasons or satisfaction they wanted to see in print. I wasn't aware of a single occasion when any one of us had been invited to the inner sanctum.

So, as I hadn't anything better to occupy my time, I made my way to the police offices immediately. In an outer office were two plainclothes detectives, with one of whom I was already acquainted.

"Morning," I said, confidently. "I understand someone wants to see me. A senior detective? Didn't get his name..."

The officer moved away from his desk. "Oh, yes," he repeated. "Detective Superintendent ..." He gave a name. "He's in his office. I'll just see if he's free."

With that he made his way to another door, and without glancing back, entered. He emerged a second later, and, expressionless, motioned me past him through the open door. A stocky, grey-haired man in a brown pinstripe suit sat behind a desk. He wasn't smiling when he looked up.

"I'm going to have your guts for garters, my lad," was his unexpected greeting.

I was so stunned, surprised by his aggressive manner, that my mouth must have dropped open in astonishment. He realised he had the advantage. He wasn't going to let go now. He proceeded to verbally lambast me, threatening, abusing me in some of the foulest language I'd heard since my Army days. As, minute after minute, his tirade continued, I tried in vain to butt in, demanding to know what was behind all this...until gradually, between the invective and the attempted intimidation, the essence of his complaint against me became clearer.

He was furious at the way I had "made fun" of his officers. And he was determined to put me in my place. But I'd had enough. I blew my top. Slamming my fist down on his desk I shouted: "Shut up, for God's sake! Who do you think you are talking to? I'm not some kid you've caught scrumping, you know. Have you gone quite mad?" (I earnestly believed at that moment he had). I went on:

"Don't you realise you're simply reinforcing anything I might have written in ridiculing some of you? I had no idea it was all down to you. Now you're simply showing your true worth, you silly little man." Suddenly his bluster subsided. His threats took on a new edge. Getting up from his chair, he leaned towards me and pointing a finger at me, said quietly: "I'm going to run you off this airport faster than your legs will carry you. So fast in fact your feet won't touch the ground."

But by now my fury had dissipated, along with anger at myself for having fallen into the trap of answering his summons in the first place. Though still shaking with frustration at my being unable to return blow for blow, his penny-dreadful clichés meant I could now laugh dismissively.

"You haven't anything to say to me that is worth listening to," I rejoined. "I find you very sad and a bit pathetic. And I don't suppose you've even considered how this little charade might look in print, either, have you?"

With that I deliberately turned my back on him and walked out, ignoring his parting shout: "Who said you could go? I haven't done with you yet." As I looked across the room at his two deputies, standing, open mouthed, I managed a grin and said: "Good morning, gentlemen. You really ought to have something done about him."

I walked back to the terminal buildings feeling pleased with myself, even though I was now thinking of a dozen more retorts I might have offered. Not for a moment did I consider going into print with the incident; I regarded it as a personal issue, and one, which I could put down to another experience in life.

My only regret is not knowing what the Detective Superintendent thought afterwards. I might have discovered just that if I'd been prepared to fly into his web a second time.

It was several months later. I was standing at the north side passenger buffet one morning drinking a cup of coffee when I turned round and caught the eye of Detective Sergeant Bert Dobbs, one of the two junior officers who had manned that outer police office. My favourite Super was seated beside him. He too spotted me. With his free hand he carefully crooked his finger at me then pointed to the floor at his feet – a distinct summons to "Come here. Now." In response, I just as deliberately repeated the gesture back to him, with one difference.

Vengefully, I continued the movement of my index finger, bringing it back up after pointing to the floor, but converting it to an unmistakeable two-finger "V" sign. Then I turned my back on him.

I never saw or spoke to the Super again. But I did speak of him and his manner to his opposite number on the uniform side of the constabulary, Superintendent Goldsack. I asked him what he thought about his plainclothes colleague. "Why?" he asked, "Have you had a run-in with him? Almost everyone has."

Then, after I'd outlined the story, he said, "I shouldn't worry about it. He's a bit intense, you know." That wasn't the word he used. My translation is less libellous. And he added intriguingly: "If you have any more trouble with him, ask him why he left his previous police job." He wouldn't enlarge on the comment either. But I just wasn't interested.

Over the next few weeks my car was flagged down by airport police three times, once for "speeding" (I wasn't. And I was just told to "watch it") and twice for "spot checks." Purely coincidental, of course.

At 6ft.7in. tall and weighing some 18 stone, Chief Inspector Trevor (Tiny) Meincken, second-in-command of the London Airport police force as immediate deputy to Supt. Goldsack, was an outstanding police officer in at least one sense. He was always visible and instantly recognisable on news reels and photographs of the Royals and other VIPs using Heathrow as he towered above them. Many of them knew him by name.

To the resident Press Corps he was a reserved and private man, though he was used to the friendly banter of the photographers complaining that they couldn't see round his portly frame. Perhaps that was why it seemed all the more shocking when Tiny went missing.

I learned of his disappearance directly from one of his colleagues, who said that Tiny's wife had telephoned the airport to report his absence from home. And my inspector friend added: "He was suspended four days ago following some irregularities in paper work." He said that he didn't want to say more at that stage as the matter was still under investigation, and that charges were being considered.

His wife Francesca was at home in Stanwell, just off the south-west boundary of Heathrow, when I called her late that evening. "I have a lot of friends in the police, and they are helping me to find him" she said. "It's unlike him to leave me in the dark about his job. I thought he was leaving for work as usual this morning. But I haven't seen him or heard from him all day."

She said she knew nothing of his suspension or the allegations against her husband other than "rumours" she had heard since reporting him missing. Colleagues said he had not reported for duty since the suspension.

Two days later, after my original story and follow-up reports by colleagues had been given wide publicity, I learned that a warrant

'Royal' policeman vanishes

By ROBERT TRAINI

THE second-in-command of the Ministry of Aviation police at London Airport, who was suspended from duty four days ago pending a police inquiry, was reported missing from home by his wife last night.

Her husband is 38-year-old Chief Inspector Trevor Meincken, who has been in attendance at the airport for most royal arrivals and departures.

He was last seen yesterday morning, when he called at his airport office.

Chief Inspector Meincken's home is in Cordelia-gardens, Stanwell, Middlesex.

Chief Inspector Meincken, who is 6ft. 7in. tall and weighs 18st., is the largest man in the Ministry's police force. His nickname is "Tiny."

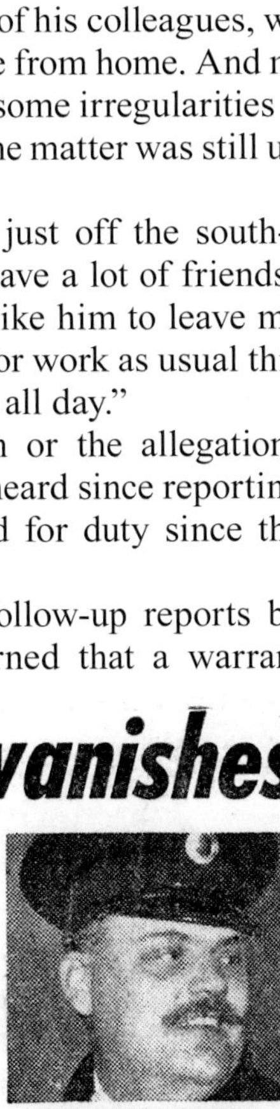

"TINY" MEINCKEN
Wife told police.

Daily Mirror

WARRANT OUT FOR AIRPORT POLICE CHIEF

Express Staff Reporter

A WARRANT was issued yesterday for the arrest of 6ft. 7in. Chief Inspector Trevor (Tiny) Meincken, deputy chief of London's Airport police.

The inspector, whose home is in Cordelia-gardens, Stanwell, Middlesex, was suspended from duty last week for an alleged infringement of the Constabulary Code.

The warrant, on a charge of forgery, was issued by the Bow-street magistrate on the application of the Ministry of Civil Aviation.

Daily Express

Suspended police chief missing says wife

By Daily Mail Reporter

A POLICE chief at London Airport who was suspended four days ago was reported missing early today by his wife.

He is Chief Inspector Trevor Meincken, of the Ministry of Civil Aviation constabulary. He was suspended pending an inquiry alleging infringements of the constabulary code.

His wife, Francesca, said at their home in Cordelia-gardens, Stanwell, early today: "I have a lot of friends in the police and they are helping me to find where he is.

Silence

"It's unlike him to leave me in the dark about his job. I thought he was leaving for work as usual this morning. But I have not heard from him or seen anything of him all day.

"I know nothing about this business apart from rumours I have heard during the day."

As second in command of Ministry police at the airport, Inspector Meincken, father of four, has been on duty at many of the royal and V.I.P. arrivals and departures.

At the airport, officials said he had not reported for duty since his suspension.

Inspector Meincken is nicknamed "Tiny"—at 6ft. 6in. he is the tallest man in the Ministry police.

Daily Mail

(all) March 1962

had been issued for Tiny's arrest on a charge of forgery. I was able to report that it had been issued by Bow-street magistrates following an application by the Ministry of Civil Aviation.

The case never came to court. Tiny Meincken was found dead in a gas-filled room at a hotel in Leighton Buzzard. At the inquest, a coroner recorded a verdict of suicide while the balance of his mind was disturbed by "certain irregularities."

In spite of an exaggerated reputation to the contrary, Heathrow has not, over the years, been a major centre for crime. One yardstick, the admittedly huge and oft-quoted £23.4m "Heathrow Brinks Mat" bullion robbery of 1983 was not, in fact, at Heathrow – but at a private trading estate two miles from the airport's administrative centre, and more than a mile from its boundary. That's almost akin to describing a break-in at a shop in Threadneedle Street as a "Bank of England" robbery. Mud sticks, whether it hits the intended target or not.

Opportunist theft from passenger baggage by airline handlers, particularly during the '70s and '80s, attracted a great deal of attention in the media because of the conviction rates in the courts. But set against the huge quantity of baggage handled, the percentage of losses was minuscule, a mere .001% in one typical reported year.

Crimes involving cargo were always more difficult to assess, because many thefts are believed to go unreported by airlines or agents. Heathrow's cargo centre is, in some ways, a closed community, and police are convinced that in many cases carriers are prepared to bear the cost of losses themselves to protect their reputation, their business and their insurance premiums.

We would have wished for the ideal situation of being able to investigate fully the occasional rumours of thefts. But without the assistance of the police, either officially or unofficially, and in the face of outright obstruction from airlines and their agents any journalistic efforts on our part would have proved time-consuming and costly. At the same time, payments to us for reporting such crimes would have been minimal in many cases because of legal restrictions.

Nevertheless, when it was possible to cover crime stories without sacrificing our bread and butter income from the airport terminals, we were only too happy to indulge ourselves. It was even more encouraging when one or more of our clients went out of their way to order coverage from us, rather than rely on their own crime specialists.

Perhaps it was because airline baggage loaders went on strike in protest against "third degree" grilling by airport police that several nationals ordered from us the story of one major robbery in December 1960. They would have been aware of our good staff and trades union contacts – and the fact that we had access to some airport areas that visiting newsmen could only view from a distance.

So I was pleased when the *Express* gave me an inside page lead across four columns and the *Daily Mail* offered a second page lead with the two-column head *(see opposite).* The story was that 27 registered mail packages had been stolen from a slashed mailbag in the cargo hold of a BEA Viscount freighter shortly before it was due to take off for Milan. Among those packages, I learned from friends in the airline's cargo department, were nearly £60,000 worth of diamonds (at least £2m in today's inflationary terms.)

The packages, all wax sealed, had been flown in from Amsterdam five days earlier, and safely moved to BEA's cargo stronghold. Later they were transferred to the Viscount airliner, due to leave for Milan in the early hours of the next day. The theft was discovered when it became necessary to unload the airliner after bad weather forced cancellation of the flight. A sealed cargo compartment had been broken into, its lock twisted off, and the slashed bag found to be empty.

The Ministry of Aviation police were called in to investigate, and they began enquiries by interrogating BEA baggage handlers. And, for the first time we could recall, the Ministry's press office at Heathrow was able and prepared to confirm the details of the break-in, though not the value of the missing consignment. They agreed that among those interviewed was 18-years-old Ted Harrington, the airline's youngest baggage handler and an orphan living in lodgings at Ashford, Middlesex, not far from Heathrow's southern boundary.

When Harrington, one of the loaders who had worked on the Viscount, returned to duty, he complained to shop stewards that he had been subjected to "undue pressure" by

Air gems vanish

Now mail bandits swoop at airport

By Daily Mail Reporter

MAILBAG bandits snatched 27 registered packets from a BEA freight plane while it was parked unattended at London Airport for 18 hours.

Early today reports from Amsterdam indicated that the missing

Daily Mail

£50,000 ROBBERY AT LONDON AIRPORT STARTS A STRIKE

Express Staff Reporter

DIAMONDS from Amsterdam worth more than £50,000 have been stolen from a mailbag in a B.E.A. Viscount freighter parked at London Airport, waiting to fly to Milan.

The theft was discovered when it became necessary to unload the plane which had been held up by bad weather

One of the mailbags was slashed. and 27 packages were missing. At once close inquiries were made. And yesterday, because of those inquiries, 200 baggage men went on strike.

They protested that one of them "was manhandled and roughed up" by airport police investigating the robbery.

This led to delays of up to two hours in outgoing flights. And last night the apron men were supported by long distance aircraft marshallers, the men who guide the planes to their parking bays.

The worker who say that he was "roughed up" is 18-year-old Ted Harrington, an orphan with digs at Park-road, Ashford, Middlesex.

TRANSFERRED

A Ministry spokesman said :—

"The packages were part of a consignment of Dutch mail that arrived at London Airport late on Friday. The mail was transferred to the B.E.A. Viscount and was due to fly on to Milan at 12.45 a.m. on Saturday.

"Bad weather held up the departure and the mail had to be taken off the plane in the afternoon. That was when the slash in the bag was noticed."

The airport strike started at 3 p.m. yesterday when Harrington—youngest member of the baggage handling staff—arrived for duty.

He at once reported to officials of the Transport and General Workers' Union that he had been questioned about the missing packets the day before. Then he made allegations about the police methods.

The men demanded the "immediate suspension" of an airport detective. The airport manager, Mr. Leslie Green, said he had no such powers.

Latest strike situation: "Hopeful." after a 2½-hour meeting.

Daily Express

300 STRIKE AFTER PLANE ROBBERY

THREE hundred baggage and freight loaders at London Airport, on strike last night, said they would not go back unless a policeman at the airport was suspended.

The policeman, they said, had questioned eighteen-year-old loader Ted Harrington about a mailbag slashing at the week-end.

Twenty-seven registered packets—their value has not been disclosed—are reported to have been taken from the mailbag on a plane.

Harrington was interviewed on Sunday, and did not leave the airport police station until three hours **AFTER** he should have been on duty, say the strikers.

Yesterday he told his shop steward, and instantly the 300 loaders — fellow members of the Transport and General Workers Union—went on unofficial strike.

The strike caused chaos. Twenty airlines were affected and 500 passengers were delayed up to one hour and a quarter.

Discussions were still going on late last night to try to settle the dispute.

Daily Sketch

(all) Dec 6 1960

£50,000 gems stolen at airport

DIAMONDS worth over £50,000 were stolen from a freight plane at London Airport during the week-end, it was revealed last night.

They were in packages of Dutch mail en route from Amsterdam to Milan.

It is believed that the Viscount freight plane, which was loaded with the mail on Friday, was left unattended for 18 hours.

The gang had smashed a lock on the compartment where the mail was stored.

Airport police were called in when one of the mailbags was found ripped open and 27 packages missing. The robbery is the biggest in the history of London Airport.

Strike

Last night London Airport's freight-handling service was in chaos because of a strike by 200 men, most of them loaders and porters.

The strikers claim that an 18-year-old fellow loader was beaten-up by an airport policeman investigating the mail-bag robbery. They are demanding the immediate suspension of the officer involved.

The youth, Ted Harrington, of Ashford, Middlesex, had complained to union officials.

Daily Herald

one detective.

Two hundred of his colleagues, the entire day shift of baggage loaders, immediately walked out in protest. Union officials called for the suspension of the police officer. They claimed that Harrington had been "roughed up" by the detective during the grilling, which had continued from Sunday afternoon well into Monday morning. Airport manager Leslie Green told me he had no power to suspend the officer.

More than a hundred other apron workers, including aircraft marshallers, joined the stoppage. Dozens of flights were disrupted. Hundreds of passengers packed the airport lounges, with flight departures delayed for up to two hours. When the strikers voted to continue their stoppage after a mass meeting, senior management officials met union leaders. Their talks ended after three hours of talks with the union agreeing to recommend a return to work. But it was later the following Tuesday before services were back to normal.

Neither the diamonds nor the contents of the other registered packets were recovered.

A year earlier, the London *Evening News* asked us to follow up a report they'd received about an attempted pay raid at a Ministry of Aviation stores depot at Hayes, Middlesex, just to the north of the airport. For once I welcomed the opportunity to escape from the news-quiet airport lounges. I picked up my car and drove over to the depot. Within minutes I was pulling up at the steel-framed entrance gates, only to be waved through unchecked by a uniformed security guard.

That was surprise No.1. The second came a moment later when I stopped again at the first office doorway I could find, only to be directed on to another when I said: "I' m here to make some enquiries about the pay raid." It was as though I was expected, and my confidence grew until I wondered if I had been mistaken for an investigating official. When I reached my destination, I was asked in, and I quickly introduced myself.

Surprise No 3. No one called for a security guard to see me off the premises. Instead, 30-years-old chief cashier John Lay stepped forward and remarked with a grin: "We knew it wouldn't be long before you chaps got here."

Proudly, he outlined to me everything he'd told the police half-an-hour earlier. Obviously at this isolated civil service outpost, he was unaware or uncaring about all the "don't talk to the Press" rules. He and his assistant, Miss Ivy Hewlett, he said, had just returned from the bank, and were making up pay slips for the 130 staff at the depot.

"The first we knew we had visitors was when there was a sudden banging on the office door. I had locked it behind me, as I always do when I bring cash in. None of the staff would bang like that."

Mr Lay said that he peered through the small glass panel of the door and glimpsed two men in the empty outer office with hats pulled down over their faces and scarves covering their mouths. At that moment one of the bandits spotted me," he said. "He pointed a snub-nosed automatic at my face – but I quickly pulled back out of his line of fire. I shouted to Miss Hewitt to get down behind her desk."

The bandits, he said, screamed and shouted at him to open the connecting door. "We kept quiet, " said Mr Lay, "And after only a few seconds, we heard the men rushing out again. They must have thought we'd called for help." Someone spotted the bandits'car number and reported it to police. Later it was confirmed that the car had been stolen.

The depot's wages bill of £2,000 remained intact. The bandits were not caught. But the *Evening News* made my story the Page One lead for at least one edition, with a heading across six columns:

Evening News Page One lead
Dec 11 1959

MINISTRY PAY RAID

Masked Gun Bandits Swoop

"Evening News" Reporter

ARMED bandits swooped on the pay office of the Civil Aviation Ministry's stores depot in Hayes, Middlesex, this afternoon.

But the raiders, their faces masked with scarves, were foiled in their attempt to snatch the £2,000 payroll and escaped in a stolen car.

The bandits had driven into the big store in Willowtree-lane. They drove up to the pay office, an isolated brick building.

Inside were Mr. John Lay, 30-year-old chief cashier and his assistant, Miss Ivy Hewlett. They had just returned from the bank and were making up pay slips for the 130 staff.

DOORS Locked

The two bandits, with their hats pulled down over their faces and scarves covering their mouths, crept through the outer door of the pay office. But they found the inner doors were locked.

Mr. Lay looked through the tiny window of one of the doors. One of the bandits immediately pointed a snum-nosed automatic at his face from the other side of the glass.

Making a clean getaway, although preferably with the loot rather than without it, is every crook's ambition. And if you can commit your crime at the airport, in theory at least it seems likely that you'd have a better chance of achieving that.

The stranger who walked up to a Heathrow passenger buffet must have planned it that way. He told waitress Elizabeth Webster: "I am the new assistant manager," and emptied her till of notes. He signed a receipt for her with a name that looked like, "A. Stibbs, asst. mgr," then walked off.

When Elizabeth realised that the direction he was taking meant he must be boarding a departing airliner, she made a 'phone call. But by the time she established there was no assistant manager called Stibbs, it was too late. The man had vanished. His total haul: just £10 in old £1 and 10 shilling notes.

Another overseas visitor was luckier, or smarter. A smooth-talking Canadian, he got chatting to late-night Heathrow cleaner Charlie Hand. Somehow, the subject came around to football pools, on which Charlie, a popular eccentric who always sported a monocle over his one glass eye, claimed to be something of an expert.

"You must show me how you do these pools" said the Canadian, "I'd like to play. Maybe we'll win something."

Charlie showed him – and promptly agreed to contribute a half-share in a five-shilling permutation they worked out together. The perm won £50,000, a real fortune in 1957. But Charlie didn't get his half-share. "The Canadian vanished," he said sadly. "And I don't know anything about him, not even his Christian name.

"He'd popped in for a cup of coffee at the buffet where I was sweeping up. He had a good-looking blonde with him." The Canadian had returned the following weekend and, said Charlie: "He was sweating and shaking. He showed me the copy coupon, and his suspicions were right. I checked it – we had twenty-four points."

The Canadian promised to return with the cheque, go to the bank with Charlie, and sign over the money, he said. He didn't.

"And," summed up Charlie, "I'm not even going to the police. There's nothing I can do

How I lost £25,000, by Charlie

Daily Sketch Reporter

MONOCLED Charlie Hand, a night cleaner at London Airport, told me last night how a smooth-talking Canadian said to him: "What about these football pools you do over here? I'd like to play. Show me how."

Charlie showed him—and gave him 2s. 6d. for a half share in a 5s. permutation they did together.

It won £50,000. But Charlie didn't get his half share. The Canadian vanished, he said.

Charlie adjusted his monocle in his glass right eye. "I don't know the first thing about the man—not even his Christian name," he said.

"He popped in for a cup of tea at the bar where I was sweeping up. He had a good-looking blonde with him."

The following Saturday night—about seven weeks ago, Charlie thinks — the Canadian came in again.

"He was shaking and sweating," said Charlie. "He showed me the copy coupon. I checked it and it was right — **TWENTY-FOUR POINTS.**"

The Canadian promised to come back with the cheque, go to a bank with Charlie and sign over half the money, he said.

He didn't.

"Nothing I could do about it," said Charlie. "Can't find him.

"In any case I haven't got any legal claim, as he signed the coupon."

Daily Sketch Feb 4 1957

Airport Post picture Feb 1957

about it. His name's on the coupon."

This was one occasion when I didn't feel justified in telling Charlie: "The publicity might help."

It would have been less than kind to refer to Keystone Cops when three Ministry of Aviation detectives spotted a man they thought was wanted on a warrant by civil police at Chelmsford, Essex. He was apparently changing currency at an airport bank in Terminal 2. When they approached him the man suddenly ran off, knocking travellers in the queue behind him in all directions. But the chase was on – down escalators, back upstairs, across a crowded lounge and into a departure hall, along a balcony and up another escalator.

Passengers scattered. Others snatched up children as detectives raced after the running man, leaping over piles of luggage and weaving through lines of trolleys. One policeman leapt 14 feet from the balcony above the first floor. He had to be taken away by ambulance. Another raced up one escalator while yet another waited at the foot of the other.

Airline staff at their desks watched the scene with me in amazement as the man raced past us several times, dodging backwards and forwards, the police copying his every turn. At last he found the only exit apparently still open to him. Turning to run down the escalator, he fell into the arms of the waiting detective.

The police officer who jumped from the balcony landed behind the airline desks. As an onlooker myself, I could have described the scene. But I turned back to the airline staff for their comments. One traffic girl told me: "He ripped his shoe and twisted his ankle. Some ambulance men came for him. I didn't realise he was a policeman – I thought he was another crook."

A colleague added: "It was like a scene from a film. It all seemed unreal." The police got their man and escorted him to a nearby police station to await an escort to Chelmsford. My eyewitness report was front paged in the *Daily Herald.*

The Heathrow police could have been accused of carelessness in the frequency of injuries received in the "line of duty." One incident was typical of several in the late 'fifties when rival gangs of youths with nothing better to do were attracted to the bright lights of the "ever-open" passenger terminals at Heathrow.

On this occasion (a few years on it might have been "Mods" and "Rockers") it was gangs of roving Teddy Boys, so named because of their Edwardian-style clothes. They found their natural tribal enemies in "Debs' Delights," wealthy young playboys also out for a good time with their high-society girlfriends. Wherever the two groups met, they clashed, with injuries on both sides.

For two or three months in 1958, airport duty officers were regularly reporting incidents involving midnight-and-later revellers thronging the terminals, at that time deserted by all but the odd delayed and hardiest early-bird passengers. Their log books recorded reports of hooligans trampling over furniture, some prancing across tables and desks with cups of tea balanced on their heads... of free standing metal ashtrays being used as battering rams... of rowdy "skiffle" and jive sessions... of emergency telephones being used for fake alarms... of wheelchairs provided for disabled passengers requisitioned for mass charges up and down escalators.

But the duty officers complained to me their reports were being ignored. "The

CHASE DRAMA AT AIRPORT

Herald Reporter

A MAN was arrested at London Airport last night after a dramatic chase up and down escalators and through airport lounges.

A detective, who leaped 14ft. from a balcony to cut off the man's escape, was taken away in an ambulance.

The chase began after three plain-clothed airport police recognised a man who was changing currency at one of the airport banks.

He was wanted on a warrant issued by police at Chelmsford, Essex.

When they approached him, the man ran. The chase was on—down through the lounge and into a departure hall, along a balcony and up an escalator.

Passengers scattered as the detectives tore after him. One policeman leapt from the balcony, one raced up the escalator and the other ran to the foot of the down escalator.

LIKE A FILM

In the first-floor lounge, airline staff looked up in amazement as the man raced across the hall in front of them.

But he found his only exit, apart from the escalator, was barred. Turning down the escalator, he ran into the arms of a detective.

The officer who leapt from the balcony landed behind the airline desks. One traffic girl said: "He ripped his shoe and twisted his ankle. An ambulance called for him.

"I didn't know he was a policeman. I thought he was another crook."

Daily Herald July 22 1959

management is burying its head in the sand," said one as the Ministry press office rejected my challenge with the words: "We don't regard it as a problem."

Even when some rowdy scenes were witnessed by senior management officials and the Ministry's chief constable, Major W. Ronnie, in an all-night "stake-out," it was stated: "No action is considered necessary at this stage. Inevitably the bright lights, the warmth and the 24-hour catering are a magnet to these people.

"But it is a public building. It has to remain open."

Then came the Teddy Boy brawl. Two rival gangs started to fight. A group of overconfident Hooray-Henrys (public school rowdies) decided to join in out of sheer bravado, and the solitary policeman on duty called for reinforcements.

Two plainclothes policemen were beaten up as they tried to part brawlers. One had to spend the night in hospital receiving treatment for his injuries. Other police were attacked as they escorted three men out of the buildings and across a car-park. Two men were arrested and charged with assault.

Too late to make the Sunday papers, the story gave me a worthwhile six-column page lead in the *Daily Mail* the following day. The *Express* used the more colourful "Skiffle in the Lounges" and "Teddy Boy picnics..." phrases in their two-column headline,...while the *Mirror* chose the harder hitting headline to say "Gangs beat up Airport Police" (*see opposite*).

An emergency meeting of senior airport management was called the following day. The police took the opportunity to complain how limited their powers were. They were able to demonstrate that unless they could prove that the safety of an aircraft had been endangered, there were very few areas where they could make an arrest without it being challenged in court, sometimes successfully. They pointed out that as airports were not public places in the legal sense, the police could often act only in accordance with by-laws which were designed mainly to safeguard the public on military airfields, where the public were specifically excluded in any case for most of the time.

Backed by a strong appeal from the management, the police eventually won the day. New by-laws were introduced to widen their powers of arrest. A few years on and the by-laws were completely revised. But it wasn't until 1974, when the need for heightened security controls led to the hand-over of policing at Britain's airports to civil police forces, that the picture was completed.

Because Heathrow, and indeed most of the major airports in the UK were still technically private property (a reality later reinforced with the privatisation of the former British Airports Authority, now BAA plc, which owns seven of them) it required an Act of Parliament to make the change. But it meant too that individual police officers at the airports, some of whom, after a short period of "refresher" training, were able to transfer to the Metropolitan or county forces, thereby continuing their unbroken airport service.

In the meantime Heathrow's Keystone Cops were still able to play a small part in arrests, by providing airport back-up for their civil colleagues bringing runaway miscreants home to face the courts and sentencing. The return of Dennis Stafford, witnessed by a big Fleet Street contingent and reported by me elsewhere is a typical example.[1]

With the notorious exception of Brazil, vividly illustrated by Great Train Robber and escaped prisoner Ronnie Biggs's success in establishing an almost lifelong bolt-hole, there are very few safe havens left for either the guilt-stricken or the unrepentant criminals fleeing the long arm of British justice.

While Fleet Street frequently alerted us to the homecoming of proud British bobbies and their charges, the airport police would sometimes take it upon themselves to hinder press photographers unnecessarily by ordering them out of camera-range. They were taking full advantage of the "no pictures of passengers under detention" ruling.[2] It mattered little to them that the photographers' passes gave them the right to be present and that pictures in most such cases were in the public interest. Usually their civil colleagues quietly but firmly advised them to back off and "let the dogs see the rabbit." They, after all, welcomed the opportunity to be seen in the newspapers bringing a criminal to justice, and had been responsible for alerting the "dogs" in the first place.

One of the earliest of these airborne "arrests" I attended was the return, in September 1951

[1] *See Chapter 4, p.90*
[2] *See Chapter 2, p.31*

Deb escorts in airport 'riot' row

THEY DANCE BAREFOOT ON ARMCHAIRS AS TEDDY BOYS SMASH UP THE LOUNGES

By Daily Mail Reporter

BAREFOOT debs' escorts pranced over the armchairs with cups of tea on their heads as Teddy Boys charged up and down the escalators with a wheelchair.

THAT, they were saying last night, was a typical Saturday night at London Airport.

Who are *they*? The duty officers who keep a day-and-night watch on the passenger buildings.

For months they have been reporting "incidents" involving midnight revellers who throng the airport's 24-hour buffets every week-end.

The skiffle groups who jive their way through the lounges—the hooligans who trample furniture and smash ashtrays.

Some of the public wash-rooms have looked like a battle-field in the cold light of morning.

The brawls

Scores of entries have been made on the rock 'n rioters in the official log-book. All were apparently ignored.

A spokesman of the Ministry of Transport and Civil Aviation said: "There is no problem."

Recently the Ministry's chief constable spent all night in the lounges with representatives of the airport management.

Afterwards it was stated: "No action is considered necessary at this stage."

But that was before the Teddy boy brawl. . . .

Two rival gangs started to fight. Two plain-clothes policemen who tried to part them were beaten up.

One, a detective-sergeant of the Ministry's police, was still receiving medical treatment yesterday. The other went on duty "wearing" his bruises.

Now the duty officers are demanding immediate action, and the police, whose powers are limited, want a review of the by-laws.

Today the airport management will hold an emergency conference to find ways of controlling the Saturday sprees.

Said one officer: "Home-going socialites from the West End give us just as much trouble as the Teddy boys.

"We have been complaining for long enough. Perhaps after this there will be second thoughts."

GANGS BEAT UP AIRPORT POLICE

DAILY MIRROR REPORTER

TWO London Airport detectives were beaten up when they tried to stop a fight between rival gangs of youths in an airport lounge at the week-end.

Yesterday one of the detectives was still undergoing medical treatment for his injuries.

The attack highlights hooliganism which has been troubling Airport officials for many months—hooliganism by society men and women as well as gangs of youths.

Recent incidents in the lounge include:

- Groups of society girls and their men friends dancing barefoot on a row of armchairs and balancing cups of tea on their heads.
- Rowdy skiffle and jive sessions.
- Furniture and wash-room equipment damaged.

An Airport spokesman said last night: "Our trouble is that we provide an all-day, all-night catering service. Youths and girls come in late at night after the coffee shops have closed.

"Society people who live out beyond the Airport drop in on the way home from London.

"We are watching the situation very carefully.

"We have never had an attack before. When we see any sign of unruly behaviour, including dancing or skiffle, the people are asked to leave."

The spokesman added that the two detectives were attacked while they were escorting three men from the passenger building across a car park.

They received cuts and bruises.

Two men will appear before the Uxbridge, Middlesex, magistrates today charged with assault.

Daily Mirror (above)
Daily.Mail (left)
(all) Feb 17 1958

SKIFFLE IN THE LOUNGES

Teddy Boy picnics upset airport

Express Staff Reporter JOHN GRANT

WEEK-END Teddy Boys and West End "bright young things" will be considered at a meeting of London Airport officials today.

Teddy Boys' picnics — they turn up for late night coffee and sandwiches in the airport lounges—have caused trouble which came to a head on Saturday night.

Two airport police were injured in an incident.

Airport officials complain of: fooling on the escalators; skiffle and jive sessions; interfering with the emergency phones and inquiry desk work.

The West Enders have also brought complaints.

The airport police chief, Major W. Ronnie, and airport manager Mr. Leslie Green, spent a night keeping watch. They decided: "It could be a problem—but no action yet."

Now that decision may be reconsidered.

BRIGHT LIGHTS

An airport spokesman said last night: "Inevitably, the bright lights, warmth and 24-hour catering are a magnet to these people.

"A section of the building could be closed. But we have to look after the comfort of travellers. And, anyway, it is a public building."

Two men will appear before the Uxbridge magistrates today following the Saturday-night incident.

Daily Express

SKYLARKING ALARMS THE AIRPORT

NEWS CHRONICLE REPORTER

REVELLERS and raiding gangs of hooligans are turning London Airport's central terminal passenger building into a bear-garden at week-ends.

The problem is assuming such proportions that senior management officials are holding an emergency conference today to find ways of stopping it.

During the week-end two plain-clothes policemen who tried to break up rival Teddy-boy gangs were beaten up when they left the brightly-lit lounges.

SKIFFLE SESSIONS

Duty officers who keep watch on the passenger buildings night and day are demanding immediate action, and the police, worried about limitations of their powers, want the airport's by-laws reviewed.

Late night revellers usually begin to congregate just before midnight every week-end and often stay far into the early hours. Gangs of skiffiers and jivers organise swing sessions in defiance of officials and police.

For months past, with the steadily-growing influx of visitors to the 24-hour buffets and restaurants, the duty officers

News Chronicle

Courtesy of ForestFM.co.uk

This picture, taken at a later date, shows the fashion and hairstyle typical of the 'Teds'. These youths were not involved in the incidents at the airport.

from Paris, of Russian-born Dr. H.A.C.Gregory, a prominent specialist, of Peterborough. Two Scotland Yard officers had flown over earlier that day to bring him back after he had been held on an extradition warrant. He was later charged with bankruptcy offences. Shortly afterwards two more Yard officers, this time from the Fraud Squad, also flew to Paris – to return with the self-styled Count Edward Johnston-Noad. He was detained under charges of false pretences and fraudulent conversion.

'THE COUNT' COMES BACK FROM PARIS

FIFTY-YEAR-OLD Edward Johnston-Noad, self-styled count, wearing a greatcoat over a brown pin-stripe suit, flies into London—escorted.

He was later detained under charges of false pretences and fraudulent conversion. The "count" was brought back to England, from Paris, by Scotland Yard Fraud Squad officers.

Daily Express April 12 1952

Man from Spain meets the CID

By Daily Mail Reporter

TWO plainclothes C.I.D. men waited for the plane from Spain at London Airport last night.

Twice they stopped surprised passengers before they found he man they wanted —swarthy John Edward Greville Alford, 28-year-old diamond merchant.

As Alford mounted a ramp to the London Airport passenger building the two burly C.I.D. men stepped up.

"We are police officers," they said. "We should like to speak to you."

He was flying home on an "emergency ticket" supplied to him on a repatriation basis by the British Consul to whom he had appealed after running out of money.

The girl he left behind him, 25-year-old Spanish night club singer Maria Jesus Val, was said to be unaware if his impending detention.

Last Thursday Maria went to help him pack at the hospital in Barcelona where he had been taken after being found unconscious at his hotel.

Alford is to appear at Bow-street today in answer to a larceny charge.

Daily Mail June 13 1960

Extradited Doctor Flies from Paris

GRIPPING a paper, Dr. H. A. C. Gregory, former London bone and muscle specialist, leaves Northolt Airport. Scotland Yard's Detective-Sergt. J. Mitchell and interpreter F. Chapborne brought him from Paris last night on an extradition warrant. They took him to West End Central police station. He was charged with alleged offences under the 1914 Bankruptcy Act. He will appear at Bow street today.

Dr. Gregory, born in Russia 61 years ago went to South Africa from his home near Peterborough in 1949. At a bankruptcy court last year a statement of affairs showed £98,000 debts. Estimated assets: £49,000.

Daily Mail Sept 28 1951

Doctor flies back

Dr. H. A. C. Gregory, of Fineshade Abbey, near Peterborough, arrived at Northolt (Middlesex) by air from Paris last night on an extradition warrant to face charges in connection with an alleged bankruptcy offence. He will appear at Bow Street today. Yard men went to Paris to execute the warrant.

News Chronicle Sept 28 1951

'Jailed sailors flown home

THREE British sailors were given sentences varying from eight years to 18 months at a court-martial aboard the frigate Wild Goose at Bahrain, in the Persian Gulf, early this month.

This was revealed by the Admiralty yesterday when the three men were flown into London Airport under escort from Fayid, in the Canal Zone.

They are under detention for "acts to the prejudice of good order and naval discipline."

The men and their sentences are: Able Seaman Brian Pettfield: eight years in prison. Able Seaman Dennis Bernard Buck: six years' imprisonment. Able Seaman Robert Irvine: 18 months' detention.

The charges against them included disobedience and drunkenness.

An Admiralty spokesman declined to give the home addresses of the men, but said that the court-martial arose from an incident on board the frigate Wren last month. It involved three junior ratings striking a senior rating.

Daily Herald Feb 13 1954

In both of these I had little to do but confirm the arrival, merely repeating the background as it had been related in Yard press releases. So I was perfectly satisfied with the two or three column inches my subsequent story warranted in the nationals. Similarly, it was only necessary to give an eyewitness account of the arrival of three British youths held in Jersey, then brought back to stand trial in Buckinghamshire on larceny charges. On this occasion nothing had been released in advance to the Press – but the incident was guaranteed publicity when their escorts decided in their wisdom to handcuff their prisoners, an unusual sight at a very public airport.

No such drastic security was thought necessary for three British sailors who were hustled back to England on a military transport flight from Fayid, in the Suez Canal zone, a few years later. Naval authorities obviously considered the two very large Royal Navy shore patrol NCOs sufficient security even for the most able-bodied seamen. The three men had been found guilty at a court martial hearing of assault on a senior officer, disobedience and drunkenness on board the frigate HMS Wren. They were to serve sentences ranging from 18 months detention at a naval correction barracks to eight years in a civil prison.

Police detention facilities at the airport were considered virtually non-existent and insecure, so the three sailors were met at their aircraft steps by a naval patrol car and driven directly to the nearest off-airport police station at Harlington. (Almost next door to Brenards' offices, this was be the same police station to provide accommodation to a Fleet Air Arm officer in a widely publicised "tug-of-love" case.[1]) There they were kept in cells to await their onward transport.

This was not a story for which we had any advance warning. My attention had been aroused by the arrival of the RAF transport aircraft, a relatively rare occurrence at Heathrow even in the 'fifties. My curiosity was rewarded by the sight of the unfortunate prisoners disembarking. But it took several 'phone calls to the Admiralty and a couple of hours' "door-stepping," metaphorically and literally, before I had sufficient information to produce a double column piece in the next day's *Daily Herald*, for example.

There was no assistance sought from the airport constabulary by the two burly Yard men who detained a London diamond merchant at Heathrow in 1960. Neither did they need to make the journey to bring him back from Spain where he had sought refuge. Twenty-eight years-old John Greville Alford was returning on an "emergency" ticket. It was supplied to him on a repatriation basis by the British Consul to whom he had appealed after running out of funds.

Alford had been taken to hospital in Barcelona after being found unconscious in his hotel room. His Spanish girl friend, a night club singer, had helped him to pack. She was unaware that police in Britain wanted to question him in connection with a charge of larceny.

Special Branch officers at Heathrow helped their colleagues to identify Alford's flight when it touched down, but they were left alone to find their man. Twice I saw them stop

[1] *See Chapter 4, p.90*

surprised passengers before they found Alford. "We are police officers," they said as he mounted a ramp to the passenger building. "We should like to speak to you."

Sometimes our attention, and that of the police of course, was focused not on a wrongdoer's homecoming (if that is the appropriate word for someone heading for jail), but the deportation of a temporary overseas resident in the UK who has incurred the wrath of his own or another country.

In 1950 the Indian Government applied to Britain for the extradition of a Pakistani millionaire. Mobarik Ali Ahmed was wanted in Bombay to answer charges of forgery and false pretences. He had been held in Brixton for three months while the Home Secretary considered the application.

Precautions to ensure the departure was kept secret were unprecedented, with special security measures enforced by the airport police at the request of the Indian Government. Driven to the airport, Ahmed was taken directly to a secluded airline office on the advice of Special Branch. With him were the Assistant Commissioner of the Bombay Police and two Scotland Yard officers, a Detective Superintendent and a Detective Sergeant. All three accompanied the millionaire on the flight – the first time the Yard had agreed to provide such an overseas escort.

Shortly before the flight took off, airport police cleared the tarmac of all but essential staff as Ahmed, surrounded by his escorts and Indian Government representatives, walked to the aircraft, his face buried in his hands. The party had left the airline office through a private door, avoiding normal passenger controls. Their names had been added to the passenger list only at the last moment.

The airport scenes gave me a five column page lead in the *Sunday Dispatch* the next day under the double headline:

PRISONER GOES BY PLANE

A middle-aged Pakistani industrialist, Mubarek Ali Ahmed, was escorted aboard an airliner at London Airport to-day by Scotland Yard detectives.

Strict security measures were taken by the airport authorities to avoid sightseers.

Ahmed, who is wanted on charges by the Indian Government, was taken out to the aircraft by car from the airline office.

His name and the names of three men travelling with him were added to the passenger list only at the last minute.

The Home Secretary, Sir David Maxwell Fyfe, announced yesterday that he had decided not to stay the extradition order for Ahmed.

Evening Standard April 19 1952

PUT ON PLANE BY YARD MEN

Mubarek Ali Ahmed, wealthy Pakistani industrialist who has been held in Brixton Jail after extradition order was made against him at request of Indian Government was escorted aboard airliner at London Airport to-day by Scotland Yard detectives.

Evening News April 19 1952

Detectives Fly To India With Extradited Pakistani

Hush-Hush Police Precautions As Millionaire Is Taken From Jail

By Sunday Dispatch Reporter

MOBARIK ALI AHMED, Pakistani millionaire who has been awaiting the Home Secretary's decision on whether he was to be sent to India to face fraud and forgery charges, was taken from Brixton Prison to London Airport shortly after breakfast yesterday.

He was escorted by Detective-Superintendent Black and Detective-Sergeant James to an Air India plane which left for Bombay at 10.30 a.m.

Precautions taken by the Indian Government and Scotland Yard to ensure his departure should be secret were unprecedented.

Shortly before the plane took off the tarmac was cleared and only passengers boarding were allowed on the field.

Mr. Ahmed, surrounded by Indian Government officials, police, and airport officers, walked to the plane with his face buried in his hands.

Before boarding the plane Mr. Ahmed said good-bye in the airport V.I.P. lounge to his 19-year-old son Iferti, who was accompanied by his Pakistani fiancée.

With them were two business friends who have been fighting to keep Mr. Ahmed in Britain since his arrest on February 27.

Father and son both distressed, embraced before Mr. Ahmed walked through a private door to the tarmac.

The police officers, at the request of the Indian Government, travelled to Bombay with their prisoner. This is the first time such action has been taken by the Yard.

the *Sunday Express* gave it two columns with the heading:

Flying Yard men guard fraud charge millionaire

Sunday Express Reporter

EXTRAORDINARY security precautions were taken at London Airport yesterday when 43 - year - old millionaire Mobarik Ali Ahmed was put aboard a plane for Bombay to answer charges of forgery and false pretences.

Mr. Ahmed, who comes from Karachi, capital of Pakistan, denies the charges. He had been in Brixton Jail since February 27.

At the airport he was put in a room with Superintendent J. Black and Sergeant James of Scotland Yard and Mr. T. Adams, Assistant Commissioner of the Bombay Police. Outside police and airport security men patrolled.

The three police officers are travelling with him to Bombay—the first time Yard men have accompanied a prisoner to his final destination.

Sunday Express (left), Sunday Dispatch (above) April 20 1952

It was the Yard's Special Branch, again, not the airport police – who took charge when a 43-years-old Greek Cypriot woman was flown to Britain for hospital treatment after she had twice been by attacked by masked gunmen at her Famagusta home. But they called on the Aviation Ministry constabulary manpower to provide a protective cordon round the steps of the BEA Viscount after it touched down.

After the first shooting, when she was left with three bullets in her body, the woman was accused on Athens radio of spying against terrorists who supported the union of Cyprus with Greece. Three weeks later another masked gunman burst into the Nicosia hospital where she was recovering, and shot her again three times. The man shouted: "That's what you get for betraying us." Troops surrounded the hospital, but failed to catch the man.

CYPRUS WOMAN GETS AIRPORT GUARD

VICTIM OF TERROR

Police guard against third attack

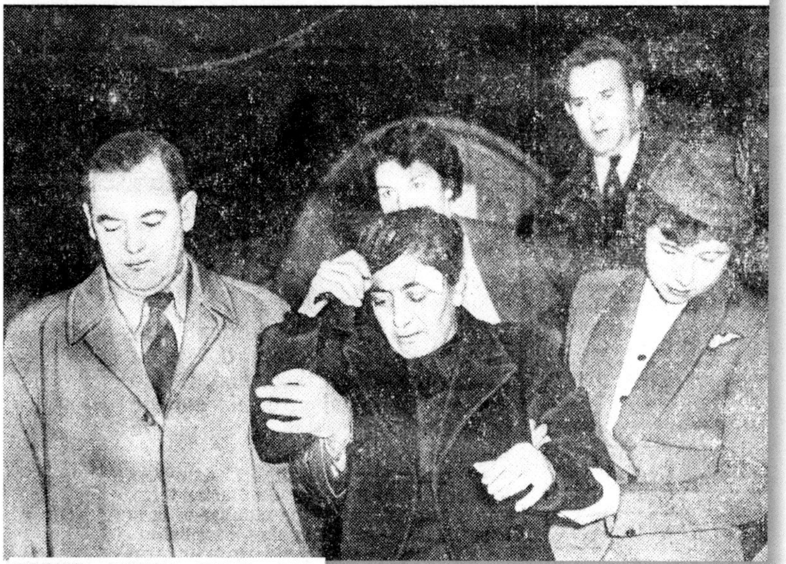

Daily Express picture

FORTY - THREE - YEAR - OLD Greek-Cypriot Mrs. Ariadne Constantinidou, who was twice attacked by masked gunmen, is helped from a B.EA. Viscount airliner at London Airport last night.

SPECIAL BRANCH officers of Scotland Yard boarded the plane and airport police ringed the steps as the woman, flown to England for treatment for her wounds, disembarked.

THE STRONG security measures were enforced to prevent any further attempts on her life by terrorists at the airport. Customs and immigration controls were relaxed to allow her to be driven straight to hospital.

MRS. CONSTANTINIDOU, who was accused by Athens radio of spying against the Cyprus terrorists, was shot at her Famagusta home six weeks ago and again three weeks later as she lay in hospital at Nicosia.

Daily Sketch (top)
Daily Express (above)

Airport guard on shot woman

POLICE ringed a Viscount airliner at London Airport last night for the arrival of a 43-year-old Greek Cypriot woman victim of two terrorist attacks—one while in hospital.

News Chronicle (all) Jan 25 1956

At Heathrow, the woman, Mrs Ariadne Constantinidou, stayed aboard while other passengers disembarked. Then the Special Branch Officers boarded, together with Customs and Immigration officers. They told her formalities were being waived so that she could be driven directly to an unnamed hospital outside London, where it was hoped to remove the three bullets.

Still wearing a plaster over her left eye where she was grazed in the second attack, the victim visibly trembled as she stepped on to the tarmac, supported on one side by a Special Branch officer, on the other by a BEA stewardess. They helped her into a waiting ambulance.

Said one police officer later: "The cordon was provided both for security and to re-assure the woman passenger, who was naturally very fearful of another attack, even on British soil."

Shortly after that incident in 1956, a much younger Cypriot woman also flew to London to escape possible retribution from EOKA (nationalists supporting union with Greece) terrorists. On this occasion there were no photographers present, and strictly no publicity. The appointed guardians of pretty brunette Drosoulla Demetriades, the British security services, decided she would be much safer if no one knew she had left Cyprus.

For Drosoulla, too, had committed the crime of dissenting from the policy of violence and terrorism after her fiancé, a special constable, was shot in the back in Nicosia's Ledra Street, the notorious "murder mile." A picture of Drousoulla kneeling by his crumpled body was flashed round the world, to be front-paged in several British newspapers.

The following day, Drosoulla, who worked for the Cyprus radio, denounced her fiancé's killers. Soon afterwards she and her family were brought to England and safety.

In February 1959 an agreement was reached between the Governments of Britain, Greece and Turkey and the leaders of Greek and Turkish-Cypriot communities, which established an independent Cyprus republic and brought an interim peace to the island. And the following May, Drosoulla also found peace – when she married an Englishman. He was 27-years-old Arnold Thomson, "Tammy" Thomson to his many friends at Heathrow, where for eight years he had been a reporter for Brenards, and my colleague. It was one of those rare occasions when a press man made the front pages himself.

The couple had met at a wine-tasting reception in London, and after Tam decided to leave journalism, they went on to become successful partners in business as well as domestically. Sadly, in the late '90s, Drosoulla died of cancer.

A prominent member of EOKA, Nicos Sampson, also a journalist and a known terrorist who had been named as the killer of Drosoulla's former fiancé, succeeded Archbishop Makarios briefly as President of Cyprus in 1974, following a coup by Greek Cypriot army officers which he supported. He died in 2001.

Tam later returned to journalism, becoming a successful travel writer.

Tammy & Drosoulla *Brenard Press picture*

It was the airport's elite corps of Special Branch officers who could be seen hovering whenever individuals or delegations associated with known Communist or Communist-affiliated organisations arrived or departed. On a number of occasions when I was interviewing or questioning leaders or members of such groups – like the so-called international "Peace" movements – I was aware of someone nearby taking more than a casual interest in what was passing between us. On turning round the curious member of the passing public would be none other than a familiar face from " the Yard."

Sometimes individual SB officers would approach reporters later, to ask specific questions about members of a delegation. For myself, I can only say that I saw no reason to hold back on any information I had already filed or was about to file as news copy – even if the Yard did decline to pay the standard linage rates.

On only one occasion, to my knowledge, did I have any direct dealings with MI5, the SB's even shadier colleagues from the Ministry of Defence. I was sitting in front of the television watching the early evening news in the summer of 1962 at my newly acquired home in Prestwick, Ayrshire. The doorbell rang, and wearily I made myself answer it. Standing side by side on the quarry-tiled front step were two men who were strangers to me. One of them produced a warrant card and introduced himself. His name escapes me, but if I remember correctly his card described him as the Chief Superintendent of Ayr County Constabulary. As we shook hands, he introduced me to his partner, describing him as "Mr Mann of the War Office" (forerunner of the Defence Ministry). He said:

"I hope you don't mind us calling on you at home, but I thought it might be more private here than at the airport. Inspector Dobbs kindly gave us your address." He had given the name of the senior officer of the Ministry of Aviation constabulary at Prestwick Airport nearby – the same Bert Dobbs, then a Detective Sergeant, with whom I had been on nodding terms at Heathrow, and who had almost been a witness to attempted intimidation by a Detective Superintendent all those months, years, earlier. The speaker paused and motioned to his companion to follow on.

Dressed in a heavy grey tweed topcoat over a blazer and flannels, with a battered tweed porkpie hat on his head, Mr Mann did not look like the stereotyped plainclothes police officer. Middle-aged, short and stocky, he wore glasses and sported a strictly military-style ginger moustache. His first name could easily have been Alexander. And with his ruddy complexion and greying ginger hair he would then almost certainly have been "Sandy" to his fellow-Scots, though I was never able to verify this.

From then on "Sandy" did all the talking.

He was pleasant and disarming in his strong Ayrshire accent, so my uncomfortable feeling of guilt over some unknown offence I must have committed quickly vanished. When I responded, he went on: "I wondered if you might be able to help me with some enquiries I'm making; whether you would answer a few questions for me?"

I replied: "So are you also a police officer, Mr Mann?"

For a moment he hesitated, then dramatically looking over his shoulder in both directions along the deserted road beyond my garden gate, he said softly, with a glance at his companion: "Actually, Mr Berry, I'm from MI5. But would you mind if we talked inside?"

I motioned them into the sitting room and both Mr Mann and the police officer perched on the edge of a couch, while I switched off the news and pulled a chair out. He then asked me if I could remember the names of two US subjects among a number of Latin Americans on board a Soviet airliner which had touched down at Prestwick en route from Havana, Cuba to Moscow some fifteen months earlier. "I understand you wrote a story on it at the time," he said, trying to be helpful.

I did remember the occasion, and said so. But I certainly couldn't remember the names. It had, in fact, again been a story by Chris Bramwell, my former colleague who had by now returned to London. He had spotted the two Americans, listed by nationality, among the 31 passengers aboard the Soviet Ilyushin 18 airliner. There were 14 South Americans on the flight, including Mexicans, Costa Ricans, Bolivians, Peruvians, Venezuelans, Paraguayans and one Cuban. The two US passport holders and 15 Russians, mainly diplomatic staff and their families, made up the remainder.

The airliner was one of a number of non-scheduled Soviet flights operating between Moscow and Cuba throughout the Cuban crisis of the early 1960s, and we were convinced that the American wire services at least would be interested in two Americans apparently working with Fidel Castro.

"Of course," I said, "We will still have the story on file. It may take a little time but I'll happily look it out for you tomorrow if you'll tell me why you want to know."

"Sandy" moved closer, lowering his voice conspiratorially. "I can't tell you very much," he said. "But I think I can tell you that the US Federal Bureau of Investigation has been making enquiries about two Americans, Mario Lopez and Mario Gonzales or Viseppo, who were believed to have passed through Prestwick on a Russian airliner from Cuba.

"I'm really only speaking to you on behalf of the FBI – as a favour to them. We… my department shouldn't really become involved. "

So saying, he produced from a folder a document clearly marked "Secret." He unclipped a photograph, then carefully replaced the document.

"Take a look at this picture," he said. Then, as I studied it: "Is this one of the two men on the flight at Prestwick?"

I looked at the picture intently. "I'm sorry," I said at last, "But I really can't answer that. It's… so long ago – more than a year. And I only saw them briefly, from a distance. I could say he looks vaguely familiar, but I might be deceiving myself... and you."

Sandy was visibly disappointed. I felt quite sorry for him. "I'll look out our original copy tomorrow," I volunteered, "Maybe that will jog my memory. But I wouldn't be too hopeful."

He didn't ask, so I didn't tell him that Chris had spotted the two names on a hand-written manifest handed over to Immigration when the passengers were shown into a transit lounge during the two-hour halt at Prestwick. The list had been erroneously left on a desk after staff had left the area, and Chris had quickly jotted down details of the various nationalities on board the flight. None of the passengers would answer his questions, and only a few of the Russians claimed to understand English.

Then I took the opportunity to ask him why the FBI were interested in the two men and whether he appreciated that I would have to report our conversation. He replied: "I'm sure you'll understand that I can't tell you the reason for the FBI's interest. I do know that you are the only people outside Cuba or Moscow who could confirm the fact that the Americans were on the flight." And he added: "I can't stop you reporting this but I must ask you not to mention my department's role in these enquiries. It could be embarrassing for us."

He didn't seem concerned when I mentioned the American wire services, except to repeat that he hoped nothing would be published in the US that would point to British security services releasing such information. I carefully avoided pointing out that the only "releasing" so far had been on my side. Soon after that my visitors departed. "I'll be in touch," said Mr Mann as I saw them to the gate.

The following day I spoke to him on the phone. He had arranged the contact through Bert Dobbs office, declining to give me a direct number to call. I told him I had traced the original story, but that the names he had given me did not correspond with ours. But he assured me that our Mario was the same Mario Gonzalez the Americans were looking for – Viseppo was in fact his middle name. The name of our second American, Jose Marcano, meant nothing to him. "But one out of two is not bad," he said.

Then, as if to indicate that he had sought advice from some higher authority, he added: "I can leave it to you to pass on whatever information you feel you should to your American clients, providing it is done discreetly, and providing they only use that information as a basis for their own enquiries in the US." (Thinking over this conversation later I couldn't help wondering how Mr Sandy Mann would have reacted if he'd known that I too had once been the subject of similar "enquiries" by his own organisation, presumably on behalf of the British Government).

Following a discussion with Ray Watts at Heathrow I agreed there was no point in trying to put together a story for British newspapers on this latest development in a situation which would hardly rank among the major "international spy scandal" stories. It was hard enough to justify advising the American wire services, but we did. Neither *Associated Press* nor *United Press International* ever returned the favour by telling us if further enquiries in the US had paid off. Neither, for that matter, did Mr Sandy Mann.

*

In complete contrast, the sudden defection some nine years earlier of British diplomats Guy Burgess and Donald Maclean was to become the most incredible spy sensation in British history. Though the scale of the infamy was not even suspected at the time, the incident opened up a can of worms which even forty years on has never been completely purged.

The *Daily Express* first broke the news on the morning of Thursday, June 7 1951. Their chief correspondent in Paris, S. L."Larry" Solon, revealed that two employees of the Foreign Office had disappeared from London. They were thought to be on their way to Moscow for "idealistic" reasons.

The following day the Foreign Office reluctantly issued a statement confirming the *Daily Express* information that the names of the two men were Donald Maclean and Guy Burgess, and that they were members of the Foreign Service. They said that they had no information on their whereabouts, but stated that they had been missing from their homes for the previous thirteen day. Both had been suspended from 1 June for being absent without leave.

In the days that followed, the efforts by British newspapers to track the movements of Burgess and Maclean – the conjoining of the names was to become as familiar as that of a music-hall double act – almost reached fever point. Reports and rumours of sightings, abounded. But very quickly so did the more authoritative and reliable eye witness reports, and the factual evidence unearthed by experienced newspaper reporters.

I clearly recall the relief we all felt when it became certain that the pair had not "escaped" straightforwardly through either Heathrow or Northolt. There was no logical reason for our concern. We were no more aware of their defection before that day in June than any other member of the public.

Nevertheless colleagues at Heathrow and Harry and I at Northolt spent several days trying to discover if the pair had caught a scheduled flight to Paris, where, it was soon discovered, they had stopped on their journey behind the Iron Curtain on their way to Moscow. When it emerged that they had driven from London to Southampton and boarded a cross-channel steamer for St. Malo... well, of course, we knew all along it would have been something like that.

We did become involved in the story again – in a small way – sooner than we expected. Donald Maclean's American-born wife Melinda, had been left behind in London by her husband with the couple's two children Fergus, 7, and 4-years-old Donald. She was also expecting a daughter, Melinda, who was born two weeks after her father's disappearance.

When she and the children flew out from Northolt for a holiday in the South of France newspapers naturally assumed she would be meeting up with her husband. But the Foreign Office, who had earlier asked her to stay in England, not only agreed to her trip but failed to oversee it. Harry reported her departure on a BEA flight.

Lady Maclean, mother of Donald, was at the airport to see them off. She told Harry: "Mrs Maclean is making no attempt whatsoever to find her husband while she is in France. This is purely a holiday."

One month later the family returned. This time I was at the edge of the tarmac as she left a BEA Viking carrying three-months-old Melinda, the two boys at her side. As two or three photographers snatched pictures, I asked her: "Did you see or hear from your husband while you were away?"

Mrs Maclean, who had twice been reported "missing" from her holiday villa while on the Riviera, replied, "I haven't seen him, I haven't heard of him and I did not expect to. I've had a wonderful holiday, and that's all it was."

Was it true she had been called back to London by the Foreign Office? "That report was an absolute lie," she said.

Carrying her baby daughter, Mrs. Melinda Maclean, with her son Fergus aged seven (seen above), landed at Northolt last night with her other son, David, 6, after a month's holiday in France. She said she had not seen or heard of her husband, missing diplomat Donald Maclean, and had not expected to. And she denied a report that the Foreign Office had ordered her home. It took her an hour to clear the Customs and Immigration offices.

MRS. MACLEAN RETURNS

MRS. MELINDA MACLEAN, American-born wife of Donald Maclean, one of the two missing diplomats, flew back to London last night with her family after their holiday in the South of France.

Before driving off from the airport to her home in Tatsfield (Surrey) she said: "The report that I had been called back to London by the Foreign Office was an absolute lie."

Daily Mirror picture (with headline & caption) News Chronicle (left) (both) Sept 17 1951

'I HAVEN'T SEEN MY HUSBAND'

MRS. MELINDA MACLEAN, attractive U.S.-born wife of Donald Maclean, one of the missing diplomats, arrived at Northolt last night after her holiday in the South of France.

When asked for news of her husband she replied: "I haven't seen him, I haven't heard of him, and I did not expect to."

Her brother-in-law, Mr. Alan Maclean, who met her at the airport, said: "She has come back under the original arrangement with the Foreign Office.

Airline officials considered whether to take the Macleans through a side door, as police and security men held back crowds of sight-seers. But Mrs. Maclean said, "No, I can take it."

As she boarded a car taking her to her Tatsfield, Surrey, home, she declared, "I had a wonderful holiday, and that's all it was.

"The report that I had been called back to London by the Foreign Office was a lie."

Mrs. Maclean and her children were on holiday at Beauvallon, near St. Tropez. Police kept a discreet vigil on her villa.

Daily Graphic

Mrs Maclean Flies Home

MRS. MELINDA MACLEAN, American-born wife of Donald Maclean, one of the two missing British diplomats, returned to London last night from the South of France. "I've had a wonderful holiday, and that's all it was," she said. In her arms as she stepped off the airliner at Northolt was her baby daughter Melinda, wrapped in a blue and white shawl. Close behind them came Mrs. Maclean's two other children, Fergus, aged 7, and Donald, 5, with her mother, Mrs. Dunbar. They drove off to Mrs. Maclean's home at Tatsfield.

Daily Mail

MRS. MacLEAN. HOME FROM RIVIERA: 'I DIDN'T SEE DONALD'

TIGHTLY clasping her shawled Baby Melinda, born after the disappearance of her diplomat husband, Mrs. Melinda Maclean stepped out at Northolt Airport last night from the plane that brought her back from a month's Riviera holiday.

Elder of her two young sons, fair-haired Fergus, aged eight, followed closely behind, clutching a "comic."

To questions about her missing husband, Donald, Mrs. Maclean replied: "I havent seen him. I haven't heard from him, and I didn't expect to."

Then she drove off in a car with her mother-in-law, her sons, the baby and Donald Maclean's brother, Allan.

Daily Herald, reconstructed from damaged original.
(all) Sep 17 1951

Mrs. Maclean home

Mrs. Melinda Maclean, wife of the missing diplomat, landed at Northolt last night after her holiday on the Riviera

Daily Express

The following year, in September 1952, the family moved to Switzerland, where Mrs Maclean told the authorities she wanted to make a permanent home. But after just one year she and her children vanished from their new home. Her mother who was staying in Geneva with them was told that they were going to spend the weekend with a friend. A few days later they were in Moscow – and were reunited with Donald Maclean.

From time to time news of both defectors emerged from behind the Iron Curtain. Both were said to be working, in different capacities, for the Soviet authorities. But I had no further contact with the names Burgess or Maclean until 1954. Then the *Daily Express* of May 10 published my report on Page One:

MACLEAN, BURGESS FLY IN

SECURITY men at London Airport looked suspiciously at two men who flew from New York yesterday.

Their names, adjoining on the B.O.A.C. passenger list, were *Mr. Donald Maclean* and *Mr. Burgess*.

The security men relaxed. No missing British diplomats for them, after all.

Said Mr. John C. (not Guy) Burgess, of Surbiton, Surrey: "I wasn't even aware there was a Donald Maclean on the flight."

Mr. Maclean? He left the airport unaware of the stir his name had helped to cause.

Daily Express
May 10 1954

A small diversion perhaps. But the reality was to return for me a further two years on when the *Daily Express* and the *Daily Herald* of September 15, 1956 carried my interview with the left-wing former Labour MP Tom Driberg on his return from a visit to the Soviet Union – to see Guy Burgess.

I asked Driberg, how he came to make contact with Burgess in Moscow when so many others had failed. "In the simplest possible way," he replied. "I wrote to him. But I'm not saying how I obtained an address for him."

He continued: "In my letter I told him I was coming to Moscow and would like to see him to talk over the whole story. To my astonishment and surprise, I received a reply. I used to know him slightly."

He had spent several hours with Burgess every day for a month, checking information for a book he was writing. He did not see Donald Maclean while he was there, because "he was away on holiday."

Driberg then went on to vigorously defend the former diplomat and his actions. "It is utter nonsense to label Burgess as a traitor," he said, "I am convinced that he acted in good faith and did nothing contrary to the interests of this country." Burgess had described allegations that he was a Communist agent as "utter rubbish," he said and added: "He has never given any secret information to the Russians."

The former diplomat, said Driburg, hoped to come back to England in due course. "I have no idea when," he said, "The job he is doing in Moscow he finds satisfying and interesting. He realises, being a realist, that he probably would not get another job with the Foreign Office and also that it is probably desirable to wait until the cold war hysteria has died down a bit.

"But he is an Englishman, and he certainly hopes and intends to return."

Driberg claimed that Burgess was employed in a foreign languages publishing house which published translations of Soviet books. "It is nonsense to suggest he is drafting important speeches. He is not doing any exalted work."

A well-known journalist as well as a politician, Driberg said that his book would not be a defence of Burgess, although he admitted: "It is rather more favourable to him than unfavourable. I do not pretend I agree with the action he and Maclean took, but I consider he was perfectly right to do what he did, feeling as he did."

Whether it was out of a sense of justice, whether it was purely for its news value, or whether it was simply loyalty to Driberg as a former staff member of the *Daily Express,* the paper's columns gave his comments considerable prominence the next day. Under a three-column heading *(below)* they ran the interview over some ten column inches, in spite of knowing only too well that the former Parliamentarian was either being very naive or had his own motives for his standpoint. Driberg's views on Burgess were the total opposite of those of the *Express* and other British newspapers which had uncovered more evidence than the British Government would ever admit to. Indeed most newspaper research in those early years merely demonstrated the total incompetence and ineptitude of the British security system while legal restraints meant that they themselves could often only hint at the guilt and complicity of others in high places.

The newspapers and the handful of MPs who were party to similar information were eventually vindicated for their claims. The former Washington-based diplomat Harold "Kim" Philby was eventually proved to be a Soviet agent. He had been wrongly cleared by Prime Minister Harold Macmillan of charges that he was the "third man" who had tipped off his two colleagues that they were under investigation. He fled to Moscow in 1963. Professor Anthony Blunt, Keeper of the Queen's Pictures and her senior art advisor confessed to being the "fourth man" in the original spy ring, and lost the knighthood he had been awarded in 1955. All four have since died.

Even the former head of MI5 himself, Sir Roger Hollis, who died in 1973, was named by a highly respected *Daily Express* investigative reporter, as being an agent of the Soviet KGB – the "fifth man." And after his death even Driberg himself was also revealed to have been a Soviet spy .

In more recent times Western investigators have poured through the freed archives of the Soviet security services in the hope of discovering their secrets. Some believe there may be yet more revelations in the future.

Driberg defends Burgess

'HE IS NOT A TRAITOR'

Express Staff Reporter

MR. TOM DRIBERG, former Socialist M.P. for Maldon, Essex, said when he arrived at London Airport from Russia last night that it was "utter nonsense" to label the missing Foreign Office diplomat Guy Burgess, now in Moscow, as a traitor.

"I am convinced," said Mr. Driberg, "that he acted in good faith and did nothing contrary to the interests of this country.

"Unless you accept that, any opposition to the foreign policy is contrary to the interests of the country."

Burgess, said Mr. Driberg, went to Moscow with Donald Maclean (in 1951) because he happened to believe what he believed politically.

Maclean was the first to have the idea.

'UTTER RUBBISH'

Said Mr. Driberg: "Burgess says 'utter rubbish' to the allegation of his being a Communist agent.

"He has never given any secret information to the Russians.'

Driberg was asked how he contacted Burgess. He said: "In the simplest possible way.

"To my astonishment and surprise, I received a reply. I used to know him slightly.

"In my letter I told him I was coming to Moscow and would like to see him to talk over the whole story."

Burgess hoped to come back to England in due course.

Said Mr. Driberg: "I have no idea when. The job he is doing in Moscow he finds satisfying and interesting.

"He realises, being a realist, that he would not get another job with the Foreign Office, and also that it is probably desirable to wait until the cold war hysteria has died down a bit.

"He is an Englishman, and he certainly hopes and intends to return.

'IT'S NONSENSE'

"He is not the sort of person who would do any work of which he was ashamed. It is nonsense to suggest he is drafting important speeches. He is not doing any exalted work.

"His work is in a foreign languages publishing house, which publishes translations of Soviet books."

Mr. Driberg, who disclosed that he was with Burgess for several hours every day for the past month, said he did not see Donald Maclean because he was away from Moscow on holiday.

Driberg said he checked information with Burgess for a book he is writing.

"It is not a defence," said Driberg. "It is rather more favourable to him than unfavourable.

"I do not pretend I agree with the action he and Maclean took, because I believe there are other ways of doing it.

"But I consider he was perfectly right to do what he did, feeling as he did."

Daily Express (both) Sep 15 1956

Burgess may come home

Guy Burgess, former British diplomat who fled to Russia with Donald Maclean, hopes to come home "when the cold war dies down," according to Mr. Tom Driberg.

The one-time Labour M P, who has been seeing Burgess in Moscow, arrived back last night at London Airport.

"He is a loyal Englishman and he certainly hopes and intends to return," he said. Mr. Driberg is planning a book on Burgess.

Daily Herald

CHAPTER ELEVEN

Modern major airports are never finished. If they were they couldn't remain major for long, and they wouldn't be modern. Demands on airport facilities change, and they in turn must constantly change to meet those demands.

Few other industries in the last eighty years have developed so rapidly as aviation. It is a growth that has placed unparalleled pressures on airports. Aircraft have become bigger and faster, routes and destinations have expanded and passenger figures have continued to increase year on year, well beyond what was thought to be the nth degree.

Arrival and departure terminals, access roads and car parks, onward ground transport, operational, security and safety services – all have had to be constantly reviewed, renewed and re-provided. The passenger service, staffing and administrative back-up needs of airlines, control authorities and a host of other essential and peripheral organisations have had to be constantly restructured to keep pace with these changes and improvements.

Over the years my colleagues and I were sorely tempted to report these changes and developments, great or small, because our working lives were so often affected by them, until we reflected and applied the acid test of "Who's interested? Who will care?" Only when we were able to establish that someone, or rather some many, among passengers or staff *would* care did we apply ourselves to the situation.

Heathrow, the world's busiest international airport, has also been described as the UK's No.1 building site (*and* the world's largest shopping mall with parking for aircraft… but that's another story). Surprisingly perhaps to the average passenger, one of the principal functions of BAA plc and Heathrow Airport Limited, as owners and landlords of this prime redeveloping property, is – constructional engineering.

Since the mid-sixties almost every single major development on the airport has been initiated, planned and designed by in-house engineers of the company or its state-owned predecessor, the British Airports Authority. Each of the three passenger terminals has seen massive refurbishment and periodic expansion. New satellite terminals have sprung up around them, along with the provision of more than sixty huge gate rooms alongside the aircraft parking bays, each one of them as large as the original departure lounges. Below ground, pedestrian subways with moving walkways were tunnelled to link the terminals with each other, with bus stations and multi-storey car parks, and with London Underground and main line rail networks.

Away from Heathrow's central terminal area, on the airport's southern perimeter and almost within hailing distance of one of the world's largest air cargo centres, the even-larger Terminal 4 was completed in the mid-eighties. Measuring 25 metres by 650 metres – the length of six football pitches – it boasts its own on-site, direct-access luxury hotel, mainline express and underground railway stations. More recently, following a long, drawn-out public inquiry, work began on an even more ambitious development, the construction of Terminal 5 on the site of the former sludge treatment works at Perry Oaks to the immediate west of the airport central terminal area. It too was finally opened by the Queen in the Spring of 2008 to cater exclusively for British Airways flights.

Whilst other airports owned by BAA have seen proportionately similar capital investments, Heathrow's assets alone at the turn of the millennium totalled £2 billion, half the value of all the company's seven airports put together.

For the first two decades of its life, the London airport, which had been conceived furtively by a wartime Air Ministry, was weaned and nurtured on taxpayers' money by enlightened post-war Governments. The mid-1950s brought the opening of the first of the permanent passenger terminals, for European and UK domestic flights, at the heart of the diamond-shaped centre of Heathrow. Now Terminal 2, it was followed seven years later by the "long-haul" Oceanic terminal, renamed Terminal 3 when British Airways forerunner, BEA, moved over into the even newer Terminal 1 in 1969.

All of these have periodically have been refurbished and added to, then extensively redesigned and rebuilt throughout the following years. Many of these early developments were to have an unhappy start in life, and some of the problems, we believed, were due rather more to weak domestic planning and severe financial restraints than to the official excuse of "teething troubles." There was an early example of bureaucratic cheese-paring which led to the cancellation, on cost grounds, of an air-conditioning system for Terminal 2, only for the original ventilation scheme to be replaced, through necessity at a later date, with a more expensive and less efficient air exchange system.

There were also the heavy-handed attempts by the old Ministry of Civil Aviation's airport management to try to compensate for this huge public expenditure by imposing unrealistic charges on airlines and other tenants for every new facility, with apparent disregard of the need for a harmonious working relationship. On one hand the tenants constantly complained that high operating costs and poor civil service management were making Heathrow the most expensive and least efficient airport in the world for them to operate from. On the other, the civil servants responded that they were charged by Government to make the airport pay for itself.

Sometimes the determination of airport management officials to make money brought ridicule from the airport staff, scorn from the media and travellers and outrage from parliamentarians – who were often themselves to blame. The original red brick and glass frontage of Sir Frederick Gibberd's award-winning Terminal 2 – or Europa Terminal as it was then – should have set the architectural standard for the full development of the central area "diamond city." Its clean, rustic lines, so in tune with the mid-fifties, cried out for his open boulevard for short-term car parking, with two or three avenues of small trees. Along one side, adjoining the terminal, would be a forecourt for 'buses picking-up and setting-down, on the other a one-way route for through traffic.

The trees were never planted. The forecourt became another congested through-route; the car park immediately came under pressure. The number of airlines using the terminal rapidly grew until there was no space for expansion. And when additional accommodation was desperately needed, the airport management was forced to make do and mend by squeezing out less essential services or by providing lower grade alternatives. Indicative of this parsimonious policy was the attempt to meet a huge increase in left luggage, which led to the erection of a temporary steel and timber structure at the centre of the Terminal forecourt. It was a decision akin to placing a builders' hut in the centre of The Mall.

We picked up on the information that Sir Frederick was formally complaining against a development which he believed, as did many others, was not in sympathy with his terminal design. He withdrew his protest only after he was assured that the prefabricated building was purely an urgent temporary provision. There was worse to come.

In no time at all a senior airport manager was tempted from his nearby office window by the view of that temporary provision's virgin flat roof now available "for exploitation," as he put it to me later. His department had been approached by an advertising agency looking for a prime site on behalf of a client, for which they were prepared to pay rather more than the going rate. The airport manager picked up his telephone and called the agency. "I think we may be able to do business..." he said.

Brenard Press picture

The "business" turned out to be whisky – or rather three giant fibreglass reproduction whisky bottles (which we had to assume to be empty) placed upright on the roof of that single-storey baggage shed. Gulliver-style at nearly twelve feet high, they raised the total height of the structure to nearly twenty feet, almost the same height as the glazed wall of the terminal they faced just a few yards away. The "bottles" carried a major distiller's familiar label with its standard text eye-catchingly inverted or mirror-imaged. Alongside were huge brilliantly illuminated panels with the message in three languages: *"There's no mistaking White Horse Whisky".*

My story in the nationals produced the expected public reaction. Words like "distasteful," even "obscene," were spluttered in the correspondence columns of the newspapers. Aviation Minister Peter Thorneycroft was asked in the House of Commons why he had sanctioned the display. He replied with just two words: "For money." At a fee of £10,000 it was one of the most expensive advertising displays of its kind in the country in 1961[1].

A few months later the bottles were quietly removed – so the full annual

[1] *Equivalent to at least £165,000 forty years on*

fee was never paid. A spokesman for the Ministry said that the display had to go because the left-luggage office was due for demolition.

The shed was still standing several years on. And the man who visualised the display site remained ever unrepentant. At that time David Livingston was deputy manager at Heathrow. Although I had first known him when he was a manager at Northolt, we became friends when a few years later he was appointed general manager of Prestwick Airport. He confessed to me then: "I don't regret my decision on the whisky display one little bit. I had been told I had to find a new way of making money, and this wasn't going to cost us a penny. I was quite prepared to take the flak for what I knew would be only a short commitment."

There weren't many similar episodes at the time. Such blatant commercialism on Crown property was usually frowned upon in those early years. Nowadays, a few whisky bottles, Gulliver-size, full or empty, wouldn't be noticed amid the range of advertising and hoardings which clutter the privatised and fully commercialised airport's central terminal, some of them just as tasteless. The difference is that all semblance of a unifying architectural theme vanished with the march of progress. The aesthetic has been sacrificed to functional market forces, to paraphrase one civil aviation critic.

It was however surprising that the Ministry didn't follow other controversial money-making ventures. Perhaps the imposition of swingeing increases on airlines that needed to operate to London was seen as less risky. "As landlords we are guardians of the public purse," a Ministry spokesman said when I put some of the complaints to him. "Many other airports in the world are subsidised by governments. In the UK we believe the industry should pay for the facilities we provide."

Few disputed the principle, even if it were quite obvious the extra costs would be born eventually by the passenger. But as one airline chief put it: "If we thought the money – our profit – was being put to good use we could understand it. But so much of it is wasted, through mismanagement of resources, through other inefficiencies, wastage and overstaffing. And so many of the charges are exorbitant and unrealistic."

*

In January 1962, shortly before my move to Scotland's Prestwick Airport, the Heathrow representatives of three major London hotel groups approached me. They wanted to tell the press of proposed charges for their basic accommodation requirements in the new Terminal 3.

As airport landlords, the Ministry of Aviation had invited three principal hotel groups to bid for prestigious positions in the terminal. Separate desks no larger than a speaker's lectern were being offered... *at a minimum rental of £2,000 a year.*[1] Measuring a mere 2ft.3ins by 1ft.6ins (685mm by 457mm), these were to form an arcade in the arrivals hall. The space allocated to each hotel desk would be wide enough to accommodate just one representative, who would then be standing literally shoulder to shoulder with a neighbouring rival.

Among the hotels approached by the Ministry were the Savoy, Berkeley and Claridges group, the May Fair, which also controlled the Grosvenor and Victoria Hotels, and the Westbury Hotel, one of the American Knott Hotels group. And I soon learnt that most of them had rejected the invitation out of hand. A spokesman for the May Fair hotel told me:

"The accommodation offered is beyond the ridiculous. It is absolutely fatuous. We are offered a bit of desk just about big enough to stand a telephone on. We have no intention of submitting a tender on such a basis. It would be cheaper to book reservations by installing a two-way radio between the hotel and a man in a car."

The Westbury said: "When we heard that the tenders could not be lower than £2,000 we were astounded." A spokesman for the Savoy group, which had the largest representation at the airport with its permanent three-man team, declined to comment publicly, but my information was that they too had rejected the chance to bid.

The story was well received, particularly by the "heavies"– with the *Times*, the *Daily Telegraph* and the *Daily Express* all giving it a double column spread alongside a single column seven inches in the *Guardian*. Popular newspapers gave similar coverage (shown reduced opposite) though curiously the *Financial Times* was unable to authenticate a double column reproduction cutting I produced for them some years on.

[1] *Or more than £33,000 at current costs*

HOTELS BOYCOTT BID FOR AIRPORT RECEPTION FACILITIES

Most of London's leading hotel groups, representing between them the City's main overseas visitors' accommodation trade, have decided to reject a Ministry of Aviation invitation to bid for reception facilities in London Airport's newest passenger terminal.

The hotels were invited to submit tenders for desks measuring only 2ft. 3in. by 1ft. 6in. at a starting price of £2,000 a year.

The Westbury Hotel, one of the American Knott hotels group, was "still considering" the invitation last night. A spokesman said: "We were unable to get a starting bid from the Ministry for our tender. When we heard the tenders could not be lower than £2,000 we were astounded."

"FATUOUS" FIGURE

A spokesman of the May Fair Hotel said: "The figure suggested for the accommodation offered is beyond the ridiculous. It is absolutely fatuous. We have no intention of submitting a tender for such accommodation on this basis. All that is offered is a small desk big enough to hold a telephone."

The May Fair was one of the first hotels to open a reception desk in the old north terminal temporary building. "Originally we were given to understand that because of our long association with the airport we would be given priority", said the hotel's public relations officer, Mr. S. Allen. "Then we found we had to bid just like everyone else. This take-it-or-leave-it attitude seems to be typical of the airport these days."

He went on: "The new passenger building was obsolete before it was opened. At any other world airport such facilities as hotel reception desks and accommodation for travel agencies would have been included in the original design of the airport. From the plans we have seen the accommodation offered us would be useless."

8 DESKS PLANNED

A spokesman for the Savoy group, which has a three-man team of receptionists on permanent duty at the airport, last night declined to comment.

Eight hotel desks were planned in the £3m. passenger building which is being opened to all long-distance flights early this summer.

The boycott by the hotels is likely to lead to second thoughts among other organizations which have asked for concessions in the big arrival hall. Already several of the five main banking concerns are said to be doubting the wisdom of spending so much on rental at the airport. One travel agency, the American Express Company, has refused accommodation offered, describing it as "an unprofitable venture". For its 20ft. of counter space the agency was being asked to pay £24,000 a year.

A Ministry of Aviation spokesman refused last night to comment on the hotel boycott. "We never discuss details of private contracts" he said. He was unable to say whether any tenders had so far been submitted. "These tenders are not due in until January 16. Until that date they are kept in a padlocked wooden box", he said.

The Times

Hotels refuse airport desks at £2,000

Nearly all the leading hotel companies in London have rejected an invitation by the Ministry of Aviation to tender for reception desks at London Airport, at a minimum rent of £2,000 a year. The desks measure 2 ft. 3 ins. by 1 ft. 6 ins.

The hotels invited include the Savoy, Berkeley and Claridge's, the Mayfair, and Westbury. Eight hotel desks were to form an arcade in the new £3 million passenger building being opened early in the summer.

The Westbury Hotel, one of the American Knott Hotels group, was "still considering" the invitation last night. But a spokesman said: "When we heard the tenders could not be lower than £2,000 we were astounded."

A spokesman for the Mayfair Hotel, which also controls the Grosvenor Hotel, said:

"The figure suggested by the airport management for the accommodation offered is beyond the ridiculous. It is absolutely fatuous. We have no intention whatever of submitting a tender for such accommodation on this basis. All that is offered is a small desk big enough to hold a telephone.

"At any other world airport such facilities as hotel reception desks and accommodation for travel agencies would have been included in the regular design of the airport. From the plans we have seen the accommodation offered us would be absolutely useless."

A Ministry of Aviation spokesman refused to comment last night on whether any tenders had so far been submitted. They are not due in until today week.

The boycott by the hotels is likely to lead to second thoughts among other organisations which have asked for concessions in the building. Several of the five main banking concerns are said to be doubting the wisdom of spending a large rental at the airport.

One large travel agency, the American Express company, has refused accommodation offered it as an "unprofitable venture." For 22 ft of counter space the agency was asked to pay £24,000 a year.

£40 week for desk at the airport

LEADING London hotels are boycotting an invitation to bid for eight hotel reception desks at the new long-distance terminal building at London Airport because—

The Ministry of Aviation say bidding must START at £40 a week.

And that, say the hotels, is too high.

A spokesman for the May Fair Hotel said last night: "We are offered a bit of desk just about big enough to stand a phone on."

The desks measure 2ft. 3in. by 1ft. 6in. The new £3,000,000 building will open early this summer.

Daily Sketch (above)
The Guardian (left)

Hotels boycott airport desks

LEADING hotels in London are boycotting an offer of reception desks at London Airport's new passenger terminal.

Daily Mirror (above)

'£40-a-week for airport desk is too much'

Daily Herald (right)

HOTELS PLAN BOYCOTT AT LONDON AIRPORT

Daily Express

HOTELS SHY FROM £2,000 FOR DESK AT AIRPORT

FIGURE CALLED "FATUOUS"

Daily Telegraph

(all) January 9 1962

Like so many of the issues between the airport landlords and their tenants, the matter was eventually resolved to the satisfaction of no one. The hotels ended up sharing a facility, which inevitably meant that their individual prestige suffered. The landlords gained one nominal rent when they might have won three or four. We gained, as observers, a considerable insight into the failure of bureaucracy to win friends and still make money for their employers, the taxpayer.

*

That insight paid off for me at Prestwick, where so many of Heathrow's "teething troubles" were to be duplicated over the next few months. My posting to the Scottish transatlantic airport came in the spring of 1962. Bill Brenard had called me to his office the previous November to discuss "a proposition."

I had no idea what it might be about, but it wasn't unusual for Bren to call in one or more of us as a sounding board for his ideas, and I always welcomed the opportunity. His enthusiasm and optimism were infectious, but when he suggested that the time was ripe to re-open a news service in Scotland, I was a little dubious.

Former Heathrow colleague Charles "Chic" Henn had made a great success of the

Brenard office at Manchester's Ringway Airport, serving the northern editions of the nationals with his locally-recruited deputy, Bernard Spilsbury. Chic's predecessor, Derek Ball, had moved on to cover Dublin Airport on his own, independently of the agency (though, it seemed with Bill's tacit agreement). But Prestwick, like the Irish Republic's Shannon Airport, had been abandoned as a Brenard outpost some years earlier, and I was never sure of the reason.

It was out of character for Bren to rake over almost dead ashes unless he believed there was a very good chance of rekindling the fire. As I should have known, he had done his homework. Glasgow's city airport at Renfrew was due to close. It was already too small for its rapidly growing UK and European traffic, and couldn't be expanded. But the decision had yet to be made: should Glasgow have a totally new airport or should domestic traffic be absorbed at Prestwick, some 30 miles from the city centre?

Bill Brenard was convinced, along with the great majority of civil aviation opinion outside Glasgow that the west coast airport was the logical choice. Its main runway was the only one north of the border that was capable of taking the largest aircraft in service. It had the best weather record of any airport in Britain. It supported a nucleus of transatlantic services to the US and Canada, and indeed was already shown as *Glasgow* airport in international airline timetables. A transfusion of domestic and European routes from Renfrew would guarantee a prosperous future for a world-class airport. It could serve not only the commercial capital of Scotland, but with improved surface transport links, also the political capital at Edinburgh *and* the industrial north-east of England.

Against Prestwick was the understandable argument that it was simply too distant from Glasgow city centre to provide it with a range of popular short-haul air routes. The principal demand of a domestic airport had to be a door-to-door fast air link with London. Heathrow was normally only an hour's flying time away with its network of air services to Europe and the rest of the world. Even a proposed new road between the centre of Glasgow and the Ayrshire coast which would cut the surface travel time to a little over 30 minutes, and the prospect of an alternative dedicated airport station on an existing rail line, failed to convince the opponents of Prestwick. And it mattered little to them that Renfrew-bound flights already had to divert to the transatlantic airport whenever bad visibility closed the city airport.

Prestwick remains unique among British airports in that it is virtually fog-free all year round. Throughout the major part of the '60s I spent there, air services were disrupted by poor visibility only once, and even then just briefly due to a passing sea mist. Thanks to the Gulf Stream, its average winter temperatures are several degrees higher than in many parts of the UK. Falls of snow are a rarity. Despite its distance from London – some 360 air miles – it was for many years a principal diversion airport for Heathrow. And a modern new terminal building was already planned.

"When Renfrew closes, Prestwick could become as important to Scotland as a whole, as Manchester Airport is to the Midlands and the North," said Bren. "We need to get back there to serve the Scottish press. And I want you to open an office for us and run the operation."

I had already begun to suspect this was the reason for the meeting. But I managed to look surprised and pleased. Before I could say anything, Bren went on: "I don't want an answer now. Go home and think it over. But I think it's a good opportunity for you – you'll be your own boss and you will be able to hire your own staff. We'll give you all the financial back-up you need to start up, and of course we'll pay for your moving and resettlement costs."

I broke in to ask the questions that had been nagging at me. "But if it's such a good prospect now, why did we close down the last operation there? It's been known for a long time that Renfrew would have to close. What if the present services move to Abbotsinch and not Prestwick?"

Abbotsinch, a Royal Navy training and sea-rescue air station which was due to close, had been named as a potential site for a new civil airport for Glasgow. Like Renfrew, it was near Paisley, to the west of the city and easily accessible. Bren was happy to respond. "Our first effort at Prestwick was a financial disaster. We couldn't persuade the Scottish papers to pay enough in retainers to make it worthwhile. And we had difficulties getting the right staff.

"But now," he went on, "The situation is quite different. We are so well regarded in Fleet Street that the Scottish news desks, particularly the *Scottish Daily Express*, the *Daily Record* and the *Scottish Daily Mail*, want us back, and have agreed to back us financially. But we must remember not to talk about retainers – it's a word that's not officially acknowledged. We'll have to call it a service fee or something."

Bren believed the dispute over the siting of Glasgow's airport had also helped the decision. "The newspaper people I've talked to there are convinced Abbotsinch won't be chosen," he said, "It's incapable of expansion operationally because of its proximity to the Clyde and densely populated areas. The short runway already runs almost up to the river.

"They would regard our presence at Prestwick as a form of insurance. They can't hope to cover it in the same way they are able to cover Renfrew, which is on their doorstep. But if the worst happened, and you were unable to settle or achieve job satisfaction there... well, you can always return south. Your role here will still be open to you."

We talked for more than an hour and I said I would think about it. Two weeks later, after much heart-searching and domestic discussion I gave him my answer: I would accept the challenge and happily transfer if the financial arrangements and other details were satisfactory and only if – I emphasised – I could take Chris Bramwell with me, if he agreed.

Chris was a few years younger than I, and we had worked together very successfully on a number of stories. He was a first class reporter and I knew we could get along very well. I recalled, in particular, our partnership on the tragic disaster of August the previous year when a twin-engined Viking airliner from Heathrow carrying 34 British schoolboys and their teachers smashed into a Norwegian mountain. They and the airliner's crew had all perished. We had laboured together for nearly 20 hours with hardly a break, sympathising with distraught parents and other relatives, and gleaning information from helpful airline staff in the face of an unyielding official news blackout.

With a new baby daughter, I had no wish to be on call twenty-four hours a day and cherished my time off. Chris, on the other hand, was still single and had no ties of which I was aware. That meant it should be much easier for him to forge the social relationships and make the contacts essential when setting up in a totally environment. When I suggested the idea, he too saw the advantages in a move away from Heathrow.

Daily Mirror

North Sea hunt for school party

3d. Thursday, August 10, 1961 No. 17,930

34 LONDON BOYS IN MISSING HOLIDAY AIRLINER

Daily Mirror

DAILY EXPRESS

THURSDAY AUGUST 10 1961

Holiday trip ends in disaster over the fiords five minutes before 'Papa Mike's' landing time

SCHOOL PLANE: 39 LOST

London boys down

Daily Express

Evening Standard

42,659 THURSDAY, AUGUST 10, 1961 3d.

Full list of names and addresses: Page Ten

Pictures of the boys: Pages Eleven and Twenty

THE PAPA MIKE DISASTER

First full story from scene of the crash

Plane hit mountain —all died instantly

From JACK HAND: Stavanger, Thursday

The terse message, "Wreckage found: no survivors," flashed by a rescue party on a mountain in Southern Norway today ended a 15-hour search for the Viking airliner which left London yesterday with 34 Croydon schoolboys and two masters

Evening Standard (left, above and overleaf) (all) August 10 1961

The *Evening Standard* report continued:

A few hours after it resumed at first light came the message from the mountain that ended the hopes of the parents of Croydon who had waited throughout the anxious night.

AT LONDON AIRPORT full emergency procedures were adopted by the airline during the night as staff in a special operations room dealt with inquiries from relatives of the boys.

One after another relatives were traced and warned that the aircraft was "overdue." One by one the scribbled names of the boys were ticked off the hastily pencilled copies of the passenger list.

The wives of the pilot, 40-year-old Captain Phillip Watts, of Camberley, Surrey, and his co-pilot, 29-year-old First Officer Reginald Smalley, who also lives in Surrey, were told.

The parents of the only girl on board, 22-year-old stewardess Susan Endicott, of Paignton, Devon, were told this morning.

Her fiance, Army officer Chris Moysey, who spent yesterday with her and saw her leave, had spent the night at the airport waiting for news.

The Viking was to have left London Airport at 9.30 a.m. yesterday. Instead it left at 2.30 p.m. after a hold-up caused by an ignition fault.

Evening Standard (extract)

One of our later contributions to the *Evening Standard* after our all-night and early morning session. *(see previous page)*

Although hesitant about the increased costs involved, Bren listened to my arguments and eventually agreed to my proposal. "Chris can go with you for the next year or two. By then you should have found someone locally to take over from him." I made one final stipulation: that if all failed, my senior status would not be affected, and that I would be free to return to Heathrow in any event if I wished after a maximum of ten years. This too was agreed.

Four months later my home in Iver, four miles from Heathrow, was sold and my family and I were on our way by air to Scotland. On an earlier recce, Chris and I had driven north, he in his Triumph Herald, I in my company Vauxhall Victor. It was a first long drive, something over 400 miles, for both of us, so we made an overnight stop en route. Arriving next day in Ayrshire reasonably refreshed, Chris sought out some digs, while I found furnished accommodation and made arrangements for my furniture to be transported and taken into storage. Now I was able to move into a single-storey cottage just 300 yards from the sea-front at Ayr, and only a few minutes drive from Prestwick airport.

Initially without an office or even a telephone, Chris and I quickly found our feet at Prestwick and were filing our first stories from public call boxes within 48 hours. Our understandable themes: the signs of growing tourist traffic and the attractions of Scotland to the first-time visitor – which contained more than a hint of personal experience. When it came to the future of civil aviation in Scotland, we were on familiar ground as we learnt that the "barbed arrow" design for the airport's proposed new £1,500,000 passenger terminal (£30 million at today's costs) might have to be scrapped, or at least completely revised.

The inside information came from a senior airport management official, Chris's first Prestwick "contact." We were able to follow up this story with the news for the Sunday papers that not a single contractor had been prepared to build the terminal at Ministry of Aviation prices. In spite of a two-months' extension on the closing dates for bids, every tender submitted to Whitehall was far in excess of Government estimates.

Site preparations and foundation work had already been completed under an earlier contract. The terminal was to have been fully operational some eighteen months later. Now it seemed the hold-up could delay the completion by at least a further six months. Even implied charges of commercial speculation could not disguise the obvious. The Government wanted an architect's design created in steel, bricks and mortar – on the cheap.

This time the news came directly from the managers of the major airlines at Prestwick. Once we had established our credentials with them they had realised the value of having a national news agency on hand. The splashes our exclusives gave us in the northern editions of English newspapers as well as the Scottish nationals and city evening papers reinforced that view and they were quick to bring us up to date on the current problems on the airport. For our part we were able to show that we had plenty of experience of commercial ineptitude or naïvety by Ministry management.

The normally laudable objective of protecting the public purse had become the standard excuse for penny-pinching over any development. The caution was even more likely if the financial returns on any proposed investment were to be long-term rather than immediate. Conversely, the number of commercial ventures which appeared to guarantee a "fast buck" return steadily increased, with apparently little thought for public service or amenity, aesthetic design or even basic good taste.

Design faults were to dog the launch of the new Prestwick terminal from Day One of its construction. Then as forecast, the completion was delayed for almost a year by the row over building costs, which finally totalled £2 million, half a million more than the original estimate in spite of drastic economies. Halfway through the delay I reported that the airport's tenants – British and foreign airlines and others – had learnt that rents for their existing "ramshackle and dilapidated" offices in the old terminal, known as the Orangefield site, could be more than doubled at the end of the following month.

The warning came in a notice to quit – a legal requirement before

Airlines fear 100 p.c. Prestwick rent rise

AIRLINES using Prestwick are fearing that rents for the airport's buildings may be more than doubled.

They expect this to be at the end of next month.

Warning of the pending increases came recently in the form of a notice to the five major airlines to quit their premises by March 31—the legal requirement before any new lease can be negotiated.

'If we quit . . .'

So far, new terms have not been fixed by the airport's "landlords"—the Ministry of Aviation.

But a senior official for one airline said yesterday: "Some of us have been led to expect the present rents to be increased by 100 or even 200 per cent.

"We are wondering what the Ministry would say if we accepted the notice to quit."

Ministry officials in Edniburgh were yesterday unable to confirm the report of a probable increase in the rents.

Said a spokesman: "Re-assessment of property for leasing purposes is done purely on an ordinary commercial basis by the Air Ministry lands branch.

"As far as we know they have not yet completed their assessments for the Prestwick accommodation."

Daily Herald (also the Scotsman - not shown) Feb 25 1963

any new lease could be negotiated. It was followed by the offer of a new lease "on terms to be negotiated later." As one of the airline managers put it: "We've been led to expect the present rents to increase by one hundred to two hundred per cent. Some of us are wondering what the Ministry would do if we all accepted the notice to quit."

It was suspected that the airport management was trying to soften the blow of even higher rents for accommodation in the new terminal through the introduction of staged increases. The proposals were quickly modified when they heard of the reaction of the airlines and other tenants. The manager of one North American airline told me: "We would expect to pay higher rents in the new terminal. It's an expensive building. But we don't like paying through the nose for our present accommodation which is decomposing through dry rot and is comparatively inefficient and unplanned."

The airlines' problems were only just beginning.

*

One of the more surprising early discoveries that Chris and I made at Prestwick Airport was that BOAC – the state-owned *British* Overseas Airways Corporation – was not seen locally as the national airline of *Scotland*. That distinction was not even awarded to the then still small but nevertheless ambitious charter company Caledonian Airways, which regarded the Ayrshire airport as its home base.

Just five major airlines then operated scheduled daily transatlantic flights in and out of Prestwick: BOAC, KLM Royal Dutch Airlines, Pan American Airways, the Scandinavian Airlines System and Trans Canada Airlines (later to be renamed Air Canada). Most of these services originated in London or on the European Continent. Although a state-owned corporation, BOAC was firmly viewed at Prestwick as a London-based, *English*-owned airline with an English manager. Its operations and its policies were dictated from London, just as KLM, Pan Am and TCA were all very much influenced by the policies and operations of their various overseas-based headquarters.

Perhaps it was that SAS, the joint national airline of Denmark, Norway and Sweden, could claim an affinity with their Scottish hosts through their ancient Viking roots. Perhaps it was because they, alone of the five, could boast an all-Scottish staff and a Scottish manager at Prestwick. Or perhaps it was that their daily transatlantic service to New York operated from a low-demand Stockholm or Copenhagen at a more convenient time and was less likely to be fully booked than BOAC's service. (The latter originated in London and picked up passengers in Manchester en route to Prestwick.) Or perhaps it was a combination of all these factors, plus an inevitable bit of Scots cussedness, that made it *their* "world's favourite" airline.

We soon discovered that we weren't the only English arrivals in Scotland to recognise this. Harry Pusey, BOAC's then recently appointed manager 'phoned one day inviting me to call at his office in the old terminal building. "There's someone here I'd like you to meet," he said, adding confidentially: "I think you'll find it interesting."

Author's collection
Ross Stainton, BOAC's western routes manager

Minutes later I was shaking hands with the general manager of BOAC's western routes, Ross Stainton. To my question: "What brings you to Scotland?" Stainton glanced across to Harry, as if inviting him to respond. He picked up the cue.

"What would you say if I told you we're planning to get SAS banned from Scotland?" he asked. It took a moment to sink in. "How?" I responded at last. And Stainton himself broke in to reply: "By getting the Government to take away their fifth-freedom right to pick up passengers here."

I wanted to say: "Are you telling me or still asking?" Instead I re-acted instinctively. "I'm horrified," I said. "I'm amazed and shocked. And I believe that's how the Scots will react." I turned back to Harry. "You know how the Scots feel about SAS," I went on, "And you know how they feel about BOAC. Surely this can only make things worse."

Stainton interrupted me. "I hear what you say. But I don't think things are as bad as all that. And if we guarantee to improve our service to Scotland to make up for any shortfall, I'm sure everyone will see the advantage to the British taxpayer if we win back passengers we are losing to a foreign operator."

It wasn't the time for a detailed discussion. There were more important questions remaining. "Are you telling me this for publication?" I asked, "And have you started the process? How soon do you hope to see them out and will you replace their flights?"

Both Scandinavian Airlines (SAS) and the Royal Dutch airline (KLM) were permitted to drop off and pick up passengers at Prestwick on their transatlantic services under rights negotiated internationally immediately after the second world war. Reciprocal so-called fifth-freedom rights for Britain through low-demand Dutch or Scandinavian airports were neither sought nor required, as they normally would be under other 'freedom-of-the-skies' agreements. Now these multilateral treaties were due for their routine five years' review by Britain and the three Scandinavian countries.

"We have been putting pressure on the Government to look again at the treaties," said Stainton. "They are very important and no British Government has so far faced up to the issue. We believe these fifth-freedom rights are very unfair to us, and we would be delighted if the Government finds the courage to do something about ending them."

He said that both SAS and the Dutch carrier, whose rights were also due to be reviewed, had been allowed to pile up traffic while BOAC was "still struggling" on the Scottish-American routes. "Surely that's the fault of BOAC," I said. "Why could you not fight the competition on a purely commercial level?"

Stainton refused to answer that directly. But he told me, "not for quotation," (at that time) that BOAC had missed its opportunities to respond when its competitors launched intensive sales campaigns in Scotland. He added, again privately: "If they are allowed to continue, these rights could cost us at least £5million a year within the next five years." He wouldn't be drawn on how BOAC would make up for Prestwick's loss of two transatlantic services other than to say: "One step at a time But I promise that the Scottish passengers won't suffer."

The Press may not have foreseen it, but the BOAC action was an ominous move which was to have major ramifications for Prestwick and Scottish aviation in the future.

I ran the story for the next day, but the results were disappointing. Only the two heavy Scottish papers, the *Glasgow Herald* and the *Scotsman*, found it significant, but the *Guardian* in Manchester ran it as a ten-inch single-column piece on an inside page

*

It was at a routine meeting with the airport commandant C.D. "Wally" Waldron at the end of September, 1962, that one interesting idea to boost the future of the airport first surfaced.

This was soon after our arrival in Scotland and long before Prestwick's new terminal was built. We had recently been sought out by Ian Imrie, the Glasgow Herald's air correspondent, and I had readily agreed with him to try to set up a regular routine meeting with Wally, something I was already planning to do myself. Ian, whose paper was one of our important and very supportive clients, was now coming to Prestwick once or twice a week, and we had a good working relationship.

Chris and I knew however that the commandant's door was open to us at almost any time to offer answers to our news questions. This meant that only rarely did we have to look for responses or comments on airport matters from an anonymous "spokesman," the aviation ministry's press officer in Edinburgh. If we declined a joint formal meeting, we would not know what Wally had

B.O.A.C. BID TO BAN FOREIGN AIR LINES

Possible Effect at Prestwick

Pressure by the British Overseas Airways Corporation to have two foreign air lines banned entirely from Prestwick Airport — or their services severely restricted—could cost the British taxpayer hundreds of thousands of pounds yearly in lost revenue and reduce the number of international air lines using the Scottish international terminal to three.

B.O.A.C. are demanding the ending of "Fifth Freedom" agreements with Scandinavia and Holland, which allow their national air lines to pick up and disembark transatlantic passengers at Prestwick.

The two air lines, Scandinavian Airlines and KLM (Royal Dutch) Airlines, have held these rights since 1946, although no British air line has, or wants, reciprocal facilities.

REDUCED INCOME

Financial losses to the taxpayer would be in the form of reduced landing fees and ground service charges paid to the Ministry of Aviation by all air lines, as it is thought unlikely that B.O.A.C. would wish to provide an equivalent frequency.

Restrictions on foreign operators could also be a further threat to the future of Prestwick Airport. If SAS—and, eventually, KLM—lost traffic rights they would be unlikely to continue using Prestwick as a transit point purely for refuelling.

©Glasgow Herald Nov 27 1963 (also the Scotsman – not shown)

Hopes for end of 'unfair' agreement

Behind-the-scenes moves by BOAC to end the situation in which foreign airlines are allowed to pick up and disembark passengers and freight at British airports are taking place during the discussions which opened in London yesterday between the British and Scandinavian Governments.

Aviation experts from Britain, Denmark, Norway, and Sweden, are making their five-yearly review of bilateral agreements on the freedom of airlines to operate services to and from each other's territory. The concern of BOAC is directed towards an agreement which has been in force since 1946—the "fifth freedom" right of the three-nation Scandinavian Airlines System to operate services from Copenhagen by way of Prestwick to New York and back, picking up and landing passengers in Scotland.

Official attitude

No British airline has—or requires—reciprocal rights in any of the Scandinavian countries. The official BOAC attitude was disclosed publicly yesterday by Mr J. Ross Stainton, general manager of BOAC's western routes. He said:

"The question of competition on the North Atlantic by fifth freedom carriers is a very important one at this time. No British Government has so far faced up to this issue. We know that successive Governments have been very much alive to the problem, as are the Americans. If they had the courage to do something about ending this unfair agreement, we would be delighted."

Mr Stainton said that SAS and the Royal Dutch Airline, KLM, which has similar rights through Prestwick due to come under review, were allowed to pile up traffic while BOAC was "still struggling" on the Scottish-American routes.

It is thought that the British airline has missed opportunities in Scotland partly because of the intensive sales campaigns of its foreign competitors.

Financial experts say that if it was allowed to continue, the "fifth freedom" rights could cost BOAC more than £5 millions a year within five years.

Guardian Nov 27 1963

discussed with Ian, or indeed whether either of us was being favoured with an exclusive. We had nothing to lose; it could only be to our advantage to attend these routine meetings which Ian intended to seek as an individual anyway.

I never really knew where the notion originated. It could have been suggested by a group of Scottish businessmen, as Wally maintained (and they could have been the managers of the five main airlines at Prestwick). It may even have been Wally's own idea. My own belief after all these years is that it sprang from the lively mind of Harry Pusey, the BOAC manager at Prestwick, who, as I've indicated elsewhere, preceded me to Scotland by only a few weeks. He was certainly aware of the proposal before it hit the headlines.

Wally outlined the plan to Ian, Chris and me, and then invited questions. Just as it had pioneered duty-free shopping for UK passengers, Prestwick, he said, was also ideally placed to become Britain's first duty free port, with its own international industrial estate. "We have the land, we have the runways, we have the roads and we have the basic infrastructure."

He pointed to the success of the duty-free industrial estate at Shannon Airport in the Irish Republic. This had been not only a principal factor in maintaining the air terminal; it had also contributed significantly to the Irish economy and labour opportunities by attracting foreign industry. With the removal of Customs restrictions, Irish and foreign manufacturers had been able to import raw materials such as parts for cameras, electronic equipment, portable radios, sewing machines, even pianos for assembly, and export the finished "manufactured" product without paying duty.

He claimed that his "group of businessmen" had been prompted to put forward the proposal by the failure of successive Governments to come to a firm decision on the future of Scottish airports. A rise in unemployment with a drift of labour south across the border, and a steady decline in the Scottish economy, had swiftly led to further support. Now they were seeking political backing for their campaign.

Behind-the-scene discussions, he said, had already taken place with politicians keen on aviation development. One prominent speaker had been expected to raise the suggestion at the recent Liberal Party conference in Llandudno, but was "hindered by the pressure of other business." And he added that the proposal had been intentionally leaked at a meeting of the Royal Aeronautical Society in Glasgow, but was not picked up. "It is generally believed," said Wally, "that in addition to giving Prestwick Airport a much-needed boost, a duty-free estate close to the airport would have far-reaching benefits for the Scottish economy generally."

Siting of the estate, he said would present no problems. "Ayr County Council have scheduled 150 acres nearby for industrial development. Offices and workshops valued at £750,000 suitable for light industry are being vacated by the National Coal Board, and other areas of ground bordering the airport could be given over to such development."

Customs and Excise authorities would have to give the scheme their backing. But he added: "It has been proved that the administration of a duty free area is not difficult. No Government department must be allowed to stand in the way of a plan to save a national economy."

The only real problem he could visualise was whether the Government would feel justified in providing inducements for foreign capital and investment as was found necessary in Ireland. Yet thanks to its proximity to the Glasgow industrial area and a huge labour pool, Prestwick could be a much better proposition to overseas manufacturers than the comparative remoteness of Shannon.

Several of these points were covered by Wally in our questions and answer session, which followed his initial announcement. Winding up, however, he emphasised that as far as personalities were concerned, everything he told us would have to be unattributable. We realised that, as a senior civil servant, he could not be giving his views on something, that might become a political issue. But he declined to be drawn on the identity of the anonymous "businessmen" behind the scheme even after we had pointed out that the publicity could only be to their advantage. If we felt we had to use direct quotes, he said, he could only be described as an unnamed supporter of the plan.

Our meeting with Wally had taken place on a Friday – not the best day for coverage in the following days' papers. Ian, quite naturally, wanted to hold back on the story for publication in Monday's *Glasgow Herald.* I told him there was no way we could afford to

COUNCILLORS MEET CUSTOMS MEN

Prestwick plan discussed

Talks between senior officials of the Customs and Excise and members of Ayr County Council were held in London yesterday on the proposals for setting up a duty-free industrial estate at Prestwick Airport. The County Convener, Mr Daniel Sim, who headed the council's delegation, said when he got back to Prestwick that the talks were "useful but not conclusive."

The meeting was the first to be held between representatives of the local authority and a Government department apart from preliminary discussions with Customs officials at Greenock some weeks ago.

Mr Sim said: "It is likely we shall require another meeting after Customs have considered our suggestions and we have considered theirs. It is clear that from the beginning there have been points about Customs administration about which we were not aware."

©Glasgow Herald *Mar 2 1963*

Customs talks on duty-free estate

Mr. Daniel Sim, Ayrshire county convener, headed a county council delegation at talks in London yesterday with Customs officials about the proposed duty-free industrial estate at Prestwick Airport. He said the talks were "useful, but not conclusive."

Scottish Daily Mail *Mar 2 1963*

miss out on Sundays' papers, and when I pointed out that Sunday news rarely seemed to affect repeat coverage the following day, he reluctantly agreed, and said he could spend the extra time following up political comments.

We could have wished for a better spread in Sunday's newspapers, particularly in the more popular papers, but the subject seemed a bit too heavy for some of them. The *Sunday Times,* the *Observer,* the *Sunday Telegraph* however, all gave us a big showing, as did most of the dailies when we followed up the story for them. On Monday I took copies of both Sunday's and Monday's papers into Wally Waldron. He confirmed he had only seen one or two. His delight was transparent. But before he could say anything he reached to answer a ringing telephone. He obviously recognised the voice on the line.

Gesturing to the open *Sunday Times* on his desk, as if his caller could see it, he yelled with glee: "We've done it, we've done it!" I thought I recognised the faint voice at the other end of the line as that of Harry Pusey...

Almost immediately the politicians, national and local, began to jump on the bandwagon, though for all we knew some of them may already have been at its steering wheel. Daniel Sim, the convener (or chairman) of the local Ayrshire County Council and a team of experts met up with Customs officials just four days later. The Chancellor of the Exchequer, Reginald Maudling, called for a report on the scheme, and initial proposals were detailed. Seven months on and the Scottish Council for Development and Industry took an active part when their vice president, Sir Robert Maclean, said he intended to sound out American industrialists for their views on a duty free estate at Prestwick.

The months passed. Occasionally we heard rumours of industrialists getting together to plan details of the estate, of talks with overseas trade missions who might be persuaded to set up assembly plants for their exports. Again and again the idea was discussed, mulled over, promoted, recalled and reviewed. Questions were asked in the House of Commons – but always, the Government of the day was noncommittal.

What did emerge more clearly than anything was the total opposition, at least locally, of Customs and Excise, who no doubt saw the proposal as a threat to their powers. Their influence on the Treasury reinforced the unwillingness of any government, Labour or Conservative, to pursue the matter seriously. It also eliminated any chance of a British government providing financial inducements to industry to establish assembly plants at such sites as the Irish government had done.

A full *twenty* years was to pass with no positive move being made. Then, in the early 1980s, under revived pressure from constituency parties, MPs, and the highly favoured right-wing financial "think-tank," the Adam Smith Institute, Margaret Thatcher's government agreed, at last, to set up a working party to look into the basic proposals.

Incredibly after so long, the working party's report was fully in favour of the establishment of the first duty free ports and trading estates in the UK. Even more unbelievably, the report's recommendations were immediately accepted in totality by the government.

Announcing this in his 1983 Budget, Chancellor of the Exchequer Sir Geoffrey Howe, said that he was introducing enabling legislation for the designation of freeport sites. "The first step is to establish free ports on an experimental basis in a limited number of locations," he added, and went on: "Widespread consultation will be needed before the sites are chosen."

There was no mention of Prestwick Airport and no indication that it might have a prior claim to be one of those chosen sites, or even that it might feature in the proposal.

George Younger, Tory Secretary of State for Scotland, was tackled on the subject by a local radio station. As the Member of Parliament for Ayr, which meant Prestwick Airport was in his constituency, he was asked why the Chancellor hadn't named Prestwick as a freeport area. He replied by pointing out that the matter was a long-term project which he recalled (accurately) had first been "suggested" twenty years earlier. He talked enthusiastically about Prestwick's chances but hurriedly referred to the rights of other areas to put forward similar claims. He forecast that the first duty free ports would be established within the next few months.

His prediction as a Government "insider," and strong supporter of the proposal, was also accurate. By February 1984 – eleven months after the Budget announcement – the first six sites in the UK were chosen. They included Prestwick.

It seemed, that now, at last, the race was on; to win over potential manufacturers, to establish the necessary infrastructure, to provide the on-site facilities and essential services. It was a race, however, which was to prove significant only for its its prohibitive bureaucratic rules and regulations, its absence of big-name industry participants, its lacklustre performances, and a total absence of newsworthy "records" in achievement.

It was also a race set for a pistol-start which was literally years too late. Overseas potential competitors had not only left the arena... but in many cases had already retired on their laurels.

The idea of free trading zones was not a new one. Duty free ports and inland trading estates had been long-established around the world. In Europe, Hamburg had been operating successfully as a free trade zone since the nineteenth century. No fewer than sixty similar zones had been established in America before the second world war. Britain had only now reached the stage of agreeing the venues – *and was still looking to catch up.*

Slowly but inevitably, the novelty of the idea wore off. Business in Britain was no longer interested (if indeed it ever had been). Perhaps that explains why, when I contacted him in 2001, Lord Howe of Aberavon, who as Sir Geoffrey Howe, Chancellor of the Exchequer in Margaret Thatcher's government, had made the original official proposals, couldn't remember what had happened to them.

"I do not recollect any formal announcement of legislation on this topic," he told me by letter, **"although we might have spoken sympathetically about the idea as deserving further study.**

"I do not think the idea was ever a serious starter." (The italics are mine.)

In reality, as a result of Lord Howe's Budget, a number of duty free trading estates were set up around Britain during the mid-1980s. For a while it even appeared that intensive efforts by enthusiastic politicians and business entrepreneurs would overcome what some supporters described as widespread obstruction by government departments and Customs and Excise.

When I last checked, at least two estates were still functioning, at Prestwick and Southampton. Their operators were reporting some success in seeking new business. Perhaps surprisingly, they were still optimistic about the future.

*

Eighteen months after reluctantly agreeing the first of a series of progressive rent increases for their old accommodation (though at a lower rate than first proposed), the airlines had to ask for a further postponement of the long-delayed move to the new terminal a quarter of a mile away. Their own cleaning, decorating and fitting of offices and check-in areas had not been completed. A voluntary 48-hour delay became a three-day wait....

RACE TO COMPLETE £2m. AIRPORT

© Evening Times, Sept 8 1964

OPENING DELAY AT PRESTWICK

The opening of Prestwick Airport's new £2m. passenger building, due to-day, has been postponed for 48 hours, it was announced last night.

Air lines, who were to have moved to-day from the 20-year-old prefabricated buildings, requested the postponement at an emergency meeting with Ministry of Aviation officials two hours earlier.

The reason, according to an airport official, is that final decorating and cleaning up of the building have not been completed and the extra time will allow kitchens and other catering facilities to come into use for the first passengers.

©Glasgow Herald

Airport opening held up

TODAY'S opening of Prestwick Airport's new £2 million passenger building has been postponed for 48 hours so that final decorating and catering arrangements can be completed.

The delay means airlines, Government Departments and shops will have only three days to prepare for the official opening by the Queen Mother on Tuesday.

In the meantime the old passenger terminal may be without some of its facilities because restaurants, bars and shops in it were due to close down today.

DELAY THREATENS NEW TERMINAL

Daily Telegraph Reporter

The opening of Prestwick Airport's £2 million passenger terminal, which was expected to be today, may have to be postponed for 48 hours. At an emergency meeting last night, two airlines asked for a postponement because catering and cargo-handling facilities may not be ready.

A Ministry of Aviation spokesman said that catering would be available. The official opening, by Queen Elizabeth the Queen Mother has been arranged for next Tuesday.

Daily Telegraph (all) Sept 9 1964

Scottish Daily Mail (left)

AIR DATE FOR QUEEN MOTHER

THE Queen Mother will formally open Prestwick Airport's new £2,000,000 passenger terminal on September 22—almost a year behind schedule.

Airlines and other companies on the airport are expected to move in a week earlier to ensure the building is operational for the Royal visit

Originally, the new passenger terminal was to have been ready last October, but the Ministry of Aviation had to revise its specification when it was found no firm was prepared to build at the official estimate

Completion dates of first spring, then summer this year were later abandoned

Sunday Mail July 5 1964

Opening date 'flexible'

Unless there are any last minute hitches, the Queen Mother will formally open Prestwick Airport's new £2,000,000 passenger terminal on September 22, almost a year behind schedule.

Airlines and other companies at the airport are expected to move in a week earlier—to ensure that the building is operational for the royal visit.

An official of the Ministry said yesterday: "Any dates we have given airlines are still flexible, though they may be confirmed shortly."

Scottish Sunday Express July 5 1964

● The Queen Mother has accepted an invitation to open Prestwick Airport's new £2 million passenger terminal this autumn. The date has been set for September 22 providing there are no last-minute hitches.

Airlines are expected to move in a week earlier to ensure that the building is operational for the royal visit. But some airport authorities believe that the terminal will be working at only half-pressure.

Originally the terminal was to have opened last October. But the Ministry of Aviation had to revise its specifications when it was found no firm was prepared to build at the official price estimates.

Scottish Daily Express July 6 1964

ROYAL OPENING OF TERMINAL "IF NO HITCHES"

Daily Telegraph Reporter

Queen Elizabeth the Queen Mother will open Prestwick Airport's new £2 million passenger terminal this autumn. The date has been set for Sept. 22, providing there are no "last-minute hitches."

Airlines will move in a week earlier, to ensure that the building is operational for the Royal visit.

But some airport authorities believe the terminal will be working at half-pressure. The building was to have been ready in October, 1963, but the Ministry of Aviation had to revise specifications when it was found that no firm would build at official estimates.

Later dates of spring and summer this year were then abandoned as more delays occurred. Yesterday, a Ministry official said: "Any dates we have given airlines are still flexible, though they may be confirmed shortly." The tenants have been growing impatient. Some face extra costs for insisting that their private contractors complete specialised construction work in time.

Daily Telegraph July 6 1964

QUEEN MOTHER FOR PRESTWICK OPENING

Queen Elizabeth the Queen Mother has accepted an invitation to open Prestwick Airport's new £2m. passenger terminal on September 22.

Air lines are expected to move in a week earlier to ensure that the building is operational for the royal visit.

©Glasgow Herald July 6 1964

Airline departures and arrivals were moved into the new terminal as aircraft took up unfamiliar positions on the virgin tarmac of its adjoining parking apron. Incoming passengers began to stream into the spacious new Customs and passport control halls. Outgoing travellers thronged round the long line of check-in desks. They were joined by even larger numbers of friends and relatives seeing them off… and an unexpected stream of visitors who had come just to see the new terminal.

Over the following few hours thousands of travellers and sightseers poured through the building. For many of them the experience was disappointing. Not one of the visitors was able to buy even a cup of tea, a glass of lemonade or a sandwich at any of the restaurants, bars, buffets or cafeterias officially open for business. Yet two days later, in September 1964, the terminal was to be officially opened by Queen Elizabeth the Queen Mother, as we had been able to forecast exclusively ten weeks earlier.

Airport manager Charles Brown said, "Some of the catering equipment broke down and the manufacturers had to send out engineers with spare parts. In other cases the catering concessionaire was unable to get equipment working even though we helped out with manpower."

Scores of passengers complained. One group of New York-bound Americans staged a sit-down strike outside a bar for 70 minutes until an airport official told them: "There's no chance of it opening yet."

At one stage it looked as if aircraft might have to leave without meals or drinks for passengers, until an emergency supply was rushed in from nearby Prestwick town. Also badly hit were airline and government department staff, many of whom had been working throughout the night moving furniture and office equipment. One airline official said: "I had to allow my staff to leave the airport in relays for coffee and meal breaks in town cafes." And an airline check-in girl told me: "The first thing we did was to go out and buy an electric kettle."

Our Sunday newspaper headlines the following day told the story:

NO CUPPA AT NEW AIRPORT

PRESTWICK Airport's £2,000,000 passenger terminal came into full use for the first time yesterday without one of its 12 restaurants, bars, buffets

Luxury airport opens—but cafes stay shut

PRESTWICK airport's luxury, modernistic £2million passenger terminal came up to full use for the first time yesterday.

down strike outside a bar for 70 minutes until an official told them: "There's no hope of it opening yet."

Sunday Mail (above)
The People (right)
(both) Sept 20 1964

Prestwick Terminal Opens But Restaurants Stay Shut

PRESTWICK Airport's luxury £2 million passenger terminal came into full use for the first time yesterday—without one of its 12 restaurants, bars, buffets, or cafeterias open.

Hundreds of passengers were unable to buy a cup of tea, a glass of lemonade, or a sandwich throughout their long wait for trans-Atlantic planes.

huts of the old terminal.

Said one airline official, "I had to allow my staff to leave the airport in relays for coffee and meal breaks in the town cafes a mile

One group of New York-bound Americans staged a sit-down strike outside a bar for 70 minutes until an official told them, "There is no hope of it opening yet."

Sunday Post
September 20 1964

£2,000,000 OF LUXURY—BUT THERE'S NO PLACE OPEN FOR A CUP OF TEA AND A SANDWICH

Prestwick's thirsty passengers stage sit-down strike

Sunday Express Reporter

THE luxurious and modernistic passenger terminal at Prestwick Airport, which the Queen Mother will open on Tuesday, went into full use for the first time yesterday—but for hundreds of passengers, sightseers and staff it was a hungry, thirsty day.

For although the £2,000,000 terminal has 12 restaurants, bars, buffets and cafeterias, not one was open to serve even a cup of tea and a sandwich.

Scores of passengers complained about the lack of catering facilities. So did their friends, who had driven miles to the airport to see them off on Transatlantic flights.

One group of New York-bound Americans staged a sit-down strike outside a bar for 70 minutes until an official told them: "There's no hope of it opening yet."

Too busy

Even harder hit were airline and Government staff, many of whom had worked throughout the night moving their office equipment from the 20-year-old prefab huts of the old terminal.

Said one airline official: "I've had to allow my staff to leave in relays for coffee and meal breaks in the town, a mile away."

An airline girl said: "First thing we did this morning was go out and buy an electric kettle. We haven't had time to protest—we've been too busy making tea and cutting sandwiches."

At one time it looked as if some aircraft might have to leave without meals or drink for passengers. But an emergency supply was arranged with only minutes to go.

A breakdown

An airport official explained: "The catering concessionaire was unable to get his equipment working in time. In addition, there was a breakdown in some cooking equipment and an engineer had to be called in."

● Members of the Scottish Council may be invited to visit the vast new terminal as guests of the Prestwick Airport Development Association because the Association feels the Council "does not fully realise Prestwick's potential as Scotland's air gateway."

Association chairman Provost Ian Foulds, of Prestwick, said this yesterday after he had complained to the Scottish Council about its huge wall map at the Industries Exhibition in the Kelvin Hall, Glasgow.

Neither the £60,000,000 atom power station at Hunterston, Ayrshire, nor the Prestwick terminal was pinpointed. After council officials had apologised to him, the provost said: "It was an oversight."

Scottish Sunday Express
September 20 1964

Forty-eight hours later the Queen Mother was able to lunch with the Ministry of Aviation's top man in Scotland and other civil servants as planned. We were assured there were no complaints. But the formality of that occasion signalled the coming of even more problems for the airport.

Within a month I was reporting that management officials were meeting to try to resolve a range of difficulties over public and passenger catering services, particularly outside peak hours. Among complaints by airlines and passengers were the high cost of meals and light refreshments, lack of choice and inconvenient opening times. Even accessibility was proving a major difficulty. The only route to the first floor catering areas was via several flights of stairs, with no lift available. That had been ruled out in the accountants' cost-cutting measures.

Over the next two days our enquiries resulted in 68 column inches of copy in the Scottish nationals and evening newspapers in Glasgow and Edinburgh. Headlines to long-running reproductions of my story included:

Terminal trouble

MINISTRY TO PROBE HIGH PRICES, POOR SERVICE AT £2m BUILDING

Scottish Daily Mail *October 12 1964*

in the *Scottish Daily Mail*, while the *Glasgow Herald* gave us:

Teething Trouble at Prestwick Airport

MEETING TO CONSIDER COMPLAINTS

©Glasgow Herald
(also Scotsman: not shown)
October 12 1964

The Sun (left)

AIR CHIEFS FACE CUPPA CRISIS

SUN REPORTER

A CRISIS meeting is on at Prestwick Airport today—to tackle the big catering problem at the £2million passenger terminal opened by the Queen Mother last month.

Senior officials of the Ministry of Aviation will be there. A Ministry expert on catering is flying in from London.

They will face a long questionnaire from airlines, and many complaints from members of the public.

High on the list is the criticism that not one of the airport's nine bars, buffets, cafeterias or restaurants is open after 11 pm.

After that not even a cup of tea can be bought.

High prices, lack of variety offered and poor service are other complaints.

Although no scheduled flights operate through Prestwick at night, bad weather can cause diversions, and charter flights are often timed to arive or depart in the small hours.

The crisis boiled up last week when 400 passengers on trans-Atlantic flights were suddenly switched there from a fog-bound London Airport.

One airline manager said: "Most of them had to wait 90 minutes for a buffet to be opened. Then a four-deep queue formed to be served by one waitress.

"I had to brew flasks of coffee on an office kettle to give my passengers a drink."

Other complaints have been made by delayed passengers unable to buy duty-free liquor "out of hours."

Thousands of pounds' worth of cooking equipment lies idle in one main buffet, and an expensively decorated bar in a departure lounge has not been used.

Only the recently-reorganised rooftop grill-room and the more expensive public restaurant are working at full pressure, serving the thousands of visitors who pour into the airport.

Ministry officials will only say that attempts are being made to overcome the problems and answer complaints.

MINISTRY INQUIRY INTO CATERING AT PRESTWICK

DAILY TELEGRAPH REPORTER

SENIOR officials of the Ministry of Aviation will meet at Prestwick Airport to-day to try to sort out some of the problems and difficulties which have beset public and passenger catering in the £2 million passenger terminal, opened three weeks ago by the Queen Mother.

A Ministry expert on catering is flying from London for the meeting, which will have before it a lengthy questionnaire from airlines, together with a mass of complaints, many from members of the public, some from overseas passengers.

Highest on the list of criticisms is that not one of the airport's nine bars, buffets, cafeterias or restaurants remains open after 11 p.m.

After that time not even a cup of tea can be bought by passengers or public.

High prices, lack of variety offered and poor service also figure in the complaints.

Although no scheduled flights operate through Prestwick at night, bad weather at other airports can cause unexpected diversions, and charter flights are often timed to arrive or depart in the small hours.

The problem came to a head one day last week when, before dawn, Prestwick was "invaded" by 400 passengers on transatlantic flights suddenly switched from fogbound London Airport.

Ministry officials will only say that attempts are being made to overcome the problems and answer complaints.

Daily Telegraph *(all) October 12 1964*

BID TO SOLVE AIRPORT FOOD SNAGS

Express Staff Reporter

SENIOR Aviation Ministry officials meet at Prestwick today to try to solve the problems which have hit catering in the new air terminal.

Probe into Prestwick complaints

TOP-level meetings opened to-day in an attempt to find solutions to "difficulties" over catering facilities in Prestwick's £2m. "showpiece" air terminal opened only three weeks ago by the Queen Mother.

Scottish Daily Express (top)
Evening Times (above)

Similar encouraging spreads were featured in the former *Daily Herald*, by now renamed *The Sun*, the *Scottish Daily Express* and in the Manchester editions of the *Daily Telegraph*, as shown here.

A government catering expert flew in from London the next day for the emergency meeting with Ministry management officials. Together they studied a lengthy questionnaire from airlines and a list of recorded complaints from passengers and visitors.

High prices, lack of variety and poor service were alleged. But highest on the list was the criticism that none of the airport's bars, buffets, cafes or restaurants remained open after 11pm, when once again not even a cup of coffee could be purchased.

Although no flights were scheduled to operate through the airport after that time, charter flights could arrive or depart in the early hours and bad weather elsewhere frequently brought unexpected diversions. Only the previous week 400 passengers on transatlantic flights switched from London had invaded the airport at little notice. Many of these had to wait 90 minutes for a buffet to be opened, forming a deep queue to be served by only one waitress.

AIRPORT'S BID TO END CUPPA CRISIS

SUN REPORTER

A ROUND-THE-CLOCK buffet service and casual staff to provide hot meals at short notice for passengers on delayed or diverted flights, were among proposals considered at a meeting of catering officials at Prestwick Airport yesterday.

A meeting was called after airline managers criticised catering facilities at the airport's passenger terminal, which was opened by the Queen Mother three weeks ago.

Mr. Charles Dive, a Ministry of Aviation catering expert, from London, and representatives of the concessionaires were at the meeting.

The Sun *Oct 13 1964*
... one day on.

Among the suggestions discussed at the meeting were a 24-hour hot meals service with staff available to provide refreshments for diverted or delayed passengers at short notice. I was able to report: "The discussions are continuing, and no firm conclusions are likely to be reached for another 24 hours." But the proposed improvements gave me "progress" headlines again, this time in the *Scottish Daily Express* and the *Daily Telegraph*.

'24-HOUR BUFFET' IS PRESTWICK CALL

Scottish Daily Express

HOT MEALS POSSIBILITY AT PRESTWICK

Daily Telegraph *(both) Oct 13 1964*

Five days after the meeting we won even further headlines in the Sunday and Monday papers when we told of the plans agreed at the talks. We were able to reveal that the proposed round-the-clock buffet service, with late-night hot meals on demand and staff available at short notice for delayed flights was to be introduced immediately. A speeded-up self-service system would replace waitress service at the buffet, and some prices were to be cut.

NEW DEAL FOR DINERS AT PRESTWICK AIRPORT

TWOPENCE off a cup of tea, round-the-clock buffet service, late-night hot meals . . .

These are just a few of the innovations resulting from top-level talks at Prestwick Airport last week to counteract complaints about catering facilities in the new terminal.

The 24-hour buffet service, with sandwiches and rolls and possibly hot snacks and salads at a later date, is the first round-the-clock catering to be introduced.

Although no flights are scheduled to operate from the airport at night, under the new system catering staff will be available to serve passengers on delayed or diverted flights at a few minutes' notice.

A new waitress "call-order" service is to be introduced tomorrow in a main cafeteria, with hot meals available until 10 p.m.

Sunday Post (above) October 18 1964

2d. off the airport tea

Sunday Express Reporter

TWOPENCE off a cup of tea, a 24-hour buffet service and late night hot meals—these innovations were announced yesterday for Prestwick Airport's new £2,000,000 passenger terminal.

They follow three days of talks between the Ministry of Aviation and the catering concessionaires to counteract complaints about facilities at the terminal.

The 24-hour buffet service, with sandwiches and rolls, and possibly hot snacks and salads at a later date, is the first round-the-clock catering to be introduced there.

Scottish Sunday Express October 18 1964

Author's collection

A few weeks on, Brooke Bond introduced their teabags through the already popular "Chimps" campaign, contrary to their previous 'loose-leaf only' policy. This was rumoured to have been inspired by a new patriotic fervour for a more accessible and 'instant' British Cuppa, perhaps as a result of the extensive news coverage.

CATERING FOR AIR PASSENGERS

Improvements at Prestwick

Twopence off the price of a cup of tea, round-the-clock buffet service, and late-night hot meals are among improved facilities to be introduced in the new passenger terminal at Prestwick Airport.

The changes were announced at the week-end by the Ministry of Aviation after talks with those responsible for the catering, which has been criticised.

The 24-hour-buffet service, with sandwiches and rolls and possibly not snacks and salads at a later date, is the first of its kind at the terminal. Although no flights are scheduled to operate through the airport at night, catering staff will be available to serve passengers on delayed or diverted flights at a few minutes' notice.

WAITRESS SERVICE

A waitress "call order" service is to be introduced to-day in a main cafeteria. Hot meals will be available until 10 p.m. A faster self-service system is to replace waitress service at the buffet.

The only price change is 6d for tea, which previously cost 8d, but a "popular" menu is being offered with success in the airport's rooftop grill room.

A Ministry official said:—"Prices and facilities will come under constant review, particularly when we have details of air line traffic plans in the future."

Airport wins 24-hour catering service

By Daily Mail Reporter

A ROUND-THE-CLOCK buffet service and late-night hot meals will be introduced at Prestwic' Airport's new passenger terminal following complaints about the catering there.

The changes were announced at the weekend by the Minister of Aviation after three days of discussions with the airport's catering concessionaire.

The buffet service is the first 24-hour catering at the terminal.

2d. off

Although no regular flights operate through the airport at night, under the new system catering facilities will be available for passengers o.. chartered, delayed or diverted flights.

A new waitress service will be introduced in a main cafeteria today with hot meals available until 10 p.m. And a self-service system takes the place of waitress service in t.ie buffet.

The only price change is the reduction in the cost of a cup of tea from 8d. to 6d.

A Ministry spok. man said: "The prices and facilities will come under constant review."

Airport starts a 24-hour plan

BIG improvements in catering facilities are an air terminal's answer to recent criticism and complaints.

The changes were announced over the week-end by the Ministry of Aviation at Prestwick Airport's new passenger terminal.

Twopence off a cup of tea, a round-the-clock buffet service and late night hot meals are among innovations.

Speeded-up

The 24-hour buffet service, with sandwiches and rolls, a future possibility of hot snacks and salads is the first round-the-clock catering to be introduced at the terminal.

Catering staff will be available to serve passengers on delayed or diverted flights at a few minutes notice — a service demanded by the critics.

A speeded-up self-service system is to take the place of waitress service at the buffet.

(from left) ©Glasgow Herald
Scottish Daily Mail
Daily Record
- also Scottish Daily Express (not shown)
(all) October 19 1964

The teacup storm may have passed by. But now there were real storms on the way.

Two months after the Royal visit, Prestwick's good weather reputation took a battering – as did the terminal itself. Winds, gusting to 50 miles an hour, pounded the terminal, tearing up roof coverings, jamming doors and threatening plate-glass windows. Passengers and visitors found all outside automatic doors locked and barred as a precaution against the gales, and had to enter and leave through a small office side-door.

An area around part of the building where tiles had been ripped away had to be fenced off when it was found that a metal supporting frame had buckled under the strain. And staff had to warn people to stay well clear of the vibrating ceiling-high windows. Soon the gales were followed by further bad weather, as my stories in the Sundays and a page lead in the *Scottish Daily Mail* the next day announced across six columns: "**Airport storm hazard**."

£2m. worth of trouble

PRESTWICK AIRPORT'S luxury £2 million passenger terminal is undergoing a "face-lift" this week—less than four months after it was officially opened by the Queen Mother.

Already, the huge glass-fronted building, which stands directly in the path of the worst Atlantic weather, is causing complaints.

Airline and Government staff say the heating is poor, and complain about draughts, badly-fitted windows, doors which won't stay shut, and leaking roofs.

Tempers which have blown hot and cold over working conditions, reached boiling point last week when the temperature in some of the building's offices fell below 47 degrees.

An evening shift of weather

Sunday Express Reporter

forecasters and their assistants staged a walk-out from the glass-walled met. office, and set up their equipment in a storeroom.

Civil servants say they have had to sit huddled over typewriters in coats and scarves. Others have been sent home from work early.

Airport management officials are viewing the complaints with concern. They have held a series of meetings with airlines and with representatives of the architects and the builders.

The airport commandant, Mr. C. Dennis Waldron, said: "I regard this as a very serious matter. The faults are now in the process of being remedied, however.

"We have already made a start on sealing all the draughts. When that is completed, we shall attempt to re-assess the heating circulation."

Scottish Sunday Express

STORM OVER THE WINDS THAT BLOW THROUGH NEW £2M. TERMINAL

PRESTWICK AIRPORT'S luxury £2 million passenger terminal is undergoing a weather-proofing "facelift" this week, less than four months after it was formally opened by the Queen Mother.

Already the huge, glass-fronted building is showing the ravages of the storms and gales of the past few weeks.

Complaints have poured in from staff about poor heating, draughts, badly-fitting windows, doors which will not stay shut, and leaking roofs.

An evening shift of weather forecasters walked out of the glass-walled met. office and set up their equipment in a store room when draughts made work impossible.

Typists have huddled over their machines in coats and scarves. Others have been sent home early because they cannot keep warm.

Critics blame the design of the building for its defects.

Normal shrinkage of new woodwork and fittings has been magnified by sudden changing temperatures.

No storm doors are fitted, and the eight public doors have to be barred to keep them shut.

Shops in the hall have had to lower their shutters to stop the wind blowing away their stock.

Airport management officials have held meetings with airlines and representatives of the architect and builders.

The airport commandant, Mr C. Dennis Waldron, said, "I regard this as a very serious matter, but the faults are now in the process of being remedied.

"We have already made a start on the task of sealing all the draughts.

"When that is completed we shall attempt to re-assess the heating circulation.

"We hope to find a solution to the problem of the outside doors within a week. Several proposals are under consideration."

Sunday Post (above)
(all) January 17 1965

Face-lift for terminal

PRESTWICK Airport's luxury £2,000,000 passenger terminal is having to undergo a weather-proofing "face-lift"—less than four months after it was formally opened by the Queen Mother.

Already the huge, glass-fronted building, which stands directly in the path of the worst Atlantic weather, is showing the ravages of the storms of the past few weeks.

Complaints have poured in from airlines and Government staff about poor heating, severe draughts, badly fitting windows, doors which won't stay shut and leaking roofs.

Tempers reached boiling point last week when the temperature in some of the building's offices fell below 47 degrees.

An evening shift of weather forecasters staged a walk-out from the glass-walled meteorological office and set up their equipment in a store room when draughts made work impossible.

No storm doors are fitted at entrances to the building and the eight public doors into its main hall have to be barred because they refuse to stay shut in the wind.

Shops in the hall have had to lower shutters to stop the wind blowing away stock.

The airport commandant, Mr. C. Dennis Waldron, said: The faults are being remedied. We hope to find a solution to the problem of the doors within a week."

Sunday Mail

PASSENGERS FACE RAIN AND COLD INSIDE £2m BUILDING

By Daily Mail Reporter

PASSENGERS picked their way through a line of flower troughs, dustbins and buckets stretching end to end across Prestwick Airport's main passenger hall yesterday.

The bins had been brought in to catch water cascading from leaks in the high roof following heavy rainfalls, spotlighting the need for a weather-proofing "face lift" being undertaken this week in the four-month-old building.

Today a team of men will move in to continue patching up holes and cracks they began to repair over the weekend.

Overcoats

Airport management officials have been studying a long list of complaints about defects in the £2 million building, many of which have been emphasised by the storms of the past few weeks.

Among them are doors that won't stay shut. Badly fitted windows, shrinking wall joints, poor heating circulation . . . and the leaks.

"Airport Storm hazard"
(Sub head only shown here)
Scottish Daily Mail
Jan 18 1965

Author's collection

Prestwick's battered new Terminal after the storm.
A solitary car is parked at the forecourt kerb alongside the only entrance - a hurriedly added 'storm porch'. The five remaining doors were all locked and barred against the strong westerly gales.

Similar spreads were given to the story in the *Glasgow Herald*, the *Scotsman*, the *Scottish Daily Express* and the *Daily Telegraph* in Manchester, which like the *Daily Herald/Sun* was ever eager to give Scottish interests a good coverage. The evidence of the leaking roof, which hardly needed privileged information or specialist knowledge, was only one of a catalogue of minor disasters I had to report. Among them were doors that wouldn't stay shut, badly fitting windows, shrinking wall joints and poor heating circulation.

The overall design of the building had been generally praised at its inception; its barbed-arrow shape lent itself perfectly to the throughput of passengers both arriving and departing, and allowed for expansion in various forms as the need arose. But the landward side of the terminal, with its immediate access from forecourt to airline check-in, faced almost directly towards the Firth of Clyde, just a few hundred yards away beyond the local golf course.

As this frontage was glazed throughout its length and height, airline staff at their desks for much of the day found themselves facing the sun whenever it chose to shine – as it did frequently on this Scottish coastline. At times it was blinding enough for air girls to complain: "We can't see the faces of passengers checking in."

But there was an even worse side to the blinding effects of the sunshine…and one which could have had a tragic outcome. Airline official Bill Cummings mistook one of the terminal's floor-to-ceiling windows as he hurried across the concourse to catch his ordered taxi on the forecourt, and tried to walk through it. He had to be treated in the airport medical centre, but fortunately, only for minor cuts.

He told me later: "I mistook the window for the open door which was right next to it. The light was shining right through the glass and causing no reflection." His head hit the glass first, then his fist, which shattered it.

CLEAR THROUGH THE DOOR— IT WAS GLASS!

A floor-to-ceiling plate - glass window at Prestwick Airport's new passenger terminal was shattered to-day when a man tried to walk through it.

The man, air-line official Bill Cummings, was treated in the airport's medical centre for slight cuts.

He said later—"I mistook the window for an open door. The light was shining through and causing no reflection — I just couldn't see the glass until I crashed through it.

"Now the airport wants to send me a bill for damage."

©Evening Times Oct 13 1964

And Bill walked right through the window

Scottish Daily Express Oct 14 1964

Transparent accident

Evening Citizen Oct 13 1964

Wall of glass shattered

Scottish Daily Mail Oct 14 1964

At other times of the year, the same exposed frontage posed more problems. Double doors opened from the terminal directly on to the forecourt. Critics complained that no allowance had been made to protect the entrances from the worst of gales and storms with porches or even a canopy. All but one of them had to be barred and locked in the strong sea winds to keep them closed .

Airport management officials admitted to me that storm-proof doors were not allowed for in the design "because they would have spoiled the look of the building." In the meantime, airline staff throughout that first winter had to keep overcoats on and wear scarves and gloves at their desks because the incoming draughts meant that the central heating system of the building was ineffective.

Surprisingly our relations with the airport management seemed unharmed by the constant bad publicity we were doling out, perhaps because we strove to be fair and gave the Ministry of Aviation every opportunity to respond to the criticisms and explain how they intended to tackle the faults. They were also hearing the same directly from the airline managers on an almost daily basis, so possibly the continuing publicity was in some way helping the airport management in their own ongoing battles with their Civil Service and political masters.

The problems of the new building were, it was claimed, mainly teething troubles – that phrase again. Even so, it was going to take several sessions of extensive dentistry, with an expensive amount of cosmetic surgery before the down-in-the-mouth anguish of increased costs could be salved, and the teeth could again take on the semblance of a smile.

There also had seemed very little to smile about in the long-term prospects of Scotland's intercontinental airport unless a favourable decision could be made soon on the successor to Renfrew. We did our best to keep the flag flying as we promoted the efforts of airlines, holiday agents and tourist and trade organisations to increase Prestwick's traffic figures – and of course to make a living ourselves.

We were happy, therefore, to report the particular efforts of at least one airline to boost its image and standing in Scotland. Contact we had made with the independent charter airline Caledonian Airways was immediately welcomed by the company at the highest level. In October 1963, the airline's chairman and co-founder, John de la Haye, phoned to tell us exclusively of a sales drive he was initiating in North America. The aim was to persuade Canadians and Americans with Scottish links to seek block bookings with the airline through social or travel club membership.

"We are sending a team of six Scottish sales representatives to the US and Canada to contact these organisations and clubs," he said. "We are confident we can capture some of

New capes for Scots air girls

● Scotland's only national air line, Caledonian Airways of Prestwick, which is leading the battle of Britain's independent air line companies to capture a share of the transatlantic passenger traffic, is now setting a novel fashion trend in the air.

Stewardesses and ground receptionists with the company are now being issued with "highwayman" kit to match their distinctive ancient Black Watch tartan uniforms.

Modelling the newly issued cape (left), specially woven in Scotland, was pretty brunette Miss Anne Ross (25), the air line's senior stewardess and sales representative in Scotland. "It's very nice and it does something for a girl," she said.

To-day Anne was on her way to New York—to demonstrate the "flying cloak" to a gathering of travel agents, Scottish tour organisers, and other air lines in America. She is to be the guest of honour at an annual convention of Scottish-American associations.

©Evening Times Jan 28 1964
Brenard Press picture

Brunette Anne Ross, Caledonian Airways's sales representative in Scotland and senior stewardess, models the company's new Black Watch tartan uniform as she prepares to set off on a major sales drive in New York.

"New Look" Tartan Outfit For Scots Air Hostesses

Sunday Post January 26 1964

Caledonian's two-year plan to buy jets

DAILY TELEGRAPH REPORTER

THE Scottish airline, Caledonian Airways of Prestwick, who last week announced the opening of a battle with Joint American Airlines over their plan for £150, 14 days, transatlantic holidays, hope to be in the market for big jets within two years.

Driving force behind the independence airline, is chairman Mr John de la Haye, 35, who disclosed this last night. At present the airline operates a relatively small flight of piston engined DC 7 C and DC 6 B.

"Handsome" profit

But next year they plan to have two prop jet Britannias as their principal flag ships. By 1966 they hope to be flying either the American Boeing 707 or its British rival, the Super VC 10.

Said Mr. de la Haye: "It may seem like crystal gazing to talk of our future aircraft fleet at this stage, but we must look ahead.

For the first time he disclosed that Caledonian Airways made a "handsome" profit in the last financial year.

He said that this financial stability meant Caledonian could attract investment "at its own terms"

Daily Telegraph (all) Sep 24 1964

SCOTS AIRLINE GOES IN FOR BIG JETS

Scottish Daily Express

Caledonian plan to buy big jetliners

Scottish Daily Mail

CALEDONIAN PLAN FOR JETS

Financial Stability

©Glasgow Herald

the market from the Americans." One of that team was pretty Annie Ross, a senior stewardess with the company and their home chief sales rep. She is seated *(previous page)* in a first picture by my newest Prestwick recruit and trainee, Charles Gordon.

Within weeks, the Caledonian boss was also telling us exclusively that his sales team had chalked up "a resounding success" by booking no fewer than 3,200 passengers on 32 charter flights from New York and Toronto, enabling them to fill seats of east-bound returning aircraft.

Mr de la Haye said that the Scots airline would soon be "coming home" by shifting its business emphasis away from London's Gatwick and making Prestwick its main operational base. Caledonian now planned to operate more than half of its programme of 116 transatlantic charter flights from the Scottish airport.

He went on to say that the company hoped to be in the market "within 2 years" for jet airliners, Boeing 707 or Douglas DC8s. Until then it would continue flying piston-engined airliners exclusively. But even more significantly he then revealed that the company had applied for a licence to operate cut-price *scheduled* services between Prestwick Airport and New York, potentially breaking the monopoly of state-owned BOAC.

Thanks to the intercession of the Scottish Council for Development and Industry, the application was being backed by Glasgow Airport's *Abbotsinch* Airport committee, as well as by the Prestwick Airport Development Association. Adding that the application also had the support of the city's Lord Provost, Peter Meldrum, the chairman of the Glasgow committee, councillor William Taylor, wrote to the Air Transport Licensing Board. "I support the view that Prestwick is under-utilised," he said. "It would be important to Scotland to have a very much increased traffic directed through and generated by this airport."

City airport chief backs cut-price flights to U.S.

©Evening Times July 7 1964

HE SUPPORTS AIR LINE'S CUT-PRICE BID

GLASGOW councillor William L. Taylor, chairman of the corporation's Abbotsinch Airport Development Committee, has come out with strong support for improving Prestwick Airport's intercontinental air links.

He has added his support and that of the Lord Provost, Mr Peter Meldrum, to an application by Scottish independent air line Caledonian Airways to operate cut - price scheduled services between Prestwick and New York.

The hearing of the application—for flights up to £30 cheaper than those of the "recognised" air lines—opens in London to-day before the Air Transport Licensing Board.

The Scottish Council (Development and Industry), the Scottish Tourist Board, and the Scottish Advisory Council for Civil Aviation have already written to the board backing Caledonian Airways, as has the Prestwick Airport Development Association.

In his letter of support, Councillor Taylor says—"I am particularly anxious to see the developments in Scotland of additional facilities for the carriage by air both of passengers and of freight.

Five days

"I support the view that Prestwick is under-utilised, and it would be important to Scotland to have a very much increased traffic directed through and generated by this airport."

Scottish Daily Mail July 8 1964

BOAC naturally opposed this "scheduled" application as soon as they learnt of it, as did two other British airlines with no direct competitive interest. Then, ten weeks later John 'phoned me to say that the application had been turned down. He didn't seem particularly disappointed, or even surprised. Then he went on to reveal that a second Caledonian application for a licence to operate all-in package holidays in America had been granted. It was soon patently obvious that the application for scheduled flights had been a red herring. Although he didn't admit it to us what he really wanted was the package tour permission *(see opposite).*

This appeared to be a major victory for the up-and-coming Scottish airline; the first, state-owned or private, to be granted such a licence on the Atlantic. Now Britons would be able to fly to America for a two weeks' inclusive holiday in luxury hotels in Boston, Washington or New York. The plan was a more structured and simplified version of a similar west-east proposal a couple of years earlier by a Canadian businessman. At a cost of about £150 a person, which included return air fare, overnight accommodation, transport between courses and green fees, the Caledonian tours would be the first of their kind planned by an airline.

A similar scheme would operate in reverse, bringing North

Luxury hotels and bus tours

HOLIDAYS IN AMERICA—AT A BARGAIN PRICE

Break through by a Scots air firm

A BIG price break through that means people from Britain will be able to fly to America for a two weeks holiday for £150 ALL-IN was reveale yesterday.

This move is expected to start a boom f "holidays in America" next year. F

Sunday Mail Page One lead *Sep 20 1964*

Scots Airline Gets OK for U.S. Holidays

TWO-WEEK holidays in the U.S. with coach tours and overnight accommodation at luxury hotels are to be offered for the first time next summer by the Scottish independent airline, Caledonian Airways—at an "all-in" price of less than £150.

This was announced yesterday in London by the airline following a decision by the Air Transport Licensing Board to grant applications by Caledonian Airways to operate two inclusive tours between London, Scotland, and the U.S.

Caledonian chairman John de la Haye described the decisioin as a major victory for his company, the first British airline to be granted such a licence.

Caledonian Airways want to offer all-in tours to Boston, Washington, and New York for Britons visiting U.S., and similar tours to Glasgow or London and excursions to the Highlands or Burns country and Stratford-on-Avon, Oxford, or Windsor to Americans.

The airline will operate 14 flights in each direction at fortnightly intervals

Sunday Post *Sep 20 1964*

American golf enthusiasts to tour courses throughout the 'home of golf'.

Confirming to us that they had granted the necessary licence to Caledonian, the first in Britain ever to be granted, the British Air Transport Licensing Board said that the company would be allowed to operate up to 14 flights a fortnight in each direction throughout the summer months. The licence would last for three years. The normal fare at this time was just over £163, and a luxury hotel would have costs £2.10s a night – without breakfast.

In its findings, the British Air Transport Licensing Board stated:

"Our decision to grant the application creates a precedent. We believe it is one that is progressive without being impudent. It is our view that the time has come for a modest experiment on this route with an inclusive tour service to meet what seems to be a genuine need and demand."

Each and every story John de la Haye or his deputy, managing director Adam Thomson passed to us exclusively was rewarded with good coverage in both Scottish and English papers. He even told us of the bad news when Caledonian's plans were brought crashing down, and the wary elation of Prestwick supporters was again short-lived. Just five weeks after learning of his successful ATLB licence bid, he called us to say he had just been advised that several leading American airlines persuaded the US government to refuse thier required approval for the package tours.

Even more disappointing was the news from London that BOAC had decided to make an eleventh-hour appeal against the ATLB's decision. In a seven-point list of objections, they claimed that the Caledonian plan would divert passengers from scheduled services.

CALEDONIAN DECISION CREATES PRECEDENT

Two-week holidays in the United States, with coach tours and overnight accommodation at hotels en route, are to be offered for the first time next summer by Caledonian Airways (Prestwick), Ltd., at an "all-in" price of less than £150.

This was confirmed at the week-end in London by the air line following a decision by the Air Transport Licensing Board to grant applications submitted by Caledonian to operate two-way inclusive tours from London and Prestwick to the U.S.

PUBLIC REACTION

The Caledonian chairman, Mr John de la Haye, described the decision as "momentous" and a major victory for his company, the first British air line, state-owned or independent, to be granted such a licence.

The licensing board regard their decision as an experiment to test public reaction to transatlantic inclusive tours.

In their findings the board say:—"Our decision to grant the applications creates a precedent. We believe it is one that is progressive without being imprudent. It is our view that the time has come for a modest experiment on this route with an inclusive tour service to meet what seems to be a genuine need and demand."

© Glasgow Herald *Sep 21 1964*

BOAC FIGHT SCOTS AIR TRIPS

AN appeal against the granting of a licence to Caledonian Airways to operate £150 all-in holiday flights across the Atlantic has been made by B.O.A.C.

The appeal, lodged with the Ministry of Aviation, could be the first of its kind to be considered by the new Minister, Mr. Roy Jenkins.

An official at the Ministry said yesterday:

"A great deal of evidence will have to be sifted."

All-in tours

B.O.A.C. originally opposed the Scottish independent firm's application to the Air Transport Licensing Board on the grounds that passengers would be diverted from scheduled flights.

Caledonian in conjunction with the Donaldson Line, of Glasgow, is offering 14-day holidays in America inclusive of luxury hotels and sight-seeing tours to British travellers.

Similar holidays in Britain are offered to American tourists.

Daily Record *Oct 30 1964*

Last-minute holiday flights appeal by B.O.A.C.

BOAC APPEAL AGAINST 'HOLIDAY' LICENCE

Scottish Daily Express (above)
Scottish Daily Mail (right)
(both) Oct 30 1964

The appeal was lodged with the Ministry of Aviation, and became the first of its kind to be considered by the incoming Labour Government's new Minister of Aviation, Roy Jenkins.[1] His press office told me: "It's impossible to say when the Minister will take a final decision. A great deal of evidence will have to be sifted."

The answer, when it did come some months later, was however in favour not of the ATLB's daring "precedent," but of the purely commercial concerns of BOAC and its big American rivals on the Atlantic. Only one of these operated services into Prestwick, and not one of them was prepared to pioneer cut-rate package tours.

The startling claim a year or two earlier that Prestwick Airport was to have a dedicated £1million luxury hotel on a reserved site adjoining the new terminal, had also raised hopes for long-term commitment to the airport, if only because the Ministry of Aviation confirmed that an agreement had been signed. Behind the project was a Canadian businessman, Douglas Henderson, who described himself as head of Sheraton Motels Ltd of Canada and London.

We learnt from Prestwick Airport air commandant C. Dennis Waldron that Henderson planned to call an all-comers' press conference the following day to announce his plan. The majority of Scottish newspapers were almost certain to attend, limiting our markets for the story, unless they asked us to cover it on their behalf. We would have to try to pre-empt the press conference with our own story that day. But as we were unable to reach the Canadian at his Edinburgh hotel, we could only give our clients an outline on the Ministry's statement and pass on the details of where they might find Henderson.

The *Scottish Daily Express* ran with our 80 words over two columns and a noncommittal comment from Henderson referring them to the announcement he planned to make the next day. The *Scotsman* fared no better but padded out a few bland comments from Henderson with some 500 words of background on the government's original hotel proposals.

The *Glasgow Evening Times* used our piece later that day and the *Scottish Daily Mail* gave us a detailed, single column the following day on the press conference statement. But as we expected, almost every other Scottish newspaper ran its own story.

Henderson's ambitious proposals included golfing-sightseeing holiday tours of Scotland for American and Canadian golfers, with accommodation at the 150-room airport hotel and a fully-illuminated hotel golf course for all-night enthusiasts. Full instruction by professionals would be available. An alternative entertainments' centre for the golfers' families would also be provided.

In answer to questions, Henderson said outside finance, which had already been promised, would provide much of the needed capital. He introduced one of the partners of a prominent company of architects, and announced the names of construction and furnishing contractors. He said that work would begin on the golf centre as soon as the land, part of the airport property, was made available. The building of the hotel would begin later that year for completion in two years.

[1] *Later Lord Jenkins of Hillhead*

'Golf by night' course for airport

By Daily Mail Reporter

TO build Britain's first floodlit golf course, so golfers can play all through the night, is a dream of 46-year-old Canadian businessman Mr. Douglas Henderson.

If the dream comes true, the course will be built at Prestwick, Ayrshire, secen of the world's first Open championship.

For Toronto-born Mr. Henderson has just signed an agreement with the Ministry of Aviation to build a luxury hotel at Prestwick Airport.

Apart from spending up to £1,250,000 on the hotel, his big plans are to :—

1. Provide a golfers' Hall of Fame with the names of 15,000 golf champions from all over the world.

Success

2. Persuade golfers from the United States and Canada to make a combined golfing-sightseeing holiday tour of Scotland at an inclusive cost of £150.

3. Build a new golf course at Prestwick and Scotland's first family golf centre, at an additional £25,000, where wives and children can be entertained while golfers are on the course.

After two year of negotiations Mr. Henderson, head of Sheraton Hotels, of Canada and London, and managing director of Golf Centres Ltd., has succeeded in winning over the Ministry of Aviation, which is giving full backing to his plan.

"The entire atmosphere of the hotel will be centred on golf. I even plan to have each of the bedrooms named after golf champions," Mr. Henderson told managers of five European and transatlantic airlines at Prestwick yesterday.

150 rooms

He is already negotiating with airlines and golfing centres over his plans for inclusive tours for Americans and Canadians.

Work on the hotel, which will be built by the Scottish firm of Crudens, will start this year.

The 150-room hotel, due to be completed by mid-1965, will be linked with the new passenger terminal at Prestwick.

Mr. Henderson has won a 99-year lease from the Ministry of Aviation on the site.

And he said work on the golf centre would begin as soon as the land, also airport property, is available.

Scottish Daily Mail April 10 1963

LUXURY HOTEL FOR PRESTWICK

A 150 bedroom luxury hotel is to be built adjacent to the new terminal at Prestwick Airport.

The Ministry of Aviation announced to-day that they have reached agreement in principle with Sheraton Motels, Ltd., of 15 Hertford Street, London, for the building and operation of the hotel.

©Evening Times April 10 1963

New hotel for airport

Express Staff Reporter

PRESTWICK Airport is to have a new luxury hotel thanks to Canadian business man Mr. Douglas Henderson, of Toronto, who describes himself as head of Sheraton Motels, Ltd., of Canada and London.

Agreement has been reached between airport landlords, the Ministry of Aviation, and Mr. Henderson, who plans to build and operate the hotel at Prestwick's new £2,000,000 passenger terminal.

A Ministry of Aviation spokesman in London said a statement was being made today. Mr. Henderson said in Edinburgh last night: "I shall make a full statement within the next 24 hours."

Scottish Daily Express also Scotsman (not shown) April 10 1963

£1.25m. hotel talks at Prestwick

CANADIAN business man Mr Douglas Henderson, who has signed an agreement with the Ministry of Aviation to build a new airport hotel at Prestwick, arrived in Glasgow from London to-day to meet the Ministry's consultant architect to the new Prestwick air terminal, Mr J. Gleave.

Mr Henderson is to have final talks with two "prominent financiers," and the financing of the £1.25m. "Palace of Golf" hotel at Prestwick Airport is expected to be settled this week-end.

"Hall of Fame"

With his personal architect, Mr Henderson will meet Mr Gleave to describe his proposals for the hotel's 162 double bedrooms, a convention hall, a golfers' "Hall of Fame" to accommodate 250 people, and a restaurant to seat 300.

In London earlier this week Mr Henderson met a representative of Crudens Ltd., the Glasgow contractors who are to build the hotel.

Under the terms of his agreement with the Ministry, Mr Henderson has to have his plans ready for approval by July 3.

...and a month later

©Evening Times May 10 1963

It simply never happened…

Just twelve months later my front-page lead in the *Evening Times* proclaimed:

EVENING TIMES

Newspaper Design Award Winner

No. 27,460 TUESDAY, APRIL 28, 1964.

Prestwick idea has run into difficulties

AIRPORT HOTEL HOPES ARE FADING

"EVENING TIMES" REPORTER

THE chances are fading that a contractor will be found to build and run a hotel at Prestwick Airport on the lines originally envisaged.

Aviation Ministry officials in London will only repeat their assurances of the past year that "negotiations with interested parties are continuing."

.. But since it was admitted that the proposal by Canadian Douglas Henderson to build a "golf

which was itself made necessary when it was realised no hotel facilities would be available this summer.

Motel instead

But an official pointed out—"The wall is light partitioning which can be removed if ever the access is required."

Some Ministry officials are believed now to be favouring the idea of an airport motel

Twelve months on.

©Evening Times (Page One lead) *April 28 1964*

The *Daily Telegraph* used a similar, shorter and muted version the next day.

Douglas Henderson's overreaching ambitions had, in fact, already vanished, a dream meeting the dawn. The story was not even referring directly to the Canadian's fantasy of a golfing Mecca but to the government's hopes of *ever* finding a contractor to take on the role of providing overnight accommodation at the airport for the traveller or his meeters and wavers....

Aviation Ministry officials tried to put on a brave front, repeating their assurances that negotiations with "interested parties" were continuing. But ever since they had been forced to admit that the Henderson proposals had been dropped, through a lack of backers and disagreements over the terms it was suggested, it was clear that these later "negotiations" were to form no basis for a new arrangement.

Some authorities believed the Ministry had been too demanding in their approaches to firms considering the airport hotel project, even though some of the original terms had been relaxed. One London hotel chain, which earlier had expressed an interest, put their case to me:

"As is so often happens, the Ministry want to have their cake and eat it. They expect a private company to take most of the risks while paying over the greater part of their revenue in ground rent and concession fees."

At the same time it was pointed out by airlines that the demand for hotel accommodation close to airports was diminishing with the changing pattern of air travel. "The big jets now arrive at a reasonable hour for making onward journeys, and arriving passengers are no longer tired out even after the longest flights," said one manager. (In reality this was not borne out by developments at other airports in later years where, after early stagnation, hotel occupancy boomed.)

AIRPORT HOTEL PESSIMISM AT MINISTRY

Daily Telegraph Reporter

After 12 months of fruitless discussions, Ministry of Aviation officials are becoming more pessimistic about their chances of ever building an airport hotel at Prestwick on the lines originally visualised.

Since the proposed "golf Mecca" project of a Canadian businessman, Mr. Douglas Henderson, was dropped, the Ministry's estates department has begun to wonder if any contractor will gamble on the future development of the airport.

Officially the Ministry will only repeat its assurances that "negotiations with interested parties are continuing." There is too much of a risk, say some contractors. One senior official of a London hotel chain said: "As is so often the case, the Ministry wants to have their cake and eat it.

"They expect a private company to take most of the risks while paying the greater part of their revenue over in ground rents and concession fees."

Daily Telegraph *April 29 1964*

For most airlines and holiday organisations that banked on the world growth in travel being reflected at Prestwick, it was an ever-similar story of frustrated ambitions and effort. The airport's official traffic figures – passenger throughput and aircraft movements – were passed to us at the end of each month, together with running half-yearly and annual totals. But however much comfort we tried to read into the periodic increases and seasonal glitches in our adviser's interpretation and with our reporting of them, the long-term future continued to look bleak.

The transatlantic airport simply wasn't sharing in either the UK or the worldwide aviation boom. Ironically, much of the investment at Prestwick had been justified by the assumed inevitability of the transfer of Renfrew's domestic traffic to the transatlantic airport, which could only boost its wider potential. In the end, that too proved to be a false assumption.

With every departure of a half-empty Boeing 707 or DC8 bringing closer the day when Prestwick's transatlantic life-line could be severed, it also became more obvious that Abbotsinch, would soon lift off as the new *Glasgow* airport, owned and operated by

Glasgow City Corporation.

That day finally arrived one day in mid-May, 1963.

After months of wrangling, the government finally confirmed that the Fleet Air Arm station was to be developed as the replacement for Renfrew after all. The argument of the combined business and city political interests of Glasgow against the prospect of their "local" airport being re-sited 30 miles out of town finally won through.

The decision was also to the particular delight of the Glasgow management of British European Airways. They apparently preferred to inconvenience Scottish transatlantic travellers by encouraging them to fly to London, almost 400 miles in the opposite direction, to catch their onward connections, only then often "interlining" them through BOAC's main rival Pan Am.

Ironically, since the significance of Abbotsinch in the future of Prestwick was my principal Scottish raison d'être, I was away when the news of the Government announcement broke simultaneously in London and Glasgow. But Chris reacted instinctively by looking for a prominent Scottish politician to comment and fortuitously chose John Bannerman, popular and respected chairman of the Scottish Liberal Party. His response: an impromptu, detailed and strongly-worded attack on what he described as "a secret deal" between the Government and Glasgow Corporation.

"I am disgusted," Bannerman told Chris. "The public must not allow the Government to get away with this without a big dust-up." He said that he objected strongly to the pushing through of the arrangement without the full knowledge and approval of the ratepayers in Glasgow and the taxpayers in the rest of the country. He pointed out that the city treasurer, who had been unhappy with the Government proposals, now appeared to be delighted, and demanded to know: "Exactly what promises have the Government made on the taxpayers' behalf that should make Glasgow Corporation so happy?"

Renfrew airport, he pointed out, made a loss of £250,000 annually. Would Abbotsinch make the same loss, and would the taxpayer also have to subsidise the new airport in addition to bearing half of the development costs of £4,300,000?

Dismissing arguments that the development would provide jobs for the unemployed in Glasgow, he said that this would be for only a short time, and that it would be better to spend £4 million on improving road and rail links to Prestwick. "The deal is being put through to clear the way for keeping Prestwick under Whitehall control."

It was to be a prophetic comment.

Chris was rewarded with a mere three inches in the *Scotsman* but big splashes in both the *Express* and the *Mail* (which produced a stock picture of a kilted Bannerman to accompany their 14 inches). But the revelation, surprisingly, was completely ignored elsewhere. The only likely explanation was that the story had to be distributed by Brenards at Heathrow rather than directly from our own office because Chris was on his own and time was against him for some long forgotten reason.

John Bannerman's instinctive reaction was not echoed elsewhere. The voices of reason and logic which for months had been so clearly supportive of the case for Prestwick, not only in the West of Scotland, but also further afield in the political capital of Edinburgh, and in the Highlands and Islands, were suddenly stilled. It was as if, with one stroke of a pen on paper, the thousands of aviation experts and enthusiasts who sincerely believed common sense would prevail, had been stunned into silence. Even the leader writers of

LIBERAL SLAMS CITY'S 'SECRET DEAL'

Express Staff Reporter

MR. JOHN BANNERMAN last night attacked the "secret deal" between the Government and Glasgow Corporation over the proposed transfer of air services from Renfrew Airport to Abbotsinch.

Mr Bannerman, chairman of the Scottish Liberal Party, and a prospective parliamentary candidate for Paisley, said: "I am disgusted.

"The public must not allow the Government to get away with this Abbotsinch deal without a big dust-up."

This is a deal being put through to clear the way for keeping Prestwick, Scotland's international airport, under Whitehall control.

PRECEDENT?

"I object strongly to the pushing through of this arrangement without the full knowledge and approval of the ratepayers in Glasgow and the taxpayers in the rest of the country.

"Exactly what promises has the Government made on the taxpayers behalf that should make Glasgow Corporation so happy? And will they be setting a precedent for similar secret deals with other municipal authorities?"

He dismissed arguments that development of Abbotsinch would provide jobs for unemployed in Glasgow. "At the most, only 300 jobs would be available, and that would be only for a short time.

"It would be far better to spend the £4 million on an improved rail and road service between Glasgow and Prestwick, which would give as many jobs and more for a longer period."

Liberal chief slams airport 'deal'

By Daily Mail Reporter

A LEADING Scottish politician attacked last night what he describes as a "secret deal" between the Government and Glasgow Corporation over the proposed transfer of air services from Renfrew Airport to Abbotsinch.

Mr. John Bannerman, chairman of the Scottish Liberal Party and a prospective Parliamentary

Scottish Daily Express (left)
Scottish Daily Mail (right)
(both) May 24 1963

several national newspapers who had rebelled against the short-sighted city interests of Glasgow, appeared lost for words.

Those voices would soon to be heard again. As I have already shown, some of the mass-circulation newspapers in Scotland had similarly failed to appreciate the BOAC threat to Prestwick's Scandinavian Airlines' services. There were already signs that this apparent apathy was fading.

The possible loss of landing fees and other support charges for the already under-used airport and the consequent threat to jobs was, however, certainly obvious to the aviation-minded Scottish public. Their fears were subsequently reinforced by my exclusive in January 1964 revealing that control of Prestwick had been suddenly taken out of Scottish hands – exactly as forecast by John Bannerman – and transferred furtively two weeks earlier to Whitehall, without any public announcement.

The change came to light when I attempted to make a simple inquiry at the Scottish division of the Ministry of Aviation in Edinburgh about Prestwick passenger traffic, only to be referred to London. The transfer was, a spokesman insisted, "a purely routine procedure" in preparation for the hand-over of Britain's major airports to an authority independent of the government. I telephoned Bannerman again for his comments. He immediately attacked the move.

"I am extremely surprised that such a step has been taken without it having been properly publicised," he said, "This is a question of taking away a cornerstone of Scotland."

This time the Scottish press – both light and heavy – reacted strongly with splashes in the *Express, Mail, Daily Herald, Glasgow Herald* and *Scotsman* (not shown):

SHOCK AS AIRPORT 'GOES SOUTH'

Scottish Daily Mail

Prestwick Airport control moves south

Express Staff Reporter

QUIETLY, and without any official announcement, control of Prestwick Airport—Scotland's only international airport—has been transferred from Edinburgh to Whitehall.

And in future, Prestwick will be one of Britain's "Big Three" airports—linked with London and Gatwick.

Yesterday Aviation Ministry spokesmen confirmed that—since January 1—Prestwick has come under London control, and the Scottish Division in Edinburgh will have no say in

Scottish Daily Express

Scotland loses control of Prestwick Airport

SCOTLAND has lost control of Prestwick Airport to London.

And last night the move was attacked by the chairman of the Scottish Liberal Party.

He said it was "a question of taking away a corner-stone of Scotland."

The transfer is the first step by the Ministry of Aviation towards the creation of an independent authority to run Britain's principal civil airports.

Officials of the Ministry's Edinburgh Division, who in the past have been responsible for administration of all of Scotland's civil airports, will no longer have a say in the operations at Prestwick.

The change-over will be completed by the end of the financial year, when accounting will also be transferred to Whitehall.

No public announcement of the change-over has been made, but a Ministry of Aviation spokesman in London said yesterday: "If and when the Airports Authority is formed, Prestwick will be regarded along with the London airports as a national airport."

Surprised

The shock news that control of Prestwick had already been handed over to London came as a surprise to many aviation experts.

Mr. John Bannerman, chairman of the Scottish Liberal Party, who last Friday attacked the plans for an airports authority controlling Scottish interests from London, said last night:

"I am extremely surprised that such a step has been taken without its having been properly publicised. This is a question of taking away a corner-stone of Scotland."

Daily Herald *Jan 14 1964*

Control of Prestwick Passes to London

From Our Scottish Air Correspondent

The management and commercial operation of Prestwick international airport passed into the hands of the Ministry of Aviation in London from the Scottish Division in Edinburgh on January 1.

The accountancy section will continue under Edinburgh control until the end of the financial year on March 31.

The technical operation of the airport—air traffic control and tele-communications—remains in the hands of the Scottish Division of the Ministry.

A parallel will be found in Abbotsinch, where Glasgow Corporation will have similar control to that London now has at Prestwick.

No legislation endorsing the transfer has yet been approved by Parliament.

In Draft Stage

Legislation to create an authority with control over London's airports and Prestwick is now in the draft stage. It was proposed several years ago in a Government White Paper, which also pointed to the taking-over of city airports by local authorities.

Because of various political contingencies it is unlikely that time will be available for this legislation to come before the present Parliament.

Mr Julian Amery, Minister of Aviation, has been criticised because of the delay in introducing legislation. The Ministry have obviously concluded that it is sufficient at present to take the necessary Departmental steps to avoid delay when legislation is introduced.

Ministry officials say that matters of high policy at Prestwick have always been referred to London from Edinburgh. One official said:—"Now, day to day routine matters can be dealt with on the spot and policy questions referred direct to London instead of channelling them through Edinburgh."

Mr John Bannerman, chairman of the Scottish Liberal Party, attacked the plan for an Airports Authority controlling Scottish interests from London on Friday. He has long advocated a Scottish Airports Authority controlling all aerodromes including Prestwick which, he claimed, could take Renfrew's services and save the £4.3m. to be spent on Abbotsinch.

© *Glasgow Herald*

Shortly afterwards I was calling John Bannerman yet again to seek his views on a proposed meeting between the two leading opponents in the still-festering Abbotsinch-Prestwick controversy. He responded by appealing publicly to the two sides to unite in supporting the integration of domestic and international air services at Prestwick under a Scottish Airports Authority – winning several more column inches in the *Glasgow*

Herald. My story concluded with his emotive key phrase:

> ***"While we Scots wrangle and divide on purely domestic issues, someone steps in and takes the prize booty from under our noses."***

The protagonists seemed to have taken the hint. I was able to reveal that the convener of Ayrshire County Council and the Lord Provost of Glasgow had arranged to meet for the first time at Prestwick. Their avowed objective was to seek ways of working together to campaign for the development and the surface links of both airports following the Government decision on Abbotsinch. And in return for Ayrshire's new support for Glasgow's right to develop a city airport, the Lord Provost, Peter Meldrum, criticised the proposals to restrict SAS and KLM services and called on the Government to switch more holiday flights to Prestwick.

Once again I was rewarded with exclusive coverage throughout the Scottish and northern editions of the English papers – the *Scotsman*, the *Glasgow Herald* and the *Guardian* all ordering in advance my coverage of the meeting.

Supports Ayr

Mr Meldrum said that if Mr Julian Amery, Minister of Aviation, had his feet on the ground and not his head in the clouds, he would see that Prestwick was used to the full by transatlantic air lines.

He gave his personal support to Ayr County Council and the Scottish Council (Development and Industry) in their fight to stop Mr Amery curtailing the Scandinavian Airlines System services through Prestwick.

Mr Meldrum desribed this as a "very futile" means of trying to bolster up B.O.A.C.

© Evening Times Jan 27 1964

Fight over Prestwick services

Mr Peter Meldrum, the Lord Provost of Glasgow, has promised Ayrshire County Council full support in its battle with the Minister of Aviation, Mr Julian Amery, over proposals to cut Continental airline services through Prestwick airport to reduce BOAC losses.

BOAC wants the ending of agreements with Scandinavia and Holland, which allow their national airlines—SAS and KLM—to pick up and disembark passengers at Prestwick. Mr Meldrum said yesterday:

"If Mr Amery had his feet on the ground instead of his head in the clouds, he would see to it that Prestwick is used to the full, instead of trying, by futile means, to bolster up BOAC's economic position."

He also urged the Minister to use his authority to persuade travel agents and air charter companies to run more holiday flights from Prestwick this summer.

Mr Meldrum was speaking at Prestwick after touring the airport's new passenger air terminal.

Guardian January 28 1964

LINKING SCOTTISH AIRPORTS

Glasgow and Ayrshire Agreement

© Glasgow Herald (also Scotsman, not shown) January 28 1964

'Airlines must use Prestwick'

Daily Telegraph January 28 1964

But other long-standing Prestwick supporters thought that the Ayrshire convener, Daniel Sim, had given up the fight for Prestwick too easily and was not committed enough to lead a continuing campaign on the airport's behalf. Two days later, at a public meeting called by Prestwick town council, the "no surrender" view was vindicated when local MPs and politicians of all parties – among them John Bannerman, shadow Scottish Secretary of State Willie Ross, and other local MPs George Younger (also a future Scottish Secretary) and Mrs Winnie Ewing, the first Scottish Nationalist MP – supported the establishment of a Civil Aviation Development Association for Scotland. Its first objective: to fight the proposed Scandinavian Airlines cuts.

MPs in talks on airport's future

SIX MPs, their opponents, and other candidates in the coming General Election have been invited to attend a meeting called by Prestwick town council next Friday to discuss the future of Prestwick Airport.

Aso invited are representatives of all local authorities in Ayrshire, the county convener, the airport commandant, and other interested people and organisations.

Five of the MPs represent constituencies in the county and the sixth, Sir John George (Unionist, Pollok), lives in Ayr.

Subjects to be discussed include the transfer of the airport's administrative control from Edinburgh to London, and Government proposals to restrict the services through Prestwick of Scandinavian Airlines.

Prestwick's town clerk, Mr. Allan Inglis, said yesterday: "These are, of course, opening questions towards a more general discussion. We are hoping for a large attendance. This is a matter of considerable importance."

Daily Herald February 1 1964

Prestwick calls talks on airport

'Airport' talks

Scottish Daily Express (top)
Scottish Daily Mail (above)
(both) Feb 1 1964

PLAN TO SAVE PRESTWICK AIRPORT GETS UNDER WAY

A WORKING party of three has been set up by the newly-formed Civil Aviation Development Association for Scotland to plan the first move of the "Scotjet" campaign to save Prestwick Airport.

First task of the "three wise men"—lawyer Allan Lockhart, Prestwick business man John Skinner, and aviation writer Raymond Berry—will be to decide the "Scotjet" campaign policy.

The 15-man main committee will decide this week whom to approach for support and how far the association's aims can be linked with those of other organisations in Scotland and throughout the U.K.

But the association has already received its first setback. Ayr county convener, Mr Daniel Sim, who led a seven-man team to London on Friday against the Ministry of Aviation's proposed cuts in Scandinavian services through Prestwick, said yesterday he was "utterly dissatisfied" with the talks.

● A working party of three has been set up by the newly formed Civil Aviation Development Association for Scotland to plan the first moves of the "Scotjet" campaign to save Prestwick Airport.

First task of the three wise men, lawyer Allan Lockhart, Prestwick business man John Skinner and aviation writer Raymond Berry, will be to decide the Scotjet campaign policy.

"When this policy has been accepted by the association's committee, we can get down to the task of campaigning support," said Mr. Lockhart

Scottish Sunday Express (right)
Sunday Post (far right)
(both) February 16 1964

The ginger group, which coined the short-form name of "Scotjet" for its campaign, appointed a three-man working party to plan its moves – local solicitor Allan Lockhart, a Glasgow businessman, Hugh Campbell, and a certain "aviation writer" called Raymond Berry.

I was unable to claim I was either publicly elected or co-opted by the Association for the important role of publicist for the new ginger group. But when the respected and widely-known Jimmy Ballantyne, local staff correspondent for the Scottish Daily Express, turned down an appeal from the body of the hall to take on the job, and no other volunteer stepped up from the ranks of local news men at the meeting, I stood up. My offer as an unknown English upstart, to promote the group's aims and activities was accepted, though with little enthusiasm.

Nevertheless, my first opportunity to be pro-active came within hours. After discovering that the BOAC case was being viewed sympathetically by the government, I telegraphed the then Aviation Minister, Julian Amery. Off my own bat but on behalf of Scotjet I made an urgent request that he pay attention to the potential loss of 10,000 overseas tourists and businessmen and the inevitable fall in Prestwick's revenue if the cuts went ahead.

'SCOTJET PLEA' IN FIGHT FOR AIRPORT

Daily Telegraph Reporter

The newly-formed "Scotjet" Committee set up to fight for the future of Prestwick Airport yesterday sent a telegram to the Minister of Aviation, Mr. Amery, expressing hopes for a mutual agreement in the Anglo-Scandinavian talks on bi-lateral air agreements.

Opening in London to-day the talks, which have been twice previously broken off, are on the Ministry's proposed restrictions against the services of Scandinavian Airlines through the Airport.

The Government wants to reduce the Scandinavian Airlines' present permitted frequency of seven flights a week to two. The Airline insists that such a low frequency would be uneconomical. Three members of the Scotjet Committee are meeting this week to plan their campaign.

Daily Telegraph Feb 17 1964

Scotjet launches fight for Prestwick Airport

THE newly-formed "Scotjet" committee, launched to fight for the future of Prestwick Airport, today wired the Minister of Aviation, Mr. Julian Amery.

The telegram expressed hopes for mutual agreement in the Anglo-Scandinavian talks which open in London today, after having been broken off twice, to discuss the Ministry's proposed restrictions in Scandinavian Airline services at Prestwick.

TELEGRAM

The telegram begins: "Respectfully submit that earnest consideration be given to the widespread views of Scottish people before uneconomic restrictions are imposed on "fifth freedom" operators at Prestwick Airport.

"Request attention be given to the obvious loss of 10,000 tourists and business men who visit Scotland on Scandinavian stop-over air tickets and the serious resultant drop in revenue to the airport."

The British Government wants to reduce the Scandinavian Airline's present permitted frequency of seven flights a week to two.

The Scandinavians insist that such a low frequency would be uneconomical.

Scottish Daily Express Feb 17 1964

Air Talks Start To-day in London

CUTS IN PRESTWICK FLIGHTS BY S.A.S.

From Our Scottish Air Correspondent

The third round of talks between British and Scandinavian representatives about traffic rights for Scandinavian Airlines System on the New York - Prestwick - Copenhagen route starts in London to-day.

The Ministry of Aviation want to reduce the frequency of S.A.S. flights through Prestwick because they claim they are in breach of existing agreements to the detriment of British Overseas Airways Corporation. Because of this view previous talks have broken down.

There is opposition in Scotland to the Ministry policy, but indications are that it is unchanged. A compromise may be reached as a result of which S.A.S. services will be reduced.

STRONG PROTEST

An Ayr County Council deputation protested strongly to Ministry officials in London on Friday about the proposed cuts and to-day a telegram will be sent to Mr Julian Amery, Minister of Aviation, from the committee of the Civil Aviation Development Association of Scotland (Scotjet) which was formed in Prestwick last week.

The telegram states:—"Respectfully submit that earnest consideration be given to the widespread views of Scottish people before uneconomic restrictions are imposed on fifth freedom operative at Prestwick.

"Request attention be given to the inevitable loss of 10,000 tourists and business men who visit Scotland on Scandinavian stop-over air tickets and the serious resultant drop in the revenue to the airport. Expressing hopes for a mutual agreement in the bilateral talks."

©Glasgow Herald Feb 17 1964

'Summit' called over SAS future at Prestwick

By Daily Mail Reporter

A "SUMMIT" meeting has been arranged to decide the future of Scandinavian Airline Services through Prestwick Airport.

The meeting, between Foreign Secretary Mr. Butler, Aviation Minister Mr. Julian Amery and Scottish Secretary Mr. Michael Noble, will be held in two weeks' time.

Until a decision is reached, the Scandinavian Governments are assuming that the present frequency of Scandinavian flights through Scotland will continue, as no official pronouncement of proposed cuts have yet been made by the British Government.

Interview

An official of Scandinavian Airlines at Prestwick said yesterday: "As far as we are concerned, nothing has been stated officially to indicate that our services will be cut down.

"We are continuing with our normal sales and advertising campaign and we shall go ahead with our planned summer operations as already published, subject to Government approval."

The Ambassadors of Denmark, Norway and Sweden are expected to make their second call of recent weeks on Mr. Butler.

While Mr. Amery has so far refused to be swayed from his intention to cut the SAS frequency to the barest minimum of two flights a week, the Foreign Secretary is likely to be more lenient in his approach to the issue.

Mr. Noble, too, is almost certain to be influenced by Scottish opinion.

Decision

In an interview in Stockholm at the weekend, Mr. Karl Nilsson, president of SAS, stated that if a unilateral decision were taken by the British Government to restrict Scandinavian Airlines, it would amount to a breach of standing international aviation agreements.

It was also suggested that such action might set a precedent throughout the world.

A telegram to the Prime Minister Sir Alec Douglas-[illegible]e, calling for his personal intervention in the dispute to reverse any curtailment decision, was dispatched by the Scotjet Committee yesterday.

The telegram accuses Mr. Amery of failing to recognise the "adverse consequences" of any decision to restrict foreign airlines and refusing to consider the necessity for maintaining Scottish air links with the world.

Scottish Daily Mail

MR BUTLER MAY HAVE CASTING VOTE

From Our Scottish Air Correspondent

Mr R. A. Butler, Foreign Secretary, is likely to have the casting vote on how many flights Scandinavian Airlines System will be allowed this summer on the Copenhagen-Prestwick-New York route.

Mr Julian Amery, Minister of Aviation, is of the opinion that the normal summer frequency of seven return services a week should be cut to two. There has been such a strong protest from Scotland that Mr Michael Noble, Secretary of State for Scotland, is likely to ask for more.

The three Ministers will hold a meeting on the subject soon after Mr Amery's return from the United States in two weeks. Mr Butler may recommend more than two services a week if he negotiates certain political concessions for Britain with the Swedish, Danish, and Norwegian Ambassadors, who are due to call on him to discuss the subject.

KLM POSITION

The Ministry of Aviation are now considering the position of

©Glasgow Herald (also Scotsman, Daily Herald, Daily Record, not shown) (all) March 4 1964

Scotjet Seek Aid of Lord Provosts

RESTRICTIONS AT PRESTWICK

Lord Provosts of five Scottish cities have been invited to join a "united front" to fight Government proposals to restrict foreign air lines from using Prestwick Airport.

The call is contained in a letter from Mr Hugh Campbell, a Glasgow business man, who is chairman of the Scotjet committee, and went out yesterday to the Lord Provosts of Glasgow, Edinburgh, Perth, Dundee, and Aberdeen, and to the convener of Ayr County Council.

Inviting them to a meeting in Glasgow on Saturday, the letter emphasises the need for Scotland to speak "with one voice" in its efforts to save Prestwick Airport's direct air links with the world.

"BRINK OF DISASTER"

Mr Campbell said:—"We believe that Scotland will be relegated to a back seat in air transport unless we fight as a nation. Our international airport, which by all expert standards is one of the best in the world, is on the brink of disaster.

"The economy and prosperity of all parts of Scotland are equally involved in this campaign."

Sir Alec Douglas-Home, the Prime Minister, has been sent a telegram by Mr Allan S. Lockhart, honorary secretary of Scotjet, objecting to restrictions on the use of Prestwick Airport by Scandinavian Airlines System (S.A.S.).

A letter of acknowledgment has been received from the Prime Minister's secretary.

©Glasgow Herald Mar 9 1964

Premier Asks Scotjet for Details

PLAN TO PROMOTE PRESTWICK

The Prime Minister, Sir Alec Douglas-Home, has asked the Scottish Aviation Development Association (Scotjet) to prepare for him a detailed account of the aims of their campaign to promote Prestwick Airport.

Reporting this yesterday, Mr Hugh Campbell, Glasgow, chairman of the association, said:—

"We are seeking support from individuals and public bodies and have had a number of letters from all parts of Scotland and, indeed, from outside, sympathising with our campaign."

Premier's Promise

The Prime Minister, he added, has promised to give full consideration to the association's views.

Referring to the decision of the Lord Provosts of Glasgow, Edinburgh, Dundee, Aberdeen, and Perth, and of the convener of Ayr County Council not to attend a Scotjet rally to-day in Glasgow, Mr Campbell said they regret the suggestions that they are not an independent, but public sponsored, body.

To-day's meeting has been postponed indefinitely.

©Glasgow Herald Mar 14 1964

No slanging, says Scotjet

The Scotjet committee refused yesterday to enter what it described as "a slanging match" with the Lord Provost of Glasgow and Ayr County Council's convener over its campaign to promote Prestwick Airport.

Chairman Mr. Hugh Campbell said last night: "We regret the inferences made against our status as an independent, but public-sponsored body. But this attitude is a typical example of the kind of national disunity we are determined to overcome."

Scottish Daily Mail March 14 1964

A few days later I was changing to my more familiar reporter's hat and revealing that a "summit" meeting was being called in London to discuss the SAS services. Foreign Secretary "Rab" Butler was being joined by the Minister of Aviation and the Secretary of State for Scotland after the ambassadors of Sweden, Denmark and Norway had made a formal protest against the threatened cuts. And I was able to add on good authority that while the Aviation Minister was echoing the BOAC view that the Scandinavians should be heavily penalised for "poaching" traffic, the Foreign Secretary was being more conciliatory.

A call by Hugh Campbell, now chairman of the Scotjet committee, to the Lord Provosts of five Scottish cities to join him in a protest to the government against the withdrawal of the SAS fifth freedom rights followed. My story on his plea quoted him directly:

"We believe that Scotland will be relegated to a back seat in air transport unless we fight as a nation with one voice. Our international airport, which by all expert standards is one of the best in the world, is on the brink of disaster.

"The economy and prosperity of all parts of Scotland are equally involved in this campaign."

The appeal was instantly either rejected outright or totally ignored by the Lord Provosts of Aberdeen, Dundee, Edinburgh, Glasgow and Perth and even by the Ayr County convener. The response from the Lord Provost of Glasgow quite incredibly dismissed Scotjet's constitution and standing, accusing it of being "unrepresentative and self-interested" – conveniently brushing aside the all-party support of elected MPs, the local Provost and councillors.

Undeterred, Hugh Campbell rejoined by refusing to enter what he called a "slanging match." With a statement for publication he told me: "We regret the inferences made against our status as an independent public-sponsored body. This attitude is a typical example of the kind of national disunity we are determined to overcome."

At the same time I was composing an even more explicit telegram of protest to the Prime Minister, Sir Alec Douglas Home in the name of Allan Lockhart, the Scotjet honorary secretary. With his acknowledgement, Sir Alec asked the association to send him a detailed account of the aims of its campaign.

To avoid accusations of being "one-issue campaigners," the Scotjet committee then spoke out over a strictly commercial aspect of Prestwick operations. It called on the airport management to favour a Scottish company when awarding new contracts for catering and duty-free sales at the airport. The first in Britain to sell duty free goods to passengers, Prestwick was now selling more whisky than any other airport – up to 3,000 bottles a day. I had been able to advise Hugh Campbell that a number of Scottish companies were already interested in tendering for the new concessions. They would be competing particularly against two major companies both of whom were already experienced in the field.

I gave the story to the nationals complete with a quote from me – as the spokesman for the Scotjet committee:

> ***"We do not presume to interfere in the Ministry's business arrangements, but we are anxious to point out the advantages of appointing a concessionaire with a close knowledge of Scottish tourist requirements and the desirability of protecting local employment,"*** I said, unashamedly.

The story was suitably given prominence in the *Daily Telegraph* and *Scottish Daily Express* – with a sympathetic nod from the *Daily Record* among others, despite a knee-jerk response from the Prestwick Airport commandant Wally Waldron, who commented:

'LET SCOTS KEEP AIRPORT BAR' PLEA

SCOTLAND'S watchdogs of aviation — the 16-man "Scotjet" committee — yesterday appealed to the Air Ministry to keep profits from sales of duty - free whisky in Scottish hands.

The committee wants the Ministry to nominate a Scottish firm for the duty-free liquor sales and catering concession in Prestwick Airport's new passenger terminal.

Tenders for the concession will be opened tomorrow.

Among the companies who have shown interest and are believed to have submitted tenders are London caterers Charles Forte and Co. and the Canadian-backed firm Skyway Hotels Ltd. Both already hold similar concessions at London's Heathrow Airport.

A number of Scottish organisations, including the present holders of the Prestwick concession, are also known to be interested.

Not interfering

A spokesman for the Scotjet Committee, which was launched earlier this month to further the development of international aviation in Scotland, said last night:

"We do not presume to interfere in the Ministry's business arrangements, but we are anxious to point out the advantages of appointing a concessionaire with a close knowledge of Scottish tourist requirements and the desirability of protecting local employment."

But Mr. C. D. Waldron, the airport commandant, said last night: "Normal Government procedure does not give preferential treatment to Scottish firms in these matters."

Despite its comparative lack of passenger traffic, Prestwick still sells more whisky than any duyt-free airport in Europe.

Scottish Daily Express

'Let Scotland keep this whisky profit'

The 16 men and women of the "Scotjet" committee want Scotland to keep the profit from the annual sale of 100,000 bottles of duty-free whisky at Prestwick Airport.

The pool asked the Ministry of Aviation to give preference to a Scottish firm for the liquor concession (estimated worth £80,000). at the new terminal. Tenders will be considered today.

Daily Record

(all) Feb 24 1964

"KEEP AIRPORT WHISKY PROFITS IN SCOTLAND"

CATERING CONCESSION PLEA

DAILY TELEGRAPH REPORTER

THE new "Scotjet" committee has appealed to the Ministry of Aviation to choose a Scottish firm when it hands out the duty-free liquor and catering concession for Prestwick Airport's new terminal this week.

About 20 British firms have been invited to tender. Sales of liquor, free of Customs duty to overseas travellers, are estimated to be worth more than £80,000 a year.

The tenders are being opened at Prestwick airport to-day. Firms who have shown interest are the London caterers Charles Forte & Co., and the Canadian-backed Skyway Hotels Ltd.

A number of Scottish firms, including the present concessionaire, are also interested.

The Prestwick airport Commandant, Mr C. D. Waldron, commented yesterday: "Of course we would be delighted if a Scottish firm were given the concession. But the normal Government procedure does not give preferential treatment to Scottish firms in these cases."

Prestwick, the first British airport to boast facilities for the sale of duty-free spirits sells more whisky than any European airport with similar facilities—up to 3,000 bottles a day during the peak summer months.

Daily Telegraph

DUTY-FREE LIQUOR CONCESSION

Prestwick Plea

The Scotjet committee, launched earlier this month to further the development of international aviation in Scotland, has appealed to the Ministry of Aviation to give preferential consideration to a Scottish firm when considering applications this week for the duty-free liquor and catering concession at Prestwick Airport's new terminal.

About 20 firms in Britain have been invited by the Ministry to tender for the combined concession. Sales of liquor, free of Customs duty to overseas travellers, are estimated to be worth more than £80,000 in revenue per year.

An official of the Scotjet committee said yesterday:—"We are anxious to point out the advantages of appointing a concessionaire with knowledge of the Scottish tourist requirements and the desirability of protecting local employment."

Prestwick was the first airport in Britain with facilities for the sale of duty-free spirits. It still sells more whisky than any other airport in Europe—up to 3000 bottles a day during the summer.

©Glasgow Herald

"Normal Government procedure does not give preferential treatment to Scottish firms in these matters."

Four days later I was able to announce that a Scottish company, Scottish Aviation Ltd., had indeed won the contract, though entirely on their own merit. No company could have been more appropriate from the standpoint of Scotjet. Scottish Aviation Ltd – now part of British Aerospace – were the founders of Prestwick Airport, and still retained an aircraft maintenance base there.

SCOTS WIN DUTY-FREE CONCESSION AT AIRPORT

SCOTTISH Aviation Ltd. has been awarded a three-year contract for the sale of duty-free whisky in the new terminal at Prestwick Airport.

The duty free liquor concession is estimated to be worth around £80,000 a year in revenue.

Scottish Aviation founded Prestwick Airport, which was finally taken over by the Ministry of Aviation in 1946. The company has held the concession for catering in the present airport hotel continuously since then.

"Delighted"

The hotel, built around Orangefield House, a seventeenth-century manor which has associations with Robert Burns, is to be demolished along with the present terminal.

But the concession for the sale of liquor free of duty to overseas passengers has been held by another company since 1959.

The combined contract was signed at the airport to-day by Mr Hugh Laughland, company secretary, of Scottish Aviation and by the airport commandant Mr C. D. Waldron on behalf of the Minister of Aviation.

Mr T. Robertson, managing director of the company said to-day:—"We are delighted to be given this concession. Iti mmediatley gives protection to some 200 staff we at present employ at the airport hotel, restaurant, and cafeteria.

"It is too early yet to say whether we shall need to recruit staff for running the duty-free liquor sales."

SCOTS FIRM TO DO ALL AIRPORT CATERING

Daily Telegraph Reporter

Scottish Aviation Ltd. yesterday won the contract for providing all catering in Prestwick airport's new passenger terminal and for the sales of duty-free liquor to overseas passengers.

©Evening Times (above)
Feb 28 1964
Daily Telegraph (far left)
Feb 29 1964
also Scotsman (not shown)

SCOTTISH AVIATION WIN CONTRACT

Diversification at Prestwick

From Our Scottish Air Correspondent

Scottish Aviation, Ltd., Prestwick, yesterday gained a contract worth about £250,000 a year in revenue under which they will provide the catering and duty-free liquor facilities for the new terminal to be opened this summer at Prestwick Airport.

As the contract was being signed in the hotel at the airport two "baby" pantechnicon vans were being demonstrated for the first time at the company's factory on the other side of the main runway.

Mr T. D. M. Robertson, managing director of Scottish Aviation, said last night the two developments were of considerable importance to the company.

©Glasgow Herald
Feb 29 1964

Meanwhile, after weeks of negotiation, the international talks finally broke down. At the end of March '64 SAS pre-empted any unilateral British decision by announcing: "Unless we hear otherwise, we are ready to reduce our Prestwick transatlantic operations to just five flights a week in each direction, subject to (British) government approval."

Then I learnt that because the bilateral agreement between the two countries had by now expired, a legal and diplomatic loophole meant that the airline could, if it wished, *increase* its seven scheduled flights without limit until new restrictions were agreed or imposed. The Ministry of Aviation reluctantly acknowledged the point when I sought their confirmation.

But the airline insisted:

"We are not looking to take advantage of this situation. We have already published our proposed timetable for the next six weeks. We are awaiting British Government approval to operate a frequency of five flights a week to New York and back."

It wasn't until April, six months after my original revelation on the BOAC plan, that restrictions on Scandinavian flights were finally detailed by the British Government. The airline would now be permitted to operate only *four* transatlantic flights a week each way between Copenhagen and New York via Prestwick, instead of a daily service. The following year, these would be cut to just *three* flights each week.

The restrictions were announced by Whitehall, and for once we had to read about them just as other members of the public did.

Airline battle springs a shock loophole

Express Staff Reporter

SCOTLAND'S airports handled more than 2,000,000 passengers last year—an increase of 12 per cent over the 1962 figures.

TURNHOUSE, Edinburgh, had increased traffic. So did **RENFREW**. Only embattled **PRESTWICK** showed a drop.

It handled 341,792 passengers in 1963, a drop of more than 8,000 on the 1962 figure.

The statistics were issued yesterday on the eve of a new turn to the tangled battle the Government is waging over Scandinavian Airline's flights through Prestwick.

EXPIRED

The Government wants to cut the number of S.A.S. flights, but from today—in theory at any rate—S.A.S. could operate as many flights as they like through Prestwick across the Atlantic.

For the five-year agreement, which allowed S.A.S. to operate a maximum seven flights a week in each direction, expired at midnight.

Scottish Daily Express

Loophole 'opens' Prestwick to SAS

By Daily Mail Reporter

FROM today Scandinavian Airlines have complete freedom to operate as many flights as they like through Prestwick Airport across the Atlantic.

But this unexpected privilege is likely to be short-lived. Within a few hours the British Government is to inform the Scandinavian Embassies in London of its decision to restrict future Prestwick operations by the airline.

At present SAS operate three flights weekly.

The five-year agreement which allowed SAS to operate a maximum of seven flights a week in each direction through Prestwick expired at midnight.

A Ministry of Aviation official confirmed: "As the company's permit to operate is unaffected, it is perfectly true that in theory at least, they may now operate any frequency they wish until our decision is made known to them."

Time-table

Last night it was thought unlikely that the airline would take advantage of the diplomatic loophole. "We have already published our proposed time-table for the next six weeks," said a spokesman. "We are awaiting Government approval to operate a frequency of five flights a week to New York and back."

Despite Ministry of Aviation assurances that the Scandinavian Embassies would be informed of the final decision over Easter, a Foreign Office official said yesterday: "We have not so far made any approach to the Scandinavians. Obviously they will have to know the decision, but it may not be for a day or two."

AIRLINE AWAITS FLIGHTS RULING

Daily Telegraph (all) Apr 1 1964 *Scottish Daily Mail*

Five S.A.S. Flights Weekly from Prestwick

FROM OUR SCOTTISH AIR CORRESPONDENT

Scandinavian Airlines System yesterday notified the authorities concerned at Prestwick Airport that they intend to operate five return flights a week on the Copenhagen-Prestwick-New York route from April 1 until May 15, subject to Government approval.

The air line will know officially by Tuesday how many flights the Government are prepared to allow them to operate on the route under a proposed new agreement.

The present five-year agreement, under which S.A.S. operated seven return flights a week during the peak summer months, ends on Tuesday night. The Ministry of Aviation, claiming that S.A.S. are taking many passengers from British Overseas Airways Corporation at Prestwick, want to cut the number of flights to two.

Pressure from the Foreign Office and Scottish Office is thought likely to have brought a compromise, but this may be not more than four flights.

With new lower fares being introduced on North Atlantic routes from Wednesday it is expected from advance bookings that considerably more passengers will use those services this summer.

It may be that S.A.S. will decide to withdraw from Prestwick altogether and fly direct from Copenhagen to New York. Apart from the dispute about the number of flights, they are faced with capital expense of about £10,000 to provide equipment in the new terminal building at Prestwick, where rents are expected to be about six times as high as in the present reasonably rented terminal.

©Glasgow Herald *March 27 1964*

Prestwick decision expected next week

By Daily Mail Reporter

SCANDINAVIAN airlines will know by Tuesday how many transatlantic flights they are to be allowed to operate through Prestwick Airport this summer.

A Ministry of Aviation spokesman said yesterday that the Scandinavian embassies were being informed of the British Government's decision over Easter.

The final decision was taken on Wednesday after a series of exchanges between the Minister of Aviation, the Foreign Secretary and the Scottish Secretary.

Though the actual number of services SAS will be allowed to operate is not officially known it is believed they will not exceed four flights a week in each direction.

AIRLINE WILL HEAR DECISION ON FLIGHTS

Daily Telegraph Reporter

Scandinavian Airlines will know by Tuesday how many transatlantic flights they are to be allowed to operate through Prestwick Airport this summer. A Ministry of Aviation spokesman said yesterday that the Scandinavian Embassies would be informed of the British Government's decision.

Though the actual number of services SAS will be allowed to operate is not yet known, it is thought they will not exceed four a week in each direction. The airline, which has operated a permitted maximum of seven flights in the summer and six in the winter, will then have to decide if four will be economically possible.

The Ministry's case against Scandinavian Airlines is contained in several pages of figures and arguments which purport to show that the airline has been "poaching" Scottish passenger traffic from BOAC. The Scandinavians produced several pages of figures disputing this argument.

PRESTWICK DECISION

SCANDINAVIAN Airlines will know next week how many Transatlantic flights they are to be allowed to operate through Prestwick Airport this summer.

A Ministry of Aviation spokesman said yesterday that the Scandinavian Embassies were being informed of the British Government's decision over Easter.

The decision was taken on Wednesday after a series of exchanges between the Minister of Aviation, the Foreign Secretary and the Scottish Secretary.

It is thought S.A.S. will not exceed four flights a week in each direction. The airline has now been operating a permitted maximum of seven flights in summer and six in winter.

Scottish Daily Mail (top left)
Daily Telegraph (top right)
Scottish Daily Express (above)
(all) March 27 1964

Although less severe than the total ban called for by BOAC – thanks to the intervention of the Foreign Secretary and the Scottish Secretary – the cuts were still a severe blow to SAS. And within days I was having to report even further cuts.

John Young, the airline's manager at Prestwick had called me to his office to give me an exclusive statement. Up to this time, contact between us or between his superiors in London and me had been discreet. Though the airline had kept me informed wherever possible, they were anxious to avoid any suggestion of collusion with Scotjet or accusations that they were trying to influence the news media during the difficult bilateral negotiations. As I was never able to quote my sources, this could have proved a drawback in reporting the talks; fortunately the accuracy of my information, sometimes passed on by third parties, sustained me.

Now, freed from these restraints, John was able to tell me that the airline was obliged to make a further cut of 25 per cent in their *unopposed* services to Scotland. This, he said, was a direct result of the restrictions on their transatlantic operations. For the first time in six years there would no longer be a direct service between Prestwick and Stavanger, Norway.

"Our summer programme between Prestwick and Scandinavia was dictated primarily by the demands of the transatlantic passengers stopping over in Scotland," he said. "The British government restrictions have severely affected this demand."

Now the headlines ran:

SCOTLAND-SCANDINAVIA AIR LINKS CUT 25 p.c.

RESTRICTIONS ON SAS

Daily Telegraph (left)

S.A.S. Cut Prestwick Services

FEWER FLIGHTS TO NORWAY

From Our Scottish Air Correspondent

Scandinavian Airlines System are reducing their local services from Prestwick Airport to Norway by 25 per cent. this summer, but during the main holiday months they will still operate a daily return service.

Thirty of 120 return flights have been cancelled. The air line had intended to operate three return flights weekly between Prestwick, Stavanger, and Bergen from May 15 to June 16 and from mid-September to the end of October.

Those flights will not operate, nor will a once-weekly service during the summer months to the same destinations. There will be no change to the daily return service from mid-June to mid-September between Prestwick, Bergen, and Oslo.

Transatlantic Traffic

Mr John Young, station manager of the air line at Prestwick, said yesterday:—"Our summer programme between Prestwick and Scandinavia was dictated primarily by the demand of transatlantic passengers stopping in Scotland.

©Glasgow Herald

Prestwick loses more overseas air links

HERALD REPORTER

SCOTLAND'S main air links with Scandinavia are to be cut by another 25 per cent. this summer following the Government's restrictions on Scandinavian trans-Atlantic routes through Prestwick.

For the first time in six years, there will be no direct service between Scotland and Stavanger, Norway.

The new cuts—60 flights from a proposed 240 services—are in addition to those already halted by the Government restrictions which reduced by 40 per cent. the Scandinavian services available from Prestwick.

Scandinavian airline manager at Prestwick, Mr. John Young, said yesterday: "Our summer programme between Prestwick and Scandinavia was dictated primarily by the demand of trans-Atlantic passengers stopping over in Scotland.

Warned

"The Government restrictions on our trans-Atlantic routes have severely affected this."

Now the only Scandinavian routes available at Prestwick will be the jet service to Copenhagen, cut from seven to four flights a week each way and the daily flights to Bergen and Oslo from June to September.

Mr. Daniel Sim, Ayr County Council convener, said last night: "This is just what we foresaw would happen and we warned the Government.

"But they rejected our evidence about trans-Atlantic stop-over passengers as being of minor importance."

Daily Herald (left)
(all) April 21 1964
also Scotsman (not shown)

SAS slash Scots bus stop flights

SCOTLAND'S "bus stop" air links with Scandinavia are to be slashed by 25 per cent this summer.

This is a direct result of the Government's restrictions on Scandinavian trans-Atlantic routes through Prestwick, which reduced the services available by 44 per cent. earlier this month.

The latest cuts will bring the number of Scandinavian flights down from 240 to 60.

Announcing the reduction yesterday, the S.A.S. manager at Prestwick, Mr. John Young, said:

"Our summer programme between Prestwick and Scandinavia was dictated primarily by the demand of transatlantic passengers stopping over in Scotland.

"The Government's restrictions on our transatlantic route has severely affected this demand."

The news brought further protests last night from Mr. Daniel Sim, the Ayr County convener, and "Mr. Scotjet," Glasgow business man Hugh Campbell, both of whom have been in the forefront of the campaign against the Government's restrictions.

"This is just what we foresaw and what we warned the Government about," said Mr. Sim.

"But they rejected our evidence about trans-atlantic stop-over passengers as being of minor importance."

Mr. Campbell said: "This could be the worst blow to Prestwick yet.

Daily Record

S.A.S. may end Scots flights

MR Vagn Christensen, general manager for Scandinavian Airlines System in Britain and Northern Ireland, indicated at Prestwick Airport to-day that his company might have to withdraw all its services between Scandinavia, Scotland, and New York at the end of this year.

He revealed that the Scandinavian Government was to ask for a complete reassessment at the end of the summer of the British Government ruling which restricts Scandinavian transatlantic flights through Prestwisck.

This reassessment would come several months ahead of the British Government's proposal to reconsider the North Atlantic passenger traffic, and the recently applied restrictions against S.A.S.

Reports denied

Mr Christensen was meeting informally with press correspondents and representatives of Scottish organisations who have been heading the campaign against the restrictions.

He said he has been authorised by Sir Anthony Milward, chairman of B.E.A., to state categorically that there was no foundation in reports that B.E.A. would replace services between Scotland and Scandinavia cut back by S.A.S.

'There is also no indication of any kind that B.O.A.C. might extend its transatlantic route through Prestwick to Scandinavia," he said.

S.A.S MAY STOP ALL PRESTWICK FLIGHTS

Mr. Vagn Christsen, General Manager of S.A.S. in U.K. and Northern Ireland said today Company would have to consider possibility of withdrawing all its services between Scandinavia, Scotland and New York at end of this year.

He revealed that Scandinavian governments proposed to ask for complete re-assessment at end of summer of British government's recently imposed restrictions on Scandinavian transatlantic flights through Prestwick.

©Evening Times (above)
Evening Citizen (Stop press) (right, top) April 23 1964

AIRLINE MAY END SCOTS SERVICES

DAILY TELEGRAPH REPORTER

SCANDINAVIAN AIRLINES system will consider withdrawing completely from Scottish air routes at the end of this year if the British Government does not change its mind

AIRLINE MAY DROP ALL PRESTWICK FLIGHTS

SCANDINAVIAN AIRLINES may have to withdraw all their services to Scotland at the end of this year if the British Government do not change their minds about restrictions they have imposed on them.

Daily Telegraph (above, centre)
Daily Herald (above) Apr 24 '64

And two days later, the airline's general manager, Vagn Christensen, on a visit to Prestwick, told me that unless the British Government eased their restrictions, SAS might have to withdraw all their services from Scotland the following year. "We will have to consider whether we can continue with just three transatlantic services a week."

This time in my "protest" story, I was able to feature both Scotjet and Ayr County Council pointing out bitterly to the government: "We told you so."

Several months were to pass before local voices were raised again over the issue. Scotjet, meanwhile, did win some plaudits for its work. Talking of the power of the media in Scotland, an Edinburgh university professor, I was informed, had proclaimed: "One of the most significant promotional campaigns in recent years has been that conducted by the Scotjet association. It has a first-class Public Relations organisation behind it..."

BOAC, perhaps understandably, played no further part in the controversy – leaving the Government to pull the plug on SAS and to take all the criticism. But the "English" airline had, it seems, failed to learn any other lessons from the public outcry it had caused.

Its recently appointed chairman, Sir Giles Guthrie, made a sudden "show-the-flag" visit to Prestwick. His objective was to meet officials of the Scottish Council for Development and Industry, whose chairman, Lord Polworth, was taking a personal interest in the airport. After the meeting he called a press conference at Prestwick to announce the appointment of an executive to act as liaison officer between the airline and Scottish tourist and industrial organisations.

But when he revealed that the new "overlord" – Sir Giles's own description, later withdrawn – was to be Robert McKean, Scottish manager of BOAC's sister airline, BEA, there was a distinct gasp of surprise among my colleagues, all of whom were local journalists and firm supporters of the transatlantic airport. Widely seen as a leading supporter of the development of Abbotsinch, BEA's principal Scottish base, if not a prime mover for it, McKean had also been an outspoken opponent of Prestwick. He had constantly rejected proposals for feeder links to the transatlantic airport, refusing to listen to proposals designed to guarantee passenger bookings. He had even unashamedly "doctored" statistics of BEA's weather diversions to Prestwick for Government consumption, as I have already shown, implying that a fog-free alternative to Abbotsinch was not important to his company's operations. The Glasgow manager's role, said Sir Giles, would be to act as a part-time line of communication between all levels of Scottish opinion and the BOAC board. But time and time again McKean had refused to listen to anyone other than Glasgow business self-interests. As far as Scottish opinion was concerned, the appointment proved to be a non-event. Sir Giles's well-meant but ill-thought-out attempt to "woo the Scots," as he put it, was given the brush-off, and we heard nothing more of the BOAC role of its chosen ally, Mr McKean.

Scotland to get air line "overlord"

SIR Giles Guthrie, chairman of B.O.A.C., indicated at Prestwick Airport to-day that he planned to make an announcement later on proposals for the appointment of a B.O.A.C.-B.E.A. "Overlord" for Scotland.

Sir Giles, who is making his first visit to Scotland since his appointment by the Mnister of Aviation, met Mr Robert McKean, Scottish manager of B.E.A., for an hour's talk last night soon after flying into Renfrew from London.

"I don't wish to say anything at the moment that might be out of context," he said to-day, "but my meeting with Mr McKean, a member of the B.E.A. Board, was perfectly natural. We exchanged pleasantries."

Statement later

He added—"I hope to say something later in connection with proposals to appoint an overlord for Scotland."

Sir Giles is holding a press conference at the airport later to-day.

©Evening Times (above)
April 15 1964

New air chief?

Sir Giles Guthrie, chairman of BOAC, on a visit to Scotland, is expected to announce today the appointment of a new "overlord" to handle the corporation's operations, sales and promotion in Scotland.

B.O.A.C. TO STRENGTHEN SCOTS SERVICES

The first move towards the integration of British Overseas Aircraft Corporation and British European Airways interests in Scotland was made yesterday when Sir Giles Guthrie, chairman of B.O.A.C., appointed a B.E.A. executive to act as a liaison officer between Scottish tourist and industrial organizations and the corporation. He is Mr. Robert McKean, B.E.A.'s Scottish manager, who will combine his new appointment with his present post.

Sir Giles, at Prestwick Airport, said he was particularly concerned in bringing the two corporations closer together. He said that B.O.A.C. had neglected Scotland in the past. Among their plans would be to provide this year, for the first time, a daily service between Prestwick and New York, summer and winter, and to meet the steadily growing demand for seats on Scottish-Canadian routes by providing extra scheduled services this summer. A new drive was being opened to attract American and Canadian tourists to Scotland.

Scottish Daily Mail (above)
The Times (left)
(both) April 16 1964

It wasn't the first time BOAC headquarters had made a

Airline starts campaign to 'woo' Scots

DAILY TELEGRAPH REPORTER

THE first move towards the integration of B.O.A.C and B E A interests in Scotland was made yesterday when Sir Giles Guthrie, chairman of B O A C, appointed an executo act as liaison officer between Scottish tourist and industrial organisations and his corporation.

The man chosen was Mr. Robert McKean, Scottish manager of B E A, who will combine his new appointment with his present post.

His task, Sir Giles said at a Press conference at Prestwick Airport, would be to act as a "line of communication" between all levels of Scottish opinion and the B O A C board. He will be responsible, in particular, to Sir Duncan Anderson, recently appointed as a part-time member of the board, to deal almost exclusively with Scottish transport needs.

No conflict

Both Sir Giles and Mr. McKean, who was present at the conference, emphasised that there was no conflict of interest between the two corporations that could not be overcome. In fact Sir Giles indicated again and again that he was particularly concerned to bring the two corporations closer together

Though he did not rule out the possibility of further B O A C appointments and management changes in Scotland, Sir Giles rejected the suggestion that Mr. McKean would take on the role of a B O A C "overlord" as had been forecast.

He went on: "We frankly admit in B O A C that we have neglected Scotland in the past." He continued: "We have not known what was wanted from us in Scotland. But we plan to change all that."

Daily service

He outlined the following major points in B O A C's coming campaign to "woo" the Scots.

Provision this year for the first time of a daily service between Prestwick and New York, summer and winter.

Daily Telegraph

BOAC to 'woo the Scots'

British Overseas Airways Corporation had neglected Scotland, but was now going to "woo the Scots," said Sir Giles Guthrie (chairman) yesterday when he announced that Prestwick was being considered as an airport for round-the-world supersonic flights.

Sir Giles announced a campaign which included the first daily service between Prestwick and New York, summer and winter; extra scheduled services this summer to meet the growing demand for seats on Scottish Canadian routes; combined sales efforts with British European Airways; and a new drive to attract US and Canadian tourists to Scotland. BOAC would set up its advertising and sales campaign in Scotland.

Prestwick's rôle

Sir Giles insisted that BOAC would always regard Prestwick as a principal airport on its world network and number one alternative to London. But he was unable to say whether it would figure in transatlantic supersonic flights. "Presumably we must operate supersonics on the so-called prestige London-New York route to begin with."

He announced he had appointed Mr Robert McKean to act as a "line of communication" between all levels of Scottish opinion and the corporation.

Airline to have Scots 'overlord'

B.O.A.C. is planning to appoint an "overlord" to take charge of sales and operations in Scotland. The move is part of a large-scale reorganisation.

As general manager for Scotland and Northern Ireland he will be based in Glasgow and will take over responsibility of co-ordinating all B.O.A.C.'s passenger, freight and operational departments in the area.

Guardian (top)
Scottish Daily Express (above)

©Glasgow Herald picture

Sir Giles Guthrie, chairman of BOAC, is seen here (right) at Prestwick greeting Mr Robert McKean, Scottish Manager for British European Airways, as his new "overlord" liaison chief.
Mr C.D. "Wally" Waldron, Commandant of Prestwick Airport, is in the background.

BOAC MOVE FOR "OVERLORD" IN SCOTLAND

Daily Telegraph Reporter

British Overseas Airways propose to appoint an "overlord" to take charge of their sales and operations in Scotland and Northern Ireland with headquarters in Glasgow. No name has yet been announced.

The corporation has been disturbed by Scottish reaction to its move to curb the traffic rights of one of its principal foreign competitors, Scandinavian Airlines.

Mr. Ross Stainton, general manager of the corporation's Western routes, said recently that it was realised BOAC had not done enough in the past to earn public appreciation in Scotland.

Daily Telegraph
(all) April 16 1964

major error in its reading of the Scottish scene. Eight months earlier, following a similar initiative by BEA for its London-Glasgow route, the airline had announced that it planned to introduce a new standby fare on the London-Prestwick route. In a press release from London, (which I received 24 hours too late to action) BOAC hailed its application to the Air Transport Licensing Board for a late-night two-guinea (£2.10p) fare on the route as "the cheapest in the world."

They should have checked with their own manager at Prestwick. When I challenged him the next day following a tip-off by a local contact he had to confirm: "We don't have any plans to operate any flights at the times proposed for the fares."

I immediately called the BOAC press relations office in London and told them what their manager had said. There was an embarrassed silence from the spokesman and a whispered consultation. "Er, I think I'd better call you back" he said at last. Two hours later he returned my call.

"It's perfectly true that we have no flights at present to which the lowest fares could apply. And we have no proposal to introduce new night schedules on the London-Prestwick route," he admitted.

Why then was the application made for night flight cheap standby fares ?

"It is a chicken and egg situation," he replied, "The application was part of a detailed revised-fare structure. Now, if we ever introduce night-flights on this route, we have established the authority to offer these low fares."

Although most newspapers carried my story, few of them gave it the prominence of their earlier reports based strictly on the press release, possibly because they had failed to investigate further themselves. The *Scottish Daily Express* had no such qualms. They gave it a prominent ten column inches *(see left)* and followed up with an editorial headed "FRUSTRATION" *(below)*.

You can put that 2-guinea air fare away!

Express Staff Reporter

B.O.A.C.'s much-publicised two guineas fare for "stand-by" passengers on night flights between London and Prestwick, will NOT come into effect this winter.

. . . Because no services are planned to operate at the times permitted.

B.O.A.C. officials in London finally admitted this yesterday — hours after the corporation had announced that the new fares, said to be the cheapest in the world, would be introduced NEXT MONTH.

Said a spokesman: "It is perfectly true that we have no flights to which the lowest fares could apply. And we have no proposal to introduce new night schedules on the London - Prestwick domestic route."

AUTHORITY

Why, then, was the application made to the Air Transport Licensing Board for night flight stand-by fares?

Said the spokesman: "It is a chicken and egg situation. The application was part of a detailed revised-fare structure. Now, if we ever introduce night flights on this route, we have established the authority to offer these low fares."

But he agreed that a further application would have to be made if B.O.A.C. wish to repeat the offer in the winter of 1964-65.

The one-way fare of two guineas would have applied only to passengers "taking a chance" on an airliner seat without making an advance booking.

A similar application was first made to the Air Transport Licensing Board by British European Airways for their London-Glasgow night services. They are still awaiting approval.

Scottish Daily Express Oct 9 '63

FRUSTRATION

WHEN B.O.A.C. announced two-guinea stand-by flights between Prestwick and London, they were hailed for their initiative. But now they admit there will be no flights to which this fare applies.

What galling absurdity!

All the frustrated traveller needs now is the news that the penny fare is to be restored on Scotland's abolished tramcars.

Scottish Daily Express Oct 10 '63

There was at least one more example of BOAC's lack of sensitivity on Prestwick's viability. The airline had promised it would continue to use the Scottish airport's under-utilised runways alongside other British airlines for its ongoing air crew training programme. That undertaking had been given in response to well-published appeals to airlines and aircraft manufacturers by the Prestwick Airport Development Association to take advantage of the airport's good weather record, its low landing fees and its remoteness from the heavily congested air lanes of the London air traffic control area (*see opposite*).

Yet I had to report just a few months later that BOAC's planned future aircrew training programme for Jumbo-jets was to be switched to Ireland's Shannon Airport – because of a twopence-halfpenny (1p) saving on aircraft fuel tax to be gained in the Republic.

No two-guinea air fares yet!

"Evening Times" reporter

B.O.A.C.'s much-publicised two-guinea fare for "stand by" passengers on night flights between Prestwick and London will not, after all, come into effect this winter . . . because no services are planned to operate at the times permitted.

This was finally admitted by B.O.A.C. officials in London, hours after the Corporation had announced that the new fares, said to be the cheapest in the world, would be introduced next month.

Said a spokesman—"It is perfectly true that we have no flights planned on which the lowest fares could apply, and we have no proposals to introduce new night schedules on the Prestwick-London route."

Why, then, was the application made to the Air Transport Licensing Board for night flight stand-by fares?

"It is a chicken and egg situation," said the spokesman. "The application was part of a detailed revised fare structure. Now, if we ever introduce night flights on this route, we have authority to offer these low fares to passengers."

The one-way fare of £2 2s would apply only to passengers "taking a chance" on an air-liner seat without making an advance booking.

©Evening Times Oct 8 1963

The early 1970s' training plan would be the biggest ever in the airline's history. Its three-year conversion programme to Boeing 747 jets for nearly a hundred senior pilots and first officers was expected to cost the airline some £5m in fuel, landing charges, accommodation and services. It would give the Irish airport, often seen as a rival to Prestwick, a big revenue boost and a clear eighteen-months' experience lead in the operation of the 400-seater giants.

Although landing and ground-handling charges at the two airports were comparable, the Irish airport had one advantage, its tax-free fuel. During the months of "circuits and bumps" training flights, the 350-ton Jumbos would be consuming nearly 30 million gallons of fuel at an estimated total cost of £2,000,000 before tax. "The British duty of 2.4 pence per gallon would increase our costs by £100,000 a year," a BOAC official told me.

I told him that the Prestwick airport management had given me a clear hint they might be able to overcome this problem. Although they had no power to waive the tax, Wally Waldron implied he would be able to consider a special deal on landing fees. To this the BOAC spokesman had no answer. "We have looked at all the possibilities for cutting costs," was all he could add.

*

The impact of Scotjet on the Scottish aviation scene began to fade when the Scottish Council gave its support the following year to the more clearly identified Prestwick Airport Development Association (PADA). Nevertheless, even this

Cheap plane hop is pie in the sky

Daily Record October 9 1963

unofficial, but highly respected, watchdog was viewed with disfavour and suspicion by the Ministry of Aviation which regarded it as something of a meddler. I readily offered my support – but this time strictly as an informant. I was able to provide up-to-date advice on airport statistics, management plans and development (or lack of it) in exchange for facts and figures, comment and campaign news. (It was PADA who told me of their appeal to all airlines to use Prestwick's runways for all future aircrew training.)

Scotjet's withdrawal from the centre of the aviation arena both coincided with and further influenced my reluctance to continue actively promoting the group. I was getting the impression that the newspapers were becoming concerned about a possible lack of objectivity in my reports. Nothing was said directly, but occasional hints were dropped in telephone conversations with the news desks and with friendly and trusted local staff correspondents.

Had I been unethical using my position as manager of a retained news agency to promote the objectives of a partisan group? I didn't believe so. Scotjet, I would have argued, was multi-political, and was formed by public demand and with public support. I played no major role in policy making. I was not being *paid* to publicise the association, and only circulated hard news about their objectives and views, as would any journalist with such a contact. Even BOAC, or at least its local management, who might have been more concerned about my role, were supportively philosophical.

As Ian Morrison, who had succeeded Harry Pusey as BOAC's Prestwick manager, put it: "I was a bit surprised at first when you offered your support to Scotjet at the public meeting. Then I realised you were only after news copy."

Air Training Scheme for Prestwick?

AIR LINES ASKED TO COME NORTH

Air lines and aircraft manufacturers throughout Britain are being asked by the Prestwick Airport Development Association to switch flying crew training to Prestwick.

The association have issued a pamphlet pointing to the advantages of the airport, which is equipped with all modern navigational and landing aids.

Mr David Reid, secretary of the association, said that Stanstead Airport, Essex, the principal centre for flying training, is now being developed as London's third civil airport.

Fog Free

He added, "Increasing traffic in the Southern Control Zone is aggravating a seasonal problem of bad weather conditions which disrupts training schedules. But Prestwick is unique in its fog-free record and an absence of intensive domestic passenger flights.

"Attracting crew training flights might not bring any great commercial benefits apart from landing fees, but it could help to spark off a revived interest in the airport's facilities for future passenger services."

At present B.E.A., British Eagle, and, to a lesser extent, B.O.A.C., are the only air lines using Prestwick regularly for training flights.

©Glasgow Herald Oct 26 1964

Move to Scotland, airlines are urged

Express Staff Reporter

AIRLINES and aircraft manufacturers throughout Britain have been asked to switch their crew training and aircraft proving flights to under-used Prestwick Airport.

The airport's Development Association has circulated a pamphlet entitled *Crew Training Without Tears* pointing to the advantages of almost unlimited and unrestricted facilties at the Scottish airport.

Mr David Reid, secretary of the association, points out that Stansted Airport, Essex, principal centre for flying training, is now being developed as London's third civil airport.

UNIQUE

He said yesterday: "Increasing traffic in the southern control zone is aggravating a seasonal problem of bad weather conditions which disrupt training schedules.

But Prestwick is unique in its fog-free record and an absence of intensive domestic passenger flights."

He added: "Attracting crew training flights might not bring any great commercial benefits to Prestwick apart from landing fees, but it could help to spark off a revived interest in the airport's facilities for future passenger services."

Only airlines to make frequent use of Prestwick for training flights are British European Airways, British Eagle and, to a smaller extent, BOAC.

Scottish Daily Express October 26 1964

Nevertheless, the formation of a new airport association with which I had no formal ties meant that I could back away from the front-line and become less directly involved. Formed under the auspices of the provost – or mayor – and town council of Prestwick, the association had grown out of the efforts of a band of local aviation enthusiasts. It already boasted a local historian and knowledgeable aviation enthusiast, David Reid, as honorary secretary. It was backed not only by the authoritative Scottish Council but also by the Scottish Tourist Board, the Scottish TUC, Scottish Aviation Ltd., chambers of commerce and other local business associations as well as a number of town councils in Ayrshire.

Prestwick provost Iain Foulds said "The Abbotsinch versus Prestwick controversy will have no part in the association's work. It will proceed entirely on the basis that Abbotsinch will go ahead as planned." And thanks to a good contact I already had with David Reid, and was now able to establish with the provost, the Prestwick Airport Development Association became for the next few years the source of a large number of stories which more than compensated for the diminished role of Scotjet.

It also had the added advantage of allowing me to work independently with local MPs such as my near-neighbour, Labour "rebel" Emrys Hughes, with the then Shadow Scottish Secretary Willie Ross and with George Younger, himself a future Scottish Secretary. I also exchanged letters and frequent telephone calls with the then only Scottish Nationalist MP, Mrs Winnie Ewing.

This frequent multi-partisan contact on the telephone or by letter, with "inside" information fed to me by PADA on one hand and airport management officials on the other, gave me a ready supply of re-active comment on almost any aviation-related issue.

Curiously, the system worked both ways as I found myself also being consulted by one or more local politicians who assumed they knew where my own political sympathies lay. I was still surprised – and not a little flattered – when one enthusiastic Scottish Nationalist, asked me, quite seriously, if I would consider standing as a parliamentary candidate for them if formally asked.

"But you must have noticed I'm an Englishman," I protested. His reply disarmed me.

"Some of our best supporters are English," he said. I thanked him but mumbled something about politics not being "my line of country." I was careful not to say which country I was talking about. Perhaps I should have added that they wouldn't be able to find a worse public speaker.

It was soon clear that Scottish tourism was still being badly hit by a fall in Scandinavian and stopover visitors. One of the human effects of the cuts was an incident when a group of 57 young American "goodwill" ambassadors to Europe had to fly home to New York via Copenhagen after their tour culminated in a lightning visit to Scotland. No one had been able to warn them that their flight from Prestwick by SAS was among those axed by the Government, and they arrived to check in only to find there was no aircraft to take them.

I stood by as SAS officials, apparently tried in vain to make an alternative booking for them on other flights, calling other Prestwick airlines in turn, only to advise the group, "Sorry, but there are no seats left." Eventually the Americans accepted an offer by SAS to re-book them on a scheduled service leaving Prestwick for Copenhagen, to connect with another SAS flight operating direct to New York, adding 700 miles and several hours to their journey.

Group leader Ira J. Hollar of Oklahoma University, told me: "This has inconvenienced us a great deal as our programme was very carefully timed. If we had known this was going to happen we would never have come to Scotland."

Glasgow's two evening papers gave considerable space to the story – the *Evening Citizen* devoting a top of the page to the spread and the dailies followed up with similar pieces.

Sorry, no room on the plane

U.S. TOURISTS FLY 700 MILES FOR CONNECTION

Evening Citizen (above)
©Evening Times (right)
(both) July 15 1964

Scots "good-will" visit backfires for 57 young Americans . . .

A group of 57 young American "goodwill ambassadors" added a day's visit to Scotland on to their two weeks' people-to-people tour of Europe—and to-day were wishing they had not.

For the girls and boys, mainly young farmers and farmers' daughters from Oklahoma, had to leave their Edinburgh hotel before dawn, drive to Prestwick, and fly 700 miles the wrong way to Copenhagen to catch a transatlantic jet home.

There was no room for them on Prestwick's direct flights to New York.

No success

The group, members of an American youth club, were originally booked to fly to New York later to-day after several hours' sightseeing in Scotland. But their flight was one of a Scandinavian air line's services cut by Government restrictions imposed on the air line in May.

Only yesterday, Mr Julian Amery, the Minister for Aviation, defended the cuts while speaking in Edinburgh, stating that they would bring extra passengers to B.O.A.C. But neither the British air line nor any other transatlantic company operating through Prestwick could offer an alternative booking for the group.

Said an official for S.A.S. at Prestwick—"All the reservations for the group were made in Kansas Coty and Copenhagen. As far as we can tell here, every effort was made to rebook the party by another air line without success."

Group leader Mr Ira J. Hollar, of Oklahoma University, said at the airport—"This has inconvenienced us a great deal. If we had known this was going to happen we would never have come to Scotland. We included it in the tour almost at the last moment, and planned to sped na lot of time in Edinburgh and at points along our approach route to the airport. Now we are spending the extra time in Denmark instead."

Pretty, blue-eyed Ann Marie Williams, aged 18, whose father owns a 1300-acre farm at Mulhall, Oklahoma, commented—"I always thought the British were logical. But it seems the height of stupidity to turn away tourists by cutting down air services."

And 17-year-old Karen Vore, from Cleo Springs, added—"I wanted to buy some cashmere sweaters and tweeds in Scotland. But there was no time to go shopping."

The *Scottish Daily Express* ran an editorial blaming Julian Amery's cuts, demanding: "Let this nonsense be ended - directly."

NO PLANE, SO U.S. TEENAGERS MISS SCOTS TRIP

A DISAPPOINTED group of young American "goodwill ambassadors" flew from Scotland yesterday after a one-day sightseeing tour had been cancelled because no direct flight home was available.

By Daily Mail Reporter

The 57 teenagers, from farms in Oklahoma, had booked to fly home by Transatlantic jet after a few hours in this country.

But they found that their flight had been cancelled because of the Government's decision to axe Scandinavian Air Lines services through Scotland. And there was no room on any other flight from Prestwick to America.

Instead they had to fly 700 miles eastwards to Copenhagen at dawn yesterday—only a few hours after arriving in Scotland—to catch a jet home.

Inconvenience

The group was concluding a two-week European goodwill tour and had added Scotland to their itinerary as an afterthought.

Their leader, Mr. Ira J. Hollar, of Oklahoma University, said as the group left Prestwck yesterday: "Our programme was very carefully timed and this has inconvenienced us a great deal.

"If we had known this was going to happen we would never have come to Scotland in the first place.

"We included it in our tour almost at the last moment and planned to spend some time in Edinburgh and at points along our coach route to the airport. Now we are spending the extra time in Denmark instead."

Karen Vore, 17, added: "I wanted to buy some sweaters and tweeds in Scotland. But there was not even time to do any shopping."

Only 24 hours earlier in Edinburgh, the Minister of Aviation, Mr. Julian Amery, had defended the airline cuts on the basis that BOAC would benefit from the extra passenger traffic.

But neither BOAC nor any other Transatlantic airline operating through Prestwick could offer the group an alternative booking yesterday.

Said a spokesman for Scandinavian Air Lines at Prestwick: "All reservations for the party were dealt with in Kansas City and Copenhagen. We made every effort to re-book the group by another airline, but had no success."

AMERY AXE STRANDS TOURISTS

HERALD REPORTER

FIFTY - SEVEN young Americans on a goodwill tour of Europe decided at the last minute to include Scotland in their itinerary.

Yesterday they were wishing they hadn't.

A flight mix-up meant they had to travel 700 miles EAST to Copenhagen before they could go 3,500 miles WEST to New York.

The group, boys and girls from farms in Oklahoma, were booked to fly from Prestwick to New York.

But their reservations had been hit by the Government's decision to axe Scandinavian Airlines' services through Scotland.

They had to catch an early-morning flight to Copenhagen and get their transatlantic jet home from there.

Neither BOAC nor other airlines operating through Prestwick could offer the Americans seats.

Only 24 hours earlier, in Edinburgh, Minister of Aviation Julian Amery had defended cutting Scandinavian Airlines' services. BOAC would benefit from extra bookings, he claimed.

Leader of the U.S. party, Mr. Ira J. Hollar, of Oklahoma University, said before they left: "Our programme was very carefully timed and this change has inconvenienced us a great deal. If we'd known this was going to happen we would never have come to Scotland."

Ann Marie Williams, 18, whose father owns a 1,300-acre farm at Mulhall, Oklahoma, said: "I always thought the British were logical. But it seems the height of stupidity to turn away tourists by cutting down air services."

Daily Herald July 16 1964

WHAT NONSENSE

A PARTY of young Americans have to fly home to the U.S. from Scotland—via Denmark.

Inconvenient and illogical they call it. Scots offer apologies to their visitors and have another word for it.

Daft.

There is no sense in Aviation Minister Julian Amery's decision to limit direct Scandinavian Airline flights through Prestwick to America.

And that goes double when—as in this case—empty seats are not available on B.O.A.C.

Let his nonsense be ended—directly.

GOODWILL TOUR HIT BY AIRLINE CUTS

Daily Telegraph Reporter

A group of 57 young American "goodwill ambassadors" had to fly to Copenhagen from Scotland to catch a jet airliner home yesterday because there was no room for them on direct flights from Prestwick Airport to New York.

The group, teenagers from farms throughout Oklahoma, had added a day's visit to Scotland to their two-week tour of Europe as an afterthought, and were originally booked to fly from Prestwick to New York yesterday. However, their reservation was hit by the Government restriction on Scandinavian Airlines' services through Scotland.

The leader of the group, Mr. Ira J. Hollar, of Oklahoma University, said: "If we'd known this was going to happen we would never have come to Scotland." The time they had planned to spend there was being spent in Denmark instead.

Scottish Daily Mail (above), Scottish Daily Express Editorial (centre), Daily Telegraph (right) (all) July 16 1964

The following day BOAC went out of their way to call me. Ian Morrison insisted: "Given fair warning we would have done our best to accommodate the party. But we were never asked.

"For such a large group we might even have provided an extra flight. After exhaustive enquiries we have been unable to trace any record of an approach to us by SAS."

BOAC: We didn't say No

NOT ASKED TO FLY OUT U.S. TEENAGERS

By Daily Mail Reporter

OFFICIALS of BOAC denied yesterday that they had been asked to provide seats on any of their Transatlantic flights for 57 American teenagers.

The young Americans—members of a "goodwill" party touring Europe—had to fly 700 miles from Scotland to Copenhagen to catch a West-bound jet flight home on Wednesday.

It was said there was no room for them on direct flights from Prestwick.

Their original booking had been cancelled as a result of Government restrictions on Scandinavian Airline Services.

A spokesman for SAS said earlier that "every effort had been made to rebook the group by another airline, without success."

The Americans complained that they had missed a day's sightseeing in Scotland because of the switch.

A BOAC spokesman in London said last night: "We would have done our best to accommodate the party, given fair warning. After exhaustive inquiries, we can find no record either in Glasgow or Prestwick of any approach to us by their airline.

At Prestwick, officials of all airlines agreed that bookings on the North Atlantic routes were "exceptionally heavy."

Practically all flights were sold out for the next few weeks.

But one added: "For such a large party, a British or American airline could have provided an extra service if they had been given sufficient notice."

Scottish Daily Mail July 17 1964

The following September the soon-to-be-outgoing Minister of Aviation, Julian Amery, was attempting to justify his decision to restrict SAS by announcing that BOAC's passenger traffic through Prestwick had increased by 30 per cent since the cuts were imposed. But as PADA's David Reid called me to point out, transatlantic traffic everywhere was booming with both Pan American Airways and KLM carrying more passengers to and from the Scottish airport.

Our story on his challenge to Mr Amery's interpretation of the traffic figures was widely recorded in both Scottish and English nationals, with phrases such as "Amery rapped," "Airport men hit out" and "Amery view contradicted" given prominence *(see overleaf)*. Yet less than a week later we had to report that now another Prestwick operator was under threat from the Minister's axe.

The Icelandic airline Loftleider, one of the few international carriers remaining outside the International Air Transport Association, had been seeking authority to switch their operations from Glasgow's Renfrew airport to Prestwick. The airline planned to introduce

Tourists didn't ask us—BOAC

BOAC officials yesterday denied that they had been asked to provide seats on any of their trans-Atlantic flights for a party of 57 American teenagers.

The Americans had to fly 700 miles from Scotland eastwards to Copenhagen to catch a West-bound jet flight home to the U.S. on Wednesday because, it was said, there was no room for them on direct flights from Prestwick.

Daily Herald July 17 1964

Airport men hit out at Amery

AVIATION MINISTER JULIAN AMERY came under fire yesterday from the Prestwick Airport Development Association.

The Association denied the claims made by Mr. Amery at the opening of the air terminal by the Queen Mother.

He claimed credit for an increase in B.O.A.C.'s traffic through Prestwick, and a general stepping-up of business at the airport from May to August, 1964.

Mr Amery also said there was growing prosperity at the airport — and, according to the Association, he inferred that this justified his action in cutting Scandinavian Airline services through Prestwick. He said this had not been done at Scotland's expense.

The Association think otherwise. Their secretary, Mr. David Reid said last night:

"All airports on the North Atlantic route enjoyed a traffic boom this summer, resulting from the introduction of cheap fares last April.

Traffic gain

"Some have traffic gains in excess of B.O.A.C. without benefit of restrictions against their competitors."

He pointed out that it was wrong to assume that B.O.A.C.'s improved results stemmed entirely from the Scandinavian cuts.

Referring directly to the Minister's statement that the gain in Atlantic traffic had not been at Scotland's expense, Mr. Reid stated:

"This cannot be said at the moment."

"The danger remains that S.A.S. could still withdraw operations from Scotland if further cuts are made."

Daily Record

PRESTWICK CHALLENGE TO AMERY

Scottish Share of Air Line Boom

The Prestwick Airport Development Association yesterday challenged statements by the Minister of Aviation, Mr Julian Amery, seeking to justify restriction imposed on the services of Scandinavian Airlines through Scotland.

Commenting on the letter Mr Amery sent to the Secretary of State for Scotland last week giving details of the increase in B.O.A.C. passenger traffic and the airport's overall increase in traffic, the association secretary, Mr David Reid, said last night:—"All air lines on the North Atlantic route have this summer enjoyed a traffic boom resulting from the introduction of cheap fares last April.

© Glasgow Herald
Also Scotsman (not shown)
(all) September 29 1964

AMERY VIEW ON AIR TRAFFIC RISE CONTRADICTED

The Prestwick Airport Development Association yesterday published a flat contradiction of statements by the Minister of Aviation, Mr. Amery, in his attempts to justify restrictions on the services of Scandinavian Airlines through Scotland.

Commenting on the letter the Minister sent to Mr. Noble, the Secretary of State for Scotland, last week, giving details of the increases in B O A C passenger traffic and the airport's overall increases in traffic, the Association's secretary, Mr. David Reid, said: "All airlines on the North Atlantic route have this summer enjoyed a traffic boom resulting from the introduction of cheap fares last April.

Daily Telegraph

The airport association points out:

1—That ALL airlines on the North Atlantic route enjoyed a traffic boom this summer following cut fares in April.

2—**That some airlines recorded even bigger gains than B.O.A.C. at Prestwick without having the help of the Amery axe against competitors.**

3—That B.O.A.C.'s increased traffic probably did not stem from the S.A.S. cuts—but from the "vigorous and long overdue" B.O.A.C. campaign to stimulate Scottish business.

"Scotland has not, in fact benefited to the full extent in the Atlantic traffic boom because of these restrictions," states the association.

Scottish Daily Express (extract)

Pilots' strike hits services

Air services between Glasgow and Iceland were brought almost completely to a standstill yesterday by an Icelandic pilots' strike.

Services operated by Icelandair were cancelled until further notice. And Loftleidir is continuing with a restricted service, using Prestwick airport.

Scottish Daily Express (right)
(reconstructed from damaged original)
June 7 1963

Canadian built CL 44 turbo-prop aircraft on the route to Keflavik, replacing their ageing Douglas DC 6Bs. They believed that the facilities at the transatlantic airport were operationally safer and more suitable for the new aircraft. They could have become the first foreign airline to transfer from another airport to Prestwick's new terminal, already deserted for much of the day.

As it wasn't in the big league of international operators, the Icelandic airline had rarely featured in our national news over the years. At Prestwick we saw their aircraft only occasionally when they were forced to divert there by bad weather. Then in June 1963 the company's pilots went on strike over working conditions and in support of a pay claim.

That meant the company's aircraft stayed on the ground wherever they were when the captains walked out. Western Scotland, and Prestwick Airport-by-the-sea, just happened to be basking in sunshine at the time, which suited most of their crews – right down to the ground. And for almost a week Icelandic cabin staff, stewardesses and stewards from several Icelandic airliners, were able to soak up the sun on the Ayrshire beach as they stayed in local hotels, all expenses paid by their airline, who were unable to get them home. The striking pilots had to make their own way back to Reykjavik at their own cost.

Sunday Post (below) June 9 1963

PILOTS GO HOME BY SEA

WHILE 12 glamorous Icelandic air hostesses took advantage of an unexpected all-expenses-paid holiday in the sun at Prestwick yesterday, their bosses, eight senior pilots of Icelandic Airlines, were driving by coach to Leith to book a sea passage home after being "disinherited" by their company.

Twenty-eight Icelandic crew members - four full crews - were stranded at Prestwick last week when their aircraft was grounded in an Icelandic nation-wide strike of airline pilots for more pay and better flying conditions. On Thursday the strike was declared official by the pilots' union.

Scottish Sunday Express,
(reconstructed from damaged original) *June 9 1963*

EIGHT PILOTS GO HOME BY SEA

STRANDED AT PRESTWICK BY AIRLINE STRIKE

EIGHT Icelandic pilots drove from Prestwick to Leith yesterday to book a SEA passage home.

They're members of four full crews who've been stranded in Scotland by a nation-wide strike of Icelandic Airline pilots.

Yesterday the pilots were told in a cable from Reykjavik, "As you are on strike your foreign station allowance ceases immediately. If you want to come home you must make your own way."

He added—"The company will have to pay our fares home as our contract states that it is their responsibility to get us home. The fact that we are on strike has nothing to do with it."

The strike is for more pay

PILOTS DITCHED

Firm says 'money stops'

EIGHT senior pilots, stranded at Prestwick by an airline strike, were last night trying to go home by sea—after being "disowned" by their company.

Sunday Mail *June 9 1963*

Strike-hit air girls spend a Sunday in the sun . . .

STRANDED—AND LOVING EVERY MINUTE OF IT

A group of the air hostesses relax on the beach . . . enjoying their unexpected holiday to the full

Scottish Daily Mail June 10 1963 — *Brenard Press picture*

Pilots' strike gives bronzed beauties a holiday in sun

By Daily Mail Reporter

TWELVE bronzed Icelandic beauties in bikinis lazed in blazing sunshine on the beach

other crew members in Scotland is expensive. If the strike goes on much longer some way must be found to get them home to Iceland."

NINE BEAUTIES RELAX AS MEN FIGHT PAY BATTLE

Express Staff Reporter

THEY say it is women who suffer when men go on strike.

But the nine lovely Iceland air hostesses who were stranded in Scotland yesterday by a pilots' strike did not complain.

And the only thing they suffered from was too much sun.

The hostesses, who should have been in New York or Copenhagen, or some other glamour spot, instead brought glamour to Prestwick beach.

In swim suits and brief bikinis they smoothed on the suntan oil and relaxed, while airline and union officials fought out the pay row in Reykjavik, 800 miles away.

Their planes have been arriving in Prestwick since Wednesday . . . and stopping there.

And while the men argued over wages and conditions, the girls were out thoroughly enjoying themselves.

WONDERFUL

The pilots, ordered home, travelled to Leith on Saturday

Scottish Daily Express June 10 1963

Air strike ends and so does holiday in the sun

By Daily Mail Reporter

THE unexpected, all-expenses paid holiday in the sun for 12 Icelandic airline hostesses stranded at Prestwick by a pilots' strike, is over.

The girls said goodbye to their week of sunbathing and swimming in a temperature of 80 degrees last night, and boarded a chartered airliner for Reykjavik.

"You can be sure it will be cold and raining when we get there," grumbled 22-year-old Gudrun Olafsdottir.

Talks

She wasn't far wrong. Weather experts at the airport said last night that the forecast for Iceland was: "Drizzle, some coastal fog and temperatures of about 50 degrees."

Strike over--Bikini girls go home

TWELVE beautiful air hostesses sadly packed their bikinis to-day and prepared to fly home—to Iceland.

For the girls, stranded at Prestwick by a pilots' strike, the all-expenses-paid haliday in the sun is over.

As they sat down to breakfast before another day on the beach, sun-soaking, the girls—members of more than 20 Icelandic air crews who were left behind at Prestwick Airport—had a phone call from the company's office in Glasgow saying the week-old strike by captains and co-pilots was over.

The pilots, who want more pay and better flying conditions, are returning to work pending negotiations with the two Iceland air lines, Loftleidir and Icelandair.

'DITCHED' GIRLS GO

THE unexpected all-expenses paid holiday in the sun for 12 Icelandic Airline hostesses — stranded at Prestwick, Ayrshire, by a pilot's strike—is over.

Last night the girls boarded a chartered airliner for the flight home to Reyjavik, Iceland.

Strike ends

The hostesses and eight other crew members learned yesterday that the strike had ended pending negotiations.

And as they said goodbye to a sizzling week of sunbathing and swimming, the forecast for Iceland was — "Drizzle, and some coastal fog."

©Evening Times (far left) June 10 1963

Daily Record (centre) Scottish Daily Mail (left) (both) June 11 1963

New row over 'pirate' air link

By Daily Mail Reporter

A NEW row over Scotland's long-distance air links is likely to break this month.

The cause—a "pirate" Icelandic airline has applied for permission to step up seating capacity on its twice - weekly cut - price Transatlantic flights to and from Scotland.

Top-level discussions between the British and Icelandic Governments open in London on October 19.

But last night there were indications that Aviation Minister Mr. Julian Amery might ban the airline from British airports or severely restrict it after seven years of successful operations with reduced fares on the Glasgow-Iceland-New York route.

'Pirate' airline plan more cut-price seats

SUN REPORTER

A ROW is looming between the British and Icelandic Governments over Scotland's long-distance air links. An application has been made by a "pirate" Icelandic airline to step up seating capacity on its twice-weekly cut-price transatlantic flights to and from Scotland.

Discussions start in London on October 19. The Icelandic Government is sending a representative.

But last night there were indications that Aviation Minister Julian Amery may ban the airline completely from British airports or severely restrict it.

The airline, Loftleidir Icelandic Airlines, one of the few international carriers outside the world airline "cartel," the International Air Transport Association, has asked the Ministry for permission to switch over from outdated American DC 6B aircraft to the bigger Canadian-built CL 44 jet-prop airliner.

More seats

For operational and safety reasons they also want to transfer services from Renfrew Airport to Prestwick.

But the new airliners, a development of the British Britannia, can carry up to 165 passengers. This means they will be offering more than twice the present seating capacity.

Said one senior Ministry official in London: "Iceland offers absolutely nothing in return for the traffic it carries into and out of Scotland."

Scottish Daily Mail (left)
Sun (above) (both) Oct 2 1964

A year on from that strike, I was able to reveal that Loftleidir had put in their transfer bid. As a routine request for operational reasons, it should have required little more than a nod from the British Government. But now the transfer was coming under closer scrutiny by those in the Aviation Ministry anxious to tighten restrictions against "non-reciprocal" foreign airlines. They argued that the case against Loftleider was even stronger than that against SAS since it involved fare undercutting with little or no local traffic to justify "poaching" of transatlantic passengers.

This time the newspapers sat up and took notice, responding to my story with, for example, eight column inches in the *Daily Telegraph*, headed:

BIGGER PLANES REQUEST MAY START NEW AIR ROW

Daily Telegraph Oct 2 1964

and ten inches in the *Glasgow Herald* with:

New Air Dispute Expected

©Glasgow Herald Oct 2 1964

We were able to follow up with a further story for the Sundays and then Monday's dailies when Chris tracked down the UK director of the airline, Mr Ronald Orme. He described as "nonsense" the

● Scottish reaction to reports that Aviation Minister Mr. Julian Amery might axe another transatlantic airline with plans to operate flights through Prestwick built up last night.

A senior official of the Scottish Council (Development and Industry) stated: "We will view with considerable misgiving any action, which unnecessarily limits the expansion of Prestwick's services on any world route.

Mr. David Reid, secretary of the Prestwick Airport Development Association, said: "If Mr. Amery persists in lopping off the weaker branches of Scottish Transatlantic services, the tree will ddie. Prestwick cannot function for only one or possibly two airlines."

Scottish Daily Mail (extract)
Oct 3 1964

PRESTWICK—A NEW BATTLE

A NEW battle over Prestwick Airport and its future flared last night. The contestants—the Ministry of Aviation and Loftleider, the Icelandic airline.

It has been suggested the company may be facing severe restrictions—or even a permanent ban — on flights into Britain by the Ministry of Aviation.

And the company have hit back at suggestions that they have given nothing in return for their eight years of cut price operations through Scotland and across the Atlantic

'IT'S NONSENSE!'

Yesterday the company's British director Mr. Ronald Orme confirmed in London that the Icelandic aviation authorities have been asked by the Ministry of Aviation to discuss the company's proposed winter schedules and routes on which they want to introduce higher density jet-prop airliners.

He added:

"If it is Aviation Minister's intention to prevent us operating through Britain he hasn't told us.

"Meantime we will continue to operate our permitted flights—two each way weekly between Britain, Iceland and elsewhere."

It was nonsense, he claimed, to say that Icelandic airline had given nothing to Scotland.

"Many of the passengers we have carried on flights through Scotland have stopped over, spending money in the country."

He emphasised, too, the thousands of dollars spent by transit passengers in duty-free purchases, souvenirs and other goods.

And he spoke of negotiations going on with Scottish travel agencies to provide Americans and Icelanders with inclusive tours of Scotland.

In addition there was the large amount of Scottish freight flown to Iceland by the company.

Sunday Mail
Oct 4 1964

argument that the airline gave nothing in return for the right it had enjoyed on its British route. He claimed that a considerable proportion of the thousands of passengers the airline carried stopped over in Scotland to spend money, and the company was planning to carry both American and Icelandic passengers on inclusive tours. He also referred to the "considerable" amount of Scottish exports carried on flights to Iceland.

Only two weeks later we had to report that talks between the Iceland and British Government on the Loftleidir request had failed. The decision meant that the airline would have to postpone its proposal to increase capacity on the service to Scotland, delaying its purchase of CL44s until the following spring. The company no longer sought to transfer services to Prestwick.

Coincidentally, on that same day we won further headlines with our exclusive from PADA who had taken exception to accusations by a Glasgow councillor of attempted "airline poaching" by Prestwick Airport. Councillor Jack Richmond claimed that at least three foreign airlines operating through Renfrew airport were considering, or had been invited to consider transferring to Prestwick before Abbotsinch was completed.

Association secretary, David Reid, called me to say that the proposals by certain airlines to transfer to Prestwick stemmed largely from the inability of Renfrew to handle modern aircraft and doubts about the marginal operational conditions for big jets of the day arising at Abbotsinch.

He went on: "Two or three of the airlines concerned formerly operated from Prestwick, and as both operate transatlantic services, they should in our view be based at Prestwick, which is officially the only Scottish transatlantic airport."

Abbotsinch, he said, was being created at considerable expense to the ratepayer and taxpayer as an airport to serve Glasgow for domestic and "certain Continental flights" only and the Government had been most specific on this point. He said that the Association would be failing in their obligations if they made no effort to attract new air services. And as one of two airports designated to serve Glasgow, Prestwick was equally entitled to cater for air services between Scotland and Europe, in addition to its transatlantic flights.

The following year the airport development association decided to appeal formally against the SAS cuts. But it was to take a general election and a change of government before there could be any hope of a relaxation. In the meantime there were new battles to be fought to try to boost Prestwick's traffic and halt the continuing decline in passengers. Each and every one of them was awarded major publicity in newspapers north and south of the border through our exclusive stories.

*

As work got under way to develop Abbotsinch, with the provision of a new passenger terminal for both domestic and international services, the fortunes of Prestwick continued to fluctuate. BOAC did fulfil its promise to step up its services, introducing extra flights on both New York and, in partnership with Air Canada, on Toronto and Montreal routes. With similar increases offered by Pan American Airways, this meant a total of 12,000 extra seats every week on transatlantic scheduled flights. But the airport's overall traffic increases fell well behind the average boom recorded for major

BAN ON 'CHEAPER FLIGHT' AIRLINE

AN airline operating cut price Transatlantic flights was told yesterday that it cannot introduce bigger, more modern jet-prop airliners.

The announcement from the Ministry of Aviation came as a blow to Loftleidir, the Icelandic airline, waiting for the green light to switch from Renfrew to Prestwick.

Said an official of the airline in Glasgow last night: "We will take up the question at a higher level — through the Foreign Ministries of Iceland and Great Britain.

BACKWARD

"The Ministry's refusal isn't logical."

Loftleidir has been operating flights between Britain and New York for eight years at fares lower than those of airlines attached to the International Air Transport Association.

It wanted to switch from piston-engined 85-seater aircraft to 165-seater Canadair CL44 airliners.

Said Ayrshire County Convener Daniel Sim: "It's a backward step to stop this airline from operating with more modern planes on longer, safer runways."

Scottish Daily Express

ICELANDIC FLIGHTS REQUEST REFUSED

Seating capacity on cut-price flights across the north Atlantic by the Icelandic airline Loftleidir is not to be increased at present.

NO LARGER PLANES FOR AIRLINE

Daily Telegraph Reporter

Seating capacity on cut-price flights across the Atlantic by the Icelandic airline, Loftleidir, is not to be stepped up.

ICELAND AIR TALKS FAIL

By Our Air Correspondent

The Ieclandic airline, Loftleidir, which wanted to introduce bigger turbo-prop CL-44 airliners on its route from Scotland to the U.S. via Iceland, will not be doing so yet.

BAN ON LOFTLEIDER SCOTTISH FIGHTS

No Larger Aircraft

Seating capacity on cut-price flights across the Atlantic by the Icelandic air line, Loftleidir, is not to be increased.

(From top) The Times, Daily Telegraph, Financial Times, ©Glasgow Herald (all) October 24 1964

PRESTWICK REPLY TO "POACHING" CHARGE

Abbotsinch Unsuitable for Big Jets?

Mr David Reid, secretary of Prestwick Airport Development Association, last night replied to charges that Prestwick was attempting to "poach" air services from Glasgow's new airport at Abbotsinch.

The charges were made by a Glasgow Progressive councillor, Mr J. Richmond, who complained that at least three foreign air lines now operating through Renfrew were considering, or being invited to consider, transferring to Prestwick before Abbotsinch is completed.

Mr Reid said proposals by air lines to transfer to Prestwick stemmed largely from the inability of Renfrew to handle modern aircraft, and doubts about the marginal operating conditions for big jets arriving at Abbotsinch.

He added that "in regard to the term 'poaching' two of the three air lines formerly operated from Prestwick, and as they fly transatlantic services they should, in the association's view, be based at Scotland's transatlantic airport."

Abbotsinch, he said, was being created at considerable expense to the ratepayer and taxpayer as an airport serving Glasgow for domestic and certain Continental flights only, and the Government had been most specific on this point.

Referring to an assurance by Mr Peter Meldrum, Lord Provost of Glasgow, that Prestwick's flights would not be "poached" by Abbotsinch, Mr Reid said "that promise referred to transatlantic traffic and followed earlier remarks about Abbotsinch taking over from Prestwick as the transatlantic airport for Glasgow.

"We would be failing in our obligations as an association if we made no effort to attract new air services. As one of two airports officially designated to serve Glasgow, Prestwick is equally entitled to cater for air services between Scotland and Europe in addition to its transatlantic flights."

©Glasgow Herald October 24 1964

airports throughout the United Kingdom, and indeed the rest of the western world.

In the meantime, PADA was asking the new Aviation Minister, Mr Roy Jenkins directly for an early review of the restrictions imposed on Scandinavian Airlines. In a statement again released only to us, David Reid and Provost Iain Foulds revealed that they had recommended that Scottish overseas routes could be safeguarded by freezing the Scandinavians for a fixed period. This would enable the two national carriers on the North Atlantic, BOAC and Pan American, to establish their requirements. Once this was known, SAS could be allowed to step up their operations in accordance with the increases in transatlantic traffic announced periodically by the Air Transport Association.

The Minister's response came after just over two weeks. Headlines – again for our exclusive report – told the story:

PRESTWICK CURB ON S.A.S. TO REMAIN

Minister Sees No Need for Urgent Talks

The Government do not intend to restore Scandinavian Airlines System services through Prestwick next summer.

Mr Roy Jenkins, Minister of Aviation, makes this clear in a letter to the Prestwick Airport Development Association, who had asked for an early review of the restrictions imposed by his predecessor, Mr Julian Amery.

The letter states:—

The Minister is, of course, most concerned to ensure that Scotland has adequate air services and that the national investment at Prestwick Airport is put to good use. He has accordingly reviewed the actions taken earlier this year over Scandinavian Airlines' services through Prestwick.

Having done so he is satisfied there is no need to reopen negotiations with the Scandinavians before the winter of 1965.

Provost Iain Foulds, Prestwick, chairman of the development association, said last night:—"Naturally I am extremely disappointed by the Minister's decision, as, I am sure, will be the majority of the people in Scotland. With a new Government I had expected some rethinking on this matter.

Loss of Trade

"Things cannot be allowed to rest. There are two unfortunate by-products to Scottish tourism and trade which have arisen from the original restrictions and from which B.O.A.C. are not in a position to benefit.

"One is the question of the tens of thousands of American and Scandinavian tourists who are now by-passing Scotland on direct transatlantic flights. The other is the considerable quantity of Scottish cargo which is now being routed via London instead of being shipped direct to and from Prestwick."

Scandinavian Airlines' transatlantic services through Prestwick were cut from seven to four a week each way last May. In October they were further reduced to three a week—the maximum number they will be permitted to operate throughout next year.

©Glasgow Herald

PRESTWICK'S AIRLINE 'FLY-OVER'

THE Government does not intend to restore Scandinavian Airlines Services through Prestwick next summer.

Minister of Aviation Mr. Roy Jenkins made this clear in a letter yesterday to the Prestwick Airport Development Association who had asked for an early review of the restrictions.

'Disappointed'

In the letter, the Minister's private secretary said: "The Minister is satisfied there is no need to reopen negotiations with the Scandinavians before the winter of 1965."

In reply to an invitation from the Association, the letter goes on to say that the Minister hopes to make an early visit to Prestwick Airport.

Chairman of the Association, Prestwick's provost Iain Foulds said last night: "Naturally, I am extremely disappointed."

Daily Record

Jenkins takes up the 'Amery axe'

LABOUR'S new Aviation Minister, Mr. Roy Jenkins, has taken up the "Amery Axe"—and is to continue his Tory predecessor's policy which slashed foreign air services in Scotland.

Scottish Daily Express

NO REVIEW OF PRESTWICK SAS LANDINGS

Daily Telegraph Reporter

The Government does not intend to restore Scandinavian Airlines (S A S) services through Prestwick next summer. The Minister of Aviation Mr. Roy Jenkins, made this clear in a letter yesterday to the Prestwick Airport Development Association which had asked for an early review of the restriction.

Mr. Jenkins said that while he was concerned to ensure that Scotland had adequate air services and the national investment at Prestwick Airport was put to good use, he was satisfied there was no need to re-open negotiations with the Scandinavians before the winter of 1965.

Prestwick's Provost Mr. Iain Foulds, chairman of the Development Association, said last night: "Naturally, I am extremely disappointed by the Minister's decision. With a new Government, I had expected some re-thinking on this matter."

Daily Telegraph
(all) November 14 1964

Mr Jenkins announced his decision in a letter to PADA, and said that he did not believe that there was 'any need' to re-open negotiations with the Scandinavians before the winter of 1965. This would be in a year's time, some eighteen months after the cuts were first ordered.

Curiously, only four days later, his Ministry then announced, to everyone's surprise, that the Scandinavian airline would be allowed to increase their three flights a week to four through Prestwick the following summer. The announcement immediately followed major speeches in the House of Commons by two politicians at opposite ends of the party spectrum. After detailed 'briefings' by PADA and me in telephone conversations and by letter, Tory George Younger, whose constituency included the airport, and Emrys Hughes, my own local MP and on the left of the Labour party, both took up the cudgels in its defence *(see opposite)*.

But the relaxation proved to be too little to enable the airline to regain its Scottish prestige position on the Atlantic. For Prestwick Airport it came too late to recover its role in Scotland. More significantly the decision became a canker which would eventually see the demise of Prestwick as a major intercontinental gateway at least for the foreseeable future, as so many aviation visionaries and local supporters had so frequently forecast.

In the meantime, we had to do some serious thinking as an agency about our future commitment and role in the west of Scotland. Chris was shortly being called back to Heathrow, where his strengths were needed in a team which had become depleted in recent months. I was left to search for at least one new recruit to take his place, and at the same time plan to establish a base at the new Glasgow airport, to meet whatever challenge it presented.

For the next two or three years, as we moved into the second half of the 60s, our output of news was somehow maintained, thanks to continuing developments in the aviation world as well as a mass of unexpected "happenings," as recorded elsewhere in these pages. But I found the pressure of building contacts at Abbotsinch and setting up communications there time and energy consuming.

The two airports were about an hour apart by road, which meant that a chunk of the working day was committed to these visits – about the same amount of time we normally allowed for daily 'phoning of news copy to clients. There was the added problem of being out of touch with news desks and news incidents which frequently seemed to occur just as Chris (initially) or I had left one airport car-park for another 30 miles away, hardly a satisfactory excuse for a lack of service to our clients.

Finding an ambitious junior to train, even someone with no experience of newspaper work whatsoever, was proving far more difficult. Though one or two seemed promising enough in their interviews, only one stayed the course for more than a year before deciding he wasn't cut out for the role of a reporter, and opted instead to join the family business. If I were to have any time off to spend with my family – from 1965 I had a son as well as a four-years-old daughter – or to establish a new base at Abbotsinch, it was important to have a deputy to rely upon at Prestwick. Eventually he or she would be a stand-in for Chris (I couldn't yet think of any new recruit in terms of a potential replacement)

That was until Bob McKenzie joined me in the late sixties.

*

Bob came to the post straight from school, the local Ayr Academy. He was bright and keen to learn. He could write well. It was not easy to give him his head and delegate opportunities to him, but it was obvious from the start that he had the potential to become a good reporter. In fact, eventually he was to move on, first to the local *Ayrshire Post*, then its "parent", the *Glasgow Herald*. Later still he joined the *Daily Express*, becoming, as I have already described, a prominent sports correspondent.

Despite the obvious relief provided by Bob's enthusiasm and ever-growing reliability, I found myself becoming more and more dissatisfied with my own role. As with many journalists I believed I was more successful when working under deadline pressure. I was never as happy dealing with what I saw as "administrative" matters and the routine of making the rounds of new contacts as I was with the immediacy, the urgency of reporting. The challenge of promoting a Prestwick fighting to gain the prominence it deserved was also fading, never to be replaced, by the promising growth of a city "bus station " air terminal, which seemed at the time to be the prospect of the new Glasgow Airport.

What was even worse for me was the slow realisation that the solidity of my 17-year marriage was also an illusion. The difficulties on the home front were not due to my work commitment, though early on this could have been a contributory factor. For more than two years I lived on a knife edge, treading warily and trying to make some sense of a devastating and bewildering situation, and refusing to believe that I could not find a way of ending the continuing tensions.

Only after the failure of several despairing and one-sided attempts at reconciliation did it finally became clear the situation was out of control. There was nothing left and there

PRESTWICK HOPES FOR MORE

Daily Telegraph Reporter

The Minister of Aviation's announcement yesterday that Scandinavian Airlines' trans-atlantic flights through Prestwick would be increased to four a week next summer, was welcomed last night by Mr. David Reid, secretary of the airport's development association.

"I hope this will be the beginning of the process for restoration of the cut services," he said, pointing out that the four flights a week was the number the airline was allowed to operate last summer and still compared unfavourably with the original seven flights operated through Prestwick.

Mr. David Reid, secretary of the airport's development association, said: "I hope this will be just the beginning of restoration of the cut services."

And he added: "I am a little surprised by the apparent change of heart at the Ministry. But we must not get this out of proportion.

"Four flights a week is the number the airline was allowed to operate last summer, and still compares unfavourably with the seven flights originally operated through Prestwick."

Daily Telegraph (top)
Scottish Daily Express (extract)

Last-ditch bid by Tory to alter airport plan

By Daily Mail Reporter

A NEW—and possibly the last — flare-up of the Abbotsinch v. Prestwick controversy is promised this week after Mr. George Younger, Conservative MP for Ayr, makes his maiden speech in the Commons today.

Mr Younger — who originally stood down at Kinross to allow Sir Alec Douglas-Home to enter the House as Prime Minister—is speaking during the second reading of the Government Bill to hand over Britain's major airports to an independent authority.

And he is taking the opportunity to raise, once again, the question of public expenditure at Glasgow's new airport at Abbotsinch and to demand a searching public review of the costs and necessity of the project.

Costs

He said yesterday: "I feel this may be the last opportunity to bring the whole subject out into the open."

At the same time, Scotland's Civil Aviation Development Association—the Scotjet committee—is returning to the battle with a meeting this week to discuss the same theme.

One member said yesterday that the entire project has been "shrouded in a veil of mystery" since contracts were signed with construction firms.

He said: "The taxpayer will have to bear the losses at Abbotsinch for several years. But even when Glasgow ratepayers are bearing those losses alone, the rest of the country will continue to pay for the ever-rising airport service costs."

It has also been pointed out that London's Gatwick airport, the fifth busiest in Europe is losing money heavily. Since Abbotsinch will never be able to take the "money-spinning" big jets, it cannot be expected to make a profit for many years.

SCOTTISH M.P.s FIGHT FOR PRESTWICK

Questions About Abbotsinch

From Our Political Correspondent

LONDON, Sunday.

The value of Prestwick Airport to M.P.s who were stranded by fog at Renfrew last week has not been lost on one of those involved, Mr Emrys Hughes, Labour Member for South Ayrshire.

He is to ask the Minister of Aviation on Wednesday to what extent Prestwick Airport is now being used as a result of other airports in Great Britain being fogbound.

Mr George Younger, Conservative M.P. for Ayr, is to ask if the Minister will increase the facilities available to foreign airlines in the use of Prestwick Airport and if he will reconsider the recent cuts made in the number of weekly flights allowed to Scandinavian Airlines System.

MAIDEN SPEECH

Mr Younger makes his maiden speech in the House of Commons to-morrow. He is speaking during the second reading of the Government's Bill to transfer control of Britain's major airports to an independent authority.

He will raise the question of expenditure at Glasgow's new airport at Abbotsinch and will demand a public review of the costs and of the necessity of the project.

He said, "I feel this may be the last opportunity to bring the subject into the open."

MONORAIL LINK

Mr Younger will have the support of a number of Labour M.P.s in his demands. He is also expected to ask the Government to consider the provision of a monorail link between Glasgow and Prestwick which is claimed to be the only place in Britain where such a transport system is financially feasible.

Scotland's Civil Aviation Development Association (Scotjet) will meet this week to discuss the same topic.

One member said to-day:—"The taxpayer will have to bear heavy losses at Abbotsinch for several years. But, even when Glasgow ratepayers are bearing the losses alone, the country will continue to pay for the ever-rising airport service costs."

He said that Gatwick, the fifth busiest in Europe, was losing money heavily and that as Abbotsinch would never be able to take the largest air liners it could not be expected to make a profit.

©Glasgow Herald (above)
Scottish Daily Mail (left)
(all) November 19 1964

was no key to turn back the clock.

With, I confess, little consideration to Bob's future, other than the conviction that he was ready to take over from me, I had to accept that my time in Scotland was up. I called Bill Brenard and asked to be allowed to return to Heathrow. Recalling our original agreement, I pointed out the company's plans for Prestwick had not worked out. Even with retainers, Scottish newspaper linage rates were too low to support sufficient staff to give the coverage for two airports, and news output from Prestwick alone would now decline. And I had completed eight of the original maximum of ten years I had agreed to spend north of the border.

Bren was understanding and sympathetic. And surprisingly he told me that he wanted me back on the 'home' team, and had been considering a reshuffle of staff. He too, it seemed, no longer believed in the long-term viability of a Scottish base. Within days, at his suggestion, I was flying to London for a meeting. Bren readily agreed to my suggestion that Bob should spend a week or two at Heathrow to gain wider experience of reporting, and on his return I began to make arrangements for my departure.

When I told my Scottish-born wife of those plans, believing that even at this late stage she might agree to come with me, she was adamant. Reminding me that she had not wanted to live in her homeland when I was offered the job, she now insisted that she had no intention of moving to England. "I am happy here now," she said. "I have my friends here. I'm staying in Scotland."

*

Unlike my marriage, Scotland's inter-continental airport was to struggle gamely on for a further incredible thirty-plus loss-making years, first under the Ministry landlords, then as the "jewel in the crown" of a long-optimistic British Airports Authority. For many of those years the airport's hopes were kept alive by the direction of all Scottish transatlantic traffic to and from Prestwick. Even this lifeline was eventually withdrawn when a Conservative Government declared an "open skies" policy which theoretically, at least, permitted such flights from any central Scottish airport.

Strangely, the policy was welcomed by the Authority's privatised successor, BAA plc, whose subsidiary company, Scottish Airports Limited, owned all three Lowland airports – Prestwick, Glasgow (Abbotsinch) and Edinburgh, as well as Aberdeen airport. It was also described as "excellent" news for Scotland by experts who should have known better, despite the fact that it meant the loss of all connections to the U.S. and Canada by the leading international transatlantic airlines.

Prestwick sadly succumbed in the mid-nineties to the decade's familiar market forces. A continuing financial loss-maker, it was sold off by BAA.

The hoped-for build-up of transatlantic and transcontinental traffic boosted by a comprehensive network of feeder routes and domestic services, had failed to materialise. Without these connections, Scotland could not hope to sustain a major intercontinental airport on the west coast in the age of 300-seater jumbo jets. By the beginning of 2001, it had been sold again to a group of Scottish businessmen. In recent years it has seen some prosperity in its air cargo traffic, and in the 21st century has offered an invaluable alternative to Glasgow Airport with a life-saving injection of "no frills" cut-rate short-haul services.

Nevertheless, I still believe the lost status of Prestwick to have been a historical calamity for Scottish aviation. I console myself with the thought that my colleagues and I played our part during the significant 'sixties to try to stave off an eventual collapse, albeit, as I have shown, almost to the point of compromising our neutrality as observer.

CHAPTER TWELVE

My return to Heathrow at the end of the sixties might have echoed my move from Northolt some twenty years earlier. In reality, the situations were a sonic barrier apart, and the similarities just as hypothetical.

Back then, I was an unfettered bachelor, still living with my parents in the family home, savouring the dream of a chosen career as it stretched out ahead of me. Now, I was a separated husband and parent myself, on the verge of divorce and a day's drive from the family. Initially homeless, I now had little idea of what the domestic future held.

Though underpaid compared with my Fleet Street contemporaries, my job, at least, was still secure. So it was not the time to make further drastic changes in that direction. My immediate concern had to be finding somewhere to live. Putting down a deposit from my meagre savings on a tiny 3-berth caravan, I was able install it temporarily on a site near Thorney, Bucks, a few miles north of Heathrow. It was an pleasant-enough lakeside setting, intended primarily for semi-permanent residential "mobile" homes. But it also offered short-term parking at a nominal rent for visitors with tourer vans.

Until the house in Scotland was sold, that caravan was to be my home. Tiny it may have been; but I was soon to share it, and in a way I least expected.

It was a Spring holiday time a few months later, and I had taken leave so that I could drive north, the caravan in tow, to tour the English-Scottish Border country with the family. I use the word advisedly because I had convinced myself that Jill would agree to come with the children and me in spite of the breakdown of our marriage. My hopes were dashed yet again. It was made clear to me that she had other plans not only for the holiday but also indeed for the rest of her life. The children and I had to drive off to Northumberland alone.

Then aged eight and four, they still remembered forty years later our visits to Alnwick castle and to the Hadrian's Wall Roman fort at Housesteads. And we coped well, on both formal overnight caravan sites and with off-road informal camping. But the brief single-parent taster hardly prepared me for the following summer.

As usual, I had planned either to drive to Scotland to pick up the children for a couple of weeks holiday or to meet them at an agreed familiar half-way point. But Jill, for once, insisted on bringing them all the way. And then, out of the blue, she dropped a bombshell. Though admitting she was not working, she informed me that it was now my turn to look after the children full-time. And hardly stopping long enough to say goodbye, she drove away back – I could only assume – to Ayrshire, leaving a bag of their clothes behind.

*

In many ways, Heathrow at the end of the "swinging 'sixties," was very different from the London Airport I'd left.

The biggest of the changes here were structural and off-airport. The opening in 1965 of a section of the new east-west motorway from West London, the M4, completely altered Heathrow's main approaches. Until the previous decade the projected South Wales Arterial Road, as it was then known, had been little more than a twinkle in the corporate eye of planners. Now the new highway had joined three historic London lifelines, the original Bath road, the Grand Union canal and the busy rail link from Paddington along the westward Thames Valley. A dedicated spur now led directly from Junction 4 of the motorway, a mile north of the old road, to the airport's central terminal access tunnel.

As well as drastically cutting road journey times, the new link meant that the airport had become for the first time part of the infrastructure of Greater London. No longer was it just an afterthought attached to the city by its apron strings.

In the same ten years, the airport's central passenger terminals had also grown up. The original diamond-shaped layout at the centre of the "star of David" complex of runways and taxiways, had been expanded by the enlargement of departure lounges and baggage halls. The addition of piers and gate rooms followed, to provide more aircraft parking space and accommodate a huge and rapidly growing increase in flights and passengers.

British European Airways, British Midland and the Irish airline, Aer Lingus moved over to the new Terminal 1 opened by the Queen at the end of 1969. Europa, the airport's first permanent passenger building, now as Terminal 2 became host to a range of foreign European airlines. Originally completed in 1962, the Oceanic Terminal was renamed Terminal 3 a few years later after further development, with arrivals and departures of transatlantic and other long distance flights now separated into two linked buildings.

The airport's new owners, the state-owned British Airports Authority, had realised that Heathrow would soon be handling more Boeing 747 "Jumbo" jets than any other European airport. At the end of the decade they launched the first stage of a redesigned layout of aircraft stands and extra taxiways to accommodate the giant wide-bodied aircraft. By closing one of Heathrow's original cross-wind runways they were able free up the necessary 30 acres of "new" land.

At the same time a number of recently provided gate rooms – passenger holding lounges at aircraft boarding points – had to be more than doubled in size, many of them becoming larger than the terminal's original main departures lounge.

The first 747 proving flight, opening the Pan American Airways Clipper service from New York, touched down at on January 12, 1970, less than 25 years after the company's first transatlantic service to Heathrow. On board were 381 complimentary passengers, including Boeing and Pan Am management and technicians, airline staff and news media representatives, more than twice the number ever seen aboard one aircraft.

London based TV and radio crews, correspondents and reporters and other guests were then invited aboard for an hour's demonstration flight over the British Isles and I was delighted to be among them. My armchair seat was in the huge airliner's forward, first class cabin immediately below the flight deck, and the privilege left me with one lasting impression. It gave me my first and only experience of peering *forward* out of an airliner's window from a passenger seat, thanks to the sharp curvature of the 747's fuselage. Not a memorable discovery anyone might think, set against all the other attributes and innovations of a world-beater. But I always did like to know where I was heading…

By the end of that year, my personal life had taken on some level of normality. The family home in Scotland, however, had not yet been sold and twice I had been obliged to upgrade our temporary accommodation, first to a larger towing caravan, and then to a 25-foot static "mobile" home on its own rented and fenced site – which I promptly set about transforming into a garden.

Bill Brenard had helpfully switched me to permanent day-time duties with free weekends, as both of the children were now at local schools. But I had to fall back on the goodwill of close relatives for essential after-school help. My brother Joe, now manager of Bren's thriving infant airport printing business, and his wife Anne picked up both children for at least a couple of hours on schooldays. For frequent weekend and occasional longer holiday stays, my younger sister Beryl, living in North London, helped out.

It was not until after my divorce and house sale – at a give-away price – that we were finally able to transfer to a small, three-bedroom terrace cottage. It needed little decorating, and with much of our split household furniture rescued from storage the three of us were able to move in among some familiar surroundings, which seemed less painful to the children than it did to me.

*

Perhaps because at the time neither Britain, nor indeed Europe, had an answer of their own to this giant of the skies, the arrival of the first Jumbo jets at Heathrow set me thinking about the beginning of the jet age some ten years earlier and its impact on civil aviation. In particular, I remembered the race to be first across the Atlantic with jets – a race won by Britain, against all the odds, by just three weeks.

In April 1937, seven years after taking out the first patent on his design, Sir Frank Whittle, an RAF engineering officer, successfully demonstrated the world's first turbojet engine. Later, in September that same year, a similar jet engine was built by a German, Dr Joachim Pabst von Ohain, a researcher and designer for the Heinkel aircraft company. Neither of the pioneers was believed to be aware of the other's work in the field.

Von Ohain's engine was installed into the world's first jet-powered aircraft, the Heinkel HE178, just before the start of the second world war. It made several flights, but a lack of political confidence in its future potential deprived the Nazi war machine of further immediate exploitation of the jet engine. Any early lead they might have had was lost.

At the same time similar official intransigence delayed practical application of the British invention. It was to be a further four years before the Whittle W.2/7000 centrifugal-compressor jet powered an aircraft, the Gloster E28/39, later re-designated the G40. Finally, in 1941, contracts were signed for 8 prototypes of a twin-engined successor, the Gloster *Thunderbolt*, which under the new name *Meteor*, later became the only jet fighter to see action with the Allies in WW2.

The Whittle jet was also handed over to the United States, where in 1942 the prototype Bell XP59A twin-jet fighter was designed around two copied engines built under licence by General Electric, and first flew that October. The first production aircraft were delivered two years later as the P59A *Aerocomet*, but were re-classified as jet fighter pilot trainers for the Lockheed P80 *Shooting Star*. The British engine also became the basis for further development of US turbojet aero-engines immediately after the war.

It was the foresight of a British Government committee set up at the height of that war in 1943 that led to the conception of the world's first civil jet airliner.

The committee, under the chairmanship of Lord Brabazon (the aviation pioneer who has already featured in these pages[1]) was required to consider recommendations for a new generation of airliners whenever the end of hostilities came. Among its conclusions was a requirement for a transatlantic mail-carrying aircraft powered by turbo jets – the first time this form of propulsion had been seriously suggested for a civil aircraft.

As soon as it was practicable, designers for the de Havilland aircraft company began to consider possible ideas for a future jet airliner. Their final proposal was for a streamlined, beautifully balanced, medium-to-long-range airliner designed to carry around forty passengers in a pressurised cabin. Its wings would be innovatively swept back, with four jet engines buried within them close to the fuselage.

But it wasn't until September 1946, more than a year after the end of the war, that work began to produce two prototypes of the aircraft, by then known as the DH106 *Comet*. It is a point of curiosity that the name was an echo of both the popular name of the Bell P59A, (*Airacomet*) in the US and the rocket-propelled German Messerschmitt 163B-1 *Komet*, an extremely short-range fighter of the mid-40s. At the same time, it should also be recalled that de Havilland had originated the name themselves in the 1930s for the DH88 *Comet* racer, a handsome and advanced twin propeller-engined aircraft .

It was early days, but Britain now had a civil airliner far more advanced than any other passenger aircraft on the drawing board. An early production line of 14 aircraft followed completion of the prototypes, and within three years the company's chief test pilot, John Cunningham made the Comet's first flight. During ground handling tests on 27 July 1949 at de Havilland's Hatfield base, north of London, he unexpectedly lifted off the runway on his third taxi run, and in a short flight over the nearby countryside reached a speed of 500 mph.

The Comet's four Ghost engines gave it a cruising speed of 490 mph and it could carry up to 40 passengers some 2,600 miles. The dawn of a new era in British aviation beckoned with a stirring advantage which put it at least five years ahead of the US.

But the story of the de Havilland Comet jet became one of triumphal achievement followed by misadventure, tragic serial disaster, and months of independent, meticulous heart-searching investigation. Relatively short-lived, the Comet 1 re-emerged in a number of celebratory sequels to that story, first through its direct successors, the Comet 2 and Comet 4, then surviving into the new millenium as the long-lived Nimrod reconnaissance aircraft.

All that was in the future. Sixteen of the original Comet 1s were ordered by the British Overseas Airways Corporation (BOAC), the first of these being delivered in December 1951. Then, on May 2, 1952, with America's Boeing Aircraft Company only just deciding to enter the race by designing and building a new turbo-jet powered airliner, the British airline opened the world's first passenger jet service between London and Johannesburg.

Sir Geoffrey de Havilland himself was among VIPs and enthusiasts who watched at Heathrow as the Comet took off on its 6,720-mile journey. Eighteen hours and forty

1 See Ch.7, p.179.

minutes later, after stops en route at Rome, Beirut, Khartoum, Entebbe and Livingstone, it touched down at the South African airport. On board were 36 pioneering passengers.

Over the next two years orders for more than 100 Comets poured in from around the world, as it constantly broke records, shrinking the globe. By this time the recognised advantages of an axial-flow design over the centrifugal compressor jet engine were being exploited, and new Rolls Royce engines employing this principle were to replace the de Havilland's Ghosts in the production line for a Comet 2. After the company announced a new, larger Comet 3, which would carry almost twice as many passengers over a greater range, the interest culminated with an order and option from Pan American Airways for a fleet of ten of the new version.

In the autumn of its debut year, a BOAC Comet 1 was involved in its first accident as it took off from Rome Airport. Happily, no one was hurt. Then in the following spring, a similar Comet of Canadian Pacific Airways crashed after take-off from Karachi. Tragically, this time five crew and six technicians died in this, the first-ever jet airliner disaster. Though no one could have suspected it, the two otherwise unrelated incidents were to signal a much more significant series of apparently inexplicable accidents and crashes involving the still-fledgling jet airliners.

Nevertheless, with an intensive pilot training programme underway BOAC were soon introducing other Comet services to West Africa, India and the Far East. Just a month after the Canadian accident, I was reporting the opening of the first BOAC London-Tokyo-London commercial jet service for the *Evening Standard* and the *Star,* among others. The Comet completed the round journey in a total of 74 hours 47 minutes, including refuelling stops en route, just 11 hours less than the time taken for the former piston-engined service.

COMET BACK FROM TOKIO IN 38 HOURS

The BOAC Comet airliner, opening the first London-Tokio commercial jet service, touched down at London Airport to-day, 38 hours 52 minutes after leaving Tokio—dead on schedule.

The Comet completed the round journey in 74 hours 47 minutes including the nine stops for refuelling.

This is 11 hours 13 minutes less than the time taken for a single outbound journey of BOAC's piston-engined Argonaut airliners.

Actual flying time for the entire 20,400 mile trip was 55 hours 59 minutes.

Four children

When the airliner reached London shortly after dawn, there were 40 passengers, including four children. Fifteen passengers were from Tokio.

Captain E. G. N. Hengle, of Kingston-on-Thames, who brought the Comet from Rome on the last stage, said that the aircraft had behaved perfectly. From the log-book he said he could tell that there had been no major snag throughout the whole trip.

Timetable for the return flight was:

Left **Tokio** 2.30 p.m. Sunday; left **Calcutta** 7.38 a.m. yesterday; left **Delhi** 10.40 a.m.; left **Karachi** 1.33 p.m.; left **Bahrein** 5.21 p.m.; arrived **Beirut** 8.25 p.m.; left **Beirut** 9.19 p.m.

Arrived **Rome** 1.3 a.m. to-day, 27 minutes ahead of schedule. Left **Rome** 2.5 a.m.; arrived **London** 5.22 on schedule.

Evening Standard

THE BOAC Comet jet airliner which left London on Good Friday returned to London Airport today, having flown to Tokio and back in three days, 20 hours, 22 minutes.

A BOAC official said the touch-down was at 5.22 am. the time taken on the return flight being 38 hours 52 minutes.

This included the nine stops which were made, and making allowance for these the flying time was 30 hours 35 minutes, including the time taken in taxiing along the ground.

Actual flying time for the entire trip — 20,400 miles — amounted to 55 hours 59 minutes.

When the airliner reached the airport there were on board 36 adults and four children.

Among the 15 passengers from Tokio were Mr and Mrs P. Vincent of Birmingham. Mr Vincent is chief accountant for the Dunlop Rubber Co in Japan and was returning on six months' leave.

The chairman of the BOAC, Sir Miles Thomas, welcoming the airliner back said: "The BOAC Comet Easter week-end trip to Tokio and back has captured the world's imagination."

Star *(both) April 7 1953*

The *Evening Standard* gave my story a two-column second lead on Page One (*left*) and the *Star* carried a similar, smaller piece also on the front page .

The aircraft was welcomed back to Heathrow exactly on schedule by the chairman of BOAC, Sir Miles Thomas, who told me: "This has captured the imagination of the world."

Then, in the following month of May 1953, and only two months after the loss of the Canadian Pacific jet, a BOAC Comet 1 suddenly fell out of the sky after leaving Calcutta and flying through a severe storm. which one local expert described as "cyclonic."

Witnesses described a bright flash in the sky and what appeared to be a wingless aircraft flying low over the trees. The airliner dived into the dried-out bed of a river 25 miles north of the airport. There were no survivors among the 43 passengers and crew on board.

My colleagues and I could only wait on the sidelines as the tragedy unfolded on the other side of the world, though I was able to contribute to reports from India in the *Sunday Express* and the *People* by describing how relatives and friends of missing passengers were swamping the switchboards at Heathrow seeking news. *(See opposite).*

Two days after the disaster, I watched as experts from de Havilland and BOAC made last minute bookings to fly from Heathrow to the scene. There were early indications that severe weather may have been responsible, and later that day, for the *Daily Telegraph,* the *Daily Mail* and the *Daily Express,* I talked to passengers on a Qantas Airways Constellation airliner arriving from Sydney. They said that they had left Calcutta 25 minutes ahead of the Comet, and had run into a brief but violent storm.

"It seemed to be partly rain and partly sand," one told me. "We were badly knocked about in mid-air. The 'plane rocked quite violently."

At a later Court of Inquiry "structural failure" of the Comet was blamed – but no explanation could be given for the cause other than the weather. Then in the following January (1954) a BOAC Comet returning to London from Singapore once again broke up suddenly in mid-air over the sea near the Mediterranean island of Elba.

LONDON PLANE MET STORM

"RAIN AND SAND"

Daily Telegraph Reporter

A Qantas Empire Airways Constellation airliner touched down at London Airport last night from Sydney, Australia, after flying across India on the same route as the Comet. It left Calcutta for Karachi 25 minutes before the Comet and, said passengers, ran into a brief but violent pre-monsoon storm.

Seven passengers from Calcutta were on board. Among them was Mr. John Bodges, an engineer, of Brixton, who said: "The storm seemed to be partly rain and partly sand. We ran into it about eight to 15 minutes out and were badly knocked about in mid-air. The plane rocked quite violently."

Another passenger, who said he was "something of an expert on local weather conditions," said: "The storm was what we call a north-wester. It was a small cyclonic storm." Both he and Mr. Bodges had tried to book passages in the Comet.

Three representatives of a rubber company said that five of their colleagues had travelled in the Comet from Singapore.

Daily Telegraph May 4 1953

...story, not ... True, there have been two accidents: one ... take-off at Rome, in October last year, when no one was hurt, and a crash at Karachi in March, in which five crew and six technicians were killed.

As news of the feared loss of the plane became known in London, London Airport was flooded with inquiries from relatives and friends flying home on Comet services. All were told: "We will phone you later." It is known that ten passengers boarded the plane at Calcutta. The plane was due in London at 7.30 a.m. today.

ALONG THE COMET'S ROUTE TONIGHT AN EXTENSIVE SEARCH IS IN PROGRESS.

TWO INDIAN AIRWAYS DAKOTAS AND A B.O.A.C. FOUR-ENGINED YORK WERE ORDERED INTO THE AIR AT CALCUTTA. A PAN-AMERICAN PLANE FLYING OVER THE SAME ROUTE CO-OPERATED IN THE SEARCH.

Signals have been sent to all police stations and military installations. More planes are being prepared to join the search at dawn.

Sunday Express May 3 1953

In London not long after the inquiry team left, there arrived a QANTAS Australian Constellation airliner, which took off from Calcutta for Karachi 25 minutes before the wrecked Comet.

From its passengers there was more news of the storm near Calcutta. Mr. John Bodges, an engineer, whose home is in Brixton, S.W., said:

"Some eight minutes after we left Calcutta we ran into a violent storm, partly rain and partly sand.

"But for us it appeared to be all over very quickly though the airliner was bumped about badly."

Two senior representatives of de Havillands, makers of the Comet, made last-minute bookings on a B.O.A.C. Argonaut which left London Airport last night for Calcutta. With them went a B.O.A.C. official, Mr. Herbert Hornblower.

Under 10,000ft.

One of the de Havilland representatives, Mr. R. M. Hare, said: "We have not attempted to form any theories on the disaster."

Daily Mail (top)
Daily Express
(both) May 4 1953

...of regular Com... ...its ...

After the B.B.C.'s 9 o'clock news last night, relatives and friends of passengers believed to be aboard the missing Comet swamped the switchboard at London Airport with inquiries. They were told: "We will phone you later."

NAMES OF THE CREW

Ten passengers were known to have boarded the plane at Calcutta, its last port of call. Several of these were flying to London, where the plane was due today.

The six ... crew ... last night ...

The People May 3 1953

A paragraph here, a paragraph there...

Local fishermen described hearing jet engines above the clouds, followed by a series of explosions. In the distance, the sun briefly glinted on a silvery object trailing smoke as it dived into the sea. It took the men many minutes to reach the scene, only to find a number of bodies in the water. Between them the fisher crews hauled them aboard and carried them to a nearby harbour.

In London, BOAC immediately grounded their Comets while they began an investigation. Airliners which were overseas were flown home empty and accommodated in hangars at the airline's maintenance base at Heathrow.

Less than four weeks later, after revealing that 50 modifications were being made, the Comet 1 fleet was reinstated by the airline. But just as full services were being gradually resumed, in April 1954 came the horrifying news that yet another BOAC jet which had left Rome 30 minutes earlier for Johannesburg, had broken up mid-air. It too dived into the Mediterranean, this time in deep water near Sicily, off the volcanic island of Stromboli. Twenty-one people died, including seven crew members, after a final radio message from the Comet reporting: "Over Naples. Still climbing."

The British Government stepped in and quickly revoked the airliner's certificate of airworthiness. The Comet was again grounded.

Royal Navy diving teams were called upon to try to recover some of the wreckage from the shallower water at the scene of the earlier Elba disaster, and eventually significant parts of the wreckage was raised. These were flown back to Britain and sent to the Royal Aircraft Establishment at Farnborough. After months of painstaking re-assembly work followed by deliberate, monitored destruction of three more aircraft, technicians were able to demonstrate that the trouble was caused by cracks in a reinforcing plate fitted to strengthen the alloy skin of the aircraft around direction-finding windows on each side of the fuselage. The weakness eventually spread, leading to a sudden and catastrophic loss of pressurisation at altitude.

The cracks were attributed to "metal fatigue," a breakdown of the physical structure of metal which can occur when it has been subjected to repeated extreme stresses. It was the first time the general public had been made widely aware of the condition, though its existence had been known to metallurgists for at least 150 years.

Indeed, the condition's potential effects on a new airliner had been explored prophetically at the end of the 1940s by author Nevil Shute in *"No Highway,"* his fictional best seller and later a successful film. Shute was himself a qualified aeronautical engineer who had once been apprenticed by de Havilland.

wikipedia license: RuthAS

A BOAC Comet 1, at London Heathrow in June 1953

wikipedia license: Arpingstone

Comet 2, Royal Air Force at Filton Bristol in 1964

wikipedia license: RuthAS

Comet 3, at Farnborough in September 1954

wikipedia license: RuthAS

Olympic Airways Comet 4B at Manchester in 1966

The research conclusions were to have an immense effect on the future design and construction of aircraft throughout the world. Until the Comet disasters, designers had not seen a need for intensive stage-by-stage testing during development. From now on a prototype of every new major aircraft planned would have to undergo ground "testing to destruction" as pioneered in the long months of Farnborough investigation. Thousands of miles of pressurised flight would have to be simulated before that coveted and obligatory airworthiness certificate could be granted.

Production of the awaited Comet 2 came to a standstill in this time, though the version did eventually emerge again as a fully modified transport aircraft for the RAF. Programmed work which was in full swing on a "stretched" Comet 3 was completely restructured to produce instead a prototype for a virtually new aircraft.

Britain's pioneering jet airliner was re-born, and the Comet 4 made its maiden flight in the spring of 1958. At any other time in aviation history its subsequent longer range versions would certainly have become a major success story, as they were to prove to be superb aircraft in their own hard-won right. But the four year gap between the grounding of the Comet 1 and its eventual successors was too great.

Two years earlier, the first Soviet jet, the Tupolev TU104, had been launched on a surprised western aviation world and flown to London on a demonstration visit. With hundreds of others, I had the chance to inspect the visitor, and was intrigued by its dated interior design, which included lace antimacassars on the seat backs. Nevertheless, for many months the Russians ruled much of the world's skies with this sole civil jet and its Pullman-style Victoriana.

By now the delay had also enabled the great American aircraft industry, with its unequalled experience in military jets, to catch up with its own first civil jet design. Others too, such as the French Caravelle, were fast approaching on the horizon.

The prototype of the Boeing 707, America's first jet airliner, made its maiden flight from the company's manufacturing plant at Seattle in July 1954. It was considerably larger than the Comet 1 or even the Comet 4. Its wingspan alone was 15 feet more, its fuselage longer by up to 17 feet and it was capable of carrying 130 passengers. It was faster and was claimed have a range of up to 4700 miles against the Comet's 2,366. Soon we had early indications that Pan American, the first airline to place an order for a fleet of the 707s, was drawing up plans to introduce its first jet passenger services on the Atlantic before the end of 1958.

BOAC had proposed to introduce the new Comet 4 on Far Eastern and Australian routes from London soon after their delivery in September that year. Faced with this American challenge, it quickly revised its programme.

In a confidential letter to pilots in June of that year, the airline finally confirmed our repeated Spring claims that it intended instead to bring the Comet 4 into service between London and New York early in 1959. Far Eastern jet services would be postponed to enable the British airline to compete directly with the Americans on the Atlantic jet routes almost from day one.

Yet already there were growing whispers that this was subterfuge on the part of BOAC; that in reality they believed they could begin transatlantic operations before the end of 1958. They were quick to deny the possibility, pointing out that they didn't yet know when they would be taking delivery of the Comet, whilst their rivals, Pan Am, would almost certainly see their first Boeing 707 in early October.

However, in the meantime we learnt that intensive British crew training on jets was quietly going ahead. By August, 22 Captains were qualified to take over the new Comets as soon as delivery began, and nearly a dozen complete crews were already standing by. Many of them had taken summer leave early to be available for final training with the Comet 4s.

BOAC expressed themselves more than pleased with the abilities and enthusiasm of their crews, and at the success of both the training and the route-proving programmes undertaken by the new jet's "understudy" Comet 2. Working with the Comet had been a great morale booster for the staff involved, as the aircraft had exceeded all expectations as a trouble-free record maker.

As if to demonstrate his faith in the new airliner's reliability, de Havilland's "Cat's Eyes" Cunningham was again at the controls when a Comet 4 flew into New York's

Idlewild (later John F. Kennedy) airport early in August. It was there to undergo a series of engine noise trials for the airport authorities and it passed with flying colours – almost exactly nine years after Cunningham's maiden flight with the Comet 1. A month later and I was reporting the arrival of the first Boeing 707 to cross the Atlantic, without passengers, to undertake parallel trials at Heathrow. And I wrote:

The Boeing ***"…slipped in like a great grey glider, the roar of its four wing jets muffled completely by the wind and slipstream."***

My story continued: ***"Only when it approached the end of its landing run did the airliner's engines appear to come to life. Then a sudden ear-shattering crash of its engines reverberated across the open airfield like a thunder clap."***

SMOKE! Comet's rival is in trouble again

News Chronicle Reporter

AMERICA'S Boeing 707 jet liner, sadly worsted by Britain's Comet IV, ran into more trouble last night.

Following the problems it faces over the noise of its four underslung engines came a new protest from local residents in the London Airport area.

Representatives of seven local councils in Middlesex and Surrey have sent a demand to the Ministry of Transport and Civil Aviation that the plane's operators, Pan American Airways, must find means of reducing its smoke stream on take-off

Complaints

The Boeing left a trail of black fumes, which settled like a smokescreen over the main runway at London Airport yesterday when it left on a local flying test.

The smoke persisted like a haze for several minutes—long after the huge jet had disappeared into the clouds and Ministry officials on the airport recorded their first telephoned complaint.

One resident demanded: "This machine should keep its wicks trimmed."

Earlier yesterday the Boeing had touched down in Paris after a direct flight from New York in seven hours five minutes assisted by 50 m.p.h tail-winds.

A record

This was a record for a commercial airliner for the 3,675 miles journey, but a Pan American spokesman in London said last night that it was "several minutes behind schedule."

News Chronicle mid-September 1958

Atlantic jet trips next month—but by U.S. planes

THE first scheduled Transatlantic jet service will be opened on October 26 by Pan-American World Airways, it was announced today in London.

There will be daily flights between New York, Paris and Rome.

"The Boeing 707 Jet Clippers will cut the flying time between New York and Paris to seven hours, reducing by four hours and 35 minutes the scheduled time of the fastest piston-engined aircraft, the DC-73," say the airline.

Daily Jet Clipper flights between New York and London ares planned to start on November 16, the statement added.

But the announcement does not mean that the Boeing 707 jet airliner has passed its noise test at London Airport.

An airport spokesman said today: "The announcement should have been conditional. They might have added 'If they let us.'"

Not known

"Results of the noise test made when the Boeing 707 visited London Airport are not known, though they are expected this week. Until then we cannot comment further about the Pan - American plan."

And an official for the American company agreed that the results of the tests had not been passed to them.

The Star September 1958

Almost before the jet had drawn to a halt on its specially reserved parking bay, the telephones began ringing with complaints. Each call was logged – though because of an administrative error, none was immediately passed on to the Ministry of Transport. There, aviation experts were analysing the readings, and for days they insisted that no one had complained about noise. And no one (including, I have to add, myself) was able to point out that the most incriminating evidence of any "noise infringement" could have been simply the brief roar of the four jets switched to reverse thrust, a safety device to assist braking of the aircraft on landing.

Just a few days later, I reported September's Pan American announcement that they would begin operating transatlantic jet services on October 26, 1958, between New York and Paris. Services between New York and London would follow in three weeks, on November 16th.

As *The Star* put it: "Atlantic jet trips next month – but by U.S. planes." A Heathrow airport spokesman commented: "The announcement should have been conditional. They might have added: 'If they let us.'

"Results of the noise tests have not yet been announced. Until a decision, based on those results is taken, the Boeing will not be able to operate full passenger services."

The start of October saw the American airline's advertising agents ignoring the gentle wrist-slap and rushing ahead to erect alongside the Bath Road one of the largest billboards ever seen at Heathrow. Against an artist's huge one-off impression of their new jet, the hand-painted board portrayed the claim, in

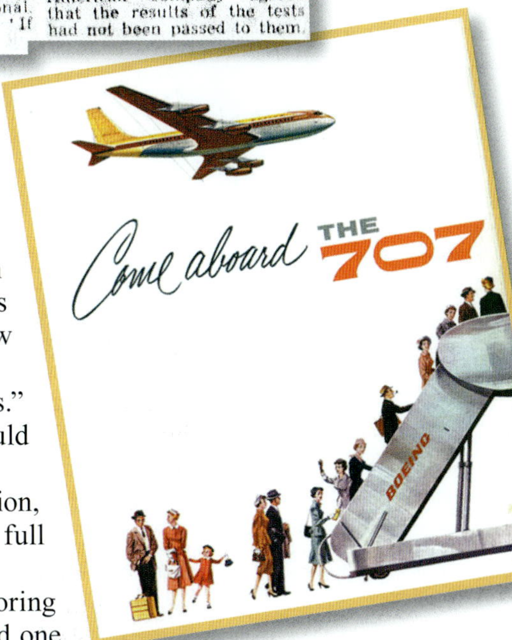

Boeing's brochure, announcing the service to a new generation of air travellers

Pan-Am's giant hoarding at London Airport makes a promise

Brenard Press Picture, Airport Post Ocober 8 1958

letters 16ins high *(above).*

Just two days later, with the painter's ladder and scaffolding still in place at the base of the billboard, a gleaming silver and white Comet 4 took off from New York for London Airport, to open the world's first-ever transatlantic passenger jet service.

Along the spotless fuselage the simple logo "***BOAC***;" high on its tail fin, a familiar *Speedbird* symbol and immediately below, the less familiar aircraft registration "**G-APDB,**" shortened, in air traffic parlance, to a highly appropriate call-sign, "Delta Bravo." The date: Saturday, October 4, 1958. The time: 7.00am Eastern Standard Time, or noon in London.

Who said "first"?

Brenard Press picture, Airport Post

BOAC receptionist Pauline Rawnsley-Curd admires one of the Comet 4 posters rushed out by the Corporation's advertising department for the departure lounge within hours of the Comet's first flight being announced.

Some two hours earlier, at 9.55 am British Summer Time, Delta Bravo's sister airliner, "**G-APDC**" (or "Delta Charlie") left Heathrow to inaugurate the westbound passenger service. Four hours out from Idlewild, the two Comets passed each other. Though their paths were some 250 miles apart, they exchanged greetings and progress reports.

On board the eastbound Delta Bravo were 16 crew members headed by Captain Tom Stoney and 28 passengers – mainly radio and newspaper journalists, specially invited to report what immediately became a civil aircraft's fastest ever-crossing of the Atlantic. With them travelled the chief executive of BOAC, Basil Smallpeice, and room was found for just five luxury fare-paying passengers. Flight number BA152 completed its 3,560-mile flight in 6 hours 7 minutes at an average speed of 580 miles an hour.

Captain Roy Millichap, a 42-years old ex-bomber pilot, was at the controls of Delta Charlie for the westbound service with a crew of 12. In this case, because of the prevailing headwinds which reached as much as 140 mph at times, the journey to New York took almost ten and a half hours – and included a halt at Gander, Newfoundland, to take on more fuel. On board was Sir Gerard d'Erlanger, who had succeeded Sir Miles Thomas as chairman of BOAC, and 34 other passengers of whom, perhaps significantly, 31 were fare paying.

*

AIRPORT BUBBLED OVER AT THE NEWS

WONDERFUL, Wonderfu Comet . . . London Airport l t e country in cheering the lant success of Britain' derplane and the ac o BOAC by defyi mists to re-conqu air routes.

Airport Post (both) October 8 1958

Picking the proverbial short straw, I wasn't present myself on *the* day at the old northside terminal to report either the historic departure from Heathrow of the first westbound flight or the arrival of the New York-London service. But I was able to contribute my own news commentary a few days later, from my own and colleagues' collective accounts. Under the heading *(left)* I wrote:

"WONDERFUL, Wonderful Comet... London Airport led the country in cheering the brilliant success of Britain's wonder plane and the achievement of BOAC in defying the pessimists to re-conquer the Atlantic air routes .

"October 4, 1958 will be remembered by thousands of Transatlantic travellers in the years to come as the day

when the first big step was taken towards bringing the two opposite shores within a day's travel."

It was a time too when the airport let itself go. Never before, throughout its twelve years of change and progress, I was able to point out, had London Airport shown so much emotion about a single event, adding:

"Excitement among the staff of thousands, which had been building up ever since the whispered news that 'BOAC might do it!' bubbled over on Friday when it was confirmed that the Comet would make the first passenger jet crossing of the Atlantic in the morning."

By late afternoon on Saturday, the thrilling news of the successful New York touch-down had stirred millions throughout Britain. Spectators in their hundreds began to flock to Heathrow, determined to catch a glimpse of the arriving Comet on its first passenger flight *from* the new to the old world.

Traditional British reserve was brushed aside as the beautiful streamlined jet touched down. A burst of intense cheering, a hundred hands, handkerchiefs, hats and even umbrellas were waved enthusiastically in salute as the record-maker swept softly by. It was a early demonstration of the kind of euphoria with which, decades later, an ecstatically proud British public were to greet every appearance at Heathrow of the Anglo-French supersonic jet Concorde, right up to its final curtain early in the second millenium.

Captain Tom Stoney, the senior BOAC pilot commanding the first London-bound flight, had a final laconic word on the news of his confirmed 6-hour 7-minute crossing. "We weren't trying for a record," he said. "With favourable tailwinds, there's no reason why an even better time shouldn't be set in the future." Some thought that Captain Stoney should have gone for broke…

At that time Captain Stoney was almost certainly thinking only of the Comet's future potential. But originally BOAC had not planned to operate their Comets on the Atlantic. They were realistic about the limitations of the early British jet, which could not compete for long with its newer, faster and higher capacity American cousins.

The production capabilities of the huge Seattle manufacturing plant of Boeing would mean fast deliveries in a guaranteed market of airline customers around the world. So BOAC, like Pan American, had already placed an order for a fleet of a longer-range Boeing 707, with more powerful engines. Neither airline was expecting delivery until the following year. When PanAm first announced an Autumn 1958 introduction on the Atlantic they were aware it could only be with the medium-range 707-120, which could be subject to intermediate stops and face a range of noise and weight limitations on the route.

So Pan American's "first jet service" between New York and London was introduced on October 26, a month earlier than planned, but a full three weeks *after* the inaugural Comet flight. Passengers on both sides of the Atlantic now checked in alongside a newly repainted billboard which proclaimed, mildly:

PAN AMERICAN STARTS DAILY JET SERVICE TO THE USA THIS AUTUMN

The single word "**FIRST**" had been carefully painted out and "**DAILY**"substituted.

*

By the mid-fifties, leading airlines in Europe and the USA were all looking at designs for jet airliners to meet their requirements in the near future. A few years on and rival jets from the drawing boards of well established aircraft companies on both sides of the Atlantic were making their debuts. Among them, was Boeing's closest US competitor, Douglas, later McDonnell Douglas, who had finally entered the fray, albeit a little tardily. Their first jet airliner, the DC 8, made its maiden flight in May 1958, almost a year behind the 707. In appearance, the two airliners, making their debuts in a variety of liveries, were almost indistinguishable .

In Britain, BOAC approached Vickers, one of the oldest and largest of the European aircraft manufacturers, with specifications for a new airliner intended eventually to replace their Comets. They were looking for a jet with a greater capacity but a similar transatlantic range to the Constellations and DC 7Cs dominating the route at the time. The aircraft company had already been working on a project to design a civil version of their Valiant bomber.

It would finally emerge as the VC10, an impressive, elegant airliner with the streamlined appearance of the Comet, but with its four engines grouped at the tail instead of interrupting the sweep of the wings as in its American cousins. The VC10 and its immediate successor, the Super VC10, were to prove extremely popular with BOAC's passengers, who liked the idea of being forward of the engines, able to enjoy less noise and vibration, and again for a while it seemed to have a promising future. But potential world interest faded in the late sixties as production of the American jets boomed and production finally ceased in 1970, though some versions flew on for many years with the RAF.

In the meantime, BOAC's sister airline, BEA (more formally the British European Airways Corporation), was ordering its own fleet of Comets. They were needed to compete directly with the Sud-Aviation's SE Caravelle, which was partly based on the Comet design. The highly regarded aircraft was already being operated by Air France and was soon to become the biggest selling European jet. As a high density operator, BEA's requirements differed from BOAC's and de Havilland were able to modify the long range Comet 4 as the 4B to carry more passengers by sacrificing some fuel capacity.

Then, in 1956 BEA co-operated with another British aircraft company to build the world's first 3-engined jet airliner, the Trident. Designed to the airline's specifications by de Havilland, the DH121 was re-designated as the HS121 following a merger with Hawker Siddeley. It won the name Trident in a contest among BEA staff.

It was while the design was still on the drawing board and well before its first flight that I talked to a group of engineers and designers from Boeing. They were leaving London after making an invited visit to the de Havilland plant at Hatfield (later, it was suggested, at the behest of the British Government).

When I asked what they had seen and what they had achieved during their visit, they told me without hesitation that they had been invited by the British company to see the drawings and specifications for the three-engined jet. "We liked what we saw," said their leader. "And we're taking all the figures back with us." Before I could explore this further, their hosts from de Havilland stepped in and hurried them away with the claim that they were "late boarding." I reported their comments, but as far as I know the story and its implications escaped the attention of news desks.

I never did discover why de Havilland appeared to be so shy of their contact with Boeing. Indeed, it was many years before I learnt of the agreement they had signed early in 1952 with America's General Electric Company for a "full exchange of knowledge and experience" in the development of jet engines, an agreement which was fully supported by the two governments *(see left).*

THE de Havilland Engine Company, Ltd., of England and the General Electric Company of the United States of America, through its overseas affiliates, the International General Electric Company, jointly announce that they have signed an agreement for a full interchange of knowledge and experience, both current and future, in the field of gas turbines for aircraft, with the exception of aircraft nuclear propulsion.

This agreement will bring together for mutual advantage the wealth of experience which the two companies have accumulated since the earliest days of practical jet engine and propeller-turbine development, in the course of which each has tended to specialise in certain directions. From now on each company will be able to benefit continuously and simultaneously from the work which the other is doing.

Both companies recognise that no one organisation is nowadays able to cover, with the necessary intensity of specialisation, every side of the entire development of the new form of power unit for aircraft, and the General Electric and de Havilland concerns have come to recognise over the post-war period that each has acquired special knowledge which is of great value to the other. Each company expects to benefit substantially from this exchange of knowledge without losing anything in the integrity and independence of its own projects.

The agreement will be implemented by the visits of key technicians across the Atlantic.

The agreement has been approved by the United States Government and the British Ministry of Supply.

Extract from the de Havilland Gazette April 1952

The revelation could have explained why a co-operation deal was also agreed with another American manufacturer which might in turn be ordering GE jet engines. A full year after the maiden flight of the Trident in January 1962, the American aircraft company Boeing unveiled its own direct competitor, the 727.

It boasted three jet engines clustered forward of the aircraft's high tailplane, one buried in the rudder, the others slung below it on both sides of the fuselage – duplicating the de Havilland design. Experts and mere observers alike around the world remarked on the American jet's "remarkable" similarity to the Trident. One authority later went so far as to describe the 727 as being *"built to the original Trident specification."*

Although it was eventually the mainstay of the BEA jet fleet and was succeeded by variations and a stretched version right through the next 25 years, the Trident could only claim limited success in other world markets. The Boeing 727, on the other hand, became the biggest selling jet airliner in history. It massively outsold the 115 or so Tridents produced, even though the British aircraft had pioneered the first automatic blind landing system at Heathrow, an aid which was to become the standard for poor visibility landings everywhere.

Two years after its launch, 500 Boeing jets had been ordered. The 727 went on to operate round the world on both schedule and charter flights in the liveries of nearly 90 different airlines.

It would be misleading to close these thoughts on the birth of the jet age without referring to another engineering development conceived in 1920, a decade *before* the Whittle jet engine. The resulting turboprop engine, a further original British achievement of the 1940-50s, ushered in a separate aviation era. Though a quieter revolution in more than one sense, and certainly seen as less glamorous, it was one which was to prove just as radical and in some cases even more immediately successful than the entry of the pure jet, at least on shorter and medium-haul high density routes.

The requirement for a turboprop – where the combustion engine gases are used mainly to drive propellers instead of providing direct thrust – was among the additional airliner types recommended by the Brabazon committee shortly before the end of World War 2. At a time when fuel costs were rising rapidly it was shown that the less powerful engines would be more efficient at their resultant slower speeds than pure turbojets.

Now one of the largest and oldest of British designers and aircraft builders, Vickers, who were already planning the piston-engine Viking, a civil version of the twin-engine Wellington bomber and just one of several successful such airliners produced in the late 1940s, was given the job of meeting the Brabazon specifications.

The prototype Vickers Viscount 630 turboprop made its maiden flight in July 1948. Two years later the world's first turboprop service was opened by BEA between London's Northolt Airport and Orly, Paris, with the 701, a larger version with increased capacity.

The Viscount proved to be the most popular British entry into world markets. Its four Rolls Royce Dart engines were quiet and economical in operation, and its lack of vibration made it a favourite with passengers. In total, 445 Viscounts were built and sold around the world, nearly 150 of them to American and Canadian airlines. Thirty to forty years later a number of the airliners were still flying on various overseas routes, having changed ownership and registrations several times.

Shortly after the introduction of the Viscount a smaller British twin-engine turboprop, the Avro 748, took off to similar world-wide success, selling in some 15 countries in various versions. Other turboprop designs by the United States, Soviet Russia and Holland were offered to meet both short and long range requirements, with the Dutch Fokker Friendship becoming probably the Viscounts' biggest rival both in Europe and America.

A worrying discovery early in 1958, when cracks appeared around vital bolts in a wing spar for the second time in two years led to 24 Viscount 701s operated by BEA, Air France and Aer Lingus being grounded. The breaking information gave me a Page One lead in the *Sunday Pictorial* and the *Sunday Express*. Much of my story was picked up by the *Express* News Editor, Arthur Brenard, brother of our founder Bill Brenard, and the

Sunday Express Jan 26 1958

SUNDAY EXPRESS

JANUARY 26 1958 Lighting-up Time 5.8 p.m. to 7.16 a.m. (Mon.). Founded by LORD BEAVERBROOK Moon Rises 9.59 a.m. Sets Midnight. PRICE 4d.

Fault found in the first batch of prop-jet airliners —but the main fleet still flies across the continents

VISCOUNTS SURPRISE

24 grounded after emergency report

by ARTHUR BRENARD and ARTHUR BRITTENDEN

TWENTY-FOUR Viscount airliners—the first batch of Britain's world-beating prop-jets off the production line —were taken out of service yesterday after the dramatic discovery by a mechanic of cracks round vital bolts in the main wing spar.

The grounded airliners belong to British European Airways, Air France, and Aer Lingus. But the main fleet of 260 Viscounts —all later models—now flying on the world's airlines, is not affected.

Photo courtesy of www.vickersviscount.net
A V.701 Delivered to BEA - their first Viscount, named 'R.M.A. Discovery'.

PAGE 2 SUNDAY PICTORIAL, January 26, 1958

Wing cracks ground Viscounts

Sunday Pictorial
Jan 26 1958

paper's air correspondent colleague, Arthur Brittenden.

The problem was happily quickly resolved, and the aircraft were already being succeeded by the 724 series and even larger and faster Viscount 800 which were unaffected. Though at first reluctant to commit itself, the British airline had already become the first to place an order for 20 of the more advanced aircraft.

The Viscount was then followed in 1959 by the Vanguard, which started out as the enlarged Super Viscount able to carry up to 140 passengers. It too joined the by now diverse stable of BEA, and more than 80 were built. But the aircraft failed to attain the status of its predecessor, partly because of the appeal of the rival American Lockheed Electra. With a faster production line and buyer-attractive financial arrangements, the Electra order book rose to nearly 150 aircraft by the time it went into service with two major American airlines – the same month as the Vanguard first appeared in BEA livery.

Artist's impression

A successor to the world-beating Viscount for BEA: it's big sister, the Vickers-Armstrong V.951 Vanguard

It was the super-quiet Bristol Britannia which appeared to hold out the brightest promise of success for BOAC, becoming, in 1957, the first aircraft to operate a non-stop Atlantic service. It too was developed to a Brabazon committee specification, as one of two types of design awarded to the Bristol Aeroplane Company.

The first of these types became the ill-fated (and with hindsight, ill-conceived) eight-engined monster, the ironically-named Brabazon. Based on an earlier bomber design, but with more powerful radial engines, the huge aircraft boasted a wing-span 36 feet bigger and a 2-deck fuselage 5ft wider than the later Boeing 747. But it offered a mere 50 to 80 fitted seats, the lowest payload capability of all time for any large airliner with a projected range of 5,500 miles. Instead, its cabin provided sleeping berths, separate dining areas – and a cinema.

The project was an idealistic luxury which proved totally unviable. Nevertheless, the Brabazon Mark 1 was built and was demonstrated at Farnborough Air Display a few days after its first flight in September 1949. It flew into Heathrow on show the following summer. But in 1952 work on a Mark 2 prototype, now with more powerful Proteus turboprop engines, was halted when no airline showed further interest, and the Government withdrew support. The following year both Brabazon prototype dreams were abandoned.

The end of the Bristol Type 167 Brabazon design nevertheless eventually boosted progress on the Type 175 Britannia programme which up to that time had been running simultaneously, as it was now possible to incorporate some of the features and facilities of the design in the new, more realistic airliner. BOAC had ordered an option on 25 of the new aircraft, later reduced, and the first of these, the series 102, made its maiden flight in August 1952.

It was to be another five years however, before they were able to enter service, because of a sorry tale of engine troubles on test flights. The frequently-recurring hold-ups, due mainly to icing problems, were persistently but responsibly reported by my late colleague Ray Watts, often in the face of denials and inexplicable accusations of "spitefulness" from airline officials. With the problems finally resolved, BOAC were able to introduce the Britannia on to their long-haul routes to Johannesburg early in 1957.

Because of the delay, it was less than a year before the airline's long range version, the Britannia 312, also became available to open the non-stop service between London and New York for BOAC. Even so, the new Whispering Giant, as it was known, was on the scene too late. The age of the pure jet on the Atlantic was about to begin, and with it the era of the jet setters. Above all, the long-distance air traveller wanted speed. Who would now want to cross the pond by turbo prop, however quiet, reliable and comfortable it might be?

*

One of the main benefits of the jet airliner over its piston-powered predecessors had to be its operational reliability. The days were passing when minor fault delays on schedule flights seemed almost inevitable. As a national news agency, for a number of years we had followed a policy of deliberately not reporting the so-called "full emergencies" and the lower-grade "standbys" of airport fire and ambulance rescue services, unless we were obliged to do so. At least eighty per cent of such precautionary alerts were for minor incidents, or down to glitches in flight-deck warning instruments. Often the resulting "bad news" of such reports could be disproportionate and thus unjustified.

The speed of travel meant a huge increase in the frequency of flights and promised a faster rate of turn-round at airports. This was now possible and indeed essential. So the new decade was to see a massive boom in popular air travel, with a steady fall in travel costs. Now there was a growing appreciation of the significance of that first principle of aviation economics which stipulates: "Aeroplanes only make money when they in the air." Happily, many of the minor alerts and "technical" groundings disappeared with the coming of jets.

As we have seen, this did not mean that the potential for serious accidents or even disasters had been eliminated either in the cross-over years from piston engines or later when jets became the standard air transport. Weather, particularly fog, snow and storms continue still to disrupt schedules on occasions. Today lightning strikes still occur, usually during ascent or descent at lower altitude through cloud, as frequently as once in every 1,000 flying hours of each aircraft. Serious damage is unlikely; *any* damage is relatively rare and often such strikes go unnoticed.

I reported my first lightning bolt in 1948, when a Swiss DC3 Dakota had a main radio transmitter put out of action in a storm near Basle. The aircraft later landed safely at London's Northolt airport, and I found that most of the 17 passengers were unaware of the incident.

Six years on, a BEA Viscount turned back to Heathrow when it was struck by lightning 20 minutes after taking off for Palma, Majorca. Among the passengers was London fashion model Gaby Young who was flying back to her Mediterranean home.

Evening Standard

40,614 THURSDAY, DECEMBER 9, 1954 Three-halfpence

LIGHTNING HITS AIRLINER

It turns back to London Airport

Evening Standard Page One lead December 9 1954

For my Page One lead in the London *Evening Standard (above)* she told me, "There was a brilliant blue flash and a bang like a rocket."

Officials for the airline said that a full examination would have to be carried out before any damage could be assessed. The passengers later set off again in a substitute aircraft. I set off on holiday, and didn't hear the assessment results…

Just eighteen months later I was again writing about lightning, though this time it involved an airliner on the ground – as it was being refuelled. A refuelling company employee, George Harris, was high on the wing of a Pan American Super Constellation airliner at the time as it was being prepared for a departure for Dusseldorf, Germany. He wasn't injured, but had to taken to an airport medical centre for treatment for shock. The aircraft was undamaged and was able to take off shortly afterwards, but the incident gave me another page one lead in the *Evening Standard* and I shared a lead in *The Star* with other weather news .

Evening Standard

MONDAY, AUGUST 6, 1956 Twopence

Great storm cancels the holiday specials

AIRLINER IS STRUCK AT LONDON AIRPORT

Evening Standard Page One lead

Airliner Is Struck: Man Injured

"Star" Reporter

THUNDERSTORMS AND TORRENTIAL RAIN OVER MOST OF SOUTH-EAST ENGLAND TODAY MADE THE BANK HOLIDAY

The Star (both) August 6 1956

It must have been a "quiet news day" to justify the spread. There were parallel incidents over the years, but only a few attracted such interest, such as the BOAC Boeing 707 bound for New York in January 1965. The jet, carrying 31 passengers had left Manchester and was making a second attempt to touch down at Prestwick in strong cross winds to pick up more passengers when it flew into a violent storm of hailstones and sleet.

At the last moment before touch down the pilot, Captain Richard Flower decided to overshoot the runway again, just as the lightning struck. He managed to make a safe landing, but a six-inch gash was discovered in the aircraft's tail plane. Said the 50-years-old Captain: "The lightning struck the nose of the aircraft as we were turning downwind. It must have gone right through the aircraft and out again at the tail, but we didn't know of the damage until after we had landed." He told how his windscreen had been blurred by scorchmarks.

Our largest coverage on this occasion was a full page inside in the *Scottish Daily Mail,* with shorter stories in the *Scottish Daily Express* and the *Sun (see opposite).* And curiously, just 30 hours later, an almost identical situation occurred with another BOAC 707 jet. This time the damage, a 30-inch gash, was to the nose cone of the aircraft. But passengers only became aware of a problem when their departure from Prestwick was delayed for six hours… for a new nose-cone to be fitted.

When in the late summer of 1958 I learnt that a BEA Viscount had been forced down in another violent storm, all three London evening newspapers ran with the story. But this time the coverage was reduced in the *News* and the *Standard* to a single column, with only the *Star* spreading it across three columns.

The airliner was carrying 45 British holidaymakers home from Majorca when it flew into the storm over France whilst heading north-west. Their pilot, Captain John Cann, decided to make an emergency landing at a quiet military airfield at Cognac, near Bordeaux. Passengers then learnt that hailstorms had shattered a flight-deck windscreen, the airliner's nose cone been dented, navigation lights had been put out and an engine cowling damaged.

Lightning hits jet

By DAILY MAIL REPORTER

AN airliner was struck by lightning yesterday as storms battered the West and North of Scotland, badly affecting road, rail and air traffic.

Trees, telephone and power lines were blown down in a day of blizzard havoc, while at sea dozens of ships had to seek shelter.

And today's forecast is that the blizzards will continue with snow and sleet in most places, especially in the West.

The airliner struck by lightning, a BOAC Boeing 707 jet, with 31 passengers aboard, was making its second attempt to land at **Prestwick Airport** in heavy cross winds.

The Boeing, on its way from Manchester to New York, was approaching the airport when it ran into a violent storm of hailstones and sleet.

At almost the last moment before touch-down the pilot, Captain Richard Flower, decided to overshoot the runway.

Blurred

One of the 31 passengers from Manchester, 19-year-old guitarist Mike Walsh, of the Four Pennies pop group, said: "We seemed to be climbing very steeply away from the airport, when suddenly there was a fantastic flash.

"The plane rocked and my first thought was that one of the engines had exploded. The cabin was flooded with light for a second—but I don't remember hearing any bang.

"Everyone was stunned for a moment, but no one seemed the least bit concerned, except me. I was scared to death."

The aircraft managed to land safely. But a 6in. gash was torn in the tail plane.

Captain Flower said later: "The lightning struck the nose of the aircraft just as we were turning down wind. There was a big flash and a terrific report. The windscreen in front of me was blurred by scorch marks or burnt paint."

After a replacement panel had been fitted, the jet left for New York, four hours late.

Scotish Daily Mail

Terror flash hits jet liner

Express Staff Reporter

A B.O.A.C. Boeing jet airliner with 31 passengers on board was struck by

Scottish Daily Express (right)

AIR LINER STRUCK BY LIGHTNING

A B.O.A.C. jet air liner was struck by lightning yesterday over Prestwick Airport.

A six-inch long tear was made in a section of the air liner's tail 'plane.

No one on board was hurt and the jet touched down safely at its second attempt to land in strong crosswinds.

The Boeing 707 jet was operating the daily Scottish Monarch service from Manchester through Prestwick to New York and was approaching Prestwick when it ran into a storm of sleet and hail.

The pilot, Captain Richard Flower, said:—

"The lightning struck the nose of the aircraft as we were turning downwind. There was a flash and a terrific report. The windscreen in front of me was blurred by scorch marks or burned paint.

"The lightning must have gone right through the aircraft and out again at the tail, but we did not know of the damage until after we landed. I tested the controls immediately and they seemed to be working normally."

Captain Flower said the air liner was flying under ground radar control and was directly beneath heavy cumulo-nimbus cloud when the lightning struck.

"I had already been forced to overshoot the runway because of the turbulent weather conditions," he said. "We had seen a line of cloud on our radar screen, but until we were hit we were unaware of the lightning."

Passenger's Story

Mike Wilsh, a guitarist with the Four Pennies "pop" group, said:—

"We seemed to be climbing steeply away from the airport when suddenly there was a flash. The air liner rocked, and my first thought was that one of the engines had exploded. The cabin was flooded with light for a fleeting second—but I do not remember hearing any bang."

The air liner, he said, had been badly buffeted throughout the flight from Manchester.

After a replacement panel had been fitted the jet left for New York four hours behind schedule.

Passengers escape as lightning hits jet

Sun (left)

LIGHTNING RIPS HOLE IN AIRLINER

By MIRROR REPORTER

LIGHTNING tore a hole in a Boeing jet airliner yesterday as it was

Daily Mirror (left)

Daily Record (below) (all) Jan 15 1965

LIGHTNING HITS A PLANE

SECOND AIRLINER IN LIGHTNING SCARE

A SECOND jet airliner was damaged by lightning on its way into Prestwick less than 30 hours after a B.O.A.C. jet was struck in a violent storm over the airport.

The airliner, a Boeing 707, flew into an electric storm at 3000 feet on its landing approach to Prestwick.

Lightning ripped a 30-inch gash in the nose of the airliner.

When the jet touched down, passengers spoke of a series of lightning flashes, but were unaware of the damage.

Engineers who examined the airliner also found scorch marks on the pilot's windscreen.

The jet's departure to New York was delayed for six hours while a replacement nose cone was flown in from London.

Sunday Post Jan 17 1965

One of the passengers told me when they returned to London aboard a relief airliner: "The hailstones were beating a tattoo on the aircraft, and a Frenchman on the ground told me they were 11 centimetres across. That's bigger than a cricket ball."

There was one lightning story the press down under was happy to report in 1956 however. It concerned the experience of a BOAC long-range

Britannia 312, whose pilot was cheerfully bragging that his aircraft had been "targeted" by lightning at least once a day every day for the past two weeks. The Captain and crew of the otherwise empty "Whispering Giant" had been taking part in an experiment for the airline and the Bristol Aeroplane company by deliberately flying into heavy storm clouds over Darwin, Australia, to test the airliner's lightning protection. "We've gained a lot of information." said Captain Howman taciturnly.

When disasters and other serious accidents have resulted from such storms, it has usually been due to fire following damage to engines or fuel lines. Modern aircraft electrical systems are protected from lightning strikes by "static wicks," the insulated rods which extend from aircraft wing leading edges and are designed to carry electrical charges safely away. Internal electrical equipment and wiring systems are also protected from lightning-induced power surges by suppressors, and the possible aircraft build-up of static is earthed on touch-down by conductive material set into rubber tyres.

Fire on board can always pose a serious threat to aircraft – and it's not only attributable to lightning. The flight-deck crew are alerted in most cases through visual and audible instruments by temperature sensors. Back as long ago as 1948 I reported the discovery of a fire in the baggage hold of a BEA DC3 about to leave Northolt for Frankfurt. Ground staff spotted smoke coming from a woman passenger's baggage as it was being loaded. The bag was removed and loaders found that a prohibited box of matches had exploded inside. The aircraft's departure was held up for just 30 minutes.

A few months later I learned of an incident aboard a BEA Viking as it returned to Northolt following an electrical fire in the wiring of a radio transmitter. "We were told the cause of the fire by the steward. But none of us was alarmed," one passenger told me. "It was put out almost immediately."

Several similar heated moments on board were recorded in my notebook over the coming years, such as the broken seal which dripped oil on to a red-hot exhaust pipe on a Constellation airliner from New York. Clouds of black smoke billowing out from the airliner as it touched down safely at Heathrow alerted fire services, who were able to damp down the ensuing fire. And a BOAC Argonaut airliner bound for Johannesburg turned back to Heathrow after an engine burst into flames 15 minutes after taking off. Among the 38 passengers on board was concert violinist Alfredo Campoli who said: "The flames from the engine were three feet long."

There was no advance warning however for either passengers or crew when fire suddenly burst out in the undercarriage of a high-wing, twin-engined BEA Elizabethan airliner shortly after it touched down at Heathrow in September 1954. Before mobile steps could be wheeled out, 41 passengers on the flight from Paris had to jump a few feet to safety from the forward exit of the piston-engined aircraft

Airliner forced down in storm

Forty-five British holiday-makers arrived at London Airport at half-past two this morning in a relief aircraft after the Viscount in which they were travelling home from Palma, Majorca, had been struck by lightning.

Evening Standard

'CRICKET BALL' HAIL STONES FORCE DOWN AIRLINER

45 holidaymakers in storm drama

FORTY - FIVE British holiday - makers arrived safely at London Airport today after their airliner was struck by lightning in a violent hailstorm and forced to land in France.

The airliner, a four-engined BEA Viscount, was bringing holidaymakers home from Majorca when it ran into the storm.

The pilot, Captain John Cann, decided to land at Cognac, South of France, after the windscreen had been cracked, the No 1 engine cowling damaged and the plane's navigation lights put out.

A relief plane brought the passengers home. No one was hurt.

One passenger, Mr Seymour of The Avenue, Tadworth Surrey, said: "The storm was very rough and had shaken us all up.

Hail 'tattoo'

"The lightning was bad, but the hail was worse. It beat a continuous tattoo on the sides of the plane.

"A local Frenchman said that at times the hailstones were 11 centimetres in size—nearly as big as a cricket ball. They made dents all over the plane."

With Mr Seymour was his wife, their married daughter Ann, their 11 - year - old, daughter, Caroline, and 17-year-old Anthony.

Star

AIRLINER HOLED IN STORM

Plane Battered With 45 Aboard

"Evening News" Reporter

A NIGHTMARE flight through a violent storm which smashed the pilot's windscreen and holed the nose of the plane was described by passengers of a Viscount

Evening News
(all) Aug-Sept 1958

Plane On Fire Turns Back

AN electrical fault caused fire to break out in the radio transmitter of a BEA Viking which left Northolt Airport early today for Oslo.

The pilot, Captain Gibbs, radioed that he was returning to Northolt and after circling 30 minutes to use up fuel he landed safely.

Miss Berit Smith-Petersen (22) one of eight passengers who was returning to Norway after a holiday in England, said:

"There was nothing to be worried about and the flames were soon quenched. We had only been flying for half an hour before we turned to come back."

Another passenger, Capt Saul, of Holmdale, Temple Sheen, East Sheen, said, "We did not realise anything had gone wrong until the steward told us that we were returning owing to the radio transfitter catching fire. None of us was alarmed."

The aircraft was taken out of service, and after a delay of about 30 minutes, passengers boarded another plane.

The Star

Plane's Radio Catches Fire in Mid-Air

Evening News

Fire on Viking airliner—eight did not know

Fire broke out in the radio transmitter of a BEA Viking which left Northolt air-port to-day for Oslo.

The pilot, Captain Gibbs, radioed that he was returning to Northolt, and after circling 30 minutes to use up fuel the aircraft landed safely.

Evening Standard
(all) October 13 1948

Flames licked the fuselage out as the aircraft drew to a halt on the tarmac.

One of the passengers, an 81-years-old Australian woman, was slightly hurt, sustaining grazes to an arm. She said later: "We all rushed to the door when we were told to leave. But someone – a man – pushed in front of me and I fell, banging my arm against the metal door frame."

Cries of "Fire!" from ground staff brought others rushing with fire extinguishers. Among the first on the scene was BOAC receptionist Valerie Seymour who was waiting to meet another incoming airliner. She told me later: "When I heard someone shout 'fire' I was standing close to a mobile fire extinguisher. I just grabbed it and ran to the 'plane and squirted where the smoke was thickest." She and other airline and airport staff managed to get the fire under control just before the airport fire services reached the scene. BEA officials said afterwards that a brake on the starboard main wheel had caught fire. The story gave me front page leads in two London newspapers… the *Evening News* and the *Star*:

WORLD'S LARGEST EVENING NET SALE

The Evening News

R3 NO. 22,631 LONDON, SATURDAY, SEPTEMBER 4, 1954 THREE-HALFPENCE

AIRLINER FIRE

41 Jump From Plane At London Airport

WOMAN FIGHTS FLAMES

"Evening News" Reporter

THE undercarriage of a B.E.A. Elizabethan airliner caught fire as the twin-engined plane landed at London Airport to-day.

Evening News (above) Page One lead

THE STAR

41 Leap Out Of Burning Airliner

FORTY-ONE PEOPLE JUMPED 5FT TO SAFETY FROM A BLAZING AIRLINER AT LONDON AIRPORT TO-DAY.

The passengers made their escape from the nose of the plane—an Elizabethan

The fire broke out in the undercarriage as it touched down.

Only one of the people aboard —Mrs Susan McClay, 81, from Adelaide, Australia — was injured. She suffered slight cuts.

The plane, which was operating BEA's "Silver Wing" luxury service from Paris, taxied towards the tarmac before airport officials saw smoke pouring from the wheels.

One of the airport staff yelled "Fire," and as people rushed forward with extinguishers the starboard wheel burst into flames.

Miss Valerie Seymour, BOAC receptionist, waiting at the edge of the tarmac to meet a plane, was one of the first to rush out with an extinguisher

Ground staff succeeded in quenching the flames.

The Star Page One lead (both) Sept 4 1954

BEA's "Silver Wing" superfast London-to-Paris luxury service, on Elizabethan airliners, offered Moet et Chandon champagne and hot lunch in its £15.19 return fare.

as well as wide coverage in the following day's Sunday newspapers.

The BOAC heroine was the same Valerie Seymour who, a few years on – as I have already described elsewhere – was to marry top British film and TV comedian Jimmy Edwards.

Curiously, and providentially for all concerned, it was the *absence* of fire which possibly saved the lives of everyone on board, including the 11 flight deck and cabin crew and 95 passengers, when a BOAC Boeing 707 jet slewed off the runway at Heathrow and sank to its portside axle in mud.

The near disaster occurred just before noon on Christmas Eve, 1960, also a Saturday, and many of the passengers on flight BA564 from Chicago, Detroit, Montreal and Prestwick, Scotland, were looking forward to joining families in the UK for the holiday. As the £3m jet gently touched down on the runway, passengers were as usual asked to remain in their seats until it had come to a halt and the seat belts warning light had been turned off.

Then suddenly, a loud grinding, scraping sound. The airliner lurched as it swerved to one side, leaving the asphalt surface of the runway, still at speed, to flounder on to the soft and rain-soaked muddy grass verge. An eye-witness said that the port side undercarriage seemed to buckle or collapse. The wing crumpled in a cloud of dust and shower of mud as the two engines skewered the ground .

As quickly as possible the passengers were required to make their way to the forward exit door which had been thrown open to allow an emergency chute to be run out, and within seconds the cabins were emptied as first they, then the crew, including three stewardesses, were hurrying through the mud to the firm ground of the runway. None was injured, though two of the passengers were later treated for shock.

I was in time to capture the front pages in at least two of the London evenings. After the late editions that day, there would be no more newspapers until Tuesday, so my market would then be limited to home and overseas news agencies. The *Evening News* and the *Evening Standard* ran with:

The Evening News

World's largest evening sale

LONDON, SATURDAY, DECEMBER 24, 1960. LATE EXTRA PRICE 3d.

Fire Engines Race To Flight 564 From Chicago

95 IN AIR ESCAPE

Evening News Page One lead

Evening Standard

42,466 SATURDAY, DECEMBER 24, 1960 3d.

Evening Standard Page One lead (both) December 24 1960

Giant Boeing 707 in London Airport mishap

95 ESCAPE AS JET GOES OFF RUNWAY

It lands up in the mud

Evening Standard Reporter

A giant BOAC Boeing 707 jet touched down at London Airport today . . . the airliner slewed off the runway . . . and the port wheel bogged down in the mud.

For the 95 pasengers it was a dramatic ending to Flight 564 from Chicago and Montreal.

No one was hurt. A fleet of coaches and lorries picked up the passengers and their luggage.

The aircraft was badly damaged.

wikipedia license: Arpingstone

Picture (inset)

BOAC Boeing 707 refuelling at London (Heathrow) Airport

The Boeing jet was severely damaged. One wing was a tangled mass of twisted metal, its underslung engine pods torn from their supports. Undercarriage props were also shorn off, and parts of the fuselage was ripped away. Fire and rescue tenders were quickly on the scene, and fire fighters escorted passengers and crew along the runway and well away from the airliner to await transport back to the passenger terminal. One senior officer told them as hundreds of gallons of foam were pumped on to the stricken airliner: "There's a terrible danger of fire. Any one of those tanks could go up."

But happily there was no fire. And later, investigators trying to establish the cause of the accident believed that combustion did not occur because BOAC were using pure kerosene fuel, which was said to have a considerably lower flashpoint than the cheaper JP4 fuel favoured by some airlines.*(see opposite)*.

There is at least one natural hazard for aircraft which has increased dramatically since the days of propeller-driven flight. A number of civil airliners have been forced down suddenly and disastrously by flying into flocks or individual birds they failed to see. Among the earliest worst incidents recorded were an Eastern Airlines Electra which lost three of its four engines when it collided with a huge flock of starlings over the US in October 1960. All but ten of the 72 passengers on board were killed in the subsequent crash.

Just two years later a United Airlines jet encountered a flight of swans at 6,000 feet. The airliner's tail stabiliser was severely damaged, and all 22 passengers and crew were killed. A carcase of one of the birds was found later to alone weigh more than 6 kilos. Other incidents involving birds have resulted in cracked or even shattered flight deck windscreens, a potential disaster in a pressurised aircraft.

Fortunately many more possible strikes are avoided, thanks to the preventive measures taken by airports around the world, measures which though relatively costly, have proved to often simple but highly effective. Among these, keeping runway grass verges at a specific height and periodically broadcasting amplified recordings of bird danger calls in the runway vicinities quickly became established practice. Though it was some years before some civil authorities came to accept that birds, particularly scavenging seagulls, were also being attracted into airport flight paths by the proximity of waste landfill sites.

Moving the sites away from that proximity and providing longer-term waste foods dumps well away from the airport, as at Scotland's Prestwick later, helped to reduce the problem, just as quickly as cutting airport grass to a specific height and playing pre-recorded bird danger calls.

My colleagues and I all had to report at various times the disproportionate damage to aircraft when birds had been accidentally ingested by jet engines. In 1962, only a month or two before I myself migrated north to Prestwick, I was reporting, from Heathrow, an emergency landing by a Canadian DC8 jet which only 80 minutes earlier had been crippled by flying into a flock of gulls as it lifted off from the Scottish transatlantic airport on its way to Cleveland, Ohio. The *Daily Express* headline the next day illustrated it: 'Seagulls 'down' jet with 128 aboard', while the *Daily Mail* presented it with: 'Gulls turn back a giant jet'.

This time were no landfill sites in the area. The sea birds were in their natural habitat, with the Prestwick runway just a few hundred yards from the shoreline. At least two gulls were sucked into an engine, damaging its rotor blades and causing it to overheat. Immediately, the pilot, Captain Eric Jokinen shut down the engine and radioed Heathrow to say he would be returning to make an emergency landing there.

Fire engines and rescue services stood by as the jet touched down safely on three engines. An official for the airline later said that the captain had decided to head for London because repair facilities and alternative flights for the 118 passengers were available there.

The broadcasting of natural bird "danger" calls to frighten flocks was pioneered with great success at Amsterdam's Schipol Airport in the 1950s. But when Heathrow ground operations staff borrowed the recorded tape, early tests proved to be less than successful. Hardly a wing was fluttered. Then it was realised that the Dutch gulls were a different breed and their warning cries were not being recognised.

Further recordings were made, this time of various cries of the large British herring gulls. Now the bird watchers, or "scarers," were able to report 100 per cent success. Hundreds of birds took off and winged away in mad panic at the first note of the warning. A similar story was reported by Chinese authorities at Beijing airport. But there it was

Plane that didn't burn

Investigators trying to find out why a Boeing 707 with 108 aboard skidded off a runway at London Airport on Christmas Eve, claimed last night that the plane did not catch fire because it was fuelled with pure kerosene.

Lord Brabazon warned recently of the dangers of the growing use of the cheaper aviation fuel JP4. British Overseas Airways Corporation, who were operating the 707, said last night: "We have no plans to change to JP4."

Daily Mail
(A few weeks later)

DC8 DELAYED ON U.S. TRIP

Gulls turn back a giant jet

A GIANT jet airliner carrying 118 passengers and a crew of 10 had to make an emergency landing at London Airport last night after colliding with a flock of seagulls.

The collision happened as the plane—a Canadian DC8—was taking off from Prestwick Airport, Scotland, bound for Cleveland, Ohio.

Two of the gulls were sucked into an engine causing it to overheat.

The pilot, Captain Eric Jokinen, immediately radioed London Airport to say he would be making an emergency landing there.

Fire-engines stood by at the airport as Captain Jokinen brought his plane down safely after a 78-minute flight on three engines from Prestwick.

MAIN BASE

A spokesman for Trans-Canada Airlines said: "Captain Jokinen headed for London because that is where we have our main base and all our repair equipment."

The 118 passengers later continued their journey in another plane.

THE WINDSCREEN of a Scandinavian Airlines' DC 8 airliner shattered as the plane came into land at Prestwick yesterday with 54 passengers. But the pilot made a perfect landing.

Daily Mail

Seagulls 'down' jet with 128 aboard

Scottish Daily Express *(both) February 5 1962*

decided that the birds recognised only local bird dialects, not Western cries. So airport operations' staff on both sides of the world had to set out to record a complete library of their own "top of the hits" local bird calls – so that the less popular sounds could be wiped from the tapes.

Writers and cinema films have for years exploited the idea of a sudden drop in air pressure aboard aircraft, visualising the loss of everything unsecured, even passengers and crew, through a broken window or otherwise damaged fuselage into the outside rarefied atmosphere. I have already referred briefly to the potential and actual danger to flight deck windscreens by lightning strikes or wayward birds, but there have been occasions where the causes of such damage have not been so obvious (such as the Comet 1 disasters).

The story of the British airliner captain who was suddenly sucked out through his broken windscreen is well documented (though not by me). His life was saved by the fast reaction of crew members. A steward who was present on the flight deck at the time grabbed the pilot's legs as he was sucked from his seat and held on to them literally for dear life. The co-pilot, who immediately took control, went into a steep dive in an attempt equalise the interior and exterior air pressures. Other crew members, who rushed in to anchor themselves helped the steward until the aircraft could be landed safely. The captain was treated for relatively minor bruises and abrasions.

Fortunately such aircraft fabric damage is rare. I can only recall two incidents, one in 1963 at Prestwick, when seconds before touch down and well below pressurised height, a cockpit window cracked on a Boeing 707 jet. The airliner was on its way from London to Toronto via the Scottish airport, but the captain immediately abandoned his runway approach and turned back to Heathrow, landing safely there. The 43 passengers on board were told of the threat to the window, but an official said that there was no immediate danger and no loss of atmosphere. Again, repair facilities were more readily available at Heathrow.

The other incident, almost ten years earlier, was certainly as dramatic, and for the passengers, considerably more distressing. This time it was a cabin window in a BOAC Stratocruiser propeller airliner which blew out without warning four miles up over the Atlantic and 200 miles west of Ireland.

In a split second, most of the air inside the cabin rushed out of a gaping 10 by 8ins hole in the window frame. The air was followed out by two overcoats and small items of hand luggage lying loose on a rack. The 33 passengers on board, many of whom were asleep, were left gasping for air and shivering in sub-zero temperatures.

Some stood up in alarm as they felt a sharp pain in their ear drums. They had been suddenly transported to the temperature and atmosphere experienced at the top of a 25,000ft mountain. The flight engineer tried to block the hole with a pillow, but it was too small, and was being dragged out. Then he wrapped a tea tray in a blanket – and the suction held it secure. Cabin crew hurriedly passed out oxygen bottles where they were needed, occasionally taking a whiff themselves.

The pilot had already acted. He put his "double bubble" four-engine Strat into a steep dive. In minutes the aircraft reached 11,000 feet, and Captain Ben Prowse finally levelled out. Twenty-seven years old stewardess Isobel Carson, from Ruislip, Middlesex, told me later: "I managed to get some of the passengers to lie stretched out on the floor and advised them to make no unnecessary movement."

My story, complete with first hand reports from some of the passengers I talked to when the airliner finally reached Heathrow resulted in big spreads in the nationals the next day, including a six-column page lead in the *Daily Mail:*

FOUR MILES UP A WINDOW GOES

Airliner girl gives oxygen and pilot dives

Daily Mail Nov 30 1954

and three columns in the *Daily Herald* with similar stories in the *News Chronicle, Daily Express, Daily Mirror, Daily Sketch* and *Daily Telegraph (see opposite).*

THERE'S DRAMA IN THE AIR

Plane window blows out at 25,000ft.

ISOBEL CARSON
Oxygen for passengers

Herald Reporter

A BRITISH Stratocruiser was flying over the Atlantic, 25,000ft. above the sea, yesterday when a window blew out.

There were 33 passengers on board.

They gasped for breath as the pressurised air in the cabin escaped, like air whistling out of a punctured inner tube, and thin-cold air replaced it.

Within seconds, everyone was shivering.

They had been transported in a flash from the warmth and comfort of a luxurious, well-heated lounge to the equivalent of the top of a 25,000ft. mountain.

It sucked two overcoats and a scarf from the luggage rack. They disappeared.

It *could* have dragged a man's body out of the window, an official said at London Airport.

Said one passenger, Mr. Angus Bruce, an Edinburgh business man, "I was asleep. I woke up and found it difficult to breathe.

"All around me, people were gasping."

Shivering

Another passenger, Mr. Johannes Dill, a South African, said: "It was minutes before we could breathe normally. By that time, I was really shivering."

Then the pilot, Captain Benjamin Prowse, put the plane into a steep dive. It went down 14,000 feet.

And an engineer fixed a tray against the blown-out window to stop the draught.

Stewardess Isobel Carson, aged 27, of Grosvenor-vale, Ruislip, Middlesex, gave oxygen to passengers who needed it.

And the Stratocruiser flew on to London.

Interestingly, and gratifyingly to me, at least three of these newspapers, the *Telegraph, Herald* and *Express*, ran another story of mine alongside, that of a BEA Elizabethan airliner which lost one of its twin nose wheels on take-off and had to return to make a difficult "nose-up" landing on only its main undercarriage wheel and emergency tail "skid" wheel. The *Herald* linked both stories with the subhead: *there's drama in the air......*

'LIE DOWN' ORDER TO 33 PASSENGERS

By Daily Mail Reporter

A WINDOW blew out yesterday in a B.O.A.C. Stratocruiser nearly four miles above the Atlantic. In a split second most of the air whooshed out of the airliner's pressurised cabin. And in that cabin were 33 people.

Pressure cabin failure . . . That, according to experts, was what caused Britain's Comet airliner to explode into countless pieces and kill all on board last January.

But yesterday there was this difference: The Stratocruiser's height was more than two miles below the height at which the Comet had been flying at the instant of disaster.

The Stratocruiser pilot knew [illegible]

Daily Mail

Plane loses window

A window blew out of a pressurised Stratocruiser flying over the Atlantic yesterday. Thirty-three passengers, including seven women and a child, awoke gasping for breath and shivering.

Immediately, Captain Benjamin Prowse, the British Overseas Airways Corporation pilot, brought the plane down from 25,000 to 11,500 feet.

The stewardess [illegible]

News Chronicle (right)

PLANE WINDOW BLOWS OUT OVER ATLANTIC

PASSENGERS' MASKS

DAILY TELEGRAPH REPORTER

A window in the pressurised cabin of a B.O.A.C. Stratocruiser, flying from New York to London Airport, blew out yesterday when the plane was at an altitude of 25,000ft and 200 miles west of Ireland. There were 43 people aboard.

Capt. B. Prowse, the pilot, reduced height by 14,000ft in a slow dive. The window, which was about 10in by 8in, was blocked up and the escape of air and heat largely prevented.

Many of the 33 passeng[illegible]

shivering.

Mr. W. Monson, an American, lost an overcoat. It was whisked through the window, which was close to a luggage rack. Another passenger, Mr. Donald Attwell, lost a coat and a scarf.

PLANE LOST WHEEL

2 Hours Circling Airport

An Elizabethan airliner bound for Amsterdam with 21 people aboard, circled London Airport yesterday with one of its two nosewheels missing. It landed after two hours. No one was hurt.

While the plane was circling to reduce the fuel load, emergency and fire services were held in readiness. Capt. J. W. Cooke, the pilot, brought the plane down with the only damage a broken wheel strut.

Daily Telegraph (above)

THERE'S DRAMA IN THE AIR

Elizabethan loses wheel

PASSENGERS in a BEA Elizabethan airliner were told to remove false teeth after the plane lost a wheel on take-off from London Airport yesterday.

The plane, with 15 passengers and a crew of five, was bound for Amsterdam.

The wheel fell off the nose.

After circling for nearly two hours, the plane, piloted by Capt. Crooke, landed on the main wheels and emergency tail wheel.

When it stopped moving the second nose wheel rolled away from the undercarriage leg.

The stewardess, 22-year-old Vera Beggs, from Belfast, said, "The passengers were calm. Before we came in for the landing we went right through the crash drill: glasses off and false teeth out and cushions at waist level."

Daily Herald

TEA TRAY PLUGS HOLE IN PLANE

By W. A. WATERTON

A STEWARD'S tray was used to plug a hole in the cabin of a BOAC Stratocruiser high over the Atlantic yesterday.

The airliner was 200 miles west of Ireland on the flight from New York to London when a window 10ins. by 8ins. blew out of the pressurised cabin.

The result was "explosive decompression"—of the same type which wrecked the Comets.

The cabin's air, at 6lb. a square inch over outside pressure, rushed out, sucking coats and some baggage with it.

ably for the rest of the flight to London Airport.

A BEA Elizabethan with 15 passengers and a crew of five was skidded down at London Airport yesterday after one of the twin wheels in the nose came off at take-off for Amsterdam. The passengers were told to take off their spectacles and brace themselves for the landing. No one was hurt.

Daily Express

BROKEN PLANE WINDOWS BAFFLE BOAC

Daily Sketch Air Correspondent

B.O.A.C. engineers were trying last night to find why a window in a Stratocruiser's pressurised cabin blew out five miles above the Atlantic.

It is the second time in four months that a window has shattered on an American-built B.O.A.C. Stratocruiser airliner.

No satisfactory explanation has been found.

The window—eight by ten inches—burst when the Stratocruiser Castol was 200 miles off Ireland yesterday.

Capt. Benjamin Prowse, aged 43, was piloting the plane at 300 m.p.h. to London from New York with 33 passengers.

The window broke with a loud crack.

Air under pressure in the cabin began to rush out.

An overcoat belonging to American passenger, Mr. W. Monson, which was on a luggage rack near the window, was sucked out of the plane.

Daily Sketch

A TEA TRAY IN THE SKY

It stopped the gap when an airliner's window blew out

Daily Mirror

(all) Nov 30 1954

After circling for two hours to use up fuel before attempting a touchdown, Captain J.W. Cooke finally brought the aircraft safely to a halt, dropping it gently forward from its nose-up stance… then the second forward wheel dropped off and rolled away from a crumpled undercarriage leg.

The stewardess, 22-years old Vera Beggs, of Belfast told me later that the 15 passengers, who were on their way to Amsterdam, had been calm throughout. "Before we came in for the landing we went right through the crash drill; glasses off and false teeth out and cushions at waist level."

Among other bizarre incidents I reported was the story of the BEA Viscount airliner which lost three of its four engines at 20,000ft , over the Bay of Biscay on a flight to London following water contamination of its fuel at Gibraltar airport.

The airliner, carrying 31 passengers and a crew of five, was 75 miles out from the French coast, heading north on January 2, 1956, when the outer starboard engine suddenly cut out. The pilot, Captain Eric Watts, 37, managed to restart it briefly, but again it cut. Then, moments later, another engine stopped. As Captain Watts turned and headed for Bordeaux a third engine, the port outer, also stopped. Immediately he put the aircraft in a steep dive.

Captain Watts and his engineering officer constantly operated the throttle controls as the engines continued to cut and restart spasmodically. At last they were able to touch down safely at the military airfield of Cazaux, near Bordeaux.

THE MIRACLE ON ONE ENGINE

By GILBERT CARTER

ERIC WATTS relaxed in the captain's seat of the Viscount on the flight from Gibraltar to London. Back in the cabin, June Crouch, 26-year-old air hostess, and Bill Duncan, the steward, were looking after the 31 passengers just finishing breakfast.

The Viscount had left Madrid on the last leg home. It was 20,000ft. over the Bay of Biscay, 75 miles from the French coast. Everything was going with the usual smoothness. Then—

NUMBER ONE engine stopped.

NUMBER TWO cut out a few minutes later.

Watts warned his crew of four—First Officer, radio operator and the cabin attendants.

And almost before Duncan and June had time to remember the emergency drill, engine **NUMBER FOUR** stopped.

THE SEARCH for an airfield

NUMBER THREE kept going. Watts brought the Viscount down from the freezing 20,000ft. level. He tried to start the three dead engines.

First one, then another coughed and spluttered. Watts and the first officer worked the engine controls like organ stops. They kept reviving and cutting out.

In the cabin, Bill Duncan and June Crouch were bright and cheerful. They asked the passengers to put on life-belts, showed them how to brace against impact, and told them: "Don't worry."

The Viscount came lower. Now it was over France and the 36-year-old pilot was seeking an airfield for an emergency landing.

THE CHANCE but only one try

He found it. A little military airfield near Çazou, 25 miles from Bordeaux.

But there could be no mistake. There was no power to climb and go in for a second try.

Watts did it. Without a bump, without damage to plane, passengers or crew, he landed the Viscount with only **ONE** engine working normally.

Last night the passengers were flown to London in a relief plane.

Watts stayed with the Viscount while B E A experts tried to find out why it happened. They believe it could have been due to water having got into the fuel.

They do not suspect sabotage at Madrid.

Daily Herald

Captain Watts

Daily Mail

1..2..3—the plane engines faded out

THREE of a British airliner's four engines cut out one after the other as the plane flew over the gale-swept Bay of Biscay on its way to London yesterday.

The thirty-one passengers aboard gasped as the plane dived steeply. But the airliner then levelled out again. For half an hour the passengers sat tense in their seats as the pilot nursed it towards France.

One of the three engines that cut out started again. The others revved only in spasms.

The plane, a Vickers Viscount of British European Airways, eventually landed safely at a French military airport at Cazaux, near Bordeaux.

Two of its engines were still out of action.

The Viscount was on its way from Gibraltar to London. It stopped at Madrid fro fuel.

It was seventy-five miles from land when the first of its engines cut out.

Last night Captain J. W. G. James B.E.A.'s flight operations director, who travelled out to inspect the Viscount, said:

"It is possible that the fuel was contaminated by water." Sabotage was NOT suspected, he added.

One of the passengers, Rear-Admiral Rover Dick, of Lowndes-street Knightsbridge, London, was asked if anyone was nervous He replied:

"Of course we were. We would all be idiots if we were not nervous"

Daily Mirror

3 ENGINES OF PLANE CUT: FUEL SUSPECT

Pilot saves diving liner

NEWS CHRONICLE REPORTER

THREE engines of a Viscount air liner stopped one by one. And there were 28 passengers on board and a crew of five.

The Viscount was 20,000 feet up over the Bay of Biscay and nearly 75 miles from the French coast when all but one of the engines cut out and only revived spasmodically and alternately.

The pilot, Captain E. R. Watts, and his engineer, working the engine controls like organ-stops, brought her to the army airfield at Cazaux, near Bordeaux, and landed safely.

Passengers said later that after the failure of the engines the Viscount went into a steep dive. "The steward and stewardess told us to put on lifebelts and brace our feet on the seats in front," said Mr. Patrick Bowen, from Holland Road, London, W

Said Rear-Admiral Royer Dick: "Nervous? Of course we were. The suspense lasted about 20 minutes. We would all have been blind idiots if we were not nervous"

News Chronicle

Fuel warning after Viscount drama

By T. F. THOMPSON

AIRLINERS refuelling at Madrid were warned last night to take extra precautions after a BEA Viscount turbo-prop airliner carrying 31 passengers force-landed at a French military airfield with three of its four

Daily Mail (right)

Did water down airliner?

Daily Sketch Reporter

ONE BY ONE three of the four engines of a Viscount airliner spluttered into lifelessness high over France yesterday.

The London-bound plane went into a steep dive and the 28 passengers were ordered to don their lifebelts and brace themselves on the seat in front.

But on only a quarter of full power the pilot pulled the airliner out of its dive and steered it into a safe landing.

Daily Sketch

(all, this page) Jan 3 1956

At Heathrow, after reporting the initial story, I spoke to Captain Jimmy James, BEA's flight operations director and former chief pilot, as with other experts he boarded a relief Viscount leaving to pick up the stranded passengers. "We have to find out what happened. It's possible the fuel may have been contaminated by water. It is certainly not the result of insufficient fuel or the wrong fuel being used in Madrid, the last port of call. And we have no reason to suspect sabotage."

One of the passengers on the crippled Viscount, Rear Admiral Royer Dick of Knightsbridge, London said later *(in a tone that implied: "Damn fool question"):*

"Of course we were all nervous. We would all be idiots if we were not nervous."

My story won good coverage in all the nationals the next day with two and three-column page leads, though I could not claim exclusivity as I must have shared some of these with the opening original reports from France. But the next day I was able to offer more column inches in an follow-up story on the arrival of water samples from the Madrid fuel depots. My exclusives in the *Daily Express, Daily Mail, News Chronicle, Daily Telegraph* and the *Daily Herald* illustrated this.

The *Express* asked:

"Riddle of the Viscount... ***WAS IT RAIN FROM SPAIN?"***

Two pints of water, one from taps at the Spanish airport and one of local rain water, were flown to London, but tests eliminated both samples from blame.

When similar tests were carried out at Gibraltar, however, salt water contamination was proved to have occurred in dockside storage barges from which fuel was carried directly to the airport. Plans were drawn up to transfer storage to specially constructed tanks at the airport as soon as practicable.

Two months after his one-engine landing, I reported meeting Captain Watts again when, with his wife, he flew back to Cazaux to present an inscribed cigarette case to the airfield controller and lighters to the ground staff. It was his personal "thank you" for the help they gave him when he was forced down.

MADRID WATER TEST IN PLANE MYSTERY

TWO milk bottles labelled "tap" and "rain" were flown into London from Madrid yesterday in an attempt to discover why three engines of a Viscount airliner faltered over the Bay of Biscay on Monday.

While the water samples were being flown to London, BEA officials in Gibraltar and Madrid denied that water could have got into the fuel — as was suspected after the incident.

Tanks checked

Mr. Anthony Caro, BEA chief in Spain said: "We had the tanks and fuel lorry checked as soon as we heard the plane was down at Cazaux, France. There is no question ...

Riddle of the Viscount

WAS IT RAIN FROM SPAIN?

Express Air Reporter

A PINT of tap water and a pint of rain water were flown yesterday to London from Madrid.

The water will be tested to see if it can help to solve the great Viscount mystery.

Other samples will be flown from Gibraltar.

For it is thought likely that there was water in the fuel of the Viscount airliner when three of the four engines cut out over the sea on the way to London on Monday.

Captain Eric Watts landed the plane (36 aboard) safely at Cazaux, near Bordeaux.

The water samples will be analysed to see if they match up with any water found in the Viscount's fuel.

It may be possible to determine whether rain seeped in—or whether water got into the fuel in some other way.

In London last night British European Airways did not know for certain what the trouble was.

The grounded Viscount has been examined in France by an investigating team who flew out from Britain.

The team found water in fuel system filters, so emptied the plane's tanks.

Daily Express (above)

BEA to try water test

By Daily Mail Reporter

TWO milk bottles containing samples of water from Madrid, one labelled "tap" and the other "rain," were flown to London last night for analysis. Other water samples are to be flown from G...

RAIN FLOWN FROM SPAIN

Two milk bottles containing samples of Madrid tap and rain water were flown to London last night for analysis.

Experts are trying to find out if water in the fuel was the cause of three of the four engines of a Viscount failing off the coast of France on Monday — and, if so, where it came from.

WATER FROM MADRID FOR PLANE TEST

VISCOUNT MISHAP

DAILY TELEGRAPH REPORTER

Two pint bottles of water from Madrid arrived at London Airport last night for analysis. It is hoped that the tests will help to explain why three of the four engines of a Viscount airliner cut out while the plane was flying from Madrid to London on Monday.

(from top) News Chronicle
Daily Mail
Daily Herald
Daily Telegraph *(all) Jan 4 1956*

Brenard Press picture
Airport Post, March 21 1956

'ONE ENGINE' ERIC THANKS FRENCHMAN

SAFE PILOT INVOLVED IN CAR ACCIDENT

Captain Eric Watts, the 37-years-old B.E.A. "one-engine" flyer who last January safely landed his Viscount airliner at a secret French military airfield when three of its engines failed, was involved in an accident with a young cyclist while on his way to London Airport on a "sentimental journey" on Monday.

With his wife Joan, Captain Watts was flying to Cazaux, the French airfield to present an inscribed cigarette case to the Controller and cigarette lighters to the groud staff as a personal "thank you" for the help they gave him when his Viscount was forced down.

Driving from his home in St. Albans, his car was in collision with a boy cyclist at Stanmore, Middlesex. The boy suffered concussion; neither Captain nor Mrs. Watts was injured.

Reaching the airport with only a few moments to spare before their Bordeaux bound airliner was due to take off, Capt Watts said "We had to wait nearly 25 minutes for an ambulance to pick up the youngster and make a report to the police."

Near misses, can also hardly be described as a natural hazard of air travel. The sky is **not** all that "crowded," except perhaps in the strictly regulated immediate vicinity of airports. And by obvious implication, the near miss (officially known as the "air miss") is the antithesis of hazardous. Avoidance of mid-air collision is safe; the keyword is "miss."

Among several incidents we covered was one at Prestwick Airport in 1963 which was more of an air-to-ground miss. Here certain collision was averted only by the quick action of the pilot of a US Air Force C118 Transport aircraft. About to touch down from West Germany with American servicemen and their families aboard, the American airliner was already on its final approach. But it had to sheer away at the last minute when a twin-engine Dakota suddenly slipped in to land ahead of it.

The Dakota, owned by a Moroccan airline, had taken off earlier on a local test flight after an engine overhaul at the Prestwick workshops of Scottish Aviation Ltd. It was believed to have had a temporary radio failure and its Moroccan crew had returned to land without being able to ask permission. "Fortunately visibility was good, and the American pilot was able to see the Dakota ahead," said an airport official.

Nearly ten years earlier in the summer of 1954, the first near miss I had to report was a hit rather than a miss, though it, too, was happily not disastrous. Two airliners brushed wing-tips 7,000ft. over Le Bourget airport. Paris. Both aircraft were damaged, and all passengers and crews survived without injury, although not to tell the tale – because all on board except the pilots were ignorant of their near escape. Perhaps their nonchalance contributed to the relative lack of interest in the incident.

Airliners' wing-tips touch

WING-TIPS of two giant airliners touched, 7,000 feet up, yesterday.

But they only brushed each other — and planes and pasengers escaped disaster by inches.

It was over Le Bourget, Paris aerodrome. Captain Ronnie Gilman had just got the control tower's order: Descend

He brought his B.E.A. Elizabethan down to 7,000 feet.

Then through the cloud he glimpsed another plane.

Capt. Gilman

Said Captain Gilman, 33, last night:

"The other aircraft—an Air France Skymaster—loomed up directly ahead of me."

None of his crew nor the 23 passengers, knew what had happened—that the Elizabethan had lost seven inches of wing tip.

But the French pilot radioed: "That was a bit close. We'll have a beer together some time."

Both planes landed safely.

News Chronicle (both) Aug 12 1954

Airliners hit each other 7,000ft up

By Daily Mail Reporter

A BEA Elizabethan airliner and a four-engined Air France Skymaster brushed wings in cloud 7,000ft. over Le Bourget Airport, Paris, yesterday.

The planes loomed up so suddenly that neither pilot had time to take evasive action. As they swept past one another their wings touched.

The wing tip of the BEA plane was crumpled and a seven-inch tip was wrenched from the French aircraft.

The French pilot radioed the BEA pilot, Captain Ronnie Gilman: "That was a bit close. We'll have a beer together sometime."

Both were able to land safely. The 23 BEA passengers going from London to Paris knew nothing about their escape—all they felt was a bump.

Daily Mail

One of the airliners, a twin-engined BEA Elizabethan, had just been given clearance by the airport control tower to descend after a flight from London, and Captain Ronnie Gilman was levelling out after bringing his aircraft with its 23 passengers down through thick cloud.

Then, through the cloud he glimpsed another airliner, a four-engined Air France DC4 Skymaster. "It suddenly loomed up in front of me," he told me on his return to Heathrow later. "I automatically took the standard avoidance action. There was a bump as we passed, but I didn't tell anyone at the time. Neither my crew nor the passengers knew what had happened. But they felt the bump."

A seven-inch gash had been wrenched from the wing tip of the Elizabethan, and the Skymaster's wing tip was crumpled. The French pilot radioed Captain Gilman: "That was a bit close." he said, cooly. " We'll have a beer together some time." Both aircraft were able to land safely.

As far as I am aware, only two British nationals, the *News Chronicle* and the *Daily Mail* ran the story *(see left).*

The passengers' ignorance on that occasion did not surprise me unduly. I once had my own experience of a similar close encounter – fortunately without the impact – on an air approach to Zurich Airport. I was one of a group of passengers on a flight leaving Heathrow in May 1960 on a two to three-day visit to Switzerland. We were aboard an inaugural Caravelle jet airliner as guests of Swissair, and the visit was being hosted jointly by the airline and the national tourist office *(see opposite).*

The captain had just advised us that he would shortly be making a descent into Zurich's airport. My companions, who were all travel specialists or blasé globe-trotting news correspondents, were happily chatting among themselves. While not forsaking the freely flowing champagne, I was anxious for my first glimpse of the Alps, and stayed in my seat, my nose glued to a port side window.

Suddenly, as we gently slid beneath the cloud, directly into my line of view and apparently not much more than 100 metres away, appeared a camouflaged jet fighter on a parallel line of flight. I sat transfixed as I watched the fighter keep pace with us. Its pilot, in helmet and goggles, was clearly visible, and his head turned several times in our direction. It was almost as if he were providing an escort. I even waved to him, but had no response. My window was only one of a dozen or more he could have seen.

I wanted to call out to one of my companions, but none was near at that time. They all seemed to be away from their seats. Then, from the corner of my eye, I watched a second, identical jet fighter move into position to the rear of its twin, but some 30 feet lower.

Keeping my eyes on the scene as far as I could with the changing angle of view, I carefully hauled myself up and called to a colleague. But when I looked back both aircraft had disappeared. With no evidence to offer I couldn't interest anyone in my sighting; no one else had apparently seen anything.

My Swissair host seemed quite unperturbed. "There's a busy military airfield nearby," was his unhelpful comment. "They were probably on their way there..."

Later, after a train ride to Lucerne in a reserved observation car, I was given a clue. We stepped from the train on to a platform smothered with flags and bunting; then into the station concourse and even more flags, the Swiss white cross and the Union Flag apparently dominating everywhere. Several of us asked: "Who's the expected VIP? Visiting royalty? A President?" only to be met by enigmatic smiles.

Swissair picture

Before my "near-miss." In May 1960 I joined *(extreme left)* **other representatives of the British national and travel trade press on an overnight tour of Switzerland as guests of the country's national airline. The trip marked the inauguration of a new Swissair London – Zurich service with the French-built Caravelle jet. With us was our host for the trip, Swissair's London PR manager, John Elliott** *(extreme right)*, **and seeing us off was W. "Bert" Unholz, the airline's manager at Heathrow,** *(in uniform at rear)* **my one-time nemesis** *(see Chapter Eight).*

As we finally reached the centre of the concourse, we found a group of grinning Swiss officials waiting to address us. They introduced themselves as "The Swiss Tourism Office." And our eyes swivelled to a huge banner suspended high above their heads which seemed to cover the entire width of the large station concourse.

It read: ***"Welcome to the British Journalists' party."***

We were the VIPs. *We* were the "royalty."

When I got to know our hosts better, at the risk of becoming a bore on the subject, I broached the question of the jets that "buzzed" our Caravelle over Zurich airport, all others present having pleaded ignorance of the incident. The closest I came to an answer was from one who insisted he remain anonymous. "Sometimes," he said, "We like to arrange a special welcome for our guests. And we have some very good contacts in the military..."

I still wonder sometimes, in spite of these assurances, if we were particularly lucky. It was only a couple of years since a BEA Viscount airliner had collided over Italy with an Italian jet fighter, killing everyone on board both aircraft. Among the victims was a Heathrow colleague, 25-years-old Brian Fogaty, a photographer with Fleet Street's *Daily Sketch* and based at the airport, who was accompanying a model on a sponsored photographic assignment.

Ironically and sadly, the pilot of the Viscount, Captain Frank Foster, who was a world champion glider pilot, was also a member of a committee set up to study ways of avoiding air collisions.

*

Crowded sky or not, terra firma can also be highly hazardous, if not dangerous, to aircraft. Bring together a huge number of them, of all shapes and sizes, on the ground, often moving about in congested areas independent of each other and incidents or accidents, will happen.

Sometimes those aircraft collide with each other or with vehicles or fixtures, resulting in anything from minor dents which nevertheless have to be checked out, to serious damage costing thousands of pounds in repair bills. They can also result in a great deal of inconvenience to everyone concerned as well as many not directly involved, and always made news.

Britannia airliner

in runway crash

A BOAC Britannia airliner with 47 passengers aboard crashed into another airliner while taxi-ing at London Airport last night. But nobody was hurt.

The Britannia's steering and brakes failed after a breakdown in its hydraulic system. The giant plane hit a two-ton generator and cannoned into an empty Pan American DC 6 airliner whose batteries were being charged from the generator.

A flailing propellor sliced open the generator's driving-cab and hood, then shattered its batteries. Gallons of acid splashed over the tarmac.

Broken pieces of the propellor peppered the DC 6's nose as the Britannia lurched into the American plane.

UNDER WING

Said one passenger: "There was no jolting in the crash—just a horrible tearing sound."

The Britannia had just been about to take off for Bahrein in the Persian Gulf.

It was more than an hour before engineers were able to separate the two airliners. The collision had locked them together.

The generator was found rammed under the Britannia's port wing.

The 47 passengers left three and a half hours late in another Britannia.

Daily Herald November 1959

Back in 1959 a BOAC Britannia with 47 passengers aboard collided with another airliner while taxi-ing for take-off at London Airport. Both aircraft were severely damaged, but no one was hurt.

The Britannia's steering and brakes failed following a breakdown in its hydraulics system. It first ran into a two-ton generator, then cannoned into an empty Pan American DC 6 piston-engined airliner whose batteries were being charged from the generator.

A flailing propeller sliced open the generator's driving cab and hood, then shattered its batteries. Gallons of acid splashed over the tarmac. Then, as I reported, the nose of the DC6 was peppered by the Britannia's broken propeller as the airliner lurched into the American 'plane.

It was more than an hour before engineers were able to separate the two airliners. The collision had locked them together. The generator was found rammed under the Britannia's wing

After they were rescued from the crippled Britannia which had been about to take-off for the Persian Gulf, one of the passengers said: "There was no jolting in the crash – just a horrible tearing sound." He and other passengers were finally able to leave, on another Britannia, three hours later, after a clear run out to the runway.

It's not always aircraft that get in the way, however. Imagine a driver having to 'phone his insurance company to claim for severe damage to his car by an airliner's propeller. *("I tried to move out of his way but he just kept coming after me!")*

That's what happened to one car driver, airline employee Peter Kirwan, who parked at the edge of the tarmac at Heathrow while on duty one October day in the early 1950s. "I had switched off and was waiting for one of my company's aircraft to meet me for some ground checks I had to do." he said. "Then I realised another aircraft was coming up from behind and was heading straight for me."

He quickly started up and swung the saloon car away in a wide sweep to the right. "I felt a jolt as the aircraft starboard propeller struck the rear of my car," he said. The blade sliced right through the luggage boot lid of the vehicle. Peter was unhurt, and was able to leave the car safely. The Canadian airliner, which was taxying out to take-off for Montreal with 33 passengers, was delayed for two hours for the fitting of a new propeller. Repairs to the car took a little longer. "The other driver must have admitted liability," said Peter "I didn't lose my no-claims bonus."

This time it was down to the Sunday newspapers to carry my story *(left).*

Car hit by plane propeller

A CAR was struck by the propeller of an airliner at London Airport last night.

Mr. Peter Kirwan a London Airport engineer, was sitting in the car on the tarmac when the airliner came up from the rear.

"I started up and put the car into a sharp right turn," said Mr. Kirwan, "but I felt a jolt as the starboard outer propeller struck the rear of the car."

The propeller ploughed into the metal of the car. The airliner, due to leave for Montreal with thirty-three passengers, was delayed for two hours.

Plane propeller hits airport car

THE driver of a saloon car escaped serious injury at London airport last night when the car was struck over the luggage boot by the propeller of a four-engined Canadian air-liner.

The car was standing on the tarmac when its driver, an airport engineer, saw the air-liner approaching from the rear on his left.

He veered the car from a standstill sharply to the right, but the starboard outer propeller ploughed through the luggage boot lid of the car.

The air-liner was taxi-ing to the tarmac before taking off with 33 passengers for Montreal. The propeller was changed.

Car Hit By Plane Propeller At Airport

By Sunday Dispatch Reporter

THE propeller of a Trans-atlantic airliner last night ploughed through a small saloon car as the aircraft taxied across London Airport.

The car was standing on the tarmac when its driver, Mr. Peter Kirwan, an airport engineer, saw the airliner coming towards him.

He started the car's engine and swung the saloon to the right. But the starboard outer propeller of the four-engined airliner tore into the luggage boot.

Mr. Kirwan escaped unhurt.

The airliner, due to leave for Montreal with 33 passengers, was delayed more than an hour while the propeller was changed.

Sunday Pictorial (above)
The People (left)
Sunday Dispatch (right)
(all) October 26 1952

Most car drivers at some time have experienced both near-misses and minor brushes with other vehicles though rarely, it must be said, when the other "vehicle" is an aircraft. One incident at Heathrow involving only a parked aircraft and no other vehicle did have more serious implications and resulted in the death of a ground worker and the permanent injury of another.

Both men were members of a gang working on a 4-engined Constellation airliner inside a BOAC hangar at London Airport in September 1954 when part of the undercarriage collapsed. A 35-years-old engineer was trapped and killed. The other man was pinned between the wing-tip of the 30-ton airliner after the port undercarriage partially retracted and crashed on to the platform where he was working.

Fellow-workers tried in vain to free the trapped men as fuel from a burst wing tank flooded round them. A wall of sandbags was built against the wing to soak up the petrol and mobile cranes were rushed in to lift the wing in a matter of minutes. But it was too late to save the engineer.

*

Back in the summer of 1952, twenty-nine passengers who had boarded a BEA Dakota at Northolt airport to fly to Glasgow found themselves an hour later sipping coffee just four air miles away, in a departure lounge at Heathrow.

For most of that hour the aircraft had circled, its undercarriage down, to use up fuel as fire services stood by after the pilot, Captain Hugh Morgan, had discovered a leak in their aircraft's hydraulics system. Then he called in a steward from the aircraft's galley and ordered four bottles of apple juice and one of water.

The passengers told me later that Captain Morgan told them the liquid was needed, not to quench a thirst but to top up the hydraulics to keep the pressure up. "It will ensure that our undercarriage operates when we touch down." he said, calmly. And soon after he did just that, safely and without complaint. The passengers later left again in a substitute aircraft. With a fresh supply of apple juice to restock the galley, presumably.

Just two days after reporting the wing-tip brush-off by two airliners over Paris, I was writing of an emergency landing of another BEA Elizabethan after a crew member gagged on fumes from a passenger's baggage.

The twin-engine airliner, carrying 46 passengers, was over Dieppe, France on its way to Nice when a steward noticed the fumes. He traced them to an accessible luggage hold, and finally to one suitcase. Opening the case he was almost overpowered as fumes poured out from a broken bottle containing about half a pint of ether.

Feeling ill, the steward reported to the captain, who immediately radioed Le Bourget airport Paris for landing facilities. A second aircraft later flew in from London to pick up the passengers, and the Elizabethan was flown back to London for cleaning. A spokesman for the airline said that none of the passengers had suffered ill effects, but the steward had been "nearly knocked over" when he opened the case. He'd had to shut it quickly.

An airline medical expert told me later: "The fact that the ether could be smelt in the cabin is significant, but without knowing how long the passengers or crew were exposed, it's difficult to say if there was a danger of them being overcome by the fumes.

"At the very least, however, they could have suffered nausea as they were in a confined space. The pilot was absolutely right to land so that they could be exposed to fresh air as soon as possible."

The *Daily Mail* gave the story a double column heading, with the *News Chronicle* and *Daily Express (latter not shown)* offering a respectable single column.

ETHER IN PLANE STOPS FLIGHT

Bottle breaks in luggage

By Daily Mail Reporter

FUMES of ether pouring from a broken bottle in a passenger's luggage caused a twin-engined BEA airliner with 46 passengers aboard to make an emergency landing in Paris yesterday.

While it was passing over Dieppe a steward noticed the fumes. He traced them to the luggage hold, and finally to one suitcase.

When he opened the case almost overpowering fumes poured out from a broken bottle containing about half a pint of ether.

The captain of the plane, which was flying from London to Nice, asked Le Bourget Aerodrome, Paris, for landing facilities.

Inquiry

A second airliner was sent to Paris to pick up the passengers who had to leave the "etherised" machine.

It is estimated that the cost of the emergency landing and the operation of the second machine will cost BEA about £500.

An inquiry is being made into the incident.

'Gassed' plane returns

AN airliner bound from London to Nice made an emergency landing at Paris yesterday after its 46 passengers complained of overpowering fumes.

The fumes were traced to a suitcase in the freight hold of the plane, a B.E.A. Elizabethan.

A steward discovered a broken bottle in the case. Feeling ill, he told the captain, who radioed Le Bourget Airport for landing facilities.

It cost £500

A second aircraft left London Airport to pick up the passengers. The diversion and the extra plane cost B.E.A. about £500.

An airline official said last night: "None of the passengers suffered ill effects from the fumes, but the steward was nearly knocked over when he opened the case. He had to shut it pretty smartly."

The Elizabethan was flown back to London later. It may take days to clear out the fumes.

News Chronicle (above)
Daily Mail (above left)
(both) August 14 1954

*

Every year scores of intending travellers make their way to the wrong airport for their departing flight. There are probably just as many "meeters and wavers" who make the same mistake when planning to see off or meet someone. Partly to blame is some airports' continuing lack of distinct identity, as I have illustrated earlier in these pages.

In the London area, there were at first two, and now no fewer than four major airports professing to serve the capital, plus the London City airport at its heart, all duplicating some services. In Scotland, two international airports competed for Glasgow's air traffic for many years and are trying to do so again.

But airline pilots, who should know better, have also gone astray on occasions.

There was the reported case of a British airline Captain who had made the same approach to Heathrow scores of times, yet found himself descending towards the A4 Bath Road when he mistook its street lights for the lights along the parallel No.1 main runway

Skymaster gets lost in London

News Chronicle Reporter

A FRENCH Skymaster flew from Paris to London with 37 passengers last night, then lost its way.

Given permission to land by London Airport control the pilot brought the plane down —*at Northolt, eight miles away.*

"Landed safely," he radioed. But London Airport officials were puzzled. They called back: "Put on your landing lights. We can't see you."

Then the phone rang: "Have you lost a plane? This is Northolt. We have it here."

So the wandering Skymaster took off again for London Airport 20 minutes later. Said its pilot: "I took a wrong turning. Both airports were using the same direction runway. My compass was out."

Said a passenger: "The stewardess told us London Airport was closed."

News Chronicle (both) Oct 15 1953

Plane lands at wrong airport

A FOUR-ENGINED Skymaster airliner with [illegible] people aboard on a routine flight to London Airport called up ground control there last night and asked permission to land.

This was given and the plane landed safely—at Northolt, eight miles away.

Until he reached the control room at Northolt the pilot was unaware he was on the wrong airfield.

And at London Airport officials were wondering how he had got lost on the runways.

The plane took off from Northolt and landed at London Airport 20 minutes after the pilot thought he had landed there. Said he, "I took a wrong turn."

Daily Herald

some 400 metres further south. It was only when he requested Air Traffic Control for permission to amend his flight direction and head for the runway approach that his error became clear.

Back in October 1953, when the air approach routes were considerably quieter, the captain of an Air France four-engined Douglas DC4 Skymaster with 37 passengers on board was given permission to land at London Airport on a routine flight from Paris. Moments later he touched down on the runway.

When he reported: "Landed safely," puzzled control officials at Heathrow replied, "We can't see you. Flash your lights." But there was no sign of the Skymaster. Then, in the Heathrow tower a telephone rang. It was a call from Northolt Airport, five miles to the north.

"Have you lost a Skymaster?" they asked. "We have it here."

Until he reached the control centre at Northolt the French captain was unaware he was at the wrong airport. To ground staff he explained that his gyro compass was seven degrees out, and he said: "I must have taken the wrong turning." With his passengers he took off again for Heathrow just 20 minutes later.

The *News Chronicle* and the *Daily Herald* gave the item a total of eight tucked-away column inches between them.

Seven years on, in the same month and eleven days later, an almost identical situation occurred. This time it involved a much bigger, much faster and much heavier problem, a Boeing 707 jet. I was on duty at Heathrow when word reached me that a Pan American flight from Frankfurt had touched down at Northolt by mistake.

My one-time favourite hunting ground had by now been returned to the Royal Air Force and had been closed to most civil traffic for more than five years. But I knew the officer appointed to act as Press Relations Officer there, and aware I could get quick access, I raced to my car to drive over. At the gate, I gave a guard the name, and after a moment I was clear to head straight for the airfield's south side passenger unit.

Seated at a desk in the adjoining operations room was the Pan Am pilot, Canadian-born Captain Warren Beall. I asked him what had happened and he said ruefully and resignedly: "It was an honest to goodness mistake. I was on radar approach through four-fifths cloud to land on London Airport's main runway.

"I was told to come straight in as soon as I was in line with the gasholder on the runway's approach. Unfortunately there is also a gasholder directly in line with Northolt's main runway."

The runway approaches for the two airports are similar, though only one can be seen at a time from approach path height.

"It wasn't until we actually touched down I realised something was amiss," added Captain Beall, a senior Pan Am pilot. "It was most embarrassing." He had to jam on his brakes, and apply reverse thrust to slow the airliner down. With a scream of protest from the tyres he finally brought it to a halt with only 100 yards of the 5,400ft runway remaining. Even in the 60s, Heathrow's main runway was more than 9,000ft.

After a few minutes I slipped into the passenger departure lounge where the 41 passengers waited to board coaches to complete their journey to Heathrow. One of them was Englishman Dr Douglas McLean of Durham.

"I knew we weren't landing at London Airport," he told me, and added, " In fact I said to the stewardess: 'This isn't London, it's Northolt.' But she just said: 'Oh, no, it is London. I know it well."

He added: "I offered to bet her a dollar it wasn't. But she just said she didn't have a dollar."

A little later the passengers, their luggage unloaded, boarded coaches for the 20-minute drive to Heathrow. And Captain Beall took off too, with his Boeing jet and his ten-strong crew, for his originally-intended destination. Scores of RAF personnel lined the apron to watch the aircraft, the biggest ever seen at Northolt at that time, quickly lift off, using every available inch of the runway. I joined the sightseers... and was pictured in

707 jetliner drops in by mistake

CAPTAIN WARREN BEALL got his gasholders mixed up yesterday—and landed his giant Boeing 707 jetliner with 41 round-the-world passengers at the wrong airfield.

BY ROBERT CUNNINGHAM

He should have brought Pan American's Flight No. 1—Istanbul to New York via Frankfort — into London Airport.

Instead he swept in over the heads of startled Service men nine miles away at R.A.F. Station, Northolt, an airfield closed to civilian traffic since 1954.

Then he climbed down, admitting sheepishly: "Most embarrassing — an honest-to-goodness mistake" and blamed the gasholders.

Vancouver-born Captain Beall, one of Pan American's senior captains, has flown into London scores of times. He was in cloud and under radar-control from the London tower as he began his approach.

Beneath the cloud it was a bright, sunny afternoon. And the controller, said the Captain gave his final instruction: "Come straight in as soon as you are in line with the gasholder"

In line

The controller meant the Southall gasholder, a London Airport landmark for pilots. It is directly in line with the Airport's main runway

But nine miles away is another gasholder, directly in line with the Northolt runway, and parallel to London Airport's. That was the one Captain Beall saw as the big Boeing broke cloud

Without hesitation he brought his 130-ton jet over the quiet R.A.F. station's boundary, set her down—and at once realised his mistake

With less than 1,800 yards of tarmac ahead—about two-thirds the length of his London runway—he braked hard and switched the four jet engines of the 707 to reverse thrust to slow it further.

The jet shrieked towards the chequered control caravan at the runway's end, and stopped with 100 yards to spare. Out from the Naafi came a crowd of incredulous airmen.

No bets

"This isn't London," said passenger Dr. Douglas McLean, of Durham. "Of course it is," said the stewardess—but turned down a dollar bet on it.

And within a few minutes Pan American was sending coaches to Northolt to carry the passengers and their luggage to London Airport.

Just over two hours later Captain Beall made a perfect take-off with his empty plane—to derisive cheers from the Servicemen and muttering from the motorists who had been held up in nearby Western-avenue in case things went wrong.

This time Captain Beall found London Airport And last night he was on his way back to the States for an inquiry—as a passenger in his own plane.

Daily Mail

BOEING LANDS BY MISTAKE

Express Staff Reporter

JUST as his wheels touched down yesterday the horrified pilot of a Boeing 707 jet airliner from Frankfort realised that he was landing at the WRONG airport—one not designed to take such huge aircraft.

He had mistaken Northolt, almost disused by civil planes, for London Airport, five miles away.

He jammed on his brakes. There was a terrific howl from the tyres and the blue and white plane finally ground to a stop with 100 yards of the 5,400ft. runway left.

After engineers had examined the Boeing it took off with its 10 crew for the flip to London Airport.

Its passengers went on by coach.

Police set up two road blocks in Western-avenue, bordering the airport. And hundreds of rush-hour cars and lorries were halted as the airliner, of Pan American Airways, thundered over at the end of the runway.

AN ERROR

The drama for Northolt and people living round about began when Canadian-born Captain Warren Beall lined up his aircraft on the wrong gasholder.

He said later: "It was an honest to goodness mistake. I was on radar approach through four-fifths cloud to land on London Airport's main runway.

"I was told to come straight in as soon as I was in line with the gasholder on the runway's approach

"Unfortunately there is a gasholder directly in line with Northolt's main runway—and that's exactly parallel to London Airport. It wasn't until we actually touched down I realised something was amiss.

"It was most embarrassing."

It was the biggest shock in years for operations men at Northolt. Said a spokesman: "The captain was flying directly into the sun and his mistake was very easy to make."

Safely up again—the 707

Wing-Commander Anthony Payne, Northolt's commanding officer, said: "I think this must be the biggest thing we've ever had in here. Our chaps in the control tower knew nothing about it until it came haring down the runway towards them."

A ROAR

Mr. Charles Evans, manager of a garage hard by the airport, said last night: "The Boeing made a terrible roar as it passed over our garage, and everybody rushed out to see what on earth was coming in."

One of the passengers, Dr. Douglas McLean, of Durham, said: "I knew we weren't landing at London Airport. In fact, I said to the stewardess: 'This isn't London, it's Northolt.' But she just said: 'Oh, no, it is London.'"

A BET

He added: "I offered to bet her a dollar it wasn't. But she just said she didn't have a dollar."

Daily Express (both) Oct 26 1960

From a safe distance your intrepid reporter sees off the unexpected visitor.
Daily Express picture by George Stroud

silhouette watching the take-off by *Daily Express* photographer George Stroud who had followed me over to Northolt.

Captain Beall was met at Heathrow by Pan Am officials who told him he had been ordered back to New York to report on the incident at an inquiry.

The Northolt visit was recorded officially a few months later when the then Air Ministry arranged for a message to pilots to be printed in huge letters on the side of the gasholder. The letters read "NO" – not a tongue-in-cheek negative to pilots who might ask "Is this Heathrow?" but simply part of an official RAF navigation code for "Northolt."

The gasholder at South Harrow in West London disappeared in the 1990s. A supermarket now stands on the site. No more need to say "No."

*

As if we hadn't enough to occupy us at Heathrow, in September 1955 I found myself reporting on another "away" incident, this time almost fifty miles away on the other side of London. Thanks to a 'phone call from a friend there I learnt that a twin engined Viking airliner of the independent airline BKS, carrying 36 homeward-bound holidaymakers from Majorca, had struck a tree on the fringe of Southend Airport as it came in to land.

The pilot immediately lifted the damaged aircraft clear and after calling for a full emergency decided to divert to Heathrow – where I was waiting to complete the story. Happily no one aboard was injured. The Viking made a safe landing, but an inspection

AIRLINER, 41 ABOARD, STRIKES TREE ON FRINGE OF AIRPORT

Pilot flies on to London, lands safely

A twin-engined Viking airliner carrying 36 holidaymakers home from Majorca struck a tree on the fringe of Southend Airport as it was landing there today. The pilot lifted his damaged airplane clear and decided to fly on to London Airport after calling for a full emergency.

Fire engines and crash tenders stood by at London Airport.

But the airliner, owned by BKS, an independent airline, landed safely.

Neither passengers nor the crew of five were injured.

Inspection of the aircraft showed that part of the port wing had been dented by the impact.

Evening Standard (both) Sept 19 1958

Holiday Airliner with 41 Aboard Hits Tree

A TWIN-ENGINED Viking airliner carrying 36 homeward-bound holidaymakers from Majorca in the Mediterranean struck a tree on the edge of Southend Airport as it was landing there early to-day.

Evening News

revealed that part of a wing had been dented by the impact. The two-airport story won treble and double-column headings for me in the *Evening Standard* and the *Evening News.*

*

With the majority of aircraft disasters, such as the Comet 1 catastrophes, inevitably occurring overseas, it often fell to us to report only the echoes and repercussions in the UK. We repeatedly witnessed sad airport scenes at UK airport arrivals terminals as families and friends of victims turned up, desperately seeking information about reported accidents. We stood by sympathetically as airline ground staff faced the unenviable task of having to tell parents or grandparents of the tragic loss of son and daughters, wives or husbands, even of children and grandchildren. And this was often only after the visitors had made innocent but puzzled enquiries about an apparently delayed arrival, or prayed for good news about a lost flight they had seen departing from the UK earlier.

I have already expressed my dismay, earlier in these pages, at having to report aviation tragedies and I was thankful not to have been involved with some major disasters over the years, among them the Manchester United crash in February, 1958 and the loss of the Trident "Papa India" at Staines, near Heathrow in 1972.

Seven players and three team officials of the world famous team were among 21 passengers who died when the BEA Elizabethan airliner crashed in a snowstorm at Munich airport on take-off for London. The specially chartered airliner had earlier flown in from Belgrade where the team had drawn 3-3 with a Yugoslav team in a European Cup match. Other victims included one member of the cabin crew and seven news media sports correspondents.

Team manager Matt Busby survived, but lay critically ill in hospital for some weeks before finally recovering. He too was well known not only for his Manchester role, but also as Scotland's World Cup team manager. But this did not stop one leading British "quality" newspaper misspelling his name in both in their front page story and a sub-heading.

Floral tributes placed at Old Trafford Football Ground on the 50th anniversary of the Munich disaster, February 6 2008.

Photographer unknown; posted uncredited on public tribute site at www.redcafe.net

The Staines disaster occurred one Sunday afternoon in June 1972, when I was taking a day off and enjoying an afternoon nap in my caravan. All 118 passengers and crew on board a Trident jet died when it dived to the ground just after take-off from Heathrow, the worst aircraft disaster in British aviation history at that time.

Although it was only a few miles away, I knew nothing of it until hearing the news on the radio early next day, and had no part in reporting either the accident or the follow-up revelations. These showed that slats on the leading edge of the airliner's wings had been retracted too soon after take-off, causing it to stall.

I have also already referred briefly in Chapter 11 to the disaster of the Viking airliner "Papa Mike," which crashed into a Norwegian mountain in the summer of 1961. Thirty four British schoolboys were among the 39 passengers and crew who lost their lives. The airliner had been specially chartered by a Croydon school, and had left Heathrow one August afternoon to fly the boys and two teachers on a holiday trip to a youth hostel near Stavanger.

Later it was learnt that the Viking, which also carried a crew of three, had run into a severe storm on its approach to its destination airport at Stavanger when ground contact with it was suddenly lost. Immediately a 15-hour search was undertaken, but it was dawn before a helicopter spotted wreckage on the side of the 1,700ft mountain. There were no survivors, and many of the victims were found still strapped in their seats in the broken-off fuselage.

Again we could only report on the scenes at Heathrow, where airline staff spent hour after hour on international telephone lines seeking news from Norwegian authorities. Colleague Chris Bramwell and I were kept constantly on our toes as snippets of information were passed to us by staff and officials and as one by one the next of kin of victims in front of us were given the sad news and confirmation they dreaded to hear.

National and evening newspapers reported the disaster with full page spreads the following day, with graphic accounts from the scene in Norway. Somewhere among the scores of column inches were the hundreds of words Chris and I had contributed. To this day I haven't been able to analyse the value of that contribution. To do so seems both irrelevant, and irreverent.

Considering the flying distance between Britain and the western seaboard of the USA, it might be thought strange that comparatively few mid-flight incidents have occurred over what is almost entirely over open sea-water. Perhaps the explanation is that we failed to hear of them, or that we weren't responsible for reporting them.

I did report one case, back in 1958, when a the pilot of a Douglas DC7C of Pan American Airways radioed an SOS from mid-Atlantic to report engine trouble. We learnt that an RAF Shackleton had immediately taken off from Ballykelly, in Northern Ireland, and was on its way to meet the airliner, which was carrying 32 passengers.

The 350mph four-engined American airliner sent out its distress call when it was five hours out from London on a polar flight from San Francisco. Later a radio call from the Shackleton reported that it was alongside, and would escort the DC7C for the rest of its flight, and ships on the route were notified. Land-based radio stations kept a constant alert for further messages from the two aircraft.

At Heathrow airport emergency services stood by as the airline reported "All we know is that one propeller has been feathered. We expect it to make a three-engine landing."

The hours passed, and I had to hand over to a colleague to report that eventual safe landing. I can't recall any undue concern on the part of airport authorities. We were well aware that three-engine landings are normally routine, but we also knew that the safety procedures had to be followed. My story made a Page One lead in *The Star* that day, *(see over)* a lead which I believe was, however, down-graded to a paragraph or two for the late editions.

In Scotland, on a Sunday evening in September 1962 just four years later, I was alerted to what appeared to be a similar situation. At first, the news that a chartered Super Constellation airliner had radioed a failure of one of its four engines over the Atlantic didn't sound too serious. But just 60 minutes later the first SOS was followed by the despairing call "I am preparing to ditch."

What could have been a routine emergency developed into one of the biggest and

Monday, May 12, 1958 STAR NEWS DESK : FLE 5000

THE STAR

No 21.753 ** 2½d

LATE NIGHT

AIRLINER SOS IN MID-OCEAN: RAF PLANE OUT TO THE RESCUE

The Star
(Page One lead)
May 12 1954

Engine failure: 32 aboard

Star Reporter

AN AMERICAN AIRLINER WITH 32 PEOPLE ON BOARD SENT OUT AN SOS OVER THE ATLANTIC TODAY.

At once an RAF Shackleton took off from Ballykelly, in Ireland, and flew out to meet the liner.

Later it radioed that it was alongside and would escort the liner on its journey.

The aircraft, a Douglas DC 7C four-engined 350 mph plane, sent out its distress call when it was five hours away from London—over mid-Atlantic.

It stated it had engine trouble.

At once ships were notified by wireless.

Radio stations kept a constant listening watch for further messages from the liner and its escorting Shackleton.

The liner, which was flying the Polar route from San Francisco, belongs to Pan American Airways.

Emergency services at London Airport were warned to stand by.

The liner was expected to land on three engines.

A spokesman for the air line said, "All we know is that one propeller has been feathered."

Among the crew of seven are two air hostesses.

picture by Jon Proctor, www.JetPhotos.net

An example of the Pan Am DC-7C Seven Seas "Clipper Ganges N747PA"

most dramatic mid-Atlantic rescue bids of all time, an operation involving a number of search aircraft and an international fleet of more than a dozen ships. They included vessels ranging from a Canadian aircraft carrier and its five escorting destroyers to ocean-going liners and assorted merchantmen, a weather ship and coastguard cutters.

The search and rescue operation was to continue throughout that night and most of the following day. It was to make evening and daily front page headlines on both sides of the Atlantic and scores of column inches around the world

The Flying Tigers Airlines Super Constellation, operating a service on behalf of the US Air Force, was carrying a total of 76 people, mainly US servicemen on their way back to bases in Europe, and some dependents. That first routine May-day call was logged at 9.29pm by the Scottish air traffic control centre at Prestwick.

Within minutes an RAF Shackleton of Coastal Command had left St Mawgan, Cornwall, to escort the airliner to the UK if possible. A USAF C54 Rescuemaster aircraft had also taken off from its base at the Scottish transatlantic airport. It reached the scene as the crippled airliner dived into the sea some 500 miles off the western Irish coast following the failure of two more of its four engines. But the Rescuemaster's pilot radioed: "Visibility is poor, and I didn't see the airliner go down. Gales are strong and waves are 10 feet high".

During those same 60 minutes I had driven back to the airport I had earlier left after a full working day. I headed directly to the USAF base on the northern side of the main runway, where I was directed to the military operations room.

The previous day my colleague Chris had left for London on holiday. I would be working on my own for the next couple of weeks, as reporter, sub-editor and copy reader combined, as on this occasion simple economics meant I didn't have the luxury of a stand-in from Heathrow. The next 18 hours were to seriously test my stamina.

In the ops room I joined several other reporters from the local offices of Scottish national newspapers, some of who had already filed their initial stories, though I was in time for the early updates on the situation at sea. But the base had become a principle nerve centre for the rescue operations and the reporters were having to take turns in the use of the only telephone the Air Force commander could spare for the media. When I told him, quite truthfully, that in view of the overwhelming media presence, my prime responsibility was to serve the British news agencies and *American* wire services however, he became conspiratorial.

"Come with me," he said, and led me along the corridor to his own office. "You won't be disturbed here," he added. I reinforced that assurance by quietly turning the key in the lock as he returned to the ops room. I was able to return to my "private" 'phone several times during the long night and day ahead, by keeping the key in my pocket… for safety of course.

It was clear that there was no possibility of "exclusives" about this operation. All the news media were getting the same information from the authorities at the same time, whether at Prestwick or any of half-a-dozen news centres co-ordinating reports across two continents. Scottish newspapers were well represented, so I decided not to try to be competitive and to concentrate on Brenards' main news markets in London, including the news agencies I'd already mentioned as my "keyword."

Prestwick Airport featured strongly in the news reports of the search and rescue. We were given an eye-witness report by Lieut. Bill Trippe, 28-years-old commander of the Rescuemaster when he flew back to Prestwick the following day and by 25-years-old Lt Joseph Lewis, pilot of a USAF C118 transport, who had himself been flying 15 American service families from Prestwick.

Trippe had been in constant touch with the first ship on the scene, the Swiss merchantman Celerina. It had approached several life-rafts with survivors on board, but reported difficulty in picking them up because of the high seas. He said he had been able to drop flares of one million candle power over the area until the ships was able to pick out the rafts with its searchlight. Lt Lewis picked up the "ditching" call just minutes from the scene, and was able to pin-point it precisely for ships in the area. Eventually 49 people were saved from the raging sea, including nine women. Eleven bodies were recovered, and two others sighted, leaving 14 unaccounted for.

My decision to lean on my London news desk, and serve only national markets helped, as it would have been too time consuming to try to feed already well-covered Scottish media. Both London evening newspapers (*The Star* had by this time been combined with the *Evening News*) carried large chunks of my copy channelled through Brenards in London, as did newspapers across the States from New York to San Francisco, via the *Associated Press* and *British United Press International* wire services.

'Sea Lit Up Like Big City' As Families Cling To Life

51 SAFE! AND MORE SIGHTED ON RAFT

Survivors Stand On Life-Rafts And Wave

"Evening News" Reporter

Parachute Doctors Fly Out To Help

"EVENING NEWS" REPORTER

MORE THAN A DOZEN SHIPS SAILED THROUGH A GALE IN MID-ATLANTIC TO-DAY IN ONE OF THE MOST INCREDIBLE RESCUE OPERA-

FOUR GIRLS IN THE CREW

THE captain and pilot of the airliner was John D. Murray, aged 44, who has a wife

Evening News & Star *Sept 24 1962*

The *Evening News* **and** *Star* **(now a combined newspaper) ran a huge optimistic banner headline, partly shown here, as did the** *Evening Standard* **among others** *(see over).*

Evening Standard

43,007 MONDAY, SEPTEMBER 24, 1962 ●●3d.

76 on rafts face 10 feet waves as mercy fleet sails to rescue

ATLANTIC MIRACLE! 50 SAVED IN SEA HELL

Evening Standard (above) (part Page One lead) Sept 24 1962

76 down in the Atlantic face 10 feet waves on rafts

50 SAVED—MERCY FLEET SEARCHES ON

Race starts to get doctors to the injured survivors

Evening Standard (left) Front Page (reduced) earlier edition 24 Sept 1962

"Flying Tiger Flight 923" picture courtesy of crash survivor F. Caruso, www.carusogroup.com

One of the most dramatic rescue operations of all time today saved 50 air-crash survivors from the Atlantic. Their life-rafts were being tossed by 10-ft. waves as rescue ships and planes closed in.

There were 76 people—including two children — aboard the Super-Constellation when it came down in darkness after three engines failed one by one.

Latest reports say more survivors have been picked up, in addition to the official figure of 50. "Many of the survivors are injured," said an Admiralty spokesman in London.

Two bodies have been found so far.

Ships and aircraft joined in a giant rescue operation after the airliner came down.

'IT'S LIKE A BIG CITY DOWN THERE'

As aircraft circled low overhead, dropping flares to light the dark Atlantic, two ships reached the scene.

They were the Swiss ship **Celerina** and the Cunard ship **Andania**.

A PILOT WHO FLEW OVERHEAD REPORTED: "THE SEA BELOW IS ILLUMINATED BY LIGHTS. IT'S LIKE A BIG CITY."

Dashing to the crash area, at full speed, are the 34,000-ton Cunard liner **Mauretania** (it has full hospital facilities aboard), the Canadian aircraft carrier **Bonaventure**, and five Canadian destroyers, two British merchant ships, the **Iron Age** and the **Manchester Progress**, and the West German ship **Transatlantic**.

THE VIGIL IN THE SKY...

Keeping a vigil in the cloudy sky above the crash area are two U.S. four-engined **Rescuemasters**, three amphibian **Albatrosses**, a U.S. patrol aircraft and three RAF **Shackletons.**

By the light of flares they searched the sea for more survivors.

It was still dark over the Atlantic and the Albatrosses could not land on the sea until daylight.

The Rescuemasters dropped huge rafts containing medical survival kit—rafts big enough to hold 20 people.

The 68 passengers aboard the Constellation, owned by the Flying Tiger company of America, were U.S. army

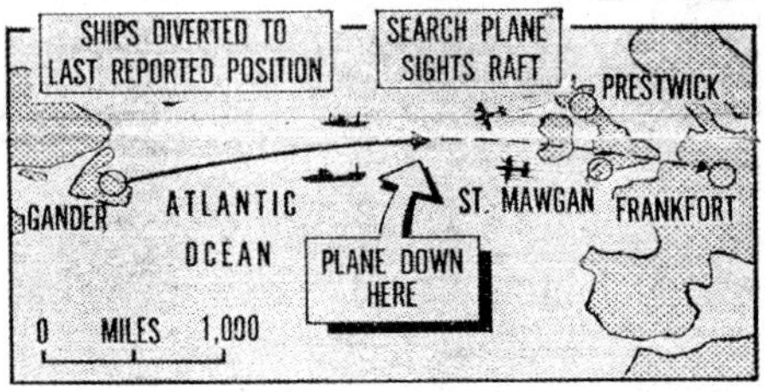

personnel and their families—including two children—flying from the United States to Frankfurt.

Three hostesses were among the crew of eight.

The first SOS from the captain, John D. Murray, 44, said one engine had cut out. Then came a message that a second engine had failed. His third message, received at the RAF air traffic control at Prestwick, reported the loss of a third engine. Then the captain radioed he was going to ditch because he had seen some shipping.

This was the timetable of the crash and the rescue:

5.10 A.M.—Super Constellation takes off at Gander, Newfoundland, for Shannon at 2 a.m.

9.29 P.M.—Prestwick Airport gets S.O.S. one engine feathered.

9.59 P.M.—SC-54 rescue airplane leaves Prestwick.

10.05 P.M.—Airliner reports second engine out of action.

10.30 P.M.—Third engine out of action.

11 P.M.—Airliner now 650 miles north-west of Shannon. Radios "Preparing to ditch in Atlantic.

11.10 P.M. — RAF Shackleton from Cornwall and U.S. Skymaster diverted to Constellation's last reported position.

11.13 P.M.—U.S. military C118 airplane contacts Super Constellation.

11.23 P.M.—Super Constellation hits sea.

11.30 P.M.—C118 bound for New York reports sighting a raft.

MIDNIGHT. — Three amphibious U.S. rescue airplanes alerted to leave Prestwick to reach area at dawn.

1.45 A.M.—Shackleton and Skymaster reach crash area.

2.46 A.M.—SC-54 rescue airplane from Prestwick arrives over area and joins other airplanes.

4 A.M.—C118 short of buel after circling crash spot for five hours giving radio "fix" returns to Prestwick.

5.30 A.M.—Celerina begins picking up survivors.

6.30 A.M.—C118 arrives Prestwick and pilot tells how passengers acted as spotters

7.15 A.M.—Radio message confirms that survivors have been picked up.

8.50 A.M.—Airplanes report that 50 people have

● **Back Page, Col. Four**

Evening Standard (above, and picture, right) earlier edition 24 Sept 1962

More survivors are spotted

From Evening Standard Reporters in Prestwick, Shannon, , St Mawgan, the Admiralty, Toronto, New York; and from Reuter, A.P., B.U.P., and Press Association despatches.

New hope in the mid-Atlantic miracle came tonight as planes from the Canadian aircraft carrier Bonaventure radioed they had spotted more survivors on a life raft in the Atlantic.

The carrier radioed: "We are hopeful of finding more survivors."

Earlier this afternoon the carrier had rendezvoused with the Swiss freighter **Celerina** which had snatched 50 air-crash survivors from a "sea hell."

Many of the survivors **are injured.** The Celerina radioed to the carrier reporting she was overcrowded with survivors and lacking medical facilities.

With the carrier is the Canadian destroyer **Athabaskan.**

Six tracker aircraft from the Bonaventure are searching for the 26 airlines passengers still missing.

The Celerina has asked that some of the survivors be moved to the aircraft-carrier.

Evening Standard (above) Sept 24 1962

Canadian aircraft carrier Bonaventure (*above*) joins the rescue mission.

MIRACLE OF THE SEA

49 live after plane dives in the Atlantic

Daily Herald (Page One Lead) and inside spread (below) Sep 25 1962

By FRANK DAWES and WILLIAM JENKINS

FORTY-NINE survivors of the Super-Constellation airliner which plunged into the icy, storm-swept Atlantic were aboard the Canadian aircraft carrier Bonaventure today heading for Shannon.

But hope faded for 21 other passengers—including two children—still missing.

Six bodies—including one woman—have been picked up by rescue ships.

It was a fantastic feat by the airliner's captain, John Murray, which saved disaster.

FEATHERED

The airliner was carrying 59 U.S. Servicemen, wives and children to Frankfurt, Germany when three of its four engines "feathered" and it was forced to ditch

Said the pilot of an R A F rescue plane: "There were waves 10ft. high

...this front-page article *(cropped)* **was expanded on an inside page** *(see right)***...**

'I SEE PEOPLE—AND THEY ARE ALIVE'

By STEWART MacLACHLAN

THE survivors of the crashed American Constellation airliner were plucked from almost certain death in mid-Atlantic yesterday—thanks to the skill and perseverance of one young pilot.

Air crews returning to Prestwick from the rescue operation last night paid tribute to 28-year-old Lieutenant Joseph K. Lewis, of Tuscoloosa, Alabama—"the man who saved the day."

For Lieutenant Lewis, pilot of a U.S. Military Air Transport Service C 118 rendezvoused with the Flying Tiger Constellation—carrying 76 people—shortly before it ditched in the Atlantic 540 miles from Ireland.

And Lieutenant Lewis orbited over the crash area for five hours, enabling air and sea rescue teams to have a spot-on bearing on the life rafts carrying the survivors.

Lieutenant Lewis, a boyish-faced father of a two-year-old baby girl, said last night: "We were flying from Paris to Newfoundland via Prestwick.

"En route to Harmon Base we got a call from a Flying Tiger aircraft that they were in distress. We intercepted him and we intended to escort him back to Shannon. Two of his engines had feathered, and he was in trouble.

"Then a third engine went 'dis' and he had to dive. At this time we were out of visual contact with him because of cloud, and we did not see him again—until we spotted the rafts.

"I estimate there were 10 minutes between the aircraft ditching and us seeing the life rafts.

"It was luck—but it was goddam lucky luck.

"We circled for five hours giving out location bearings until our fuel forced us to return to Prestwick."

Slim, modest, crew-cutted Lieutenant Lewis, spoke of the calm, almost unreal conversations he had with 44-year-old Captain John Murray, captain of the stricken Constellation. "He was calm, collected and knew what to do. He did it."

HE SAVED THE DAY

THE first of the air rescue crews of the 63rd Air Rescue Squadron returned to their base at Prestwick a few hours later.

Lieutenant Bill Trippe, aged 28, of Baltimore, captain of the Rescuemaster, said: "That MATS C 118 saved the day. That young pliot took hours off the rescue operation—and God knows how many lives he saved.

"When we reached the area shortly before the MATS aircraft left we could see numerous small lights—lights from rafts. It was cloudy and pretty dark. The sea was pretty mean.

"We were circling about when suddenly one of the crew shouted: 'I see people—and they're alive.'

"I asked them if they were sure—and they said they were definite. That was the best news I had heard in a long, long time.

"RAF Shackletons kept company with us and circled low on to the sea, dropping one million candle power flares which enabled us to spot three rafts.

"A Swiss ship, the Celerena, was about forty miles away and we guided her to the spot by radio.

(all) Sep 25 1962

THE BEWILDERED 49

FIRST DRAMATIC MESSAGE

Survivors are all cheerful

Scottish Daily Mail

The *UP* city desk later 'phoned Brenards to thank us for our contributions with a "Good work" comment and the *Evening News* said: "Well done!"

In later editions, the *Evening Standard* accredited their coverage to their *"...own reporters in Shannon, Prestwick, St Mawgan, the Admiralty, Toronto and New York; and from Reuter, AP, BUP and Press Association despatches."*

Of course, my total contribution, measured in the percentage of headlines and column inches, hardly compensated for the time and effort expended. It wasn't by any means the only occasion that I wondered if the effort had been really justified.

*

Here and there throughout these pages I have slipped into the aviation vernacular of referring to individual civil aircraft by a phonetic representation of their registration codes. In most countries – a notable exception is the USA – the registration is represented by a letter or letters identifying the operator's nationality, followed by other letters individual to each aircraft. For ease of radio and verbal communication such registrations are often shortened to the final two letters.

The use of phonetic spelling of difficult names and words probably began with Alexander Graham Bell more than a hundred years ago. Later, in World War 1, poor communications with the battle front may have led to the first widespread use of phonetic alphabets. But it took another world war and the following emergence of mass civil air travel to formalise a wide variety in such aids.

The current internationally-recognised phonetic representation of aircraft codes, based on the English language, was drawn up (not without some criticism of illogical choices) in the mid-1950s. The registrations do nothing to help the average observer identify a particular aircraft by type or airline, although dedicated collectors of such data, aware of the history and allocation of particular sequences of letters, might dispute that.

The combination of letters in aircraft registration can often represent something more personal to the owner or operator, as with "cherished" car licence plates. Some have been chosen just for fun such as the UK registrations G-GEES, G-HOST or G-IANT, G-IDDY or G-IPSY. Sometimes by association or circumstance, others have achieved a special significance…

*

I was sitting at the bedside of my then wife, Jill, as she lay recovering from a major operation at West London's Harefield Hospital when a voice screeched: *"Ooh, look! That's you…!"*

The cry came from a fellow-patient in the adjoining bed behind my chair. She was propped up on one elbow staring past us watching a television set at the end of the ward. I half turned to look over my shoulder and followed her wide-eyed gaze.

There, on the huge projection screen, was a larger-than-life black and white stills picture of me earnestly scribbling in a notebook as I listened to a tale told by two stoical fur-clad Englishwomen. The three of us were standing on a rain-swept concrete taxiway at Heathrow. They were under a shared umbrella. I wore a soaked cloth cap which, with the raised collar of my belted raincoat did nothing to stop the rain pouring down my neck. The television sound had been turned down – but we could just make out the voice of a BBC newsreader describing the scene at the airport earlier that day.

Moments before the photograph was taken, the two women, Ena Bailey from London, and her friend, Norah Keenan, from Harrogate, Yorkshire, had been on their way to Rome. They were among passengers aboard a British European Airways Viscount airliner which crashed at Heathrow before it had even reached the threshold of the take-off runway.

In the gloom of low cloud and poor visibility, the turbo-prop airliner had taken the wrong turning on to another, disused runway. It had then ploughed through a five-foot high steel barrier at more than sixty miles an hour.

The airliner's nose-wheel and main undercarriage were completely sheared off. Two of its four engines were torn from their wing mountings and hurled aside. The Viscount belly-flopped on to its fuselage and skidded across the concrete for more than a hundred yards before slicing through a four-wheel trailer vehicle and a stack of steel girders. It demolished a contractor's tool shed, then spun completely round, finally slewing to a halt facing the way it had come.

Severely shaken by the impact, the two women, along with twenty-nine other passengers and aircrew, had nevertheless been able to step directly to the ground through their aircraft's shattered doorway. Two of the passengers were slightly hurt in the accident, but the pilot, Captain Eric Waits, was detained overnight in hospital.

This was January 1955. Only weeks earlier BEA had switched its operations from nearby Northolt airport to the prefabricated buildings of the old north side terminal at Heathrow. The opening of the airport's new central terminal, with its first permanent passenger building, now Terminal 2, still some months away.

The Viscount had moved out from the aircraft stands alongside the old terminal and turned right on to the taxiway which ran parallel to the No.1 northern runway. The airport control tower, also then on the north side of the airport, instructed Captain Waits to continue westwards to what was then the end of the perimeter track and turn on to Runway 6 for take-off. This runway, running south-east/north-west, formed part of the Star of David pattern of runways which existed at Heathrow at that time.

But in the gloom of low cloud and rain Captain Waits turned left too soon, on to the threshold of what had been a parallel runway, No.3, recently closed as part of the redevelopment of the central area. Given permission to take-off – there was then no ground radar at the airport, and the Viscount was no longer visible to controllers in the tower – he revved his engines and gathering speed, began his take-off run.

He saw the obstruction in his path too late. The Viscount rammed the steel barrier just as Captain Waits slammed on his brakes and cut his turbo-prop engines.

The screech of metal being torn to shreds, the scream of brakes, the howl of protesting engines and the repeated crashing and grinding as they were torn from their wing sockets alerted us all, even in the enclosed walls of the barrack-like prefabricated passengers buildings. Along with airline ground staff, who only too quickly had established for me which flight and aircraft had been involved, I raced outside to attempt to peer in vain through the gloom to the distant central terminal area.

Back inside, I hurriedly called my news desk with a flash for circulation. *"Possible casualties but no confirmation,"* I added in a note for newspaper news desks. Then: "I'm on my way there," as I dashed off to my second-hand '49 Ford Anglia parked alongside the terminal's main entrance.

After racing to the scene through the tunnel, recently completed but not yet in public use, I had found the passengers from the Viscount waiting in the teeming rain to be "rescued." All around was strewn the twisted remains of the engines and undercarriage, intermingled with builders' detritus and equipment, creating a huge metal scrap yard right at the centre of the airport, in full view of the nearby control tower. I found the two women standing to one side, sheltering together under their one umbrella.

Calmly and quietly, as if talking about a film they had seen on a recent visit to the cinema, the women told me how the cabin crew had taken charge as soon as they realised the aircraft had been in a severe collision. The steward called out to the passengers to keep their seats as one of the stewardesses operated an emergency door release. "Then we found ourselves just stepping out on to firm ground," said Mrs Bailey. "It was just like stepping off a bus."

For several minutes we talked, the women telling me of the shock of the impact seconds after the airliner had picked up speed. Their view from the oval-shaped window alongside their seats was almost totally obscured by the driving rain and low visibility. "We seemed to swerve violently to one side after this violent grinding noise," said her friend, adding: "Then we appeared to drop suddenly and the whole aircraft swung round again as if we were on a turntable. And there were more crashes and bumps before we came to a complete stop. Then everything went suddenly quiet, and the lights went out.

"Everyone just sat there, without moving. There was no sign of panic – we were all too stunned. Everything happened so quickly. Then the crew took charge."

From the corner of my eye I could see that a bus had pulled up some sixty yards away and other passengers were being guided aboard. I pointed my two women in the right direction and managed to hurry away. Now I would have to make my way back to the terminal and if possible ahead of them, wherever they were being driven. But I also had to try to find the Captain of the flight or at least a crew member – and get to a 'phone.

Passing the tail-plane I casually glanced up at the registration of the aircraft painted on its fuselage. I had learnt the usefulness of using the last two registration letters in news stories and conversations with airport staff who use them regularly in referring to individual aircraft. The Viscount's registration, I noted, ended in "OK." Ignoring the irony, I quickly scribbled down the phonetic "*O*bo King" for reference (this was before international standardisation was to introduce the substitute "*O*scar *K*ilo"). Then, in a classic double-take, I immediately turned back to look again. And I saw that for once the phonetics were unnecessary.

PA-Reuters picture, Jan 16 1955

Two stoical Englishwomen face up to dismal weather to tell me calmly how, minutes earlier, they had stepped from a crashed airliner at Heathrow.
In the gloom of low cloud and poor visibility, their Rome-bound Viscount airliner had tried to take off from a runway closed for redevelopment of the airport's cenrtal area. The airliner collided with waist-high steel barriers which sheered off its undercarriage.

The official, full, registration of the Viscount which had lost its way, I realised, was…G-AMOK.

Getting back to the Northside with my notes was going to take me far longer in reality than it did in writing here. Police or airport operations staff, or both, had decided to restrict access to the crash site and had closed the gateways in otherwise impenetrable wire barriers on my way back. Now I would have to do a wide circuit even to return to my car which I could just glimpse through the fence a couple of hundred yards away.

Some 20 minutes later, on the far side of the construction area, I finally found another

Courtesy of www.vickersviscount.net

Another registration in the sequence, G-AMOI, can be seen below on the tailfin of a British European Airways Viscount, photographed at Heathrow carrying Winston Churchill in 1955

route out from my "pen" and after wearily trudging back to the car, returned to the north terminal. I called my newsroom and hurriedly dictated some opening words to follow my earlier flash.

As I spoke, I was interrupted to be told that two colleagues were also on the story, and had beaten me by some fifteen minutes. One was already standing by to dictate his closing "add." All I could do was to withdraw gracefully and ask my copy-taker to pass on my hard-won quotes, for what they were now worth.

The quotes failed to see the light of day. And neither did my reference to the Viscount which had run, *Gee, amok…* It seems that not one of my colleagues had been aware of the prop-jet airliner's registration. And, of course in operational parlance it was only referred to then as *"Viscount Obo King ."*

There was one final twist to the tale of phonetic shorthand.

Two or three years after the Viscount's expensive adventure, the registration letters of another airliner, this time a four-engined Bristol Britannia of BOAC, had its own moment of glory. It was suddenly taken out of service, "re-licensed" and given a new, out of sequence, registration number. And all because I had given some publicity in the national press to comments by the airline's own staff about the old one.

In January 1958 the Britannia "Bravo Golf" (as it would be known today) had been provided to fly the Prime Minister of the day, Harold Macmillan, back to London after an official Commonwealth visit. As I returned to the terminal from his brief press conference, two BOAC passenger officers called me over. "Did you notice the registration of the PM's aircraft?" asked one. Before I could say I hadn't, his colleague answered with a grin: "His Government's all no bloody good – the aircraft says so."

Pressed by the first speaker, I went back outside to see for myself. Just as the two claimed, the registration read: *"G-ANBG."*

I wondered what BOAC would think of it all, and called their London press office. A senior spokesman was horrified, but not for the obvious reason. "How childish can you get?" he demanded. "Haven't you anything more serious to write about?" When I told him that it was two of his airline's own staff, hardly children, who had brought the matter to my attention, he hung up.

Two months later the same spokesman strongly denied that BOAC had bowed to the pressure of disparaging remarks and taken the unusual step of applying for a new registration "It would be so unusual" he said. "We've heard stories like this before. They've never been true."

This time it was. The new registration: the harmless *"G-ANLL"* – Lima, Lima. Or perhaps *Laugh, Laugh?* Or just *Lampoon, Lampoon?*

The *Sunday Pictorial* was amused enough to run the story across four columns.

Mac's plane NBG—so its number is up

PIC NEWS SNACK BAR

IT wasn't very respectful—the way some people referred to the Britannia airliner that brought Mr. Macmillan home from his Commonwealth trip.

For the Britannia's registration number was G-ANBG. And when the Prime Minister came in to land, airport staff were heard to say: "Here comes Government—all N.B.G."

The crack caught on. Passengers began to repeat it.

But yesterday B.O.A.C. changed all that.

Embarrassed officials confessed that G-ANBG has been rechristened G-ABLL.

The new number is out of sequence with the rest of the fleet. But SOME-ONE'S blushes have been spared....

Sunday Pictorial
March 16 1958

CHAPTER THIRTEEN

Because these memoirs are generally recalled by events, rather than on a time scale, it is inevitable that at times the telling will appear erratic.

Such a flexible framework means that my mind clock appears to be operating to a programme of its own. But it is a device which enables me suddenly to switch back in time now and then to introduce a number of related situations. Threaded together, they combine to add a few more assorted patches to an almost completed coverlet. So once again we open with the late nineteen-forties-early 'fifties...

*

Harry Pollitt was a Bolshie - and one of Lenin's lads... The campfire ditty from my early teens ran through my mind as the leader of Britain's communists grasped my arm aggressively. He pulled himself between me and my target.

"Do you know who I am?" he demanded. I answered with a reluctant: "Of course, Mr Pollitt," but he waved a black leather pocket notebook in front of my nose and snapped: "I've told you once and I won't tell you again. Go away and leave him alone."

Was this short, rounded, red-faced challenger I was looking down at really the bogie man of the extreme left?

He stood beneath the portals, a'quaking at the knees... they were only the words of a mocking lament. Perhaps I smiled at the memory. In any event, he was obviously losing his patience. "Right," he said, thrusting a hand in the pocket of his raincoat and pulling out a stub of pencil. He flicked open the pages of the pad dramatically. "You've really spoilt yourself for the future, my lad. You'll be going down in my little black book...."

The general secretary of the British Communist Party was well aware that I had been waiting to talk to a senior member of his party, the leader of Britain's coal miners, Arthur Horner. Though sharing the same extreme politics, and both physically short, the two men could hardly have appeared more different in temperament. As general secretary of the National Union of Mineworkers at this time (the late nineteen-forties to early 'fifties) Horner was a tireless worker on behalf of his thousands of members and a jovial and popular figure. He was grudgingly respected even in the right-wing media of the day.

Both the London *Star* and the *Evening Standard* had ordered the coverage of Horner's departure for Moscow. He had been offered treatment for his high blood pressure, a familiar gesture by the health-proud Soviets to those foreign nationals they recognised as sympathisers, as I've described before.[1] Travelling with him was his wife, and seeing them both off were their married daughter, their 11-years-old grandson Julian... and Pollitt. One of the news desks had advised me that the party leader would be present, though it was, after all, only Horner I was interested in.

But as I approached the former miner in London Airport's north side check-in hall Pollitt intervened. "No questions," he ruled, raising his arm protectively between me and my target. "Mr Horner won't answer any questions. He's not well and doesn't want to be bothered."

Arthur Horner for his part was nonetheless taking charge at the airline desk and was chatting quite cheerfully with the check-in clerk. So as he and his wife collected their boarding cards, I asked him how he was feeling. He replied cheerfully and we were able to exchange a few more words. There was no resentment and no indication at all that my questions might not be welcome, or that I was intruding. Lightly I asked him if the trip to Moscow meant a course of political re-education for him. The union leader laughed out loud at the suggestion. "I rarely need it," he said. "When I do, I have a quiet word with Harry here. I'm just going to prove the value of Soviet medicine. I intend to come back cured."

It was at this point that Harry broke in with his "black book" threat, deliberately moving in front of me. "Mr Horner seems to be perfectly capable of looking after himself," I protested, but the moment had passed. I don't believe the invalid had heard Pollitt's "labour camp" threat to me – if that's what it was to be when the Glorious Revolution came.

1 *See Ch.5, p105*

MR. HORNER GOES TO MOSCOW

Mr. Arthur Horner, the miners' secretary, leaving his home at Kenton, Middlesex, to-day, to fly to Russia. With him are his wife and daughter. See: Visit to Russia.

Visit to Russia

LEANING heavily on the arm of a friend, Mr. Arthur Horner, Communist General Secretary of the National Union of Mineworkers, boarded an airliner for Brussels at London Airport to-day. He is on his way to Moscow for six weeks' health treatment. He is suffering from high blood pressure.

Seeing him off was Mr. Harry Pollitt, General Secretary of the Communist Party, Mr. Horner's married daughter, and his grandson, Julian, aged 11.

Mr. Horner laughed at the suggestion that his trip to Moscow meant a course of political re-education. "I rarely need it," he said. "When I do I just have a quiet chat with Harry here.

'Exhausted'

"I am going to prove the value of Soviet medicine. I intend to come back cured."

Mr. Horner's daughter said that her father was "completely run down."

"He has not had a holiday in years," she said. "He is exhausted."

Evening Standard picture April 27 1953

HORNER OFF TO MOSCOW

LEANING heavily on the arm of a friend, Arthur Horner, Communist general secretary of the National Union of Mineworkers, stumbled through the Customs Hall at London Airport today to board a plane for Brussels on his way to Moscow for six weeks' health treatment.

At the airport to see him off were Harry Pollitt, general secretary of the Communist Party, Mr Horner's married daughter and his 11-years-old grandson Julian.

Mr Horner laughed at a suggestion that his trip to Moscow meant a course of political re-education.

"I rarely need it," he said. "When I do I just have a quiet chat with Harry here. I'm going to prove the value of Soviet medicine. I intend to come back cured."

Mr Horner's daughter said that her father was "completely run down." She added: "He hasn't had a holiday in years. He's completely exhausted."

Boarding the same plane were three parties of British delegates to May Day celebrations in Moscow, Bucarest and Sofia.

The Star April 27 1953

Happy Horner

Mr. Arthur Horner, the miners' union general secretary, back home from his health cure behind the Iron Curtain, said at London Airport: "Soviet doctors looked after me marvellously. I'm as happy as a sandboy and fighting fit."

Daily Express June 22 1953

The communist party chief moved away towards the Customs barrier, giving me a final glare. So I turned to the family instead. Horner's daughter was just as polite as he. She said her father hadn't had a break in years. "He badly needs a holiday," she said, "And that's how he's looking at this trip. He's exhausted."

Both papers used the story the next day, with accompanying agency pictures of an unsmiling Mr and Mrs Horner. I was relieved that I had been able to introduce a little humanity into the story. I was glad too that I hadn't abused my privileges by reporting Harry Pollitt's threats, though if Arthur himself had been just as unpleasant I would have been sorely tempted – if only to cover my failure to get a decent "quote."

Two months later I was able to report Arthur's return. As far as I am aware, only one paper, the *Daily Express*, carried my story, in just eight lines. The miners' leader told me: "Soviet doctors looked after me marvellously. I'm as happy as a sandboy and fighting fit."

This time my efforts went unrecorded in the revolutionary annals. His political "boss" wasn't present to pencil in the occasion for posterity.

It was fully ten years later that I was able to reveal that the overseas travel plans of another prominent British communist had been suddenly disrupted as he was about to leave for America. Willie Gallacher, 81-years-old former president of the British communist party and MP for West Fife in Scotland for fifteen years until 1950, had planned to visit his 75-years-old sister in America. She had emigrated to the US with her husband 50 years earlier, and was convalescing after spending some time seriously ill in hospital. She and her brother had not met for 12 years.

Mr Gallacher booked his seat on a BOAC flight leaving Prestwick for Chicago one Friday in July, 1963. He had applied in the usual way to the US Consulate in Glasgow for an American visa. When he was advised that because of his politics his application was likely to be turned down, he made a direct appeal to the US State Department explaining that he wanted the visa for personal, not political reasons.

After a week's delay the visa was granted, but only on the proviso that he reported his movements to the US authorities during his conditionally-limited three-week stay.

But then, on the day of his planned departure, the Americans changed their minds. Willie Gallacher's visa was revoked, without explanation. I learnt this as I checked his booking with BOAC. "The booking has been cancelled," said an official. "We were advised in a telephone call last night from the US Consul General's office that the visa had been revoked. Today this was being confirmed by letter.

"In view of this we had no choice but to cancel the booking. We could face a heavy fine if we carried any passenger who was not in possession of a visa. We are not the only airline to be advised of this. We understand all transatlantic companies at Prestwick were notified."

The US Consul General, Wallace Holbrook, refused to confirm that the visa had been revoked, and would only tell me: "The matter is still under consideration." But his letter to BOAC and other airlines confirming the earlier 'phone call was delivered shortly afterwards by special messenger.

I wasn't happy with the situation. The story was open-ended and needed an explanation for the change of mind in Washington. It also needed a reaction from Willie himself – and I could get no reply from his home near Glasgow. But there were also evening edition times to consider. I had to go ahead with what I had.

The Glasgow *Evening Times* were happy enough to lead their front page with the story, under an "*Evening Times* Reporter" byline.

EVENING TIMES
Newspaper Design Award Winner
No. 27,212 FRIDAY, JULY 12, 1963. 3d

Visa revoked for visit to sick sister

U.S. SAYS 'NO' TO WILLIE GALLACHER

"EVENING TIMES" REPORTER

AN AMERICAN VISA issued to 81-year-old Communist ex-M.P. Willie Gallacher has been revoked.

The information leaked out after a telephone call from the U.S. Consul-General in Glasgow to five international air lines at Prestwick Airport to-day.

This decision has now been confirmed by a letter delivered to all air offices in Glasgow and to ticket desks at the airport.

B.O.A.C. officials at the airport said later that Mr Gallacher's booking had been cancelled and that when passengers for the flight were called he did not appear.

The chief of the visa section at the U.S. Embassy in London said that he could make no comment. The law provides that anything to do with a visa was confidential.

Mr Gallacher, former M.P. for West Fife, was booked to fly out for Chicago on a B.O.A.C. flight this afternoon.

Special appeal

He had made a special appeal to the U.S. State Department explaining that he did not want to enter America for political reasons but to visit his sister, 75-year-old Mrs Agnes Wilson, whom he has not seen for 12 years.

Mrs Wilson, who emigrated to America with her Scots husband 50 years ago, recently left hospital, but is still ill at home.

Mr Gallacher's visa was issued after a week's waiting, but it required him to report his movements to the American authorities during a limited three-week stay.

Born in Paisley

Mr Gallacher, who lives at 68 Rowan Street, Paisley, has been a leading member of the Communist Party and the Communist International since 1920.

He became president of the British Communist Party in 1956, and was M.P. for West Fife from 1935 until 1950.

Mr Gallacher, who was born in Paisley, was chairman of the Clyde Workers' Committee during the First World War.

©Evening Times (Page One lead)

Courtesy Maxton Collection
Gallacher at the height of his career, outside the Soviet Embassy

MR. GALLACHER'S U.S. VISA IS REVOKED

ISSUED IN ERROR, SAYS EMBASSY

VETERAN COMMUNIST CANCELS FLIGHT

An American visa issued to Mr. William Gallacher, British Communist Party " elder statesman ", to enable him to visit his sick sister in Chicago, has been revoked by order of the United States Government.

The information leaked out through a telephone call made by the United States Consul-General's office to the five major transatlantic airlines at Prestwick.

Mr. Gallacher, who lives in Paisley and was formerly M.P. for West Fife, was booked to fly on a Chicago-bound B.O.A.C. airliner yesterday. He is 81. His sister, Mrs. Agnes Wilson, aged 75, has not seen him for 12 years.

He made a special appeal to the American State Department, explaining that he did not wish to enter America for political reasons. His visa, which was issued after a week of waiting, was for a stay of three weeks and required him to keep in touch with American authorities.

The booking was cancelled only 30 minutes before take-off time.

An American Embassy official said in London last night that the visa had been issued in the first place through an administrative error.

The Times

©Glasgow Herald (below)

U.S. REVOKE VISA TO FORMER COMMUNIST M.P.

U.S. bars Gallacher from sister

Daily Herald

(all) July 13 1963

The following day the London *Times,* which with the *Scottish Daily Mail* had ordered my story after seeing the evenings, ran with it on an inside page, as did the *Daily Herald*, the *Scotsman* and the *Glasgow Herald (see previous page).* All three quoted the Consul as saying that the visa had originally been issued in error.

Just five days on, however, Chris Bramwell was reporting the departure of Mr Gallacher for Chicago after all. The US State Department, which originally had indicated that the decision to revoke the visa was "unlikely to be reversed," had changed its mind again, on the personal intervention this time (it was reported from Washington) of Secretary of State Dean Rusk himself.

At Prestwick a number of American tourists among fellow passengers on his re-booked flight recognised him from photos carried alongside my earlier story. Their reactions varied. One elderly American told an airport official: "If that man's going on my 'plane then I'm not going." But he said it with a grin and willingly preceded the Scotsman into passport controls.

Two others, Mrs Ruth Flax and Mrs Ruth White, both from New York, walked forward and grabbed the startled Scotsman's hands, wishing him a happy stay in America… he seemed bowled over by the attention. "I fail to understand why anyone is interested in an old man like me, or in my sister, who is nearly as old," he told Chris. "We're quite harmless, you know."

Mr Gallacher revealed that he would also be visiting a nephew, in Iowa, during his visit... at the suggestion of the Americans. "They must have done some research on me," he said impishly. "Out of the blue they wrote making it clear that I could visit my nephew as well. I hadn't told them he existed."

Three weeks later Chris (I was away) was able to record the traveller's homecoming at the very limit of his visa's duration. And it was a beaming Willie Gallacher who told him: "My arms are aching from the pumping they have had. I could scarcely believe they would give me such a warm welcome. I was overwhelmed by American hospitality."

As Chris reported for the Scottish *Sunday Mail:*

The Americans really went to town on ex-Communist MP Willie Gallacher, the man they at first wanted to ban. There were press interviews, TV speeches... and SMILES when 81-years-old Willie arrived in the States...

The headlines, first in the Sundays, then again in Monday's papers, told the full story.

WILLIE PRAISES U.S. HOSPITALITY

SCOTLAND'S most famous prodigal, 81-year-old Communist Willie Gallacher, flew into Prestwick Airport to-day after his much discussed three-week trip to the U.S., "overwhelmed" by American hospitality.

The former Communist M.P. for West Fife, whose American visa was granted on the direct order of the American Secretary of State, Mr Dean Rusk, to enable him to visit his sick sister in Chicago, went on — "I could scarcely believe they would give me such a warm welcome. My arms are aching from the pumping they have had.

"My sister's phone hardly stopped ringing with invitations to visit people and with good wishes from complete strangers."

Sucking a familiar—but empty—pipe, Mr Gallacher stepped from a trans-Canada jet at Prestwick in pouring rain, his green sports shirt open at the neck.

Of his sister, 75-year-old Mrs Agnes Wilson, with whom he stayed in Chicago, he said—"She is a very sick woman, though not as bad as I expected. And she is still hoping to come home to Scotland, though it may not be until next year."

His American visa, issued after an earlier one had been revoked, allowed him to stay only three weeks and expired at midnight last night. "No one asked me to talk politics," he said.

"They all realised that my visit was personal, not political."

And he added — "The security people left me alone, too. Nobody followed me."

©Evening Times August 10 1963

WILLIE'S HOME— WITH A SORE ARM!

MR WILLIE GALLACHER (81) flew home yesterday after his three-week trip to the United States—"overwhelmed" by American hospitality.

The former Communist M.P. for West Fife, whose American visa was granted on the personal order of the American Secretary of State to enable him to visit his sick sister in Chicago, said, "I could scarcely believe they would give me such a warm welcome.

Sunday Post August 11 1963

VIP Willie is a hit in America

THE Americans really went to town on ex-Communist M.P. Willie Gallacher, the man they at first wanted to ban.

There were Press interviews, T.V. speeches . . and SMILES when 81-year-old Willie arrived in the States.

And yesterday, back home in Paisley after his three-week visit, Willie said:

"I was greeted like a long lost brother everywhere."

Friendly

British M.P.s protested when Willie was refused a visa by the American State Department to visit his 75-year-old sister Agnes, ill in a chicago hospital.

The American Secretary of State, Dean Rusk intervened —and the visa was granted.

Willie said: "The authorities

'MAIL' REPORTER

—and everyone else—could not have been nicer.

"After leaving a crowd of reporters and photographers at Prestwick when I flew out, I was greeted with an even bigger crowd of officials, press and TV men when I arrived in America.

"They certainly gave me the V.I.P. treatment, and the authorities coud lnot have been more friendly.

"They went out of their way to make things easy and pleasant.

Sunday Mail, Aug 11 1963

WILLIE COMES BACK —ALL SMILES

Scottish Daily Express, Aug 12 1963

chapter thirteen

Industrial unrest became a tedious and unrelenting feature of life in Britain throughout much of the 'forties and 'fifties. Many of the problems were centred on the public sector, in the nationalised resources such as mining and in newly created service and transport bodies. Expectations of a new management-workforce relationship in many of these reborn organisations were initially high in the aftermath of war and such discord was seen by many as a complete negation of the essence of public ownership.

My introduction to dissatisfaction in the workplace came in my early days as a cub reporter when I had to report disruption of public catering services at London's Northolt airport following a walk-out by restaurant and buffet staff. The stoppage here was in support of a simple double pay demand for Sunday working. It was quickly resolved when airline ground staff, members of an opposing trade union, stepped in to help out, defiantly ignoring the "blackleg" jibes of their erstwhile colleagues.

The following months brought frequent wildcat strikes, disruptively timed walk-outs, carefully planned go-slows and even more subtle workings-to-rule, affecting telephone switchboard staff, Heathrow road-tunnel builders and Customs officers, among others.

Essential airline staff had also quickly discovered their negotiating strength. Airline stoppages became significant, directly affecting an increasing number of travellers for the first time. As early as 1948, 850 British European Airways' maintenance engineers and electricians defied their unions and walked out at Northolt. They were followed just two days later by baggage-handlers at the airline's town terminal. The disputes were unrelated.

Less than three years on, at the height of summer, BEA's flights to and from Northolt were grounded by a strict but short-lived work-to-rule policy declared by 300 senior and specialist engineers, members of the prestigious Association of Supervisory Staff, Executives and Technicians, in support of a pay claim. And in 1952 came the first major demarcation row.

When an electronic gauge was introduced into BOAC aircraft maintenance workshops, a stoppage by 1,500 engineering workers threatened to hit long-distance Comet jet and Stratocruiser services. The Amalgamated Engineering Union said their members should operate the gauge. But the Electrical Trades Union claimed: "It's our job." And 50 instrument workers walked out in protest. It took several days of talks involving national officers of both unions before the problem was resolved and a strike avoided.

By the mid-'fifties the aircraft maintenance staff of BOAC, now numbering several thousand, had become the largest single-employer workforce at Heathrow, with their opposite numbers at BEA a close runner-up. The maintenance teams embraced a wide range of abilities including executive and management engineers, mechanics, electronics technicians, electricians, sheet metal workers and even upholsterers and carpenters.

Inevitably, clear definition and separation of such skills and workshop responsibilities were seen by the trade unions as essential in the interests of both safety and individual job security. But the task of those unions at local level was to ensure that this multi-faceted workforce should speak with one voice to management. Strength through unity was the key phrase and demarcation issues and similar internecine disputes had to be avoided whenever possible.

The result was the establishment of a joint shop stewards' committee headed by a nucleus of experienced negotiators who would represent a wide range of shop floor interests. Sid Maitland was one such leader. A branch official of the old ETU, he was an avowed Communist and a skilled orator who had come to BOAC from the catering company of J. Lyons. His leading role in the decisions of thousands of maintenance workers to take disruptive action in protest against a range of management proposals over coming months was often bitterly resented by national officers of the unions concerned, most of whom refused publicly to recognise the committee.

They argued that major disputes could only be resolved through the national joint council for civil air transport, a body recognised by both unions and employers. The shop stewards' committee, it was said, was unconstitutional and therefore unofficial. This view was shared by the government and British airline managements. The latter, nevertheless, had to be realistic, often dealing directly with the shop stewards on a daily basis. National officers of the unions were often seen to be merely 'rubber-stamping' agreements reached at these lowly levels, even though the decisions taken might affect members of those unions in unrelated industries, throughout the country.

The huge expanse of concrete alongside the hangars and workshops of Heathrow's aircraft maintenance bases became a verbal battleground between the unions' generals and their sometime opponents, the rebel elements of those same unions. In front of them, awaiting their "orders" were the massed ranks of the comparatively silent foot soldiers. Yet though he was openly opposed to many of those generals' policies – or their apparent lack of action – Maitland was usually able to avoid public confrontation with them on that battleground, either by planning or by the intuitive accident of absence.

As he had earlier supported industrial action, one such absence by Maitland couldn't have been more obvious. On this occasion in 1954, two national officers, one of whom was Jim Matthews, a senior official of the General and Municipal Workers union, appealed directly to 2,000 BOAC engineers to call off an eight-weeks' old dispute. The men were refusing to work on restoring six airliners the state-owned airline had sold to two private air firms. They believed the two companies would be in direct competition with BOAC, and that working conditions under the new owners would not be up to standards established by BOAC.

For once the foot soldiers were far from silent. I reported that the union officials had to fight their way through an apparent minority of angry, shouting workers after a mass meeting voted 2-1 in favour of *ending* their blacking of the aircraft. The men, and a handful of women, had crowded into an aircraft hangar, a venue agreed by the airline because of the bad weather. In the centre of the row from the moment the giant hangars clanged shut behind me, as a last-in "stranger," was grey-haired, bespectacled Miss Ann Godwin, chairman of the union side of that much-maligned national joint council. Over and over again, her voice often drowned by protests, she appealed for silence as Matthews, secretary to the council, asked the engineers to accept the "peace" resolution.

Schoolmistress-like, she parried every protest. She ignored demands that the six aircraft remained "cocooned" in their protective web. She brushed aside allegations that the meeting was "unconstitutional." With her hands thrust deep into the pockets of her overcoat, she bulldozed the workers into a straight vote in favour of ending their boycott. Then drawing an imaginary line through the centre of the throng with her hand, she called for the vote: "On the left: *For*. On the right: *Against*."

After the majority vote there was another storm of protest when she refused to accept an amendment from the floor which claimed that Matthews had "distorted facts" about working conditions in the two independent airlines. Some of the engineers mobbed Matthews as he hurried away from the meeting, claiming the decision to call off the two-months' action was illegal. Shop stewards said they would hold another meeting to consider the legality of the vote.

But the day was won. The boycott was called off.

The story of the battling schoolmarm standing up to an angry throng appealed to the dailies, even though the dispute was a relatively minor one unlikely to have any obvious impact on airline operations. The *Daily Express* gave it a two-column heading *(left)* while the *Daily Sketch* homed in on the human angle:

AIRLINE MEN MOB UNION LEADER

UNION officials had to fight their way through scores of angry shouting workers after a mass meeting of 2,000 B.O.A.C. engineers, at which a two-to-one vote favoured beginning work immediately on "mothballed" Hermes airliners which are being sold to private charter companies.

In the centre of the row from the moment the giant hangar doors were clanged-to on the meeting was grey-haired, bespectacled Miss Ann Godwin, chairman of the union side of the National Joint Council.

Over and over again—her voice often drowned by protests—she appealed for silence as burly Jim Mathews, secretary to the council, asked the engineers to accept the resolution.

SHE PARRIES

Schoolmistress-like, she parried every protest. She refused to accept an amendment which said that Mr. Mathews had "distorted facts."

Indicating a line through the centre of the throng with her hand, Miss Godwin called for the vote—"On the left, for. On the right, against."

But the opposition protested that the decision was unconstitutional. They mobbed Mr. Mathews as he tried to reach his car outside the hangar demanding another hearing.

Miss Godwin waited calmly for the crowd to disperse. "All I want is a cup of tea," she said.

Daily Express

MISS GODWIN QUELLS AIRLINES ROW

Daily Sketch Reporter

A 56-YEAR-OLD woman, grey-haired and bespectacled, played school-marm with scores of angry, shouting engineers yesterday — and ended an eight-week-old dispute.

It happened at London Airport, where the engineers have been refusing to work on six Hermes airliners which B.O.A.C. have sold to private air firms.

Two thousand men crowded into a hangar to hear union officials plead with them to work on the planes. In front of them stood Miss Ann Godwin, chairman of the union side of the National Joint Council for Civil Air Transport.

With her hands thrust deep into the pockets of her green coat, she bulldozed the engineers into a straight 2-1 vote in favour of a resolution ending the boycott.

There was a storm after the vote was taken. Those against the resolution claimed that the meeting was unconstitutional.

Jim Mathews, E.T.U. official, who had pleaded for the engineers to work on the planes, came in for rough treatment when he tried to leave.

Engineers who voted against the resolution mobbed him as he tried to reach his car, gripping him by the arms.

They accused him of "distorting the facts" when describing working conditions for employees of Airwork and Britavia, the companies who have bought the Hermes.

Daily Sketch
(both) May 18 1954

HERMES MEN VOTE: BACK TO WORK TODAY

TWO thousand B.O.A.C. engineers ended a stormy meeting at London Airport last night by voting 2-1 to return to work today on Hermes aircraft.

Thus ended, officially, a two-month-old row which began over the proposed sale by B.O.A.C. of 19 Hermes to independent firms at £90,000 each. The engineers feared that working conditions under the private firms would not be up to B.O.A.C. standards.

Most of yesterday's meeting was a running battle of shouts between union leaders and the rebels who wanted the last six of the Hermes to be kept "cocooned."

In the centre of the catcall battle was grey-haired spectacled Miss Ann Godwin, chairman of the Air Unions panel. It was she who insisted on a vote and she got her way.

Some members said the vote was illegal, but Mr. Jim Matthews, national organiser of the Union of General and Municipal Workers, said: "So far as we are concerned the whole issue is closed."

TWO-TO-ONE VOTE ENDS PLANE STRIKE

TRADE UNION officials had to fight their way through scores of angry, shouting workers at London Airport yesterday when more than 2,000 BOAC engineers voted 2—1 in favour of beginning work immediately on the six remaining "cocooned" Hermes aircraft sold by BOAC to independent airlines.

Miss Ann Godwin, chairman of the union side of the National Joint Council, appealed for silence as Mr. Jim Mathews, Electrical Trades Union official and secretary on the National Joint Council, asked the engineers to accept the resolution to return to work.

Drawing with her hand an imaginary line through the centre of the crowd, Miss Godwin called for the vote—"On the left, **For**. On the right, **Against**." The resolution was carried.

Shop steward Mr. Ted Anderson said that another meeting will be held today to consider the legality of the vote.

News Chronicle (far left)
Daily Mail (left)
(both) May 18 1954

A few years later Sid Maitland gave up his front-line activities as chairman of the shop stewards' committee following his promotion by BOAC. He went on to win an appointment as a senior official of BALPA , the British Airline Pilots' Association, strangely finding himself on the same team as Norman Tebbitt, a BOAC pilot and BALPA officer. Later, Tebbitt was to become the right-hand man, (some might say *extreme* right-hand) to Margaret Thatcher.

But there were always other left-wingers (some might say *extreme* left!) ready to step into the shoes of departed activists. In January 1961, the *Evening Standard* devoted their Page One lead to my story of another mass meeting:

Hats by Edward Mann — Always making fashion news

Evening Standard

42,474 — THURSDAY, JANUARY 5, 1961 — 3d.

Jim Matthews slams the walk-out strikers

AIRPORT MEN VOTE 'BACK TO WORK'

But they say 'No overtime'

By ALAN JOHNSON

The strike which has paralysed State airline services is over.

Evening Standard
(Page One lead)
Jan 5 1961

An hour before the meeting, which would be attended by 1,000 of a possible 3,000 maintenance staff, Matthews condemned a four-hour stoppage in support of a wage demand as the "height of irresponsibility". He ordered those members of his own union involved to return to work immediately.

Tempers flared when the meeting was told that four men, who'd joined the stoppage the previous day, had been suspended for a day without pay. There were immediate demands for a full strike. But unofficial strike leaders, among them Sid Maitland's successor Billy Benson, made it clear they did not want a major stoppage over the suspensions on the eve of renewed pay-talks they had been promised. The workers finally agreed to return to work later that day but insisted on adopting another resolution, to ban all overtime for the day.

I spoke to Benson after the meeting. A self-proclaimed communist ("I've been a member for 13 years") he confirmed he was a former shop steward for the Sheet Metal Workers' Union. He then strongly criticised the managements of both BEA and BOAC for the suspensions. "I have searched though the constitution and found nothing that allows them to take this course," he said. "The managements have always proposed suspension without pay as an alternative to the sack.

"The unions have never agreed to it."

Speaking at the same meeting was another communist, Fred Gore, chairman of the BEA shop stewards. To an appeal from the floor that the overtime ban be extended indefinitely, he replied:

"Let's be realistic. We have an overwhelming majority not to work overtime today. But we want these (pay) talks to re-open without any restrictions on either side." And to another question, he replied: "If the management refuse to allow any suspended men to start work when their shift re-opens, we will be out. There's no question about that."

Later Gore told me: "It's impossible to say what our next step will be. Everything depends on the outcome tomorrow. Our protest was a token one, and it has achieved the desired objective of making sure that the wage claim is discussed tomorrow.

"Until last night we were unable to get that information from the management."

The dispute gave me a bonus, another front page lead, this time in the *Evening News,* as I was able to report for the early editions:

The Evening News & STAR

World's largest evening sale

No. 24,574 LONDON, FRIDAY, JANUARY 6 1961 PRICE 3d.

Betting Shops Will Have To Live Up To Councils' Odds (P3) — Should August Bank Holiday Be Scrapped? (P11) — The U.S. Finds 1961 Is An Upside-Down Year (P5)

After A Strike Grounds Airliners For 44 Hours

BEA IS FLYING AGAIN

But Only 17 Aboard Giant Viscount

"Evening News" Industrial Reporter

THE FIRST BEA PLANE TO LEAVE LONDON AIRPORT FOR 44 HOURS TAXIED TO THE RUNWAY TO-DAY.

It was a Viscount airliner bound for Oslo and Stockholm. Only 17 passengers were on board the 57-seater flight, but many of the empty seats were filled with mail.

Said one reservations clerk: "It seems that most of the passengers were frightened off by the news of the past two days.

"Many other BEA services due to leave earlier were cancelled through the after-effects of the lack of maintenance. It will be some hours before services are completely back to normal."

Services were resumed after 860 BEA engineers and maintenance men reported for duty.

Earlier there had been fears that the day shift men might not turn up because "get tough", air chiefs continued to suspend men after the 5 p.m. return to work yesterday.

BOAC, whose services were also disrupted by yesterday's unofficial strike, were gradually clearing the backlog of delayed flights to-day.

PAY TALKS

Are Resumed

BEA men went back to work a few hours before pay talks were due to be resumed in London. It was the claim of 6d. an hour that led to the four-hour token strike on Wednesday which sparked off the trouble.

The claim affects 10,000 aircraft engineering and maintenance workers, including the 3,000 BOAC and BEA men involved in the London Airport dispute.

When union leaders met the civil airline employers just before Christmas an offer described as "final" was made.

Skilled grades were offered 3d. an hour (10s. 6d. a week), intermediate grades 2¾d. (9s. 7d.) and unskilled 2½d. (8s. 9d.).

Evening News (Page One lead) Jan 6 1961

"The first BEA plane to leave London Airport for 44 hours taxied to the runway today," I wrote. Services had been resumed after a shift of 860 engineers and other maintenance staff had reported back for duty.

Earlier however, there had been fears that the day shift men might not turn up because "get tough" airline chiefs had continued to suspend staff after the previous day's return to work. The BEA men went back to work only a few hours before the pay talks were due to start in London. It was a claim for 6d (2 ½ p.) an hour which had led to the 4-hour token stoppage.

The claim affected 10,000 aircraft engineering and maintenance workers throughout the UK, including the 3,000 BEA and BOAC staff at London Airport. BOAC, whose services had also been disrupted, had to spend the next 24 hours slowly clearing a backlog of delayed flights.

Such disruptive actions were hugely costly to the airlines in lost revenue from cancelled and delayed flights (though, it must be added, the financial loss to the workers was just as significant to them, a simple truth often ignored). Yet the managements concerned rarely, if ever, sought to put their case before the public. Only when they were challenged by the news media, seeking answers to some of the claims and allegations made by union speakers at their mass rallies would they respond, and then only with the barest of information. Even less frequently did individual executives involve themselves publicly in industrial clashes by appearing on the battlefield in person.

The only exception I can recall was Peter Masefield, aviation pioneer and chief executive of British European Airways (who had head-hunted my brother Harry). On at least two occasions, to the consternation of local shop stewards, branch and national trade union officers and significantly, some of his own management, he insisted on making personal appeals to the massed assembly of disgruntled maintenance workers.

One of these involved the dismissal of an engineering union shop steward, Jack Peters, who had defied a BEA ruling restricting his union activities during working hours. Three hundred engineers voted for an overtime ban in protest against "unfair restrictions of trade union activities." But BEA rejoined: "We offered him two and a half hours' paid time a day for his trade union activities."

Peters later appealed against his dismissal. While that was being considered, Masefield addressed the maintenance men, electricians and engineers by loudspeaker from a public platform, where Miss Anne Godwin joined him. Jack Peters's appeal was turned down by the airline's local chief maintenance engineer, but he was allowed to take the matter higher to the "supreme court" of BEA chief engineer Beverley Shenstone.

Two months later the trade union officer was given his job back by the chairman of BEA, Lord Douglas, as an "act of grace." Far from being grateful or even gracious in return, the engineers however immediately called for the resignation of both Lord Douglas and Peter Masefield for what they described as a "deplorable handling of the dispute." They demanded an inquiry as a step towards improving future labour relations. And they condemned Jim Matthews for his role in the dispute.

In a later incarnation some 20 years on, Masefield, by now *Sir* Peter and chairman of the British Airports Authority, again intervened personally in an industrial dispute. He joined his personnel department's negotiators in an attempt to resolve a situation involving the Heathrow fire service.

Hundreds of incoming and outgoing air services were cancelled or diverted and thousands of travellers suffered when the airport was brought to its knees by a strike of fire fighters. The men, who some weeks earlier had accepted a pay offer by the airport authority, were now demanding pay parity with their opposite numbers in neighbouring civil fire brigades. It was the first stoppage of its kind, completely closing the airport operationally. Provision of a full on-site fire service is a keystone in the licensing of a civil airport.

Robert Christie picture

Sir Peter Masefield, (*above*) former BEA Chief Executive, who later became Chairman of the British Airports Authority. Pictured here at Prestwick Airport, which he described as the "jewel in the crown" of British airports, Sir Peter ponders his answers to a reporter's questions.

With Chris Bramwell, my former colleague who was now reporting for the *Daily Telegraph*, and Gerald Seymour[1] for *Independent Television News*, I was incarcerated for many hours in a small office at the Heathrow main fire station while joint and separate talks continued. The three of us found ourselves acting as periodic go-betweens as proposals were passed between the sides. It was three days before the dispute was settled. The BAA boss may have played a significant role. I don't believe, however, that as "mediators" we three had any input to the final successful outcome.

Gerald Seymour

The biggest single-day coverage I won for an industrial row was in October 1958, when I broke the news to the dailies of an unofficial stoppage at midnight by 300 night-shift BOAC engineers. I had been alerted earlier to the move by a union contact. It was a walk-out which was to bring the airline to a standstill for more than a week.

The *Daily Express,* the *Daily Mail,* the *News Chronicle* and the *Daily Sketch* all led their early editions with my exclusive story, carrying the Page One banners right through

[1] *Now the best-selling thriller author*

DAILY EXPRESS

No. 18,161 — TUESDAY OCTOBER 14 1958 — 3 a.m. forecast: Cloudy, some rain — Price 2½d.

Striking engineers are told: Go back to work

BOAC STANDSTILL

Warning at 1 a.m.: Hundreds delayed

LONDON AIRPORT MEN DEFY 'SACK' ULTIMATUM

NIGHT STRIKE STOPS BOAC PLANES

MIDNIGHT STRIKE STOPS BOAC

Daily Sketch Reporter

HUNDREDS of passengers were held up at London Airport last night after engineers went on strike.

BOAC cancelled flights by six big airliners to Johannesburg, Singapore, Lagos, Montreal and New York (two).

The engineers have been keeping up an overtime ban and work to rule since Wednesday.

'Join us' call

When the night shift downed tools last night, it was said to be in answer to an ultimatum by BOAC chief executive Mr. Basil Smallpeice.

If the strike continues when the day shift arrives to-day, 4,000 engineers, electricians and maintenance men will be affected.

BEA men may be asked to join them.

BEFORE the strike, hundreds of passengers were held up for anything between two and 24 hours.

The go-slow meant late departures—and that also slowed incoming planes.

Last night three airliners delayed from 8 p.m. were expected to leave at midnight.

Then half an hour before passengers were due to be called through Customs, they were sent to the ticket desk and told of the cancellations.

Said a BOAC official: "Some asked for transfer to other airliners, but most are being accommodated at hotels by us."

BEFORE the strike, Mr. Smallpeice told the men their overtime ban was "irresponsible."

And: "Refusal to work overtime without reasonable explanation constitutes misconduct."

The trouble began over a pay claim.

BOAC told the men: Anyone refusing to do overtime is liable to be sacked immediately.

The union countered promptly with a thinly veiled threat: "If any disciplinary action is taken against our members as a result of the ban and work to rule, we shall take the only course left open to us."

By midnight, pickets had been posted around entrances to BOAC headquarters, buildings and hangars

Daily Sketch Page One lead (right) and Back Page lead (above) Oct 14 1958

Daily Mail

MORNING SPECIAL

NO. 19,434 — © Associated Newspapers Ltd., 1958. — FOR QUEEN AND COMMONWEALTH — TUESDAY OCTOBER 14, 1958

2 am NEWS — Sack threat brings crisis at airport

STRIKERS STOP BOAC

Passengers held up in row over overtime

By Daily Mail Industrial Correspondent

A STRIKE grounded the BOAC fleet at London Airport early today after a row over the reported sacking of five maintenance engineers who refused to work overtime.

As the night shift maintenance men downed tools BOAC said it was unable to operate any services out of London for the time being.

Passengers waiting for planes already delayed by an overtime ban were called to the ticket desk and told of the cancellations. Some asked to be transferred to other airliners, but most were put up at hotels.

The cancellations included flights to Johannesburg, Singapore, Lagos, Montreal, and two to New York.

Pickets were posted round the hangars where BOAC's, Britannias, DC 7Cs, and Stratocruisers are serviced.

They planned to stay on guard throughout the night to warn men coming on duty for the first day shift at 6.30 a.m.

If the strike goes on 4,500 engineers, electricians, and other maintenance men will be out. They are being called to a mass meeting this afternoon.

Daily Mail Oct 14 1958

the night.

At 1.00am I followed with a statement from BOAC.

"The corporation is unable to operate any services out of London for the time being," it said, "Every effort is being made to minimise inconvenience to passengers by arranging with other airlines for them to be carried to their destinations." Every newspaper gave space to my detailed background to the dispute. The maintenance staff had walked out at midnight after a day-long battle between their local representatives and the corporation. Almost a dozen flights

Daily Mirror

TUES OCT 14 1958

2d THE BIGGEST DAILY SALE IN THE UNIVERSE

No. 17,055

Air chiefs called to crisis meeting

1 a.m. NEWS

STRIKE GROUNDS B.O.A.C.

BRITISH Overseas Airways Corporation announced at 1 a.m. today that all its flights from London Airport were cancelled following a lightning strike by maintenance engineers.

The announcement came as senior officials rushed by car to the B.O.A.C. headquarters building at the airport for an emergency management meeting.

If the strike continues today, some 4,000 engineers and electricians will be affected.

As strike pickets guarded hangars where the airline's Britannias, Stratocruisers and DC7Cs are serviced, passengers were called to the ticket desk and told of the standstill.

Many were found rooms in local hotels for the night.

A statement from the Corporation said: "Every effort is being made to minimise inconvenience to passengers by arranging with other airlines for them to be carried to their destinations."

The dispute arose out of an overtime ban by B.O.A.C. maintenance men on a pay dispute.

Downed Tools

Yesterday afternoon B.O.A.C. asked **FIVE** of the day shift men to work overtime.

The rest of the maintenance men on duty immediately downed tools.

Later 300 engineers and electricians of the night maintenance staff went on strike when told by union officials that the five men had been **SACKED.**

But B.O.A.C. denied that anyone had been dismissed.

A B.O.A.C. spokesman said early today: "A number of employees were instructed yesterday evening to work overtime on aircraft required for outgoing services today.

"They were informed that if they did not work overtime in accordance with their contract of employment they would be dismissed.

"However, before the shift ended and overtime could begin, all hourly-rated engineering employees on duty withdrew their labour.

"No dismissals have taken place."

'Go Back' Plea

A **UNION** official said: "The decision to stop work immediately was taken at a mass meeting."

He added that pickets would remain on guard through the night to tell employees arriving for the first day shift at 6.30 a.m. of the dispute.

An urgent appeal to the strikers to resume normal working was made early today by Mr Jim Matthews, secretary of the Trades Union side of the National Joint Council for Civil Air Transport.

He said: "I would remind them (the strikers) that an appeals procedure exists to deal with the question of any dismissals, and that in any event any dispute should be put through the constitutional process."

Daily Mirror Oct 14 1958 (reconstructed from damaged original)

and hundreds of passengers had already been affected by a two-day overtime ban over the size of a pay award. Then, in a public statement, the management had warned its 4,000-strong force of engineers that the ban was "unconstitutional and wholly irresponsible." The BOAC notice added: "The refusal to work overtime without any reasonable and acceptable explanation constitutes misconduct."

Copies of the warning, signed by Basil Smallpeice, the airline's managing director, were handed out to all the maintenance staff. I had spotted Mr Smallpeice in a Heathrow arrivals terminal the previous day. He told me then:

"We never thought the ban would affect us so soon. I shall call some meetings in the morning." His warning came soon after those meetings.

The engineers' shop stewards re-acted swiftly. "If any disciplinary action is taken against our members as a result of the ban and work-to-rule we shall take the only course open to us," they said.

Five men were approached by a supervisor who asked them to stay on for overtime work. They refused, despite a threat of dismissal. The skeleton nightshift of 300 walked out after being told the five had been dismissed. But BOAC insisted: "No one has been sacked. The men stopped work before the shift ended and before the overtime could begin."

First flights to be cancelled that night were those which had been delayed by the ban. They included two services to New York and others to Singapore, Lagos and Montreal. Some of the passengers were transferred to other airlines. Most were accommodated in nearby hotels.

Shop stewards posted pickets around the hangars where BOAC's Britannias, DC7s and Stratocruiser aircraft were serviced. They planned to stay on guard to warn 4,500 engineers, electricians and other maintenance staff of their action as they reported for their day shift at 6.30am.

The picketing was far from necessary. News of threatened sackings had spread like wildfire overnight, thanks in no small way to my headlined story. Ironically, from now on

I could only read of the dispute in those same newspapers when I was suddenly laid low by a severe bout of 'flu. It was down to my colleagues to report the next day that the wildcat walk-out had become a total stoppage. Defying the pleas of national union officers a mass meeting of maintenance workers voted overwhelmingly in favour of industrial action.

Twenty-four hours later an emergency session of the national joint council called at the request of BOAC failed to resolve the issue. And such was the anger of trade union members of the council at what they called "waffling" by management representatives, it was felt that the strike might even be made official. Secretary of the trade union side Jim Matthews, who had opposed the walk-out, was quoted as saying that he was not prepared to lift a finger to help end it until the management were prepared to negotiate properly.

Within hours, when it appeared likely that maintenance staff of BEA, who had already given their moral and financial support to the BOAC workers, might join the strike, the Conservative government stepped in. The Minister of Labour called in both sides for talks, and the Minister of Aviation met the chairmen of the two airlines.

But it was not until the government agreed to set up a court of inquiry to examine the causes of the dispute that direct discussions re-opened between the employers' and unions' representatives. And just as I returned to work we learned that more than 4,000 men had decided at another mass meeting to end their strike. With only one dissenter, they accepted a resolution put to them by the shop stewards' chairman, Sid Maitland, who described it as an honourable and just solution. It included a promise by the management that the wage claim would be considered further and that there would be no victimisation "on either side."

An earlier £5-a-head challenge by Mr Matthews to airport union officials to name the five workers they claimed had been sacked was not taken up, to "protect them and their families" from harmful publicity...

*

It seemed unlikely, back in the mid-1950s, that news about the problems of the nation's railways would ever feature very highly in our attempts to keep Britain's airports in the headlines. In the 21st century, with a rail and underground network paying such an important role in onward surface transport needs of the air traveller, it might be a different story.

But when thousands of railwaymen throughout the country withdrew their labour in support of a pay claim I won an unexpected bonus of front page leads in all three London evening newspapers. I was alerted early in the day at the end of March, 1955, by the sight of a twin-engined Viking airliner of the RAF Queen's Flight being prepared for departure from the north side aircraft marshalling apron, just a hundred yards from the old Royal Lounge. This was puzzling, because no royal flight had appeared in the day's VIP operations programme. The Queen herself was taking her annual holiday in Balmoral, and no royal engagements had been announced for the day which involved Heathrow. Nevertheless, once I had discovered that the Royal Lounge was being prepared for use, I began making serious inquiries.

Very soon I learnt that the royal aircraft was standing by for an unscheduled departure for Aberdeen, according to the Queens Flight ground staff. But who were the passengers? That was a different matter. "We don't know," they said.

Said the airport press office: "It's a secret. We haven't been told, and we won't know until they – if it is they – arrive at the VIP suite."

At last I discovered that the special flight had been arranged for a government deputation, though my sources couldn't, or wouldn't provide names. I could only speculate – and that meant linking the deputation and Balmoral...

The railway strike was already hitting at food supplies to the shops. Now it was threatening coal supplies to industry and power stations. The national press was suggesting that a State of Emergency might have to be called. I rang the Brenard photo desk and told them of the planned departure. "I think it may have something to do with the government seeking emergency powers," I said. "I've no idea who will be in the deputation, but they may well make a picture."

My guess proved right. The deputation was made up of members of the Privy Council. Headed by Lord Salisbury, the Council's Lord President, it included the Minister of Fuel and Power, Mr Geoffrey Lloyd, and Mr W.G.Agnew, clerk to the Council. They were joined at the aircraft steps by Lord Munster, Minister without Portfolio.

Lord Salisbury confirmed that he and his party were indeed flying to Balmoral, but would add nothing. My story took the newspapers by surprise. But within minutes of the deputation's departure, it was confirmed in London that the Prime Minister had asked the Queen to proclaim a State of Emergency to ensure the continuation of the country's essential services, a request that required the Council to seek an audience. But any Privy Council group would normally have been expected to travel by train. The occasion was sufficiently newsworthy to provide me with front-page spreads in all three London evenings, suitably illustrated by the airport's resident *PA-Reuter* photographer. Our own photographer, Tony Hewson ran out of film slides after one shot…

WORLD'S LARGEST EVENING NET SALE

The Evening News

NO 22,836 LONDON, TUESDAY, MAY 31, 1955 TWOPENCE

EMERGENCY ORDER TODAY

Ministers Fly to See the Queen—and Eden Returns to London

By STANLEY DOBSON
"Evening News" Political Correspondent

A ROYAL Proclamation declaring a state of emergency during the rail strike is expected within a few hours.

Lord Salisbury, Lord President of the Council, Lord Munster, Minister without Portfolio, and Mr. Geoffrey Lloyd, Fuel Minister, flew from London Airport to Balmoral to-day.

They were accompanied by Mr. G. W. Agnew, Clerk to the Privy Council.

The party, who travelled in a Viking of the Queen's Flight, are due back at London Airport at 5.30 p.m.

Lord Salisbury will report to the Prime Minister, who was returning from Chequers to No. 10, Downing-street this afternoon.

The Royal Proclamation was being signed by the Queen at a special meeting of the Privy Council.

Evening News
May 31 1955

After an unhelpful "No comment" from members of the Privy Council, I try to dodge an intrusive lens and share a long-forgotten joke with Lord Salisbury *(centre)* and Mr Geoffrey LLoyd, leaving for Balmoral.

Brenard Press picture

Evening Standard

40,737 TUESDAY, MAY 31, 1955 Twopence

RAIL STRIKE: Ministers fly to see the Queen

EDEN ASKS FOR A STATE OF EMERGENCY

Orders in Council to be introduced

Evening Standard Political Correspondent GEORGE HUTCHINSON

Sir Anthony Eden has asked the Queen to proclaim a state of emergency. Members of the Privy Council, headed by Lord Salisbury, are meeting today at Balmoral, where the Queen is staying.

Lord Salisbury, who is Lord President of the Council, left London Airport this morning in a Viking of the Queen's Flight. With him were Mr. Geoffrey Lloyd, Minister of Fuel and Power, Lord Munster, Minister without Portfolio, and Mr. W. G. Agnew, clerk of the Council.

Arrangements for the flight were made in secret. Until the Privy Councillors arrived at the airport—with Lord Salisbury carrying a red Government despatch case—only senior officials and the pilot of the aircraft knew who the passengers were to be.

The Viking reached Dyce Airport, Aberdeen, at 11.30 a.m. Lord Salisbury and his colleagues were taken to Balmoral by Royal car.

All four are expected back in London tonight. Chauffeurs were warned to stand by at the airport.

Evening Standard
May 31 1955

THE STAR

The Star
May 31 1955

Emergency Order Today

Queen Signing At Privy Council

Ministers Fly To Balmoral

"Star" Reporter

THE QUEEN ARRANGED TO SIGN A ROYAL PROCLAMATION DECLARING A STATE OF EMERGENCY TODAY. ...

Balmoral Castle by Stuart Yeates, Flickr.com

*

Five years after Labour's landside victory in 1945, Prime Minister Clem Attlee again went to the country. He believed the party could hold on to a large majority for a second term following its successful introduction of the hugely popular National Health Service and the Welfare State. But that overall majority of 146 seats crashed to a majority of only 5 overall, the closest election result since 1847.

Labour Party left-wingers in the new Parliament, led by Michael Foot, called on the Government to follow-up its nationalisation of the mines and implement immediately its pledge to take into public ownership the nation's water, cement and sugar industries as proposed in the party's manifesto. But his demands were received coolly by the leadership, anxious to avoid controversial legislation which could unite the Tories and a handful of Liberal MPs. And as if to pre-empt any protest movement activity, deputy leader Herbert Morrison said that there was no scope in the party for indulging in "the luxury of revolts" against the Government. Solidarity would be vital.

A mere nineteen months later, Attlee decided to seek a further public mandate for his government's policies. Within hours of his announcement of a date for the General Election, the *Tribune* published a pamphlet entitled "Going Our Way," which fiercely criticised Trades Union leaders for ignoring their members' views and attacked the Budget and the Chancellorship of Hugh Gaitskell. In the spring of 1951 Bevan himself had resigned from the Government front bench in protest against the high level of defence spending in the Budget, and also against the introduction of prescription charges. Bevan had described right-winger Gaitskell as a "desiccated calculating machine." In telling Attlee of his resignation he described the government's policies as "repugnant."

In October the country again went to the polls. And this time despite a huge increase in the total Labour vote, the Tories under Churchill converted a Labour majority of 5 seats into a Conservative majority of 17, due mainly to some two million Liberal voters switching their allegiance to the Conservatives. The Labour party establishment and their supporters, the right wing trade union leaders, blamed the disruptive left. For their part, the Bevanites blamed the failure at the polls on the leadership's "betrayal of socialism."

They had no intention of letting the "betrayers" off the hook. In March the following year, the Labour Opposition decided not to oppose the Tory Government's defence proposals. But Bevanites in the House led a revolt of 57 Labour MPs to vote against the government on the issue, defying their own party whips.

The left versus right rows looked as if they might continue right through the course of the new parliament. By October 1952, after accusations by his supporters that he was dithering, Attlee finally hit out. He branded the Bevanites as "wreckers," and accused them of trying to run a party within a party.

A majority of Labour MPs finally approved a motion banning unofficial groups within the party, and a few days later the Bevanites decided to suspend their operations. Bevan himself lost the deputy leadership of the party to his right-wing rival Herbert Morrison by a large margin of votes. But at the same time the left obstinately strengthened its position when grass root members throughout the country voted two more centre-left "names," Richard Crossman and Harold Wilson, on to the policy-making National Executive of the party.

*

The *Press Association* had asked us for coverage of the departure for New York on October 2, 1952 of Sir William Lawther, president of the powerful National Union of Mineworkers. He was due to attend a convention of American miners in Cincinnati as a fraternal delegate, and I was not expecting any world-shattering comments when I approached him at the BOAC check-in desk.

Nevertheless I asked routinely how he had reacted to Nye's olive branch appeal to his union "friends" of a few days earlier, and if he had anything to add. His response set me rocking back on my heels.

"If this situation in the party goes on much longer," he affirmed angrily, "there will be a complete and utter split." And he went on:

"I shall tell the American miners the facts about Bevan. I know they will be extremely interested to hear how an ex-miner can talk so much nonsense in so short a time."

He said that the average trade unionist was not concerned with "petty squabbles raised by tub-thumpers," and added: "If he has a grievance he takes it through the normal channels."

Sir William cooled a little as a patient receptionist interrupted to ask for his ticket. Then, referring to the Bevanites as "these people," he went on: "They want to get their way by means which have no relation to reality. If we in the trade union world did the same the balloon would go up.

"They talk about industrial action. It's easy for them sitting up there in the House of Commons. They have got their money safe and sure."

As I scribbled madly, Sir William referred to Bevan's description of the American capitalist "decadence."

The American miners' minimum wage was the dollar equivalent of a pre-decimal £6.5s (shillings) per shift, he said, compared with the £7.3s *per week* underground minimum for the British miner. "In a five-shift week the American miner can earn £23 more than his British opposite number. Is **that** decadence?" And as he boarded his airliner, the miners' leader made one more parting thrust at the Bevanites. He said: "These fellows are like a spectator at a football match or the chap at the ringside. They can always say how many goals could be scored or when the knockout blow should fall.

US miners drawing money in advance of payday, in Kentucky.
DoI records, NARA

"But they soon realise the difficulties when they get an atom of responsibility."

The BOAC Monarch service took off for New York as scheduled a few minutes later at 8 pm. There was still an hour or two to spare before the deadline for the early editions of the dailies. But I wanted to give the newsdesks plenty of time to mull over my copy, and it was not a story that required any structuring; everything was there in the quotes. All I had to do was dictate from my notes, including a word or two of natural background and my job was done. It was all too easy....

My reward came with the first editions of those dailies the next day, a Friday. The *Daily Express* was the most impressive, its banner headline splashed across the top of the front

DAILY EXPRESS

No. 16,313 FRIDAY OCTOBER 3 1952 CONTROLLING SHAREHOLDER LORD BEAVERBROOK Weather: Dull, brighter later

ICE-CAP Stranded men tell of dinner party PUZZLE Eight ships chartered for Soviet grain STALIN I won't attack the West MOSSADEG Pay up or get out' ultimatum

LAWTHER FEARS 'UTTER SPLIT'

IF BEVAN DRIVE GOES ON

Daily Express, Page One lead (all) October 3 1952

page *(above)*.

The *News Chronicle* also made it the page one lead story. The 2-line headline was enigmatically overlined: "Fight to the finish planned"...

NEWS CHRONICLE

FRIDAY, OCTOBER 3, 1952

Fight to the finish planned

UNIONS SPURN BEVAN WOOING

Lawther talks of utter split

News Chronicle Page One lead

LAWTHER HITS BEVAN 'NONSENSE'

'It May Utterly Split Party'

By Daily Mail Reporter

SIR WILLIAM LAWTHER, the miners' president, last night blamed Mr. Bevan for bringing the threat of a complete split in the Labour Party.

Sir William, who is flying to the United States to address American miners, said before leaving London Airport that he would give them "the facts about Bevan."

"They will be extremely interested to hear how an ex-miner can talk so much nonsense in so short a time," he said.

Commenting on the Socialist Conference at Morecambe, Sir William said: "The average trade unionist is not concerned with petty squabbles raised by tub-thumpers. These people want to get their way by means which have no relation to reality. If we in the trade union world did the same the balloon would go up.

£30 a week

"They talk about industrial action. It's easy for them sitting up there in the House of Commons. They've got their money safe and sure.

"Mr. Bevan spoke about the decadence of the American capitalistic system. The American miner's minimum wage is £6 5s. a shift, compared with £7 3s. per week underground minimum for the British miner. In a five-shift week the American miner can earn £23 more than his British opposite number—is that decadence?"

Daily Mail

Lawther to tell America

SIR WILLIAM LAWTHER, President of the National Union of Mineworkers, left London last night for New York as fraternal delegate from the Miners' International, to the conference of the American miners.

He had this to say on Mr. Aneurin Bevan and Bevanism:

"I know American miners will be extremely interested to hear how an ex-miner can talk so much nonsense in so short a time.

"These people (Bevanites) want to get their way by means which have no relation to reality. If we in the trade union world did the same the balloon would go up.

"My view is that if this situation goes on much longer there will be a complete and utter split in the Labour Party.

"But these fellows are like the spectator at a football match or the chap at the ringside.

"They can always say how many goals could be scored or when the knockout blow should fall. But they realise the difficulties when they get an atom of responsibility."

Daily Herald

LAWTHER FORESEES COMPLETE SPLIT

Sir William Lawther, miners president, referring to Bevanism when he left London Airport last night for the U.S., said:

"If this situation goes on much longer there will be a complete and utter split in the Labour Party.

"These fellows, like football spectators, can always say how many goals should be scored, but realise the difficulties when they get responsibility."

Daily Graphic

The *Daily Mail* and the *Daily Herald* both gave the story considerably less prominence, somewhat irrationally since they represented opposing elements of the political spectrum. They each reduced it to a single column, though still on the front page. The tabloid Tory *Daily Graphic* cut the miners' leader down to a mere three paragraphs.

A few hours later my story was totally eclipsed... by the late edition page one news that Britain had exploded its first atomic bomb. Which somehow seemed to put the squabbles into the right context, even though they were far from settled.

I met Nye and his wife, the popular Jennie Lee, who for several years was also a Labour MP, on a number of occasions during his turbulent '50s. One such time I have already described, though it went unrecorded at the time.[1] At the end of March 1953, a year before his final protest against the party's defence policies, the couple flew to Paris to attend the International Socialist Conference. They were deputising for Attlee, who was in hospital recovering from an appendicitis operation. "I have been asked to talk of my visit to India and Pakistan," said Bevan.

But the couple confused at least one newspaper, which was apparently aware of the Paris appointment – by deciding to fly first to Milan to visit friends before the meeting in France. The *Evening News* reduced my story of the Bevans' departure for *Italy* to one paragraph as part of an Easter holiday rush report. In the very next column they also printed four unrelated lines under the heading "BEVAN FLIES TO PARIS" *(opposite)*.

1 *See p.38*

Two years after our first encounter I found myself again interviewing Sir William Lawther, by now a miners' union ex-President This time he was flying out as a fraternal delegate to the German Trades Union Congress in Frankfurt. Once more he launched into an attack almost before I had pulled out my notebook.

Referring to Bevan's latest criticism of trade union leaders at the previous week's Labour party conference in Scarborough, he said : "As one ex-miner to another ex-miner, I suggest to Mr Bevan he would learn much more by paying more attention to his farm than by going on at the T.U.C.

"Mother Earth can still teach even politicians some lessons and maybe it would be better for him to wield in future the hoe rather than the muck rake."

He said that at the German conference he would attempt to dissipate any mistaken conclusions which may have arisen from statements by Mr Bevan on ther part trade unions played in Britain. "We are neither bullies nor dumbbells," he said and he added: "We do not accept that anyone, however important he may believe himself to be, is the custodian of the wisdom of the ages. We do not accept in the Trade Union movement any political Buchmanites."[1]

In a complex analogy, he compared Bevan to the US Republican Senator Joe McCarthy, who had become notorious for his anti-communist witch-hunt in the mid-'fifties and was regarded by the Democrats as their most valuable election asset. "Mr Bevan is fast achieving that claim for our Tory party," he said.

As I left him to board his flight I moved away to telephone my story of Sir William's departure with a strong sense of déja vu. Of course I recalled the previous year's interview, but it was only then that I remembered that it too had occurred shortly after the annual Labour Party conference. I asked my news desk to check back in the files of old copy and tell me the date of my previous encounter with the miners' president. (Fortunately, though rarely needed, thse files were retained, carefully tabulated for several years, if only for legal reasons.) I was intrigued to learn that the two dates were exactly two years and a day apart. Simply co-incidence – or was it planned?

As far as I can recall, only three newspapers carried my story the second time around. The best coverage was that of the *Daily Mirror (below)* while The *Daily Sketch*, and the *Daily Telegraph's* respectful single column tied at equal second.

Bevans for Paris

Socialist conference

Mr. Aneurin Bevan and his wife left London Airport to-day for Milan, on the way to Paris, where they will attend the International Socialist Conference. They are deputising for Mr. Attlee, who is recovering from an appendicitis operation.

Said Mr. Bevan: "I have been asked to talk of my visit to Pakistan and India."

The Bevans will spend a few days in Milan before going to Paris.

Evening Standard

Big Air Rush

Hundreds of school children, weighed down with luggage, led the air rush to the Continent.

From London Airport alone more than 30 flights were leaving for Paris from dusk to-day until nearly midnight, 21 of them extra services.

Air France was operating for the first time between London and Paris to-day its new 85-seater giant Provence airliner, scheduled to make two return flights between Orly and London Airport. British European Airways put on almost their full fleet of Elizabethan airliners on the London-Paris route.

Other extra services operated to Switzerland, Italy and the South of France.

Among the travellers from London Airport were Mr. Bevan and his wife, Miss Jennie Lee, bound for Italy.

At Northolt 96 services operated to-day, leaving every few minutes. Solidly booked, the air-liners will have carried nearly 3,000 by to-night.

FURTHER OUTLOO[K]
Weather forecast for Sunday/ Monday is "unse[...]

BEVAN FLIES TO PARIS

Mr. Bevan and his wife, Miss Jennie Lee, left London Airport to-day for Paris, to attend the international Socialist conference.

Evening News
(all) March 1953

The magic of air travel?

SIR W. LAWTHER HITS AT Mr. BEVAN

BUCHMANITE CHARGE

Sir William Lawther, former President of the National Union of Mineworkers, replied at London Airport yesterday to Mr. Bevan's attack on trade union leaders at the Labour party conference last week. Sir William is attending the German Trades Union Congress as a fraternal delegate.

He said he would attempt to dissipate any mistaken conclusions which might have arisen from statements by Mr. Bevan on the part trade unions played in Britain. British trade union leaders were "neither bullies nor dumb-bells."

"We do not accept that anyone, however important he may believe himself to be, is the custodian of the wisdom of the ages. We do not accept in the trade union movement any political Buchmanites."

ATTENTION TO FARM

As one ex-miner to another, he suggested that Mr. Bevan would learn a good deal more "if he paid more attention to his farm than by going on at the T.U.C."

It would be better for him to wield the hoe rather than the muck rake. In the United States Senator McCarthy was regarded as the Democrats' most valuable asset in an election. Mr. Bevan was fast achieving that claim "for our Tory party."

In 1952, when leaving shortly after the Labour party conference to attend a miners' convention in the United States, Sir William delivered a similar attack on Mr. Bevan. He called him a "tub-thumper" and the new Labour party leaders "youngsters."

By October 1954 much of the fire had gone out of the left. Bevan had resigned from the shadow cabinet over Labour's defence policy. By a twist of politics, he was succeeded by Harold Wilson who had resigned from the government with Bevan three years earlier.

A few months later I went to see off the Bevans on their departure for Cairo at the start of a tour of the Middle East. While I talked to Nye, Jennie Lee slipped away to a book stall to buy her husband a paperback for the journey. I glimpsed its cover as she handed it over. It was a mystery entitled: "Man in the Dark."

'STOP MUCK RAKING,' BEVAN IS TOLD

SIR William Lawther, former miners' leader, told Mr. Aneurin Bevan, M.P., to "stop muck raking" in a sharp attack last night.

Trade union leaders were "neither bullies nor dumb-bells," he said.

"We do not accept that anyone — however important he may believe himself to be—is the custodian of the wisdom of the ages."

'Even Politicians'

Referring to Mr. Bevan's Labour Party conference speeches in Scarborough last week, Sir William added:

"As one ex-miner to another ex-miner, I suggest to Mr. Bevan he would learn a good deal more by paying more attention to his farm than by going on at the T.U.C.

"Mother Earth can still teach even politicians some lessons and maybe it would be better for him to wield in future the hoe rather than the muck rake."

And to round things off, he declared that Bevan was reaching the position when he was "the most valuable asset to our Tory Party."

Sir William was leaving London Airport to go to the German Trade Union Congress as Britain's fraternal delegate.

Daily Mirror

LAWTHER ATTACKS FARMER BEVAN

SIR WILLIAM LAWTHER, former miners' union leader, yesterday attacked Mr. Aneurin Bevan, who attacked union leaders at the Labour Party's Scarborough conference last week.

"We are neither bullies nor dumb-bells and we do not accept that anyone, however important he may believe himself to be, is the custodian of wisdom," said Sir William.

"We don't accept in the trade union movement any political Buchmanites.*

"He'd learn a good deal more if he paid more attention to his farm than by going on at the T.U.C. Mother Earth can still teach even politicans some lessons, and maybe it would be better for him to wield in future the hoe rather than the muckrake.

Sir William was leaving London Airport for Frankfurt to attend the German T.U.C. as Britain's fraternal delegate.

* Sir William's definition of a Buchmanite: "One who considers himself beyond criticism of any kind and above normal every-day failings."

Daily Telegraph (top)
Daily Sketch
(all) October 4 1954

My last contact with a Bevan – and that with Jennie Lee, not her husband – came in 1957, when he was once again deputy leader of the Labour Party. Two years earlier, on the retirement of Attlee, Hugh Gaitskell had beaten both Bevan and Herbert Morrison for

1 *Sir William's definition of the founder of the Moral Re-armament movement was: "One who believes himself beyond criticism of any kind and above everyday failings."*

the leadership, by a huge margin of votes (Gaitskell 150, Bevan 70 and Morrison only 30). Bevan had pledged his loyalty to the new leader, following Gaitskell's plea for unity.

Now a reception fit for a Prime Minister awaited him at Heathrow, where he was due home after an extensive tour of India and the Middle East. Photographers, TV cameras, reporters, airport officials and his wife waited to greet him, as my story in the *Daily Express* among others recorded. But when the BEA Elizabethan airliner touched down, he was not on board. The stewardess told me: "Mr Bevan left the aircraft in Rome."

Why? Said Miss Lee: "Don't ask me. It's a mystery and I can't understand why he hasn't let me know." In fact, as newspapers reported the next day, Nye had flown from Rome to Paris, only returning to the UK a day late. I don't believe anyone asked why; except perhaps Jennie.

*

It was autumn, another year on. And I wasn't in the least surprised to see the name "Sir William Lawther" yet again in our news diary for 1955. What was surprising was that this time he was arriving back in Britain – not departing.

I caught up with him at the Customs barrier when he flew in from Southern Rhodesia[1] after a three weeks' visit to the copper belt. The date: October 2 – exactly a year on from our last meeting. I couldn't resist the cliché as I greeted him: "We can't go on meeting like this, Sir William. Someone might think we were conspiring."

He nodded noncommittally. I went on: "Do you realise I have approached you on either the second or third of October three times over the last four years?"

He replied: "Oh, yes. I was well aware of that," but declined to be drawn further. I suppose I half expected him to take the opportunity again to reinforce his views about left-wingers in the Labour Party. Instead he chose to criticise anonymous politicians who went out to Africa on "lost weekend" visits and came back knowing all the answers.

European trade unionists had given up certain responsibilities and tasks intended to be for the benefit and welfare advancement of the Africans, he said.

"This process will undoubtedly mean a better outlook and improved development. There is no easy solution to the race and labour problems and no more harm is done than by those visitors who go out on a lost weekend journey and then know all the answers." And he added that the colour bar evident in Britain could not easily be explained away to the African workers.

The *Daily Herald* was, I believe, the only newspaper to use this latest pronouncement. It headlined my two-column 150-word hat trick.

And it would seem that Sir William finally gave up on me as a personal publicist. I never met him again.

Lawther attacks 'lost' week-enders

POLITICIANS who go out to Africa for "lost week-end" visits and come back knowing all the answers were rebuked by Sir William Lawther last night.

The former miners' leader said at London Airport after a three-week visit to the Rhodesian copper belt:

"There is no question that the European trade unionists have given up certain responsibilities and tasks for the advancement of Africans. This process will undoubtedly mean a better outlook and improved development.

"There is no easy solution to the race and labour problem and no more harm is done than by those visitors who go out on a lost week-end journey and then know all the answers."

He said that the trade union colour bar evident in Britain could not easily be explained away to the African workers.

Daily Herald ***October 3 1955***

*

The world of ballet would seem to be light years away from politics, domestic or international. Yet ballet, like classical music, featured prominently in Soviet ideology weaponry during the cold war years as an example of how a classic art form could flourish as popular culture under a communist system. So the defection of one of its most revered icons was a severe blow to that ideology just at the time when the Soviet Union was capitalising on its already proven technological superiority by now successfully sending the first man into space.

From past experience I was well aware that the arrival in Britain of Leningrad's prestigious Kirov ballet company was unlikely to make headline news for me. I could only try to gather as much information as possible and hope that something would emerge. At the Customs exit in Heathrow's Terminal 2 the hosts for their London theatre season were waiting to greet the dancers and I sought them out for details of the visit and names of the principals. I also wanted to establish whether a Russian interpreter was among the greeters, or if it was known if any English speakers would be among the visitors' management team.

After a few minutes we were joined at the barrier by press photographers, returning from the tarmac where they had tried to picture the dancers leaving the aircraft after

[1] *Now Zimbabwe.*

their flight from Paris. They seemed impatient and agitated and one, a leading agency photographer, complained to everyone at large: "Someone in the group told them all to keep moving just as we were trying to line them up. We couldn't even get the leading dancers to pose."

When the doors from the Customs hall opened the visitors suddenly appeared as a disorganised, impatient flood, almost tripping over each other in their haste to get clear of the building as quickly as possible. Somewhere at the centre of the throng I could see the British party trying to greet individuals, but in many cases they too were being brushed aside. Swept along by the tide, I asked in vain if anyone near me could speak English, but I was ignored.

At last I was able to buttonhole one of the British hosts. "What's happened?" I asked. "What's wrong? Why are they in such a hurry?" Briefly he replied as we hurried together down an escalator: "There's been some trouble in Paris. They won't talk about it but it seems as if one of their principal dancers has run away. Or defected. We don't know who and we don't know any more details."

Outside the terminal, as the ballet company boarded their private 'bus I tried again to question the Russians. If they understood me, none of them showed it. They simply shook their heads or turned away. Finally I gave up. I rushed to a telephone and called my news desk.

"Call the *Express* news desk," I said. "Ask them if they know anything about a Russian ballet dancer defecting in Paris. I'll stand by here. But call me back, please, as soon as you can."

I didn't have long to wait for the 'phone to ring.

"The *Express* said yes. It's true," came the reply. "A male dancer called Rudolf something or other. They said not to worry. They have the full story from Paris airport."

My contribution to the headlined stories that appeared everywhere the next day was completely negative. I could only describe the Kirov's arrival, their members' unwillingness to share their shameful secret, their haste to reach the safety of their private coach. My clients would, understandably regard the one comment from their welcoming committee, as innocuous.

So, like most of the country, I didn't hear the full story until the next day. The Kirov's leading male dancer, Rudolf Nureyev, I read, had broken away from the company as it was about to board its London-bound flight at Le Bourget Airport. He ran towards a number of French police officers shouting, "Protect me! Protect me!"

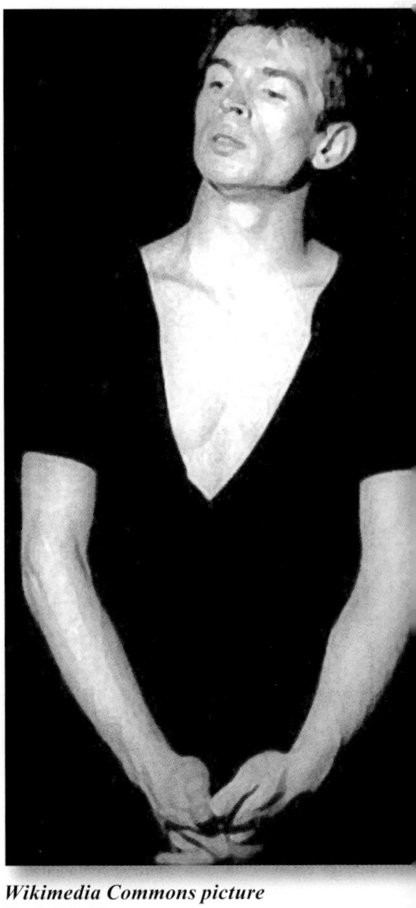

Wikimedia Commons picture
Rudolph Nureyev

In spite of strong protests from the Kirov management, the 23-years-old dancer was escorted protectively to a private room where he told police two Soviet officials in the Customs hall had intercepted him. He said the officials had told him he must leave the company and return to Moscow immediately. When he refused to go with them, he said, he had been threatened. It was at this point he ran up to the policemen.

Shortly afterwards, in the presence of French government representatives and police, Nureyev agreed to see Soviet Embassy representatives. They had known about his wish to defect for some time, they said. This was why he was being ordered back to Moscow. They tried to get him to change his mind, but their efforts were in vain. The dancer said he had asked the French for political asylum.

Almost immediately, the Soviet propaganda machine, now rejoicing in their shattering space success with Yuri Gagarin, found time to launch a clumsy whispering campaign against his Nureyev's achievements and abilities, making him a pariah in his homeland.

A prominent Russian diplomat, proud of his cultural contacts, told me confidently on one occasion: "Well, you know, Nureyev was no great loss to us. He was never a great dancer...." This of the man who the Soviets themselves had once described as "a second Nijinsky."

In the UK where the dancer, who in the meantime had applied for and had been granted Austrian citizenship, nevertheless formed a seemingly unlikely but hugely successful partnership on stage with our own prima ballerina Margot Fonteyn. By the mid-sixties, he had become an icon for the adoration of Sadlers Wells's balletomanes.

The popularity of Dame Margot herself had long been established with the ballet goers, the critics, the onlooking general public and press alike. On her many comings and goings

Wikimedia Commons picture
Margot Fonteyn, 1948

through London's airports, she was ever charming and co-operative with both reporters and photographers. In 1955 she had married Dr Roberto Arias, then Panamanian Ambassador to London.

Wittingly or unwittingly she became embroiled in South American politics as he actively opposed a new military regime in Panama. Even after he was crippled in a shooting incident she remained cool and unruffled, caring for him constantly and travelling with him whenever her theatre engagements permitted. At one point she was detained and spent a day in a Panama City jail accused of assisting her husband in an attempted coup, before convincing police of her innocence. Though I won little copy from her later return, I was pleased to renew our acquaintanceship and felt privileged to be attending her welcome-home press conference.

In an ideal world, sport, like ballet, should be far removed from politics, and certainly from party politics. Then think of the Olympic Games, international football tournaments, tennis, golf, even boxing contests and ponder how much nationalism, and consequently politics, is part of the process of international competition.

Hours before a 60-strong Soviet athletics squad was due to fly home after competing successfully in an international meeting in London, a warrant was issued for the arrest of 27-years old discus-thrower Nina Ponomareva. She had been accused of stealing five hats worth together £1.12s.11d (less than £1.65) from a department store in London's Oxford Street, but had failed to appear in court.

Unable to find her, Scotland Yard detectives waited outside the Russians' Lancaster Gate hotel as the rest of the team left in two coaches to drive to Heathrow. We had been asked to cover the departure and to watch out for Nina joining them at the last minute. But I learnt that only 59 names of athletes and officials had been listed for the specially chartered KLM Constellation airliner. The seventeenth name on the list, that of Nina Ponomareva, had been deleted following a late night telephone call from the Soviet Embassy.

A KLM official told me: "No reason was given for deleting the name, and no revised booking was made." But he had been able to confirm that Nina's luggage had been checked in with the rest of the squad's baggage.

The few English-speaking members of the group simply shrugged their shoulders when I asked what had happened to Nina. And shortly afterwards the chartered airliner

Evening Standard picture

THE RUSSIANS LEAVE —WITHOUT NINA

Evening Standard Reporter

Fifty-nine Russian athletes and officials left London Airport today in a specially chartered KLM Constellation airliner for Helsinki, Finland, on their way home.

But there was no sign of the 27-year-old discus-thrower Nina Ponomareva, who, last week, was accused of stealing five hats valued at £1 12s. 11d. from an Oxford Street store. She failed to appear in court and a warrant for her arrest was issued.

Name cancelled

Sixty names were in a list of passengers for the airliner, but Nina's name—17th in the list—was cancelled by the Russians in a telephone message last night to the London office of KLM.

An airline spokesman said today: "No reason was given by the Soviet Embassy for the deletion of her name. No new booking has been made for her."

When the Russians left their Lancaster Gate hotel in two coaches for the airport, two Scotland Yard detectives sat in a police car on the opposite side of the street.

Nina's luggage, which had remained in the hotel, went on with the rest of the athletes baggage.

'Back soon hope'

The few members of the team who spoke English only shrugged their shoulders when asked about her before they set out for the airport.

The deputy team manager,

Evening Standard
September 3 1956

took off for Moscow without her. And what did happen to her – in terms of the alleged shoplifting offence? Emulating her fellow athletes, I too have to shrug my shoulders. My recollection is that to avoid further publicity and to end an embarrassing incident, the Soviet Embassy, through the Foreign Office, pleaded "guilty" on Nina's behalf and arranged for the payment of a subsequent fine and legal costs. But I may be wrong...

*

Late in December, 1962, the *Scotsman,* the *Scottish Daily Express* and the Manchester edition of the *Daily Herald* carried our brief report from Prestwick Airport about the expected arrival that day of a Soviet Ilyushin airliner on its way from Moscow to Havana, Cuba.

What was significant about the flight? We had, after all, witnessed, and on occasions reported almost a dozen similar such non-scheduled flights touching down at the Scottish airport during the year – among them the one Chris had discovered to be carrying two American nationals who were of much interest to the FBI and MI5, as I have already described.[1] The turboprop airliner could only make the long transatlantic crossing by topping up its fuel en route. But as this would be via the Canada-US seaboard after taking the short northerly crossing of the Atlantic, the Russians were also obliged to pick up Canadian or American navigators for part of the journey.

Mystery Reds fly to Cuba

While the mass departure of Soviet technicians and their families by sea from Cuba continues, an Ilyushin 18 airliner carrying a crew of 12 and 59 "mystery" passengers was expected to touch down at Prestwick today on its way to Havana.

Routed from Moscow, via Halifax, Canada, the turbo-prop airliner is calling at Prestwick to refuel.

But special permission has been obtained for the passengers to land in Scotland and spend 17 hours on the ground. "We understand the Russians will be awaiting the arrival of Canadian navigators for their flight to Halifax," said one airport official.

'Mystery' flight

Preparations were being made last night at Prestwick Airport for the arrival of a Russian Ilyushin 18 air liner from Moscow. The plane, en route to Havana with 59 "mystery" passengers, was calling to refuel.

Daily Herald (top)
Scottish Daily Express
also Scotsman (not shown)
(all) December 28 1962

The difference was that this new arrival would be the first to touch down since the Cuban missile crisis. It was due a mere eight weeks after the head-to-head Soviet-American confrontation which had brought the world the closest it has ever been to nuclear war.

American spy-planes had discovered that Soviet medium-range missiles were being installed at a number of sites throughout the island of Cuba, which at its closest is less than 150 miles from the mainland US coast. President Kennedy had immediately ordered warships to blockade international waters of the mid-Atlantic. They halted and turned back at least one of several Soviet supply ships, which could clearly be seen to be carrying only partially-hidden missiles and other rocket spare parts on their decks. The Soviet leader, Nikita Khruschev, had finally agreed to dismantle the sites and return the missiles to Russia only after two weeks of intense verbal exchanges with his American opposite number and after both sides had talked openly of nuclear war.

National Park Service picture,
Wikimedia Commons licence
Khruschev and Kennedy, June 1961

Normally we wouldn't have dreamed of informing our clients in advance of such a potential story, but we had reason to believe that on this occasion at least two local newspaper correspondents were aware of the expected flight. It was possible that an advance story would be the only way we, as an agency, would "make" the news pages.

In fact it was to be a very different story, which won us exclusive headlines the next day. When we inquired at the desk of the handling agent for an estimated arrival time for the Ilyushin 18 turboprop, we were told: "It's been delayed indefinitely." And privately we were advised: "The Foreign Office are still considering whether to permit it."

Chris put through a call to the Foreign Office news department in London. I called the Aeroflot manager at Heathrow, an old contact that I knew would have to have details of the flight even though his only direct responsibility was his daily scheduled service between Moscow and London. He was able to confirm the number of passengers on the proposed flight, and he told me: "They are all members of a delegation of agriculturalists, architects and people from various trades and industries." But an hour or two later when I called him back to ask if he'd been given a revised arrival time for the flight he said that he now knew that all 59 passengers on board were "Russian tourists" who had chartered the flight to Cuba.

At last the Foreign Office confirmed that it had refused permission for the flight to land in Britain, the first time such action had been taken. A spokesman stated: "This is a reciprocal action. In the past Britain has requested flying rights beyond Moscow. This has repeatedly been refused.

[1] *See Ch.10, p.237-238*

BRITAIN BARS SOVIET CUBA-BOUND PLANE

NORMAL NOTICE OF FIVE DAYS NOT GIVEN

By MICHAEL HILTON,
Daily Telegraph Diplomatic Correspondent

BRITAIN has refused permission for a Russian Ilyushin 18 airliner, flying between Moscow and Cuba, to overfly Britain and land at Prestwick. The airliner would have been carrying 59 passengers and was due at Prestwick yesterday.

Permission for the overflight was requested by the Russian Embassy in London on Wednesday. The normal minimum period for such requests is five days.

In the past few months Russia has requested, and been granted, permission for overflights for 11 aircraft flying between Moscow and Havana.

Evidently, it has occurred to the authorities in London that this was beginning to take on the appearance of a regular service.

In 1961, Britain asked Russia for permission to establish a regular service for flights beyond Moscow to the Far East. Permission was refused.

LONDON SERVICE
Separate agreement

Russia is not a member of the International Civil Aviation Organisation, for members of which there are certain reciprocal overflying and refuelling rights.

This means that permission has to be sought for each individual flight, except the London-Moscow service, for which there is a separate agreement.

Passengers on the cancelled flight had been listed as "a large delegation of agriculturists, architects, and people from various trades and industries." A spokesman for Aeroflot, the Russian airline, said yesterday that so far as they knew the flight had been delayed for 24 hours.

Daily Telegraph

BRITAIN BARS RED PLANE FOR CUBA

HERALD REPORTER

THE Foreign Office yesterday refused to allow a Russian Ilyushin 18 turbo-prop airliner to land at Prestwick Airport.

The plane, flying 59 "mystery" passengers from Moscow to Cuba, was scheduled to land at the airport early yesterday.

The Russians were to stop over for 17 hours to refuel and pick up the necessary Canadian or American crew.

But the Foreign Office turned down their application to land.

Turned down

A Foreign Office spokesman said last night: "The Russians in the past have turned down requests from us to permit planes on non-scheduled flights to fly beyond Moscow.

"Now we have turned down their application for this trip. It's as simple as that."

In London, a senior official to the Russian airline, Aeroflot, described the passengers as "a large delegation of agriculturalists, architects and people from various trades and industries."

The flight would have been the first passenger service from Moscow to Havana since the Cuba crisis

ALAN CLARKE writes:

There is no doubt, too, that the very vague information the Russians have given about the Ilyushin's passengers, has reinforced the decision not to allow the flight through Prestwick.

At the height of the Cuban blockade it was foreseen that the Russians might attempt to send weapons and military personnel to Cuba by air, and Britain took precautions to ensure that Prestwick was not used as a refuelling point

Daily Herald

WORLD NEWS SPOTLIGHT

SCOTS NO TO RED AIRLINER

BRITAIN has banned a Cuba-bound Russian airliner from flying over this country.

Daily Mirror
(all 6) December 29 1962

"Landing rights for this aircraft were requested only two days ago – and on a Bank Holiday. We have an agreement which requires at least five days notice for unscheduled flights." He added: "We've been in touch with the Russian Embassy for more information about the passengers on board the aircraft and they have given us only limited information – though this was not a factor in the refusal."

The *Daily Telegraph* gave us a second lead on page one – but attributed it to their diplomatic correspondent, Michael Hilton, who added his own conclusions to our basic story *(left)* but the single-column headlines of other newspapers followed a similar pattern:

Airport ban on Soviet plane

By Daily Mail Reporter

A RUSSIAN Ilyushin 18 airliner was refused permission by the Foreign Office to land at Prestwick yesterday on its way to Cuba.

Scottish Daily Mail

Britain bans Cuba-bound airliner

Scottish Daily Express

BRITAIN BARS RUSSIAN PLANE

BRITAIN has banned a Cuba-bound Russian airliner from flying over this country.

Daily Record

It was made quite clear to us, in spite of Government denials, that one reason for the ban was American pressure. Washington feared the Russians might use such flights to carry small arms and continue to send military technicians and advisers to Cuba, even though intelligence and other reports from Havana had indicated a big increase in the evacuation of Soviet personnel by sea.

Those fears were reinforced some three months later when we earned page leads in two Sunday newspapers. The Scottish tabloid *Sunday Mail* gave us some 500 words of copy under a Page One 3-line banner, and the widely-circulated *Sunday Post*, also a tabloid, asked: "WAS CZECH 'PLANE CARRYING ROCKET PARTS TO CUBA?" *(See both, opposite).*

We had been warned by Wally Waldron, the airport commandant, about the proposed police swoop when making enquiries about the expected arrival of the Czech Airlines 'plane, the first ever to visit the Scottish airport. He said that when the aircraft touched down, a security check would be carried out – "on the instructions of the Foreign Office." He agreed that it was the first time he had ever heard of such a requirement, but privately he confirmed my guess that the search was intended to ensure that no weapons or other military equipment was being carried.

On board the airliner, a British-built turbo-prop Britannia, similar to those operated by BOAC, but displaying the Czech flag on its tail and bearing the inscription *"Ceskoslovenske Aerolinie,"* were 45 passengers including women and children. They were believed to be mainly Russian nationals and all were bound for Havana, Cuba. But before they were allowed to disembark to enable their aircraft to take on fuel for the Atlantic crossing, the aircraft was boarded by a senior plain-clothes police officer from

AIRLINER IN SCOTS POLICE PROBE DRAMA

SENIOR police officers boarded an airliner flying from Czechoslovakia to Cuba, when it touched down at Prestwick Airport yesterday.

On board the airliner, a British-built turbo-prop Britannia with the Czech flag painted on the tail, were 45 passengers including women and children—believed to be mainly Russian nationals.

At Prestwick, all officials would say was that a security check was being carried out "on the instructions of the Foreign Office." The plane was held up for over three hours.

Police stand by

A plain clothes senior officer of the Ministry of Aviation Constabulary went aboard the aircraft

He spent a few minutes speaking with the pilot, and examined the passenger cabin, freight and baggage holds.

Then, accompanied by a crew member, he inspected the lower part of the airliner's fuselage from ground level, as uniformed police stood by.

Later the police officer said: "I can make no statement. All enquiries should be made at Ministry of Aviation headquarters."

A Home Office immigration officer also boarded the aircraft.

They wouldn't talk

The passengers lunched on salad and ice-cream at the airport, then waited in a transit lounge. Many bought picture postcards of Scotish views, souvenirs, and duty-free Scotch whisky.

NOT ONE OF THEM WOULD DISCUSS THEIR JOURNEY.

Early last month, the Foreign Office refused the Soviet airline, Aeroflot, permission to land an Ilyshin airliner at Prestwick for refuelling on its way to Cuba.

It was then suggested that the ban was the direct result of American pressure to ensure no new build-up of Soviet military activity in Cuba.

Not warned

Yesterday it was understood that the Czech airline had approached Britain for permission to operate some of its Havana services through the United Kingdom.

But at Prestwick an official for B.O.A.C., who handled the flight, said: "We have no knowledge of any future flights by the Czech airline through Prestwick.

"We were not warned of this particular flight until a few hours before it touched down."

And in London, a Ministry of Aviation official could not say why the flight was re-routed to refuel at Prestwick.

Later last night a Foreign Office spokesman said: "The airliner was given permission to over-fly the country as long as it landed at Prestwick for inspection."

He refused to say what the police officers were looking for.

It is believed the Foreign Office instruction for the security check stems from American fears that Red civil aircraft were used to transport rocket parts and other military equipment to Havana during the Cuban crisis.

Sunday Mail (Page One lead)
March 31 1963

WAS CZECH 'PLANE CARRYING ROCKET PARTS TO CUBA?

Mystery Search At Prestwick Airport

SECURITY police officers boarded a Czechoslovakian airliner flying from Prague to Cuba when it touched down at Prestwick Airport yesterday.

On board the airliner were 45 passengers, including a number of women and children. At Prestwick it was stated the security check was being carried out on the instructions of the Foreign Office.

It is believed the Foreign Office instructions to airport officials to carry out a security check stemmed from American fears that civil airliners from behind the Iron Curtain were used to transport rocket parts and other military equipment into Cuba.

An aviation expert said last night "This kind of stipulation by the British Government amounts to little less than a British blockade of Cuba."

A plain-clothes recruitment officer of the Ministry of Aviation Constabulary spent a few minutes speaking with the police.

He examined the passenger cabin and the freight and baggage holds. He inspected the lower part of the airliner's fuselage from ground level as uniformed police stood by.

A Home Office Immigration officer also boarded the aircraft.

Later the police officer said, "I can make no statement. All inquiries should be made at the Ministry of Aviation headquarters."

A Foreign Office spokesman said, "The airliner was given permission to overfly the country as long as it landed at Prestwick for inspection."

He declined to say what the officers were looking for.

Sunday Post
March 31 1963

Passengers re-board the Czech airliner with their whisky and Scottish souvenirs

Sunday Post, March 31 1963
Brenard Press picture

the Ministry of Aviation constabulary.

He spent several minutes speaking with the Czech captain and then examined the passenger cabin and the freight and baggage holds. Accompanied by a crew member, he then inspected the lower part of the airliner's fuselage from ground level as other police officers stood by. A Home Office immigration officer also boarded the aircraft and checked the passports of passengers and crew.

Later the plain-clothes officer said: "I can make no statement. All inquiries should be made at Ministry of Aviation headquarters."

The passengers were taken to the airport restaurant where they were joined by the Britannia's grey-uniformed aircrew for a lunch of salad and ice-cream. Several of them bought Scottish souvenirs, picture postcards and duty free Scotch at an airport shop. None of the passengers would discuss their journey, but a member of the crew said: "This is a scheduled service between Prague and Havana. Normally we fly to Shannon Airport in Ireland and Gander in Newfoundland. I have no idea why we have come to Prestwick."

The aircraft spent nearly four hours on the ground at Prestwick before being allowed to take off to continue its flight to Gander and Havana.

When we called the Foreign Office news department to ask if the police were looking for arms, a spokesman replied: "You'll have to ask the Ministry of Aviation that. It's nothing to do with us." But he then agreed, grudgingly: "The airliner was given permission to overfly this country as long as it landed at Prestwick for inspection.

POLICE CHECK ON RED AIRLINER

Sunday Express Reporter

SENIOR police officers boarded a Czech airliner when it touched down at Prestwick Airport yesterday.

The plane, a British built turbo prop Britannia, was bound for Cuba from Prague with 45 passengers, many of them women and children.

A plain clothes member of the Ministry of Aviation constabulary boarded the aircraft for talks with the pilot and to examine the passenger cabin freight, and baggage holds.

Uniformed police stood guard when he inspected the fuselage, accompanied by a member of the crew.

A Home Office official also boarded the aircraft. The search lasted four hours. The plane then took off for Gander.

Lunch

The passengers, believed to be mainly Russian nationals and the grey-uniformed members of the crew, were taken to the airport restaurant for lunch during the check. A member of the crew said: "This is a scheduled service to Havana. Normally we fly vit Shannon Airport and Gander. I have no idea why we have come to Prestwick.

An airport official said they had been warned about the flight only a few hours before the plane touched down.

A Foreign Office spokesman said last night: "The Czech airliner was given permission to overfly the country, provided it landed at Prestwick for inspction.

"This is routine procedure for an uncheduled flight."

Scottish Sunday Express
March 31 1963

"This is a routine procedure for an unscheduled flight," he stated. He again refused to say what the police officers were looking for and implied that details of the search were the responsibility of the Aviation Ministry.

But few of the London and Manchester-based Sunday newspapers gave it the prominence of their Scottish counterparts. And the *Scottish Sunday Express* news desk in Glasgow told me after it had published just nine inches of the story on an inside page: "We had planned to use this on Page One until the Foreign Office claimed it was a perfectly routine procedure which is carried out frequently by the Ministry of Aviation. We couldn't get through to you to tell you this or to ask for your comments."

It seemed to me we might have a new angle for what would have been a standard follow-up for Monday's papers. I telephoned the press officer for the Ministry of Aviation's Scottish Division at his home near Edinburgh and told him exactly what the Foreign Office had said. He listened without comment until I had finished.

I was left thinking that perhaps he hadn't understood what I was saying. The Foreign Office seemed to be denying responsibility for the action taken against the Czech airliner. It insisted that the procedures were routine and was implying that the Ministry of Aviation had been too zealous in its interpretation of the "inspection" requirement. But at last he said: "Give me little while to look into this and to call my Controller. Then I'll call you."

When the call came it was not the official spokesman on the line but the Scottish Division Controller himself. He appeared calm but determined. (His spokesman later told me: "He was absolutely furious with the Foreign Office.) "I want to give you a full statement to clarify some of the misinformation you have been given," he said. "Can you take it down?"

I replied: "Certainly. But do I attribute it to you personally?" I could have bitten my tongue. I shouldn't have asked. I felt sure he would want to be quoted directly

"No," he replied, "Perhaps not. Attribute it to our official spokesman . I'll give him a copy and he can then deal with any further inquiries."

He went on to say: "The Czech airliner was searched for arms or weapons of war when it landed for a 'technical stop' at Prestwick.

"Our police boarded the airliner on instructions from the Foreign Office. The airline agreed to the security search when permission to operate the flight through the UK was granted.

"This was an unscheduled service operating between Czechoslovakia and Cuba. The US has denied the Czechs landing rights for such flights. Following customary international usage, the Czechs asked for normal flying rights through the United Kingdom, including facilities for a technical stop. In such cases it is customary for the UK Government to specify which airport is to be used for such a stop and Prestwick was specified.

"Under an agreement drawn up between member countries of the International Civil

Aviation Organisation, a search may be carried out on any aircraft which may reasonably be suspected of carrying weapons of war. This was the condition being implemented at Prestwick with the full knowledge of the Czechoslovakian Government and the airline."

He would not comment further, but agreed that he too had never heard of a previous occasion when a non-scheduled airliner had been required to undergo a security check of this kind at a British airport. And he said that it could be safely inferred that the search was a direct result of American pressure to ensure there was no new build-up of Soviet military activity in Cuba.

Monday's dailies carried a muted version of my follow-up story. It had clearly been "talked down" by the Foreign Office.

ARMS SEARCH ON AIRLINER

POLICE who searched a Cuba-bound Czech airliner at Prestwick had been ordered by the Foreign Office to look for arms, an Aviation Ministry spokesman said last night. It is believed that the Czech airline had been told the plane could land at Prestwick only if it agreed to the search—the first of its kind in Britain.

Scottish Daily Express also Scotsman (not shown)

CZECH PLANE SEARCHED FOR ARMS

By Daily Mail Reporter

A CZECH-OWNED Britannia airline was held up for three hours at Prestwick at the week-end while a search was made for arms.

Senior Ministry of Aviation policemen carried out the check.

The plane was on a flight from Czechoslovakia to Cuba. Most of the passengers are understood to be Russians.

A Ministry of Aviation spokesman said in Edinburgh last night that instructions to carry out the search came from the Foreign Office.

Last month the Foreign Office refused the Russians permission to refuel an Aeroflot air liner at Prestwick on its way to Cuba.

Scottish Daily Mail (both) April 1 1963

Editor's collection
The Ceskoslovenské Aerolinie timetable from 1962 *(left)* ...and the updated version from November '63 *(right)*, perhaps to show there was nothing hidden in the undercarriage...

*

Early in October 1963 we learned that Soviet cosmonaut Yuri Gagarin, who as the first human to escape the gravity chains of Earth had won so many plaudits for the Soviets' space age pioneering achievements, was shortly to visit Prestwick. He would be flying from Moscow via New York to Mexico to attend an international space conference and routine permission was being sought for his turbo-prop Ilyushin airliner to refuel at the Scottish airport.

But two days after reporting this news I had to reveal that the Soviet airline Aeroflot had still not received clearance from the UK government for the two-hour halt. Officials of BOAC, which normally handled Aeroflot flights through Prestwick, then advised me that Gagarin's aircraft had made an unscheduled stop at Riga, Latvia, some four-and-a-half hours' flight time from Scotland, with a "mechanical fault," but in fact awaiting clearance permission. But the Foreign Office said: "We are still considering this matter. We normally require 5 days notice for such a request."

Yuri flies in to-morrow

THE world's first spaceman, Yuri Gagarin, will be at Prestwick Airport to-morrow.

Yuri, on his way to a space conference in Mexico via New York, is flying in an Ilyushin jet air liner which will make a refuelling halt at Prestwick and is due to arrive at 12.30.

If time permits, the Russian spaceman will visit Burns Cottage and Museum at Alloway.

The flight has been delayed for 27 hours.

Yuri will be joined on the aircraft at Havana, Cuba, by spacegirl Valentina Tereshkova, who is also on the way to the conference.

YURI DUE ON FLYING VISIT

SPACEMAN Number One Yuri Gagarin is to make his first visit to Scotland tomorrow — for two hours.

He is flying in a Soviet airliner from Moscow to Cuba —by way of Prestwick.

Gagarin will join space girl Valentina Tereshkova in Havana and both will go on to a space conference in Mexico.

An airline official at Prestwick said yesterday: "The airliner with Gagarin was due to arrive tomorrow, but we have been told it will not leave Moscow until Wednesday morning."

© Evening Times, Oct 8 and Scottish Daily Express, Oct 9 1963

The Soviet aviation authorities had applied on October 3rd for permission to land at Prestwick on the 8th. Two days later a revised application asked for the 9th. Further amendments to the request, other than the arrival date, were made on the 7th. When the date for the touch down came and went, the Foreign Office finally admitted to me that the Soviet application was being rejected because of a failure to meet all the "routine conditions." At the same time a spokesman was telling news desks of the national press in London that permission had been refused because British flights were refused similar over-fly facilities in the Soviet Union.

Hours later, after speaking to Aeroflot's manager at Heathrow, Ivan Smernov, I was able to break the news that the Foreign Office had relented. Gagarin's aircraft would be allowed into Prestwick after all. But the decision had come too late. As I reported for Friday's papers, (October 11) the cosmonaut had already returned to Moscow from Riga.

MIX-UP CATCHES YURI IN MID-AIR

THE Foreign Office yesterday left Soviet astronaut Yuri Gagarin "up in the air"—because his Mexico-bound airliner did not land at Prestwick to refuel.

Said an official of the Soviet airline, Aeroflot: "We have approached the Foreign Office for permission to operate the aircraft through Prestwick, but so far have received no answer."

Said a Foreign Office spokesman last night: "The Government normally requires five days' notice of the flight."

Meanwhile, late yesterday British Overseas Airways, who normally handle Russian flights through Prestwick, were notified that Gagarin's aircraft had made an unscheduled landing at Biga, the Baltic port 500 miles west of Moscow, to await clearance permission.

Scottish Daily Express (both) October 10 1963

GAGARIN'S PRESTWICK STOP DIFFICULTY

The Foreign Office are expected to decide today whether a Russian airliner carrying Colonel Yuri Gagarin, the Russian cosmonaut, can refuel at Prestwick on its way from Moscow to Mexico.

The Russians wanted to touch down in Scotland yesterday but failed to get permission. It was learnt last night that the airliner had made an unscheduled stop at Riga, Latvia—four-and-a-half hours' flying time from London—with a "mechanical fault".

The Times

BRITAIN MAY BAN GAGARIN'S PLANE

HERALD REPORTER

A plane carrying Russian cosmonaut Yuri Gagarin may be banned from refuelling in Britain on its way to Mexico.

The Foreign Office are stalling over whether to allow the aircraft to refuel at Prestwick.

Officials of the Russian airline Aeroflot said in London yesterday: 'We have received no answer so far to our application for permission."

FRANCIS MOIR, Herald Diplomatic Correspondent, writes: A decision on whether the Russian plane can land at Prestwick will be made early today, and last night it looked like permission would be refused.

Daily Herald (above)
©Glasgow Herald (above, right)
Evening Citizen (right)
also Scotsman (not shown)
(all) October 10 1963

Gagarin *(front left)* meets astronauts Edward H. White II & James A. McDivitt in June 1965. Seated, US Vice President H.H. Humphrey and standing, French Premier Georges Pompidou
NASA picture

GAGARIN'S PLANE DELAYED

—And No Permit for Prestwick

A Russian air liner flying the Soviet cosmonaut Yuri Gagarin, which was expected to touch down at Prestwick Airport yesterday to refuel before flying on to Mexico

GAGARIN'S FLIGHT DELAYED

FOR the second time in 36 hours, a Russian airliner flying Soviet cosmonaut Yuri Gagarin from Moscow to Mexico was delayed again today.

A further two and a half hours was added to the expected departure time of the flight

Smernov confirmed: "We have received authority for the aircraft to land and refuel at Prestwick. But it is now quite possible that the cosmonaut will travel by some other route.

"Using a larger aircraft, he could now fly directly from Moscow to Cuba and continue from there."

The *Daily Herald* gave the story the best spread, with a headline across four columns, while *The Glasgow Herald* used a detailed explanation from a diplomatic correspondent of why the

Ban on Gagarin's plane dropped

Herald Diplomatic Correspondent

THE airliner carrying Soviet spaceman Yuri Gagarin to Mexico can, after all, land at Prestwick Airport to refuel before flying the Atlantic.

Five hours after announcing that permission would not be given, on tit-for-tat diplomatic grounds, the Foreign Office changed their mind.

IN MOSCOW

This followed "further representations in Moscow — maybe from Mr. Kruschev himself—that the refusal would stop Gagarin getting to Mexico in time for the International Aviation Festival opening.

The original Whitehall turndown was based on the long-standing refusal of Moscow to allow British aircraft to land for refuelling in Russia.

"We agree to make one more exception," said the nal announcement, "and to accord the facilities requested."

In response, it was hoped that the Soviet Union would discuss, soon, some return for transit facilities granted by Britain over the past two years.

But signals sent from Prestwick to Riga, Latvia, from which Gagarin's plane was due to fly, brought no reply last night. Prestwick had asked for a flight plan.

And in London an official of Eeroflot, the Russian airline, said Gagarin had returned to Moscow following the initial refusal for his plane to land here.

CHANGE OF MIND ON GAGARIN'S FLIGHT

From Our Diplomatic Correspondent

LONDON, Thursday.

Britain to-day refused permission for a Russian aircraft carrying the cosmonaut, Colonel Yuri Gagarin, to land at Prestwick en route for Cuba and Mexico—and later withdrew her refusal.

Britain had rejected the request on the grounds that Russia does "not give us reciprocal facilities." This refers to the fact that she has never been willing to agree to civil aviation facilities for British air lines at points beyond Moscow.

The dispute blew up last December when Britain barred a Soviet aircraft carrying 59 Russians to Havana from landing at Prestwick.

Exceptions have been made. Soviet Foreign Minister Gromyko's aircraft refuelled at Prestwick last month on the way to the U.S. Some time during the day Colonel Gagarin was elevated by the Foreign Office to the status of an exception.

©Glasgow Herald

BACK IN MOSCOW

Last night an official of Aeroflot, the Russian air line, said that Gagarin was now back in Moscow. He returned there from Riga, Latvia, when permission for his Ilyushin aircraft to operate through Prestwick Airport was originally refused.

Confirming that the air line had since received authority for the aircraft to use Prestwick as a refuelling stop on its way to Cuba, the official said:—"It is now possible that Colonel Gagarin will travel by some other route. Using a larger aircraft he could fly direct to Cuba."

There was every possibility, he added, that Colonel Gagarin and the spacewoman, Valentina Tereshkova, would return to Moscow via Prestwick in about a week's time.

Valentina Tereshkova
NASA picture

YURI CAN LAND —BUT IT'S TOO LATE

Express Staff Reporter

WHITEHALL changed its mind last night about not allowing a Russian plane with spaceman Yuri Gagarin aboard to land at Prestwick on its way to Mexico.

At first the Foreign Office sent a Note to the Russian Embassy saying "No."

Reason: No reciprocal facilities are ever granted by Russia in allowing British planes to fly beyond Moscow.

But last night a spokesman said: "Since it now appears from further representations in Moscow that our refusal would prevent Major Gagarin from

Scottish Daily Express

Daily Herald (left)
also Scotsman (not shown)
(all) October 11 1963

TRIP BACK

The official said: "It is now quite possible that Colonel Gagarin will travel by some other route. Using a larger aircraft, he could fly direct from Moscow to Mexico. We are not likely to know his movements in London until the morning."

But he said there was every possibility that Colonel Gagarin and space girl Valentina Tereshkova would return to Moscow via Prestwick in about a week.

The Russian Ilyushin aircraft carrying Gagarin was forced to make an unscheduled stop at Riga on its flights from Moscow to Prestwick because of a mechanical fault. It returned to Moscow yesterday.

application was refused under my story. The *Daily Record* was more outspoken when it headlined my two column story: "Britain snubs space couple" *(right).*

Then it assumed, wrongly it seemed, that Valentina Tereshkova, the world's first woman in space, would be travelling with him, as she was attending the same conference in Mexico. I could have told them, courtesy of Smernov, she was already in Cuba, having flown separately to Havana.

The *Scottish Daily Express*, and the *Scottish Daily Mail* both used similar stories, adding their own contributions as further information followed from Government sources. Some revealed that the British Ambassador in Moscow had carried a message directly from the British Foreign Secretary, Lord Home, sanctioning the refuelling stop.

The following day I called Smernov again to try to establish if the Soviet spaceman had indeed made alternative arrangements to fly the Atlantic. As a result I was able to advise the newspapers that Gagarin was already on his way directly from Moscow to Cuba by a longer-range jet aircraft.

Three days later, at my request, the Aeroflot manager informed my Heathrow news desk as soon as he had confirmation of the cosmonaut's return flight home and its proposed route. They quickly alerted me and once again I was able to jump the gun by reporting that both Gagarin and Tereshkova would be calling at Prestwick on their way *back* to Moscow the following day – a mere four days after the aborted visit.

I ran the story first for the evening newspapers, following up with the dailies, once again winning exclusive coverage. Attributing my information directly to Smernov, in each case I ended my piece with a reference to Valentina's newly announced engagement to fellow cosmonaut Andriyan Nikolayev. I had a hunch that it might be relevant....

There has to be a footnote to this story of conflicting information (or misinformation through conflicting interests). In my monthly report on our

Britain snubs space couple

BRITAIN changed her mind last night about a snub to two Russian space pioneers . . . but it was too late.

The world's first spaceman, Yuri Gagarin, and the first spacewoman, Valentina Tereshkova, were already on their way back to Moscow.

The trouble started when the Russians asked permission for a plane carrying the two to refuel at Prestwick.

The plane, a turbo-prop was taking Gagarin and Tereshkova to the International Aviation Federation Conference in Mexico.

'Exception'

The Foreign Office **REFUSED** permision for the Prestwick touch-down.

This, they explaned, was a "tit for - tat" move because Russia refused to grant British planes similar facilities in the Soviet Union.

Then last night the Foreign Office **RELENTED.**

They said they would make an "exception" and allow the plane to land.

But by this time the stranded space couple were on their way back to the Soviet capital.

Their plane had stopped overnight at Riga, on the Baltic, for mechanical repairs."

When news of the Foreign Office ban was received the plane headed back to Moscow.

A Russian official in London said last night: "It is now quite possible that Colonel Gagarin will travel by some other route.

"Using a larger aircraft he could fly direct from Moscow."

But he said it was possible that Gagarin, and Tereshkova would return to Moscow via Prestwick in about a week's time.

Announcing their change-of-mind, the Foreign Office said it was because they had been told the ban could make the space couple miss the opening of the Mexico conference.

Daily Record October 11 1963

Yuri misses out Britain

Soviet cosmonaut, Yuri Gagarin, eft Moscow Airport early yesterlay for Cuba—and will not after ıll visit Prestwick Airport.

This was stated in London by a enior official of Aeroflot, the Russian air line. He added: Colonel Gagarin has taken a lirect flight to Cuba. In Havana ıe will be joined by Valentina Tereshkova.

Daily Herald Oct 12 1963

GAGARIN FLIES FROM MOSCOW

Not for Prestwick

Soviet cosmonaut Yuri Gagarin left Moscow Airport yesterday for Cuba—and will not, after all, visit Prestwick Airport.

This was stated in London by a senior official of Aeroflot, the Russian air line. He added:—"Colonel Gagarin has taken a direct flight to Cuba. In Havana he will be joined by Valentina Tereshkova, who will then fly on with him to Mexico."

The two Russians are attending a space conference which opens in Mexico to-day. Prestwick airport officials had no knowledge of the latest change in plans following the reversal of an earlier Foreign Office decision to ban Gagarin's original flight.

© Glasgow Herald Oct 12 1963

SCOTS STOP FOR VAL AND YURI

THE first girl in space, Valentina Tereshkova, is paying her first visit to Britain to-morrow, when she flies into Prestwick Airport.

She and the world's first spaceman, Yuri Gagarin, will be "dropping" into Prestwick Airport on their way back from Mexico after attending the International Aviation Federation.

Their Russian Ilyushin 18 air liner is making a two-hour refuelling stop at Prestwick.

Said an official of the Russian air line Aeroflot — "We have received permission from the Foreign Office for the air liner carrying the cosmonauts to land at Prestwick."

He was unable to say if the "space twins" had permission to visit nearby Burns Cottage.

Last week the Foreign Office refused permission for Gagarin's flight from Moscow to land at Prestwick. They later reversed the decision, but by then Gagarin was on board a direct flight from Moscow to Cuba.

Valentina's engagement to third cosmonaut Andrian Nikolayev was announced recently while she was in Cuba.

©Evening Times

SPACE GIRL WILL DROP IN AT PRESTWICK

THE first girl in space, Valentina Tereshkova, is paying her first visit to Britain tomorrow when she flies into Prestwick airport. With the world's first spaceman, Yuri Gagarin, she will be on her way home to Russia from Mexico after attending the International Aviation Federation.

Their Ilyushin 18 airliner is making a two-hour refuelling stop at Prestwick.

Said an official of the Russian airline Aeroflot "We have received permission from the Foreign Office for the airliner to land." He was unable to say if the cosmonauts had permission to visit Burns's cottage.

Evening Citizen

Valentina drops in

The first girl in space, 26-year-old Valentina Tereshwova, pays her first visit to Britain tomorrow. She and number one cosmonaut Yuri Gagarin will spend two hours at Prestwick when a Russian airliner flying them home from Mexico touches down to refuel.

TWO-HOUR SCOTS VISIT FOR YURI AND VALENTINA

Express Staff Reporter

FIRST space girl Valentina Tereshkova (26) is to pay her first visit to Britain tomorrow.

She and spaceman No. 1 Yuri Gagarin will spend two hours at Prestwick, where a Russian airliner flying them home from Mexico is to touch down for re-fueling.

They have been attending a meeting of the International Aviation Federation in Mexico.

Said an official of Aeroflot, the Russian airline, in London yesterday: "We have received permission for an Ilyushin 18 airliner carrying Colonel Gagarin and Miss Tereshkova to land at Prestwick on Thursday."

Last week the Foreign Office refused permission for an airliner carrying Gagarin to land in Britain. The decision was later reversed—but by that time Gagarin was on board a direct flight from Moscow to Cuba.

Valentina's engagement to third Russian spaceman Andrian Nikolayev was recently announced in Moscow.

Scottish Daily Express (above)
Daily Herald (left) (all) Oct 16 1963

Space girl Valentina lands at Prestwick tomorrow

By Daily Mail Reporter

THE first girl in space, 26-year-old Valentina Tereshkova, is to visit Scotland tomorrow.

She and No. 1 cosmonaut Yuri Gagarin will spend two hours at Prestwick Airport where a Russian airliner flying them home from Mexico is to refuel.

Cosmonette and cosmonaut have been attending a meeting of the International Aviation Federation in Mexico.

Burns

An official of Aeroflot, the Russian airline, said in London yesterday: "We have received permission from the Foreign Office for an Ilyushin 18 airliner to land at Prestwick tomorrow and can now confirm the arrival time of the aircraft."

He was unable to say if a request would be made by the couple to be allowed to leave the airport to visit Burns's Cottage near by, a favourite pilgrimage for Russians flying through Prestwick.

Last week the Foreign Office refused permission for an airliner carrying Gagarin to land in Britain. The decision was later reversed but by this time Gagarin was already on board a direct flight from Moscow to Cuba.

Scottish Daily Mail Oct 16 '63

Space girl here

THE first girl in space, Valentina Tereshkova, 26, will pay her first visit to Britain tomorrow.

She and No. 1 cosmonaut Yuri Gagarin will spend two hours at Prestwick Airport, where a Russian airliner flying them home from Mexico will touch down for refuelling.

They have been attending an International Aviation Federation meeting in Mexico.

Daily Record *October 16 1963*

Prestwick operations, I put in a word of thanks to colleagues at Heathrow who had provided invaluable assistance in passing on messages between Smernov, the Foreign Office, the Ministry of Aviation and me. As I said in my letter to news director Ray Watts:

'...the Aeroflot quotes *(in my news reports)* were taking precedence over Foreign Office indecisiveness. We were not only supplying the newspapers with the only reliable information on Gagarin's whereabouts, but the Ministry of Aviation and BOAC as well. Our stock shot up because we were the only people to be in contact with Smernov, and the only people to know the facts before officials.

'The airport manager *(at Prestwick)* said he was being so misled by his own Ministry, he was telephoning me periodically for information. He said in front of the airport commandant and a number of local press boys that Brenards' were the only people to know what was going on, and that he'd rather rely on us than any official source!'

The following day the world's news media descended on Prestwick for what was to be one of the largest press conferences ever seen at the Scottish airport. If we had been professionally promoting the Soviet space achievements rather than simply reporting them we would have chalked up a major PR success. Every national in the UK was directly represented, as were radio and TV organisations.

For us, it was *too* successful. Hardly any news markets were still left open to us for covering the event as a news agency. Indeed, I believe we had only one advance order from a client and that, from the *Press Association*, must have been a form of insurance as they too were directly represented.

I had half expected this. As I told myself, the arrival in Britain of the first man and the first woman in space would have attracted a great deal of media attention whether I had provided all the advance information or not. So I had to be satisfied with our income and prestige from all the advance exclusives.

Surprisingly, Colonel Yuri Gagarin himself failed to appear at the press conference. He stayed aboard his Ilyushin airliner. He was, we were told, still fast asleep, though some of us believed he might be expressing his irritation over the earlier diplomatic problems, a suggestion hastily denied by Embassy officials.

Engaged cosmonauts Valentina Tereshkova and Andriyan Nikolayev, however, did appear at the door of the airliner to step on to British soil together. My hunch had proved correct, to the delight of the waiting photographers. They posed agreeably and talked freely about their space flights and their romance. Someone asked about their marriage plans, the possibilities of a moon honeymoon and whether they hoped to have children.

But it was my question to Tereshkova, which drew the quote of quotes at the press conference. "Would you like your first baby to be a cosmonaut as well?" I asked the couple. If my memory is correct, Valentina replied: "We would like him, or her, to travel with us in space." Her fiancé went one step further. "He could become the first *lunartik*," he said.

For a moment there was silence. Then a burst of laughter from the unashamed media corps. The couple looked puzzled, and the tension was only cleared when an Embassy interpreter stepped in with a brief lesson in English semantics. The headlines the next day said it all. Not one of them was mine....

*

Official Soviet picture

(left) **The official, autographed Soviet picture of the first man in space, Colonel Yuri Gagarin, given out to well-wishers waiting to greet him at Prestwick Airport in 1963. But when he finally touched down on Scottish soil, he failed to appear to meet his fans. Colleagues said that he was still on board... sleeping.**

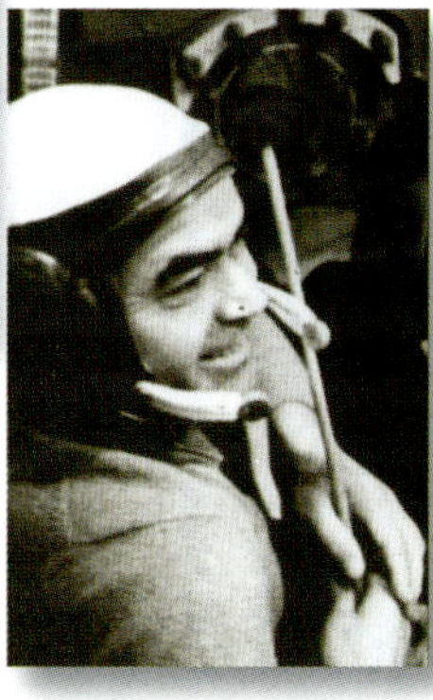

(right) **a NASA picture of Andriyan Nikolayev, and Valentina Tereshkova who was immortalised on a Russian postage stamp**

After all the fuss had died down and the cosmonauts had left on the final leg of their journey home, I recalled a relevant earlier involvement with the space age. It was back in January 1956, less than two years before the launch of the Soviet Sputnik, the world's first artificial satellite. We had been advised that Dr Richard van der Riet Woolley, Britain's newly appointed Astronomer Royal, was flying into Heathrow from Sydney to take up his appointment.

Two or three of our clients, including the *Times* and the *Press Association*, had ordered coverage of his arrival. Dr Woolley, 49-years-old Director of the Commonwealth Observatory at Canberra, Australia, was now succeeding Sir Harold Spencer Jones at the Royal Observatory at Herstmonceux Castle, Sussex.

As I waited at the Northside arrivals customs barrier, I was joined by Val Banyard, the *Daily Telegraph's* resident reporter at Heathrow, also there to cover Dr Woolley's arrival.

Greeting him and congratulating him on his appointment, we both questioned him on his work and what he saw as his objectives as Astronomer Royal. He said that he hoped to get England back to the forefront in astronomy and astro-physics.

"There was a time, about 100 years ago, when the English were pre-eminent among the world's astronomers, not only for theoretical work but for observing," he said, "There has been a tendency of late for this headquarters to be in California."

After he had talked about a new 90-inch telescope at Herstmonceux, and his interest in the question of stars in relation to nuclear physics, I broke in to ask for his view on the prospect of interplanetary travel. His reply was to come back to haunt him.

"Utter bilge," he pronounced. "That's what I think about all this present talk. Utter bilge."

He went on: "I'm a straightforward scientist and I don't believe anybody will ever put up enough money to do such a thing. It would be enormously expensive, but if the next war could be won by the first chap getting to the moon and by that alone, some nation might put up the enormous amount required."

He couldn't give any idea how much it would cost, but it would be a very large sum indeed. "It's all rather rot. I don't think anybody will go anywhere in the ordinary way."

Headlines for the following day, including the *Times* from my story, and the *Telegraph* from Val's, were unanimous in their legitimate selectiveness of Dr Woolley's comments. Although frequently misquoted, 'Space travel - Utter bilge,' would be the phrase which was to plague him for the rest of his life. One quasi-scientific magazine even attributed its misrepresented "utter *bunkum*" to his predecessor, Sir Harold Spencer Jones.

The British Interplanetary Society, understandably, were among many who reacted strongly to Dr Woolley's views, by maintaining that space travel was "inevitable" though no one apparently disagreed with his views about the costs involved.

The universal censure he suffered could have explained an incident some two years later when he was again at Heathrow to see off two Russian astronomers who had been his guests at the Royal Observatory. "Shut up! Don't say a word," he snapped at the two bemused visitors, hustling them towards passport controls as I approached them.

The Russians, Professors Mitrofan Zverov and Andre Severny, stepped back with embarrassed grins on their faces. When they were on their way to their Moscow plane without the angry doctor, however, the Russians enjoyed themselves. As I wrote for a news diary column, Professor Zverov jokingly covered his face with a brief case and called out "No pictures" to a waiting cameraman. Then, waving a greeting, he posed willingly beside his smiling colleague.

The good Doctor, by now Sir Richard, died aged 80 in 1986, still protesting that his "bilge" remarks had been taken out of context. Leading science fiction author and fellow scientist Sir Arthur C. Clarke gallantly and generously tried to excuse Dr Woolley's comments on no less than three occasions in later years. He pointed out that the Royal Astronomer's estimates on the costs involved had proved to be on target. Such costs certainly have been close to prohibitive for most countries, and could even be equated to one side's budget for a major war.

But Sir Richard was not to know that the costs of putting man on the moon would be no higher than the cost of Cold War competitiveness and national pride... and apparently just as affordable to the wealthiest nation on earth.

SPACE TRAVEL "UTTER BILGE"

ASTRONOMER ROYAL ON COST

Professor Richard van der Riet Woolley, the newly appointed Astronomer Royal, said on his arrival at London Airport yesterday from Australia that the prospect of interplanetary travel was " utter bilge." Professor Woolley, who is 49, succeeds Sir Harold Spencer Jones. He has been director of the Commonwealth Observatory at Canberra and took up his duties yesterday at the Royal Observatory at Herstmonceux Castle, Sussex.

He described himself as a " straightforward scientist " and continued his comments on space travel by saying:—" I don't think anybody will ever put up enough money to do such a thing.

" It would be enormously expensive, but if the next war could be won by the first chap getting to the moon and by that alone, some nation might put up the enormous amount required. I cannot give any idea how much it would cost, but it would be a very large sum indeed. It is all rather rot. I don't think anybody will go anywhere in the ordinary way."

REPLY ON " FLYING SAUCERS "

Asked about " flying saucers," he said that he did not believe in them, and added: " I have an amusing story about ' flying saucers.' I was awakened about 3 a.m. by the R.A.F., no less, who asked about an object at 3,000ft. due west. I hopped out of bed and had a look, and then I missed my chance. I should have said: ' Take off, boys, it's the Russians.' Instead, I had to tell them it was the planet Mars."

Referring to his work at Herstmonceux Castle, Professor Woolley said: " There was a time, about 100 years ago, when the English were pre-eminent among the world's astronomers not only for theoretical work but for observing.

" There has been a tendency of late for this headquarters to be in California, but we hope to make some attempt to get England back to the fore in scientific astronomy and astro-physics. There is a new telescope, the Isaac Newton memorial telescope, with a diameter of 90in. What we are interested in is the question of stars in relation to nuclear physics, and the interior of the stars. We have much work to do."

With the two largest telescopes in Australia and South Africa, the British Commonwealth had an advantage over America, in that some objects could be seen only in the southern hemisphere.

Commenting on Professor Woolley's remarks on the future of interplanetary travel, Mr. Kenneth W. Gatland, a member of the council of the British Interplanetary Society, said: " Space travel is inevitable." It was bound to come as a sequel to the exploration of the upper atmosphere with rockets and the launching of artificial satellites during the International Geophysical Year.

The Times
January 3 1956

CHAPTER FOURTEEN

It's a truism recognised by every flyer. Air travel is stressful and airports are potentially nerve-racking. Even the twenty-first century business executive, able to avoid ticketing and baggage hall queues with an electronic reservation and solitary hold-all, can be disturbed when the routine is broken.

Airports are notorious for passenger heart attacks, and were among the first public assembly points internationally to recognise that lives can be saved by portable defibrillators, now usually available in emergency situations.

Even so, such precautions are not always enough, and many deaths at the start or the end of a journey still occur. At Heathrow we rarely heard of them quickly enough to be able to report them. Medical staff there interpreted their patient-confidentiality requirements so literally that they were known on occasions to order willing relatives not to talk to the press. Some senior medical staff over the years even refused to pass information internally to their own managements, in the proclaimed but misguided belief that the sole function of press and public relations staff was to seek publicity when answering legitimate media inquiries.

In Scotland, just weeks after we re-launched Brenards' news service from Prestwick Airport following a ten year gap, we experienced the statistically unlikely occurrence of two unrelated sudden deaths of passengers within minutes of them stepping from separate transatlantic airliners. Both were women and both were returning to Scotland to visit relatives after many years in North America.

An ambulance raced on to the tarmac after the pilot of a BOAC Boeing jet from Toronto radioed an SOS saying that Miss Jessie Ogilvie, aged 59, had suffered a heart attack during the east-bound flight.

On her way to stay with a relative in Edinburgh, she recovered sufficiently by her arrival to be wheeled across the tarmac in a wheelchair, and was even able to wave cheerfully to her sister, waiting in the public enclosure. But after examination by an airport doctor, Miss Ogilvy collapsed again. She died on her way to a local hospital.

The second woman, Mrs Davina Brown, 69, of Erie, Pennsylvania, was returning to Scotland for the first time in more than 20 years with her husband Robert for a reunion with her family. The couple disembarked from a Scandinavian airliner, and on exiting the Prestwick Customs hall spotted relatives who had driven across Scotland from Fife to meet them. Then, as she excitedly hurried forward, Mrs Brown suddenly collapsed and fell to the floor. She died before a doctor could reach her.

The tragedies led to a front page lead in the Glasgow *Evening Times (below)* and an eight-inch single column in the rival *Evening Citizen (left).*

2 WOMEN DIE AT PRESTWICK AIRPORT

TWO middle-aged women, both returning to Scotland to visit relatives after many years in North America, collapsed and died at Prestwick Airport today after leaving separate trans-Atlantic flights.

A radio S O S call from the pilot of a B.O.A.C. Boeing jet airliner brought an ambulance racng out to meet the first flight as it touched down from Toronto.

One of the passengers, 59-year-old Mrs Jessie Ogilvie, had had a heart attack during the journey.

Helped from the airliner by a doctor, Mrs Ogilvie, on her way to Edinburgh, was wheeled across the tarmac in an invalid chair.

She waved . . .

She was able to wave cheerfully to a sister and other relatives waiting in the public enclosure. But after examination by the doctor, Mrs Ogilvie collapsed.

She died a few moments later in an ambulance as she was being driven to Heathfield Hospital, Ayr.

The second woman, 69-year-old Mrs Davina Brown, of Erie, Pennsylvania, was travelling with her husband, Robert, for her first reunion with her family in more than 20 years.

. . . and she rushed

But as the couple left the Customs hall, Mrs Brown rushed forward to greet her sister, Mrs Mary Scott, of 14 Kirkland Road, Methil, Fife.

Suddenly she fell in the corridor and died before a doctor could be contacted.

Evening Citizen July 10 1962

EVENING TIMES

Britain's Best-Designed Evening Newspaper.

No. 26,898 TUESDAY, JULY 10, 1962.

Two women flew to visit relatives for first time in years, then . . .

TV Page 8

DOUBLE DEATH DRAMA AT AIRPORT

©Evening Times (Page One lead) July 10 1962

TWO WOMEN DEAD AT AIRPORT

Two women travelling to visit relatives in Scotland collapsed and died at Prestwick Airport yesterday within minutes of stepping from separate transatlantic air liners.

A radio call from the pilot of one air liner brought an ambulance and a doctor out to meet the flight as it touched down from Toronto.

DEATH DRAMA AT SCOTS AIRPORT

Scottish Daily Express (above)

© Glasgow Herald (left), (both) July 11 1962

WOMEN FLY HOME...AND DIE

TWO women died at Prestwick Airport yesterday, shortly after leaving separate transatlantic airliners. Both were returning to Scotland to visit relatives after spending many years in North America.

An ambulance went to meet a B O A C Boeing as it touched down from Toronto.

The pilot had radioed that a passenger, Miss Jessie Ogilvie, 59, had suffered a heart attack during the journey.

Daily Herald

2 WOMEN FLY IN—TO DIE

YEARS in Canada, years in the U.S. . . . and yesterday, at Prestwick airport, two women were to meet their kinfolk again.

Fifty - nine - year - old Mrs. Jessie Ogilvie had become ill on the flight from Toronto.

On the way to the ambulance, she caught sight of her Edinburgh relatives. She waved, and collapsed.

For Mrs. Daviut Brown it was to be the first reunion since 1942 with her sister Mrs. Mary Scott, of Kirkland-road, Methil, Fife.

Mrs. Brown, aged 69, over from Erie, Pennsylvania, collapsed at the airport. In minutes she was dead.

Daily Record (above)

Scottish Daily Mail (right)

(all) July 11 1962

'HOME AGAIN' WOMEN DIE AT AIRPORT

By Daily Mail Reporter

TWO women came home to Scotland yesterday to visit relatives neither had seen for many years.

But within minutes of stepping off separate Transatlantic air liners the women collapsed and died at Prestwick Airport.

I have not claimed personal authorship for those reports, or the similar stories carried in six national newspapers the following day, partly because I can't remember having any involvement. Although we shared coverage on some stories, I believe this was one of the many occasions my colleague Chris Bramwell was solely responsible, as he was for a follow-up two days later *(right).*

When another death at Prestwick just four days later made front page news on both sides of the Atlantic I was, however, very much involved.

SON'S AIR DASH AS MOTHER DIES

MR WILLIAM BROWN, the 35-year-old American-born son of Mrs Davina Brown, one of the two women travellers who died after arriving at Prestwick Airport yesterday, flew into Scotland today from New York.

Still wearing his working clothes, he had come straight from his job in Erie, Pennsylvania, after hearing of his mother's death.

Mrs Brown, aged 69, collapsed and died as she was greeted by relatives at the airport on her first visit home to Scotland for 29 years. Her husband, Robert, spent the night with her family in Methil, Fife.

The other woman who died was Mrs Jessie Ogilvie, who was on her way to relatives in Edinburgh.

Daily Herald July 12 1962

Never an early riser by choice, preferring late-night work, I nevertheless usually managed to get to my place of work in time for the first transatlantic arrival. If not, I was lucky enough to catch up with anything I might have missed. Contrarily, on this occasion, if I had been on time I might have missed the opportunity to win two front pages in the principal Glasgow evening papers, as well as large spreads in the following day's Sunday newspapers *and* coverage throughout the Untied States.

My first surprise was seeing the district staff correspondent of the *Scottish Daily Express* and *Sunday Express*, Jimmy Ballantyne, emerging from an airline office as I walked through the old Prestwick passenger terminal building. It was early in the day for any reporter from a morning newspaper to make an appearance at the airport – unless news was breaking. If it were, he must have believed he had an exclusive, or he would have left it to us.

At several levels we were friends and colleagues, as the *Express* had given us more encouragement than almost any other Scottish newspaper. Unlike at least one other local reporter, Jimmy apparently never saw us as a threat to his position. But we were also potential rivals by serving evening newspapers particularly and daily newspapers other than the *Express* with information he might have believed was exclusively his own.

Nevertheless we passed the time of this day together and if I was careful not to show my curiosity over his presence, he was just as careful not to give anything away. He very quickly went on his way, and I took the opportunity to trace his steps back to the BOAC office. And before I could ask a question, someone piped up: "About time you got here. We've just been telling Jimmy Ballantyne. You know we had a death here during the night?"

I had less than half-an-hour to the first evening edition times, so I quickly noted down everything I was told, with two or three of the BOAC staff joining in the conversation and adding information as they answered my questions. Then I had to dash away to seek out others with direct knowledge.

It emerged that soon after 3:40 that morning, a Super Constellation of the American charter airline, Flying Tigers, had touched down safely on the Prestwick runway in good night visibility after a flight from Frankfurt, Germany. At the controls was the co-pilot, who had just switched his four propellers to reverse pitch to give added braking power, when he suddenly slumped forward in his seat… and died.

The airliner was still moving at speed, but immediately the senior pilot, Captain Frank Morrow, took over the controls. He taxied off the runway and brought the airliner safely to a standstill with more than half of the 9,000ft runway to spare. Then he radioed for medical assistance as he tried unsuccessfully to rouse his colleague. Within moments a police car appeared bringing a nursing sister from the airport medical centre. An ambulance followed close behind.

With Captain Morrow on board the airliner, a sister ship of one that was to dive into the Atlantic just a few weeks later, were two flight engineers, a navigator and a third qualified pilot, but no passengers. The airliner was being flown empty to Scotland to pick up 118 members of a Glasgow sports and social club who had chartered it for a flight to New York.

I found Captain Morrow in the lobby of the old airport hotel, as he awaited a transatlantic telephone call from his airline. He told me that he had been flying with his co-pilot, Russell Rodriguez, at 39 just one year older than the Captain himself, for the previous 11 years. "He was one of the sharpest pilots I have known," he said. "He made a beautiful landing but then he collapsed. I could see it was something serious by the way he fell. But I had no time to think about it.

"He appeared normal and perfectly fit throughout the 3,200-mile crossing. I had no reason to suspect his health. If I had, of course I would not have allowed him at the controls."

Captain Morrow, from Little Silver, New Jersey, said that Captain Rodriguez had formerly flown with the Royal Canadian Air Force, and as a pilot with BOAC. "He had to give up working for the British airline because of his US citizenship," he added.

A Flying Tiger slip crew was already standing by at Prestwick to take the charter passengers to New York. The Super Constellation, a sister ship of the one that was to dive into the Atlantic a few weeks later, was originally due to leave the previous Wednesday. The departure had been postponed several days, partly because of bad weather in the US, and partly because of the airline's heavy commitment programme.

The passengers, who had already been taken on a coach tour on Friday to pass the time, now learnt of a further hold-up while police carried out their inquiries into the death of Captain Rodriguez. They were finally able to leave that day, six hours late. My front page leads followed:

You can rely on DORMIE MENSWEAR Hire SERVICE
Evening Citizen
No. 30,619 SATURDAY JULY 14 1962 PRICE 3d.
LATE CITY
BELL'S SCOTCH WHISKY THE CELEBRATION SCOTCH
Tragedy as airliner flies to pick up club members
HOLIDAY PLANE PILOT DIES AT CONTROLS

Evening Citizen (Page One lead)

...ran the banner heading in the *Evening Citizen,* with the *Evening Times* tabloid repeating:

EVENING TIMES
Britain's Best-Designed Evening Newspaper.
No. 26,902 SATURDAY, JULY 14, 1962. 3d

© Evening Times (Page One lead) (both) July 14 1962

Captain takes over when death strikes as air liner lands
CO-PILOT DIES AT CONTROLS

Passengers at Prestwick watch drama

A Constellation airliner

THE pilot of a Fair holiday charter airliner died at the controls seconds after touching down today at Prestwick Airport to pick up 118 Scots passengers for New York.

The senior pilot, Captain Frank Morrow, took over and brought the plane — a Constellation belonging to the United States airline Flying Tiger — in safely.

Evening Citizen (Page One lead cont.)

Drama at Prestwick

AS a four-engined Constellation air liner from New York rolled along the tarmac at Prestwick Airport to-day the co-pilot died at the controls.

The 'plane, one of the Flying Tiger Line of America, was still moving, and the co-pilot had switched the four propellers to reverse pitch to give added braking power, when he slumped forward.

Immediately the senior pilot, Captain Frank Morrow, of New Jersey, who was seated beside co-pilot Captain Russell J. Rodriguez, took over full control.

He brought the aircraft to a halt, taxied off the runway and radioed for medical assistance. Police cars, an ambulance, and medical staff raced out.

There were no passengers on the flight. The aircraft was being ferried in from New York to pick up 118 Scottish passengers, members of the Legbrannock Sports and Social Club, who had chartered it for a "reunion" flight to the United States.

"No time"

With Captain Morrow and his co-pilot was a third qualified pilot, two flight engineers, and a navigator.

Said Captain Morrow after leaving the aircraft — "Russell had made a beautiful landing and was at the controls, reversing the propellers, when he slumped forward I could see it was something serious by the way he fell.

"But I had no time to think about it—I took over control and brought the aircraft to a halt with more than half of the 9000ft. runway to spare."

Captain Morrow said his first officer had appeared perfectly normal throughout the 3200 miles crossing of the Atlantic.

"I had no reason to suspect anything was wrong—if I had, of course, I would not have allowed him at the controls. But he seemed perfectly fit. He was one of the sharpest pilots I have ever known—I have been flying regularly with him for the past 11 years."

Delays

The Legbrannock charter was originally planned to leave Prestwick on Wednesday, but the flight was held up partly by bad weather

(Continued on Back Page)

Pilot dies at controls

(Continued from Page 1)

in the United States and partly because the Flying Tiger fleet was fully committed.

Passengers who checked in at Prestwick Airport yesterday for the revised departure time were told of a further delay and were taken on a coach tour of the Burns country.

The aircraft was scheduled to leave Prestwick at 3 a.m. to-day but touched down from New York at 3.43 a.m. The departure was delayed a further six-and-a-half hours to allow police inquiries and air line reports to be completed.

Airman

Said Captain Morrow—"Captain Rodriguez formerly flew with the Royal Canadian Air Force and later as a pilot with B.O.A.C. He had to give up working for the British air lines because of his U.S. citizenship."

A slip crew was taking the aircraft back to New York from Prestwick, but Captain Morrow flew with the aircraft to Gander, Newfoundland.

Flying Tiger Airlines was formed in 1948 by a group of American ex-Service men who named the company after the insignia of their squadron of fighter aircraft.

The air line operates some scheduled services within the U.S. and a number of regular charter flights across the Atlantic, as well as cargo services.

© Evening Times (Page One lead cont. above, and right)

(all) July 14 1962

London's evening edition newspapers also carried the story, though it was understandably given less prominence than in Scotland, and I was later sent clippings from a number of American papers.

British Sunday newspapers, from the *Sunday Times,* the *Observer* and *Sunday Telegraph,* right through to the *People,* the *News of the World* and the *Sunday Post* all gave extensive coverage to the story. The *Sunday Express* naturally ran Jimmy Ballantyne's story.

AIRLINER PILOT DIES AT CONTROLS

Evening Standard July 14 1962

Pilot dies as liner lands

THE co-pilot of a four-engined Constellation airliner collapsed and died at the controls just as the plane was touching down at Prestwick Airport, Scotland, yesterday.

Immediately the captain of the airliner took over full control and brought the plane safely to a halt.

PILOT DIES AT PLANE TOUCH-DOWN

SUNDAY TELEGRAPH REPORTER

THE co-pilot of a Constellation airliner died at the controls as the plane was touching down

Sunday Telegraph

Pilot Dies as He Lands Airliner

Captain Russell Rodriguez, aged 39, co-pilot of a Constellation airliner, collapsed and died

Sunday Times (all) July 15 1962

Airliner pilot dies at controls

News of the World (above)
Observer (left)

PILOT DIES LANDING AT PRESTWICK

A 39-YEAR-OLD U.S. co-pilot, Captain Russel J. Rodriguez, died at the controls of his plane yesterday, seconds after making a safe landing at the end of a 3200-mile crossing of the Atlantic to Prestwick.

The drama was watched by 118 members of a Lanark-

Pilot of airliner dies as he touches down

AN airliner pilot died at the controls yesterday

People

Sunday Post (left)

2 DOCTORS PROBE MYSTERY OF DEAD PILOT

By Daily Mail Reporter

TWO Service doctors were called in by the Ministry of Aviation yesterday to conduct the post mortem on the American pilot who died at the controls of an air liner.

The doctors, Wing-Commander J. K. Mason, of the RAF Medical Service, and Captain Froed, of the U.S. Air Force, flew from London to Prestwick Airport.

Their flight followed a telephone discussion between the Ministry's chief medical officer and the Ayr fiscal, Mr. J. Cruikshank.

Before driving to Heathfield Hospital, Ayr, to carry out their autopsy, Wing-Cdr. Mason said:

"Cases such as this are very rare but not unknown. It is standard practice for the Ministry to call in a service pathologist on sudden deaths aboard aircraft, because of the aspects of aviation medicine that may have a bearing on the case.

"But, of course, we don't yet know what killed Captain Rodriguez.

"International air agreements require all pilots to undergo strict medical examination periodically. The dates of such examinations are recorded on their licences."

'Perfectly fit'

The dead pilot was said to be "perfectly fit" at his last examination six months ago.

The American doctor was asked to take part in the post mortem because of the U.S. nationality of Captain Rodriguez. Full reports are being forwarded to the Ministry of Aviation and the U.S. authorities.

Captain Rodriguez, 39, of Newark, New Jersey, died at the controls of a Super Constellation air liner seconds after landing it safely at Prestwick Airport.

The aircraft, owned by Flying Tiger Airlines, of America, was being ferried in to pick up 118 members of the Legbrannock Sports and Social Club, Lanarkshire, who had chartered it to fly to New York.

The senior pilot on board, Captain Frank Morrow, 38, took over the controls just in time to bring the aircraft to a halt.

Doctors probe pilot's death

HERALD REPORTER

TWO Service doctors—one British and one American—were called in yesterday to carry out a post-mortem examination on Captain Russell Rodriguez, the American pilot who died at the controls of an airliner.

Capt. Rodriguez, 39, died seconds after landing a Super Constellation at Prestwick Airport, Ayrshire, on Saturday.

The senior pilot aboard took over just in time to halt the plane which was not carrying passengers.

Daily Herald (above)
Scottish Daily Mail (left)
(both) July 16 1962

And the following day Chris was able to file a follow-up when two aviation pathologists, one American and one British, flew to Scotland to conduct a joint post-mortem examination. In due course they were able to confirm what was suspected – that Captain Rodriguez had suffered an unsuspected and sudden heart attack.

Over the years, the stress of travel has often manifested itself as a fear of flying. Airlines have sought the advice of psychologists and spent thousands of pounds in helping passengers to overcome what is sometimes seen as irrational. On one occasion a Geneva-bound passenger, a dark-haired young Englishwoman, took her seat on board her airliner at Heathrow, then suddenly jumped up and screamed: "I must get off."

The aircraft engines were switched off, aircraft steps were wheeled up, and the woman, who carried just hand-baggage, disembarked. She left the airport refusing to say anything.

Similarly, just three minutes before an Irish airliner was due to take off from London Airport for Dublin, one of the 34 passengers turned to officials and told them: "I've changed my mind. I don't want to fly."

As he was escorted back through controls the passenger, a young man, told me: "I've just lost my nerve."

The airliner took off without him, but carried his baggage, unaccompanied, to Dublin – something that security wouldn't allow today. Now, such baggage would have to be unloaded, a process which would delay departure by at least an hour. Ever optimistic, the airline re-booked the reluctant passenger on the same flight the next day. Unsurprisingly, he failed to show up. Some passengers, of course, are stressed by their anxiety to get aboard, like the South African businessman who jumped from his departure lounge seat when his flight was announced, grabbed his overcoat - and dislocated his shoulder. Solomon Segal had to have it set in an airport medical centre as his airliner left for Johannesburg without him. He *did* fly the next day.

It may have been financial problems behind the stress which a few months earlier had led a woman passenger suddenly to gasp for a doctor at Heathrow. Seconds after flying in from Belgium, she headed for the exit door of her airliner and made her dramatic appeal directly to the aircraft's captain. Then she suddenly clutched a hand to her side. A four-inch blood stain appeared on her jacket and spread over her fingers. As a stewardess helped her back to a seat, the pilot, Captain Deltour quickly radioed for medical aid.

Miss Mary Mason, a young, attractive English woman from Grimsby, Hull, told airport officials she had undergone an operation in a Belgian hospital only 24 hours earlier. "They were charging me £6 a day while I remained in hospital," she said. "They told me I would have to stay at least two more weeks there. I just couldn't afford it so I walked out."

Miss Mason was taken to nearby Hillingdon Hospital. Later it was said there that she was "comfortable, and not in any danger." The *Daily Mirror* thought it justified a page lead and only the *Daily Express* and *Daily Mail* gave the story "straight" headlines the following day:

AIRPORT DRAMA—WOMAN GASPS 'FETCH A DOCTOR'

Daily Mirror

and there were similar reports in the *Daily Sketch,* the *Daily Herald* and *News Chronicle (see opposite).*

Britain's *free* National Health Service had, of course, only been functioning for seven years. Which might explain a suggestion of national chauvinism in the coverage.

THE PATIENT
Flies to London day after operation

Daily Mail (above)

Woman from hospital ill at airport

Daily Express, (all) July 19 1954

Operation girl flies from 'too-dear' hospital

Daily Sketch Reporter

A YOUNG woman walked up to an official at London Airport yesterday and asked: "Can I see a doctor, please?"

As she spoke, a big blood-stain appeared on the jacket of her costume and she clutched her side in pain.

An ambulance was called and she was rushed to hospital.

The woman, who gave her name as Mrs. Mary Mason, of Grimsby, had just landed from Brussels. She said she had been operated on in Brussels only 24 hours previously.

She should have stayed in the hospital for a fortnight but, she said, "They were going to charge me £6 a day.

"I just couldn't afford it so I walked out."

At Hillingdon (Middx) Hospital last night she was said to be "not in any danger."

Daily Sketch

Fees too dear

SO WOMAN FLED AFTER OPERATION

Daily Herald

Too costly to be ill abroad

AN attractive young woman stepped off a Brussels airliner at London Airport yesterday and asked an official:

"Can I see a doctor?"

Then she clutched a hand to her side. A four-inch blood-stain appeared on her jacket and spread over her fingers.

News Chronicle
(all) July 19 1954

*

It was also back in the Spring of 1955 I learned of one of those strange newsworthy mysteries which from time to time prove frustrating because somehow they are never journalistically "wrapped up."

A young woman with dark brown hair and in her early twenties had checked in for a flight to Switzerland. She asked to be allowed through passport controls immediately and into the departure lounge of Heathrow's new European terminal. This was occasionally permitted in the pre-security days, even though passengers would not normally clear controls for their flights until 40 minutes before take-off. And the young woman, who spoke with a foreign accent and gave her name as "Miss Seitz" was six *hours* early.

But after only an hour or two into her long wait, as she sat reading calmly and quietly in the departure lounge, she was approached by an immigration officer and an airline receptionist to be told: "Two gentlemen have been asking for you and want to talk to you. They are waiting at a ticket desk in the other lounge. We said we'd take a message, but they insisted it was important. They had to see you." One of the men was about 38 years old and fair-haired, well dressed and well spoken.

The passenger looked horrified. "Don't let them near me," she pleaded. "I might be in very great danger if you do. Please, I beg you – don't let them near me."

After calming her, the Home Office man and the airgirl returned to the check-in area to tell the two men of her refusal to see them. Police were called when the men persisted in their demands to be allowed through controls, then twice attempted to "crash" a nearby barrier. They refused to give the police any reason for trying to contact the woman. "They became very aggressive and unpleasant," an airline man told me later.

Two police officers then spoke to the passenger. She would only tell them: "I'm terribly tired, but please don't let me go to sleep. I will have terrible nightmares." Pressed to say why she was so frightened, and what danger she believed she faced from the men, she said: "I might get my throat cut. And I can't tell you any more than that."

Later the young woman was taken out with other passengers to board her Swissair flight for Geneva. The two police officers saw her safely aboard. As the airliner lifted from the runway, the police advised the two men, still waiting in the pre-controls area, that the passenger had left the country, and there was no reason for them to wait. They drove off towards London.

I was on a late duty that day and only learned of the drama from an airline man minutes before Miss Seitz boarded. I was able to approach her only after the police and an airgirl waiting with her vouched for me. By then she was calm and appeared unafraid. She told me her first name was Jacqueline and confirmed her surname. But she declined to answer any other questions. After she had gone that I discovered what she had told the police.

As far as I was concerned, it remained an unsolved mystery, and I could only tell it "as it happened." But that was exactly how the Sunday papers viewed the story as well, with the *Sunday Graphic* sensational: **'THEY WILL MURDER ME'** *(see overleaf)* echoed by the *News of the World* and the *People*.

I wasn't able to discuss the case the next day with the airport staff involved, as not one of them was back on duty. But they would have been as surprised as I when the mystery took an even stranger turn with the arrival of *another* Miss Seitz as a passenger on a flight

Terror at the airport

A TERRIFIED girl pleaded for a police guard at London Airport yesterday as she waited for a plane to New Zealand. Two men kept trying to contact her.

She begged airport officials not to let the two men near her. "I might be in very grave danger if you did," she cried.

But what lay behind the strange drama was still a mystery as the plane left.

The girl, pretty, dark haired and aged about 25, was named in the passenger list as Miss Seitz. She spoke with a foreign accent.

She went through all Customs and immigration formalities six hours before the plane left. Then she went into the final departure lounge, where only passengers are allowed

People
March 13 1955

'THEY WILL MURDER ME' ... CRIES GIRL IN AIRPORT DRAMA

Sunday Graphic

GUARD ON GIRL AT AIRPORT

A MYSTERY woman, who claimed that her life was in danger, pleaded for police protection yesterday at London Airport, where she was waiting for a plane to Switzerland.

She refused to explain why she was afraid, but police barred attempts by two men to approach her. She was given an escort until her plane took off. Then the men left the airport and drove away towards London.

The woman was aged about 25, pretty, and dark-haired. Her name was given in the passenger list as Miss Seitz. She arrived at the airport six hours before her plane left, and asked to be let through the Customs early, though Officials agreed, though passengers are not normally allowed to clear controls until 40 minutes before they are due to take off.

The woman was sitting in the final departure lounge when she was told, "Two gentlemen are trying to contact you — they're waiting in the other lounge."

"Don't let them near me," she pleaded. "I might be in very great danger — please don't let them near me."

The two men were turned back at the entrance to the Customs hall, and were ordered also from another entrance.

The woman told the officials, "I'm terribly tired, but please don't let me go to sleep. I would have terrible nightmares."

When questioned about her danger, she said, "I might get my throat cut."

Several minutes before the other passengers went on board, the woman was escorted to her plane by two airport policemen. An air girl stayed with her on the plane until she was joined by the other passengers.

News of the World *(both) March 13 1955*

THE SCARED GIRL MYSTERY DEEPENS AS No. 2 FLIES IN

Daily Sketch

FRIGHTENED WOMAN: A NEW RIDDLE

Express Staff Reporter

A FRIGHTENED Miss Seitz flew from London to Geneva at the week-end. Within 24 hours a calm Miss Seitz flew from Geneva to London.

The question last night: Was it the same woman?

The first Miss Seitz, dark-haired, about 20, called herself **Jacqueline.** She drove to London Airport six hours before the Geneva plane was due to leave and huddled in the departure lounge.

Two men tried to see her. She asked for police protection. "I might be in great danger," she said. "Please don't let them near me."

Police stopped the men. Miss Seitz flew off to Geneva.

The **second Miss Seitz** called herself **Michele.**

A NOTE

When she flew into London from Geneva there was a note against her name on the passenger list: "No information to be given on inquiries regarding this passenger," it said.

All she would say was that she was collecting some luggage in London before returning to Geneva.

Then she drove to a block of flats in Chelsea.

In Switzerland last night the Seitz family said that it was Michele who flew from London to Geneva. And it was Michele who flew back. She "just changed her mind."

Michele, they said, has a cousin named Jacqueline who travelled from London to Geneva 10 days ago, then went off to Paris.

But threats by mystery men at London Airport? "It sounds crazy to us," said the family.

Daily Express
(both) March 14 1955

from Switzerland to London.

This time I really was too late with my latest discovery to seek an answer from the passenger. She had already left the airport. And the airline could only tell me that there had been a note against her name on the passenger manifest stating: "No information to be given on inquiries regarding this passenger." I was able to establish only that the new Miss Seitz was called Michele, aged 20, and that she was thought to be Jacqueline's younger sister. All she would tell airport staff was that she was in London to collect some luggage and would be flying straight back.

Possibly scenting a solution, the following days' newspapers traced Michele to an apartment house in Sloane Gardens, London, after I'd advised them she was heading for Chelsea. They reported that shortly afterwards luggage labelled "Miss J Seitz" and addressed to Basle, Switzerland, was hastily removed from a flat and loaded into a cab.

Miss Seitz herself – Jacqueline or Michele – declined to answer any questions, apart from apparently saying she was leaving for Geneva, *not* Basle, and was taking the luggage with her. And in Switzerland, her family insisted it was not Jacqueline but Michele who made the *original* flight to London, and had changed her mind about staying. Jacqueline was not her sister, they said, but a cousin who had travelled to London ten days earlier but had then flown to Paris.

And of the threats by two men at London Airport? That was just dismissed by the family as "crazy."

At this point, I silently agreed. And I too gave up.

*

More than four years after the opening of the first stage of Heathrow's Central Terminal in the mid-1950s, long distance airlines were still using the prefabricated huts of the original north-side terminal alongside the A40 Bath-road. The M4 Motorway and its airport spur were a planner's dream for the future, but traffic from the Bath-road entrance to the centre of the airport was increasing rapidly, and it was necessary to enlarge the junction.

Engineers decided that a block of low-roofed offices and store rooms would have to be demolished. The site was needed to construct a large roundabout at a junction of five roads just inside the entrance gateway. Workmen moved in, erected route indicators and barriers, and the buildings started to come down.

They were about to bulldoze one tiny buff-painted hut when someone had an Awful Thought. The little hut would have to stay – because a clause in the airport contracts said so. The reason: a sign over the door which stated simply "Gentlemen." The buff-coloured hut was the only facility of its kind within a stipulated distance of the nearest occupied working offices.

A high level meeting was called; the best engineering minds were engaged. "We'll just have to build round it," decided Authority at last. And that's exactly what they did, building a 4-road roundabout to completely encircle the little hut. The last kerbstone was eventually laid, the last road sign painted, the barriers came down and almost immediately, the traffic bottlenecks were relieved by the new roundabout.

The planners were happy with the results. Not so happy were those nearest office workers. As one of them put it to me: "It's a very inconvenient convenience. It's an island haven in a sea of traffic. None of us would dare cross those busy roads."

The little hut that the world passes by

By Daily Mail Reporter

A WORKMAN finished putting the last coat of paint on the little prefabricated hut, and, defying the blaring of car horns, stepped back to admire the job.

London Airport's "memorial to inconvenience" was no longer an eyesore, even if it was inaccessible.

For the little yellow hut and the simple inscription "Gentlemen," has been completely cut off in the centre of a new roundabout.

Until a few weeks ago the hut was one of a block of office buildings and store rooms overlooking the busy bottle-neck at the airport's congested main gates.

Then the planners stepped in with the idea of converting the junction of five roads into a complex roundabout.

They began to sweep the site clear—until an official found a clause in the work contract which said the little hut must stay because it was the only facility of its kind in the area.

High level meetings were called. "We'll just have to build round it," the planners decided.

"It's just an island haven in a sea of traffic," an airline official said yesterday. "None of us would dare cross those busy roads."

Daily Mail

SO THE LITTLE HUT STAYS

PLANNERS at London Airport decided that a block of prefabricated offices and store-rooms would have to be demolished.

The site was needed to make a traffic round-about near the main gates.

Workmen moved in, and the building started to come down.

They were about to start on one little, yellow-painted hut with the word "Gentlemen" on the door, when someone Had An Awful Thought.

TRAFFIC

He was right! That particular hut would have to stay where it was.

A clause in the airport contracts stipulated that a little hut marked "Gentlemen" must be on that site.

And there it stays, while the traffic whirls round the round-about.

But it's a very inconvenient convenience. The traffic round the round-about is so heavy that no-one dares to cross the road to the sign marked "Gentlemen."

Daily Herald (both) Oct 1959

IT'S JUST A MATTER OF CONVENIENCE

A WORKMAN splashed the final undercoat of paint on to the stucco-finished walls of the little prefabricated hut on Friday, and defying the blare of motor horns, stepped back to admire his work. London Airport's "memorial to convenience" was no longer an eyesore—even if it was an inconvenience.

For the little yellow building with its shoulder high frosted windows and simple white-painted inscription "Gentlemen" has lost its once-proud place in the Airport's architecture. Once part of a block of busy offices flanking the main entrance to the airport, the building is now sadly isolated in the centre island of a new traffic roundabout designed to ease traffic congestion at the North Terminal's busiest bottleneck.

Brenard Press picture
"....an island haven in a sea of traffic."
Airport Post, Oct 29 1959

Fast forward to 1963 and Prestwick Airport, where officialdom proved it could be just as naïvely bureaucratic as its London counterparts. My interest was first aroused when we learnt that two 90-seater Viscount airliners had been chartered by the War Office, forerunner of the Ministry of Defence, at a cost of £500 (about £7,500 in 2008) to fly just 40 senior Army officers to the Scottish airport, and back again to London a few hours later.

The reason for the visit: the officers were to attend a "cloak and dagger" rehearsal for a proposed secret NATO launch for Britain's newest super tank, the Chieftain, a few days later.

One of the two airliners was simply a back-up and would fly empty, both ways. A fleet of luxury coaches, all of which had been stripped of seats and floorboards in a search for possible terror bombs, stood by to whisk the officers to a tank testing ground somewhere in Scotland.

All of the passengers were full colonels or above, but when they chose to travel together, *six* of the seven coaches remained empty in an operation covered by a security blackout. Holiday traffic on adjoining coastal routes was held up as special escort police cars guided the mainly empty convoy of coaches. Other roads to the testing ground near Kirkcudbright on the Solway Firth were guarded by patrols instructed to stop traffic attempting to overtake. On the return journey similar security was enforced.

We filed the story to the Sunday newspapers and were rewarded with recognition in the

Sunday Times and an inside page lead in the Scottish *Sunday Mirror*. The latter's headline writers provided a prophetic pun on initials with their:

A V.I.P. DAY FOR COLONELS

Sunday Mail ***July 17 1963***

In spite of the air of secrecy surrounding those rehearsals, many high ranking officers were said to have talked freely about the programme, making a mockery of any security. Nevertheless it was one of the lessons learnt from that rehearsal which led to the real Chieftain demonstration for government politicians and NATO defence experts becoming almost a public event two months later, by an all-too obvious attempt to maintain "secrecy."

Once again, two airliners were quietly chartered by the War Office to fly the guests to Scotland for the tank demonstration. They included, from Britain, Government Minister James Ramsden, the Under-Secretary of State for War, top soldier General Sir Richard Hull, Chief of the Imperial General Staff and, from the U.S. and Europe, senior NATO army officers, military strategists and technicians.

At Prestwick senior airport officials waited. Operations managers decided that the two airliners should be parked on the far side of the parking apron, several hundred yards from the passenger terminal, though still in sight of public areas. A small fleet of luxury cars and coaches was again already lined up in full view to carry the VIPs off to the tank demonstration site 60 miles to the south.

But now, on a grass verge just a few yards from where the aircraft were to come to a halt, was a newly erected sackcloth screen, billowing freely in the wind. It soon became obvious to onlookers that the screen was to be the one successful concession to secrecy – or at least the privacy – of the VIP passengers. It came into its own as the be-medalled generals and umbrella-armed Whitehall civil servants queued at its flapping "door" before boarding their onward transport.

And the screened enclosure became the number one embarrassment of the day for officials when they were asked to explain why an ordinary field latrine, hessian, servicemen, for the use of, could possibly be necessary at a major transatlantic airport, and only a short distance from similar, more conducive facilities.

A Ministry of Aviation spokesman responded: "I can't say a thing about it." The Army was similarly tongue-tied, with a Scottish Command officer, finally commenting seriously: "It was provided for the convenience of passengers.

"Whose idea was it? Well it certainly wasn't my office who suggested it."

I MEAN ... ER, EVEN V.I.P.s ARE HUMAN

Express Staff Reporter

THE mighty top brass of the British Army and of the Nato countries of Europe were coming. And Prestwick Airport was prepared.

Senior airport officials waited; a fleet of luxury cars and coaches was lined up to whip the V.I.P.s off to a secret demonstration of Britain's Chieftain tank; and . . . and . . . how on earth did THAT get there?

IT stood, in all its sackcloth glory, amid the windswept open grassland between the airport's web of runways and taxiways . . . one ordinary . . . well . . . ahem . . . Service men, for the use of **LATRINE.**

IT proved rather an embarrassment as bemedalled generals and umbrella-carrying Whitehall officials queued to board the fleet of cars and coaches for their long drive to the testing ground near Kirkcudbright, 60 miles away.

Not us!

Said a Ministry of Aviation official: "I can't say a thing about it."

Said a serious-faced Scottish Command spokesman: "It was provided for the convenience of passengers. Whose idea was it? Well, it certainly wasn't my office that suggested it."

Later, airport officials tactfully pointed out that the War Office passengers—among them Mr. James Ramsden, Under-Secretary of State for War, and the Chief of the Imperial General Staff, General Sir Richard Hull—might not have had the opportunity to make full use of the facilities of their airliner during the 75-minute flight from London—and that "a change of altitude can affect different people different ways."

Last night IT was still standing at the edge of the tarmac. "It will remain until the V.I.P. flights leave," said an official.

Scottish Daily Express

All so convenient for Top Brass..

IT stood amid the windswept open grassland between Prestwick Airport's web of runways.

IT appeared a few hours before two special War Office charter planes touched down at the airport from London bringing British Army and N A T O Top Brass to a demonstration of the new secret tank, the Chieftain, at a Scottish testing ground.

IT was inspected by senior officials who drove out to meet the special planes.

Can't say . . .

IT came into its own as the bemedalled generals and umbrella carrying Whitehall officials queued in full view of a public enclosure before they drove to the testing ground near Kirkcudbright, 60 miles away.

But IT became the number one embarrassment of the day for War Office and airport officials when they were asked to explain why an ordinary latrine, hessian, cervicemen, for the use of, was required at a principal transatlantic airport.

Said a Ministry of Aviation official: "I can't say a thing about it."

Said a Scottish Command spokesman: "It certainly wasn't my office that suggested it."

The V I Ps included Mr. James Ramsden Under Secretary of State for War, and the Chief of the Imperial General Staff, General Sir Richard Hull.

Last night, Prestwick Airport's own Clochmerle was still standing at the edge of the tarmac. "It will remain until the V I P flights leave" said an official.

Daily Herald (all) July 18 1963

DEFENCE EXPERTS IN SCOTLAND

Secret Tank Tests

Senior Army officers and defence experts from Britain, the Commonwealth, and Nato countries flew yesterday from London to Prestwick Airport to attend a full-scale demonstration of Britain's new secret tank, the Chieftain, at a testing ground near Kirkcudbright to-day.

The Government is hoping to secure orders valued at £100m. for the Chieftain, which is of revolutionary design and is said to be able to "swim" underwater and to be driven on paraffin, diesel oil, or petrol.

©Glasgow Herald

Later, an authorised airport manager tactfully pointed out to me that the passengers might not have had the opportunity to make full use of the facilities aboard their airliner during the 75-minute flight, and that "a change of altitude can affect different people different ways."

Prestwick's very own sackcloth-screened "Clochemerle" was finally dismantled and restored to its contracted providers. The VIPs were not inconvenienced. They had left the airport.

*

Producers and directors of film and television drama with airport settings will often go to the trouble of hiring uniforms and paying extras to walk on as passing aircrew – usually consisting of at least one pilot and two or three stewardesses. In reality, airline captains or their First Officers rarely appear in passenger areas of major airports whilst on duty. On departing flights they are usually too busy studying last-minute weather reports, checking ground maintenance of their aircraft or running through pre-flight lists.

And while their passengers are shuffling forward in ticket desk queues, coping with security checks or shopping in duty free malls, cabin crews too are already active aboard their aircraft, checking their stocks of food, drinks and gifts, studying passenger-needs information and ensuring everything is ship-shape and prepared before the flood gaterooms are opened to a rushing flow of their hundreds of travelling souls.

Even after touchdown and on completion of their journey, flight deck and cabin staff head off in a direction completely different from that taken by passengers. They are then responsible for clearing their aircraft and themselves through a dedicated aircrew customs office - and formally "handing over" that aircraft to their company operations officers.

The same is of course true of non-airline aircrew, those travelling as passengers, those who fly as pilots for others or in their own private aircraft, making use of Heathrow if they are able to find "slots" in the crowded daily timetable of the world's busiest international airport. Among these have been the world solo record makers, such as the first lone Atlantic flyer Charles Lindberg, long-distance pioneers like the late Jim Mollison or Sheila Scott, the first woman to fly solo round the world in the mid-sixties, at the start of her many such achievements. Lindbergh, the first non-stop solo flyer of the Atlantic after the pioneering crossing by Alcock and Brown, only appeared at Heathrow as a flying businessman.

Other pilots, like Captain O.P. Jones, who commanded the first flight for the newly formed BOAC, Captain Brian Trubshaw, test pilot for the British Aircraft Corporation and of the British supersonic Concorde became airport legends for their personalities as well as their achievements. And there are still to be found a handful of "hands-on," pilots, reminiscent of Monique Agazarian, who as chief pilot and managing

Jim Mollison (above), pioneering point-to-point air record setter, both solo and with his wife Amy Johnson, herself a long-distance record breaker.

Charles Lindberg (left), pilot of the first solo transatlantic flight, New York - Paris, 1927
Library of Congress picture

Multiple world record-breaker Sheila Scott with her Piper Aztec "Mythre", 1971 (above).
(NASA picture)

On 9 April 1969 Brian Trubshaw (above), chief test pilot, landed Concorde impeccably after its first flight - despite the failure of two radar altimeters.

Captain O.P. Jones (above), later legendary chief pilot of both Imperial Airways and its sucessor BOAC, seen here in the 1920-30s at Shoreham airfield, where he learnt to fly.

director of Island Air Services, provided a valuable and popular joy flight service from the ground public enclosure at London Airport in the late 1940s.

picture by Mick West

Island Air Services. The Rapides would blast straight across the grass to the runway and slot into the traffic pattern at the Tower's discretion. Note high tech security fence, left.

Monique had joined the company after spending the war as one of those heroines of the Air Transport Auxiliary, ferrying aircraft from factories on wartime delivery. She was later joined by her husband-to-be, Ray Rendall, a captain with British European Airways, who became her managing director when Monique was appointed Chairman.

Her tiny airline operated twin-engined Rapide biplanes, reliable workhorses which, with their fixed undercarriages and handful of passenger seats, introduced many thousands of trippers (including me) in complete confidence to their first or early flights. I've already told how honeymooners Elizabeth Taylor and Michael Wilding were among those joy riders, though I doubt if they were first time flyers.

I recently came across another pilot, "old school" in temperament if not in years, flying for the My Travel airline. His name escapes me even though I thought I'd made a mental note of it when my hands were full and I couldn't reach my usually available notebook. That of course is the danger of depending on a notebook for a lifetime… memory alone becomes totally unreliable. But as he personally greeted all of us on boarding and joined his cabin staff to say goodbye on arrival at our destination, other travellers may recall him, particularly as his in-between public address chat was both attention-grabbing and constantly witty.

During the journey he made at least two personal appearances after announcing himself from behind a bulkhead curtain, and kept us all in fits with his self-deprecating patter, and his professed envy of his pampered and "wealthier" passengers.

That was in recent years. And there was at least one other airline Captain fifty years earlier whose name stood out for his sense of harmless fun.

Some tales told of his "exploits" may well be mythical; others were reputedly vouched for by cabin staff, who both respected and admired the flyer. In common with other airline Captains of the day, Panda frequently left his flight deck in the care of his co-pilot to walk through the cabin to pass the time of day with his passengers. On one such occasion his sleeve was plucked by an elderly woman passenger, on a late evening flight, who asked him:

"Captain, could you explain to me how you know the way when you're flying in the dark?"

Panda gently stepped back and asked the passenger to join him in the gangway. Taking her elbow he crouched slightly and pointed through a cabin window to the starboard wing-tip of the Viscount airliner. "Do you see that light flashing on the end of the wing?" he asked. When the passenger agreed, he turned and pointed to the opposite port wing-tip. "Do you see the light on the other side?" Again, the elderly traveller concurred.

"Right," said Panda. "Well, providing I keep the aeroplane flying directly halfway between those two lights, I know I'm on course." The old lady took her seat again, apparently quite happy with her lesson in navigation.

On another occasion, with their hand luggage safely stowed and their seat belts secured, passengers waited patiently for their airliner to start up. Then came an announcement from the chief stewardess or hostess, as they were then known. "Ladies and gentlemen," she began. "We are very sorry for the delay, but our Captain has been unavoidably delayed.

"I am pleased to say, however that he is on his way, and we will be taking off shortly."

Soon there was a flurry of activity at the open passenger door as someone slowly mounted the steps. The newcomer, wearing a loose fitting beige raincoat and dark glasses, entered the cabin and made his way forward, tapping his route with a white stick. Reaching the door to the flight deck, he groped for the handle, and entered. The door closed behind him.

Moments later, the public address system came alive again. "Good evening, ladies and gentlemen. This is Captain Watson speaking. Thank you for your patience. I am glad to tell you that we are now cleared for take-off."

Then the airliner's engines came to life. It seems that Panda probably didn't need those navigation lights after all, even when he could clearly see them.

When a mongoose being carried in the hold of a Seaboard and Western freighter from India died suddenly during the flight, two hundred monkeys, also on board, set up a fearful wailing. For a time, the complaining American crew suffered the funeral dirge, but eventually it became too much. A radio message was sent to the nearest Indian airport asking permission to jettison the body of the mongoose into the Indian ocean.

Airport control officers who picked up the message were puzzled. They decided the crew were suffering from a touch of the sun and asked for a repeat. To them the message plainly read:

"Mangus dead. Permission to jettison." And Mangus, they knew, was the name of the pilot.

My colleague's story might have ended there. But he and I jointly spent almost three weeks trying to track down Captain Mangus to confirm it, only to hear from him eventually: "Sorry fellows, but it just didn't happen.

"We did have a dead mongoose, and the monkeys did make a heck of a fuss about it. But the rest of the story was tacked on by a co-pilot of mine who thought it would be a good laugh."

There were, of course, many other pilots whose names would have been easily remembered by both travellers and non-travellers. Some of them were regular visitors to Heathrow, as passengers or to meet friends, like legless RAF ace Sir Douglas Bader. He once was invited to formally open and name a new bar in the airport's Terminal 1. He told me he was "very tickled" to learn that the bar was to be called: "The Pilots' Arms."

Courtesy www.acesofww2.com.

242 Squadron's Douglas Bader *(l)* & Willie McKnight *(r)* admire their unit's unofficial motif.

Another contemporary pilot who almost certainly would have appreciated the joke was the 43-years old Luftwaffe fighter commander and himself a wartime ace, General Adolf Galland. I once met him when he flew into Heathrow in 1955 on his way to the Farnborough air show as a civilian industrial adviser. Though they were later peacetime associates, some say as "bar buddies," Bader too first met the German in completely different circumstances. The British flyer had become a prisoner of war in Germany after being shot down, and Galland had come to talk to him. He had abandoned his artificial legs to escape from his burning aircraft, and the German pilot asked him how he had managed it.

He was quoted as saying he couldn't remember much about it. "One never does," replied his Iron Cross opponent, explaining: "I know. One of your pilots once shot *me* down."

Adolf Galland.

Over the years there were a number of our clients who seemed to pop up regularly to make the news pages. Though most of these were celluloid celebrities, there were many from "show business" generally, specifically from television, film, the theatre, ballet, and music worlds at all levels and tastes. There were other personalities from other arts, politics, and from a range of sporting activities. And there were also some household names I was thankful only to have to meet once, and who, even if they were regular travellers, rarely featured either in the gossip diaries or the news columns.

Sir Winston Churchill's son Randolph inherited much of his father's bullish reputation, making it his own, apparently without any of the wartime premier's redeeming, more admirable, characteristics. A journalist himself, he never appeared to be a popular figure among his peers, frequently earning "a bad press" for his views and attitudes. On the one occasion I had to approach him, it was with a question the *Daily Express* news desk asked us to put to him on his return from an overseas trip.

The particular question I no longer recall, but it begged a comment from Churchill on something written about him by another well-known commentator of the day. It was unlikely he had heard of the item while abroad, so I wasn't expecting a positive response. Nevertheless, notebook in hand, I approached him as he emerged from the arrivals' Customs Hall in Heathrow's Terminal 2, and introduced myself politely as he strode the few yards to a downwards escalator. He grunted dismissively and failed to stop. I followed him.

Hurrying forward to the moving stair he suddenly stumbled. He reached for the rail to recover himself, turned back to me and snarled: "You pushed me!"

I responded automatically. "I'm sorry Mr Churchill, but you're mistaken. I haven't touched you. I was at least three feet behind you." But he wasn't listening. "Don't be so bloody rude," he snapped. By this time we had both reached the bottom of the escalator. But I couldn't let this go. I hadn't put the *Express* question to him. "Sir," I said quietly, and perhaps sulkily, "I don't have your reputation for being rude…"

As I said it, I recalled two similar occasions, both recorded in these pages, when I had been similarly impatiently rejected, on those occasions by showbiz personalities. Now once again there was a sudden conversion. Randolph Churchill stopped in his tracks, turned, and faced me. "Very well," he said, politely but coldly, "What do you want from me?"

I explained the newspaper's request, and repeated what I'd been told. As I thought, he was unaware of the report, and he said calmly: "There is no way I am going to respond through a third party to something I haven't even read. Even if I had read it I might choose to ignore it.

"Now I must go. But thank you." Fair enough, I thought. I would have done the same, as I told the *Express*, and as they agreed. I saw no published follow-up next day. All it could have been from me was: *"Mr Churchill declined to comment."*

Since 1945 almost every US President has visited Britain on either an official or an informal visit at least once during his term (the exceptions being Lyndon Johnson and Gerald Ford, both being succeeding vice-presidents). Such visits have increased in frequency in recent years due partly to the speed and ease of travel.

When a major media occasion has been provided for a Presidential airport arrival, with massive security and access restrictions, contact with the press has always been minimal. Usually it is a "photo-call" only, with perhaps, a prepared "no questions" address by the visitor for reporters. The White House press corps, honoured and highly influential in the US, is ever present, often travelling on the presidential "Air Force One" airliner.

The Boeing 707 – without bunting, but otherwise 'dressed overall' as Presidential airliner 'US Air Force One' was the first jet to take on this role. The picture was taken during President Carter's 1977 London visit.

Official US Air Picture

But American presidents in office, like Britain's monarch, have no direct casual contact with the news media of the host country on arrival, unlike some other heads of state. Although I witnessed the arrival or departure of most of the US leaders over the years, as a news man I only met one, Dwight Eisenhower, and that was before he entered politics as a Presidential candidate. Jimmy Carter exchanged a couple of words with me in 1977, but I had by then moved on myself to my airport management role, later to plan and oversee the reception arrangements for his successor, Ronald Reagan.

Presidential *families* were different. I came across Patricia Lawford, sister of recently-elected President Jack Kennedy, in 1961 at Heathrow as she and her husband, 38 years-old British actor Peter Lawford changed 'planes on their way home to Los Angeles. The couple had been visiting Mrs Lawford's father, Joseph Kennedy, at his villa in the South of France. They were expected to stay a further two weeks, but suddenly left for London.

As they waited in a departure lounge, Mrs Lawford put through a call to the White House. Her call had to be routed via Paris, as direct transatlantic

Peter Lawford in *'Royal Wedding'* (1951)

Patricia Kennedy, circa 1948 ***Courtesy of JFK Presidential Library, Boston***

lines were busy. Then, near to tears, she told me: "My baby is undergoing an operation in five to six hours."

I said stupidly: "I hope it isn't too serious." She replied, as she hurried out to a Los Angeles-bound airliner with her grim-faced husband: "It's serious enough."

Later, an airline official said that the pilot of her aircraft had been asked to give the couple all help possible if they wanted news of the baby during the flight. As the 707 jet neared the American coast, a message was flashed to Washington to ask "How's the baby?"

The following day's newspapers carrying my report were able to provide the answer. The baby, Robin Elizabeth, was making good progress after a major but successful abdominal operation. In her mid-forties, she is now a respected marine biologist in New York.

PAT LAWFORD
A call from the sky

Daily Express picture

Kennedy's sister in drama of phone call and her baby

Express Staff Reporter

FROM a blue and white Boeing 707 airliner over the North Pole last night a radio message flashed to the White House in Washington.

It asked: "How is the baby?"

Aboard the giant plane flying to Los Angeles from London was President Kennedy's sister Patricia and her husband, British-born actor Peter Lawford.

As they flew home an operation was performed on the Lawfords' five-week-old baby daughter—their fourth child.

Mrs. Lawford and her 38-year-old husband, who is now an American, had been visiting Mrs. Lawford's father, Mr. Joseph Kennedy at his villa in the South of France.

They were expected to stay another fortnight. Suddenly, yesterday, they flew into London from Nice.

SERIOUS

They spent an hour changing planes. As they waited, Mrs. Lawford put in a call to the White House.

Operators told her that Trans-atlantic cables were busy, and her call was routed through Paris.

Then, close to tears, she said: "My baby is undergoing an operation in five or six hours."

Was it serious?

"Serious enough," she said as she hurried along beside her grim-faced husband.

Then they went aboard for their Polar flight.

An airline official said: "The airliner pilot has been asked to give them all help possible if they want news of the baby during the flight."

Hollywood message: The Lawford baby - her names are Robin Elizabeth - is in hospital for an operation for a major abdominal obstruction. The operation was successful. And Robin Elizabeth "is making good progress."

Daily Express
Circa Aug 10 1961

When 30-years old Edward Kennedy, President Kennedy's younger brother, flew into London from Paris a few months after his sister, he found London taxi-cab drivers rather less helpful than the Lawfords' airline crew.

Mr Kennedy, soon to seek successful election to the American senate, was on a European fact-finding tour on behalf of the President, and had three hours to spare at Heathrow before catching an onward flight to Dublin. He decided to attend mass at a Roman Catholic church in nearby Hounslow West, but the embassy car sent to take him had punctured a tyre.

So Mr Kennedy strode from the forecourt of Terminal 2 to a nearby taxi rank. Eight cabs stood by. There was no driver in the first; nor in the second. So he and his embassy escort climbed into the third. Almost immediately a group of drivers appeared. "Hounslow West and fast," said the embassy man to the nearest in the group.

"Not in this one," said the driver.

"Why not? " asked the President's brother.

"We're waiting. We'll call another cab up." said the driver, ignoring the five taxis behind him. And despite the protests from Mr Kennedy's escort, one of the group went off to find the driver of the last taxi on the rank. While they waited, the two travellers were told of the taximen's "fare share" system. Under this, the passenger could only take the first cab in a rank. But if the journey was a short one, the intending passenger would be passed on to the last cab in the line-up.

picture by Cecil Stoughton
Courtesy of JFK Presidential Library, Boston

Edward Kennedy, 1963.

Mr Kennedy and his companion had to wait another five minutes for the eighth driver, Mr Monty Marks, to appear. Then he kept his passengers waiting even longer while he hurried into the terminal to buy cigarettes. The fare to Hounslow West cost the embassy official a total of ten shillings, (50p) including a "keep the change" tip of 2s.3d (about 12p). My story on the incident (with a diplomatic "No comment" from the future Senator) and the follow-up repercussions won wide coverage in the nationals, as well as overseas *(see overleaf)*. But it took *Daily Express* cartoonist Giles to visualise a similar situation involving a prominent Commonwealth statesman who at the time was accusing the British Government of "treachery" over the break-up of the Central African Federation.

The across-the-page cartoon shows a gloomy Heathrow with a taxicab pulling away from the rank in heavy snow, the driver apparently nursing a black eye and a bloodied nose. Huddled in the cab is a disgruntled Federation Prime Minister and ex-boxer, whose gloves are off (but secured to his luggage). Nearby is a group of dismayed cab-drivers.

Kennedy's brother turned out of taxi

PRESIDENT'S brother or not, 30 - year - old Edward Kennedy found out yesterday, you can't budge a London cabby if he doesn't want to go.

Mr. Kennedy, who is on a European fact - finding mission for the American President, discovered this particular fact when he flew into London Airport from Paris, on his way to Dublin.

With three hours to spare before continuing the flight, Mr. Kennedy decided to attend Mass at a Roman Catholic church in Hounslow West. But the embassy car sent to take him punctured a tyre.

So the President's brother and an embassy man hurried over to a taxi rank. Eight cabs stood there.

Not in No. 3

There was no driver in the first. Nor in the second. They climbed in the third and a group of drivers walked over. "Hounslow West and fast," ordered the embassy man.

"Not in this one," said the driver.

"Why can't we have one of these?" asked the President's brother.

"We are waiting. We will call another cab round," replied the driver.

Protests from the embassy man did not perturb the cabbies. Calmly they put into operation their "fare shares" system. Under this the passenger must take the first cab—unless the journey is short. Then Cabby No. 1 passes him on to the last in the line.

The No. 8 cabby yesterday was 32 - year - old Monty Marks from Streatham. And he kept Mr. Kennedy waiting even longer while he bought cigarettes.

A 2s. 3d. tip

Finally, seven minutes after arriving at the rank Mr. Kennedy was off to church. Fare for the four-mile journey: 7s. 9d. Monty got 2s. 3d. tip.

One of the other drivers said: "We didn't know it was the President's brother, but if we had it would have made no difference."

Mr. Jim Francis, secretary of the Transport Union cab section, said last night: "It's time the authorities stopped this kind of thing.

"It's bad for the trade. There has been similar trouble at the airport before. It is not right that these drivers should refuse fares in this way."

The regulations require taximen to take a passenger up to six miles "on the clock." A police spokesman explained: "If a cabby refuses the passenger can report him to the police."

Daily Express Feb 26 1962

World copyright © Express Newspapers Ltd *Daily Express, Feb 27 1962, Cartoon by Carl GILES*

The cartoon's caption reads: *"The taxi driver who ordered President Kennedy's brother to the end of the rank should watch it if they try the same thing with Sir Roy Welensky."*

The taxi story didn't end there. Exactly one month later I had to report that 75 cab drivers at London Airport had suddenly stopped work and parked up. They were, they said, on strike in protest against the "first come, first served" rule which they claimed was unfair. And thousands of taxi drivers throughout London were warned by their unions: "Don't blackleg."

The trouble started when a Ministry of Aviation police inspector ordered drivers to obey the regulations and take the first fares to come along. "The rule means that the cab-drivers who have waited longest for a fare might have to accept a very short journey, only to face going to the end of the queue when they return to the airport." explained one driver to me, as he abandoned his cab and joined others on picket duty at the cab-rank.

And John Kavanaugh for the Owner Drivers' Association told me: "We instituted our own system of fare-sharing. Until now the airport management turned a blind eye to us operating this way. We say it has resulted in a better service to the public.

75 cabbies strike at air port

LONDON'S 10,000 taxi drivers got a "grape-vine" message last night: "The airport boys are on strike. Don't be a blackleg."

And at London Airport, seventy-five taxis stood idle as angry passengers complained to police and airport officials.

The trouble began when a Ministry of Aviation police inspector warned drivers to obey regulations and take the first fares that came along.

'Brewing'

Said one of the cabbies' spokesmen, Mr. John Kavanaugh, of the Owner-Drivers' Association:

"This row has been brewing up for a long time. But it really came to a head in an incident involving Mr. Edward Kennedy, the American President's brother.

"We have our own system of fare sharing, which allows the last man on the rank to take the short journeys.

"The airport management have turned a blind eye and allowed us to operate this system, which we say has given the public a better service."

Airport taxis in Kennedy strike

By GERARD KEMP

ALL 75 taxi drivers at London Airport stopped work last night in protest against a ruling that they must take the first fare that came along.

Daily Mail (all) Circa March 26 1962

AIRPORT TAXI DRIVERS STRIKE

TAXI drivers at London Airport went on strike yesterday in protest against the "first come, first served" regulations.

Seventy-five taxis stood idle while stranded passengers queued to telephone for Mini-cabs or hire cars.

The drivers formed pickets and hung a notice beside the main approach tunnel: "Don't blackleg."

Trouble has been brewing among the cabbies since Mr. Edward Kennedy, the U.S. President's brother, was involved in an incident at the airport last month.

Daily Herald (above)
Daily Mirror (left)

"The row came to a head over the incident involving Mr Kennedy. All we want from the airport management is a clarification of the regulation."

It took a series of meetings over several months before the dispute was resolved to everyone's satisfaction.

There are always of course, many ordinary passengers from the less dramatic walks of life, the unsung achievers, the unlikely heroes and the totally mundane, making their quiet way through the airports, with or without needing a taxi. Some may have won fame through their own endeavours. Some would have had fame thrust upon them, by accident or association. Some simply commanded attention for a comparatively fleeting moment, only to be remarked upon again so many years later.

One such legitimate one-off traveller was the unlikely absent-minded professor with the "washing machine." It was the early 1950s, and I discovered him in the check-in hall of the northside terminal buildings as he was about to set off on a flight to Paris. I watched in puzzled fascination as he moved between other passengers, stopping briefly every few yards to place his burden, cylindrical and about the size of a small dustbin, in front of him on the carpeted floor.

For I moment I thought it was because his object was heavy. Then I realised that each time he halted he bent over it, fiddled with what appeared to be a dial, and jotted down a reading. At last he appeared satisfied. He put away the notebook he had taken from his pocket and, planting the "washing machine" in front of him, took a seat in the corner of the crowded lounge. It was my chance.

While other passengers looked on curiously, I asked the man if he would mind telling me what he was doing. "Oh, nothing wrong, I assure you ," he replied in a strong French accent. "And I do 'ave permission… I always ask first. See…" Reaching into his pocket, he added, defensively: "I 'ave a letter."

I don't know who he thought I was but it was my turn to do the reassuring. Then he explained. His name, he said, was Professor Jean Martin, and he was a French physicist. His £3,000 "washing machine" was used to measure gravity, and he was taking readings on behalf of the British Greenland expedition. The obvious questions were already forming: "What for?" and "Why here at Heathrow for an expedition to Greenland?" But the Professor anticipated them.

"Unless you 'ave all day – and I 'aven't anyway – it would be pointless to try to explain," he said. He did try, but I was happy to take him at his word when his flight was suddenly called. And as I recalled this anecdote, I couldn't help thinking what a wonderfully innocent world it was before any such situation in an airport terminal would have immediately alerted the armed police patrols, permission or not…

There were some visitors, too who were neither celebrities nor passengers, but who quickly became part of the airport scene for up to a decade. One was the man who said he was a Roman Catholic priest but claimed to be looking for his daughter among the daily hundreds of thousands of passengers. He kept up his vigil for two or three years, visiting terminals at both Heathrow and Northolt sometimes as often as two or three times a week.

Police, medical staff and airline and airport employees had him under almost constant surveillance, but he was no trouble to anyone, and kept himself to himself, a very sad and lonely figure. Apparently not even the airport chaplains could help him.

The woman in white was another familiar figure. On her regular visits to Heathrow in the late 'fifties, she told staff that she was waiting to meet her fiancé who was returning home after several years overseas. The description was not of her attire, but of her features,

KENNEDY TAXI ROW ENDS IN STRIKE

Express Staff Reporter

NINE THOUSAND London taxi-drivers were told last night: "The boys at London Airport are on strike. Don't blackleg." And it was all over a regulation that affected President Kennedy's brother.

At the airport 75 empty taxis were crammed in a tiny car park while their drivers went on picket duty.

The strike began after a police inspector warned drivers that they must obey airport regulations and take the first fare. But the drivers claim he said they could do what they liked when his back was turned.

Mr. John Kavanagh, representing the owner-drivers' association, said: "This row came to a head over the incident involving Mr. Edward Kennedy."

Had to wait

Mr. Kennedy was refused service by several cabbies last month under their rota system. They told him he must wait for a man who was buying cigarettes.

"All we want from the airport management is a clarification of the regulation," said Mr. Kavanagh.

"Our system of fare-sharing allows the last man on the rank to take the short journeys and it has resulted in a better service."

Daily Express
circa March 26 1962

JFK Presidential Library
Edward Kennedy, here aged 4, presumably did not have to queue for this lift from big brother Jack.

NO MYSTERY

THROUGH the crowds in London Airport's departure lounges last night pushed dapper Professor Jean Martin with his "washing machine."

In a corner of the lounge he set down his machine and turned on a switch. The crowd waited silently.

The little French physicist bent over the machine, nodded, switched off, picked up the machine and elbowed his way out again.

"I'm making gravitational readings to aid the British Greenland expedition. Pointless to explain," he said cheerfully, as he boarded a plane for Paris.

Sunday Pictorial

News in brief

His 'washing machine' costs £3,000

IT was "rush hour" at London Airport last night when a dapper little man with what seemed to be a "washing machine" entered the crowded departure lounges.

Finding a quiet corner, he put his machine on the ground, turned a knob. Silence fell. Then the little man explained.

He was Professor Jean Martin, French physicist. His £3,000 machine measures the time that things take to fall to the ground—the "pull of gravity."

Sunday Express
(both) Aug 10 1952
This equates to well over £62,000 today

which were painted a startling, unrelieved white. The paint, or make-up, which blended totally with her shoulder-length white hair, extended into its roots at her forehead and covered her ears and neck.

We soon learnt that she was Joan Abery, a 70-years-old former pharmacist who had become a recluse after her fiancé jilted her. But it wasn't until she died alone in the early 1990s that it was revealed that after the death of her mother 30 years earlier, she had moved into the garden of the bungalow they had shared in Reading, Berkshire. As with her mother before her it was several weeks before her body was discovered under dozens of boxes, tree branches and colourful open umbrellas which she had apparently made her home.

Airport detectives had made searching enquiries about both the "priest" and the painted lady, then decided to take no action as both were considered harmless and able to care for themselves. But the same police did go to considerable lengths to investigate and warn off another frequent loiterer seen chatting to staff and travellers in busy airport areas. His principle offence was his wearing of a fake airline uniform, with the apparent insignia of a Captain or first Officer on his sleeves and epaulettes.

Airgirls claimed that he often misled passengers and public with false information about flights. What was worse was that he was frequently seen propping up a public bar with a stiff drink in his hand.

As one passenger officer put it: "Travellers are often aware of the strict rules airlines have about aircrew not drinking and flying. Some were very upset to see what they thought was a pilot drinking spirits while apparently on duty."

Inevitably there were also regular travellers in those early days, just as there are today, who were famous mainly for… being famous. As if illustrating Andy Warhol's oft-repeated "fifteen minutes of fame," the last of these are among the most difficult to document. Where now are the likes of the Dockers (motor magnate Sir Bernard and his Lady) who seemed to be always on the diary pages? Where are the international playboys of the calibre of Prince Aly Khan – father of the present Aga – and Grand National rider and motor racing driver the Marquis Alfonso de Portago, to name a few who come quickly to mind ?

No hairdresser is so well established or so colourful as TV's first, Raymond "Mr Teasy-Weazy" Bessone. Perhaps now he would have to be a TV chef. And how many remember the elegant Lady Beatty, or her travelling pseudonym "Mrs O'Connor," despite her widely reported romance with the late Frank Sinatra?

The self-styled rodeo ring-master Buffalo Bill II, better known to his mother as the English-born Captain Edward Gray; his look-alike, Colonel Sanders of the secret Kentucky chicken sauce recipe fame; the Persian millionaire Nubar Gulbenkian son of the world's wealthiest man and his gold taxi (in reality a luxuriously fitted black cab with a basket-weave gold overlay); they were ever among the more eccentric travellers through Heathrow.

Jackie Collins

Competing for the title of most frequent well-known passengers throughout the 1980s and 1990s were Sir David Frost, sometime TV mogul, talent spotter, serious interviewer, chat-show host, comedian and presenter, and Joan Collins, British star of a long-running Hollywood soap opera. It's not often remembered now that Joan was a J.Arthur Rank charm-school starlet and played a range of less glamorous leading roles in British films some forty years earlier. Even then she was a seasoned air traveller, as I have already described elsewhere.

Not so well known then, in spite of her efforts to the contrary, was Joan's younger sister, Jackie.[1] As I have written, in later years she was to find *her* forte in writing racy novels based on her experiences and observations in Hollywood where once she had hoped to emulate her sister. I met her at a book signing for one of those novels and reminded her that she had once told me she had changed her surname to "Douglas" to escape frequent comparison to Joan.

"Did I?" she asked, Then: "Yes, I probably did. I think I changed it several times. It didn't make any difference!"

She may not have remembered. But she did remember me… well at least, she *said* she did on the fly-leaf of her book she autographed.

[1] *See Chapter Five, p.118*

The names of Italy's Gina Lollobrigida and Swedish-born Mai Zetterling are not ones you might expect to come naturally together when flicking through the photo stills' portfolios of cinematic memories. But the flashing-eyed Latin looks and temperament of the one and the Nordic pertness of the other will both be associated in my mind for the most unlikely of reasons. Both were successful at being ordinary, unglamorous, plainly dressed and completely unrecognisable in a crowd. Well, almost unrecognisable.

They had something else in common. For many years they were airport "regulars," always flying in and out to discuss new films, to pick up a potential script, to start or finish a picture or to attend a premiere, though not, I must add, together. On these occasion we were, of course, alerted to their travels by their respective agents or film promoters who were then regularly rewarded with the standard flattering photo-shoots in an airport corridor or at the steps of their respective airliners.

Then came one day when we were not alerted in advance – the day I spotted what I was convinced was a familiar face in a very unfamiliar guise of unglamorous headscarf and glasses, little make-up, flat shoes and an unfashionable coat belted around a generous waistline. She recognised me at the same moment, and immediately tried to hide herself behind a countless number of shopping bags she carried in both hands. She turned to me resignedly as I addressed her hesitantly: "Miss Lollobrigida…"

Sighing audibly, she acknowledged me bravely and asked: "How did you know…who told you…?"

I could only say: "But I would, *anyone* would, recognise you anywhere, Miss Lollobrigida," while wondering if that was really what she wanted to hear. For a few minutes only we chatted before I excused myself and she made her way through departure controls. Neither of us touched on what could have been the embarrassing subject of her appearance, her ordinariness. The closest she came to it was to say: "I've just been here privately to do some shopping."

She might have added: "In disguise," to forestall any potential revelations from me. I couldn't be that unkind. But I couldn't help pondering what the fans of one of the world's most beautiful women, or indeed what all those film producers would have thought if they had seen the glamorous Lollo as she appeared to me that day. And would she have posed for a picture?

For the lovely Mai, though it too involved shopping, the setting was quite different and for that reason, probably even more unsettling for her. I was making my way into the town air terminal of British European Airways in London's Kensington High Street to head for the airport and had just emerged from the Underground exit between the two then well-known department stores of Pontings and Derry and Toms. I turned sharply to the left as I reached the public footpath… and walked straight into the outstretched arms of Mai Zetterling. She lost her balance and dropped her shopping bags.

With a heartfelt: "I'm sorry, Miss Zetterling. Let me help you," I bent down to retrieve her bags with her. She was obviously startled to be addressed by name and glanced quickly in my direction as our heads almost clashed, but said not a word. I repeated: "I'm so sorry. Perhaps I wasn't looking where I was going," but she was already hurrying away. I don't believe she wanted to be recognised. She too was casually and simply dressed, and could have been any one of a thousand women out shopping. *She* obviously didn't remember or didn't wish to know me.

Norma Sykes was a name as unfamiliar to newspaper readers of the mid-fifties as it would be today. Yet everyone would have then recognised the curvaceous figure and blonde bombshell looks of the girl who had shot to fame as Sabrina on British television black and white screens for doing absolutely nothing, and for saying even less. The nineteen-years-old had been "discovered" by the popular comedy actor Arthur Askey and given the name and a regular walk-on part in his weekly show, carrying all before her.

Her fling with Hollywood actor Steve Cochran had begun three months earlier when he escorted her to a film premiere. It elevated her to the columns of the national Press again as she clung to his arm and wept when he left her at Heathrow to catch a flight to Lisbon.

"We're just good friends," she insisted, unwittingly echoing the catchphrase of the

As she might have preferred to be seen – and recognised: "La Lollo" pictured here at a film reception.

Mai Zetterling

SABRINA WEEPS AS STEVE FLIES AWAY

DAILY MIRROR REPORTER

SABRINA, the curvaceous girl from Blackpool who became a television star without saying a word, dabbed a tear-stained cheek yesterday.

She was saying farewell at London Airport to Hollywood film star Steve Cochran, who was flying off to Lisbon.

Nineteen - year - old Sabrina—real name Norma Sykes—had driven him to the airport.

Since he escorted her to a film premiere nearly three months ago they have often been seen together.

Take-Off Delayed

Soon after Steve boarded the air-liner yesterday the passengers were told that a technical fault would delay the take-off for thirty minutes.

All but one of them filed back to the airport building for refreshment.

All but one — husky Steve Cochran.

An airline official explained: "Mr. Cochran was not feeling very well and didn't want to move."

Last night Sabrina said to me:

"Why was I crying at the airport? Well, Steve was taking my dog, Shane, with him to Lisbon.

"I thought I wouldn't be seeing my darling doggie again. . . ."

Sabrina added: "I don't want Steve to think that I am moping for him. There is no romance."

She added:

"But Steve is ringing me up tomorrow. Really he is!"

And her eyes lit up.

Such sweet sorrow for Sabrina

JUST GOOD FRIENDS

By DAVID NATHAN

WHEN the He-man of the screen parts from the She-woman of T V and there are tears on the tarmac—remember they are *only friends*.

It was like that yesterday when Steve Cochrane, the Hollywood star, flew from London to Lisbon, leaving behind Miss Norma Sykes, better known as Sabrina.

Sabrina dabbed at her eyes as she waved to the taxi-ing plane. Then she left in the car in which she had driven Mr. Cochrane to the airport.

His publicity-mongers had tried to stop photographers picturing him with Sabrina.

How could there be anything in it, they asked, when Mr. Cochrane's name was linked with Lisbeth Scott's, "with whom, incidentally, he has just made a picture?" Mr. Cochrane and Miss Sykes *are just friends*, said one.

But parting is hard, even for *just friends*. When Sabrina had gone Mr. Cochran's plane was delayed.

Daily Herald (above)
Daily Mirror (left), (both) Dec 28 1955
Daily Mirror picture

decade, "I'm crying because he is taking my little doggy with him to Portugal and I'm not sure when I shall see him – my doggy, that is – again." And she added: "I don't want Steve to think I'm moping for him. There is no romance."

She was supported by Cochran's publicity representatives, who had tried to stop photographers taking pictures of them together. "There's nothing to it," they said, "His name is currently linked to Lisbeth Scott and yes, he's just made a picture with her."

I have also referred in earlier chapters to London criminals like gang boss Jack Comer, and to con-man, fraudster and armed thief Dennis Stafford. The first, better known as Jack Spot, appeared to be an acknowledged superior of the unknown lesser thug who had once threatened me and trailed me, a cub reporter, across London. The latter, Stafford, presented me with a scoop over my Fleet Street colleagues when, as an escapee from Wormwood Scrubs he was hauled back from Trinidad under arrest, only to escape gaol a second time shortly afterwards. A few years on and he was sentenced to prison again after being found guilty of murdering a fellow director of a fruit machine company.

The international underworld has long held a fascination for some leading lights of show-business. Frank Sinatra and George Raft both had well-documented links with the US Mafia. Sophie Tucker, self-styled "last of the Red Hot Mamas" and the great Judy Garland both revelled in their acquaintanceship with gangsters on both sides of the Atlantic. Here, our own Barbara Windsor, popular *Carry On* screen comedy star and later TV soap opera actress, was a former girl-friend of Charlie Kray, loyal brother to the infamous twins Ronnie and Reggie. She described the brothers later as "so polite." Her marriage shortly afterwards to Ronnie Knight, also a known criminal who at one time was arrested for murder though acquitted, lasted twenty years.

Diana Dors, originally Britain's answer to Marilyn Monroe and who was to become a much acclaimed serious actress, also associated with criminals for much of her working life. And British screen actor, hard man Stanley Baker, listed "Big Albert" Dimes, leader of the underworld's "Italian mob" and the Richardson brothers, rivals to the Krays, among his friends.

When Hollywood actor Jose Ferrer flew to London in 1952 it was to a welcome unlike anything anyone had seen at the airport before – or since. He was here for the world premiere of his British musical *Moulin Rouge,* (the original version) a loose biopic of the love life and times of French impressionist Henri de Toulouse Lautrec.

Jose Ferrer

Eddie Chapman

Lining both sides of Heathrow's single-storey original northside arrivals terminal, waiting to greet him like a guard of honour, were around 20 of London's most notorious gangsters. I immediately recognised pre-Kray era underworld boss Billy Hill, who had recently split from his close associate Jack Spot. With him was convicted safe-blower Eddie Chapman, who a year or two earlier had been honoured for bravery as a wartime double agent, inside Germany for Britain and, with the knowledge of the secret service, also "spying" on his home country for the Germans, who had first trained him.

There were several others whose faces were familiar, though I couldn't put a name to them and who unsurprisingly declined my request for identification. And at one stage I spotted Special Branch officers of Scotland Yard moving among them, making notes. Then, seconds before the screen actor made his appearance the visitors all donned false beards and odd-shaped unfashionable hats, and *all of them went down on their knees.* In his Oscar-nominated role as the diminutive artist, Ferrer had played Lautrec by "walking" on his knees, strapped into specially made shoes.

Ferrer's reaction to his welcoming "committee" as he emerged from the Customs-controlled baggage hall was to roar with laughter. He gleefully shook hands with some of those in the line-up, and I had to barge my way through the crowd to ask him if he knew of the reputation of some of them. He would only say: "But these are all my friends. Of course I know them. Their reputations? I don't know what you mean. A lot of that is exaggerated."

*

Whenever I am asked what kind of people I most disliked interviewing, I have to reply, "sports players and competitors." Then to counteract the usual reaction of surprise, shock and even horror, I invariably have to hasten to admit that the fault is usually mine; not the subjects'.

With a few exceptions, such as when I am proud to claim a form of affinity with my home soccer club Arsenal, or I become caught up in patriotic euphoria over some international sporting achievement, or with an event which has some significance for me, most sport, particularly team sport, leaves me cold. This means, of course, that when it was necessary to seek up-to-date information from some celebrated sports personality – I was usually the least informed of reporters. Invariably I had to do some urgent research. Mostly there simply wasn't time.

Brenard Press picture *Sept 5 1972*

Mark Spitz, seven times US swimming gold medallist in the 1972 Olympics, seeks a team official's advice before answering a question from a radio reporter at Heathrow. He was on his way home early from the Games on the day of the Arab terrorist raid on the Israeli team quarters. Spitz, who was also Jewish, was the world's leading Olympian gold medal winner until overtaken at the Beijing Games in 2008 by another US swimmer, Michael Phelps, with 9 golds.

Which may have explained why Glasgow Celtic football boss Jock Stein, one of Scotland's greatest-ever team managers, sighed out of sheer exasperation when I once asked him what I thought was a perfectly reasonable, if innocuous question.

In reply he demanded of no one in particular: "Why is it they always send me someone who knows nothing about the game and asks the most stupid questions?" Though taken back, I was able to respond at last: "I'm sorry, Mr Stein. But sometimes the most stupid questions earn the best answers. To be honest, I wasn't being deliberately stupid. I just don't know enough about football.

"And I have to tell you, no one sent me – I'm here all the time. I also know little about coal mines, but less than an hour ago had some interesting responses to my questions from a miners' union official."

Brenard Press picture *Sept 5 1972*

A youthful-looking Stirling Moss strides through Heathrow

Not usually known for his affability or patience, Stein was then surprisingly conciliatory, and gave me a detailed and tolerant response. But perhaps unsurprisingly, neither question nor answer appeared in print the next day, and today I have no recollection of what they were.

Among the few sports people I felt reasonably comfortable with were track and field athletes, perhaps because of the diversity of events they represented. I could also face up to motor racing drivers, (all of them I found to be extremely friendly, engaging and polite) prominent golfers, and boxers, both professional and amateur (all of course, predominantly individual competitors).

The latter are, like show business celebrities, almost always anxious to promote themselves, and many have excelled at their own PR even when their fight promoters seemed to prefer to relate directly to the news media themselves. One exception was the 1930s Italian world heavyweight champion, Primo Carnera, a giant of a man and the first prominent fighter I ever met. By this time a leading wrestler, he had lived in the US since the late '40s, and in Italy he was regarded as a hero for his anti-fascist stand there during the war.

His response to questions was often a monosyllabic grunt, which presumably led a well-known, small-of-stature London evening sports writer to greet the "Man Mountain" at Heathrow with the words: "Hello, Primo. Are you as punch-drunk as ever?"

I was directly in the line of fire for a swinging cross, so I mentally and physically winced at this ill-mannered challenge. Primo thankfully totally ignored me and, roaring back incomprehensibly at his would-be interrogator… strode away.

Strangely, Muhammed Ali, who as Cassius Clay was world-renowned as an amateur Olympic champion before becoming boxing's most acclaimed professional and biggest ever self-publicist in and out of the ring, could also be modest, polite and unassuming when free of an array of microphones and movie or TV cameras. In one brief question and answer session I once snatched with him, his calm responses were so quiet I had to ask him to repeat them for me to ensure accuracy.

SOLOMONS IS ANGRY

FIGHT promoter Jack Solomons said yesterday at London Airport, when he arrived back from New York, that unless he can get a guaranteed attendance of at least 70,000 there is little chance of another Turpin-Robinson fight in London.

"We need a crowd of 100,000 before it is really worth while," he said.

Of Turpin's statement that he would retire next September, Solomons said: "I've heard it all before. If we do have a return match in London it won't be until next June, and I can't see Turpin leaving the ring almost immediately afterwards."

Asked for his opinion of referee Ruby Goldstein's verdict, Solomons snapped: "It was absolutely wrong. The Yanks are too pernickety. The moment someone gets more than two punches they think there is going to be a death."

He said that Robinson was "dead" from the eighth round.

Solomons' judgment

Jack Solomons arriving at London Airport last night said that unless he got a guaranteed attendance of at least 70,000 there was little chance of another Turpin-Robinson fight in London.

His verdict on the verdict: "It was absolutely wrong. The Yanks are too pernickety. The moment someone gets more than two punches they think there is going to be a death."

He is the only British expert at the ringside to express this view.

Page Seven: "Turpin Robbed" is just gutter talk.

Reynolds News (above)
The People (left)
Sunday Express (below)
(all) Oct 16 1951

UNLESS he gets a guaranteed attendance of at least 70,000 spectators, promoter Jack Solomons said yesterday that there was little chance of another Turpin-Robinson fight in London. "We need a crowd of 100,000 to make it really worth while," said Solomons, as he stepped from a New York plane at London Airport.

Asked for his opinion of the referee's verdict, Solomons replied: "It was absolutely wrong. The Yanks are too pernickety. The moment someone gets more than two punches they think there is going to be a death.

"Robinson was 'dead' from the eighth round."

Among British fight promoters, Jack Solomons was probably the most active and well-known for "big fights" of the post-war years. He was never reluctant to express his views on the outcome of his bouts or the contestants. After America's Sugar Ray Robinson (whom Muhammed Ali is said to have described as "The Master,") won back his world middleweight title from Britain's Randolph Turpin in 1951 after only 3 months, he told me: "It was absolutely wrong. Robinson was dead from the eighth round."

It was a view challenged by many of the boxing pundits of the day. And two years on Turpin was criticised by Solomons for his 15-round points defeat by American Carl Bobo Olson. Turpin's close friend and second Mick Gavin gave an early clue to the boxer's mental state when he flew home. He told me: "The only words Randy said to me during the fight when I challenged him on his attitude were 'Micky, I'm fed up.'" And of Turpin's poor ring performance Solomons said that the former champion should be brought before the stewards

Statue of Randy Turpin, In his home county, Warwick

'I'm fed up,' said Turpin

The only words Randolph Turpin spoke during his fight against Bobo Olson last Wednesday in New York were: "I'm fed up."

They were quoted by 47-year-old Mick Gavin, one of the boxer's oldest friends and his second in the fight, when he reached London Airport last night. "Randolph must conquer his apathy," said Gavin. "I shall try to make him see sense, but I don't hold out much hope."

News Chronicle (left) Oct 26 1953

BOXING: Turpin's second says—

'I'LL TRY TO MAKE RANDY SEE SENSE'

RANDOLPH TURPIN is finished as Britain's hope—unless something or someone can be found to snap him out of his apathy towards the fight game.

That is the opinion of Randy's oldest friend, his second Mick Gavin.

Gavin said at London Airport yesterday, when he flew back from New York: "The only words Randy said to me during the fight when I challenged him on his attitude were, Micky, I'm fed up."

He had found Turpin in "good shape" physically before the fight, but mentally "on edge."

Gavin hopes to persuade Turpin to spend some weeks resting at his home in Warwick. "I shall have another good go at him to try to make him see sense," he said.

Daily Mirror *October 26 1953*

[illegible] inquiry into Turpin[illegible] [illegible] to this fight then I, for one, will be very much dissatisfied with the board.

Promoter Jack Solomons, home yesterday, sternly insisted: "Turpin must be brought up before the stewards to account for his behaviour."

Among all the blether of words about Turpin's future comes a coldly candid opinion from 47-year-old Mick Gavin, who has acted as second to Turpin in all but two of his big fights.

Gavin reckons Turpin is finished as a British fight hope unless something can be found to shake him out of his present mood and revive his interest in the boxing business.

Gavin confirmed what I had suspected—that Turpin wanted to quit halfway through the fight with Olson. Gavin says: "When I told him to snap out of it he replied, 'I don't want any more. I'm fed up.'"

Grey-haired Micky said he would have one final try to make Turpin see sense, but added sadly: "I am not holding out much hope."

Daily Express (extract)
Oct 26 1953

to account for his behaviour.

But the promotor was also quick to defend the reputation of British heavyweight champion Don Cockell who retained his Empire title with merely a points win in Johannesburg over South Africa's Johnny Arthur. Although many critics were disappointed, Solomons described it as a "fine performance" when he flew back to London.

"A win on points was the most we could expect," he said blaming the altitude. "I'd like to see Rocky Marciano do better in those conditions."

Solomons undoubtedly won the respect of many more of "his" boxers for the loyalty he showed them. This was clearly demonstrated when three of America's greatest boxing champions, heavyweight Maxie Baer, cruiserweight Gus Lesnevich and featherweight Henry Armstrong flew to London together in 1958. They had been invited by Solomons to attend the farewell party he was organising at the Harringay Arena, the north London venue of so many decisive world title bouts, which was about to close for good.

The promoter was at the London Airport arrivals' barrier to greet them personally, and as they spotted him thet rushed forward. Lesnevich by now a businessman, and Armstrong by now a Baptist preacher who at one time had held three titles simultaneously pumped both of their host's hands, planting a a smacking kiss on his cheek . Baer, who excused himself for a few minutes to plant a kiss on every airgirl in sight, then enclosed Solomons in a bear hug with a cry of: "Howdy, old money bags!"

Harry "The Horse" Levene, Solomons rival as a fight promoter, was just as astute as a publicist. But he was more circumspect with his opinions both before and after a big fight. He regularly telephoned us directly to tell us of potential champions he was tempting to Britain to meet British contenders in his rings. And the newspapers readily lapped up our often-exclusive stories on the subsequent arrivals. So we both gained.

Other fighters, particularly Ingemar Johansson from Sweden, who took the world heavyweight championship from America's great Floyd Patterson in 1959, were able to look after their own corner, promoting themselves in news terms with expertise. I first met him some three months after the title fight in New York. The articulate and likeable Swede flew in from his home in Gothenburg to switch on the sea-front seasonal

Brenard Press picture
Evening Standard Dec 28 '53
Don Cockell

COULD ROCKY DO BETTER?

—Jack Solomons

BRITISH heavyweight champion Don Cockell's points win against Johnny Arthur to retain his Empire title at Johannesburg on Saturday disappointed South African critics, but last night Promoter Jack Solomons described it as a "fine performance" when he arrived back in London by air.

"If an English boxer doesn't go out and kill someone, everybody is disappointed," he said. "A win on points was the most we could expect and it was a wonderful result.

La Starza signed

"I'd like to see Rocky Marciano do better out there. How many of our boys can go out to South Africa and win? Even I get breathless in that altitude."

Mr. Solomons said he had already signed up American heavyweight Roland La Starza to fight Cockell in London on March 30 as an eliminator for Rocky Marciano's world heavyweight crown.

Daily Sketch *Feb 1954*

EX-CHAMPS

THREE champs flexed their muscles and strode into London last night —arms thrown back, chests out, and making with the wise-cracks. Like old times.

They had come to say a fond farewell to Harringay Arena—the spacious, echoing hall where they saw their moments of triumph and defeat.

There was Maxie Baer—boisterous, beefy and prosperous. The one-time "Clown Prince of Boxing" is now 49, and famous in America as a showman and television star.

He enclosed promoter Jack Solomons in a bear-hug, planted a smacking kiss on his cheek with a cry of: "How-do, old money bags."

Evangelist

Henry "Homicide Hank" Armstrong, the only man to hold three world titles at once, was comparatively quiet.

The gentle Negro from Missouri conducted himself as befits a respected Baptist evangelist.

And there was glorious Gus Lesnevich, now 43, whose battles with our Freddie Mills earned them both a place in the ring history books. Gus—a Russian-American from New Jersey—is now an executive with a trucking company.

Party spirit

****

INTO London Airport from New York last night flew Gus Lesnevich, Maxie Baer, and Henry Armstrong—three of the fighters whose fists helped to build the legend of Harringay They're here for tonight's farewell party when the famous arena closes for good.

Organiser, of course, is the man who has run so many shindigs there in the past: Jack Solomons. He was at the airport to meet his guests.

Said Lesnevich, who fought historic cruiser-weight battles with Freddie Mills: "It's great to be here, but it was a big surprise to hear about Harringay. Why are they letting them do it?"

Armstrong, the man who once held three world titles at the same time, is now a Baptist minister in Columbus, Mississippi.

Baer, one time world heavyweight champion, who now has his own television show, was playing the showman when he got here. He kissed every air girl in sight—even kissed and hugged Solomons

It should be a good party.

cuttings' (above, right) sources unidentified *Oct 28 1958* lights at Morecambe, Lancashire, and I asked him the one question everyone wanted the answer to. When was he meeting Patterson in a return match?

"Not until they've paid me for the last one," was his reply. "And not under any conditions until at least ten weeks until after they've paid me." He went on: "I was supposed to get 20 per cent of everything. Yet so far I haven't even heard when they propose to pay me. At this moment the New York Boxing Commission is working on it for me."

Johansson denied he was bound by contract to fight Patterson again early. "When everything is cleared up I want to meet him again. I am in training and my right hand is still working good." After the Morecambe event he was flying back straight back to Sweden, where he was due to meet up former champion Jack Dempsey, promoter of the New York fight, to discuss the return.

The interview made both news pages and sport columns of the London evenings and the dailies the following day. But in fact it was not until the following Spring that Johansson was able to continue the conversation. Photographer Pete Ward and I caught up with him and his manager Eddie Ahlquist, in a transit lounge at Heathrow and he revealed that a date had finally been fixed for the fight in June, almost exactly a year since he won the title *(see below)*. Patterson won back his title in that return fight. I hope he was well compensated for his long wait for payment.

When a Scottish Amateur Boxing team set off for a tournament in Rumania in 1959, I believed I was on hand just to witness a departure and confirm it to the *Press Association* who had ordered it. The last I expected was a story, even though the 10-strong group included British Olympic champion Dick McTaggart.

Why don't they pay me?—Ingo

INGEMAR JOHANSSON wants the cash for his first fight with Floyd Patterson, and won't take a return date until ten weeks after he has been paid his £30,000 plus purse.

Sweden's new world champion, who landed at London Airport from Gothenburg yesterday, said:

"I have not had a penny from that fight. I was supposed to get 20 per cent. of everything, but so far I haven't even heard when they propose to pay me."

Johansson was here to switch on the Morecambe (Lancs) illuminations in place of the Duke of Bedford.

Johansson is making a double air dash, back home to-morrow for talks

By STEVE FAGAN

with Jack Dempsey on his return world title bout, payment for the first fight and will fly here again to See Henry Cooper and Erskine in next Wednesday's fights at Porthcawl.

Here is what Ingo had to say on his world title war:

On CHALLENGERS: "I am ready to fight Henry Cooper or anyone else after my return with Patterson. Everyone wants to fight me as world champion."

FLOYD PATTERSON: "I want to meet him again, but I'm not bound by any contract to fight on September 21. There can be a return when everything has been cleared up and explained to me."

JUST SILLY

FIGHT "FIXING": "Do I look the type to allow any 'fixing' of the Patterson fight. Who wanted me to win, anyway?

"It was the worst thing that could have happened to the Patterson people. I don't believe anyone takes this idea of a 'fixed' fight seriously. It is plain silly."

JACK DEMPSEY: "I had a telegram last night saying he was coming to Gothenburg. I want to meet him and I hope to see him before I fly back here on Tuesday."

Cash before return insists Ingemar

WORLD heavyweight champion Ingemar Johansson flew into London yesterday from Gothenburg and delivered this verbal "one-two" to Floyd Patterson and Rosensohn Enterprises — the company which promoted the first contest between the Swede and Patterson: "I will not meet Patterson for a return match under any conditions until at least ten weeks after I have been paid for the title fight. I haven't received a penny yet."

Johansson, in England to switch on the illuminations at Morecambe, said: "I was supposed to get 20 p.c. of everything. So far I have not heard when they will pay me. At the moment the New York Boxing Commission is working on it for me."

He insisted that he was not bound by any contract to meet Patterson before September 21, as has been stated.

In training

But he added "When everything is cleared up I want to meet Patterson again. I am in training and my right hand is still working good."

The champion is coming back to Britain on Tuesday. He will watch Wednesday's Empire title fight between Henry Cooper and Gawie de Klerk at Porthcawl, but is expected to meet Jack Dempsey, managing director of Rosensohn Enterprises, in Sweden before he makes the trip.

Of world light heavyweight champion Archie Moore's "million-dollar" offer or a possible fight with the winner of the British Cooper-Erskine fight Johansson said "Everyone wants to meet the champion. I would like to meet Patterson first—then Moore or anyone else—including Henry Cooper."

Dempsey is due in Sweden today. In New York yesterday a spokesman for Dempsey said that if agreement is reached for the return fight the announcement will be made from Gothenburg. "Johansson is champion and the announcement should come from his home town."

Evening News (above)
Daily Mirror (left)
(both) September 1959

THE EVENING NEWS, THURSDAY, MARCH 3, 1960

World Title Return Fight Date Is Settled

INGO SAYS JUNE 22

Ingemar stays 35 minutes —but names THE DAY

World heavyweight champion INGEMAR JOHANSSON at London Airport today. He was there just 35 minutes while changing aircraft on his way from America to the Middle East. But during that time he announced that his return world title fight with Floyd Patterson was definitely fixed for June 22 in New York.

Johansson's trip to the Middle East is for a series of exhibition matches for United Nations troops who are stationed there.

Later, Johansson plans a tour of American bases in Europe.

The world champion was joined in London for his flight by manager Eddie Ahlquist who had flown on to London ahead of him.

After his tours, Johansson will return home for training.

"I expect to be back in America about seven or eight weeks before my fight with Patterson," he said.

Evening News (far right),
Brenard Press picture
Evening Standard (right)
(both) March 3 1960

Cooper Must Wait For His Chance

By REG GUTTERIDGE

INGEMAR JOHANSSON, the world heavy-weight champion, will have his return fight with former title-holder, Floyd Patterson, on June 22 in New York. So he said at London Airport to-day.

Johansson, flying from America to the Middle East, spent 35 minutes in London changing flights. He is to give a series of exhibition bouts during a ten-day visit to United Nations' troops stationed in the Gaza Strip. Then he plans a tour of U.S. bases in Europe.

"After the tour I shall go back to my gymnasium near my home in Geneva to start really hard training," he said.

"I expect to be back in the United States about seven or eight weeks before the fight.

Fit Now

"I am perfectly fit now. I am never out of training. These exhibitions keep me on top."

Johansson was joined for his flight to Beirut by his adviser, Swedish sports-paper owner, Eddie Ahlquist, who flew to London ahead of the champion tc arrange sparring partners for the training spell in Switzerland.

Champion and adviser have a strong allegiance to Jack Solomons. They like the way Solomons does fight business; they like England — and British boxers.

It seems to me that Henry Cooper will eventually get his world-title crack—he fought Johansson for the European crown—but not before Ingo has gone in again with Patterson.

That would be something to hope for when the team returned to the UK with perhaps a "result." The same probably applied to the corps of airport resident photographers, who were to follow me to Heathrow's Terminal 2 departures a few minutes later. They would be simply taking what they would describe as "library shots."

The team were already seated when I arrived in the lounge. I spotted McTaggart immediately. He was playing cards with three other boxers and team coach Hugh Ferns as they sat at a small, round coffee table killing time as they waited for their flight to Bucharest. On the table, alongside a couple of coffee cups, were a few copper coins.

After a few minutes I was joined by three or four photographers but none of them made a move to take pictures. They wanted a simple group shot as the boxers boarded their aircraft and I was only waiting with them to make sure the team caught its flight.

Suddenly the doors from the passport control area burst open and two airport police officers, a sergeant and an inspector, burst in. Ignoring us, they marched up to the boxers. For a moment I thought they were asking for autographs. Then one of them snatched up the stack of cards and a handful of coins. The other pulled out a notebook and took down the names of McTaggart, Hugh Ferns and the three other boxers, Danny Lee, Ernie Piper and Willie Fisher.

We were too far away to hear what was said, and a few of the photographers and I walked quickly over to the group. I don't know if the police saw us approaching, but after a final brief word with the team, they decided to take no further action. They then left, with the cards and the coins.

The boxers angrily turned on us. The photographers and I were accused of a "set-up" One of them shouted: "You reported us for gambling. You called the police for the sake of a story." We were only able to calm them after we pointed out that we weren't even aware what the police had said to them. And McTaggart told me: "We were fed up with waiting about so some of decided to play cards. The police said we were gambling, but none of us bet anything. The only money changing hands was a halfpenny on each wrong card."

He said the boxers had first been approached by plain-clothes officers (none of us was aware of this). They were told they were committing an offence by "gambling in a public place." About two shillings (10p) in old halfpennies, pennies and threepenny pieces were confiscated.

Said Hugh Ferns: "The police are being absolutely childish about this. The boys haven't any money to gamble with.

"We were playing dominoes using cards because we had exhausted every other form of entertainment the airport had to offer." The story made most of the following day's newspapers, with the *Daily Sketch* and *Daily Herald* providing three-column headlines.

AIRPORT POLICE RAID HA'PENNY GAME

FOUR amateur boxers and a coach had their names taken by police who broke up their card game at London Airport last night.

The players were members of the Scottish ABA team, killing time in a lounge as they waited to fly off for a match with a Rumanian amateur team.

Dick McTaggart, Scottish Olympic champion, had his name taken.

Fed up

He said later: "We've been on the airport for nearly six hours after flying down from Glasgow. We've looked in every shop window, and we found the airport news cinema had been closed down.

"We were fed up with hanging about—so we started playing cards. The police said we were gambling—but none of us was betting and the only money that was changing hands was a ha'penny on each wrong card."

The pack of cards and about two shillings, mainly in coppers and threepenny bits, were confiscated by the police.

Other boxers in the card party were Danny Lee, Ernie Piper and Willie Fisher.

Absolutely childish

They were first approached by plain-clothes officers who told them they were committing an offence by "gambling in a public place." Then a police-sergeant and an inspector appeared.

"The police are being absolutely childish about this," said the team's coach and trainer, Hugh Ferns. "The boys haven't got any money to gamble with anyway.

"We were only playing dominoes with cards because there was nothing better to do."

Daily Mail (above)

Daily Sketch (left)

CARD 'RAID' AT AIRPORT

Daily Sketch Reporter

THE coach and four members of the Scottish Amateur Boxing Association had their names taken by police at London Airport last night—for playing cards.

One of them was Olympics champion Dick McTaggart, who was waiting with the rest to fly for a match against Rumania.

He said: "We were fed up hanging about, so we started playing.

"The police said we were gambling—but none of us was betting.

"The only money that was changing hands was a halfpenny on each wrong card."

The cards, and about 2s. in coppers and 3d. bits, were confiscated by the police.

Other boxers in the card party were Danny Lee, Ernie Piper, and Willie Fisher.

'NO MONEY'

"The police are absolutely childish about this," said the team's coach and trainer, Hugh Ferns. "The boys haven't got any money to gamble with.

"We were playing dominoes with cards because we had exhausted every other sort of entertainment the airport had to offer."

Olympic boxer in card game swoop

OLYMPIC boxing champion Dick McTaggart had his name taken by police at London Airport last night —for playing cards in an airport lounge.

Five of the 10-strong A B A team were passing the time before flying off to a match in Rumania.

Dick McTaggart said: "We've been on the airport for nearly six hours after flying down from Glasgow. We've looked in every shop window and found that the airport news cinema was closed.

GAMBLING

"We were fed up with hanging about—so we started playing cards. The police said we were gambling. But none of us was betting and the only money that was changing hands was a halfpenny on each wrong card."

The pack of cards and about 2s., mostly in coppers, were confiscated by the police who also took the names of three other boxers, Danny Lee, Ernie Piper, Willie Fisher, and the team coach, Hugh Ferns.

Daily Herald (all) circa July 1959

Five, Five Five—For 24 Hours

FIVE American businessmen stepped from an airliner at London Airport today, gathered round a table in the passenger lounge and brought out a pack of cards. With the table piled high with American 10 and 5-dollar bills they continued their 24-hour non-stop poker game.

The five men started their game a few minutes after leaving San Francisco for London on their way to Tel-Aviv. They refused to be interrupted even during the 40-minute refuelling stop at London Airport.

A fellow passenger said: "Hundreds of dollars had changed hands—but no one seemed to be losing. They money just keeps going around the table."

As they went out to board their airliner for their flight to Israel, one of the five players said: "We've got quite a few hours left to play. Someone's got to win."

The Star
(both) circa May 1958

POKER GAME GOES BY AIR

It lasts 24 hours

Five American businessmen stepped from an airliner at London Airport today, gathered round a table in a passenger lounge, and brought out a pack of cards. With the table piled high with money they continued a 24-hour non-stop poker game.

The five poker players started their game a few minutes after leaving San Francisco for London on their way to Tel Aviv.

A fellow passenger said: "None of them stopped playing for a moment during the journey. Hundreds of dollars have changed hands but no one seems to be losing. The money just keeps going round the table."

Evening Standard

Only a year earlier I had reported a similar card game, which on this occasion had somehow escaped the attention of the airport's vigilant police force. A group of five American businessmen had stepped from an airliner at Heathrow during a refuelling stop, gathered round a table in the transit lounge and brought out the pack of cards.

With their table piled high with American 10- and 5-dollar bills they continued with a round-the-clock non-stop poker game they had started just minutes after leaving San Francisco, 6,000 miles away. Now they had some 40 minutes to go before departure for their final destination, Tel Aviv, and they were able to pick up the game where they had left off.

A fellow passenger told me: "Hundreds of dollars have changed hands, but no one seems to be losing. The money just keeps going round the table." When their flight was finally called someone swept up the cards in order, face down, and one of the players said: "We've got quite a few hours left to play. Someone's got to win..."

*

The woman passenger in front of me was expensively, if fussily dressed and was displaying the then unfashionable bright red lipstick and pink cheeks of a slightly artificial English rose complexion. We unexpectedly came face to face at the entrance to Heathrow's Terminal 2 departures lounge, soon after its opening in 1955, and recognition was mutual. Which was just as well as we had almost collided head-on.

"Hello, how are *you*?" we both said, almost simultaneously. And she turned to her husband, just a pace behind her.

"Gerald, come and meet the man who made me famous." Then, as she made the introduction, she told him: "I owe it all to him…"

With hindsight I should have pleaded: "Not guilty, " immediately. Instead I mumbled, "Not at all. Not at all." I had, after all only reported the incident, even though it had elevated Mrs Gerald Legge from the occasional gossip-column description of "socialite," and "daughter of prolific novelist Barbara Cartland" to a media-perceived aristocratic caped crusader. It was in reality by her own efforts that the former Raine McCorquodale, marginal member of the 1950's "Princess Margaret set" eventually became Countess Spencer, stepmother to the much-loved Diana, Princess of Wales.

We had first met a year earlier, in November 1954, in the less luxurious setting of another departures lounge, the huts of Heathrow's original northside terminal. I was about to make my way on a routine recce there from the check-in area when a British European Airways' passenger officer hailed me.

"If you put your skates on you'll be in time to witness a passenger blowing her top about dirty tea-cups," he explained as he caught up with me. "She's a Mrs Gerald Legge – she told me she's a friend of Princess Margaret – and she's off to Paris.

"But you'll have to hurry. We were about to call the flight."

I hurried across the Customs baggage hall and through passport controls to the departure lounge. It was emptying slowly as passengers boarded, stopping only to show their boarding passes, but airline staff willingly pointed out the fur-coated figure at the back of the queue. As soon as I told her what I'd heard, she confirmed her outburst.

"I was ashamed for Britain at the disgusting condition of the lounge," she said. "I marched up to the coffee counter and said: 'Come out of there and clear up.' The girl told me: 'Oh, I haven't got time. I'm very busy and I've a lot to do.'"

The passenger had then asked two barmen at an adjoining counter to clear the tables in the lounge, but said they replied: "It's not our job."

Angrily she went over to an airline desk at the departures door holding up a half-empty cup of coffee and a brimful ashtray and demanded: "Is no one going to clear this disgraceful mess?"

With Mrs Legge, a Westminster Tory councillor, were a number of friends, including, she told me, the Vicomtesse de Ribes who had been visiting her in London, the Duke and Duchess of Montoro, and the Comtessa de Rivera. As she hustled them out to the 'plane ahead of her she said: "When we entered the lounge the tables were absolutely covered with filthy coffee cups, everybody's cigarette ash and dirty cigarette ends. I was downright ashamed to let them see the condition of our airport. I've never been so shocked.

"I tried to complain to a charming man who said: 'It's not me, it's BOAC,' and sent for the BOAC man. But I can't wait for him because they've called the flight. They've done that on purpose. But I shan't let it rest there. I shall see someone high up when I return."

As the last passengers left the lounge, I approached the buffet attendant, Eileen Wells, a BOAC catering employee, for her reaction. She was busy washing cups.

"The woman was being very unfair," she said. "We had a delayed flight in here, and when the passengers on the BEA flight came into the lounge it became very crowded.

"I had been very busy serving teas and coffees on my own, but had started to clear away used cups when the woman burst in. She was obviously trying to impress her friends by the way she was throwing her weight around. I didn't answer her back. I told her very politely that I had collected some cups up and was busy washing them. I said I would clear some more when I had finished serving.

"But she wasn't listening to me. She was being totally unreasonable. We can't clear tables by waving a magic wand. She shouted at the barmen who were clearing and washing down their counter: 'Come out of there and clear up.' They're not supposed to leave the bar. But one of them would have given me a hand once the lounge emptied again."

Before filing my copy for the dailies, which with Eileen's comments seemed to me to be reasonably balanced. I checked with BOAC, who staffed and operated the buffet. Then I called the airport press office of the Ministry of Civil Aviation, responsible at that time for general cleaning of the buildings, including the clearing of ashtrays.

Said a BOAC spokesman: "We understand a planeload of passengers had left the lounge only moments before Mrs Legge entered. It is quite unreasonable to suggest that dirty cups should be cleared away simultaneously with the passengers." And a Ministry man added: "We're always on our toes to keep the airport tidy, but you can't help those moments when things are lying about."

Every daily newspaper, including the "heavies", ran with my story the next day, each of them rummaging through their photo libraries for suitable pictures of the 25-years-old former debutante. The *Daily Sketch* supported their front-page coverage with an oversized studio portrait of the subject above the headline:

SOCIETY WIFE IN DIRTY CUP STORM

THE beautiful Mrs. Gerald Legge, Society leader and friend of Princess Margaret, was the centre of a storm—in a coffee cup—at London Airport last night.

A dozen passengers were sitting quietly in the departure lounge waiting for their planes when in burst a blonde tornado — a voluble tornado in the form of the fur-coated Mrs. Legge, one of Britain's best-dressed women.

She entered the lounge from the immigration hall with a party of friends, including French socialite the Contessa de Riber, who has been staying with her. Then, with a cup of coffee in one hand, a brimful ash-

⇨ *Back Page*

Daily Sketch (left, front page), (below, continuation)

Society wife in airport scene

⇨ *From Page 1*

tray in the other, she stalked to the air line desk.

In a voice that echoed from end to end of the lounge she demanded: "Is no one going to clear up this disgraceful mess?" She pointed to tables littered with half-empty cups and stub-filled ash-trays.

"I'm absolutely ashamed that this is a British airport," she stormed.

Then she turned to the buffet. "Can't you do something," she queried. And to the bar attendant, "Come out from there and clear up."

Said Westminster Councillor Mrs. Legge later: "I had a party of foreigners with me and I was downright ashamed to let them see the condition of our airports. I travel quite a bit but I've never been so shocked. Continental airports are spotless by comparison."

The B.O.A.C. and the Ministry of Civil Aviation are jointly responsible for clearing cups and keeping the airport lounge clean.

Airline representatives telephoned for a Ministry official, but before he could appear Mrs. Legge's flight to Paris was called.

Said a B.O.A.C. official: "We understand a plane load of passengers had left the lounge only a moment before Mrs. Legge entered.

"It is quite unreasonable to suggest that dirty cups should be cleared away simultaneously with the departure of passengers."

Mrs Gerald Legge shakes the airport

'FILTHY LOUNGE MADE ME ASHAMED'

From ALAN HUMPHREYS : Paris, Monday.

ONE voice silenced the passengers' conversation in the lounge of London Airport today—the voice of Mrs. Gerald Legge, Mayfair hostess and Westminster councillor. She was angry, shocked, embarrassed. In a five-minute volley of criticism, she told the airport staff why.

Clean up this lounge, said Princess's friend

Daily Mail *Daily Mirror* *(all) November 16 1954*

The *Mirror* used a head and shoulders from the same portrait, the *News Chronicle* gave the story the full length of a column, and the *Telegraph* described the story as a "PROTEST OVER AIRPORT 'FILTH'".

The *Daily Express* gave one of their leading writers, Anne Edwards, the opportunity for a boxed and highlighted comment above my story:

Anne Edwards *says—Here's a woman who deserves a medal for conspicuous bravery. A few more women with the courage to stand up and blast a whole Government service, and we will get this country to run its restaurants at least as efficiently and cleanly as most women run their homes.*

Mrs. LEGGE ROCKS AIRPORT

Named as the winner of that Anne Edwards' medal is socialite Mrs. Gerald Legge. And this is how the citation might read . . .

IT was coffee time at London Airport. A dozen passengers sat in the departure lounge. All was quiet after yesterday's fog delays.

Then up to the airline desk stormed Mrs. Legge, 24, fur-coated and angry.

In a voice that echoed through the lounge, she demanded: "Is no one going to clear up this disgraceful mess?" She pointed to tables littered with half-empty cups and stub-filled ash-trays.

I'm absolutely ashamed that this is a British airport. I have never seen such filth in all my

MRS. GERALD LEGGE

life," she declared. Next—to the buffet . . . "Come out from there and clear up," she ordered.

Airline men phoned for a Ministry of Civil Aviation official. But before he could appear Mrs. Legge's flight to Paris was announced.

"They have done that on purpose," she said. "But I shall see someone high up when I return."

Westminster councillor Mrs. Legge explained: "I have a party of foreigners with me and I am ashamed to let them see the condition of the airport. Continental airports are spotless by comparison."

Then silence as the leading lady of this year's society show "The Frog" swept off-stage through the exit door.

And the Mintstry man who missed Mrs. Legge? Said he: "It is difficult at the best of times to maintain the high state of cleanliness we would like to see ourselves."

Daily Express (all) November 16 1954

Mrs. LEGGE KICKS UP A FUSS

Over dirty cups and ashtrays

By James O'Driscoll

FUR-COATED Mrs. Gerald Legge gazed at the half-empty tea and coffee cups in the departure lounge at London Airport yesterday.

She glared at the stub-filled ashtrays and raised her voice in a battle-cry: *"Is nobody going to clear up this disgraceful mess?"*

News Chronicle

PROTEST OVER AIRPORT 'FILTH'

MRS. GERALD LEGGE'S CRITICISMS

Before flying to Paris yesterday afternoon, Mrs. Gerald Legge, a member of Westminster City Council, stood in the London Airport departure lounge and said to officials: "I am absolutely ashamed that this is a British airport."

A few travellers were sitting in the lounge when Mrs. Legge entered with a party of friends. She pointed to tables littered with half-empty cups and filled ashtrays, and asked:

"Is no one going to clear up this disgraceful mess? I've never seen such filth in all my life."

Later she said: "I had a party of foreigners with me and I was downright ashamed to let them see the conditions of our airport. I travel quite a bit myself but I have never been so shocked. Continental airports are spotless by comparison."

B.O.A.C. REPLY

British Overseas Airways Corporation, which is jointly responsible with the Ministry of Civil Aviation for keeping the airport lounge clean, said: "We understand a plane-load of passengers had left the lounge only a moment before Mrs. Legge entered.

"It is quite unreasonable to suggest that dirty cups should be cleared away simultaneously with the departure of passengers." A Ministry official added: "It is difficult at the best of times to maintain the high state of cleanliness we would like to see ourselves.'"

Daily Telegraph

UNTIDY BRITAIN

¶ The woman traveller who made a rumpus at London Airport about dirty coffee cups and cluttered ashtrays may have been a bit hasty with B.O.A.C. and t. Ministry of Civil Aviation, who apparently share responsibility for keeping these waiting rooms tidy. Fairly wide experience of London Airport at all hours and all seasons inculcates the conviction that there is a real and sustained endeavour to keep these rather dismal hutments in spick-and-span order.

Evening News (editorial)

BAA archive picture

Before Mrs Legge's "tea party."
This was the way the original Northside departure lounge at Heathrow normally looked when empty of passengers. The exit to aircraft (not shown) was to the right of this picture; the passengers' bar and cold snacks buffet can be seen to the left .

Up to that point I'd had no strong feelings about the rights and wrongs of the argument. But I couldn't help thinking Anne Edwards was a little too hasty. Her comment appeared to be based entirely on an edited version of the story which gave little emphasis to the waitress's response. The no-doubt unintentional implication that Mrs Legge could be included among "most women who run their own homes" was laughable. The views were echoed and enlarged upon the following day in the London *Evening News,* though it did concede that the incident was not typical of the general cleanliness standard of the airport. To say I was disappointed with the coverage would be an exaggeration. The echoes of Mrs Legge's outburst went on for months, even years afterwards. There was the inevitable spate of newspaper cartoons. One by Artie in the *Express* showed a fur-coated figure approaching a kerbside coffee stall. The caption: *"Quick, Bert, clear the cups and empty the ashtrays. Here comes Mrs Gerald Legge."*

Osbert Lancaster's Pocket Cartoon, also in the *Express*, showed two of his "regular" characters seated in an airport lounge under a "Refreshments" sign as a waitress marched by, ignoring them. The text read: *"It's no good, darling. Mrs Legge's probably told them you're a messy feeder!"*

ARTIE'S HEADLINE

"Quick, Bert, clear the cups and empty the ash-tray—here comes Mrs. Gerald Legge!"

POCKET CARTOON
by OSBERT LANCASTER

"It's no good, darling, Mrs. Legge's probably told them you're a messy feeder!"

(both) Daily Express Nov 17 1954
World copyright
© Express Newspapers Ltd.

Daily Express cartoonists "Artie" and "Osbert Lancaster" added their own party pieces by way of biting comment the following day.

And as with my Jane Russell-Tommy Kavanagh scoop, the story of Mrs Legge and the dirty tea cups was picked up by stage and radio comedians and featured as a topical gag in comedy shows for months afterwards.

I continued to feel some responsibility, however, for the one-sided interpretation of the incident. Perhaps I had over-emphasised Mrs Legge's role and failed to give sufficient support to the counter-argument myself. I hadn't named the waitress in my copy, even though she had featured in another story of mine some eighteen months earlier. At that time a group of delayed, impatient passengers had rebelled after she confessed to them in exasperation that she had run out of cups.

For weeks she and other waitresses at two buffet counters, serving up to 3,000 cups of tea or coffee a day, had protested to their superiors: "We can't give good service with only 41 cups between us."

On that occasion Eileen Wells was threatened by BOAC with a disciplinary court and was warned she could face dismissal. The charges were eventually withdrawn and the stock of available crockery quickly increased. This time BOAC were more gallant. They appeared to be giving their waitress their full support in their responses to my questions.

Three years on, a telegram reached me from a couple of television researchers, Pauline and Larry Forrester, who said they were gathering material for a new television

She faces storm over the teacups

MRS. EILEEN WELLS. Irish-born waitress at a London Airport buffet, will face a disciplinary "court" tomorrow—because she told irate customers that the buffet had only eighteen cups.

The "court" will comprise senior B.O.A.C. catering and staff executives, and Mrs. Wells's "lawyer" will be a trade union official. The result might be reprimand, suspension or even dismissal for "Paddy" Wells.

For weeks waitresses at the airport's TWO buffets, which serve up to 3,000 cups of tea and coffee a day, had protested to passengers: "We cannot give good service with only forty-one cups between us."

The *Daily Mirror* was told that three weeks ago passengers on three delayed flights had to wait twenty minutes to be served.

One of the customers demanded to know why—and Mrs. Wells told him.

Next day a supply of nearly 200 cups was rushed in.

Daily Mirror (above)
Daily Herald (right)

3,000 teas —and only 41 cups

WHY, demanded a customer, was there a 20-minute wait for a cup of tea at one of London Airport's two main tea-and-sandwich buffets? The waitress replied that there were only 18 cups.

That was three weeks ago. Now the waitress, Mrs. Eileen Wells, is to be interviewed by senior BOAC catering and personnel executives. A trade union official will be present.

For weeks waitresses who serve up to 3,000 cups of tea and coffee a day at the two buffets had protested: "We can't give good service with only 41 cups between us."

The day after Mrs. Wells explained to the customer the reason for the delay, 200 cups were sent.

A BOAC official said yesterday: "We understand Mrs. Wells is to appear at an interview. We cannot say at the moment what it is about."

Waitress in storm over the tea-cups

IN one of London Airport's two tea buffets tempers were fraying. Three planes had failed to take off to schedule and the delayed passengers crowded into the buffet.

"Tea, please," they ordered, and waited . . . and waited . . . and waited.

Twenty minutes later came the first explosion from an angry customer.

It was then that dark-haired Mrs. Eileen Wells, Irish-born waitress, explained: "We've only got 18 cups."

And because she did so Mrs. "Paddy" Wells has been ordered to face a disciplinary "court" to-morrow.

3,000 daily

Judge and jury will be senior B.O.A.C. catering and personnel executives.

Conviction would result in a severe reprimand, suspension or even a dismissal, for "Paddy."

For weeks waitresses at the two buffets—they serve up to 3,000 cups of tea and coffee a day—had protested: "We can't give good service with only 41 cups among us."

But the day after the customer objected, a new supply of 200 cups were rushed in.

Mrs. Wells's colleagues say it was only because they complained publicly.

Daily Sketch
(all) July 27 1953

parlour game entitled *"Place the Face."* The proposal was that a celebrity would be asked to remember people connected with some incident in his or her life. Would I be prepared to go along and play a "mystery face" as the reporter who helped to pin the tag "campaigner" to the name of Mrs Gerald Legge?

I could – perhaps I *should* – have told them that this was one celebrity who would certainly remember her "stalker". She had already spotted me once. But I said I would be delighted. This could be my big opportunity to tell a few million viewers that everything was not quite as it seemed, and that that here was one crusader who may have gone in with all guns blazing without asking her target to put up her hands.

Sadly, my opportunity never came. Pauline Forrester had told me: "We have a number of people to consider and we may not need your help. We'll let you know."

They obviously didn't need me. But neither did they let me know. Possibly because, as far as I am aware, no face was ever placed by any celebrity. The game was scratched.

Strangely, I was approached again, early in 1959, by another researcher, this time on behalf of the television journalist Daniel Farson. He wanted to know the background to the dirty tea-cups for a planned interview with Mrs Legge, by now Lady Lewisham, for his ITV series, *"Success Story."*

Shortly before the programme was due to be shown, the television company screened a promotional trailer which highlighted their guest's version of the Heathrow incident. In it Lady Lewisham said the publicity from the story had contributed more than anything in her life to her fame as a "crusader." Yet although television trailers are usually made up from significant extracts designed to promote interest in the final programme, all reference to the tea-cups had apparently been edited out when the interview was eventually screened.

Some time before his death in the late '90s, I tried unsuccessfully several times to contact Daniel Farson to ask why the incident had been cut from the screened version of the interview. I had also written to the subject of the interview, by now Countess Spencer and a "near-neighbour" of mine in Northamptonshire, asking if she could provide the answer. In reply she sent me a picture postcard of Althorp, her home as the wife of Earl Spencer, father of Princess Diana of Wales.

In an almost unintelligible scrawl she wrote (I think): "Sorry, I can't help you at present… just going away. Also just moving house…" She invited me to call again the following month, adding: "I can answer any questions then."

After three separate telephoned attempts to get past an assistant, and one second-hand, unfulfilled promise that the mistress of the house would call me back, I gave up. It wasn't that important. Or was it?

Eighteen months after the tea-cups episode Mrs Legge chose to patronise the airport's northside public restaurant for lunch. Apparently warned in advance of her arrival, (by whom, I have no idea) an airport official conducted her in full ceremony to a table where she graciously received in turn, the restaurant management, senior Ministry of Civil Aviation executives and even BOAC officials who wanted to pay their respects.

She must have felt gratified that her few words in the departures lounge had been remembered so well, if only for their sting, as I commented at the time in my airport newspaper column. When I pumped her for a revised verdict on her surroundings, she was diplomatically careful not to commit herself for the future.

"It's all very nice," was all she would say. "I *have* enjoyed myself."

I learned much later that on this occasion her reserve might have been because public catering at Heathrow had recently been taken over by the Forte organisation. In one of her many interviews Mrs Legge had revealed that she had been friends with the company's founder Charles Forte, later Lord Forte, "since his milk bar days."

It seems unlikely that she could have laid claim to a similar relationship with the Soviet Government or with the management of the Russian airline, Aeroflot. A few days later Mrs Legge called at Heathrow hoping to join VIPs invited to make a conducted tour of the airline's first jet, the Tupolev TU104. The airliner was making its debut in London, but she could only watch with sightseers from the edge of the tarmac.

"I know nothing of her. Who is Mrs Legge?" asked the Aeroflot manager when I spoke to him. He even looked puzzled when I said she had been a Westminster councillor, and was then a member of the Greater London Council…

As I have already referred to four separate identities for the tea-cups crusader, sometimes with little explanation, I should spell them out in a little more detail. The lady in question seems unlikely to disappear completely from the gossip columns.

Just as a reminder, she was born Raine McCorquodale in 1929, the daughter of prolific romantic novelist, the late Barbara Cartland, also known for an extravagant sense of style. In 1948 she married the Honourable Gerald Legge, becoming Lady Lewisham when her husband's father later inherited a peerage. Her husband then succeeded to the title of 9th Earl of Dartmouth, with Raine as his Countess, following the death of his father in 1962. A divorce followed in 1976, but she retained her title of Countess by marrying the late Earl "Johnny" Spencer, father of the then young Lady Diana.

About a year after Johnny's death in 1992, Raine married an allegedly penniless French aristocrat, Jean-Francois de Chambrun, and reverted to the simple title of Madame. The couple were divorced in 1996. Other less welcome epithets were awarded over the years, notably "the wicked stepmother" by Princess Diana, and "Acid Raine," by other members of her family.

But it was back in 1961, while still Lady Lewisham, she had next come to our attention. That Easter she was once more passing through Heathrow, or trying to. This time she was just one of a number of holiday travellers held up while trying to negotiate a jammed car-park. "We were stuck in a queue for ten minutes unable to move an inch," she told a colleague.

"All that time some horrible little man with a uniform too big for him was denting the roof of the car as he banged it with his fist, and shouting at us to get a move on. I've never seen anything so ridiculous."

But the car-park problem was not the only thing to upset her that day. When she finally managed to check in for her flight, she found the Comet jet had been delayed an hour "for technical reasons."

"With all that money we tax-payers put into research in this country, why can't we build an aeroplane that flies?" she demanded. "This always happens to me when I fly. Now I shall arrive in Athens too late for dinner."

I never had the doubtful privilege of meeting Raine in person again. But in October 1985, long after I had given up reporting and joined the soon-to-be privatised British Airport Authority, Alan Proctor, the Heathrow Airport Director, asked me as his deputy public relations manager to provide him with a thumb-nail sketch of Countess Spencer. He told me she had been involved in an argument with security guards, and he wanted to know something of the person he might be dealing with. As a former public relations manager for the Authority himself he was aware of my earlier experience with the Countess.

Later Alan was to pass on to me details of the security incident for our PR information log, to enable us to deal with news media inquiries *if they arose.* Volunteering any information to the news media was, it always seemed, anathema to my boss, the chief Heathrow public relations manager, unless it was blatantly good publicity (my word, not his, it must be said) for the BAA. It was this avowed policy I was required to follow, so our log entry remained undivulged.

Four days later part of the story inevitably leaked out and, I hasten to add, I was not responsible, though I have my suspicions who was. The *Sunday Express* discovered that Countess Spencer had angrily refused to be frisked by security guards at Heathrow before a flight to Paris.

In time-honoured fashion, Princess Diana's stepmother was reported to have demanded: "Don't you know who I am?" when she was stopped at a random check point.

Two security officers were called in when she repeated her refusal to undergo a search. They explained that the security procedures were laid down by Parliament, which at that time required individual searching of ten per cent of all passengers. The Countess was then informed that numerically she was part of this ten per cent, and was obliged to submit to a body search. She only gave in when she was told she would not be allowed aboard the flight unless she agreed, and she was finally led to a cubicle by a woman security officer and frisked.

The *Sunday Express* report was apparently picked up by several newspapers overseas. It prompted one American from Johnson City, New York, to pen a hurried note to the airport PR office to say: ***"...when I read of this incident in my local paper I felt gratified***

indeed because I've always believed everyone gets a 'fair do' anywhere in good old democratic England, and especially at the best-run airport in the world – Heathrow!! Good Show!!"

I don't believe it would be accurate to attribute the *Express* story directly to our log entry. But I suppose that it could still be described as blatantly good publicity.

What the *Express* didn't know and what I couldn't tell them at the time was that rules or no rules, the Countess wasn't won over. During the body search, she voiced her strong objections to what she called "lesbian hands" touching her. She had pleaded: "I'm not a terrorist and I'm only on a day trip," and moved away towards the departures area.

Called back, she still objected to a public searching but finally agreed to go to a discreet cubicle, where a female supervisor with a different woman guard standing by, attempted another search. The countess, Alan told me, again protested about "lesbian hands" and said she would take the matter further. Only then did she finally submit to a routine frisk.

It lasted all of five seconds. Strangely enough, no infringement of security was reported.

*

Lady Lewisham must have been pleased to learn, just ten weeks after she first found fame over a Heathrow tea counter, that her "good friend" Charles Forte, the milk bar king, was to take over public catering in the airport's brand new passenger terminal when it opened in the spring.

Mr. Piccadilly gets new job as air host

THE milk-bar king whom they call "Mr. Piccadilly" will soon be giving thousands of overseas visitors their first taste of British catering.

For 47-year-old Mr. Charles Forte, head of a chain of milk bars and restaurants, is to take over the four buffets and restaurants in the new London Airport passenger buildings opening in March.

The Ministry of Transport and Civil Aviation confirmed last night that his firm has been chosen from 59 catering organisations invited to tender.

According to other catering chiefs, the Ministry's conditions include a 10 per cent. cut of the takings. On this basis, they say, Mr. Forte will be running it for prestige only.

But at his office last night Mr. Forte said: "I don't agree that those are the terms. We have every hope of making a reasonable profit."

Italian-born Mr. Forte became known as Mr. Piccadilly after gaining control of 1½ acres around the Eros statue.

Daily Herald *Jan 25 1955*

Not that there was any connection between the two events, but it may have occurred to her that in any similar situation at the airport in the future she could just lift a telephone…

She would have learned the news from my story in the newspapers in January 1955 when I revealed that Mr Forte's company had been chosen from 59 catering organisations invited to tender for the contract to run the buffets, bars and restaurants in the new building, later to become Terminal 2. It was the first of many contracts and concessions "Mr Piccadilly" was to win at and around Heathrow. The nickname had been given him by a newspaper after he gained control of 11 acres of land adjoining London's Eros statue.

According to other caterers, the Ministry's conditions included a 10 per cent cut of his airport turnover – not just of his profit. On this basis, they claimed, the selected contractor would be operating in the airport terminal just for the prestige. But from his office Mr Forte said: "I don't agree those are the terms. We have every hope of making a reasonable profit."

As I couldn't help commenting in my airport newspaper column: *"I'm thinking of opening my own refreshments buffet on the airport, providing I get enough support to meet the Ministry rents. I shall call it Forty Two."* [1]

A day or two later I discovered that Mr. Forte was having a quiet lunch in the northside public restaurant, still run by BOAC at that time. I approached him and introducing myself, I asked: "Would you say you were spying out the land?" .

"Well yes, getting the feel of the place," he replied. Was he happy with the story I'd given him over his airport contract? "Was that you?" he asked. "Well, I certainly was. It must have been the biggest splash I've had to date. Next time I visit the airport you must let me buy you dinner."

Although he visited his much expanded airport "empire" on a number of occasions in the future, I never ran into him again. Neither was I ever his guest at dinner. Later I half wished I had told him how our life paths had been co-incidentally linked, albeit only fragilely, by my slightly sad daydreams of his early Black & White Milk Bars in Fleet Street, and even earlier war-time Dulverton, in Somerset.

I'm glad I didn't, because in reality there never was such a link.

The discovery came while checking his memoirs many years later for background information for this final chapter. I learned that in fact Lord Forte had never owned the Black and White milk bars chain. That was founded and owned by an Australian, the

[1] *A few years on, a restaurant in West London was advertised as "A Forty Restaurant." It opened on the Western Avenue A40.*

Honourable Hugh D. Macintosh. As a customer in the Fleet St. milk bar Charles Forte was impressed with its business potential. In 1934 he wrote to Macintosh offering to invest in exchange for a partnership… and suggested improvements to the limited menu. Both ideas were rejected.

The 26-years old businessman went away and after spending weeks searching for the right premises, opened his own milk bar in Upper Regent Street with financial help from his family and friends. The Australian with the Scottish heritage and the Italian-born adopted Scotsman were now rivals.

But Charles Forte moved on from those milk bars. Knighted in 1970 and made a life peer in 1982, he went on to become the head of one of the world's largest hotel chains – including several adjoining Heathrow.

THE AFTER WORDS…

In the mid-1970s I too moved on, in a more modest way. And mine was the shorter journey in every sense. Acutely aware of my own finances, or rather the lack of them, and the writing on the wall for future financial security in the world of newspapers I decided it was time to consider new accountablilities.

A couple of years earlier I had responded to a recruitment advertisement by the then British Airports Authority for a new Heathrow Airport Public Relations Manager (mainly a Press Relations responsibility.) Unfortunately my CV apparently wasn't even worthy of a reply.

Undaunted, two years on I again applied to the BAA for an advertised vacant post of Senior P.R.O. This time I was advised that "owing to a very large response" the Authority was no longer accepting applications. Nevertheless the same post was re-advertised six months later at an increased salary. I again applied, and this time was successful – at an even higher salary rate.

Many years later I discovered that only two applicants had been interviewed the previous March. When both rejected the salary offered and pulled out, BAA chairman Sir Norman Payne insisted on the increased offer.

At 44 years of age I was about to start a new career.

Index of names